P9-DUY-965

Developments in Wireless Network Prototyping, Design, and Deployment:
Future Generations

Mohammad A. Matin
Institut Teknologi Brunei, Brunei Darussalam

WITHDRAWN
UTSA Libraries

Information Science
REFERENCE

Managing Director:	Lindsay Johnston
Senior Editorial Director:	Heather A. Probst
Book Production Manager:	Sean Woznicki
Development Manager:	Joel Gamon
Development Editor:	Myla Harty
Acquisitions Editor:	Erika Gallagher
Typesetter:	Deanna Zombro, Nicole Sparano
Cover Design:	Nick Newcomer, Lisandro Gonzalez

Published in the United States of America by
Information Science Reference (an imprint of IGI Global)
701 E. Chocolate Avenue
Hershey PA 17033
Tel: 717-533-8845
Fax: 717-533-8661
E-mail: cust@igi-global.com
Web site: http://www.igi-global.com

Copyright © 2012 by IGI Global. All rights reserved. No part of this publication may be reproduced, stored or distributed in any form or by any means, electronic or mechanical, including photocopying, without written permission from the publisher. Product or company names used in this set are for identification purposes only. Inclusion of the names of the products or companies does not indicate a claim of ownership by IGI Global of the trademark or registered trademark.

Library of Congress Cataloging-in-Publication Data

Developments in wireless network prototyping, design, and deployment: future generations / Mohammad A. Matin, editor.
       p. cm.
   Summary: "This book highlights the current design issues in wireless networks, informing scholars and practitioners about advanced prototyping innovations in this field"-- Provided by publisher.
   Includes bibliographical references and index.
   ISBN 978-1-4666-1797-1 (hardcover) -- ISBN 978-1-4666-1798-8 (ebook) -- ISBN 978-1-4666-1799-5 (print & perpetual access) 1. Wireless communication systems--Design and construction. I. Matin, Mohammad A., 1977-
   TK5103.2.D496 2012
   621.39'81--dc23
                                   2012002870

British Cataloguing in Publication Data
A Cataloguing in Publication record for this book is available from the British Library.

All work contributed to this book is new, previously-unpublished material. The views expressed in this book are those of the authors, but not necessarily of the publisher.

Library
University of Texas
at San Antonio

Editorial Advisory Board

B. S. Sharif, *Newcastle University, UK*
Mohd Alauddin Mohd Ali, *National University of Malaysia (UKM), Malaysia*
Kun-chan Lan, *National Cheng Kung University, Taiwan*
John Hale, *University of Tulsa, USA*
Mahbub Hassan, *University of New South Wales, Australia*
Yichuang Sun, *University of Hertfordshire, UK*
Asrar Ul Haq Sheikh, *King Fahd University of Petroleum & Minerals (KFUPM), Saudi Arabia*
Mauricio Papa, *University of Tulsa, USA*
Ignas G. M. M. Niemegeers, *Delft University of Technology, Netherlands*
Romano Fantacci, *University of Florence, Italy*

Table of Contents

Section 5
Services and Applications

Detailed Table of Contents

Section 1
Fundamentals and Security Issues

> *M. A. Matin, Institut Teknologi Brunei, Brunei Darussalam*

Wireless networks offer mobility and elimination of unsightly cables and utilize radio waves or microwaves to maintain communication. It is rapidly growing in popularity for both home and business networking. Wireless technology keeps on improving and at the same time the cost of wireless products are continuously decreasing. The demand for ubiquitous personal communications is driving the development of wireless networks that can accommodate mobile voice and data users who move throughout buildings, cities, or countries. The objective of this chapter is to provide the fundamentals of wireless networks so that the general readers can be able to easily grasp some of the ideas in this area.

> *Md. Zahurul Islam Sarkar, Queen's University Belfast, UK*

Nakagami-m fading channel is chosen to analyze the secrecy capacity for fading channels since the Nakagami-m distribution can model fading conditions, which are more or less severe than that of Rayleigh and has the advantage of including Rayleigh as a special case. At first, secrecy capacity is defined in case of full channel state information (CSI) at the transmitter, where transmitter has access to both the main channel and eavesdropper channel gains. Secondly, secrecy capacity is defined with only main channel CSI at the transmitter. Then, optimal power allocation at the transmitter that achieves the secrecy capacity is derived for both the cases. Moreover, secrecy capacity is defined under open-loop transmission scheme, and the exact closed form analytical expression for the lower bound of ergodic secrecy capacity is derived for Nakagami-m fading single-input multiple-output (SIMO) channel. In addition, secrecy capacity is defined for the AWGN channel in order to realize the information-theoretic security of wireless channels with no fading. Finally, analytical expressions for the probability of non-zero secrecy capacity and secure outage probability are derived in order to investigate the secure outage performance of fading channels.

Peter J. Hawrylak, The University of Tulsa, USA
John Hale, The University of Tulsa, USA
Mauricio Papa, The University of Tulsa, USA

Radio frequency identification (RFID) devices have matured to the point where they are now expanding beyond the retail supply chain and public transit fare management systems. RFID technology provides a low power and economical method to link remote sensors to larger control systems. In these cases, the RFID protocols provide the communication link between the sensor and larger control system. Security solutions designed for the retail and transit fare management systems are not sufficient for these new control systems. New avenues of attack are available, and attackers have different goals. Therefore, the security of these RFID protocols must be re-examined in order to identify those vulnerabilities that are not significant in the retail or fare applications, but could be exploited in these new settings. This chapter analyzes the ISO 18000-6 Type C protocol to identify potential security vulnerabilities. This protocol is one of the major RFID protocols for passive RFID systems.

Andrea Vesco, Istituto Superiore Mario Boella, Italy
Riccardo Scopigno, Istituto Superiore Mario Boella, Italy

This chapter presents a novel weakly synchronous and distributed coordination function, called Time-Division Unbalanced Carrier Sense Multiple Access (TD-uCSMA). TD-uCSMA relies on synchronization among nodes and the contextual switching of channel access parameters to enable resource management and Quality of Service (QoS) provisioning over CSMA/CA wireless access networks. The TD-uCSMA operating principles and issue of synchronization are presented in detail. Moreover a signalling architecture is here designed, for the first time, to enable dynamic and distributed resource reservation over the wireless network by means of two protocols: the Resource Reservation Protocols with Traffic Engineering (RSVP-TE), properly extended to work in TD-uCSMA networks and the new Resource State Management Protocol (RSMP). The TD-uCSMA operating principles and the signalling architecture are then validated by simulation over many scenarios comprising multi-hop wireless access networks. Finally the chapter addresses the issue of prototyping TD-uCSMA by open source IEEE 802.11 legacy drivers.

Section 2
Coding for Wireless Systems

Giulio Bartoli, University of Firenze, Italy
Francesco Chiti, University of Firenze, Italy
Romano Fantacci, University of Firenze, Italy
Dania Marabissi, University of Firenze, Italy
Andrea Tassi, University of Firenze, Italy

Network coding (NC) is a promising technique recently proposed to improve network performance in terms of maximum throughput, minimum delivery delay, and energy consumption. The original proposal highlighted the advantages of NC for multicast communications in wire-line networks. Recently, network coding has been considered as an efficient approach to improve performance in wireless networks, mainly in terms of data reliability and lower energy consumption, especially for broadcast communications. The basic idea of NC is to remove the typical requirement that different information flows have to be processed and transmitted independently through the network. When NC is applied, intermediate nodes in the network do not simply relay the received packets, but they combine several received packets before transmission. As a consequence, the output flow at a given node is obtained as a linear combination of its input flows. This chapter deals with the application of network coding principle at different communications layers of the protocol stack, specifically, the Medium Access Control (MAC) and physical (PHY) Layers for wireless communication networks.

Chapter 6
Ahmed Bannour, Higher School of Communications of Tunis Sup'Com, Tunisia

Mohamed Lassaad Ammari, Higher School of Communications of Tunis Sup'Com, Tunisia

Yichuang Sun, University of Hertfordshire, UK

Ridha Bouallegue, Higher School of Communications of Tunis Sup'Com, Tunisia

The Algebraic Space Time Codes (ASTC) are constructed based on cyclic algebras; they showed a good spectral efficiency, a full diversity, and a full rate under non selective channel condition. However, the radio - mobile channel is a selective channel whose features vary during the time. This selectivity is owed to the multi-path phenomenon and generates interferences between symbols (IES). The overall objective of this chapter is to proof that ASTC is adapted to channel selectivity, in order to analyze and improve its performances in wide-band system.

Chapter 7
Elsadig Saeid, Universiti Teknologi PETRONAS, Malaysia

Varun Jeoti, Universiti Teknologi PETRONAS, Malaysia

Brahim Belhaouari Samir, Universiti Teknologi PETRONAS, Malaysia

Future Wireless Networks are expected to adopt multi-user multiple input multiple output (MU-MIMO) systems whose performance is maximized by making use of precoding at the transmitter. This chapter describes the recent advances in precoding design for MU-MIMO and introduces a new technique to improve the precoder performance. Without claiming to be comprehensive, the chapter gives deep introduction on basic MIMO techniques covering the basics of single user multiple input multiple output (SU-MIMO) links, its capacity, various transmission strategies, SU-MIMO link precoding, and MIMO receiver structures. After the introduction, MU-MIMO system model is defined and maximum achievable rate regions for both MU-MIMO broadcast and MU-MIMO multiple access channels are explained. It is followed by critical literature review on linear precoding design for MU-MIMO broadcast channel. This paves the way for introducing an improved technique of precoding design that is followed by its performance evaluation.

Section 3
Network Design

Chapter 8

A key component for Vehicular Ad-Hoc Network (VANET) simulations is a realistic vehicular mobility model, as this ensures that the conclusions drawn from simulation experiments will carry through to the real deployments. Node mobility in a vehicular network is strongly affected by the driving behavior such as route choices. While route choice models have been extensively studied in the transportation community, the effects of preferred route and destination on vehicular network simulations have not been discussed much in the networking literature. In this chapter, the authors describe the effect of route choices on vehicular network simulation. They also discuss how different destination selection models affect two practical ITS application scenarios: traffic monitoring and event broadcasting. The chapter concludes that selecting a sufficient level of detail in the simulations, such as modeling of route choices, is critical for evaluating VANET protocol design.

Chapter 9

Designing future computer networks dictates an eclectic vision capable of encompassing ideas and concepts developed in contemporary research unfettered by today's operational and technological constraints. However, unguided by a clear articulation of core design principles, the process of network design may be at stake of falling into similar pitfalls and limitations attributed to current network realizations. This chapter presents CORM: a clean-slate Concern-Oriented Reference Model for architecting future computer networks. CORM stands as a guiding framework from which several network architectures can be derived. CORM represents a pioneering attempt within the network realm, and to the author's knowledge, CORM is the first reference model that is bio-inspired, accounts for complex system characteristics, and applies a software engineering approach to network design. Moreover, CORM's derivation process conforms to the Function-Behavior-Structure (FBS) engineering framework, which is credited to be applicable to any engineering discipline for reasoning about, and explaining the process of design.

Section 4
Cognitive Radio Networking

Chapter 10

Cognitive radio (CR) is a new technology introduced to deal with the issues of spectrum scarcity and underutilization. Since the spectrum is limited, the unlicensed secondary users (CR users) opportunistically access the underutilized spectrum allocated to the licensed primary users (PUs) of the network.

This chapter first gives a brief overview on spectrum sensing and its impact on the system throughput in a cognitive radio network. Later, cooperative relays are introduced in the network to improve spectrum efficiency and mitigate interference to PU. A detailed analysis of power allocation is demonstrated where the transmit power of CR is kept within such limit so that it can maintain low interference to PU. This optimal power allocation can achieve high throughput, which is also presented in this chapter.

Danda B. Rawat, Eastern Kentucky University, USA
Gongjun Yan, Indiana University-Kokomo, USA
Bhed Bahadur Bista, Iwate Prefectural University, Japan

The rising number and capacity requirements of wireless systems bring increasing demand for RF spectrum. Cognitive radio (CR) system is an emerging concept to increase the spectrum efficiency. CR system aims to enable opportunistic usage of the RF bands that are not occupied by their primary licensed users in spectrum overlay approach. In this approach, the major challenge in realizing the full potential of CR systems is to identify the spectrum opportunities in the wide band regime reliably and optimally. In the spectrum underlay approach, CR systems enable dynamic spectrum access by co-existing and transmitting simultaneously with licensed primary users without creating harmful interference to them. In this case, the challenge is to transmit with low power so as not to exceed the tolerable interference level to the primary users. Spectrum sensing and estimation is an integral part of the CR system, which is used to identify the spectrum opportunities in spectrum overlay and to identify the interference power to primary users in spectrum underlay approach. In this chapter, the authors present a comprehensive study of signal detection techniques for spectrum sensing proposed for CR systems. Specifically, they outline the state of the art research results, challenges, and future perspectives of spectrum sensing in CR systems, and also present a comparison of different methods. With this chapter, readers can have a comprehensive insight of signal processing methods of spectrum sensing for cognitive radio networks and the ongoing research and development in this area.

Raza Umar, King Fahd University of Petroleum and Minerals, Saudi Arabia
Asrar U. H. Sheikh, King Fahd University of Petroleum and Minerals, Saudi Arabia

Cognitive radio (CR) has emerged as a smart solution to spectrum bottleneck faced by current wireless services, under which licensed spectrum is made available to intelligent and reconfigurable secondary users. CR technology enables these unlicensed secondary users to exploit any spectrum usage opportunity by adapting their transmission parameters on the run. In this chapter, the authors discuss the characteristic features and main functionality of CR oriented technology. Central to this chapter is Spectrum sensing (SS), which has been identified as a fundamental enabling technology for next generation wireless networks based on CR. The authors compare different SS techniques in terms of their sensing accuracy and implementation and computational complexities along with merits and demerits of these approaches. Various challenges facing SS have been investigated, and possible solutions are proposed.

Section 5
Services and Applications

Chapter 13

Cheng Guo, Delft University of Technology, The Netherlands
R. Venkatesha Prasad, Delft University of Technology, The Netherlands
Jing Wang, Delft University of Technology, The Netherlands
Vijay Sathyanarayana Rao, Delft University of Technology, The Netherlands
Ignas Niemegeers, Delft University of Technology, The Netherlands

Context awareness is an important aspect in many ICT applications. For example, in an intelligent home network, location of the user enables session transfer, lighting, and temperature control, et cetera. In fact, in a body area sensor network (BASN), location estimation of a user helps in realizing realtime monitoring of the person (especially those who require help) for better health supervision. In this chapter the authors first introduce many localization methods and algorithms from the literature in BASNs. They also present classification of these methods. Amongst them, location estimation using signal strength is one of the foremost. In indoor environments, the authors found that the signal strength based localization methods are usually not accurate, since signal strength fluctuates. The fluctuation in signal strength is due to deficient antenna coverage and multi-path interference. Thus, localization algorithms usually fail to achieve good accuracy. The authors propose to solve this problem by combining multiple receivers in a body area sensor network to estimate the location with a higher accuracy. This method mitigates the errors caused by antenna orientations and beam forming properties. The chapter evaluates the performance of the solution with experiments. It is tested with both range-based and range-free localization algorithm that we developed. The chapter shows that with spatial diversity, the localization accuracy is improved compared to using single receiver alone. Moreover, the authors observe that range-based algorithm has a better performance.

Chapter 14

Kun-chan Lan, National Cheng Kung University, Taiwan
Zhe Wang, University of New South Wales, Australia
Mahbub Hassan, University of New South Wales, Australia
Tim Moors, University of New South Wales, Australia
Rodney Berriman, National ICT Australia, Australia
Lavy Libman, National ICT Australia, Australia
Maximilian Ott, National ICT Australia, Australia
Bjorn Landfeldt, National ICT Australia, Australia
Zainab Zaidi, National ICT Australia, Australia
Ching-Ming Chou, National Cheng Kung University, Taiwan

Wireless mesh networks (WMN) have attracted considerable interest in recent years as a convenient, new technology. However, the suitability of WMN for mission-critical infrastructure applications remains by and large unknown, as protocols typically employed in WMN are, for the most part, not designed for real-time communications. In this chapter, the authors describe a wireless mesh network architecture to solve the communication needs of the traffic control system in Sydney. This system, known as SCATS and used in over 100 cities around the world — from individual traffic light controllers to regional computers and the central TMC —places stringent requirements on the reliability and latency of the data exchanges. The authors discuss experience in the deployment of an initial testbed consisting of 7 mesh nodes placed at intersections with traffic lights, and share the results and insights learned from measurements and initial trials in the process.

Preface

The Wireless Communication Network is developing at an accelerated pace enabling real-time multimedia services. The last few years have experienced a rapid growth in research on wireless networks having attractive outcomes. Researchers are currently envisioning different attractive properties of wireless networks. The expectations are increasing about what the current and future generation wireless network can do for a wide range of applications. Successful design and deployment of wireless networks, thus, call for technology advances. This book offers the basics as well as advanced research materials for wireless networks. The book highlights the current design issues, which put the reader in good pace to be able to understand more advanced research and make a contribution in this field for themselves. It is believed that the students who seek to learn the latest development in wireless technologies will need this book.

Chapter 1 provides the fundamentals of wireless networks so that the general readers can be able to easily grasp some of the ideas in this area.

Chapter 2 focuses the most recent research on secure communications where a legitimate user communicates with a legitimate receiver in the presence of an eavesdropper. Perfect secrecy is achieved when the transmitter and the legitimate receiver can communicate at some positive rate, while insuring that eavesdropper gets zero bits of information.

Chapter 3 analyzes the ISO 18000-6 Type C protocol, which is one of the major radio frequency identification (RFID) protocols for passive RFID systems to identify potential security vulnerabilities. RFID provides a low power and economical method to link remote sensors to larger control systems. Security solutions designed for the retail and transit fare management systems are not sufficient for these new control systems. New avenues of attack are available and attackers have different goals. Therefore, the security of these RFID protocols is re-examined in this chapter.

Chapter 4 presents a novel weakly synchronous and distributed coordination function, called Time-Division *Unbalanced* Carrier Sense Multiple Access (TD-uCSMA). TD-uCSMA relies on synchronization among nodes and the contextual switching of channel access parameters to enable resource management and Quality of Service (QoS) provisioning over CSMA/CA wireless access networks. The TD-uCSMA operating principles and issue of synchronization are discussed in details.

Chapter 5 deals with the application of network coding principle at different communications layers of the protocol stack, specifically, the Medium Access Control (MAC) and physical (PHY) Layers for wireless communication networks. Network coding (NC) is a promising technique recently proposed to improve network performance in terms of maximum throughput, minimum delivery delay, and energy consumption. Recently, it has been considered as an efficient approach to improve performance in wireless networks, mainly in terms of data reliability and lower energy consumption, especially for broadcast communications.

Chapter 6 presents Algebraic Space Time Coding (ASTC) to frequency selective channels. The authors consider the MIMO-OFDM system with Algebraic Space Time Coding (ASTC), threaded algebraic space-time (TAST) and Diagonal Algebraic Space Time (DAST) coding. The OFDM technique allows overcoming the channel selectivity. Thus, the ASTC codes can still maintain their properties and achieve good capacity under frequency selective channels.

Chapter 7 describes the recent advances in precoder design for multi-user multiple input multiple output (MU-MIMO) and introduces a new technique to improve the precoder performance. MU-MIMO is expected to adopt for future wireless networks.

Chapter 8 provides a realistic vehicular mobility model in order to have a holistic view of the network functioning. Mobility model deals with the realistic representation of vehicular movement including mobility pattern.

Chapter 9 presents Concern-Oriented Reference Model (CORM) for architecting future computer networks. CORM stands as a guiding framework from which several network architectures can be derived. CORM represents a pioneering attempt within the network realm, and to the best of the authors' knowledge, it is the first reference model that is bio-inspired, accounts for complex system characteristics, and applies a software engineering approach to network design. Moreover, CORM's derivation process conforms to the function-behavior-structure (FBS) engineering framework, which is credited to be applicable to most of the engineering discipline for reasoning about, and explaining the process of design.

Chapter 10 first gives a brief overview on spectrum sensing and its impact on the system throughput in a cognitive radio (CR) network. Later on, the chapter provides a detailed analysis of power allocation to achieve maximum throughput. Cognitive radio is a new technology introduced to deal with the issues of spectrum scarcity and underutilization. It has emerged as a smart solution under which licensed spectrum is made available to intelligent and reconfigurable secondary users.

Chapter 11 outlines the state-of-the-art research results, challenges and future perspectives of spectrum sensing in CR systems, and also presents a comparison of different methods. It provides a comprehensive insight of signal processing methods of spectrum sensing for cognitive radio networks and the ongoing research and development in this area.

Chapter 12 compares different spectrum sensing techniques in terms of their sensing accuracy, implementation, and computational complexities, along with merits and demerits of these approaches and proposed possible solutions.

Chapter 13 first introduces different localization methods and algorithms which are available in the body area sensor networks (BASNs) literature and later on presents their own approach for localizing person. The location estimation of a user in a BASN helps in realizing real-time monitoring of the person for better health supervision.

Chapter 14 describes wireless mesh network architecture to solve the communication needs of the traffic control system in Sydney. This system, known as SCATS and used in over 100 cities around the world — from individual traffic light controllers to regional computers and the central TMC —places stringent requirements on the reliability and latency of the data exchanges.

It is hoped that this book serves as a comprehensive reference for graduate students and that it will be a useful learning tool for research in this exciting field.

Mohammad A. Matin
North South University, Bangladesh

Section 1
Fundamentals and Security Issues

Chapter 1
Introduction to Wireless Networks

M. A. Matin
Institut Teknologi Brunei, Brunei Darussalam

ABSTRACT

Wireless networks offer mobility and elimination of unsightly cables and utilize radio waves or microwaves to maintain communication. It is rapidly growing in popularity for both home and business networking. Wireless technology keeps on improving and at the same time the cost of wireless products are continuously decreasing. The demand for ubiquitous personal communications is driving the development of wireless networks that can accommodate mobile voice and data users who move throughout buildings, cities, or countries. The objective of this chapter is to provide the fundamentals of wireless networks so that the general readers can be able to easily grasp some of the ideas in this area.

INTRODUCTION

Wireless networks have been a crucial part of communication in the last few decades and a truly revolutionary paradigm shift, enabling multimedia communications between people and devices from any location (Figure 1). It brings fundamental changes to data networking, telecommunication, and is making integrated networks. It has made the network portable because of digital modulation, adaptive modulation, information compression, wireless access and multiplexing. It supports ex-

citing applications such as sensor networks, smart homes, telemedicine, and automated highways. Early users of wireless technology primarily have been the military, emergency services, and law enforcement organizations. As the society moves toward information centricity, the need to have information accessible at anytime and anywhere takes on a new dimension. With the rapid growth of mobile telephony and networks, the vision of a mobile information society (introduced by Nokia) is slowly becoming a reality. It is common to see people communicating via their mobile phones and devices. With today's networks and coverage, it

DOI: 10.4018/978-1-4666-1797-1.ch001

Copyright © 2012, IGI Global. Copying or distributing in print or electronic forms without written permission of IGI Global is prohibited.

is possible for a user to have connectivity almost anywhere. The growth in commercial wireless networks occurred primarily in the late 1980s and 1990s. The huge competition in the wireless industry and the mass acceptance of wireless devices have caused costs associated with the terminals and air time to come down significantly in the last 10 years.

BENEFITS OF WIRELESS NETWORKS

Wireless networking is potentially a quick, easy and economical alternative that works between nodes and is executed without the use of wires around our home or office. It also opens up pos-

sibilities for connecting buildings which are up to several kilometres apart. It offers consistent and effectual keys to a number of instant applications therefore at present it is used under numerous diverse platforms such as health care, education, finance, hospitality, airport, and retail. The usage of wireless network increases day by day, because it has significant impact on the world. Therefore its uses have appreciably grown-up. The benefits of wireless networks are summarized as below:

- User can move about and get access to the wireless network while working at an outdoor location.
- User can send information over the world using satellites and other signals through wireless networks.

Figure 1. Typical networking scenario of a person with various personal devices (Source: WiMedia, Ecma International 2010)

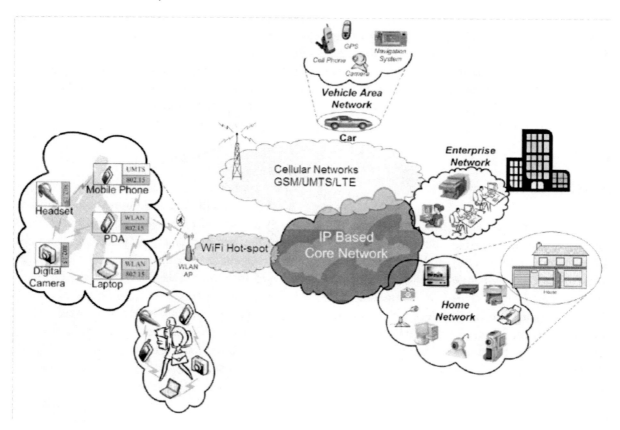

- Now-a-days, wireless network is used in emergency services like police department where wireless network is utilized to communicate significant information rapidly.
- The growth of wireless network is increasing both in people and businesses to send and share data swiftly in a small office or across the world.
- Wireless networks offer high speed internet is as a cheap and compatible with peer-to-peer mode.
- Wireless networks make easy of file sharing, the use of printer and other documents with high security.
- Wireless network makes this world a global village in real.

WIRELESS DATA SERVICES

A wireless network joins two or more computers by means of communication without using any wires. It has different functional parts such as radios base stations and mobile networks and utilizes spread-spectrum or OFDM depending on the technology being used. Wireless networks enable a user to move about within a wide coverage area and still be associated to the network. There are different types of wireless networking such as wide area network, local area network and personal area network. UWB and Bluetooth can be used as wireless personal area network. Wireless network now has been a Broadband wireless with great invention of Wi-Fi and WiMAX networks. Wi-Fi, cellular and WiMAX offer fast and reliable connection, but each has a different set of strengths and weaknesses. For short range and for access to local area networks for internet, Wi-Fi is the obvious choice (see also Figure 2). On the other hand, WiMAX and cellular allow connecting to internet without the need to search for a new hotspot and are considered a huge improvement over a slow dial up internet services.

Wireless Wide Area Network (WWAN)

Wireless wide area networks technologies (Ghosh et al 2010) (3GPP.org, WiMax forum) provide broadband Internet access to mobile subscriber and typically cover large areas, such as between neighbouring towns and cities, or city and suburb. These networks can be used to connect branch offices of business or as a public internet access system. The wireless connections between access points are usually point to point microwave links using parabolic dishes on the 2.4 GHz band. Emerging heterogeneous WWANs can provide increased availability of mobile data connectivity with increased data rates.

Cellular Mobile Wireless Systems

Several broadband wireless data services are the extension of cellular mobile technology. The earliest phones were only good for voice calls, but as each new generation was introduced, mobile telephony offered more and better features. The recent exponential growth in cellular systems throughout the world is directly attributable to new technologies of the 1970's, which are mature today. Figure 3 describes the various generations. The great advantage of a mobile broadband service is that it covers a much wider territory than any Wi-Fi base station. For people who use their computers away from their home or office, are connected to the Internet without the need to search for a new hot spot and the use of a different access account in each new location. Now-a-days, it is possible to keep the same connection alive in a moving vehicle. Each of the major wireless broadband services offers coverage in most metropolitan areas. The 2G standards are the first set of wireless air interface standards to rely on digital modulation and sophisticated digital signal processing in the handset and the base station. Even with relatively small user data rates, 2G standards are able to support limited internet browsing. Of course,

Figure 2. The IEEE 802.22 standard relative to other IEEE 802 wireless data transmission standards (Stevenson et al. (2009))

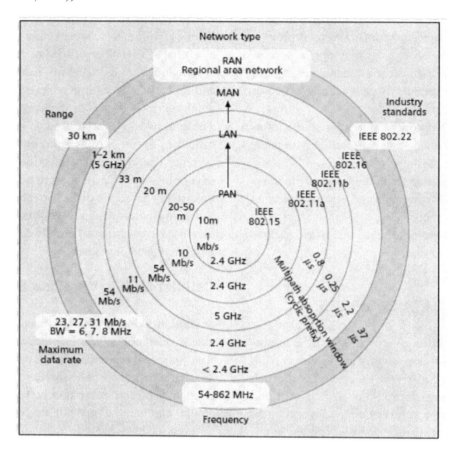

computer technology has also been improving at the same time, so today's 2.5G and 3G mobile telephones often incorporate enough computing power to allow them to double as pocket-size Internet terminals (as well as cameras and media players) and broadband data adapters that use 2.5G and 3G technology can attach to a laptop or other portable computer and provide a direct wireless connection to the Internet. Companies developing 3G equipments envision users having the ability to receive live music, conduct interactive web sessions, and have simultaneous voice and data access with multiple parties at the same time using a single mobile handset at any time, any where. Today, most cellular broadband wireless services offer credit card–size adapters that connect to your computer through the PC Card

socket on the side of a laptop or into the front or back panel of a desktop computer. Many new laptops will come in near future with internal adapters and integrated antennas for both Wi-Fi and 3G wireless or WiMAX that mount directly on the motherboard, just as they contain internal Wi-Fi adapters and dial-up modems today. 4G is the fourth generation of cellular wireless standards. It is a successor to the 3G and 2G families of standards. In 2009, the ITU-R organization specified the requirements for 4G standards, setting peak speed requirements for 4G service at 100 Mbps for high mobility communication (such as from trains and cars) and 1 Gbps for low mobility communication (such as pedestrians and stationary users). It is expected to provide all IP-based mobile broadband solution.

Figure 3. Different generations of cellular mobile

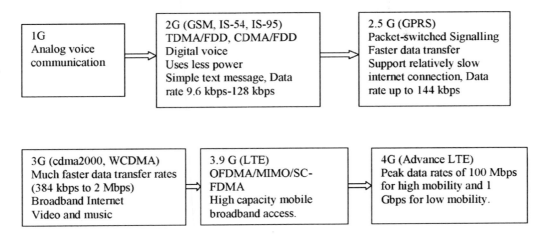

WiMAX

Worldwide Interoperability for Microwave Access (WiMAX) is an IP based, wireless broadband access technology for distributing broadband wireless data and provides performance similar to 802.11/Wi-Fi networks with the coverage and QOS (quality of service) of cellular networks. It is intended for wireless "metropolitan area networks" that typically uses one or more base stations that can provide service to users within a 30-mile (50 Km) radius. The IEEE 802.16 specification contains the technical details of WiMAX networks. WiMAX, 3G cellular data services, and metropolitan Wi-Fi networks will compete for the same commercial niche such as wireless access to the Internet through a service that covers an entire metro-politan area. Each WiMAX service provider uses one or more licensed operating frequencies somewhere between 2 GHz and 11 GHz. A WiMAX link can transfer data (including handshaking and other overhead) at up to 1Gbps for fixed station, but most commercial WiMAX services are significantly slower than that. In addition, more and more users share a single WiMAX tower and base station, some users' report that their signal quality deteriorates. Unlike the cellular broadband wireless data services that piggyback on existing mobile telephone networks, WiMAX is a separate radio system that is designed to either supplement or replace the existing broadband Internet distribution systems. In practice, WiMAX competes with both 3G wireless services and with Internet service providers that distribute Internet access to fixed locations through telephone lines and cable television utilities. The more recent Long Term Evolution (LTE) standard is a similar term describing a parallel technology to WiMAX that is being developed by vendors and carriers as a counterpoint to WiMAX. Home and business subscribers to a WiMAX service usually use either a wired LAN or Wi-Fi to distribute the network within their buildings. Figure 4 shows a typical WiMAX-3GPP2 Interworking Network architecture.

Wireless Local Area Network (WLAN)

Wireless local area networking (WLAN) products conform to the 802.11 standards upon which wireless networking devices are built. The gear a person needs to build wireless networks include network adapters (NICs), access points (APs), and routers. The WEP technology used in WLAN elevates the rank of security. WLANs have expanded well-built status in a different kind of markets during the last

Figure 4. WiMAX-3GPP2 interworking network architecture (Source: WiMAX Forum)

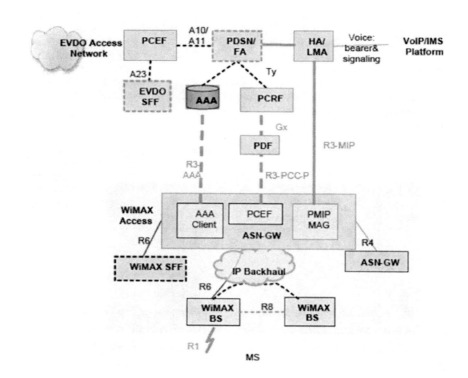

decade and set up to offer wireless connectivity within a limited exposure area which may be a hospital, an university, airport, health care provider or a gas plant. The technology used in WLANs is Spread Spectrum developed by the military offer secure and reliable services. Frequency-hopping spread-spectrum maintains a single logical channel and Direct-Sequence Spread Spectrum offers chip pattern to make it more effective to be used infrared technology. Wireless LAN adapters are necessary for regular computer platforms. The benefits of WLAN are high range and coverage, high throughput, resist to mulitpath interference, integrity, interoperability with wired infrastructure, interoperability with wireless infrastructure, simplicity and ease of use, security, low cost, scalability and, safety which make a wireless network in real, a great platform.

Table 1 summarizes some of the features for the 802.11 standards.

In general, 802.11b/g devices will usually cover a house quite well, but there are no guarantees. In addition, for 802.11g, the connection speeds will drop in order to get a reliable link. In fact, 802.11g product with up to 54MB provides similar performance to an old 802.11b device which is only up to 11MB speed. This technology uses frequency-hopping spread spectrum and direct-sequence spread spectrum approaches for data transmission. The signal of this technology penetrates better through wooden floors and ceilings than through brick walls, and has no chance at all through concrete or stone. The use of an access point in the loft connected to a directional antenna pointing down from the rafters has proved to be an effective way to get full coverage in a typical house. 802.11a/5GHz radio, although costing a little more than 2.4GHz products is the future for wireless networking in buildings as it can give improved non-line-of-site (NLOS) capabilities over 2.4GHz devices.

Table 1. 802.11 standards

Standard	Max. Data Rate	Frequency	Modulation	features
802.11a	54 Mbps	5.1-5.8GHz	OFDM	Popular for outdoor links. The large number of non-overlapping channels compared with the 2.4GHz band might end up making 5GHz more popular for 11n WiFi.
802.11b	11 Mbps	2.4GHz	DSSS	Suitable for both internal and inter-building applications
802.11g	54 Mbps	2.4GHz	OFDM, DSSS	OFDM 2.4GHz standard gives much the same functionality as 802.11b but at higher data rates. The OFDM standard is supposed to give improvements over the older 11b products for indoor (non-line-of-site) use. Most WiFi nowadays uses 11g.
802.11n	Up to 600 Mbps	Available for 2.4Ghz and 5GHz frequencies	OFDM	Uses 40MHz wide channels though devices normally have the option to use single stream 20MHz WiFi channels. Due to pressures from the WiFi chip manufacturers 11n is looking like becoming the de-facto standard in the next few years.

Figure 5. Potential application scenarios of UWB (Oppermann, 2004)

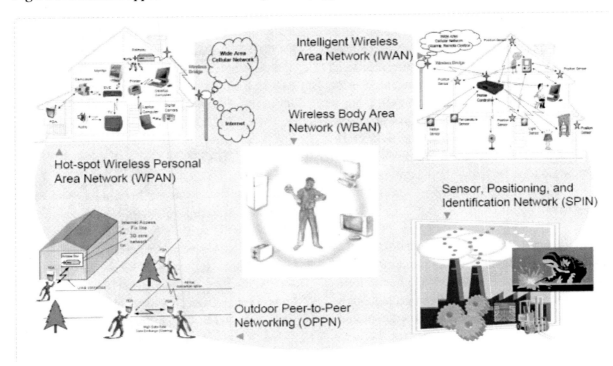

Wireless Personal Area Networks (WPAN)

UWB

UWB and Wi-Fi are seen as complementary technologies for the most part because Wi-Fi is a wireless local area network (WLAN) while UWB is a wireless personal area network (WPAN). The only area in which there is an overlap between these two technologies is in wireless video applications. Currently, Wi-Fi is not an effective method to distribute video applications wirelessly, because the peak transfer rate of 54 Mbps is much too slow for video applications (Matin M A (2010)). UWB is a superior technology in video applications because it peak transfer rates are in excess of 100 Mbps (see also Figure 5). The global interest in this technology is huge especially in communications environment due to the potential delivery of ultra high speed data transmission, coexistence with existing electrical systems (due to the extremely low power spectrum density) with low power consumption using a low cost on-chip implementation. The spectrum allocation for UWB is in the range of 1.99 GHz-10.6 GHz, 3.1 GHz- 10.6 GHz, or below 960 MHz depending on the particular application.

Bluetooth

Bluetooth wireless networking technology uses radio signals to replace the wires and cables within the person's personal workspace. Bluetooth devices connect a computer or a mobile telephone to peripheral devices, such as a keyboard, a mouse, or a set of speakers and transfer data between them. It uses low power levels and generally does not require a license for spectrum use. Each Bluetooth radio channel has a 1 MHz bandwidth and hops at a rate of approximately 1600 hops per second. Bluetooth is not practical for connecting a computer to the Internet because the maximum data transfer rate is only about 2.1 Mbps which is low, and it has a very limited signal range (most often about 33 feet, or 10 meters, or less). The standard has been designed to support operation in high interference environmets and relies on a number of forward error control (FEC) coding and automatic repeat request (ARQ) schemes to support a raw channel bit error rate (BER) to prevent interference between Bluetooth and Wi-Fi signals.

ZigBee

ZigBee is built on IEEE 802.15.4 standard and uses small, low-power digital radios for WPAN applications such as wireless light switches, electrical meters with in-home-displays, and other consumer and industrial equipment. The zigbee devices typically require low power and are deployed in the 2.4 GHz frequency. ZigBee has a defined rate of 250 kbps best suited for periodic or intermittent data or a single signal transmission from a sensor or input device (embedded-computing.com).

CONCLUSION

In the past few decades, there has been a rapid growth in wireless networks which consists of wireless wide area networks (WWAN), wireless local area networks (WLAN), and wireless personal area networks (WPAN). Devices used for this exciting technology have become small, low power and low cost which in turn accelerated their widespread use in hospital, organizations, universities, airports, health care departments, stores, and much more. The concluding remark is wireless network have made this world a global village in real.

REFERENCES

Ghosh, A., Ratasuk, R., Mondal, B., Mangalvedhe, N., & Thomas, T. (2010). LTE-advanced: Next generation wireless broadband technology. *IEEE Wireless Communications Magazine*, *17*(3), 10–22. doi:10.1109/MWC.2010.5490974

Matin, M. A. (2010). Ultra wideband preliminaries. In Lembrikov, B. (Ed.), *Ultra wideband*. Intech Publisher. doi:10.5772/10059

Oppermann, I. (2004). *An overview of UWB activities within PULSERS*. Paper presented in Ultra- Wideband Seminar in Singapore.

Stevenson, C. R., Chouinard, G., Lei, Z., Hu, W., Shellhammer, S., & Caldwell, W. (2009). IEEE 802.22: The first cognitive radio wireless regional area network standard. *IEEE Communications Magazine*, *47*(1), 130–138. doi:10.1109/MCOM.2009.4752688

Chapter 2
Secure Communications over Wireless Networks

Md. Zahurul Islam Sarkar
Queen's University Belfast, UK

ABSTRACT

Nakagami-m fading channel is chosen to analyze the secrecy capacity for fading channels since the Nakagami-m distribution can model fading conditions, which are more or less severe than that of Rayleigh and has the advantage of including Rayleigh as a special case. At first, secrecy capacity is defined in case of full channel state information (CSI) at the transmitter, where transmitter has access to both the main channel and eavesdropper channel gains. Secondly, secrecy capacity is defined with only main channel CSI at the transmitter. Then, optimal power allocation at the transmitter that achieves the secrecy capacity is derived for both the cases. Moreover, secrecy capacity is defined under open-loop transmission scheme, and the exact closed form analytical expression for the lower bound of ergodic secrecy capacity is derived for Nakagami-m fading single-input multiple-output (SIMO) channel. In addition, secrecy capacity is defined for the AWGN channel in order to realize the information-theoretic security of wireless channels with no fading. Finally, analytical expressions for the probability of non-zero secrecy capacity and secure outage probability are derived in order to investigate the secure outage performance of fading channels.

1. INTRODUCTION

This chapter is concerned with the study of secrecy capacity and secure outage performance for the wireless channels, focusing on the recent research of secure communications where a legitimate user communicates with a legitimate receiver in the presence of an eavesdropper. Perfect secrecy is achieved when the transmitter and the legitimate receiver can communicate at some positive rate, while insuring that eavesdropper gets zero bits of information. Specifically, two different channels, such as fading and additive white Gaussian noise (AWGN) channels are considered for the study. The open nature of wireless communication network makes it susceptible to eavesdropping and fraud. As a result, the privacy and security

DOI: 10.4018/978-1-4666-1797-1.ch002

Copyright © 2012, IGI Global. Copying or distributing in print or electronic forms without written permission of IGI Global is prohibited.

in wireless communication networks have taken on an increasingly important role, as these networks are used to transmit personal information. Moreover, the problems of cryptography and secrecy systems furnish an interesting application of communication theory. Traditionally, channel fading has been viewed as a source of unreliability of communication. Therefore, the natural problem of great interest is, how we can achieve high data rates with reliability in spite of the harsh wireless channel subject to the fading, limited power and bandwidth resources. Since the goal of this work is to achieve reliable communication at the maximum possible data rate, the relevant information-theoretic measure is secrecy capacity (i.e. the maximum transmission rate at which the eavesdropper is unable to decode any information) of the channel. The probability of non-zero secrecy capacity and secure outage probability are the measures of secure outage performance for the relevant channel model. Moreover, security issues arising in wireless communication networks include *confidentiality*, integrity, authentication and nonrepudiation. Confidentiality is the measure of reliability which guarantees that legitimate receiver successfully receives the intended information from the source node, while eavesdroppers are unable to decode any information from the intended information. Integrity guarantees that original information sent by the source node

is not modified by the eavesdroppers during its transmission. Authentication ensures that a recipient of information i.e. legitimate receiver is able to identify the sender of received information i.e. the source of original information from which the information has been sent. Nonrepudiation ensures that a sender of information is not able to deny having transmitted that information and the recipient is not able to deny having received the information.

1.1 Information-Theoretic Analysis of Cryptosystem

The conception of *information-theoretic security* was first introduced by Shannon (Shannon, 1949) to characterize fundamental limits of secure communications over wireless channels. Shannon considers a scenario as shown in Figure 1 where transmitter end contains two information sources such as a message source and a key source. The message source produces a message W which is enciphered to a cryptogram E by a key K shared by the transmitter and receiver. The cryptogram E is sent to the receiving end by a possible interceptible means and the key K is produced by a key source which is transmitted to the receiving end by a messenger. The key must be transmitted by non-interceptible means from transmitter to the receiving point. Sometimes it must be memorized.

Figure 1. Schematic diagram of a cryptosystem

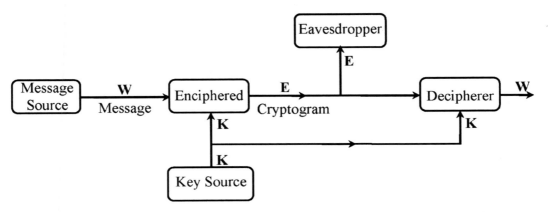

So it is desirable to have the key as small as possible. An eavesdropper, which knows the family of encryption functions (keys) and the probability of choosing keys, may intercept the cryptogram E. At the receiver end the cryptogram E and the key K are combined in the decipherer to recover the original message.

Condition of Perfect Secrecy: The system is considered to be perfectly secure if the *a posteriori* probabilities of W given E are equal to the *a priori* probabilities of W for all E, i.e. $P_E(W) = P(W)$. In other word, the condition of perfect secrecy can be summarized as follows;

Theorem 1. *For any possible message W and cryptogram E, a necessary and sufficient condition for perfect secrecy is that*

$$P_W(E) = P(E) \tag{1}$$

That is, $P_W(E)$ must be independent of W, where $P_W(E)$ is the conditional probability of cryptogram E if message W is chosen and $P(E)$ is the probability of obtaining cryptogram E from any cause.

Proof: Let us suppose the possible messages W are finite in number $W_1, \ldots, W_n$ and have the *a priori* probabilities $P(W_1), \ldots, P(W_n)$ respectively. The messages are enciphered into the possible cryptograms E expressed as the finite number in $E_1, \ldots, E_k$. Then, from Bay's theorem, we have

$$P_E(W) = \frac{P(W) P_W(E)}{P(E)} \tag{2}$$

where, $P_E(W)$ = *a posteriori* probability of message W given E.

$P(W)$ = *a priori* probability of message W.

$P_W(E)$ = conditional probability of cryptogram E if message W is chosen.

$P(E)$ = probability of obtaining cryptogram E from any cause.

For perfect secrecy $P_E(W)$ must be equal to $P(W)$ for all E and W. Thus from (2), we have the result.

It was also shown in (Shannon, 1949), if the number of messages is finite, the same number of possible keys is required to achieve the perfect secrecy. If the message is thought of as being constantly generated at a given rate R (to be defined later), key must be generated at the same or a greater rate to ensure the perfect secrecy.

1.2 Information-Theoretic Security in Wireless Communications

The basic idea of information-theoretic security in wireless network is to transmit confidential messages to a legitimate receiver without using an encryption key and to use the inherent randomness of the physical medium including noises and channel fluctuations due to fading. In this approach, a transmitter intentionally adds structural randomness called stochastic coding to prevent potential eavesdroppers and attackers from intercepting useful information while guaranteeing that a *legitimate receiver* can obtain the information reliably. Figure 2 illustrates a system that exploits the information theoretic security in wireless communications. A legitimate user named Alice wants to send confidential messages to a legitimate receiver named Bob in the presence of an eavesdropper named Eve. The channel between transmitter and legitimate receiver is known as *main channel* and that between transmitter and eavesdropper is known as *eavesdropper channel*.

Advantages of information-theoretic security over cryptosystems: Ensuring perfect secrecy in the wireless communication systems, information theoretic security approach possesses the following advantages compared to the contemporary cryptosystems.

Figure 2. A confidential communication system with transmitter, receiver, and eavesdropper

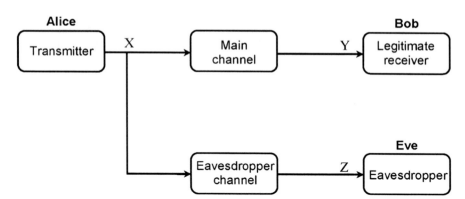

- Information-theoretic security approach eliminates the key management issue which results significantly lower complexity and saving in resources.
- Compared to public-key algorithms for key management in the hybrid cryptosystems, the information-theoretic security approach is less vulnerable to the main-in-the middle attack (Lai et. al., 2009, Maurer, 2000, Rosenbaum, 1993, Walker, 1990) due to the intrinsic randomness shared by terminals.
- Information theoretic security approach exploits the physical layer attributes of channel randomness for secure communications and this approach can be applied to existing cryptosystems to add an additional level of protection for information transmission or to achieve key agreement including key generation and distribution for the remote terminals.
- Information-theoretic security approach achieve provable security which is robust to powerful eavesdroppers possessing unlimited computational resources, knowledge of the communication strategy employed coding and decoding algorithms, and access to communication systems either through perfect or noisy channels.

Related works: Recently, Barros et al. have characterized information-theoretic security in terms of outage probability in (Barros and Rodrigues, 2006) for quasi-static Rayleigh fading channels where both the transmitter and receiver are equipped with single antenna. In the case when transmitter does not know the eavesdropper channel, they define the probability of transmitting at a target secrecy rate R_s bigger than the secrecy capacity C_s (i.e. the outage probability) as the probability that the information theoretic security is compromised. They compute this probability, and also show that the probability of positive secrecy capacity can actually be positive even when the eavesdropper has a better average SNR than the legitimate partners. They extend their work in (Bloch et. al., 2008), and consider the cases when Alice has either imperfect or perfect knowledge of the eavesdropper channel. The ergodic secrecy capacity for Rayleigh fading single-input single-output (SISO) channel was derived in (Gopala et. al., 2008). Based on the concept of (Barros and Rodrigues, 2006, Bloch et. al., 2008, Gopala et. al., 2008), the secrecy capacity of Rayleigh fading SIMO channel was defined in (Sarkar and Ratnarajah, 2011) under different assumptions of transmitter CSI, such as (i) full CSI at the transmitter (ii) only main channel CSI at the transmitter and (iii) open-loop transmission scheme.

The objective of this chapter is to study the measures of information-theoretic security in the fading wireless channels. Traditionally, channel fading has been viewed as a source of unreliability of communication. Therefore, the natural problem of great interest is, how we can achieve high data rates with reliability in spite of the harsh wireless channel subject to the fading, limited power and bandwidth resources. Since our goal is to achieve reliable communication at the maximum possible data rate, the relevant information-theoretic measure is *secrecy capacity* of the channel. In this chapter, Nakagami-m fading channel has been used to generalize the definition of secrecy capacity and to investigate the *secure outage performance* of fading channels. Because, Nakagami-m distribution provides more flexibility in matching experimental data than the Rayleigh, log-normal or Rician distributions. It has the advantage of including Rayleigh as a special case and it can model fading conditions which are more or less severe than that of Rayleigh. Moreover, Nakagami-m distribution has been found to be very good fitting for the mobile radio channel (Suzuki, 1977, Beaulieu and Cheng, 2005). At first, secrecy capacity is defined for full CSI case, where transmitter has access to both the main channel and eavesdropper's channel gains, then secrecy capacity is defined in case of only main channel CSI available at the transmitter. In both the cases, optimal power allocation at the transmitter that achieves the secrecy capacity has been characterized in terms of channel gains. Then, the secure outage performance of fading channels has been analyzed under open-loop transmission scheme using the concept of (Bloch et. al., 2008). The secrecy capacity of AWGN channel has also been discussed in order to realize the information theoretic security of wireless channels with no fading.

2. SECRECY CAPACITY

The secrecy capacity of fading channel which is defined as the maximum transmission rate ensuring that the eavesdropper gets zero bits of information from the main channel can be characterized under (i) full CSI at the transmitter (ii) only main channel CSI at the transmitter and (iii) open-loop transmission scheme. The secrecy capacity under full CSI assumption serves as an upper bound while the secrecy capacity under open-loop transmission scheme might be a lower bound to the secrecy capacity and exists only when the signal-to-noise ratio (SNR) of main channel is greater than that of eavesdropper channel; otherwise the secrecy capacity is zero (Sarkar and Ratnarajah, 2011).

2.1 Expression of Secrecy Capacity for Discrete Memoryless Wiretap Channel

Based on a secure communication system with sender, receiver and eavesdropper as shown in Figure 2, a general expression of secrecy capacity for the discrete memoryless channel can be derived as follows. Suppose X is the transmitted signal and Y and Z are the received signals at the legitimate receiver and eavesdropper, respectively. For a general discrete memoryless wiretap channel with transition probability $\Pr\left(y, z \,\middle|\, x\right)$, a single-letter expression for the secrecy capacity is given by (Liu and Shitz, 2009),

$$C_s = \max_{f(u,x)}\left[I\left(U;Y\right) - I\left(U;Z\right) \right] \qquad (3)$$

where $f\left(u, x\right)$ is the input distribution and U is an auxiliary random variable that satisfies the Markov relation $U \rightarrow X \rightarrow \left(Y, Z\right)$. From (3), the upper bound of the secrecy capacity can be derived as shown in Box 1.

Box 1.

$$C_S \leq \max_{f(u,x)} \left[I(U;Y,Z) - I(U;Z) \right]$$
$$= \max_{f(u,x)} \left[I(X;Y,Z) - I(X;Z) - \left\{ I(X;Y,Z|U) - I(X;Z|U) \right\} \right]$$
$$\leq \max_{f(x)} \left[I(X;Y,Z) - I(X;Z) \right] = \max_{f(x)} I(X;Y|Z)$$

Box 2.

$$I(X;Y|Z) = H(X|Z) - H(X|Y,Z)$$
$$= H(X|Z) - H(X|Y)$$
$$= \left\{ H(Z,X) - H(Z) \right\} - \left\{ H(Y,X) - H(Y) \right\}$$
$$= \left\{ H(X) + H(Z|X) - H(Z) \right\} - \left\{ H(X) + H(Y|X) - H(Y) \right\}$$
$$= \left\{ H(Y) - H(Y|X) \right\} - \left\{ H(Z) - H(Z|X) \right\}$$
$$= I(X;Y) - I(X;Z)$$

Using the chain rule, we have the formula in Box 2.

Therefore, the secrecy capacity for a discrete memoryless channel is given by,

$$C_s = \max_{f(x)} \left[I(X;Y) - I(X;Z) \right] \qquad (4)$$

2.2 Secrecy Capacity of Nakagami-m Fading Channel

A schematic diagram of confidential communications through *Nakagami-m fading channel* is considered as shown in Figure 3 to characterize secrecy capacity in the presence of an eavesdropper.

The channel between transmitter and legitimate receiver is referred to as main channel and that between transmitter and eavesdropper is known as eavesdropper channel. The channel gains of main and eavesdropper channel are assumed to be the sum of magnitudes of complex Gaussian random variables so that the envelop of each

channel is Nakagami-m with different integer values of fading parameter, *m*, and the average SNR, Ω. The transmitter has single antenna while legitimate receiver and eavesdropper are equipped with n_R and n_E antennas, respectively. The received signals at the legitimate receiver and eavesdropper are given by,

$$\mathbf{y}_M(t) = \mathbf{h}_M x(t) + \mathbf{z}_M(t) \qquad (5)$$

and

$$\mathbf{y}_E(t) = \mathbf{g}_E x(t) + \mathbf{z}_E(t), \qquad t = 1, 2, 3, ..., n \qquad (6)$$

respectively, where n is the length of transmitted signal. $\mathbf{h}_M$ is a $n_R \times 1$ vector i.e. $\mathbf{h}_M = [h_1, h_2, ..., h_{n_R}]^T$ denotes the channel gain from transmitter to legitimate receiver (main channel) and $\mathbf{g}_E$ is a $n_E \times 1$ vector i.e.

15

Figure 3. The Nakagami-m fading channel with an eavesdropper

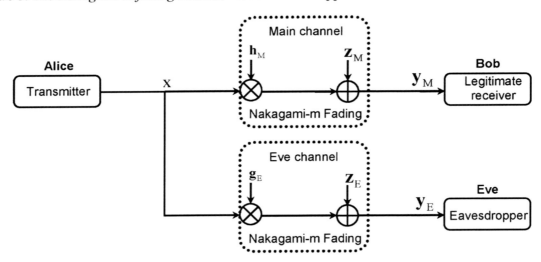

$g_E = [g_1, g_2, ..., g_{n_E}]^T$ denotes the channel gain from transmitter to eavesdropper (eavesdropper channel). $z_M(t) \sim CN(0, \sigma_1^2 \mathbf{I}_{n_R})$ and $\mathbf{z}_E(t) \sim CN(0, \sigma_2^2 \mathbf{I}_{n_E})$ are the complex noises imposed on legitimate receiver and eavesdropper, respectively. Both the vectors $\mathbf{h}_M$ and $\mathbf{g}_E$ are the sum of magnitude of complex Gaussian random variables, so the envelops, $\left\| \mathbf{h}_{M_i} \right\|$, $i = 1, 2, ..., n_R$ and $\left\| \mathbf{g}_{E_j} \right\|$, $j = 1, 2, ..., n_E$ are Nakagami-m with different integer values of m, and with Ω_M and Ω_E, respectively, where Ω_M and Ω_E are the average SNRs for different subchannels of main and eavesdropper channels, respectively.

2.2.1 Full CSI at the Transmitter

In order to define the secrecy capacity with full CSI at the transmitter, it is assumed that channel gains remain constant during each coherence interval and change independently from one coherence interval to the next. At the beginning of each coherence interval, transmitter knows the channel states of the intended user and the eavesdropper perfectly. When the channel gains of main and eavesdropper channels are known at the transmitter, then one would expect the optimal scheme to allow for the transmission, only when the main channel is better than eavesdropper channel, and to adapt the transmitted power according to the instantaneous values of main channel and eavesdropper channel gains. Under the assumption of full CSI at the transmitter, the instantaneous secrecy capacity of the channel model shown in Figure 3 is defined as seen in Equation 7, and the ergodic capacity is given by Equation 8.

Where $r_1 = \sum_{i=1}^{n_R} \left\| h_{M_i} \right\|^2$, $r_2 = \sum_{j=1}^{n_E} \left\| g_{E_j} \right\|^2$, $P(r_1, r_2)$ is the allocated transmit power for given CSI $\{r_1, r_2\}$ and P_T corresponds to the power constraint. When r_1 and r_2 are both known at the transmitter, then the transmitted power is allocated according to the instantaneous values of r_1 and r_2 to allow the transmission only when $r_1 > r_2$. Let Equation 9 be when $r_1 > r_2$, then,

Equation 7.

$$C_{S}^{(\text{Full})} = \max_{\mathbb{E}[P(r_1,r_2)] \leq P_T} \left[\log_e \left(1 + \frac{P(r_1,r_2)}{\sigma_1^2} \mathbf{h}_M^\dagger \mathbf{h}_M \right) - \log_e \left(1 + \frac{P(r_1,r_2)}{\sigma_2^2} \mathbf{g}_E^\dagger \mathbf{g}_E \right) \right]$$

$$= \max_{\mathbb{E}[P(r_1,r_2)] \leq P_T} \left[\log_e \left(1 + \frac{P(r_1,r_2)}{\sigma_1^2} \sum_{i=1}^{n_R} \left\| \mathbf{h}_{M_i} \right\|^2 \right) - \log_e \left(1 + \frac{P(r_1,r_2)}{\sigma_2^2} \sum_{j=1}^{n_E} \left\| \mathbf{g}_{E_j} \right\|^2 \right) \right]$$

$$= \max_{\mathbb{E}[P(r_1,r_2)] \leq P_T} \left[\log_e \left(1 + \frac{P(r_1,r_2)}{\sigma_1^2} r_1 \right) - \log_e \left(1 + \frac{P(r_1,r_2)}{\sigma_2^2} r_2 \right) \right]$$

Equation 8.

$$\left\langle C_{S}^{(\text{Full})} \right\rangle = \max_{\mathbb{E}[P(r_1,r_2)] \leq P_T} \mathbb{E} \left[\log_e \left(1 + \frac{P(r_1,r_2)}{\sigma_1^2} r_1 \right) - \log_e \left(1 + \frac{P(r_1,r_2)}{\sigma_2^2} r_2 \right) \right]$$

$$= \max_{\mathbb{E}[P(r_1,r_2)] \leq P_T} \int_0^\infty \int_{r_2}^\infty \left[\log_e \left\{ \frac{1 + \frac{r_1 P(r_1,r_2)}{\sigma_1^2}}{1 + \frac{r_2 P(r_1,r_2)}{\sigma_2^2}} \right\} \right] f_{r_1}(r_1) f_{r_2}(r_2) dr_1 dr_2$$

Equation 9.

$$R = \int_0^\infty \int_{r_2}^\infty \left[\log_e \left(1 + \frac{P(r_1,r_2)}{\sigma_1^2} r_1 \right) - \log_e \left(1 + \frac{P(r_1,r_2)}{\sigma_2^2} r_2 \right) \right] f_{r_1}(r_1) f_{r_2}(r_2) dr_1 dr_2$$

$$\mathrm{f}\left(P(r_1,r_2) \right) =$$
$$\log_e \left(1 + \frac{P(r_1,r_2)}{\sigma_1^2} r_1 \right) - \log_e \left(1 + \frac{P(r_1,r_2)}{\sigma_2^2} r_2 \right) \tag{10}$$

is concave in $P(r_1,r_2)$. Thus, by using the Lagrangian maximization approach for solving (8), we get the following optimality condition:

$$\frac{\partial R}{\partial P(r_1,r_2)} =$$
$$\frac{r_1}{\sigma_1^2 + P(r_1,r_2) r_1} - \frac{r_2}{\sigma_2^2 + P(r_1,r_2) r_2} - \lambda = 0 \tag{11}$$

Condition 1: When $r_2 > 0$, the solution of Equation (11) is given by,

$$P(r_1, r_2) =$$

$$\frac{1}{2}\sqrt{\left(\frac{\sigma_2^2}{r_2} - \frac{\sigma_1^2}{r_1}\right)\left(\frac{4}{\lambda} - \frac{\sigma_1^2}{r_1} + \frac{\sigma_2^2}{r_2}\right)} - \frac{1}{2}\left(\frac{\sigma_2^2}{r_2} + \frac{\sigma_1^2}{r_1}\right) \tag{12}$$

and the optimal power allocation policy at the transmitter is given by Equation 13.

Condition 2: When $r_2 = 0$, the optimal power allocation policy at the transmitter obtained from (11) is given by,

$$P^*(r_1) = \left(\frac{1}{\lambda} - \frac{\sigma_1^2}{r_1}\right)^{+} \tag{14}$$

where, λ is a constant that satisfies the power constraint $E\left[P(r_1, r_2)\right] \le P_T$ with equality. Therefore, corollary 2 summarizes the optimal power allocation that achieves the secrecy capacity of Nakagami-m fading SIMO channel with full CSI at the transmitter.

Corollary 2: *Under the full CSI assumption, the optimal power allocation that achieves the secrecy capacity for Nakagami-m fading SIMO wiretap channel defined by (5) and (6) is given by Equation 15 where,* $\left[x\right]^{+} = \max\left\{0, x\right\}$ *and the parameter* λ *is a constant that satisfies the power constraint* $E\left[P(r_1, r_2)\right] \le P_T$ *with equality.*

Probability density functions of r_1 and r_2:

The probability density function (pdf) of the envelop of $\mathbf{h}_{M_i}$ denoted by γ_{M_i} follows the Nak-

agami-m distribution given by (Magableh and Matalgah, 2007),

$$f_{\gamma_M}\left(\gamma_M\right) = \frac{2m^m \gamma_M^{2m-1}}{\Gamma(m)\Omega_M^m} \times e^{\frac{-m\gamma_M^2}{\Omega_M}} \tag{16}$$

Define

$$\chi_M^2 = \sum_{i=1}^{n_R}\left\|\mathbf{h}_{M_i}\right\|^2 = \sum_{i=1}^{n_R}\gamma_{M_i} \tag{17}$$

where χ_M denotes the distribution of the square root of the summation of squared subchannel gains. In case of independent and identically distributed (i.i.d.) Nakagami-m fading channel, the pdf of χ_M is given by (Magableh and Matalgah, 2007),

$$f_{\chi_M}\left(\chi_M\right) = \frac{2\left(mn_R\right)^{mn_R}\chi_M^{2mn_R-1}}{\Gamma\left(mn_R\right)\left(\Omega_M n_R\right)^{mn_R}}e^{\frac{-m\chi_M^2}{\Omega_M}} \tag{18}$$

Using random variable transformation, the pdf of $r_1 = \chi_M^2$ is given by,

$$f_{r_1}(r_1) = \left.\frac{f_{\chi_M}\left(\chi_M\right)}{2\chi_M}\right|_{\chi_M = \sqrt{r_1}} = \frac{r_1^{mn_R-1}\exp\left(-\frac{r_1}{\beta_M}\right)}{\Gamma\left(mn_R\right)\beta_M^{mn_R}} \tag{19}$$

where $\beta_M = \dfrac{\Omega_M}{m}$. Similarly, defining

Equation 13.

$$P^*(r_1, r_2) = \left[\frac{1}{2}\sqrt{\left(\frac{\sigma_2^2}{r_2} - \frac{\sigma_1^2}{r_1}\right)\left(\frac{4}{\lambda} - \frac{\sigma_1^2}{r_1} + \frac{\sigma_2^2}{r_2}\right)} - \frac{1}{2}\left(\frac{\sigma_2^2}{r_2} + \frac{\sigma_1^2}{r_1}\right)\right]^{+}$$

Equation 15.

$$P^*\left(r_1, r_2\right) = \begin{cases} \left[\frac{1}{2}\sqrt{\left(\frac{\sigma_2^2}{r_2} - \frac{\sigma_1^2}{r_1}\right)\left(\frac{4}{\lambda} - \frac{\sigma_1^2}{r_1} + \frac{\sigma_2^2}{r_2}\right)} - \frac{1}{2}\left(\frac{\sigma_2^2}{r_2} + \frac{\sigma_1^2}{r_1}\right)\right]^+, & \text{if} \quad r_2 > 0 \\[12pt] \left[\frac{1}{\lambda} - \frac{\sigma_1^2}{r_1}\right]^+, & \text{if} \quad r_2 = 0 \\[12pt] 0 & \text{otherwise}. \end{cases}$$

$$\chi_E^2 = \sum_{j=1}^{n_E} \left\|\mathbf{g}_{E_j}\right\|^2 = \sum_{j=1}^{n_E} \gamma_{E_j}, \tag{20}$$

the pdf of $r_2 = \chi_E^2$ is given by,

$$f_{r_2}(r_2) = \frac{f_{\chi_E}(\chi_E)}{2\chi_E}\bigg|_{\chi_E = \sqrt{r_2}} = \frac{r_2^{mn_E - 1}\exp\left(-\frac{r_2}{\beta_E}\right)}{\Gamma\left(mn_E\right)\beta_E^{mn_R}} \tag{21}$$

where $\beta_E = \dfrac{\Omega_E}{m}$.

Upper bound on the secrecy capacity with full CSI assumption:

Let us rewrite the secrecy capacity of (8) as

$$C_S^{(Full)} = \max_{P(r_1, r_2)} \mathbb{E}_{r_1 > r_2}\left[\log_e\left\{\frac{1 + \frac{r_1 P\left(r_1, r_2\right)}{\sigma_1^2}}{1 + \frac{r_2 P\left(r_1, r_2\right)}{\sigma_2^2}}\right\}\right] \tag{22}$$

and denote the achievable secrecy rate as $R_{p,q}^{(Full)}$ under the full CSI assumption. Consider a delay limited transmission of secure data through fading channel (Bloch et. al., 2008), and define Equation 23 and

$$R_q^{(Full)} = \min_{(r_1, r_2)}\left[\log_e\left\{1 + \frac{P\left(r_1, r_2\right)}{\sigma_1^2} r_1\right\}\right] \tag{24}$$

For a given power allocation scheme $P\left(r_1, r_2\right)$

$$R_{p,q}^{(Full)} \le R_p^{(Full)} \tag{25}$$

for any achievable secrecy rate $R_{p,q}^{(Full)}$, since imposing delay constraint can only degrade the performance. Also, for a given $P\left(r_1, r_2\right)$,

$$R_{p,q}^{(Full)} \le R_q^{(Full)} \tag{26}$$

since imposing secrecy constraint can not increase the achievable rate. Then, combining (25) and (26), and maximizing over $P\left(r_1, r_2\right)$,

$$R_{p,q}^{(Full)} \le \max_{P(r_1, r_2)} \min\left\{R_p^{(Full)}, R_q^{(Full)}\right\}$$

Therefore, under full CSI assumption, the secrecy capacity of Nakagami-m fading SIMO channel is upper bounded by

Equation 23.

$$R_p^{(Full)} = \int_0^\infty \int_{r_2}^\infty \left[\log_e \left\{ \frac{1 + \dfrac{P\left(r_1, r_2\right)}{\sigma_1^2} r_1}{1 + \dfrac{P\left(r_1, r_2\right)}{\sigma_2^2} r_2} \right\} \right]^+ f_{r_1}\left(r_1\right) f_{r_2}\left(r_2\right) dr_1 dr_2$$

$$C_S^{(Full)} \le R_{p,q}^{(Full)} \le \max_{P(r_1, r_2)} \min \left\{ R_p^{(Full)}, R_q^{(Full)} \right\} \tag{27}$$

such that $\mathbb{E}\left[P\left(r_1, r_2\right)\right] \le P_{\mathrm{T}}$.

At high SNR regime, using $\log_e(1 + x) \approx \log_e x$, we get the secrecy capacity as follows:

$$C_S^{(Full)} \approx \mathbb{E}_{r_1 > r_2} \left[\log_e \left(\frac{\sigma_2^2 r_1}{\sigma_1^2 r_2} \right) \right] \tag{28}$$

As shown in (28), at high SNR regime, the secrecy capacity of the wiretap channel converges to a certain value and the power allocation strategy is completely ineffective.

Lower bound on the secrecy capacity with full CSI assumption:

The following result establishes a lower bound on the secrecy capacity under full CSI assumption. The key idea is to share a private key between **Alice** and **Bob** without being constrained by the delay limitation. Then, this key is used to secure the delay sensitive data to overcome the secrecy outage phenomenon. In the steady state, the key renewal process takes place by superimposing the key on the delay sensitive traffic. Let $q(r_1, r_2)$ and $R_n(r_1, r_2)$ are the arbitrary chosen functions satisfying

$$q(r_1, r_2) \ge r_2 \text{ for all } r_2 \tag{29}$$

$$\mathbb{E}\left[R_n\left(r_1, r_2\right)\right] \le \mathbb{E}\left[\log_e \left\{ \frac{1 + \dfrac{r_1 P\left(r_1, r_2\right)}{\sigma_1^2}}{1 + \dfrac{q\left(r_1, r_2\right) P\left(r_1, r_2\right)}{\sigma_2^2}} \right\} \right]^+ \tag{30}$$

and Equation 31.

Then, under full CSI assumption, the secrecy capacity is lower bounded by

$$C_S^{(Full)} \ge \max_{P(r_1, r_2), q(r_1, r_2)} \left[\min_{\{r_1, r_2\}} \left\{ R_m\left(r_1, r_2\right) + R_n\left(r_1, r_2\right) \right\} \right]$$

such that

$$\mathbb{E}\left[P\left(r_1, r_2\right)\right] \le P_{\mathrm{T}}. \tag{32}$$

where we get the formula in Box 3.

2.2.2 Only Main Channel CSI at the Transmitter

Under this assumption, transmitter knows only the CSI of main channel at the beginning of each coherence interval. This case corresponds to the situation where eavesdropper is passive and malicious attacker in the wireless network. In this case, transmission occurs at a variable rate according to the instantaneous value of main chan-

Equation 31.

$$\mathbb{E}\left[R_n\left(r_1,r_2\right)\right] \le \min\left[\log_e\left\{1+\frac{P\left(r_1,r_2\right)}{\sigma_1^2}r_1\right\},\log_e\left\{1+\frac{P\left(r_1,r_2\right)}{\sigma_2^2}r_2\right\}\right]$$

Box 3.

$$R_m\left(r_1,r_2\right)=\left[\log_e\left\{\frac{1+\frac{r_1P\left(r_1,r_2\right)}{\sigma_1^2}}{1+\frac{r_2P\left(r_1,r_2\right)}{\sigma_2^2}}\right\}\right]^+ - \left[\log_e\left\{\frac{1+\frac{r_1P\left(r_1,r_2\right)}{\sigma_1^2}}{1+\frac{q\left(r_1,r_2\right)P\left(r_1,r_2\right)}{\sigma_2^2}}\right\}\right]^+ .$$

nel gain which relies on the assumption of large coherence intervals. When only the main channel CSI is available at the transmitter, then the instantaneous secrecy capacity for Nakagami-m fading SIMO channel is given by Equation 33, where $P\left(r_1\right)$ is the allocated transmit power for given CSI $\left\{r_1\right\}$. During each coherence interval, transmitter transmits codewords at a rate $\log_e\left(1+\frac{P(r_1)}{\sigma_1^2}r_1\right)$ with the optimal power allocation policy $P\left(r_1\right)$ at the transmitter, and the variable rate scheme ensures that the mutual information of the eavesdropper channel is upper bounded by $\log_e\left(1+\frac{P(r_1)}{\sigma_1^2}r_1\right)$, if $r_1 > r_2$. Otherwise, the mutual information of the eavesdropper channel will be $\log_e\left(1+\frac{P(r_1)}{\sigma_2^2}r_2\right)$. In this case, the ergodic secrecy capacity is given by Equation 34.

The objective function is not a concave function of $P\left(r_1\right)$. Therefore, using the Lagrangian formulation, we only get the following necessary KKT conditions for the optimal point (see Equation 35).

Upper bound on the secrecy capacity with only main channel CSI at the transmitter:

Let

$$R_s^{(M)} =$$
$$\mathbb{E}\left[\log_e\left(1+\frac{P\left(r_1\right)}{\sigma_1^2}r_1\right)-\log_e\left(1+\frac{P\left(r_1\right)}{\sigma_2^2}r_2\right)\right]^+$$

(36)

$$R_d^{(M)} = \min_{r_1}\left[\log_e\left(1+\frac{P\left(r_1\right)}{\sigma_1^2}r_1\right)\right]^+ \quad (37)$$

and $R_{s,d}^{(M)}$ denotes the achievable secrecy rate with only main channel CSI at the transmitter. Following the same argument as that of the full CSI scenario with the power allocation scheme $P\left(r_1\right)$ we have

Equation 33.

$$C_S^{(\mathrm{M})} = \max_{\mathbb{E}[P(r_1)] \le P_T} \left[\log_e \left(1 + \frac{P(r_1)}{\sigma_1^2} r_1 \right) - \log_e \left(1 + \frac{P(r_1)}{\sigma_2^2} r_2 \right) \right]$$

Equation 34.

$$\langle C_S^{(\mathrm{M})} \rangle = \max_{\mathbb{E}[P(r_1)] \le P_T} \mathbb{E} \left[\log_e \left(1 + \frac{P(r_1)}{\sigma_1^2} r_1 \right) - \log_e \left(1 + \frac{P(r_1)}{\sigma_2^2} r_2 \right) \right]$$

$$= \max_{\mathbb{E}[P(r_1)] \le P_T} \int_0^\infty \int_0^{r_1} \left[\log_e \left(1 + \frac{P(r_1)}{\sigma_1^2} r_1 \right) - \log_e \left(1 + \frac{P(r_1)}{\sigma_2^2} r_2 \right) \right] \mathrm{f}_{r_2}(r_2) \mathrm{f}_{r_1}(r_1) \, dr_2 dr_1$$

Equation 35.

$$P(r_1) \left[\lambda - \frac{r_1}{\sigma_1^2 + r_1 P(r_1)} + \int_0^{r_1} \left(\frac{r_2}{\sigma_2^2 + r_2 P(r_1)} \right) \mathrm{f}_{r_2}(r_2) \, dr_2 \right] = 0,$$

$$\lambda \ge \frac{r_1}{\sigma_1^2 + r_1 P(r_1)} - \int_0^{r_1} \left(\frac{r_2}{\sigma_2^2 + r_2 P(r_1)} \right) \mathrm{f}_{r_2}(r_2) \, dr_2, \quad \mathbb{E}[P(r_1)] \le P_T.$$

$$R_{s,d}^{(M)} \le R_s^{(M)} \tag{38}$$

$$R_{s,d}^{(M)} \le R_d^{(M)} \tag{39}$$

Then, combining (38) and (39), and maximizing over $P(r_1)$,

$$R_{s,d}^{(M)} \le \max_{P(r_1)} \min \left\{ R_s^{(M)}, R_d^{(M)} \right\}$$

Therefore, with only main channel CSI at the transmitter, the secrecy capacity of Nakagami-m fading SIMO channel is upper bounded by

$$C_S^{(M)} \le R_{s,d}^{(M)} \le \max_{P(r_1)} \min \left\{ R_s^{(M)}, R_d^{(M)} \right\} \tag{40}$$

such that

$$\mathbb{E}[P(r_1)] \le P_T.$$

Lower bound on the secrecy capacity with only main channel CSI at the transmitter:

The following result establishes a lower bound on the secrecy capacity with only main channel CSI at the transmitter. Since the achievability scheme for this scenario is different from the full CSI scenario, therefore, the channel uses is divided into super-blocks. Then each super-block is further divided into block and the data is transmitted using one-time pad encryption. More specifically, the achievable secure rate is utilized within a block only in order to generate the secret key. The generated key is decoded at the end of each super-block whereas the data packets are still decoded block by block using the key sent in the previous super-block. Let Equation 41 show with only main channel CSI at the transmitter, the secrecy capacity of Nakagami-m fading SIMO channel is lower bounded by

$$C_s^{(M)} \geq R_{s,d}^{(M)} \geq \max_{P(r_1)} \min \left\{ R_s, R_d^{(M)} \right\} \qquad (42)$$

such that

$$\mathbb{E}\left[P\left(r_1 \right) \right] \leq P_{\mathrm{T}}.$$

2.2.3 Open-Loop Transmission Scheme

The performance of open-loop transmission scheme is much worse than the schemes that employ rate adaptation. Therefore, the performance curve for the open-loop transmission scheme might be a lower bound to the secrecy capacity. In this case, transmitter transmits at a constant rate P_T and the secrecy capacity exists only when the SNR of main channel is greater than that of eavesdropper channel, otherwise the secrecy capacity is zero (Bloch et. al., 2008). Let $\gamma_{\mathrm{M}} = \dfrac{P_T}{\sigma_1^2} r_1$ and $\gamma_{\mathrm{E}} = \dfrac{P_T}{\sigma_2^2} r_2$ are the SNRs of main channel and eavesdropper channel, respectively.

Then, the following definition characterizes the lower bound of secrecy capacity for Nakagami-m fading SIMO channel.

Definition 1: *The lower bound of secrecy capacity for Nakagami-m fading SIMO wiretap channel is given by Equation 43.*

Defining,

$$I_{\mathrm{M}} = \log_e \left(1 + \gamma_{\mathrm{M}} \right) = \log_e \left(1 + \rho_{\mathrm{M}} r_1 \right) \qquad (44)$$

and

$$I_{\mathrm{E}} = \log_e \left(1 + \gamma_{\mathrm{E}} \right) = \log_e \left(1 + \rho_{\mathrm{E}} r_2 \right) \qquad (45)$$

where $\rho_{\mathrm{M}} = \dfrac{P_T}{\sigma_1^2}$ and $\rho_{\mathrm{E}} = \dfrac{P_T}{\sigma_2^2}$. In order to find the analytical expression for the lower bound of ergodic secrecy capacity, it is necessary to find the probability density functions (pdfs) of I_{M} and I_{E}. Since, the distribution of mutual information is related with the distribution of channel gain, therefore, following proposition is used to find the pdfs of I_{M} and I_{E}.

Proposition 1 (Sellathurai et. al., 2007): *Let $t \sim \chi_{2n}^2$ and the probability density function of t is denoted by* $\mathrm{f}(t)$. *Then the probability density function of* $I = \log_e(1 + \theta t)$ *is given by,*

$$q\left(I \right) = \frac{e^I}{\theta} \mathrm{f}\left(\frac{e^I - 1}{\theta} \right) \qquad (46)$$

Equation 41.

$$R_s = \mathbb{E}\left[\log_e \left(1 + \frac{P\left(r_1 \right)}{\sigma_1^2} r_1 \right) - \log_e \left(1 + \frac{P\left(r_1 \right)}{\sigma_2^2} r_2 \right) - R_{s,d}^{(M)} \right]^+$$

Equation 43.

$$C_{\mathrm{S}}\left(\gamma_{\mathrm{M}},\gamma_{\mathrm{E}}\right) \geq \begin{cases} \log_e\left(1+\gamma_{\mathrm{M}}\right) - \log_e\left(1+\gamma_{\mathrm{E}}\right), \text{if} \quad \gamma_{\mathrm{M}} > \gamma_{\mathrm{E}} \\ 0 \qquad\qquad\qquad\qquad\qquad \text{otherwise} \end{cases}$$

Proof: We have $I = \log_e\left(1+\theta t\right)$. The pdf of mutual information, I, can be written as (Sellathurai et. al., 2007),

$$q\left(I\right) = \int \delta\left(I - \log_e\left(1+\theta t\right)\right) \mathrm{f}\left(t\right) dt \qquad (47)$$

The following mathematical facts have been used for this proof (Ratnarajah and Vaillancourt, 2005);

i) $\delta\left(z\left(\kappa\right)\right) = \sum_{\nu} \dfrac{\delta\left(\kappa - \kappa_{\nu}\right)}{\left|\dfrac{dz}{d\kappa}\right|_{\kappa_{\nu}}}$, where κ_{ν} are the

   zeros of $z\left(\kappa\right)$, i.e. $z\left(\kappa_{\nu}\right) = 0$;

ii) $\int_a^b \delta\left(\kappa - \kappa_1\right)\delta\left(\kappa - \kappa_2\right)d\kappa$ for $\mathrm{a} < \kappa_1, \kappa_2 <$ b; and

iii)

$$\int_V z\left(\kappa\right)\delta\left(\kappa - \kappa_0\right) d\kappa = \begin{cases} z\left(\kappa_0\right), & \kappa_0 \in V \\ 0 & \text{otherwise.} \end{cases}$$

Assuming $\kappa = 1 + \theta t$, we have

$$z\left(\kappa\right) = I - \log_e \kappa \text{ and } \frac{dz}{d\kappa} = -\frac{1}{\kappa}.$$

Now from $z\left(\kappa_{\nu}\right) = 0$, $\kappa_{\nu} = e^I$ and $\left|\dfrac{dz}{d\kappa}\right|_{\kappa_{\nu}=e^I} = \left|-\dfrac{1}{\kappa}\right|_{\kappa_{\nu}=e^I} = \dfrac{1}{e^I}$. Using the above

mathematical facts and from (47), we have Equation 48 where $\delta\left(.\right)$ is a delta function.

From Proposition 1 and (44) the pdf of I_{M} is given by,

$$q\left(I_{\mathrm{M}}\right) = \frac{e^{I_{\mathrm{M}}}}{\rho_{\mathrm{M}}} \mathrm{f}\left(\frac{e^{I_{\mathrm{M}}} - 1}{\rho_{\mathrm{M}}}\right) \qquad (49)$$

Similarly, from Proposition 1 and (45) the pdf of I_{E} is given by

$$q\left(I_{\mathrm{E}}\right) = \frac{e^{I_{\mathrm{E}}}}{\rho_{\mathrm{E}}} \mathrm{f}\left(\frac{e^{I_{\mathrm{E}}} - 1}{\rho_{\mathrm{E}}}\right) \qquad (50)$$

Using (19) in (49), the pdf of I_{M} is given by,

$$q\left(I_{\mathrm{M}}\right) = \frac{e^{I_{\mathrm{M}}}\left(e^{I_{\mathrm{M}}} - 1\right)^{mn_R - 1}}{\Gamma\left(mn_{\mathrm{R}}\right)\left(\rho_{\mathrm{M}}\beta_{\mathrm{M}}\right)^{mn_R}} \times e^{-\frac{e^{I_{\mathrm{M}}} - 1}{\rho_{\mathrm{M}}\beta_{\mathrm{M}}}} \qquad (51)$$

Similarly, using (21) in (50), the pdf of I_{E} is given by,

$$q\left(I_{\mathrm{E}}\right) = \frac{e^{I_{\mathrm{E}}}\left(e^{I_{\mathrm{E}}} - 1\right)^{mn_{\mathrm{E}} - 1}}{\Gamma\left(mn_{\mathrm{E}}\right)\left(\rho_{\mathrm{E}}\beta_{\mathrm{E}}\right)^{mn_{\mathrm{E}}}} \times e^{-\frac{e^{I_{\mathrm{E}}} - 1}{\rho_{\mathrm{E}}\beta_{\mathrm{E}}}} \qquad (52)$$

The lower bound of ergodic secrecy capacity is given by Equation 53.

The analytical expression for the lower bound of ergodic secrecy capacity obtained from equations (51), (52) and (53) is given in theorem 1.

Theorem 1: *For an i.i.d. Nakagami-m fading SIMO channel, the lower bound of ergodic secrecy capacity under open loop transmission scheme is given by Equation 54.*

Proof: we have

Equation 48.

$$q(I) = \int \delta\big(z(\kappa)\big)\mathrm{f}(t)\,dt = \int \frac{\delta\big(\kappa - \kappa_\nu\big)}{\left|\dfrac{dz}{d\kappa}\right|_{\kappa_\nu}}\mathrm{f}(t)\,dt = \int \frac{\delta\big(1 + \theta t - e^I\big)}{\dfrac{1}{e^I}}\mathrm{f}(t)\,dt$$

$$= \int e^I \delta\big(1 + \theta t - e^I\big)\mathrm{f}(t)\,dt = e^I \int \delta\left(\theta\left(t - \frac{e^I - 1}{\theta}\right)\right)\mathrm{f}(t)\,dt$$

$$= \frac{e^I}{\theta}\int \delta\left(t - \frac{e^I - 1}{\theta}\right)\mathrm{f}(t)\,dt, \quad \text{since} \quad \delta(cx) = \frac{1}{|c|}\delta(x)$$

$$= \frac{e^I}{\theta}\mathrm{f}\left(\frac{e^I - 1}{\theta}\right), \quad \text{since} \quad \int \delta(x - x_0)\mathrm{f}(x)\,dx = \mathrm{f}(x_0)$$

Equation 53.

$$\langle C_S \rangle \geq \int_0^\infty \int_0^\infty \left[\log_e\left(\frac{1 + \rho_M r_1}{1 + \rho_E r_2}\right)\right]\mathrm{f}_{r_1}(r_1)\mathrm{f}_{r_2}(r_2)\,dr_1 dr_2$$

$$= \int_0^\infty \int_0^\infty (I_M - I_E)q(I_M)q(I_E)\,dI_M dI_E, \quad \text{if} \quad \gamma_M > \gamma_E$$

$$\langle C_S \rangle \geq \int_0^\infty \int_0^\infty \left[\log_e\left(\frac{1 + \rho_M r_1}{1 + \rho_E r_2}\right)\right]\mathrm{f}_{r_1}(r_1)\mathrm{f}_{r_2}(r_2)\,dr_1 dr_2$$

$$= \int_0^\infty \int_0^\infty \big\{(I_M - I_E)q(I_M)q(I_E)\big\}\,dI_M dI_E$$

$$= \underbrace{\int_0^\infty \int_0^\infty I_M q(I_M)q(I_E)\,dI_M dI_E}_{=C^{(1)}}$$

$$- \underbrace{\int_0^\infty \int_0^\infty I_E q(I_M)q(I_E)\,dI_M dI_E}_{=C^{(2)}} \tag{55}$$

Using the value of $q(I_M)$ and defining $z = \dfrac{e^{I_M} - 1}{\rho_M \beta_M}$, we have Equation 56.

Using the following identity of Equation 57 we have Equation 58 (Gradshteyn and Ryzhik, 2007, eq. (4. 222. 8)).

Replacing the value $q(I_E)$ in (58) and using the following identity of (Gradshteyn and Ryzhik, 2007, eq. (3.351.3)),

$$\int_0^\infty x^n e^{-\mu x}\,dx = n!\,\mu^{-n-1} \tag{59}$$

we have Equation 60.

Following the similarly procedure of $C^{(1)}$, we have Equation 61.

Finally, substituting the values of $C^{(1)}$ and $C^{(2)}$ in Equation (55), we have the result.

Example 1

(a) (*Symmetric antenna configuration*) Consider $n_R = n_E = n_c$. From Theorem 1, the lower bound of ergodic

Equation 54.

$$\langle C_{\mathrm{S}}\rangle \geq \sum_{k_1=0}^{mn_{\mathrm{R}}-1} \frac{1}{\left(mn_{\mathrm{R}}-k_1-1\right)!}\left[\sum_{k_2=1}^{mn_{\mathrm{R}}-k_1-1}\frac{\left(k_2-1\right)!}{\left(-\rho_{\mathrm{M}}\beta_{\mathrm{M}}\right)^{mn_{\mathrm{R}}-k_1-k_2-1}}-\frac{\exp\left(\dfrac{1}{\rho_{\mathrm{M}}\beta_{\mathrm{M}}}\right)\mathrm{Ei}\left(-\dfrac{1}{\rho_{\mathrm{M}}\beta_{\mathrm{M}}}\right)}{\left(-\rho_{\mathrm{M}}\beta_{\mathrm{M}}\right)^{mn_{\mathrm{R}}-k_1-1}}\right]$$

$$-\sum_{v_1=0}^{mn_{\mathrm{E}}-1}\frac{1}{\left(mn_{\mathrm{E}}-v_1-1\right)!}\left[\sum_{v_2=1}^{mn_{\mathrm{E}}-v_1-1}\frac{\left(v_2-1\right)!}{\left(-\rho_{\mathrm{E}}\beta_{\mathrm{E}}\right)^{mn_{\mathrm{E}}-v_1-v_2-1}}-\frac{\exp\left(\dfrac{1}{\rho_{\mathrm{E}}\beta_{\mathrm{E}}}\right)\mathrm{Ei}\left(-\dfrac{1}{\rho_{\mathrm{E}}\beta_{\mathrm{E}}}\right)}{\left(-\rho_{\mathrm{E}}\beta_{\mathrm{E}}\right)^{mn_{\mathrm{E}}-v_1-1}}\right]$$

$$\text{nats/symbol, if } \rho_{\mathrm{M}}\beta_{\mathrm{M}} > \rho_{\mathrm{E}}\beta_{\mathrm{E}} \text{ and } n_R \geq n_E.$$

Equation 56.

$$C^{(1)} = \frac{1}{\Gamma\left(mn_{\mathrm{R}}\right)}\int_0^\infty q\left(I_{\mathrm{E}}\right)\left[\int_0^\infty \log_e\left(1+\rho_{\mathrm{M}}\beta_{\mathrm{M}}z\right)z^{mn_{\mathrm{R}}-1}e^{-z}dz\right]dI_{\mathrm{E}}$$

Equation 57.

$$\int_0^\infty \ln\left(1+ax\right)x^b e^{-x}dx = \sum_{i=0}^b \frac{b!}{\left(b-i\right)!}\left[\frac{\left(-1\right)^{b-i-1}}{a^{b-i}}e^{\frac{1}{a}}\mathrm{Ei}(-\frac{1}{a})+\sum_{k=1}^{b-i}\frac{\left(k-1\right)!}{\left(-a\right)^{b-i-k}}\right]$$

secrecy capacity for an i.i.d. Nakagami-m fading SIMO channel under open loop transmission scheme is given by Equation 62.

(b) *(Single-input single-output (SISO) channel)* Consider $n_{\mathrm{R}} = n_{\mathrm{E}} = 1$. From Theorem 1, the lower bound of ergodic secrecy capacity for Nakagami-m fad-

ing SISO channel under open loop transmission scheme is given by Equation 63.

(c) *(Rayleigh fading channel)* Consider $m = 1$. From Theorem 1, the lower bound of ergodic secrecy capacity for Rayleigh fading SIMO channel under

Equation 58.

$$C^{(1)} = \sum_{k_1=0}^{mn_R-1} \frac{1}{(mn_R - k_1 - 1)!} \left[\sum_{k_2=1}^{mn_R-k_1-1} \frac{(k_2 - 1)!}{(-\rho_M\beta_M)^{mn_R-k_1-k_2-1}} - \frac{\exp\left(\frac{1}{\rho_M\beta_M}\right)\mathrm{Ei}\left(-\frac{1}{\rho_M\beta_M}\right)}{(-\rho_M\beta_M)^{mn_R-k_1-1}} \right] \times \int_0^\infty q(I_E)\, dI_E$$

Equation 60.

$$C^{(1)} = \sum_{k_1=0}^{mn_R-1} \frac{1}{(mn_R - k_1 - 1)!} \left[\sum_{k_2=1}^{mn_R-k_1-1} \frac{(k_2 - 1)!}{(-\rho_M\beta_M)^{mn_R-k_1-k_2-1}} - \frac{\exp\left(\frac{1}{\rho_M\beta_M}\right)\mathrm{Ei}\left(-\frac{1}{\rho_M\beta_M}\right)}{(-\rho_M\beta_M)^{mn_R-k_1-1}} \right]$$

Equation 61.

$$C^{(2)} = \sum_{v_1=0}^{mn_E-1} \frac{1}{(mn_E - v_1 - 1)!} \left[\sum_{v_2=1}^{mn_E-v_1-1} \frac{(v_2 - 1)!}{(-\rho_E\beta_E)^{mn_E-v_1-v_2-1}} - \frac{\exp\left(\frac{1}{\rho_E\beta_E}\right)\mathrm{Ei}\left(-\frac{1}{\rho_E\beta_E}\right)}{(-\rho_E\beta_E)^{mn_E-v_1-1}} \right]$$

open loop transmission scheme is given by Equation 64.

The **rate adaptation scheme** provides higher secrecy rates than open-loop transmission scheme. Therefore, the performance curve for the open-loop transmission scheme is a lower bound to the secrecy capacity and exists only when the SNR of main channel is greater than that of eavesdropper channel, otherwise the secrecy capacity is zero as shown in Figure 4. Moreover, the secrecy rate under full CSI assumption is higher than that of only main channel CSI at the transmitter as one expects.

2.3 Secrecy Capacity of Additive White Gaussian Noise Channel

The Gaussian wire-tap channel, in which the outputs at the legitimate receiver and eavesdropper are corrupted by the additive white Gaussian noise, was precisely studied in (Leung and Hellman, 1978). Consider a Gaussian wire-tap channel as shown in Figure 5, where transmitter, legitimate receiver and eavesdropper are equipped with single antenna. Based on this system model, the characterization of secrecy capacity in case of real and complex AWGN channels are discussed.

Equation 62.

$$\langle C_S \rangle \geq \sum_{k=0}^{mn_c-1} \frac{1}{(mn_c-k-1)!} \left[\left[\sum_{\tau=1}^{mn_c-k-1} \frac{(\tau-1)!}{(-\rho_M \beta_M)^{mn_c-k-\tau-1}} - \frac{\exp\left(\frac{1}{\rho_M \beta_M}\right) \text{Ei}\left(-\frac{1}{\rho_M \beta_M}\right)}{(-\rho_M \beta_M)^{mn_c-k-1}} \right] \right.$$

$$\left. - \left\{ \sum_{\tau=1}^{mn_c-k-1} \frac{(\tau-1)!}{(-\rho_E \beta_E)^{mn_c-k-\tau-1}} - \frac{\exp\left(\frac{1}{\rho_E \beta_E}\right) \text{Ei}\left(-\frac{1}{\rho_E \beta_E}\right)}{(-\rho_E \beta_E)^{mn_c-k-1}} \right\} \right]$$

nats/symbol, if $\rho_M \beta_M > \rho_E \beta_E$

2.3.1 Real AWGN Channel

Assuming communication between Alice and Bob over a standard real AWGN channel with noise power N_M and Eve's observation is also corrupted by Gaussian noise with power N_E. Eve's receiver has lower SNR than Bob's receiver i.e. $N_E > N_M$. In this model, the channel input–output relationship for one channel use is given by,

$$y_M = x + z_M \tag{65}$$

$$y_E = x + z_E, \tag{66}$$

where y_M and y_E are the received signals at the legitimate receiver and eavesdropper, respectively. The noise variables z_M and z_E are the Gaussian random variables with respective variances N_M and N_E. The noise is independent and identically distributed over channel uses. The channel input is subject to an average power constraint P_T, i.e.

$$\frac{1}{n} \sum_{t=1}^{n} \mathbb{E}\left\{ |x(t)|^2 \right\} \leq P_T \tag{67}$$

Equation 63.

$$\langle C_S \rangle \geq \sum_{i_1=0}^{m-1} \frac{1}{(m-i_1-1)!} \left[\frac{(-1)^{m-i_1-2}}{(\rho_M \beta_M)^{m-i_1-1}} \exp\left(\frac{1}{\rho_M \beta_M}\right) \text{Ei}\left(-\frac{1}{\rho_M \beta_M}\right) + \sum_{i_2=1}^{m-i_1-1} \frac{(i_2-1)!}{(-\rho_M \beta_M)^{m-1-i_1-i_2}} \right]$$

$$- \sum_{i_1=0}^{m-1} \frac{1}{(m-i_1-1)!} \left[\frac{(-1)^{m-i_1-2}}{(\rho_E \beta_E)^{m-i_1-1}} \exp\left(\frac{1}{\rho_E \beta_E}\right) \text{Ei}\left(-\frac{1}{\rho_E \beta_E}\right) + \sum_{i_2=1}^{m-i_1-1} \frac{(i_2-1)!}{(-\rho_E \beta_E)^{m-1-i_1-i_2}} \right]$$

nats/symbol, if $\rho_M \beta_M > \rho_E \beta_E$

Equation 64.

$$
\begin{aligned}
\langle C_S \rangle \geq &\sum_{\phi_1=0}^{n_R-1} \frac{1}{\left(n_R - \phi_1 - 1\right)!} \left[\sum_{\phi_2=1}^{n_R-\phi_1-1} \frac{\left(\phi_2-1\right)!}{\left(-\rho_M \beta_M\right)^{n_R-\phi_1-\phi_2-1}} - \frac{\exp\left(\dfrac{1}{\rho_M \beta_M}\right) \mathrm{Ei}\left(-\dfrac{1}{\rho_M \beta_M}\right)}{\left(-\rho_M \beta_M\right)^{n_R-\phi_1-1}} \right] \\
&- \sum_{\delta_1=0}^{n_E-1} \frac{1}{\left(n_E - \delta_1 - 1\right)!} \left[\sum_{\delta_2=1}^{n_E-\delta_1-1} \frac{\left(\delta_2-1\right)!}{\left(-\rho_E \beta_E\right)^{n_E-\delta_1-\delta_2-1}} - \frac{\exp\left(\dfrac{1}{\rho_E \beta_E}\right) \mathrm{Ei}\left(-\dfrac{1}{\rho_E \beta_E}\right)}{\left(-\rho_E \beta_E\right)^{n_E-\delta_1-1}} \right]
\end{aligned}
$$

nats/symbol, if $\quad \rho_M \beta_M > \rho_E \beta_E$

Figure 4. The secrecy rate versus average transmit power under rate adaptation and open-loop transmission schemes for Nakagami-m fading channel with $n_R = 2$, $n_T = n_E = 1$ and $m = 2$

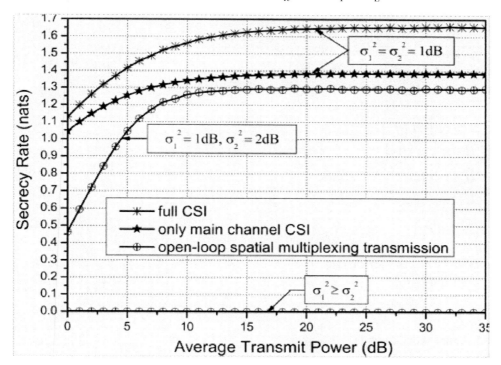

Figure 5. The additive white Gaussian channel with an eavesdropper

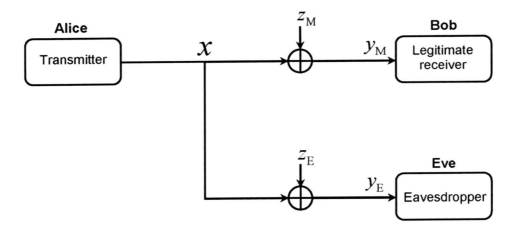

where t denotes the symbol time (i.e. channel use) index. For this instance, the secrecy capacity is given by,

$$C_{\text{S}} = \max_{f(x)} \left[I\left(x; y_{\text{M}}\right) - I\left(x; y_{\text{E}}\right) \right] \tag{68}$$

where $I(x, y_{M})$ denotes the mutual information of the main channel (i.e. channel between Alice and Bob) and is given by

$$
\begin{aligned}
I\left(x; y_{\text{M}}\right) &= H\left(y_{\text{M}}\right) - H\left(y_{\text{M}} \big| x\right) \\
&= H\left(y_{\text{M}}\right) - H\left\{\left(x + z_{\text{M}}\right) \big| x\right\} \\
&= H\left(y_{\text{M}}\right) - H\left(z_{\text{M}} \big| x\right) \\
&= H\left(y_{\text{M}}\right) - H\left(z_{\text{M}}\right) \\
&= \frac{1}{2}\log_2 \pi e\left(N_{\text{M}} + P_{T}\right) - \frac{1}{2}\log_2 \pi e N_{\text{M}} \\
&= \frac{1}{2}\log_2 \pi e\left(1 + \frac{P_{T}}{N_{\text{M}}}\right), \quad \text{bit/sec/Hz}
\end{aligned}
$$

(Since x and z_{M} are independent)

Similarly, $I(x, y_{E})$ denotes the mutual information of the eavesdropper channel (i.e. channel between Alice and Eve) and is given by

$$
\begin{aligned}
I\left(x; y_{\text{E}}\right) &= H\left(y_{\text{E}}\right) - H\left(y_{\text{E}} \big| x\right) \\
&= H\left(y_{\text{E}}\right) - H\left\{\left(x + z_{\text{E}}\right) \big| x\right\} \\
&= H\left(y_{\text{E}}\right) - H\left(z_{\text{E}} \big| x\right) \\
&= H\left(y_{\text{E}}\right) - H\left(z_{\text{E}}\right) \\
&= \frac{1}{2}\log_2 \pi e\left(N_{\text{E}} + P_{T}\right) - \frac{1}{2}\log_2 \pi e N_{\text{E}} \\
&= \frac{1}{2}\log_2 \pi e\left(1 + \frac{P_{T}}{N_{\text{E}}}\right), \quad \text{bit/sec/Hz}
\end{aligned}
$$

(Since x and z_{M} are independent) and $f(x)$ denotes the input distribution. Therefore, the secrecy capacity for real Gaussian channel obtained from (68) is given by,

$$
\begin{aligned}
C_{\text{S}} &= \max_{f(x)} \left[\frac{1}{2}\log_2 \left(\frac{1 + \dfrac{P_{T}}{N_{\text{M}}}}{1 + \dfrac{P_{T}}{N_{\text{E}}}} \right) \right] \\
&= \frac{1}{2}\log_2 \left(\frac{1 + \dfrac{P_{T}}{N_{\text{M}}}}{1 + \dfrac{P_{T}}{N_{\text{E}}}} \right), \quad \text{bits/sec/Hz}
\end{aligned}
\tag{69}
$$

2.3.2 Complex AWGN Channel

In this subsection, we consider both the main and eavesdropper channels are complex AWGN channels, i.e. transmit and receive symbols are complex and both additive noise processes are zero mean circularly symmetric complex Gaussian. Since each use of the complex AWGN channel can be viewed as two uses of a real-valued AWGN channel, the secrecy capacity of the complex wiretap channel follows from (68) is given by,

$$C_S = \log_2 \left(\frac{1 + \dfrac{P_T}{N_M}}{1 + \dfrac{P_T}{N_E}} \right) \text{ per complex dimension} \tag{70}$$

3. SECURE OUTAGE PERFORMANCE OF NAKAGAMI-M FADING CHANNEL

Outage analysis quantifies the level of performance (in this case secrecy capacity) that is guaranteed with a certain level of reliability. As the measures of outage analysis the analytical expressions for the probability of non-zero secrecy capacity and secure outage probability are derived in this section for the Nakagami-m fading SIMO channel. The analytical expressions for the probability of non-zero secrecy capacity and secure outage probability in case of Rayleigh fading channel are also shown as a special one.

3.1 Probability of Non-zero Secrecy Capacity

Invoking independence between the main channel and the eavesdropper channel, we may define the probability of existence of a non-zero secrecy capacity as,

$$\Pr\left(C_S > 0\right) = \Pr\left(\gamma_M > \gamma_E\right)$$
$$= \Pr\left(I_M > I_E\right) = \int_0^\infty \int_0^{I_M} q\left(I_M\right) q\left(I_E\right) dI_E dI_M \tag{71}$$

where γ_M and γ_E are the SNRs of main and eavesdropper channels, and I_M and I_E are the corresponding mutual information of the main and eavesdropper channels, respectively.

Replacing the values of $q\left(I_M\right)$ and $q\left(I_E\right)$ in (71) and performing integration, the probability of non-zero secrecy capacity for Nakagami-m fading SIMO channel is given by Equation 72.

Example 2

(a) (*Symmetric antenna configuration*) Consider $n_R = n_E = n_c$. From (72), the probability of non-zero secrecy capacity for Nakagami-m fading SIMO channel is given by Equation 73.

(b) (*SISO channel*) Consider $n_R = n_E = 1$. From (72), the probability of non-zero secrecy capacity for Nakagami-m fading SISO channel is given by, Equation 74.

(c) (*Rayleigh fading channel*) Consider $m = 1$. From (72), the probability of non-zero secrecy capacity for Rayleigh fading SIMO channel is given by, Equation 75.

3.2 Secure Outage Probability

The secure outage probability that the instantaneous secrecy capacity is less than or equal to a target secrecy rate ε_S, is defined as,

Equation 72.

$$\Pr\left(C_S > 0\right) = 1 - \sum_{\alpha=0}^{mn_E - 1} \frac{\rho_M^\alpha \left(mn_R + \alpha - 1\right)!}{\alpha! \left(\beta_E \rho_E\right)^\alpha \Gamma\left(mn_R\right) \beta_M^{mn_R}} \times \left(\frac{1}{\beta_M} + \frac{\rho_M}{\rho_E \beta_E}\right)^{-(mn_R + \alpha)}$$

Equation 73.

$$\Pr\left(C_S > 0\right) = 1 - \sum_{k=0}^{mn_c - 1} \frac{\rho_M^k \left(mn_c + k - 1\right)!}{k! \left(\beta_E \rho_E\right)^k \Gamma\left(mn_c\right) \beta_M^{mn_c}} \times \left(\frac{1}{\beta_M} + \frac{\rho_M}{\rho_E \beta_E}\right)^{-(mn_c + k)}$$

Equation 74.

$$\Pr\left(C_S > 0\right) = 1 - \sum_{i_1=0}^{m-1} \frac{\rho_M^{i_1} \left(m + i_1 - 1\right)!}{i_1! \left(\beta_E \rho_E\right)^{i_1} \Gamma\left(m\right) \beta_M^m} \times \left(\frac{1}{\beta_M} + \frac{\rho_M}{\rho_E \beta_E}\right)^{-(m + i_1)}$$

$$P_{out}\left(\varepsilon_S\right) = \Pr\left(C_S \le \varepsilon_S\right), \qquad (76)$$
where $\varepsilon_S > 0$.

The significance of this definition is that when the secrecy rate is set to ε_S, the confidential communication will be ensured only if $C_S > \varepsilon_S$, otherwise the secure transmission will not be guaranteed. From the total probability theorem of Equation 77.

We see that $C_S = 0$ when $I_M \le I_E$ i.e. $\Pr\left(C_S \le \varepsilon_S \middle| I_M \le I_E\right) = 1$. Then, Equation 77 can be written as Equation 78.

Substituting the values of $q\left(I_M\right)$ and $q\left(I_E\right)$ in (78) and performing integration, we have Equation 79 where $\xi = \dfrac{\rho_E \beta_E e^{\varepsilon_s} + \rho_M \beta_M}{\rho_M \rho_E \beta_M \beta_E}$

Example 3

(a) (*Symmetric antenna configuration*) Consider $n_R = n_E = n_c$. From (79),

the secure outage probability for Nakagami-m fading SIMO channel is given by Equation 80.

(b) (*SISO channel*) Consider $n_R = n_E = 1$. From (79), the secure outage probability for Nakagami-m fading SISO channel is given by Equation 81.

(c) (*Rayleigh Fading Channel*) Consider $m = 1$. From (79), the secure outage probability for Rayleigh fading SIMO channel is given by Equation 82.

Figure 6 shows the secure outage probability for Nakagami-m fading channel with $m = 1$ (Rayleigh fading channel) as a function of ρ_M for selected values of n_R and ρ_E. We see that secure outage probability decreases with n_R. This is because, improved receive antenna diversity by increasing n_R helps the main channel to combat

Equation 75.

$$\Pr\left(C_S > 0\right) = 1 - \sum_{\delta=0}^{n_{\mathrm{E}}-1} \frac{\rho_{\mathrm{M}}^{\delta}\left(mn_{\mathrm{R}} + \delta - 1\right)!}{\delta!\left(\beta_{\mathrm{E}}\rho_{\mathrm{E}}\right)^{\delta}\Gamma\left(n_{\mathrm{R}}\right)\beta_{\mathrm{M}}^{n_{\mathrm{R}}}} \times \left(\frac{1}{\beta_{\mathrm{M}}} + \frac{\rho_{\mathrm{M}}}{\rho_{\mathrm{E}}\beta_{\mathrm{E}}}\right)^{-\left(n_{\mathrm{R}}+\delta\right)}$$

Equation 77.

$$\begin{aligned} P_{out}\left(\varepsilon_S\right) &= \Pr\left(C_S \le \varepsilon_S \big| \gamma_{\mathrm{M}} > \gamma_{\mathrm{E}}\right)\Pr\left(\gamma_{\mathrm{M}} > \gamma_{\mathrm{E}}\right) + \Pr\left(C_S \le \varepsilon_S \big| \gamma_{\mathrm{M}} \le \gamma_{\mathrm{E}}\right)\Pr\left(\gamma_{\mathrm{M}} \le \gamma_{\mathrm{E}}\right) \\ &= \Pr\left(C_S \le \varepsilon_S \big| I_M > I_{\mathrm{E}}\right)\Pr\left(I_M > I_{\mathrm{E}}\right) + \Pr\left(C_S \le \varepsilon_S \big| I_M \le I_{\mathrm{E}}\right)\Pr\left(I_M \le I_{\mathrm{E}}\right) \end{aligned}$$

Equation 78.

$$\begin{aligned} P_{out}\left(\varepsilon_S\right) &= \Pr\left(C_S \le \varepsilon_S \big| I_{\mathrm{M}} > I_{\mathrm{E}}\right)\Pr\left(I_{\mathrm{M}} > I_{\mathrm{E}}\right) + \Pr\left(I_{\mathrm{M}} \le I_{\mathrm{E}}\right) \\ &= \Pr\left(I_{\mathrm{M}} > I_{\mathrm{E}}\right) - \int_0^{\infty}\int_{I_{\mathrm{E}}+\varepsilon_S}^{\infty} q\left(I_{\mathrm{M}}\right)q\left(I_{\mathrm{E}}\right)dI_{\mathrm{M}}dI_{\mathrm{E}} + \Pr\left(I_{\mathrm{M}} \le I_{\mathrm{E}}\right) \\ &= 1 - \int_0^{\infty}\int_{I_{\mathrm{E}}+\varepsilon_S}^{\infty} q\left(I_{\mathrm{M}}\right)q\left(I_{\mathrm{E}}\right)dI_{\mathrm{M}}dI_{\mathrm{E}} \end{aligned}$$

Equation 79.

$$P_{out}\left(\varepsilon_S\right) = 1 - \sum_{k_1=0}^{mn_{\mathrm{R}}-1} \frac{e^{k_1\varepsilon_s + \frac{1-e^{\varepsilon_s}}{\rho_{\mathrm{M}}\beta_{\mathrm{M}}}}}{\left(\rho_{\mathrm{E}}\beta_{\mathrm{E}}\right)^{mn_{\mathrm{E}}}\Gamma\left(mn_{\mathrm{E}}\right)\left(\rho_{\mathrm{M}}\beta_{\mathrm{M}}\right)^{k_1}} \sum_{\zeta_1=0}^{k_1} \frac{\left(1-\frac{1}{e^{\varepsilon_s}}\right)^{k_1-\zeta_1}\left(mn_{\mathrm{E}}+\zeta_1-1\right)!}{\zeta_1!\left(k_1-\zeta_1\right)!\xi^{\left(mn_{\mathrm{E}}+\zeta_1\right)}}$$

Equation 80.

$$P_{out}\left(\varepsilon_S\right) = 1 - \sum_{k=0}^{mn_c-1} \frac{e^{k_1\varepsilon_s + \frac{1-e^{\varepsilon_s}}{\rho_{\mathrm{M}}\beta_{\mathrm{M}}}}}{\left(\rho_{\mathrm{E}}\beta_{\mathrm{E}}\right)^{mn_c}\Gamma\left(mn_c\right)\left(\rho_{\mathrm{M}}\beta_{\mathrm{M}}\right)^{k_1}} \sum_{\zeta_1=0}^{k_1} \frac{\left(1-\frac{1}{e^{\varepsilon_s}}\right)^{k_1-\zeta_1}\left(mn_c+\zeta_1-1\right)!}{\zeta_1!\left(k_1-\zeta_1\right)!\xi^{\left(mn_c+\zeta_1\right)}}$$

Equation 81.

$$P_{out}\left(\varepsilon_S\right) = 1 - \sum_{i_1=0}^{m-1} \frac{e^{i_1\varepsilon_s + \frac{1-e^{\varepsilon_s}}{\rho_M\beta_M}}}{\left(\rho_E\beta_E\right)^m \Gamma\left(m\right)\left(\rho_M\beta_M\right)^{i_1}} \sum_{\zeta_1=0}^{i_1} \frac{\left(1 - \frac{1}{e^{\varepsilon_s}}\right)^{i_1-\zeta_1} \left(m + \zeta_1 - 1\right)!}{\zeta_1!\left(i_1 - \zeta_1\right)!\xi^{\left(m+\zeta_1\right)}}$$

Equation 82.

$$P_{out}\left(\varepsilon_S\right) = 1 - \sum_{k_1=0}^{mn_R-1} \frac{e^{k_1\varepsilon_s + \frac{1-e^{\varepsilon_s}}{\rho_M\beta_M}}}{\left(\rho_E\beta_E\right)^{mn_E} \Gamma\left(mn_E\right)\left(\rho_M\beta_M\right)^{k_1}} \sum_{\zeta_1=0}^{k_1} \frac{\left(1 - \frac{1}{e^{\varepsilon_s}}\right)^{k_1-\zeta_1} \left(mn_E + \zeta_1 - 1\right)!}{\zeta_1!\left(k_1 - \zeta_1\right)!\xi^{\left(mn_E+\zeta_1\right)}}$$

fading which in turn causes the improvement of secrecy capacity and makes it possible to achieve a positive secrecy capacity even when the eavesdropper channel is better than main channel i.e. $\rho_E > \rho_M$. So, it is more attractive to achieve information-theoretic secrecy in the fading wireless channels by using multiple antennas at the legitimate receiver. On the other hand, secure outage probability increases with ρ_E but decreases with ρ_M. Therefore, the better the main channel the smaller the secure outage probability.

Outage secrecy capacity: The ε-outage secrecy capacity is defined as the largest secrecy rate such that the outage probability is less than or equal to ε and can be found,

$$P_{out}\left(C_{S,out}\left(\varepsilon\right)\right) = \varepsilon \tag{83}$$

It is hard to find the outage secrecy capacity analytically since the outage probability is a complicated function of the secrecy rate, ε_S. But it is possible to compute its value numerically based on the equation of outage probability.

4. FUTURE RESEARCH DIRECTIONS

In this chapter, an overview of research on information theoretic security with a focus on the problem of secure communication through fading channel is discussed. Although intensive work has been done on this topic in recent years, quite a few important issues still remain unresolved. Some of these issues are discussed below.

The study of achievable secrecy capacity region with dirty paper coding (DPC) scheme is an important issue for the various fading network scenarios, including broadcast, multiple-access, interference and relay networks. Only a few studies (e.g. (Liu and Poor, 2009)) have addressed the development of secrecy capacity region with DPC.

The secure outage performance for the fading relay networks when CSI is not available at the transmitter is also an open problem, and study of it could yield practical applications for such networks. A very few papers are available in the literature in which the secrecy capacity of relay networks (Aggarwal et. al., 2009) has been studied in the presence of single as well as multiple eavesdroppers.

Practical code design to achieve secrecy needs to be further explored, in particular, for the cases

Figure 6. Simulation and analytical results of the secure outage probability for Nakagami-m fading channel with $m = 1$ (Rayleigh fading channel) as a function of ρ_M for selected values of n_R and ρ_E.

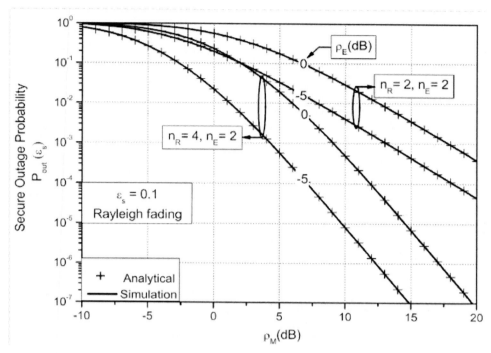

in which both the main channel and eavesdropper channel are noisy. Structured code approaches based on lattice codes, as a counterpart of linear codes, are very useful for implementing many information theoretic techniques such as binning technique, dirty-paper coding, and Wyner-Ziv coding (see e.g., (Erez et. al., 2005)). These approaches may be powerful for secure code design for continuous channels and/or channels with large alphabets.

5 CONCLUSION

In this paper, secrecy capacity is defined for Nakagami-m fading channel under different assumptions on the available transmitter CSI. Since Nakagami-m distribution can model fading conditions which are more or less severe than that of Rayleigh and includes Rayleigh as a special case, therefore the study of secrecy capacity for Nakagami-m fading channel is a generalized one. In order to analyze the secure outage performance of fading channels, analytical expressions for the probability of non-zero secrecy capacity and secure outage probability are derived for Nakagami-m fading channel. This work considers the system model with multiple antennas at the legitimate receiver and eavesdropper, therefore the analysis includes SISO channel as a special case. Analytical expressions are verified via Monte-Carlo simulation and some numerical results are shown to clear the insight of derived expressions. Results show that multiple antennas at the legitimate receiver makes it possible to achieve a positive secrecy capacity even when the eavesdropper channel is better than main channel. Therefore, it is more practical and attractive to achieve information-theoretic secrecy in wireless networks by using multiple antennas at the physical layer.

REFERENCES

Aggarwal, V., Sankar, L., Calderbank, A. R., & Poor, H. V. (2009). Secrecy capacity of a class of orthogonal relay eavesdropper channels. *EURASIP Journal on Wireless Communications and Networking*, 2009.

Barros, J., & Rodrigues, M. R. (2006). Secrecy capacity of wireless channels. In *Proceedings of the IEEE International Symposium on Information Theory (ISIT2006)*, (pp. 1054–1059). Seattle, USA.

Beaulieu, N. C., & Cheng, C. (2005). Efficient Nakagami-m fading channel simulation. *IEEE Transactions on Vehicular Technology, 54*(2), 413–424. doi:10.1109/TVT.2004.841555

Bloch, M., Barros, J., Rodrigues, M. R. D., & McLaughlin, S. W. (2008). Wireless information-theoretic security. *IEEE Transactions on Information Theory, 54*(6), 2515–2534. doi:10.1109/TIT.2008.921908

Erez, U., Litsyn, S., & Zamir, R. (2005). Lattices which are good for (almost) everything. *IEEE Transactions on Information Theory, 51*, 3401–3416. doi:10.1109/TIT.2005.855591

Gopala, P. K., Lai, L., & Gamal, H. E. (2008). On the secrecy capacity of fading channels. *IEEE Transactions on Information Theory, 54*(10), 4687–4690. doi:10.1109/TIT.2008.928990

Gradshteyn, I. S., & Ryzhik, I. M. (2007). *Table of integrals, series, and products* (7th ed.). San Diego, CA: Academic.

Lai, L., El Gamal, H., & Poor, H. V. (2009). Authentication over noisy channels. *IEEE Transactions on Information Theory, 55*, 906–916. doi:10.1109/TIT.2008.2009842

Leung-Yan-Cheong, S. K., & Hellman, M. E. (1978). The Gaussian wire-tap channel. *IEEE Transactions on Information Theory, 24*, 451–456. doi:10.1109/TIT.1978.1055917

Liu, R., & Poor, H. V. (2009). Secrecy capacity region of a multiple-antenna Gaussian broadcast channel with confidential messages. *IEEE Transactions on Information Theory, 55*(3), 1235–1249. doi:10.1109/TIT.2008.2011448

Liu, T., & Shitz, S. S. (2009). A note on the secrecy capacity of the multiple-antenna wiretap channel. *IEEE Transactions on Information Theory, 55*(6), 2547–2553. doi:10.1109/TIT.2009.2018322

Magableh, A. M., & Matalgah, M. M. (2008). Capacity of SIMO system over non-identically independent Nakagami-m channel. In *Proceedings of the IEEE Sarnoff Symposium*, (pp. 1–5). Princeton, NJ.

Maurer, U. (2000). Authentication theory and hypothesis testing. *IEEE Transactions on Information Theory, 46*, 1350–1356. doi:10.1109/18.850674

Ratnarajah, T., & Vaillancourt, R. (2005). Quadratic forms on complex random matrices and multiple-antenna systems. *IEEE Transactions on Information Theory, 51*(8), 2976–2984. doi:10.1109/TIT.2005.851778

Rosenbaum, U. (1993). A lower bound on authentication after having observed a sequence of messages. *Journal of Cryptology, 6*(3), 135–156. doi:10.1007/BF00198462

Sarkar, M. Z. I., & Ratnarajah, T. (2011). Secrecy capacity and secure outage performance for Rayleigh fading SIMO channel. In *Proceedings IEEE 36th International Conference on Acoustics, Speech and Signal Processing*, Prague, Czech Republic.

Sarkar, M. Z. I., & Ratnarajah, T. (2011). Secure communication through Nakagami-m fading MISO channel. In *Proceedings of IEEE International Conference on Communications (ICC 2011)*, Kyoto, Japan.

Sellathurai, M., Ratnarajah, T., & Guinand, P. (2007). Multirate layered space-time coding and successive interference cancellation receivers in quasi-static fading channels. *IEEE Transactions on Wireless Communications*, 6(12), 4524–4533. doi:10.1109/TWC.2007.060399

Shannon, C. E. (1949). Communication theory of secrecy systems. *The Bell System Technical Journal*, 28, 656–715.

Suzuki, H. (1977). A statistical model for urban radio propagation. *IEEE Transactions on Communications*, 25(7), 673–680. doi:10.1109/TCOM.1977.1093888

Walker, M. (1990). Information theoretic bounds for authentication schemes. *Journal of Cryptology*, 2(3), 131–143. doi:10.1007/BF00190800

Xiao, L., Greenstein, L., Mandayam, N., & Trappe, W. (2008). A physical-layer technique to enhance authentication for mobile terminals. In *Proceedings IEEE International Conference on Communications (ICC)*, (pp. 1520–1524). Beijing, China.

Chapter 3
Security Issues for ISO 18000-6 Type C RFID:
Identification and Solutions

Peter J. Hawrylak
The University of Tulsa, USA

John Hale
The University of Tulsa, USA

Mauricio Papa
The University of Tulsa, USA

ABSTRACT

Radio frequency identification (RFID) devices have matured to the point where they are now expanding beyond the retail supply chain and public transit fare management systems. RFID technology provides a low power and economical method to link remote sensors to larger control systems. In these cases, the RFID protocols provide the communication link between the sensor and larger control system. Security solutions designed for the retail and transit fare management systems are not sufficient for these new control systems. New avenues of attack are available, and attackers have different goals. Therefore, the security of these RFID protocols must be re-examined in order to identify those vulnerabilities that are not significant in the retail or fare applications, but could be exploited in these new settings. This chapter analyzes the ISO 18000-6 Type C protocol to identify potential security vulnerabilities. This protocol is one of the major RFID protocols for passive RFID systems.

INTRODUCTION

Radio frequency identification (RFID) devices are becoming pervasive in our world and play a key role in the deployment of the Internet of Things (IoT). This chapter focuses on security issues of the ISO 18000-6 Type C (International Organization for Standardization, 2010) protocol stack, which is based on the EPCglobal Gen-2 protocol (EPCglobal, 2008). This protocol stack is becoming particularly relevant in distributed process control systems, also known as SCADA (Supervisory Control and Data Acquisition)

DOI: 10.4018/978-1-4666-1797-1.ch003

Copyright © 2012, IGI Global. Copying or distributing in print or electronic forms without written permission of IGI Global is prohibited.

systems. In particular, the ISO 18000-6 Type C protocol supports the use of sensors in SCADA systems used in the operation of various critical infrastructures such as the oil & gas industry and the electric power sector.

This chapter presents a brief introduction to RFID architectures and an overview of the ISO 18000-6 Type C protocol. Next, threats to RFID systems are described and analyzed in the context of the protocol stack, the messaging structure, and the state transitions of RFID network nodes. This analysis provides the basis to present interruption, modification, and fabrication attacks on such systems. In particular, a series of scenarios are presented to illustrate the relevance of security issues identified in this chapter. Possible solution paths and mitigation strategies for these issues are presented to help system users and designers mitigate the negative effects that these attacks may have. The chapter concludes with a section highlighting the security challenges facing RFID and the necessary areas of research to overcome these issues.

RFID BACKGROUND

RFID provides a means to remotely identify and monitor assets. Initially used for monitoring retail inventories, supply chain management, automatic toll collection (e.g. EZ-Pass), and keyless entry systems, RFID is now being coupled with sensors to monitor the asset's condition (Todd, Phillips, Schultz, Hawkins & Jensen, 2009; Law, Bermak & Luong, 2010). The attachment of sensors increases the value and applicability of the information provided by the tag. Wireless sensors offer many advantages for monitoring conditions in hard to access places and machinery because wiring is minimal and minimal infrastructure is required for wireless sensor systems. As a result, RFID systems are being investigated for use as the communication medium for edge devices to sense conditions for critical infrastructures such

as the Smart Grid (next generation power grid). This increase makes RFID systems a target for or a tool in the use of a malicious cyber-attack. Thus, the security of the communication protocols employed to connect RFID devices together must be investigated.

RFID systems are comprised of four major components: RFID tags, RFID readers, RFID middleware, and backend software. The backend software controls the overall system and provides the repository of information for the tags. An enterprise resource planning (ERP) software package is one example of backend software. The RFID middleware sits between the backend software and RFID reader. Sometimes the RFID middleware is contained within the RFID reader itself. The RFID middleware provides the functionality of a device driver to link the RFID reader to the network and ultimately to the backend software, and filters or prunes the information sent to the backend software. This helps to reduce the amount of data transmitted over the network. The RFID reader is the edge device providing the last mile network connection between itself and the RFID tag. RFID tags are attached to the asset. RFID tags contain a unique identification number and possibly some additional memory that may read only or read-writable. Some RFID tags, termed a *license plate tag*, contain only the unique identifier that is used to access a record in a database maintained by the backend software. More advanced tags offer additional memory that can store or record additional information, such as expiration date or to track information over the asset's lifetime.

One general classification for RFID tags is based on how they are powered. There are three types of tags using this classification: passive, battery-assisted passive (BAP), and active. Passive tags have no on-board battery and must harvest their operating energy from the environment. A group of passive tags are shown in Figure 1.

The most common method is to harvest energy from the RFID reader's RF transmission. Other energy harvesting methods include thermal,

Figure 1. Passive RFID tags

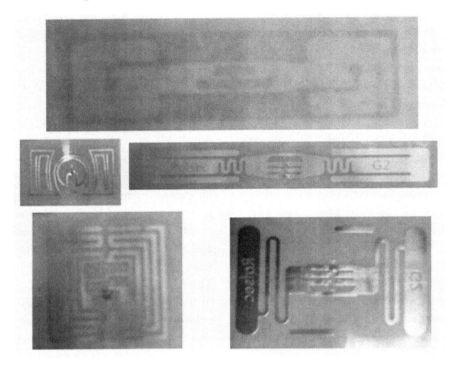

solar (O'Connor, 2011), and piezoelectric (vibrations) materials. Passive tags do not need to have their batteries replaced and by attaching simple sensors can be used to monitor conditions. Passive tags communicate using backscatter communication by modulating the amount of energy of the reader's signal they reflect back to the reader. BAP tags have a battery and are typically built using passive tag that includes a sensor. The battery provides energy to power the sensor and microprocessor, but not the communication. A BAP tag still uses backscatter communication. This allows the sensor to record information continuously, not just when being interrogated (powered) by the reader. Further, because the tag does not have to use part of the reader's signal to power itself and can use all of the energy in that signal for communication, it can communicate over longer distances compared to a passive tag. BAP tags can be used to monitor conditions of items, such as temperature, in the cold chain, e.g.

frozen food and pharmaceutical supply chain (Emond, 2008). Active tags have a battery that powers the entire tag, including communication hardware. Energy consumption of active tags is critical and must be evaluated to make the best use of this limited resource (Hawrylak, Cain, & Mickle, 2007). While the batteries in most active tags can be replaced, this is costly in terms of time and labor. Active tags and to a lesser degree BAP tags are susceptible to an energy draining attack (Raymond, Marchany, Brownfield & Midkiff, 2009) where an attacker infiltrates the system to cause tags to stay active (awake) or perform more work than normal in order to deplete their battery reserve.

The wireless nature of RFID has led to a significant amount of research in the areas of preventing tracking and ensuring privacy. Juels presents a thorough overview of these issues (Juels, 2006; Juels, & Weis, 2009). RFID has been investigated as a method to deter counterfeiting of Euro banknotes. This presents a problem because the same technology can be used to track the movement of a particular banknote and its owner (Juels & Pappu, 2003).

As RFID expanded beyond the initial use of differentiating between friendly and unfriendly military assets, identify friend or foe (IFF) technology, the security requirements have changed (Rieback, Crispo, Tanenbaum, 2006). RFID is being employed to verify identification documents such as passports. As a result the ability to clone and authenticate the RFID tags in the documents is important (Koscher, Juels, Brajkovic, & Kohno, 2009). Misuse of the RFID protocol can cause significant problems in these applications, such as increasing processing times at border crossings.

As RFID technology becomes more widespread, attackers have at their disposal a multitude of new vulnerabilities to exploit (Rotter, 2008; Mirowski, Hartnett, & Williams, 2009; Mitrokotsa, Rieback, & Tanenbaum, 2010). This chapter explores the ISO 18000-6 Type C protocol in detail and describes how the protocol can be manipulated to conduct attacks against RFID systems. These attacks in themselves are nothing more than a nuisance to the system, but when combined with other actions can represent serious threats to the larger system.

OVERVIEW OF THE ISO 18000-6 TYPE C PROTOCOL STACK

The ISO 18000-6 Type C (International Organization for Standardization, 2010) protocol (standard) defines operation of passive RFID systems operating in the 860 MHz to 960 MHz range worldwide. ISO 18000-6 Type C defines the lower layers of the OSI communication stack for the reader and tag, provides a description of the tag operation (finite state machine for the tag), and the memory organization of the tag. The physical link, medium access control (MAC), and network layers, as well as parts of the transport

and session layers are described in this standard. Due to local regulations (e.g. FCC, ETSI, etc.) there is not a single frequency available worldwide for this protocol. The protocol is based on simple amplitude shift keying (ASK) or phase shift keying (PSK) modulation for the reader to tag link and ASK modulation for the tag to reader link. The tag to reader link employs backscatter communication. Details about the physics behind RFID tag operation can be found in (Finkenzeller, 2003; Mickle, Mats & Hawrylak, 2008; Hawrylak, Cain & Mickle, 2008). Hawrylak and Mickle (Hawrylak & Mickle, 2009) present an overview of the physical layer of the EPC Gen-2 (EPCglobal, 2008) specification which ISO 18000-6 Type C is based on.

ISO 18000-6 Type C tag memory, illustrated in Figure 2, is divided into four categories or *banks*: reserved, unique item identifier (UII), tag identification (TID), and user memory. Reserved memory contains passwords for accessing the higher level functions (e.g. read and write) and to disable or kill the tag.

The UII memory bank includes a unique serial number for the tag, information about tag capabilities, and associated error detection information (e.g. checksum or CRC). The UII can be a single number or can be divided into several fields to encode information such as manufacturer ID or country of origin. These fields provide a means to search tags based on their UII's and then to identify those tags that are of interest from a larger group. EPCglobal has published a specification describing a number of different UII structures for RFID applications (EPCglobal, 2010).

The TID memory contains information to identify the type of the tag and the standard used to encode the UII information. The TID provides the reader with information about what fields are present in the UII and where they are located. The TID also contains a list of the optional commands and features supported by the tag.

Figure 2. ISO 18000-6 Type C memory layout

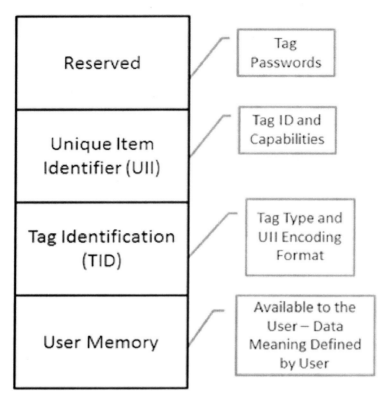

User memory is a blank memory whose structure and meaning is defined by the user of the tag. Not all tags have user memory. One use of user memory is to store sensor readings or maintenance history for parts on airplanes (Bacheldor, 2009).

ISO 18000-6 Type C defines a three stage reader to tag communication sequence: Selection, Inventory, and Access. During the Selection phase the tags of interest are identified from the population of tags within range of the reader. This enables the reader to focus the Inventory phase on only those tags of interest. For example, the Selection phase can be used to identify all tags linked to medical contrast die (Lavine, 2008) out of all tagged items in a medical cabinet. This will speed up the Inventory phase and reduce the number of collisions. During the Selection phase

tags do not send any response to the reader, but alter one or more flags in the tag.

The Inventory phase is used by the reader to collect the UII (identification information) of each tag participating in the Inventory phase. The UII provides a link between the tag and an entry in a database that contains more detailed information about the asset the tag is attached too. Often, this is all that is required and in this case, the tag is referred to as a *license plate* tag. However, there are a number of cases where this is not the case, such as, a remote area where a connection to the central database is not available. In this case, the tag must store the critical information locally and provide the reader access to that information.

The Access phase is when a reader communicates with a single tag; in the Selection and Inventory phases the reader communicates with all tags within range. During the Access phase the reader will read or write the tag's non-volatile memory, adjust memory protection levels (lock or unlock), and deactivate, or *kill*, the tag. For example, the expiration date for a perishable item could be stored in the tag memory and the Access phase is when that information would be retrieved by the reader.

The exchange of commands and responses in a typical ISO 18000-6 Type C exchange is illustrated in Figure 3. The Selection phase is composed of one or more Select commands to identify the tags that are of interest. The Inventory phase is composed of one or more inventory commands: Query, QueryAdjust, QueryRep, ACK, and NAK to retrieve each tag's UII. These commands are used to manage the Aloha based anti-collision mechanism and the selection and order of commands used impacts the time required to retrieve all UIIs (Maillart, Kamrani, Norman, Rajgopal & Hawrylak, 2010; Ravilla, Ogirala, Murari, Hawrylak, & Mickle, 2011). The Access phase requires the RN16 that the tag generates and transmits once its slot counter reaches zero. The RN16 is used in the Req_RN command to cause the tag to

generate a new random 16-bit number, which is used as a handle in later higher level commands. The handle is similar to a file handle and enables the tag to verify that the higher level command is addressed to itself and not another tag.

Selection Phase

The reader transmits a series of Select commands to identify those tags that match the request. This is similar to the SQL select command used to search database tables. The matching information is maintained by a set of flags in the tag that are altered based on the results of the Select commands. These flags are then used in the Inventory phase to eliminate those tags that are not of interest. The tag maintains a total of five flags that are used during the Selection and Inventory phases. Four of those flags, S0, S1, S2, and S3, deal mainly with the Inventory phase and one, the *Selected Flag*, deals mainly with the Selection phase.

The Select command is composed of seven parameters: target, action, membank, pointer, length, mask, and truncate. The target and action parameters specify the flag affected by the Select

Figure 3. A typical ISO 18000-6 Type C exchange

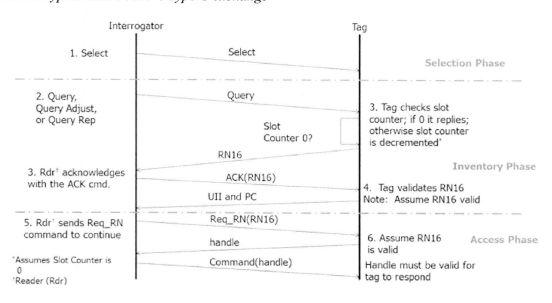

command and the action to take with that flag. The membank, pointer, and length parameters specify the location of the data stored in the tag that will be compared to the mask data to determine whether or not the tag matches the request. Select commands can access any memory bank, including user memory. The truncate parameter instructs the tag whether or not to return the full UII or only the UII portion not included in the mask. Multiple Select commands can be chained together to perform complex searches involving the standard logical operations: AND, OR, and NOT.

The Select command can search tags based on their physical capabilities, the commands they support, their UII, and their data. The UII can be encoded in the EPCglobal format or in the ISO (International Organization for Standardization) formats. The EPCglobal format is primarily focused on identifying retail goods on the sales floor or on tracking goods through the supply chain. EPCglobal has defined a series of UII encodings (EPCglobal, 2010) which divide the UII into fields based on the particular application. The ISO format provides a similar field definition. These fields enable the user to search tags based on specific items, such as manufacturer, owner, and asset type that can be encoded in the UII (International Organization for Standardization, 2009; EPCglobal, 2010). Hawrylak and Mickle (Hawrylak & Mickle, 2009) describe how to use the Select command to speed up reading tags in the EPCglobal format by identifying the tags of interest for the inventory round.

For example, if a reader wishes to identify all tagged medical contrast die with an expiration date in the current month stored in user memory, it could issue two Select commands using the AND operation. The first Select command would identify all tags having the appropriate UII field for medical contrast die and the second Select command would identify all tags having user memory (not all tags support user memory). By setting the action parameter of the second Select

command to AND the tags whose Selected Flag are asserted after the second Select command are those related to medical contrast die and have user memory. Such tags are termed *selected tags*.

Inventory Phase

The tag's UII is retrieved during the Inventory phase. During the Inventory phase multiple tags are communicating with a reader and a framed Aloha based anti-collision system is employed. The Inventory phase is divided into a series of Inventory Rounds where the tags respond to the reader in order to transmit their UII. Inventory Rounds are initiated by the Query command. The Query command determines which tags will participate in the new Inventory Round, using the Select and Inventory Flags.

ISO 18000-6 Type C supports four sessions each maintaining one of the four Inventory Flags. This enables multiple readers to inventory the same tag by using different sessions. The Query command specifies which session to use, whether the Select Flag must match or not, and the value of the Inventory Flag. Only those tags matching these parameters will participate in the new Inventory Round. Time is divided into slots in each Inventory Round and the reader moves to the next slot by issuing a Query, QueryRep, or QueryAdjust commands. The number of slots is determined by the Q parameter that is specified in the Query command. The number of slots in each round is 2^Q and each tag will select a random number between 0 and 2^Q-1, termed the *slot counter*. Tags respond by sending a 16-bit random number, termed *RN16*, when the slot counter is equal to zero. This RN16 is used by the reader as a handle for retrieving the UII from the tag. A tag that has had its UII successfully read by the reader is termed *acknowledged*. Collisions occur when two or more tags respond during the same slot. Often one of these tags has a signal that is strong enough to drown out the other tags replies (Maguire & Pappu, 2009). This allows the reader to retrieve only one of the replies. Using advanced signal processing techniques it is possible to recover multiple replies (Sun, Hawrylak, Mao, & Mickle, 2010), thus providing a throughput of greater than one tag per slot.

A Query command starts a new Inventory Round causing all tags matching the Query parameters to select a new slot counter. The QueryRep command indicates the start of the next slot and all tags will decrement their slot counters. QueryAdjust causes the tags to generate a new slot number and can change the Q parameter by one in either direction. However, the QueryAdjust command does not start a new Inventory Round and only un-acknowledged tags will participate. These three commands have different lengths in order to speed up the Inventory Round. QueryRep is the shortest command because it will be sent the most, Query is the longest, and the length of QueryAdjust is between QueryRep and Query.

The ACK command is used to acknowledge the receipt of the RN16 from the tag causing the tag to send its UII and PC information to the reader.

Access Phase

The Access Phase provides an opportunity for the reader to retrieve or alter data stored in the tag's memory, adjust tag memory security settings, disable the tag, or reinitialize the tag. The Write and BlockWrite commands provide the capability to write data to the tag. The Write command allows one 16-bit word to be written and the BlockWrite command provides the capability for multiple 16-bit words to be written with a single command. The Read command provides the ability to read a variable amount of data from the tag. The BlockErase command provides the reader with the ability to erase data stored in the tag's memory. However, the erase method the tag uses is not specified by ISO 18000-6 meaning that erasure could be simply marking the memory as available rather

than remove or overwrite the data to be erased. The tag memory can be secured to prevent future reading (for passwords) and writing. The Lock and BlockPermalock commands can be used to adjust these settings. Memory can be protected against writing either from only the Secured state or not at all, but reading cannot be disabled. Passwords provide control over both reading and writing capabilities. The read and write controls for the password data are linked together, either both are allowed or both are disallowed. It is also possible to lock memory so that it can always be written to (never locked) and that the password can always be read and written.

Tags may implement an access password that is required to access the Secured state. Only in the Secured state can the Lock and BlockPermalock commands to change the memory security settings be executed. An access password of all 0s indicates that the access password option is not being used and tags enter the Secured state after receiving a valid Req_RN command (International Organization for Standardization, 2010). The access password is 32-bits and is transmitted in two successive 16-bit transfers. Before each part of the 16-bits is transferred the reader requests a new handle. The 16-bit portion of the access password is exclusive ORed (XORed) with the handle and then sent to the tag. This provides some security requiring the attacker to monitor the communication to obtain both handles. After sending the first 16-bits of the access password, the reader must request a new handle using the Reg_RN command and repeat the process to transmit the second 16-bits. The tag enters the Secured state only if both 16-bit halves are correct and the required process was followed.

The BlockWrite, BlockPermalock, BlockErase, and Access commands are defined as optional commands in ISO 18000-6 Type C (International Organization for Standardization, 2010) and are not supported by all tags.

ISO 18000-6 TYPE C PROTOCOL BASED THREATS

Rogue Select Command

Selecting a tag population is the first step in the select, inventory and access cycle that dictates interactions between tags and interrogators. This process, which may involve use of one or more Select commands, determines which subset of accessible tags will participate in the inventory round where tags are identified in preparation for further access. The ability to interfere with this process is the first opportunity an attacker may have to adversely affect the RFID environment. It is important to note that interrogators also have the ability either attempt to inventory not selected tags or to completely ignore the fact that a tag is selected (the selected state in a tag is stored in the SL flag). The attacks described in this section assume the system follows common use patterns where the interrogator inventories and accesses those tags that have been selected. The main goal behind the attacks is to affect the selection process with varying degrees of impact. Clearly, the most extreme three attacks would seek either selection of all or none of the tags or the complement (NOT) of the interrogator's set operators. However, by manipulating Select parameters it is also possible for an attacker to have very granular control of the tags that will participate in the inventory and access phases.

Although Select is a single command, the fact that it can be used in succession using seven different parameters (target, action, membank, pointer, length, mask and truncate) make it a very versatile command. During selection, the interrogator successively applies union (OR), intersection (AND), and negation (NOT) operators to update a tag's state to either selected or not selected (via the SL flag). The target parameter indicates whether the Select may modify a tag's SL flags and the action parameter indicates how it would be modified. The final result of an action determines what is done by matching and not matching tags. Those tags that conform to parameters membank, pointer, length and mask are considered to be matching.

An attacker with the ability to observe the selection process may gain valuable information about what an interrogator's intentions are and may use this information to dictate any further actions. For instance, an attacker might be able to find out TID values of interest to the interrogator (the same applies to UII).

In addition, the Select command provides an attacker with the ability to use information gleaned from the command to search the tag's memory and infer information from those searches. An attacker can search for tags from a particular company or for a particular type of item based on their UII because the UII is typically encoded in the EPCglobal (EPCglobal, 2010) or the ISO format. Alternatively, an attacker can use the Select command to search for specific items in the tag's user memory. These items may include a part of a data record such as a phone number or a sensor value. The attacker can then use the Inventory Process to determine the set of tags matching their request. From this information they can infer information about those tags and the assets to which they are attached. These tags can be targeted by the attacker in future attacks.

An attacker could also have the ability to insert Select commands and manipulate the tag population that will respond to the Inventory. For instance, rogue Select commands with actions 110 and 111 could be used to alter or augment the tags currently selected by the attacker by having non-matching tags assert or negate the SL flag. On the other hand, action 000 could be used by an attacker to de-assert the SL flag in matching tags with the SL flag set. In other words, this type of attack would effectively remove tags from the set the interrogator has already selected. Rogue Select commands could also be used to change the tag's inventoried flag to A or B for non-matching tags.

In one scenario, the rogue Select command can be used to identify tags that are linked to high-value assets. The goal of this attack could be to identify a group of assets to steal or a group of tags to try to further compromise, e.g. by planting false information. Here the Select command can be used by the attacker to search the tag's user memory bank for specific information, such as a medical condition or a material safety data sheet (MSDS) to identify hazardous compounds. This type of attack is possible if information is stored in a standardized format, similar to the definitions for the UII (EPCglobal, 2010). Such standardization is required for a given RFID tag to be interoperable with systems from various vendors; otherwise, users will be forced to employ multiple RFID tags (one for each type of system supported), which is very costly and inefficient. After the appropriate string of Select commands has been sent, the attacker uses the Inventory Phase to determine the tags (through their UII) matching the criteria. This information can be used to target future attacks against specific assets that may be less secure or more valuable to the attacker. An alternative embodiment of this attack can use the Inventory Phase for those tags that are *not* selected. This may help to disguise the true targets of the attack. In this case, the attacker ignores those tags that respond and focuses on those that did not respond. The attacker will most likely use this information to target a particular set of physical assets (e.g. a group of containers or a particular truck).

Denial of Service (DOS) Attacks: Inventory Round

The Inventory phase, or *Inventory process*, is divided into a series of Inventory Rounds. The mix of commands sent by the reader during the Inventory process directly impacts the throughput or amount of time required to retrieve the UII from all tags present (Maillart, Kamrani, Norman, Rajgopal & Hawrylak, 2010; Ravilla, Ogirala, Murari, Hawrylak, & Mickle, 2011). There are a number of attack vectors available to delay or

stop the Inventory process. The attack vectors differ in their ease of detection by the defender.

Simplistically, an attacker can jam the communication by transmitting noise or random data in the vicinity of the reader and tags. This is known as a *jamming attack* and will disrupt the tag-to-reader link, but is easily detected by the defender. Most likely, this attack would be interpreted as environmental noise present in that location. However, if the environment does not normally experience this level of noise or the noise does not cease after a short time the defender can infer that a jamming attack is underway. The transmitter emitting the jamming signal must be removed or disabled to restore normal communications. This attack is easily detected but is effective in stopping the Inventory process for a time.

A variation of the jamming attack is to use a rogue tag to conduct the jamming. Such a tag is known as a *blocker tag* (Juels, Rivest & Szydlo, 2003; Juels, & Brainard, 2004) and is intended to protect privacy by preventing one's RFID tags from being read clandestinely. The blocker tag responds in every slot, thus causing a collision, to obscure legitimate tags. However, an attacker could place blocker tags in the vicinity of the reader to delay or stop the inventory round. In one scenario, an attacker can place a few rogue blocker tags on items. Until these rogue blocker tags are removed these items can cause disruptions when they are within range of an RFID reader. This attack would appear at first to be a defective tag that responds in every slot. The presence of the blocker tag would quickly be discovered because a tag that complies with the ISO 18000-6 Type C standard will not respond in every slot. Countermeasures include using signal processing techniques to remove the blocker tag's signal (Rieback, Crispo, & Tanenbaum, 2005; Sun, Hawrylak, Mao, & Mickle, 2010) or physical removal of the blocker tag devices. The method of Sun *et al.* (Sun, Hawrylak, Mao, & Mickle, 2010) can be employed to remove the randomized blocker tag proposed by Rieback *et al.* (Rieback, Crispo, & Tanenbaum, 2005), and retrieve information from legitimate tags.

The previous two attack vectors are based on RF jamming and are easy to detect. Physical security is the best option to counter these attacks as both require placement of a device within range of the reader and tags. This range is limited to 3-10m.

More subtle attacks include those that use the commands in the protocol to disrupt the Inventory process. These attacks, when used sparingly, can easily blend in with other commands issued by legitimate readers. The Query command can be injected during an Inventory Round to cause the tags to start a new Inventory Round. This will cause those tags that have already been Acknowledged (sent their UII to the reader) to reenter the Inventory Process, thereby, reducing throughput. Injection of the QueryRep command can move through the slots too quickly, before the reader can respond to those tags that replied (tag's whose slot counter was zero and sent their RN16 value) during the previous time slot. These tags will reset (roll over) their slot counter to all 1's (maximum value) and will not respond for another 65,536 slots. This may cause the legitimate reader to miss those tags. In an inventory tracking system, this can result in incorrect inventory reports. For example, a hospital may under-estimate the quantity of goods in inventory leading to them ordering unnecessary supplies. In another example, not reading all of the tags may cause a supplier to include extra items in a shipment due to the undercount. The QueryAdjust command can be used to cause the tags to select new slot numbers and to adjust the value of the Q parameter. Both may result in a decrease in the throughput of the Inventory Process by deviating from the optimal action for a given situation (Maillart, Kamrani, Norman, Rajgopal & Hawrylak, 2010; Ravilla, Ogirala, Murari, Hawrylak, & Mickle, 2011). Another goal of a DOS attack can be to slow but not stop the RFID communication. One use of RFID is in the supply chain to sort and track items as they move through the processing facility or distribution warehouse. With the just-in-time inventory systems being employed slowing down the distribution process could result in supply disruptions.

Tag Status Modification

Higher-level features (changing tag settings, reading data, or writing data) require the tag to be in the Open or Secured state. However, there are a number of ways to cause tags to exit these states. Causing a tag to revert back to one of the Inventory process states: Ready, Arbitrate, or Reply requires that the reader go through the Inventory process to obtain the tag's UII again. This causes a delay in processing a tag and even to that tag being overlooked in the process. These attacks can be particularly problematic if they interrupt an exchange where data is being written (or updated) to the tag. If interrupted before the write or update is complete the tag will have corrupted or incorrect data (part new and part old). In the worst case the tag may move out of range of the reader before the reader can re-establish communication and complete the write or update.

The Query command can be used to force a tag to return to the Ready state. This occurs regardless of whether or not the malicious Query command matches the session used in the previous Inventory Round. This feature is required in the protocol to prevent a tag from becoming stuck in the Open or Secured states and not being able to communication with multiple readers. The QueryRep and QueryAdjust commands can also be used but the session parameter must match the session used in the previous Inventory Round. However, there are only four session parameters and these are two of the shortest commands so it is relatively simple for an attacker to transmit four of these commands each using a different session. After these four commands all tags that were in the Open or Secured states will return to the Ready state. Both commands are frequently used in the protocol, with QueryRep probably accounting for the majority of commands. Because of this, the attacker issuing these four commands can blend into the normal network traffic relatively easily.

The Select command is another method of carrying out this type of attack. Unlike the QueryRep and QueryAdjust methods, the Select command does not need to match the session of tag. Thus, a single rogue Select command will cause all tags to return to the Ready state.

Writing Fake Data to Tag

Information is stored on RFID tags using "Write" and "BlockWrite" command. While mechanisms and features in RFID exist that give implementers the ability to control data writes to tags, the ISO 18000-6 Type C Protocol itself does not entail any a cryptographically robust authentication system or provide an integrated authorization model to mitigate the threat of false data insertion by malicious readers.

Memory on tags is logically separated into four distinct banks: Reserved, UII, TID and User. The Reserved bank contains user access and kill passwords. The UII bank stores information identifying the object to which the tag is attached, contains the storedCRC and storedPC values, and holds other meta data about the tag regarding protocol and tag characteristics. The TID bank holds information that expresses the custom characteristics, commands and features of the tag. The User memory bank is available as optional storage on the tag.

The Lock and BlockPermalock commands can be used to prevent (lock) memory locations from reading and/or writing. This feature should be used by tag owners to protect important pieces of information on the tag such as the Access Password, Kill Password, and UII. The BlockPermalock command enables locking of individual blocks of User Memory, but is an optional command for tags. Other solutions include writing encrypted data with a CRC (or some other error detection method) to the tag so that only authorized users can decrypt and verify the information. This is similar to methods used to digitally sign emails to verify contents and the sender's identity.

To process a Write or BlockWrite message, a tag must be in the Open or the Secured states. Transition to the Secured state is predicated on a successful RN_Req message interchange between reader and tag in which the reader requests and receives a new RN16 handle from the tag. The handle is intended to be used in subsequent communications between the pair as means if mutual authentication. The handle is sent in the clear. Thus, an adversary can acquire it through eavesdropping and use it to issue write commands from an authorized reader (i.e. one other than the reader that issued the RN_Req message) that would then be accepted by the tag. The only mitigating element herein is that the adversary must position a reader close enough to the tag to capture the tag's backscatter communication signal.

A handful of primitive protection mechanisms are built in to the ISO 18000-6 C protocol for guarding against unauthorized access of tag data. Write commands use a cover coding technique to obscure data in transit. Memory regions on the user memory bank can be segmented into blocks as a basis for partitioning access patterns and permissions. Readers can issue commands to lock, unlock, and even permanently lock or permanently unlock the tag memory banks and regions. A 32-bit access password, when non-zero, is required to transition to the Secured state, allowing the reader to execute the locking commands on the tag. The Secured state also allows a reader to write to locked memory.

False Data Insertion to the Reader

In RFID systems, readers serve as a conduit for data transfer between tags and backend software. Readers acquire data from tags via read commands that transmit the contents of tag memory back to the readers. By inserting false data into the reader, adversaries can corrupt and compromise the integrity of information that will ultimately reside in enterprise resource planning software and other applications tied to RFID networks. At a high level, there are two avenues for using tags to inject false data into readers: (1) legitimate tags can be subverted and false data written into them, and (2) bogus tags can take the place of legitimate tags in a RFID system. Inasmuch as the first avenue calls for writing false data to tags (described above) and legitimate communications beyond that, the focus of the discussion here is on the second approach.

Bogus tags can either be introduced into a RFID system as part of a supply chain attack, or they can be introduced by surreptitiously replacing a legitimate tag active in the network. The former method preys upon weaknesses in the system engineering process, while the latter method relies on an attacker's ability to represent communications from the bogus tag as originating from a legitimate tag. This typically requires eavesdropping on tag-reader communications to acquire the RN16 handle. For instance, should a reader issue a Req_RN message to a legitimate tag using a handle known by the bogus tag, the bogus tag may reply with a new RN16 of its own to the reader. At this point, a new handle is established for communication between the bogus tag and reader, who believes it is talking to the legitimate tag. A secondary tactic here is to disable the legitimate tag, e.g., by means of a kill command if the password is known. Once the legitimate tag is disabled, the bogus tag can use the stolen handle freely to accept and respond to read requests, masquerading as a legitimate tag to the reader.

SOLUTION PATHS

Early RFID deployments in the airline baggage tracking and retail environments were concerned with being able to communicate (read) the tags and prevent someone from changing the UII. Advances in technology have solved the first issue, in many cases, and the ability to lock rewritable memory or the use of write-once memory has solved the second issue. However, as RFID is deployed in different application domains new security issues arise. The three major security issues resulting in these new application domains are privacy or confidentiality, accuracy of information, and availability of the system.

Authentication

Strong authentication of readers and tags prevents many of the attacks described in this chapter. For example, by responding to only Select commands from authenticated readers, rogue searching of tag memory and the DOS attack using a rogue Select command can be averted. However, strong authentication is difficult for RFID networks because they will be distributed, often in locations having limited connection to the central network. Without a reliable connection to a central network standard private/public key methods for authentication, such as those used by the Internet, are not feasible. In addition, the list of authenticated readers will be large and this could be prohibitive for ISO 18000-6 Type C tags, which are passive. Adding large memories increases the cost and operating power requirements, thus reducing read range, of the tag. Another drawback is that such an RFID system will be limited to a set number of readers and will not be widely usable as the system will be a closed-loop type system. One solution to this issue is to define a limited set of operations for un-authenticated readers, such as limiting them to accessing only the UII and TID portions of the tag. This would force the un-authenticated readers to retrieve information about the tag (and the asset it is attached to) from the back-end system. Accepted security practices can be employed on the back-end system to authenticate the un-authenticated reader. This also limits the size of the authenticated reader list that must be stored on the tag.

Encryption

Encryption addresses confidentiality of the data by preventing un-authorized entities from understanding the information. Encryption can be used to protect sensitive data, such as medical records, while they are stored on the tag. The encryption and decryption of this information can be performed entirely on the reader or back-end system where accepted security practices are more easily implemented. Having the back-end perform all encryption and decryption operations is probably the best option because it is typically the most secure system. From a physical security stand-point the back-end system (central database) can be much easier secured against physical attack than a network of readers deployed around the world. This also offloads the requirement that the tag or reader support encryption as they will view the encrypted data as a format they do not understand. Strong, but power and resource intensive, encryption methods, such as elliptic curve cryptology, can be employed by the system. Now the tag is simply a storage facility for this encrypted data and the reader provides the means to transfer that encrypted data from the back-end to the tag or vice versa. Encryption can also address authentication because only a legitimate and authenticated entity will be able to access the proper decryption key from the back-end system to decrypt the data. Encryption allows multiple entities to store data in the same tag and limit access to that information by deciding who receives the keys needed to decrypt that information. This enables competitors to store information in the same tag that can only be understood by themselves or their business partners. However, this method does not prevent the DOS attacks from rogue readers such as the rogue Select command.

Encryption is can also be used to counter the writing of fake data to a tag by providing a means to digitally sign data. With such a digital signature, for example an encrypted CRC (cyclic redundancy check), tampering of data can easily identified.

FUTURE RESEARCH DIRECTIONS

Future research is required to identify, document, and understand the threats facing RFID systems as they expand to applications beyond the supply chain. The DOS type attacks are particularly problematic because they can be easily introduced and require physically removing the rogue reader. Strong physical security following accepted principles (Department of Defense, 2006) can prevent and deter such attacks. However, not all installations can be secured to the required level and other techniques need to be incorporated into the protocol or tag to prevent such attacks. Because of the limited resources of the tag any solution will address some DOS attacks, and raise the bar for the attacker, but will not offer a full-proof solution.

Countermeasures developed to address identified threats must consider operational context and practical limitations in RFID systems. Security services that overlay existing protocols and memory architectures must be developed and validated. Research in developing energy efficient encryption, e.g. low power AES (Lee, Vo, Huynh, Hong, 2011), access control and authentication solutions must be pursued to enhance the security services resident in passive and low energy tags. The spatial aspects of RFID network communications call for the exploration of architectures that weave cyber and physical security services to yield a comprehensive solution.

New hardware technologies, more robust memory architectures, and increasingly sophisticated communication protocols are integrated into RFID systems all increase the menu of threats posed to RFID systems. However, these advances also create new opportunities for the design and implementation of enhanced security services within tags and readers. Research must continue to follow these advances, both to track emerging threats and to spur the development of novel security architectures for RFID systems.

These new technologies will require redesign of tags and readers to accommodate the new security features. Analysis of the effect of a DOS type attacks can be determined from simulation. For example, the work of Maillart, *et al.* (Maillart, Kamrani, Norman, Rajgopal & Hawrylak, 2010) investigating development of the optimal tag inventorying algorithms can be used to benchmark the effect of a particular DOS attack on a population of tags. Simulations for other protocol aspects and enhancements can be employed. FPGAs can then be used to prototype new hardware that implements the security enhancements studied in simulation. FPGAs offer the ability to estimate the added overhead of the new security measures verses the original protocol and the hardware resources required. Finally, commercial tools can be used to move from the FPGA design to an ASIC design.

CONCLUSION

The use of RFID solutions in environments where availability, integrity and confidentiality are relevant features, requires careful analysis of the underlying architecture. While the use of cryptographic primitives in ISO 18000-6 Type C standard certainly contributes to strengthen its security posture, there are a number of other places that can be used to exploit this type of solutions. The stateful nature of the architecture presents ample opportunity to affect how tags respond to the reader (interrogator). In particular, we have shown that an attacker might be capable of gathering valuable intelligence by simply observing Select commands that identify the set of tags of interest to the application or interrogator. If the capability to insert Select commands is added, then an attacker can easily alter the selected set of tags by adding or removing tags from the set that would otherwise be selected. This type of attacks can be used to support sophisticated attacks that may eventually include fake tag responses. One of the goals of this work is to raise awareness of

simple attacks that may take advantage of the state transitions the ISO 18000-6 Type C standard for the selection, inventory, and access phases. By identifying the vulnerabilities present in the protocol appropriate solutions and countermeasures can be designed and implemented to defend against or eliminate these vulnerabilities.

REFERENCES

Bacheldor, B. (2009, February 2). Tego launches 32-Kilobyte EPC RFID tag. *RFID Journal*. Retrieved June 1, 2011, from http://www.rfidjournal.com/article/view/4578

Department of Defense. (2006). *National industrial security program operating manual*, February 2006.

Emond, J. P. (2008). The cold chain. In Miles, S. B., Sarma, S. E., & Williams, J. R. (Eds.), *RFID technology and applications* (pp. 144–156). New York, NY: Cambridge University Press. doi:10.1017/CBO9780511541155.012

EPCglobal. (2008) *EPC™ radio-frequency identity protocols class-1 generation-2 UHF RFID protocol for communications at 860 MHz – 960 MHz version 1.2.0*. EPCglobal Inc.

EPCglobal. (2010). *Tag data standards version 1.5*. EPCglobal Inc.

Finkenzeller, K. (2003). *RFID handbook: Fundamentals and applications in contactless smart cards and identification*. Chichester, UK: John Wiley & Sons Ltd.

Hawrylak, P. J., Cain, J. T., & Mickle, M. H. (2007). Analytic modeling methodology for analysis of energy consumption for ISO 18000-7 RFID networks. *International Journal of Radio Frequency Identification Technology and Applications*, 1(4), 371–400. doi:10.1504/IJRFITA.2007.017748

Hawrylak, P. J., Cain, J. T., & Mickle, M. H. (2008). RFID tags. In Yan, L., Zhang, Y., Yang, L. T., & Ning, H. (Eds.), *The Internet of things: From RFID to pervasive networked systems* (pp. 1–32). Boca Raton, FL: Auerbach Publications, Taylor & Francis Group. doi:10.1201/9781420052824.ch1

Hawrylak, P. J., & Mickle, M. H. (2009). EPC Gen-2 standard for RFID. In Y. Zhang, L. T. Yang, & J. Chen (Eds.), *RFID and sensor networks: Architectures, protocols, security and integrations* (pp. 97-124). Boca Raton, FL: Taylor & Francis Group, CRC Press.

International Organization for Standardization. (2009). *ISO/IEC 18000-7 Information technology -- Radio frequency identification for item management -- Part 7: Parameters for active air interface communications at 433 MHz.*

International Organization for Standardization. (2010). *ISO/IEC 18000-6:2010 FDIS information technology -- Radio frequency identification for item management -- Part 6: Parameters for air interface communications at 860 MHz to 960 MHz.*

Juels, A. (2006, February). RFID security and privacy: A research survey. *IEEE Journal on Selected Areas in Communications, 24*(2), 381–394. doi:10.1109/JSAC.2005.861395

Juels, A., & Brainard, J. (2004). Soft blocking: Flexible blocker tags on the cheap. In *Proceedings of the 2004 ACM Workshop on Privacy in the Electronic Society*, (pp. 1-7).

Juels, A., & Pappu, A. (2003). In Wright, R. (Ed.), *Squealing Euros: Privacy-protection in RFID-enabled banknotes* (*Vol. 2742*, pp. 103–121). Lecture Notes in Computer Science Berlin, Germany: Springer.

Juels, A., Rivest, R. L., & Szydlo, M. (2003). The blocker tag: Selective blocking of RFID tags for consumer privacy. In *Proceedings of the 10th ACM Conference on Computer and Communications Security*, (pp. 103-111).

Juels, A., & Weis, S. A. (2009, November). Defining strong privacy for RFID. *ACM Transactions on Information and System Security, 13*(1). doi:10.1145/1609956.1609963

Koscher, K., Juels, A., Brajkovic, V., & Kohno, T. (2009). EPC RFID tag security weaknesses and defenses: Passport cards, enhanced drivers licenses, and beyond. In *Proceedings of the 16th ACM Conference on Computer and Communications Security* (CCS '09), (pp. 33-42). New York, NY: ACM.

Lavine, G. (2008, August). RFID technology may improve contrast agent safety. *American Journal of Health-System Pharmacy, 65*(15), 1400–1403. doi:10.2146/news080064

Law, M. K., Bermak, A., & Luong, H. C. (2010, June). A sub-W embedded CMOS temperature sensor for RFID food monitoring application. *IEEE Journal of Solid-state Circuits, 45*(6), 1246–1255. doi:10.1109/JSSC.2010.2047456

Lee, J.-W., Vo, D. H. T., Huynh, Q.-H., & Hong, S. H. (2011, June). A fully integrated HF-band passive RFID tag IC using 0.18-μm CMOS technology for low-cost security applications. *IEEE Transactions on Industrial Electronics, 58*(6), 2531–2540. doi:10.1109/TIE.2010.2060460

Maguire, Y., & Pappu, R. (2009, January). An optimal Q-algorithm for the ISO 18000-6C RFID protocol. *IEEE Transactions on Automation Science and Engineering, 6*(1), 16–24. doi:10.1109/TASE.2008.2007266

Maillart, L. M., Kamrani, A., Norman, B. A., Rajgopal, J., & Hawrylak, P. J. (2010). Optimizing RFID tag-inventorying algorithms. *IIE Transactions, 42*(9), 690–702. doi:10.1080/07408171003705714

Mickle, M. H., Mats, L., & Hawrylak, P. J. (2008). Resolution and integration of HF and UHF. In Miles, S. B., Sarma, S. E., & Williams, J. R. (Eds.), *RFID technology and applications* (pp. 47–60). New York, NY: Cambridge University Press. doi:10.1017/CBO9780511541155.005

Mirowski, L., Hartnett, J., & Williams, R. (2009, October). An RFID attacker behavior taxonomy. *IEEE Pervasive Computing / IEEE Computer Society and IEEE Communications Society, 8*(4), 79–84. doi:10.1109/MPRV.2009.68

Mitrokotsa, A., Rieback, M., & Tanenbaum, A. (2010). Classifying RFID attacks and defenses. *Information Systems Frontiers, 12*(5), 491–505. doi:10.1007/s10796-009-9210-z

O'Connor, M. C. (2011). Ultracapacitor offers 75-foot read range for passive tags. *RFID Journal*. Retrieved July 6, 2011, from http://www.rfidjournal.com/article/view/8565

Ravilla, S. R., Ogirala, A., Murari, A., Hawrylak, P. J., & Mickle, M. H. (2011). Anti-collision policy for RFID systems: Fast predict tags in field algorithm. *International Journal of Radio Frequency Identification Technology and Applications, 3*(3), 215–228. doi:10.1504/IJRFITA.2011.040995

Raymond, D. R., Marchany, R. C., Brownfield, M. I., & Midkiff, S. F. (2009, January). Effects of denial-of-sleep attacks on wireless sensor network MAC protocols. *IEEE Transactions on Vehicular Technology, 58*(1), 367–380. doi:10.1109/TVT.2008.921621

Rieback, M. R., Crispo, B., & Tanenbaum, A. S. (2005). Keep on blockin' in the free world: Personal access control for low-cost RFID tags. In B. Christianson, B. Crispo, J. A. Malcolm, & M. Roe (Eds.), *Proceedings of the 13th International Conference on Security Protocols* (pp. 51-59). Berlin, Germany: Springer-Verlag.

Rieback, M. R., Crispo, B., & Tanenbaum, A. S. (2006, March). The evolution of RFID security. *Pervasive Computing, 5*(1), 62–69. doi:10.1109/MPRV.2006.17

Rotter, P. (2008, April-June). A framework for assessing RFID system security and privacy risks. *IEEE Pervasive Computing / IEEE Computer Society and IEEE Communications Society, 7*(2), 70–77. doi:10.1109/MPRV.2008.22

Sun, Y., Hawrylak, P. J., Mao, Z.-H., & Mickle, M. H. (2010, March). Collision resolution in ISO 18000-6c passive RFID. *Applied Computational Electromagnetics Society (ACES) Journal, Special Issue: Computational and Experimental Techniques for RFID Systems and Applications, 25*(3).

Todd, B., Phillips, M., Schultz, S. M., Hawkins, A. R., & Jensen, B. D. (2009, April). Low-cost RFID threshold shock sensors. *IEEE Sensors Journal, 9*(4), 464–469. doi:10.1109/JSEN.2009.2014410

KEY TERMS AND DEFINITIONS

Access Phase: Final stage of communication where higher-level operations, e.g. read and write, are carried out.

Inventory Phase: This is the second stage of communication where the reader determines the unique item identifier (UII) for all tags within range. The reader has the option to inventory subgroups of this tag population based on the tags' Selected Flag. The Selected Flag is determined during the Selection Phase.

ISO 18000-6 Type C: RFID protocol for passive RFID tags operating between 860-960 MHz.

Passive RFID Tag: Type of RFID tag that uses backscatter to communicate and does not have an on-board battery. This type of tag harvests energy to power itself, typically from the reader's signal.

Physical Security: Aspect of security that deal with preventing physical access and modification to an asset.

RFID: RFID stands for Radio Frequency Identification and is a system of tags and readers used to monitor and identify people and assets.

RFID Reader: A device that communicates with RFID tags wirelessly. The RFID Reader provides the link between the RFID Tag and the application software. It is sometimes called an RFID Interrogator.

RFID Tag: A device that is attached to a person or asset, and that communicates wirelessly with an RFID reader.

Selection Phase: This is the first part of the ISO 18000-6 Type C protocol where the tags of interest to the reader are identified. This helps to reduce the number of tags participating in later stages of communication to only those that are of interest.

Chapter 4
A Weakly Synchronous and Distributed Coordination Function for QoS Management in CSMA/CA Wireless Access Networks

Andrea Vesco
Istituto Superiore Mario Boella, Italy

Riccardo Scopigno
Istituto Superiore Mario Boella, Italy

ABSTRACT

This chapter presents a novel weakly synchronous and distributed coordination function, called Time-Division Unbalanced Carrier Sense Multiple Access (TD-uCSMA). TD-uCSMA relies on synchronization among nodes and the contextual switching of channel access parameters to enable resource management and Quality of Service (QoS) provisioning over CSMA/CA wireless access networks. The TD-uCSMA operating principles and issue of synchronization are presented in detail.

Moreover a signalling architecture is here designed, for the first time, to enable dynamic and distributed resource reservation over the wireless network by means of two protocols: the Resource Reservation Protocols with Traffic Engineering (RSVP-TE), properly extended to work in TD-uCSMA networks and the new Resource State Management Protocol (RSMP). The TD-uCSMA operating principles and the signalling architecture are then validated by simulation over many scenarios comprising multi-hop wireless access networks. Finally the chapter addresses the issue of prototyping TD-uCSMA by open source IEEE 802.11 legacy drivers.

DOI: 10.4018/978-1-4666-1797-1.ch004

Copyright © 2012, IGI Global. Copying or distributing in print or electronic forms without written permission of IGI Global is prohibited.

INTRODUCTION AND MOTIVATION

The use of wireless technologies for broadband access networks is relatively new and raises new challenges. The benefits of wireless solutions in the access tier are clear but leave several open issues, mainly concerning the capability of supporting a wide range of applications, in a flexible and scalable fashion. This indeed requires a solution that combines resource management capabilities and Quality of Service (QoS) provisioning.

Several solutions exist for the arbitration of channel access in wireless networks, spanning from OFDMA to CDMA, CSMA/CA or TDMA. Each of them brings its own benefits, such as QoS, scalability and distributed coordination.

The CSMA/CA-based solutions are becoming more and more popular thanks to their low cost and their ability to work without any central coordination. Basically this is the reason why CSMA/CA has been adopted also in Wireless Mesh Networks (IEEE 802.11s) (IEEE, 2011) and in Vehicular Ad-hoc Networks (IEEE 802.11p) (IEEE, 2010). The main point of strength in CSMA/CA is that the decision process is distributed among all the nodes consequently, each node determines individually when to access the channel, relying on the principle of random access. Thus the solution is indeed scalable, distributed and easy to implement, therefore it represents a likely candidate for a widespread and ubiquitous broadband wireless access. Unfortunately, CSMA/CA suffers from performance degradation to sub-optimal access decisions, hence to a higher number of collisions. As a result it performs poorly when strict QoS is required. Moreover, CSMA/CA performances get even worse in multi-hop scenarios because (*i*) node density increases access delay and reduces the overall throughput (*ii*) queuing and access delay at each hop additively contributes to the end-to-end delay and (*iii*) the number of possible hidden terminals and hidden collisions grows as well.

In order to support the increasing demand for QoS the IEEE 802.11e (now in IEEE 802.11 standard) was proposed. The standard introduces the *Hybrid Coordination Function* (HCF) and two channel access mechanisms are managed under the same HCF umbrella: the *HCF Controlled Channel Access* (HCCA) and the *Enhanced Distributed Channel Access* (EDCA).

The EDCA coordinates channel access in a distributed fashion and provides a flexible and scalable solution for differentiated QoS provisioning. It introduces the access class (AC) concept to classify and differentiate traffic whereas it differentiates service by prioritizing channel access using AC-specific EDCA parameters. Several works assess the EDCA performances (Mangold et al., 2003) and propose further optimizations (Zhu et al., 2004; Romdhani et al., 2003; Pries et al., 2008) to minimize contention delays and collision rates, hence improving throughput and delays. Other works study the issue of tuning the EDCA parameters (Casetti et al., 2004) to provide good service differentiation in specific traffic scenarios.

However this solution provides statistical service guarantees and it is not clear yet how to manage EDCA parameters to implement scalable resource management.

The HCCA offers a deterministic, TDMA-based channel access, which is centrally arbitrated by the hybrid controller (HC). The HC manages reservation requests and coherently splits time into a *contention-free period* (CFP) and a *contention period* (CP). Any node, willing to transmit in a CFP, has to negotiate with the HC channel access during a negotiation EDCA-based phase. The HC offers transmission opportunities (TXOPs) in response, if enough resources are available to meet QoS requirements. Thus HCCA avoids collisions that can lead to breaking established QoS and degradation of the overall performances and allows the HC to implement bandwidth reservation policies enabling parameterized QoS provisioning. However the need for a centralized HC potentially increases the complexity of the solution, it faces scalability issues in multi-hop networks and as a matter of fact, has never been implemented.

For these reasons, alternative solutions attempt to guarantee QoS with TDMA approaches where nodes access the network at well-defined instants avoiding contentions and preventing collisions. This approach is successfully adopted in (Baldi et al., 2009; Carlson et al., 2004; Carlson et al., 2006; Borgonovo et al., 2004; Scopigno et al., 2009) where the limitation due to a centralized coordination function is overcome and reservation is managed in a distributed fashion. However such solutions still suffer from the intrinsic stiffness of a reservation mechanism that hardly copes with variable traffic profiles; additionally they require proprietary extensions to the standardized MAC layer, which are very likely to hinder their deployment.

Altogether, an effective and scalable broadband wireless access subtends some requirements. First (*i*) the solution should be preferably based on CSMA/CA, so to leverage on its potential for ubiquitous deployment then (*ii*) a mechanism for bandwidth and traffic management is required. Such a mechanism should enable bandwidth reservation and re-use in order to exploit the entire available bandwidth and prevent resource waste, especially when dealing with variable traffic profile. Nonetheless the bandwidth reservation should be practically viable both in terms of algorithms and signalling. In particular (*iii*) the solution should work in a distributed way and in multi-hop networks. Additionally, (*iv*) the reservation should be managed by a signalling protocol, in order to enable dynamic network configuration and re-configuration; possibly signalling should be compatible with already existing standards.

A recent work proposed a novel, weakly synchronous and distributed coordination function called Time-Division *Unbalanced* Carrier Sense Multiple Access (TD-*u*CSMA). It is meant to provide CSMA/CA with a mechanism for bandwidth (and traffic) management over single-hop (Vesco et al., 2009) and multi-hop (Scopigno et al., 2011) broadband wireless access networks. TD-*u*CSMA relies on a weak synchronization among nodes and the time-driven periodic switching of channel access contention parameters inside network nodes. In such a way, it combines the advantages of TDMA (bandwidth management and QoS provisioning) with the ones belonging to CSMA/CA (scalability and bandwidth re-use). The results in (Vesco et al., 2009; Scopigno et al., 2011; Vesco et al., 2011) show that TD-*u*CSMA is a good candidate to satisfy the above mentioned requirements, avoiding a centralized architecture and without requiring relevant changes to the standardized MAC layer. The proposed solution is not merely a new coordination function, but includes also a signalling suite that improves the overall flexibility in QoS management. The subtended signalling architecture well suites and integrates with existing standard solutions for QoS management and may be deployed by custom extensions to them. Moreover, TD-*u*CSMA is expected, as confirmed by some recent tests, to be implementable by simple modification of the actual open source IEEE 802.11 legacy drivers, adding TD-*u*CSMA specific functions.

TIME-DIVISION UNBALANCED CARRIER SENSE MULTIPLE ACCESS (TD-UCSMA)

The TD-*u*CSMA has been recently proposed in (Vesco et al., 2009) and (Scopigno et al., 2011). It is a weakly synchronous and distributed coordination function that provides a viable solution for resource management and QoS provisioning over CSMA/CA wireless access networks.

Considering its operating principles, discussed hereinafter, it does not require major changes to the standardized MAC layer. This has two beneficial effects. First, some Wi-Fi stations are likely to be software-upgradable to the new coordination function. Second, it is facilitated the coexistence between Wi-Fi legacy stations and TD-uCSMA

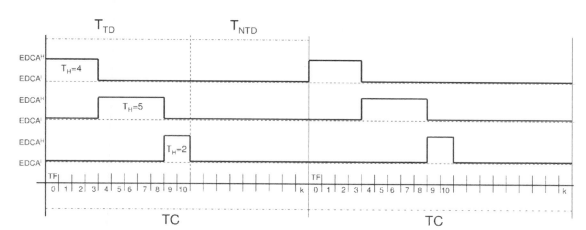

ones as showed in (Vesco et al., 2011). In fact, they can simultaneously operate within the same wireless access networks, without heavy, undesired effects.

Operating Principles

In a TD-uCSMA network all nodes are synchronized with a common time reference (CTR) whose structure is depicted in Figure 1. The CTR is a periodical time structure in which the time frame (TF) constitutes the time unit and k TFs are grouped in a time cycle. The time cycle dimension provides the periodicity of the CTR structure. Both the time frame duration T_f and the length - measured in TFs - of the TC are configurable system parameters.

Worthily, the time structure deployed in TD-uCSMA is the one typical of TDMA, but the decision on channel access is distributed among all nodes, following the CSMA/CA rules.

In TD-uCSMA each node maintains two main settings of the EDCA configurable parameters (*AIFS, TXOP*, CW_{min} and CW_{max}); additionally, all the nodes share these common settings. The two configurations are referred to as *high-prior-*

ity set ($EDCA^H$) and *low-priority* set ($EDCA^l$). The EDCA parameters are *unbalanced* in the two sets. More formally:

$$AIFS^H < AIFS^l$$
$$CW_{min}^H \leq CW_{max}^H < CW_{min}^l \leq CW_{max}^l$$

such that node i, contending for channel access in accordance to $EDCA^H$, has *almost* strict priority on node j using $EDCA^l$ settings.

The rationale behind TD-uCSMA is to synchronize the contextual switching of EDCA parameters at each node so that:

- Only one node contends for channel access in accordance to $EDCA^H$ during a TF;
- All nodes maintain $EDCA^H$ for a predefined periodical time interval. The time period, during which node i operates in accordance to $EDCA^H$, is referred to as T_H^i.

Figure 1 also shows an example of time-driven contextual EDCA parameters switching inside three nodes sharing the collision domain.

Figure 2. Two possible designs of node implementing TD-uCSMA; queues (rectangles) and logical entities for coordination function (circles). Best-effort (left) and differentiated service discipline support on the background traffic.

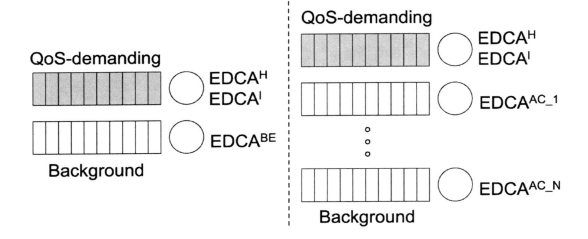

As a direct consequence of TD-*u*CSMA operating principles, a node *i* is very likely to gain access to the channel and to maintain it for the full period T_H^i. However, it is worth highlighting that the nodes gain channel access due to CSMA/CA mechanisms, even though enforced by the unbalanced setting chosen for $EDCA^H$ and $EDCA^{l\,1}$. By converse, channel access is not due to a predefined access order as in TDMA-based solutions. This is expected to have important benefits on TD-*u*CSMA, giving the stations the possibility to exploit unused but reserved resources.

In principle, the EDCA parameters are switched over time, node by node, and each node handles QoS-demanding traffic as a single aggregate. Thus, bandwidth management is performed on a per-node base too, simply leveraging on the allotment of distinct T_H to the nodes in the same collision domain. Since TD-*u*CSMA preserves the CSMA/CA nature, if a node *i* does not have enough traffic to be sent, before the end of its T_H^i, any other node can gain channel access. Hence bandwidth re-use is easily and intrinsically imple-

mented and bandwidth wasting, as side effect of reservation, is avoided.

However a subset of TFs can be left un-allocated to let nodes send background traffic, in accordance to the either best-effort or differentiated service discipline, as addressed in (Vesco et al., 2011). More in details, Figure 1 shows that the time cycle can be divided into two periods, T_{TD}, in which TFs are allocated to nodes and T_{NTD} during which TFs are left un-allocated.

In a possible design, two back-off entities can be implemented within a node, to provide QoS and best-effort services, in an integrated way, as depicted in Figure 2 (left).

The back-off entity working in accordance to TD-*u*CSMA principles (referred to as TD-*u*CSMA entity) contends for channel access, to send QoS-demanding traffic, using $EDCA^j \quad \forall j = H, l$ settings. The back-off entity working in accordance to CSMA/CA principles (referred to as CSMA/CA entity) contends for channel access, to send background traffic, using $EDCA^{BE} = EDCA^l$ settings. Remarkably, TD-*u*CSMA back-off entity works in accordance to

$EDCA^l$ during T_{NTD}. Moreover, since TD-uCSMA preserves backward compatibility, legacy CSMA/CA nodes can still join the network, contending for channel access using low-priority contention parameters.

The background traffic can be further differentiated at each node, as depicted in Figure 2 (right). In this design the background traffic is delivered by parallel back-off entities that are prioritized using the contention parameters specific of their respective Access Classes (AC), as from EDCA specification (Mangold et al., 2003).

Bandwidth Management Model

This section devises a bandwidth management model, providing a simple and viable solution to reserve bandwidth to the QoS-demanding traffic, in a TD- uCSMA network. The work in (Vesco, 2009) demonstrated two important properties of the TD-uCSMA coordination function:

1. Basically only node i gains access to the channel during T_H^i, consequently the congestion windows in $EDCA^H$ can be minimized to reduce back-off time between two consecutive transmissions. As a result bandwidth utilization is increased, without affecting the collision probability;

2. If node i tends to use its T_H^i with poor efficiency, due to short packets, this does not affect the transmissions of the other nodes in their respective T_H periods, unlike what happens with CSMA/CA.

Thus, given the congestion windows in $EDCA^H$ as $CW_{min}^H = CW_{max}^H = 1$ and neglecting the propagation delays, the theoretical bandwidth G_{id}, available for reservation, can be expressed as the efficiency in channel utilization, considering only the protocol overheads, as follows:

$$G_{id} = \frac{R \cdot t_p}{t_p + AIFS^H + 2 \cdot t_{plcp} + t_h + SIFS + t_{ack}} \tag{1}$$

where R is the line-rate, t_p and t_h are the MAC payload and header transmission times, t_{plcp} is the transmission times of PLCP header and preamble and t_{ack} is the acknowledgment transmission time.

In TD-uCSMA bandwidth reservation is performed, on a per-node base, by allocating to a node the TFs to contend for channel access in accordance to $EDCA^H$. Therefore to node i can be reserved a bandwidth

$$G_i = \frac{T_H^i}{TC} \cdot G_A \tag{2}$$

where G_A is the available bandwidth. It was experimentally verified in (Vesco et al., 2009; Scopigno et al., 2011) that nodes sending QoS-demanding traffic experience very few collisions, basically taking place at the boundaries of their T_H. As a consequence G_A can be fairly estimated by G_{id}, with a tolerance of about 10% in the typical application scenarios of wireless access networks.

Therefore, reverting Equation (2), it is possible to compute the number n_i of TFs to be allocated to node i, to reserve the required bandwidth G_i:

$$n_i = \frac{T_c}{T_f} \cdot \frac{G_i}{G_A} = \frac{k \cdot T_f}{T_f} \cdot \frac{G_i}{G_A} = k \cdot \frac{G_i}{G_A} \tag{3}$$

Each node on a multi-hop route can exploit Equation (1) to estimate the available bandwidth G_A and Equation (3) to calculate the number of TFs, whose allocation is required for reserving a bandwidth G, independently of the other nodes.

In principle, the Equation (1) can be applied only with constant packet length. However, as demonstrated in (Scopigno et al., 2011), the mean packet size alone provides itself a good approximation of the reservation requirements. It has been also demonstrated that the reservation model based only on average packet-size can be further improved if the standard deviation of the packet-size distribution is estimated; standard deviation can be included as a second-order correction term, which can be omitted in most cases. Moreover the detailed nature of the packet-length distribution (*e.g.*, Gaussian, Uniform, Two-State) has only a third-order effect on TD-*u*CSMA's reservations and, as a result, can be practically neglected.

Altogether Equation (1) and consequently Equations (2) and (3) can be generalized in a straightforward way, to work with variable packet lengths, in the following way:

$$G_{id} = \frac{R \cdot T_p}{T_p + AIFS^H + 2 \cdot t_{plcp} + t_h + SIFS + t_{ack}}$$

(4)

where $T_p = \mathrm{E}[t_p]$ is the mean value of the MAC payload transmission time.

TD-UCSMA AND THE ISSUE OF SYNCHRONIZATION

The TD-*u*CSMA relies on the time-driven switching of contention parameters, inside nodes, coordinated by the Common Time Reference (CTR) structure in Figure 1. The synchronization plays an important role in TD-*u*CSMA, this hypothesis, poses two crucial questions for the viability of the proposed coordination function: (*i*) how much critical is the precision in synchronization? (*ii*) How should/could synchronization be provided?

The first answer is that synchronization is not particularly critical for at least two reasons:

1. The required clock rate is not critical and it can be easily achieved and guaranteed with the needed accuracy since it works at low rate. In fact, while in TDM-based networks synchronization has to reach the bit-level, in TD-*u*CSMA the time base is the TF, which is expected to be up to 10^4 bigger than bit-time. Even more, the TF duration is normally wider than the transmission time of a maximum length packet to let TD-*u*CSMA work properly;

2. The synchronization of nodes is mandatory and critical for a correct network operation in TDM-based networks, while the underlying CSMA/CA mechanisms provide an intrinsic resilience in TD-*u*CSMA networks. More explicitly, the TD-*u*CSMA coordination function does not completely fail in case of loss of synchronization because it may be held-on by local clock, providing almost unaltered operation, or the network can still operate in accordance to CSMA/CA as in plain Wi-Fi networks.

Altogether, summing up, the requirements on synchronization can be considered *weak* (or *soft*), in opposition to the *hard synchronization* schemes subtended by carrier-grade TDM networks[2]. These points answer the first question, on the required clock precision, and also justifies why TD-*u*CSMA is defined a *weakly synchronous coordinated function*.

The second answer is that multiple solutions apply to the TD-*u*CSMA synchronization requirements.

In principle, synchronization can be provided either by the Global Positing System (GPS) or by Galileo in near future. In this design nodes are synchronized to an external and absolute time reference called Coordinated Universal Time (UTC). This solution, indeed, provides synchronization with high accuracy and do not require the exchange of additional information on data path that might decrease the resource's utilization and increase the control overhead. However it involves additional hardware - with impact on costs – and can work only outdoor, additionally, only where the satellite reception can be guaranteed. Moreover it delivers an absolute synchronization whose precision is far beyond the requirements of TD-*u*CSMA[3]. In conclusion, it represents a possible solution in certain cases, but they also seem too expensive and largely more overly precise than required.

This conclusion motivates search for alternative solutions relying on the concept of clock tree. In these solutions it is common to logically organize a multi-hop topology in a rooted tree one. Then the local clock of the root node is elected as the time reference and it is distributed – hence shared – among all the network nodes. Here the synchronization is not absolute but, nevertheless, it is shared, hop-by-hop, across all the nodes as in Timing-Synch Protocol (TPSN) (Generiwal et al., 2003), which is an evolution of the Network Time Protocol (NTP) (Mills, 1991). The Flooding Time Synchronization Protocol (FTSP) (Maròti et al., 2004) uses broadcast communications and MAC layer time-stamping, following the same approach as TPSN, but further enriching it with additional features, like clock skew compensation, dynamic topology adaptation and root failure recovery.

Also these solutions can be applied to the synchronization in TD-uCSMA networks, however they do not represent the most flexible and suitable solution. A step toward the definition of a fully distributed synchronization solution came from the Average TimeSync Protocol (ATS) (Schenato et al., 2007). It exploits a consensus algorithm proved to achieve a time reference agreement by averaging local time information. ATS compensates clock skew and offset at each node to synchronize them with a virtual time reference that depends on the local clock skews and offsets. The Leaderless Time Synchronization Protocol (LTSP) (Vesco & Abrate, 2011) has recently extended this approach. In LTSP all nodes refer to a common notion of time, in order to deploy the common time reference structure (synchronous

beat of time frames) and to locate themselves therein (identification of the current time frame). The solution convergence has been demonstrated under reasonable hypotheses that largely hold in the case of TD-*u*CSMA. Moreover LTSP seems particularly promising for TD-*u*CSMA for the following reasons:

- It works in large multi-hop networks under indoor and outdoor conditions;
- Synchronization traffic can be broadcasted in a different channel from the main data channel reducing overhead;
- It is robust to node failures since it is leaderless and completely distributed;
- It works properly also when packets broadcasted for synchronization purpose experience losses. Packet losses have major effect on the convergence time, rather than on convergence itself;
- Synchronization is not expensive and the accuracy is magnitudes higher than the accuracy required by TD-*u*CSMA. The accuracy of the synchronization is affected but it is still sufficient to fulfil the TD-*u*CSMA requirements when synchronization traffic experience delay and delay jitter.

Altogether, the distributed leaderless approach is, in the Author's opinion, the best solution to achieve the *weak* and non-critical synchronization required by TD-*u*CSMA.

A PROTOCOL ARCHITECTURE FOR DISTRIBUTED BANDWIDTH MANAGEMENT AND QOS PROVISIONING

State of the Art of Cross-Layer QoS and Perspectives on TD-uCSMA

The Open Systems Interconnection (OSI) reference model (ISO/IEC, 1994) defines a hierarchical architecture that logically partitions the functions required to support system-to-system communication. It has served as a fundamental element of computer networking since its inception in 1984; the reasons for its long-lasting success are connected to the several advantages offered by the layered approach. By separating networking functions into smaller logical pieces, network problems can be solved more easily, through a divide-and-conquer methodology. Then, a protocol stack subdivides a problem into small problems, and communications take place mainly between *adjacent layers* and according to a minimum set of *primitives*. As a result, most of the available network solutions adhere to the layered model and can easily interwork, thanks to it.

However, quite recently (Shakkottai et al., 2003; Zhang et al., 2005; Carneiro et al., 2004) the stiff paradigm of the OSI communications model has started to show some limitations. The doubt that arose in the scientific community is that a stronger coordination between (traditionally separate) layers may be needed to efficiently cope with problems such as QoS, error-correction and reliability, energy saving and security. This does not mean that a layered approach should be completed upset, but only that performances might be improved overtaking it in some cases.

An example may help the understanding. The problem of providing a)exible and strict QoS service to an IP)ow intrinsically, impacts on multiple OSI layers. However, the classical layered OSI model can encounter some problems and hinder the deployment of a coherent solution across all layers. For instance:

- A QoS-aware function may be available at multiple layers. It may be statically - and probably separately - con□gured, within each layer or dynamically configured but only at certain layers;
- Different QoS-aware functions may be available at different layer. In some cases QoS decisions made at a given layer are not compatible with functions available at lower/upper layers;
- Different views of the QoS requirements and network resources are available at different layers. Often the QoS requests are even not passed across all layers, because the required Service Access Points (SAPs) are not defined.

These points lead to the identi□cation of a fundamental problem: some layers in the protocol stack are not provided with QoS information and thus interact poorly with the others, instead of positively contributing to QoS.

However, it is common view that strict QoS cannot be provided without resource reservation in the network and reservation cannot work without an appropriate routing with traffic-engineering capabilities and efficient scheduling. All these functions are spread over multiple layers hence QoS is necessarily configured at multiple layers. The specific case of cross-layer optimization toward resource management and QoS provisioning, suits particularly well the dynamical setting of TD-uCSMA as here discussed.

From a practical point of view, bandwidth management in TD-uCSMA may be carried out node-by-node (manually or through a central management system) or dynamically (defining a proper signalling architecture). The protocol architecture, depicted in Figure 3, is proposed to support dynamic resource management and QoS provisioning over wireless access networks. It comprises TD-uCSMA at MAC layer to provide QoS and two signalling protocols at MAC control layer to drive TD-uCSMA operations, hence to implement dynamic resource management.

The signalling architecture includes, first of all, the Resource State Management Protocol (RSMP) to automatically flood the allocation states and to maintain the consistency of the information among nodes. Effectively TD-uCSMA does not only need to know *how many* free TFs are available on each channel, but also *which* ones

Figure 3. Protocol architecture for distributed resource and traffic management and QoS provisioning over CSMA/CA networks

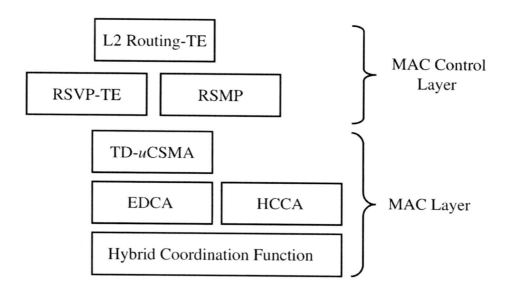

are free. Obviously this information should be flooded throughout the collision domain and timely updated.

The second protocol of the signalling architecture must be a reservation protocol. Here the Resource Reservation Protocol with Traffic Engineering (RSVP-TE), properly extended to make it compatible with TD-*u*CSMA wireless access networks, is proposed.

This choice has the benefit of exploiting an available and consolidated protocol (RSVP-TE) and, what is non-negligible, to help future integration with Multi-Protocol Label Switching (MPLS) backbone. In fact, paths in TD-*u*CSMA networks may follow the same rationale of Label Switched Path in MPLS networks.

Both signalling protocols are designed to follow the soft-state reservation approach. The soft-state rationale is coherent with the initial hypotheses of per-aggregate TD-*u*CSMA operating principles, which imply almost static (or at least not fast changing) reservations setup and tear down.

On the top of the signalling architecture (RSMP and RSVP-TE) there is a dynamic routing proto-

col. Such a routing protocol can exploit the traffic engineering information available from RSMP and integrate it in its routing process achieving traffic-engineering capabilities. Thus, whenever a new QoS-route is established, specific primitives can call the RSMP and RSVP-TE daemons to coherently proceed with the reservation and announcements.

The proposed architecture, indeed subtend a cross-layer rationale and optimization for the following motivations:

- The traffic-aware routing is made possible, with *network* capabilities of QoS. In fact, while the RSMP and RSVP-TE manage the reservation states on the wireless medium a layer-3 routing protocol with traffic engineering capabilities, such as OSPF-TE (Moy, 1998; Katz et al., 2003), can work on the top of them. This is coherent with the analysis carried out in (Facchini et al., 2010);

- The routing is either an upper-layer mechanism which makes the reservation intrinsically cross-layer between TD-uCSMA and layer-3 routing or cross layer, if it is active also at layer-2 by exploiting Optimized Link-State Routing Protocol (OLSR) (Clausen et al., 2003). In both cases there are cross-layer interactions within the stack;

- The RSMP and RSVP-TE made the reservation dynamic and compatible with layer-2 thanks to TD-uCSMA. As a result, a reservation can be started at layer-3 and acts also at layer-2. A QoS-aware SAP can be defined between the two layers;
- The architecture is largely compatible with MPLS that is often considered cross-layer. It acts between layer-2 (L2) and layer-3 (L3), sometimes it is said to be L2.5.

The blocks of the signalling architecture are described in details in the following sections.

Resource Reservation Protocol with Traffic Engineering (RSVP-TE)

The Resource Reservation Protocol (RSVP) (Braden et al., 1997; Wroclawski, 1997) was designed in 1997 to reserve bandwidth or, more in general, scheduler attributes and to distribute labels to identify traffic flows and implement label swapping on routers. Then RSVP was extended to support Traffic Engineering in 2001. The resulting RSVP-TE (Awduche et al., 2001) is however flexible enough to be further extended to support additional attributes, such as the ones involved by TD-uCSMA's reservation procedure.

The signalling procedure starts when a source node, willing to reserve a bandwidth G toward a destination node, sends a PATH message to the next node on the route. The subsequent nodes on the route, upon receiving the PATH message, check if enough resources, *i.e.*, TFs, are available to satisfy the reservation request by means of Equations (1), (2) and (3). If enough resources are available they forward the PATH message to the next node toward the destination, otherwise they discard the PATH message.

When the destination node receives the PATH message, it sends back a RESV message to the source node throughout the same nodes traversed by the PATH message. The subsequent nodes on the route back to the source node, upon receiving the RESV message, check again the availability of the resources. If enough resources are still available to satisfy the request they allocate the required TFs within the time cycle. Thus, node-by-node the RESV message travels back and, as soon as, it reaches the source node, the bandwidth reservation is established.

The application of RSVP-TE to TD-uCSMA, with exception of the resource to be reserved, does not deeply differ from classical use of the reservation protocol. However, in the case of two (or more) reservation requests simultaneously cross the TD-uCSMA network through the same nodes, resource contention may happen. When a node on a selected route receives a RESV message and not enough resources are still available to satisfy the request, it discards the RESV message. This causes the repetition of the reservation request when a reservation timer T_{RTR} expires at the source of the reservation requests and the expiration of possible reservations on the preceding node after a time-out T_{TO}. Both timers are addressed in details in section Protocol Timings. This procedure is equivalent to solve the contention with a simple FIFO approach, *i.e.*, the resources are allocated to requests which RESV message coming back first.

A source node can repeat a reservation request for a maximum of Retry-Count (RC) times otherwise the request is definitively rejected. Thus, it is required that each PATH and RESV message couple contains a unique identifier (UID) to keep trace of the reservation request.

The UID can be carried within a new Object, called TUNNEL_MAC. This Object is here proposed as a sub-object of the standard SESSION

Object (Braden et al., 1997; Wroclawski, 1997) following the same rationale used to extend it in RSVP-TE to support tunnel setup. The TUNNEL_MAC Object is applied to the PATH and RESV message in this TD-*u*CSMA-aware extension, but it is optional with respect to RSVP-TE specification. The format is depicted in Figure 4.

The TUNNEL_MAC sub-object comprises:

- **MAC Tunnel end-point**: The main address of the node acting as end-point of the reservation;
- **UID**: The unique identifier.

Each node on the route can compute the number of TF required to satisfy the bandwidth request independently of the other nodes, thanks to TD-*u*CSMA's operating principles, as already discussed. The information strictly required is the bit-rate and the average packet length, as demonstrated in (Vesco et al., 2009; Scopigno et al., 2011). This information must be included in the PATH and RESV messages and can be specified using the SENDER_TSPEC and FLOWSPEC Objects, respectively defined in (Braden et al., 1997; Wroclawski, 1997). They already include two 32-bit long parameters (Peak Data Rate [p], Maximum Packet Size [M]) that can easily fit this purpose.

Each node on the route, from destination to source, informs the subsequent nodes about the TFs they have already allocated to the current reservation request. This is meant to minimize the probability of misallocation, *i.e.*, allocation of the same TFs to different nodes sharing the same collision domain, before RSMP announcements can be updated with the new TF allocation. Operatively the node informs the subsequent nodes by means of a new object called ALLOC_TF.

The ALLOC_TF Object is applied to the RESV message in this TD-*u*CSMA-aware extension, but it is optional with respect to RSVP-TE specification. The ALLC_TF Object maintains the format of the general RSVP Object specified in (Braden et al., 1997; Wroclawski, 1997) as depicted in Figure 5.

The ALLOC_TF Object comprises:

- **Length**: The total length of the object (in byte) including the header;
- **Class-Num**: The object type;
- **C-Type**: The sub-object type;
- **Object Contents**: Tn the form of a tuple **<Node><TF><Timestamp>** containing the main address of the node, the TF allocated and the relative Timestamp, which is the absolute time at which the TF has been allocated. Each node, traversed by the RESV message, adds a tuple for each TF allocated to the current reservation request.

The RSVP-TE, here extended, can be effectively deployed also if multiple non-overlapped channels coexist in the TD-*u*CSMA network. In this scenario a node, traversed by a reservation request directed toward a node on a different chan-

Figure 4. TUNNEL_MAC sub-object format

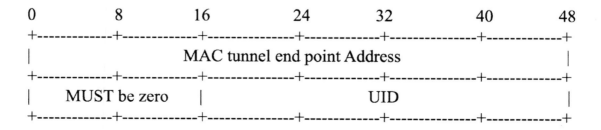

Figure 5. ALLOC_TF Object format

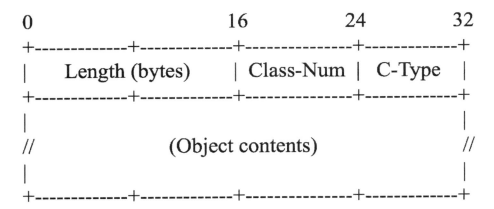

nel, must initialize a new ALLOC_TF Object and send it to the next node within the RESV message if the bandwidth requirements can be satisfied on the next channel.

In accordance to the soft-state approach, the reservation at each node needs a periodic refresh, which is carried out by the same PATH and RESV messages used for the initial setup. The timer T_{RFS}, running at the source node of the reservation request, handles the transmission of the PATH messages refreshing the reservation. If the reservation refresh fails for RC times, then the reservation expires within the time-out T_{TO}. All the PATH and RESV messages issued for refresh purpose contain the same UID of the related reservation request.

Finally, in accordance to the RSVP-TE rationale and to the general asymmetric nature of aggregate traffic, a bidirectional path can be split in two distinct setups originated by the two end nodes.

Resource State Management Protocol (RSMP)

The RSVP-TE was designed to work in backbone networks with point-to-point link between each pair of routers. As a consequence, the PATH and RESV messages reserve scheduler attributes consistently along all the routers traversed. On the contrary, the operation of TF allocations in wireless access networks is not straightforward due to the shared nature of the wireless medium. In this scenario, the main question is how far the allocation information should be propagated through the network, to avoid misallocations without flooding the wireless network of signalling traffic.

The typical protection techniques, adopted in TDMA-based solutions, propose to propagate this information up to two-hop neighbours by PATH and RESV messages as in (Baldi et al., 2009). This design indeed provides strong protection but it is hard to be maintained and comes at the cost of much explicit signalling, as addressed in (Carlson et al., 2004). In a different design, the allocation information is propagated up to one-hop neighbours (Carlson et al., 2006). In this design a node receiving allocation information by another node avoids three TFs: the actual receive TF, the preceding receive TF of the node transmitting the message and the receive TF of the node preceding the transmitting node. This design indeed reduces overheads but may lead to TF under-utilization.

The Resource State Management Protocol (RSMP) has been designed to maintain the consistency of the allocation information among nodes

Figure 6. RSM base structure

TF	Status (F/R/C)	Node	UID	Latest Refresh
1				
2				
:	:	:	:	:
k-1				
k				

in the same collision domain, while assuring high network utilization and low signalling overhead.

Each node is supposed to maintain a RSM Base whose structure is depicted in Figure 6. The number of rows coincides with the time cycle dimension - measured in TF - and the row i stores information about the state of TF i as a tuple:

- **TF**: The time frame number within the time cycle;
- **Status**: The time frame status. *free* if it is available for allocation, *resv* if it is allocated hence not available for allocation. In case of misallocation, *i.e.*, the same TFs is allocated to different nodes, the TF status is *collision*;
- **Node**: The main address of the node the TF is allocated to. In case the status of the related TF is *collision* this field is set to a well-known address (for instance 0) whereas it is empty when the TF is *free*. Each node may choose what address should be used as node address in resource management, *e.g.*, the address of one of the TD-uCSMA interfaces;
- **UID**: Unique identifier of the PATH and RESV messages, *i.e.*, of the reservation request, allocating the TF;
- **Latest Refresh**: The absolute time at which the latest refresh message has refreshed the TF status. This field is refreshed only by node mastering the allocation or detecting the collision.

Moreover a time-out T_{TO} is associated to each entry of the RSM Base. A new T_{TO} starts as the entry is refreshed, whereas the entry is purged and the relative TF released, *i.e.*, the status becomes *free*, if the information is not refreshed before T_{TO} expiration.

Each node periodically sends a RSM message to the neighbours in broadcast to update their RSM Bases. The timer T_{RSM} handles the sending periodicity. A RSM message reports the information about the status of TFs as seen by the originator node.

The message content, depicted in Figure 7, organizes the information as a tuple:

- **TF**: The time frame number within the time cycle;
- **Status**: The time frame status except status *free* since information about available TFs is not updated;
- **Node**: The main address of the node the TF information is related to;
- **UID**: Unique identifier of the PATH and RESV messages, *i.e.*, of the reservation request, allocating the TF;
- **Timestamp**: Coincides with the Latest Refresh field in the RSM Base.

The RSM messages are created starting from the RSM Base. A row is added to the RSM message for each TF whose status is either *resv* or *collision*. Thus the message has as many lines

Figure 7. Content of the RSM message

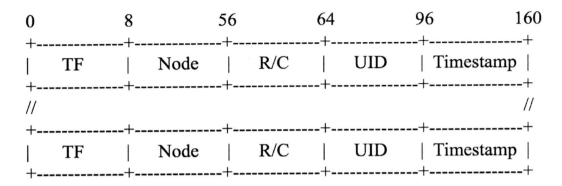

```
0             8            56            64            96           160
+--------------+--------------+--------------+--------------+--------------+---------------+
|    TF        |    Node      |    R/C       |    UID       |  Timestamp   |
+--------------+--------------+--------------+--------------+--------------+---------------+
//                                                                                      //

+--------------+--------------+--------------+--------------+--------------+---------------+
|    TF        |    Node      |    R/C       |    UID       |  Timestamp   |
+--------------+--------------+--------------+--------------+--------------+---------------+
```

as the number of TFs that are not perceived *free*. Moreover the Timestamp field is always set to the value in Latest Refresh field of the RSM Base.

Each node aggregates RSM messages received during the time interval T_{RSM} and processes them to upgrade the RSM base. For each announced TF, if the Timestamp is more recent than the value Latest Refresh stored in the RSM Base, the node upgrades the status of the TF, the main address of the node the TF is allocated to, the UID and it refreshes the Latest Refresh field by setting it to the Timestamp value reported by the RSM message.

Here a remark is particularly important. Since the Timestamp in the RSM message coincides with the Latest Refresh field in the RSM base and only the node mastering the allocation or detecting the collision refreshes the Latest Refresh field, it is not possible for information to survive beyond its expiration time, as a side effect of logical loops in the protocol.

If a node detects a misallocation by means of a RSM message, it releases the TFs and sets their status to *collision* in the RSM Base. In this case the Latest Refresh field in the RSM Base is set to the current time, that is the time of collision detection. Otherwise, if the status *collision* is reported by the RSM messages but does not affect that specific node, the Latest Refresh field in the RSM Base is set to the most recent Timestamp value

reported. A TF whose status is *collision* is not available for allocation until the state changes to *free* due to T_{TO} expiration.

In principle, each node creates and broadcasts a RSM message every time T_{RSM} expires. However, in a possible design, a node may broadcast a RSM message to the neighbours also when a TF is allocated by a RESV message to minimize the probability of misallocation.

The information in the RSM Base is easily mapped onto the TD-uCSMA at MAC layer. A node contends for channel access in accordance to $EDCA^H$ during those TFs whose status is *resv* and are allocated to it, and in accordance to $EDCA^l$ during all the TFs whose status is *free* and *collision* and during all the TFs allocated to different nodes.

The RSMP can work also with multiple non-overlapped channels. All TD-uCSMA interfaces sharing the same collision domain have to maintain the same vision of the TF allocations to prevent multiple nodes to contend for channel access in accordance to $EDCA^H$ during the same TFs. However the same TF can be re-allocated on different channels, hence a node with multiple TD-uCSMA interfaces on different channels, creates and maintains a RSM Base for each interface and must not propagate information about one channel to the others.

Resource Reservation Flavours

The proposed extension to RSVP-TE and the cooperation with RSMP do not affect the main features of RSVP-TE. Thus, RSVP-TE can enrich the solution with additional features that are already available in its architecture, such as options for Path Priority, Fast Reroute and Pre-emption. In addition RSVP-TE also provides messages to announce situations such as path errors and forced tear down, which may be required also in TD-uCSMA reservation. Moreover path setup can be both explicit and hop-by-hop, either on-demand or unsolicited.

Thus, a network operator can explicitly reserve bandwidth over a route specifying the nodes to be traversed. This solution lets operator plan the routes which traffic should take and, consequently, implements its traffic and resource management policies by dynamic signalling. This is implemented by exploiting the EXPLICIT_ROUTE Object (Awduche et al., 2001) that contains the list of nodes in the route. This step is independent of how bandwidth is reserved thus it can be implemented in a TD-uCSMA network.

However, to exploit capability of routing protocols to dynamically react to changes in network topology and traffic load, reservation can be implemented hop-by-hop to enable effective dynamic traffic and bandwidth management. The reservation signalling can be mastered by the decisions made by a layer-2 routing protocol, such as OLSR, as depicted in Figure 3.

Interestingly, the subtended soft-state signalling approach can easily support the dynamic adaptation to network changes. Since PATH and RESV messages are *idempotent*, when a route changes, the next PATH message will initialize the reservation on the new route, and future RESV messages will establish there the reservation while the reservation on the previously used segments will time out in accordance to RSMP rationale. Thus, whether a message is new or a refresh it is determined separately at each node, depending upon the existence of UID information in the RSM Base at that node.

Finally, the possibility of implementing the RSMP rationale is envisioned as an extension to OLSR to further minimize overhead. In this way, while maintaining the consistency of the information about allocated TFs among nodes, it may be possible to exploit the bandwidth availability information with the ones already maintained by OLSR to build a Traffic Engineering Base. This may be a first step toward the implementation of traffic engineering policies over wireless access networks.

Protocol Timings

The proposed signalling architecture subtends a strong interaction among RSMP, RSVP-TE and the RSM base. All blocks imply timers and general rules are required to match all the timers to let everything work robustly. The basic idea is that each node can refresh the entries, in RSM Base, that refer to allocation mastered or collisions detected by node itself, whereas they can update the others based on the time carried inside the RSM messages it receives. While a relation between the timers is inferable, a precise synchronization is not strictly required. The main four timers involved in the signalling architecture are:

1. T_{RSM}: Drives the RSMP refresh messages to announce updates in the allocations. A possible rule is to choose T_{RSM} so that (*i*) its propagation across the collision domain is lower than T_{RSM} itself to avoid inconsistencies, (*ii*) multiple RSM messages are sent between two consecutive RSVP-TE refreshes, thus preventing misallocations and (*iii*) despite possible errors in RSM messages broadcasting, a RSM message must be received before the successive RSVP-TE refresh to assure the coherence among RSM bases;

2. T_{RFS} : Drives the regular transmission of RSVP-TE refresh messages between signalling neighbours to maintain the reservation states. Normally refresh times are supposed to be set as high as possible to facilitate network scalability;

3. T_{RTR} : Drives the reservation request repetition. Its configuration must be coherent with the typical round-trip-time experienced by reservation setup;

4. T_{TO} : Drives the age of the allocation information in the RSM Base. Since RSVP-TE refresh frequency is normally set at a lower bound it is acceptable to have multiple T_{RFS} periods before erasing an entry in the RSM Base. In this way the possible loss of both RSM and RSVP-TE messages is counteracted. This approach is facilitated by the intrinsic bandwidth re-use enabled by TD-uCSMA.

However, the timer configuration must suit a typical application scenario of TD-uCSMA, which subtends a dynamic but not fast-changing wireless access network. The performances coming from different timer configurations are assessed by simulation in the following Sections.

SIMULATION ANALYSIS

Simulation Setups

All the blocks of the protocol architecture, depicted in Figure 3, have been implemented within the NS-2 network simulator. Then simulations were run to validate the capability of supporting QoS (thanks to TD-uCSMA) and dynamic resource management (by the signalling architecture). The multi-hop wireless access network, depicted in

Figure 8, constitutes the setting chosen for the simulations. In the proposed scenarios, the number of nodes does not exceed sixteen and all the nodes share the same physical channel. In the authors' view this is coherent with the goal of the proposed technology that manages QoS in a per-aggregate basis. In fact, if a higher number of nodes were involved, additional channels would probably be required to satisfy all the reservation requirements.

In practice, one-hop neighbours correctly demodulate all the transmissions, unless collisions take place, whereas the interference range is changed across the experiments, to assess the performance under different interference conditions. In all the simulation scenarios the data rate R is set to 54 Mb/s (auto-fall-back disabled), the basic data rate is set to 6 Mb/s, $SIFS$=16 μs and the slot time at physical layer $slotTime$ = 9 μs to comply with IEEE 802.11a standard. Moreover, the PLCP preamble and header are 96 and 24-bit-long respectively, the MAC header length is 34 bytes and ACK length is 14 bytes. The MAC payload size is 1500 byte.

Concerning the TD-uCSMA back-off entity handling QoS-demanding traffic, the following settings are used:

$$AIFS^i = SIFS + AIFSN^i \cdot slotTime \quad \forall i = H, l$$

where $AIFSN^H = 2$ and $AIFSN^l = 7$, $CW_{min}^H = CW_{max}^H = 1$ whereas $CW_{min}^l = 31$ and $CW_{max}^l = 1023$.

Moreover the time cycle is divided into 100 TFs of duration equal to 1 ms, whereas T_H in each node is changed throughout the simulations experiments.

The QoS-demanding traffic is simulated as long-lasting aggregates according to the hypothesis of stationary traffic conditions subtended by TD-uCSMA applications.

Figure 8. The topology used in the simulations here discussed

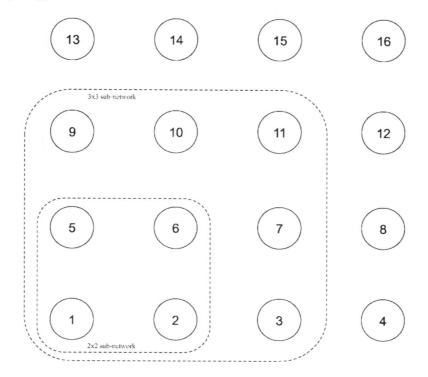

Simulation Results

QoS with Static Bandwidth Management

The TD-*u*CSMA's performances and its static resource management capabilities have already been assessed in single-hop scenarios (Vesco et al., 2009; Vesco et al., 2011) and in multi-channel scenarios where multi-hop routes are made of multiple single-hop collision domains (Scopigno et al., 2011). New simulation results are here presented to consolidate the understanding of the underlying bandwidth management principles and assess the QoS provided by TD-*u*CSMA in a worst-case scenario, when multi-hop routes coexist over a single collision domain.

The first set of simulations considers the single-hop 2x2 wireless grid in Figure 8. The available bandwidth $G_A \approx 32$ Mb/s as estimated starting by Equation (1) with a tolerance of 10%, in accordance to the simulation setups. The four nodes exchange 8 traffic aggregates; two aggregates of 8 Mb/s, one of 6 Mb/s, one of 4 Mb/s, two of 2 Mb/s and other two aggregates of 1 Mb/s. A share of the available bandwidth is statically reserved to each aggregate, by means of Equation (2), in accordance to their bit-rate. The bit-rates of the traffic aggregates are increased up to their maximum values to simulate different offered traffic loads.

Figure 9 (a) shows the goodput (at MAC layer) as function of the offered traffic load. This graph highlights that the four nodes can completely exploit their respective bandwidth reservations, even when the offered load reaches the network saturation rate (given by G_A). On the contrary, CSMA/CA cannot attain the same result, especially when the bandwidth requirements are significantly unbalanced among the traffic aggregates, as in this scenario. Figure 9 (b) shows that CSMA/CA negatively affects the goodput of the aggregates with higher bit-rates, whereas TD-*u*CSMA is able to guarantee the reserved bandwidth. This is further confirmed by the analysis of end-to-end delay experienced by single packets in Figure 9 (c). When the offered load reaches 24 Mb/s, CSMA/CA is not able to get through the offered traffic. The queues within the nodes start saturating and the delays grow high. On the contrary, TD-*u*CSMA keeps both the mean and the maximum delays bounded; which are less than 25 ms also when saturation is reached.

The second set of simulations is about the multi-hop 3x3 wireless grid in Figure 8. The available bandwidth $G_A \approx 32\,Mb/s$, in accordance again to the simulation setups. Each traffic aggregate consumes a share of the entire available bandwidth, at each traversed hop. As a result, in the proposed scenario comprising multi-hops routes, the nine nodes exchange 5 traffic aggregates, each crossing two hops; one aggregate of 8 Mb/s, one of 4 Mb/s, one of 2 Mb/s and other two aggregates of 1 Mb/s. A share of the available bandwidth is statically reserved to each aggregate, by means of Equation (2), in accordance to their bit-rate. The bit-rates of the traffic aggregates are increased up to their maximum values to simulate different offered traffic loads. In these simulations the interference range is changed.

Figure 10 (a) and (d) shows the goodput (at MAC layer) as function of the offered traffic

Figure 9. Simulation results assessing the TD-uCSMA performance in the single-hop 2x2 wireless grid scenario: (a) Aggregated goodput; (b) Per-aggregate goodput at the network saturation point; (c) End-to-end mean and maximum delay at the network saturation point

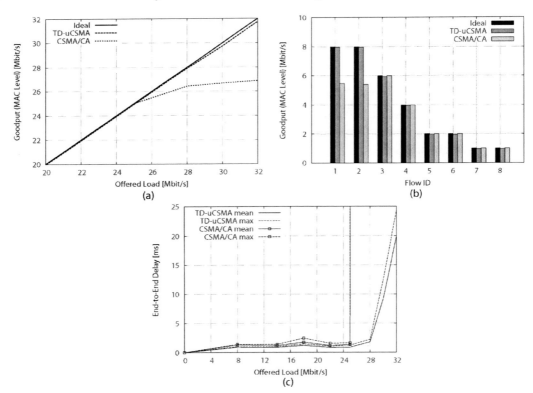

Figure 10. Simulation results assessing the TD-uCSMA performance in the multi-hop 3x3 wireless grid scenario. The interference range coincides with the one-hop neighbours (left) and with two-hops neighbours (right). (a) Aggregated goodput; (b) Per-aggregate goodput at the network saturation point; (c) End-to-end mean and maximum delay at the network saturation point; (d) Aggregated goodput; (e) Per-aggregate goodput at the network saturation point; (f) End-to-end mean and maximum delay at the network saturation point.

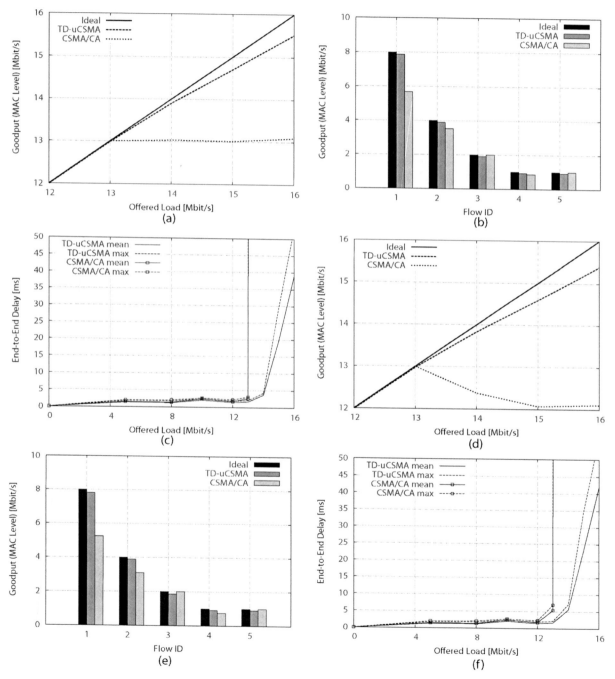

load, when the one-hop neighbours and two-hops neighbours fall within the interference domain respectively. The TD-uCSMA performs properly and outperforms CSMA/CA in both cases. The comparison demonstrates also that the performance of TD-uCSMA is only slightly degraded, when the interference grows, whereas CSMA/CA is heavily affected by it. This means that TD-uCSMA intrinsically protect the traffic aggregate. Thus, the traffic aggregate is somehow *isolated* over a multi-hop network, leading to higher resource utilization than with CSMA/CA. This feature is particularly important for wireless access networks, since bandwidth is at the same time a precious but scarce resource. The results depicted in Figure 10 (b) and (e) further confirm the TD-uCSMA capability of guaranteeing the reserved bandwidth also over multi-hop networks. Moreover, the analysis of delays depicted in Figure 10 (c) and (f), confirms that the maximum and mean end-to-end delay are still upper-bounded with TD-uCSMA, less than 50 ms, even under saturation.

Eventually, these results clearly show the effectiveness of the bandwidth management capability of TD-uCSMA and of Equation (2) with (3) in providing a simple and viable bandwidth reservation model.

Distributed and Dynamic Bandwidth Management

The third and final set of simulations aims at assessing the performances of the dynamical reservation signalling architecture over the entire wireless access network in Figure 8. Hence the RSMP and RSVP-TE protocols are now enabled on the NS-2 simulator. Each node issues a reservation request for 2 Mb/s toward a node randomly; hence the reservation requests cross a different number of hops during the same simulation. The reservation requests adhere to a Poisson process with mean arrival rate λ whereas the holding times are statistically independent and exponentially distributed with mean holding time $1/\mu$=120 sec. The mean arrival rate is changed throughout the simulations to assess the performances under different reservation load condition $\rho = \lambda/\mu$. The timers are configured as follows: $T_{RSM} = 500$ ms, $T_{RFS} = 5$ sec, $T_{RTR} = 1$ sec and $T_{TO} = 15$ sec. The sources of the reservation requests are configured to retry a request (for reservation and/or refresh purpose) up to 10 times.

Figure 11 (a) shows the percentage of reservations accepted, rejected and blocked over the entire simulation. The line labelled *accepted* refers to the reservations correctly operated for the entire life of the traffic aggregate; the line labelled *blocked*, instead, refers to the reservations successfully operated that are then blocked during the data transmission phase; finally, the line labelled *rejected* refers to the reservation requests dispatched without success. The analysis of the simulation results revealed that no reservations are rejected or blocked due to the loss of RESV and PATH messages; hence, the *rejected* statistic shows the percentage of requests that experienced the lack of resources in the network; similarly the *blocked* statistic shows the percentage of reservations correctly operated that are then torn down due to a misallocation of one or more TFs as detected and reported by RSMP.

The blocking happens when two nodes issue reservation requests on different routes but at the same time. In this case both the reservations can be correctly operated but the same TFs may be allocated to both reservations, at different nodes; in this case the RSMP can propagate the information only when the misallocation is detected and, then, the reservation is blocked. This means that the time required to propagate the allocation information through the network should be related with the minimum inter-arrival time of two reservation requests. On the contrary, rejection depends on ρ and the number of resources, *i.e.*, TFs, in the network.

However the main result in Figure 11 (a) is that for $\rho=\lambda/\mu < 3$, hence $\lambda <3\mu$, up to 95% of the reservations are accepted and the traffic is correctly forwarded by TD-uCSMA at MAC layer. This result is coherent with the initial hypothesis of TD-uCSMA, which is meant to manage almost static (or at least non-fast-changing) reservation requests (setup and tear down). Moreover Figure 11 (b) shows that setup delay is very low, lower than 25 ms, in the region of interest, whereas Figure 11 (c) highlights that the protocol overhead is almost negligible, with respect to the very high bandwidth exploited thanks to TD-uCSMA.

PROTOTYPING OF TD-UCSMA WITH OPEN SOURCE DRIVERS

Recent effort has been spent in addressing the issue of the prototyping the TD-uCSMA, exploiting an open source Linux distribution for embedded devices, called OpenWRT (Baker et al., 2011) and running it on router board with IEEE 802.11 miniPCI cards based on an Atheros AR5k series chipset.

OpenWrt provides a fully writable filesystem with package management. This frees the developer from the application selection and configuration provided by the vendors and permits the customization of the devices through the use of packages to suit any application. Moreover the

Figure 11. Simulation results assessing the dynamic signalling capabilities provided by the RSMP and RSVP-TE properly extended: (a) Percentage of requests accepted, rejected and blocked; (b) Mean end-to-end delay experienced by reservation requests correctly operated; it also comprises the delay experienced by blocked reservations; (c) Signalling overhead

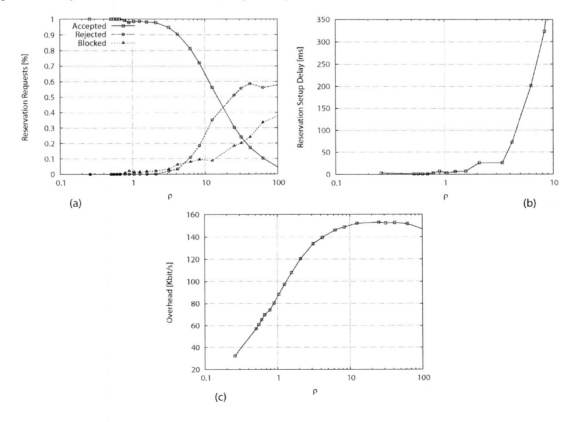

IEEE 802.11 Atheros drivers are open source and implemented by the ath5K kernel module within OpenWRT. The ath5k kernel module is an open source driver to control the ath5k wireless chipset family in the Linux kernel. The module gives the kernel the capability to load and unload the PCI board and control the inner functioning of the chip. It is not used to handle the 802.11 MAC level of the TCP/IP stack, since that task is handled both by the hardware and the mac80211 kernel module as depicted in Figure 12.

Basic Operations

The ath5k kernel module is implemented through several files, each of them used for a very specific function. However only some of them are really relevant to the goal of TD-*u*CSMA prototyping:

- **ath5k.h:** The header file contains definitions of constants, such as the channel ac-

cess parameters proper of (legacy) IEEE 802.11. These parameters are defined as constants and used throughout the implementation of the module. Moreover, the module includes the definition of functions used to perform basic register I/O on the Atheros chipset and the libraries for the interaction with the rest of the kernel, through the ath common layer and the mac80211 layer;

- **base.h:** The header file defines the Software Carrier structure called *ath5k_softc*. This structure is passed to various functions throughout the module and keeps track of the driver state associated with an instance of a device;

- **base.c:** The implementation file defines the functions to load and unload the ath5k kernel module from the kernel. It also implements several functions used to handle the PCI (to probe, unload, suspend and re-

Figure 12. TCP/IP stack within OpenWRT

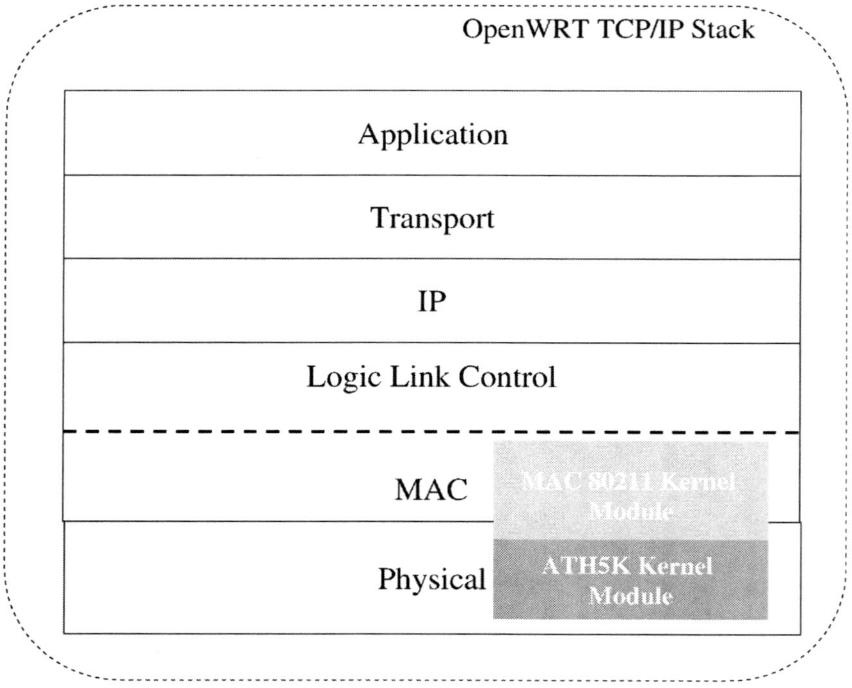

sume). These functions are used to define an entry point to the whole driver and to perform the initial setup of the module;

- **qcu.c:** Tthe implementation file defines the functions handling both data and control queues; it also implements functions used to initialize, reset, query and manipulate individual and group of queues. Among them is the reset function, which associates the default channel access contention parameter (defined in **ath5k.h**) to each of the queues, whenever a reset operation occurs;

- **reg.h:** The header file defines the memory addresses used to read and write specific registers on the Atheros chipset, such as the ones storing the channel contention parameters. Thus it becomes possible to change the channel access parameters by writing these registers at runtime. This file is highly relevant to the implementation of the TD-uCSMA since the switching of

channel access parameters is one of the main operating principles in TD-uCSMA.

The ongoing attempt to implement TD-uCSMA is extremely simple and is depicted in the block scheme of Figure 13. The implementation consists of two files, **tducsma.h** and **tducsma.c**, included within the ath5k kernel module.

The **tducsma.h** file contains the definition of the *td_ucsma structure*. It basically includes the channel access parameters in the $EDCA^H$ and $EDCA^l$ sets; the current TF and time cycle and their respective duration; a timer and an array representation of the time cycle containing the TF allocations. The elements of this array are equal to 1 if the related TF is allocated to the node and 0 otherwise.

The **tducsma.c** file contains the implementation of three functions that are called at different times, during the execution of the ath5k kernel

Figure 13. A block scheme of the TD-uCSMA implementation

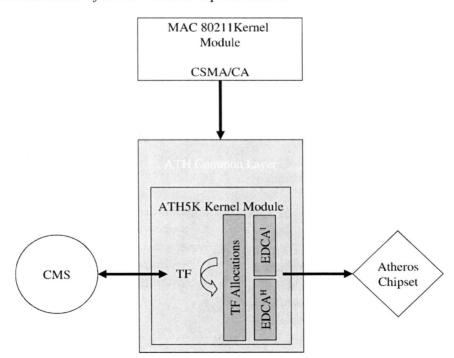

module, to implement the TD-uCSMA operating principle:

- **tducsma_setup()** is called as soon as the kernel module is loaded into the kernel and initializes the *td_ucsma structure* with default values (defined in the **tducsma.h**) and perform other initial operations;

- **tducsma_localization()** is used to determine in which TF and time cycle the node is located to achieve synchronization with the other nodes participating in the network;

- **tducsma_callback()** is called at the beginning of each TF. It writes the channel access parameters in accordance to the TF allocation array on the Atheros chipset. The node contends for channel access in accordance to $EDCA^H$, during the TF allocated to it and according to $EDCA^l$ otherwise. The operation is performed using the register write functions defined in **ath5k.h** and the registers' addresses defined in **reg.h**. This function also schedules the next execution of the callback at the beginning of the next TF. The timer is implemented by using the Linux 2.6.x kernel built-in *hrtimer* (Corbet, 2006) that permits a greater precision than other legacy solutions.

The pointer to the *td_ucsma structure* is added the *ath5k_softc structure* within the **base.h** file so that it is possible to access it from any function of the ath5k kernel module.

As soon as the ath5k module is loaded into the kernel, the **tducsma_setup()** function is called by the entry point defined in **base.c** file. Then the kernel module performs a reset of the wireless card, calling the reset implemented in the **qcu.c** file. During this operation the function **tducsma_localization()** is called in order to achieve localization within the CTR structure, as described in the next section, and start the subsequent scheduling of TFs. Thus, the function **tducsma_callback()** is called at the beginning of each TF to write the correct values of the channel access parameters into the registers of the Atheros chipset (through the **ath5k_hw_reg_write()** function defined in **ath5k.h file**) and to schedule the beginning of the next TF.

It is worth observing that the proposed implementation of the TD-*u*CSMA only foresees minor changes to the ath5k kernel module, to enable the switching of the channel access contention parameters over time. Conversely, the basic CSMA/CA operations implemented by the mac80211 kernel module are not altered and the same is for the underlying wireless card's hardware. This fact itself further confirms that TD-*u*CSMA preserves the typical benefits of a distributed approach (efficient resource utilization and scalability) and does not require changes to the standard 802.11 MAC Layer.

Time Synchronization

The TD-*u*CSMA nodes refer to a common notion of time, in order to deploy the CTR structure (synchronous beat of time frames) and to locate themselves therein (identification of the current time frame). In this first prototype the common time coincides with the system time at each node. Hence the local clocks are maintained synchronized with the others using the NTP (Mills, 1991) by relying on a single, "out of band" connection to a local NTP server to reduce the latency hence synchronization errors.

The **tducsma_localization()** function perform the operations for identifying the current time frame within the CTR structure depicted in Figure 1. The function, after reading the system time τ calculates the current TF as follows:

$$TF = \mathrm{mod}\left(floor\left(\frac{\tau}{T_f}\right), \quad TC\right) \qquad (5)$$

where TC is the time cycle dimension measured in TFs. Afterwards each node has to schedule the beginning of the next TF after a period of time T_{comp} as follows:

$$T_{comp} = ceil\left(\frac{\tau}{T_f}\right) - \tau \qquad (6)$$

Finally, the **tducsma_callback()** function schedules the beginning of each subsequent TF, every time a TF beat occurs. Moreover each node has to maintain its time-localization within the time cycle by incrementing the number of the initial TF at the beginning of each time frame.

Each node beats the subsequent TFs according to its local clock. As a consequence, the TF beating of nodes progressively get un-synchronized. For this reason, after a given number of time cycles, all nodes have to resynchronize the TF beat. This is achieved by calling again the **tducsma_localization()** function from within the **tducsma_callback()** when needed.

Central Management System

A central management system (CMS) has been implemented as well, to facilitate the remote configuration of TD-*u*CSMA related parameters on all the nodes (*e.g.*, time frame duration and time cycle dimension; the channel access parameters in $EDCA^H$ and $EDCA^l$ sets. Moreover the CMS enables the static allocation of TFs within all the nodes.

All the above parameters are stored, as variables, within the *td_ucsma structure* in the ath5k kernel module. Thus, the *sysfs* file system (Corbet, 2003) is exploited to enable the remote CMS to change these variables simply by writing the desired values into specific files mapped to the variable themselves. This solution permits to interact with TD-uCSMA at run-time, and to reserve bandwidth over single routes, through the use of the CMS.

CONCLUSION

This chapter has presented a novel weakly synchronous and distributed coordination function, called Time-Division *Unbalanced* Carrier Sense Multiple Access (TD-*u*CSMA). The TD-*u*CSMA relies on synchronization among wireless nodes and the contextual switching of channel access parameters to enable resource management and QoS provisioning over CSMA/CA wireless access networks. The TD-*u*CSMA operating principles and issue of synchronization have been presented and simulation results have validated the operating principles.

Moreover a signalling architecture enabling dynamic and distributed resource reservation over the wireless network has been discussed. Simulations results have shown that RSMP and RSVP-TE properly extended correctly operate on a TD-*u*CSMA networks with almost negligible overhead.

Finally the issue of prototyping TD-*u*CSMA by open source Atheros drivers has been addressed to show that few and simple modifications to the IEEE 802.11 legacy driver are required to implement TD-*u*CSMA. This interesting result confirms that TD-*u*CSMA is compliant to the standard 802.11 MAC Layer

REFERENCES

Awduche, D., Berger, L., Gan, D., Li, T., Srinivasan, V., & Swallow, G. (2001). *RFC 3209 (proposed standard), RSVP-TE: Extensions to RSVP for LSP tunnels.* Retrieved from http://www.ietf.org/rfc/rfc3209.txt

Baker, M., & Rozema, G. (2011). *OpenWRT, wireless freedom*. Retrieved from https://openwrt.org/

Baldi, M., Giacomelli, R., & Marchetto, G. (2009). Time-driven access and forwarding for industrial wireless multihop networks. *IEEE Transactions on Industrial Informatics, 5*(2), 99–112. doi:10.1109/TII.2009.2017523

Borgonovo, F., Capone, A., Cesana, M., & Fratta, L. (2004). AdHoc MAC: New MAC architecture for ad hoc networks providing efficient and reliable point-to-point and broadcast services. *Wireless Networks, 10*(4), 359–366. doi:10.1023/B:WINE.0000028540.96160.8a

Braden, R., Zhang, L., Berson, S., Herzog, S., & Jamin, S. (1997). *RFC 2205 (proposed standard), resource reservation protocol (RSVP) – Version 1 functional specification*. Retrieved from http://www.ietf.org/rfc/rfc2205.txt

Carlson, E., Bettstetter, C., Karl, H., Prehofer, C., & Wolisz, A. (2004). *Distributed MAC for real-time traffic in multi-hop wireless networks*. IEEE Conference on Sensor and Ad Hoc Communications and Networks (SECON 04).

Carlson, E., Prehofer, C., Bettstetter, C., Karl, H., & Wolisz, A. (2006). A distributed end-to-end reservation protocol for IEEE 802.11-based wireless mesh networks. *IEEE Journal on Selected Areas in Communications, 24*(11), 2018–2027. doi:10.1109/JSAC.2006.881633

Carneiro, G., Ruela, J., & Ricardo, M. (2004). *Cross-layer design in 4G wireless terminals* (pp. 7–13). IEEE Wireless Communication Magazine.

Casetti, C., & Chiasserini, C. (2004). Improving fairness and throughput for voice traffic in 802.11e EDCA. *IEEE Personal, Indoor and Mobile Radio Communications Symposium (PIMRC 04)* (pp. 525-530).

Clausen, T., & Jacquet, P. (2003). *RFC 3626 (experimental), optimized link state routing protocol (OLSR)*. Retrieved from http://www.ietf.org/rfc/rfc3626.txt

Corbet, J. (2003). *Kobjects and Sysfs*. Retrieved from http://lwn.net/Articles/54651/

Corbet, J. (2006). *The high-resolution timer API*. Retrieved from http://lwn.net/Articles/167897/

Facchini, C., Granelli, F., & Fonseca, N. L. S. (2010). Identifying relevant cross-layer interactions in cognitive processes. *IEEE Global Telecommunications Conference (GLOBECOM 2010)* (pp. 1-6).

Ganeriwal, S., Kumar, R., & Srivastava, M. B. (2003). Timing-sync protocol for sensor networks. *ACM International Conference on Embedded Networked Sensor Systems (SenSys 2003)* (pp. 138–149).

Hightower, P. (2008). Motion effects on GPS receiver time accuracy. *Instrumentation Technology Systems*. Retrieved from http://www.itsamerica.com/

IEEE. (2010). *IEEE 802.11p standard, wireless access in vehicular environments*.

IEEE. (2011). *IEEE 802.11s draft 8.0, draft amendment: ESS mesh networking*.

ISO/IEC International Standard 7498-1. (1994). *Information Technology – Open systems interconnection – Basic reference model: The basic model*.

Katz, D., Kompella, K., & Yeung, D. (2003). *RFC 3630 (proposed standard), traffic engineering (TE) extensions to OSPF version 2*. Retrieved from http://www.ietf.org/rfc/rfc3630.txt

Mangold, S., Sunghyun, C., Hiertz, G., Klein, O., & Walke, B. (2003). *Analysis of IEEE 802.11e for QoS support in wireless LANs* (pp. 40–50). IEEE Wireless Communication Magazine.

Maròti, M., Kusy, B., Simon, G., & Lèdeczi, A. (2004). The flooding time synchronization protocol. *ACM International Conference on Embedded Networked Sensor Systems (SenSys 2004)* (pp. 39–49).

Mills, D. (1991). Internet time synchronization: The network time protocol. *IEEE Transactions on Communications*, *39*(10), 1482–1493. doi:10.1109/26.103043

Moy, J. (2008). *RFC 2328 (Standard), OSPF version 2.* Retrieved from http://www.ietf.org/rfc/rfc2328.txt

Pries, R., Menth, S., Staehle, D., Menth, M., & Tran-Gia, P. (2008). Dynamic contention window adaptation (DCWA) in 802.11e wireless local area networks. *IEEE International Conference on Consumer Electronics (ICCE 08)* (pp. 92–97).

Romdhani, L., Ni, Q., & Turletti, T. (2003). Adaptive EDCF: Enhanced service differentiation for IEEE 802.11 wireless ad-hoc networks. *IEEE Wireless Communications and Networking Conference (WCNC 03)* (pp. 1373–1378).

Schenato, L., & Gamba, G. (2007). A distributed consensus protocol for clock synchronization in wireless sensor network. *IEEE Conference on Decision and Control (CDC 07)* (pp. 2289–2294).

Scopigno, R., & Cozzetti, H. A. (2009). Mobile slotted aloha for VANETs. *IEEE Vehicular Technology Conference (VTC Fall 2009)* (pp. 1-5).

Scopigno, R., & Vesco, A. (2011). A distributed bandwidth management scheme for multi-hop wireless access networks. *IEEE Communications Society Conference on Sensor, Mesh and Ad Hoc Communications and Networks (IWCMC 2011)* (pp. 534–539).

Shakkottai, S., Rappaport, T. S., & Karlsson, P. C. (2003). Cross-layer design for wireless networks. *IEEE Communications Magazine*, (n.d), 74–80. doi:10.1109/MCOM.2003.1235598

Vesco, A., Abrate, F., & Scopigno, R. (2011). Convergence and performance analysis of leaderless synchronization in Wi-Fi networks. ACM Workshop on Performance Monitoring, Measurement, and Evaluation of Heterogeneous Wired and Wireless Mobile Networks (PM2HW2N 2011), in conjunction with ACM International Conference on Modeling, Analysis and Simulation of Wireless and Mobile Systems (MSWiM 2011).

Vesco, A., & Scopigno, R. (2009). Time-division access priority in CSMA/CA. *IEEE Personal, Indoor and Mobile Radio Communications Symposium (PIMRC 09)* (pp. 1–6).

Vesco, A., & Scopigno, R. (2011). Advances on time-division unbalanced carrier sense multiple access. *IEEE Workshop on Flexibility in Broadband Wireless Access Networks (FlexBWAN 2011), in conjunction with IEEE International Conference on Computer Communications and Networks (ICCCN 2011)* (pp. 1–6).

Wroclawski, J. (1997). *RFC 2210 (proposed standard), the use of RSVP with IETF integrated services.* Retrieved from http://www.ietf.org/rfc/rfc2210.txt

Zhang, Q., Yang, F., & Zhu, W. (2005). Cross-layer QoS support for multimedia delivery over wireless Internet. *EURASIP Journal on Applied Signal Processing*, (n.d), 2005.

Zhu, H., Cao, G., Yener, A., & Mathias, A. (2004). EDCF-DM: A novel enhanced distributed coordination function for wireless ad hoc networks. *IEEE International Conference on Communications (ICC 04)* (pp. 3866–3890).

ENDNOTES

[1]   The transmission opportunity (TXOP) parameter is not exploited in TD-uCSMA. In fact, if a node were delayed in its channel access, TXOP would enforce this delay:

hence the delay would be propagated, with a disruptive effect on the underlying TD-uCSMA operating principles.

2 *Tight* (or *Hard*) Synchronization applies, for instance, to pure Sonet/SDH fixed networks. Their prerequisite is a synchronization spanning over the network and so precise to limit the occurrence of positive or negative *justifications*. In SDH justification is called the mechanism adjusting the number of bits multiplexed from different links onto a same link, in order to compensate for limited clock precision and/or clock drifts.

3 With a known position, the receiver does not have to calculate a positional fix to update the clock phase (the so called "1-pulse-per-second" or "1PPS"). In turn, a rapid and accurate control of the phase error is facilitated and the difference between the real GPS time and the equipment tick can be kept very low (Hightower, 2008) even when only one satellite is being tracked.

Section 2
Coding for Wireless Systems

Chapter 5
MAC and PHY-Layer Network Coding for Applications in Wireless Communications Networks

Giulio Bartoli
University of Firenze, Italy

Francesco Chiti
University of Firenze, Italy

Romano Fantacci
University of Firenze, Italy

Dania Marabissi
University of Firenze, Italy

Andrea Tassi
University of Firenze, Italy

ABSTRACT

Network coding (NC) is a promising technique recently proposed to improve network performance in terms of maximum throughput, minimum delivery delay, and energy consumption. The original proposal highlighted the advantages of NC for multicast communications in wire-line networks. Recently, network coding has been considered as an efficient approach to improve performance in wireless networks, mainly in terms of data reliability and lower energy consumption, especially for broadcast communications. The basic idea of NC is to remove the typical requirement that different information flows have to be processed and transmitted independently through the network. When NC is applied, intermediate nodes in the network do not simply relay the received packets, but they combine several received packets before transmission. As a consequence, the output flow at a given node is obtained as a linear combination of its input flows. This chapter deals with the application of network coding principle at different communications layers of the protocol stack, specifically, the Medium Access Control (MAC) and physical (PHY) Layers for wireless communication networks.

DOI: 10.4018/978-1-4666-1797-1.ch005

Copyright © 2012, IGI Global. Copying or distributing in print or electronic forms without written permission of IGI Global is prohibited.

INTRODUCTION

Network coding represents one of the main topic for future communication technology. It permits to maximize the information flow in the network, leading an increased throughput with low complexity increase. NC concept can be applied to different layers of the protocol stack. Traditional NC has been proposed at the network level of wired systems. However, in some cases the achievable gains with this approach are limited (Liu, 2006). For this reason NC has been extended also to other communication layers in order to exploit link-layer or physical layer information, especially when used in wireless networks.

Despite the underlying theory of NC is attractive, many practical aspects need still to be addressed in order to understand the actual performance and benefits of this technique in wireless communications. In particular, large part of the works in the literature considers wireless links reliable like the wired ones. However, the propagation medium is very different and should be carefully addressed: theoretical concepts need to be revised and adapted to real environments. After a state of the art review, some open research issues concerning with link reliability and wireless propagation channel are addressed in this chapter and deeply investigated considering NC integration at different protocol stack layers, namely MAC and PHY.

MAC layer NC (MAC-NC) schemes are based on the features provided by this layer - basically (un)acknowledged communications - and do not require to identify the sessions to which packets fragments belong to, while effectively managing the resources. Likewise, Physical Layer NC (PLNC) schemes are inspired by the basic NC principle to remove the constraint that different information flows have to be transmitted in separated channels. In particular, for PLNC schemes the definition of efficient approaches concerning cancellation or detection of collided packets at the final receiving ends is the main design goal.

For both approaches this chapter offers a critical review of the state of the art and then outlines new solutions that overcome classical methods.

The MAC-NC has been adopted to achieve better performance for connection oriented services, i.e., acknowledged communications, in terms of end-to-end packet delay in the presence of lossy links. The focus is usually on a network model where source nodes broadcast packets to a group of two or more sink nodes over error prone wireless channels. Three different alternatives have been considered in order to assure a reliable data multicasting, namely: a classical random linear network coding (RLNC) scheme, a linear network coding combined with a basic ARQ or, alternatively, with a soft combined ARQ scheme. Performance comparisons provided by means of analytical and numerical results clearly highlight that the best solution is to adopt the last alternative.

In addition, it has been investigated the feasibility of applying MAC-NC to unreliable wireless communications scenarios (i.e., without explicit acknowledgment of packet reception outcome) in which the transmitted power level of different network nodes is optimized with the aim of minimizing the number of NC packets transmitted on a link basis, thereby lowering the end-to-end delay and the overall power consumption.

Also PLNC has been addressed. One of the most interesting topic concerning the PLNC deals with the Two-Way Relay Network (TWRN) where a pair of nodes exchange information through a third node with relaying function. The two main approaches of PLNC coding are Amplify and Forward (AF) and Decode and Forward (DF). Generally the latter approach works better in AWGN (Additive White Gaussian Noise) channel because the noise is not forwarded by the relay. However in actual multipath fading channels this approach has several limitations due to channel variations that have impacts on the relay demodulation, the knowledge of the channels involved in the communication and the power balancing to name a few. In this chapter the attention is focused on DF approach. Issues related to channel knowledge, channel inversion and resource allocation are investigated. In particular, different solutions to counteract channel non ideality and suitable subcarriers and power allocation schemes based on actual channel knowledge are presented, showing the benefits in terms of bit error rate and throughput.

BACKGROUND

In order to introduce NC concepts this section starts with an overview of the traditional NC approach and then focuses on its extensions to lower communications layers in wireless links.

In particular an overview of the state of the art of MAC-NC and PLNC in wireless links is provided: each subsection gives a description of the NC approach in the specific protocol stack layer, focusing on critical issues that need to be investigated.

The Digital Network Coding (DNC) technique has been proposed for the first time in (Ahlswede, 2000); in order to clarify the general idea underling this communication technique consider the so-called "butterfly network" (Yeung, 2006), reported in Figure 1.

Figure 1 shows a communication network where a slotted time access to the communication links is assumed:

- There are two nodes that are unit rate traffic sources (represented by the nodes number *one* and *two*) generating one symbol per time slot directed to a pool of receiving nodes (the nodes number *five* and *six*);
- Each link has the capacity of one symbol per time slot.

It can be easily seen that nodes *five* and *six* are not able to receive at the same time, both transmitted symbols (*a* and *b*): two disjoined paths interconnecting each traffic source to both the receivers do not exist in the network. The DNC overcomes these limits allowing nodes *five* and *six* to receive two symbols per time slots.

When network communications rely on DNC, the intermediate nodes in a path between the data sources and the destination nodes combine the incoming traffic flows and forward them. In particular in the considered butterfly network, in a time slot the node *three* performs a linear combination of symbols *a* and *b* (for instance represented by the symbol $a + b$) and sends it toward the receivers. This strategy leads the nodes number *five (six)* to receive *a* (*b*) in addition the linear combination of *a* and *b* (*a+b*). In that way receiving nodes can recover both transmitted symbols. In this simple example the DNC made possible the communication at the maximum rate of two symbols per time slot to each receiving node.

This simple example can be generalized to more complex networks. Let $G = (V, E)$ be a directed and acyclic graph with the set of vertices V and the set of edges $E \subseteq V \times V$ (with a capacity of one symbol per time slot) the main theorem of DNC (Fragouli, 2007) states what follows:

Main Theorem of DNC. Let $S \in V$ be a node connected to h unit rate traffic sources (i.e., h sources transmitting one symbol per time slot), and $R = \{R_1, R_2, ..., R_n\} \subset V$ a set of receiving nodes, assuming that the number of disjoined paths between S and R_i ($\forall i \in \{1, 2, ..., n\}$) is h, it can be found a DNC transmission scheme defining the recombining operations performed by the intermediate nodes of the network in order to made possible a delivery rate to each receivers equal to h. □

Linear combination of the symbols is performed by means suitable coding vectors. A message that has to be sent to one or multiple destination nodes, is composed of q symbols defining a vector $L = \{L_1; L_2; ...; L_q\}$. Given a coding vector g (of length q), in each time slot a coded symbol $u = L \times g$ is sent (jointly to the coding

Figure 1. A butterfly network topology

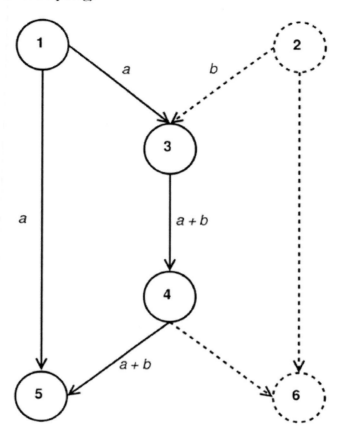

vector itself). At the receiver side each received symbol $\hat{u}_i$ represents an element of the vector $\hat{U} = \left\{\hat{u}_1; \hat{u}_2; \ldots; \hat{u}_q\right\}$ and the corresponding coding vector represents a column of the matrix $G = \left\{g_1; g_2; \ldots; g_q\right\}$. When the rank of G is equal to the number of the linear independent symbols, the original q symbols can be decoded as:

$$L = \hat{U} \times G^{-1}$$

A set of theoretical frameworks have been developed (in addition to the information theoretic one) in order to easily face to the DNC. Fragouli (2007) presents the strengths of each model that are:

- **The Line-Graph Framework** (Koetter, 2003): Where each vertex represents a network link, for this reason the operations performed by the intermediate nodes can be rewritten in a more compact way with respect to the classical representation of a network by a directed graph;
- **The Combinatorial Framework** (Fragouli, 2004): Where the DNC is considered as a packing problem of trees (defined as subgraphs in the communication network) rooted at an intermediate node performing coding operations;
- **The Linear-Programming Framework** (Papadimitriou, 1982): Where the DNC problem can be modelled as the maximization of flow in a network between a source node and a pool of destination nodes.

Should be noted also that the generation of the coding vector problem can been addressed in several ways (Ho, 2008) but from a practical point of view there are two main strategies:

- **The Random Linear Network Coding (RLNC)** (Chou, 2007): Where the coding vectors are randomly chosen and each transmitted symbol must be delivered jointly to the coding vector used to compute the coded symbol itself (Lucani, 2008);
- **The Non-Coherent Random Network Coding (NRNC)** (Kötter, 2008): That is an extension to the classical RLNC approach characterized by a reduced overhead because a coding vector is represented as an element of the vector subspace holding all received packets. For this reason the coding vector can be recovered in a distributed manner at the receiver side.

MAC-NC

Unfortunately the DNC scheme presented before from the information theoretic point of view, cannot be merged as it is into a real communication standard with a minimal effort because:

- The classical DNC scheme combines communication streams composed by elements that belongs to a finite field. Each element can be considered as a packet flowing in the network. In particular in a classical *full IP* (Kurose, 2006) communication network the packet concept takes different meanings depending on the considered layer of the protocol stack;
- Each communication pattern derived from the classic DNC requires a signalization protocol to practically synchronize the state of the traffic source and sink nodes. For example a sink node should send an

acknowledgment message to the source node to communicate that it has collected a sufficient number of linearly independent packets, etc.

For these reasons the general concept of DNC must be adapted to the specific communication layer in which it is adopted, facing with its peculiarities and specific functionalities. This is particularly valid for wireless communications. In the literature many works have demonstrated the advantages of DNC in different scenarios (Yeung, 2008), (Cui, 2004) but original investigations are mainly focused on wire-line networks. Only recently DNC has received attention for applications in wireless networks. In particular NC in wireless systems is considered a way of improving network capacity and coping with unreliable wireless links (Towsley, 2008; Fragouli, 2007). In fact, wireless channels are inherently error prone with a time varying packet error rate (PER) resulting in packet erasures. These topics are directly related to the problem of delivering real-time media applications with QoS constraints (for e.g., in terms of available bandwidth and delay constraints) across the network itself that is managed by the MAC layer. In the past many solutions have been proposed to deal with link reliability at MAC layer, ranging from basic retransmission schemes as Automatic Repeat reQuest (ARQ) (Comroe, 1984) or even Hybrid ARQ (HARQ) (Lin, 1984) types. DNC can represent a valid solution: this challenging issue can been addressed developing specific DNC based communication schemes at the MAC layer. In particular the MAC-NC has been adopted in the broadband wireless communication standard jointly to the specific Automatic Repeat reQuest (ARQ) scheme in use (Jin, 2008) or it operates in a cross layer manner with a Hybrid ARQ policy (Tran, 2009). Nevertheless, the exact evaluation of the reliability gain of NC, or the comparison with (Soft) ARQ schemes for different load and error conditions are still open issues.

PLNC

As stated before, Network Coding has been originally introduced at higher layers (e.g., transport and network layers) to optimize network capacity, while recently its concept has been extended also to the physical layer (Katti, 2007; Zhang, 2006). PLNC approaches exploits the PHY layer information, in particular the broadcast nature of the propagation channel in order to improve the network throughput.

In order to understand the PLNC approach we can focus on a simple cooperative network where two nodes exchange information but are not in radio visibility and, hence, an intermediate node acts as relay (Zhang, 2006). Assuming a Time Division Multiple Access (TDMA) system, a traditional network, i.e., not using NC, needs four time slots for a bi-directional communication: two time slots are used by the source nodes to transmit their packets to the relay and two time slots are used by the relay to forward the packets to destination nodes. This is because the simultaneous transmission of different signals on the same time slot can be disruptive. PLNC overcome this concept considering the interference as a mean to increase the system throughput: the collision of two signals transmitted on the same time slot is nothing but the sum of the two signals. Hence if the destination node knows the interfering signal, it can recover the intended signal. In that way PLNC reduces the needed time slots to two.

In particular, in PLNC systems the relay node forwards to the destination nodes a signal obtained by the composition of the two original transmitted signals. Two approaches are possible:

Amplify and Forward (AF) - the relay node amplifies and forwards the received signal that is the arithmetic sum of the analog signals transmitted by the two source nodes without any additional elaboration: the signal composition is made by the channel (Katti, 2007). This approach is often referred as Analog Network Coding.

Decode and Forward (DF) - the relay node performs a suitable decoding of the signal, then it maps the result of the decoding in a new signal that could be interpretable by both the destination nodes. In particular, the signal received by the relay node is a superimposition of the signals transmitted from the source nodes, hence the relay node cannot correctly decode the two signals. However, the relay node can extract useful information to forward. Assuming for the sake of simplicity an antipodal modulation, the relay can distinguish between two cases: transmission of the same symbol or antipodal symbols. These two cases are encoded and transmitted to the terminal nodes. (Zhang, 2006). This method is often referred as *DeNoise and Forward* (DNF) because not a real decoding is performed at the relay. Some papers extend this concept also to higher order modulations (Koike-Akino, 2009; Zhang, 2006).

The first approach is less performing because the noise level is amplified together with the useful signal. In (Maric & Goldsmith, 2010) it is shown the AF approach is effective only in high-SNR (Signal to Noise Ratio) channels. In AWGN channel DF approach presents better performance (Popovski & Yomo, 2006). However, in actual channels where multipath fading occurs each link experiences a different channel gain and the DF approach presents poor performance because of the decoding at the relay node is based on the assumption that two interfering signals are received with the same power.

For this reason many papers on PLNC in the literature concern with the AF approach and with solutions to solve its drawbacks. Among them, Gao (2009) presents an efficient method for estimating channel parameters required for data detection that maximize the effective SNR. In (Gacanin, 2010) the performance of an AF scheme is investigated in frequency selective channels adopting advanced equalization techniques. Moreover Li (2009) shows the effects of timing errors in frequency selective channels. Finally Shiqiang (2011) presents a joint rate and power adaptation that increases the performance of Analog Network Coding.

A limited number of papers is present in the literature dealing with methods to improve the DF performance in multipath fading environments. Most of them propose methods based on ideal pre-equalization of channel (Ding, 2009; Koike-Akino, 2009; Cui, 2008).

However the proposed methods do not take into account the complexity of channel inversion operation needed for channel pre-equalization. In addition they do not take into account realistic hypothesis concerning with the power constraints. When the signal experiences deep fading attenuation, the pre-equalization requires a significant amplification of the signal in the transmission phase and this cannot be acceptable. For this reason DF technique is considered quite inefficient.

Another important aspect that limits the actual implementation of the DF approach is the signalization overhead. In (Peh, 2008) an interesting solution to overcome the fading problem is presented where power control is jointly applied at both source nodes. However the paper does not take into account the signalization overhead required because each node should know both channels state.

LOWER LAYERS NC ADAPTATION FOR WIRELESS ERASURE CHANNELS

MAC-NC for (Un)Reliable Links

With the aim of properly integrating NC at MAC layer an investigation has been conducted about the overall end-to-end delay performance of different schemes for reliable communications over a lossy wireless network, on the basis of the same model proposed in (Ghaderi, 2008).

Differently from previous works on this subject in (Chiti, 2010) it is assumed that the correctly received packets are stored in an buffer at the sink node side and sent to the application layer as soon as the original sequence has been completed. That buffer is called "re-sequencing buffer" and the additional latency experienced by the packets is consequently called "re-sequencing delay".

The most important reliability schemes can be summarized as follows:

1. The basic linear NC scheme – where the intermediate nodes, whenever possible, send out packets that are random linear combination of previously received packets belonging to independent data streams;

2. The combined ARQ-NC scheme – where the intermediate nodes linearly combine packets belonging to independent streams with the same sequential number. In particular an ideal ARQ scheme, where the outcome of any packet transmission attempt is immediately known, has been considered. In this case, differently from the previous one, the intermediate nodes continue to send out exactly the same combined packet till an error-free reception occurs;

3. The combined Soft ARQ-NC scheme (SARQ-NC) – that is equivalent to the ARQ-NC scheme except for the soft combining of the last received copy of a packet with all possible previous incorrect copies. This scheme relies on the Chase's principle (Chase, 1985), (Fragouli, 2006), instead of merely discarding them.

The network model adopted in (Chiti, 2010) to derive analytical and numerical results is shown in Figure 1 and it is consistent with the classical scheme introduced in (Ahlswede, 2000) to point out the advantages of the network coding approach. In particular, it consists of two source nodes broadcasting independent data to two sink nodes. In this model all the links are bidirectional and nodes are ideally capable of simultaneously receiving packets. Time reference for each link is slotted and all links are assumed to be synchronous. In addition, links are affected by independent errors, which makes a packet erroneously received to be retransmitted until an error-free reception occurs.

The acknowledgment messages (ACK) are assumed to be instantaneously received after the packet transmission completion and error-free. Moreover, the packet loss probability P_e has been assumed equal for all the wireless links and independent from links or transmission attempts. As a consequence, the random variables p representing the probability of success in delivering a packet (such that $P_e = 1 - p$) are identically distributed whatever the link is involved and the same is valid for the associated delivery delay.

The probability distribution of the overall end-to-end delay is derived hereinafter, under the assumption of a negligible queuing and processing delay at the transit nodes. This means that the network is low loaded (i.e., $\rho \to 0$, where ρ is the so called loading factor (Bose, 2002)), as in a more general scenario each node can be properly modeled as a G/G/1 system.

Note that, according to this model, intermediate nodes have to perform combinations of packets belonging to individual input data flows having the same sequence number. As a consequence, packets are sent out to the application layer at the sink nodes according to their original order, hence there is no need of re-sequencing.

Finally, an ideal MAC scheme has been considered, in which packets could be received simultaneously without collisions. In fact, an eventual delay in accessing the shared medium should affect in the same way all the investigated reliable schemes.

Path $1 \to 3$: the distribution of delay $\tau^{(3)}$: τ in delivering packet a from node 1 (source) to node 3 follows a shifted geometric distribution[1] such that:

$$\Pr\{\tau = m\} = p(1-p)^{m-1}$$

with $m \geq 1$ representing a particular discrete value of delay. The same occurs for delay distribution over path $2 \to 3$.

Path $(1 \to 3) \cup (2 \to 3)$: the latency $\tau^{(3)}$ for collecting both packets a and b at node 3 can be expressed as it follows:

$$\Pr\{\tau^{(3)} = m+1\} = \sum_{l=1}^{m}\left(\tau_{m+1}\tau_l + \tau_l\tau_{m+1}\right) + \tau_{m+1}\tau_{m+1}$$

where $m \geq 1$. It is worth noticing that the previous equation does not take into account collisions occurring within the same time slot.

Path $1 \to 3 \to 4 \to 5$: the latency θ for collecting packet a+b at node 5 (sink) is a random variable such that:

$$\theta = \tau^{(3)} + \tau + \tau = \tau^{(3)} + \tau^{\Sigma}$$

where the latency τ^{Σ} can be expressed as the addition of delays over two independent links as it follows:

$$\tau^{\Sigma} = \tau + \tau$$

In addition, it is possible to show that:

$$\Pr\{\tau^{\Sigma} = m\} = \sum_{l=2}^{m}\left(\tau_{m-l}\tau_l\right) = (m-1)p^2(1-p)^{m-2}$$

with $m \geq 2$. Thus, it follows that:

$$\Pr\{\theta = m\} = \sum_{l=1}^{m}\left(\tau^{(3)}_{m-l}\tau^{\Sigma}_l\right)$$

where $m \geq 2$ and $\tau^{\Sigma}_0 = \tau^{\Sigma}_1 = 0$

Path $(1 \rightarrow 3 \rightarrow 4 \rightarrow 5) \cup (1 \rightarrow 5)$: finally, the overall delivering latency $\tau^{(5)}$ for collecting packets a and $a+b$ at node 5 (sink) is a random variable such that:

$$\Pr\left\{\tau^{(5)} = m+1\right\} = \Pr\left\{\max\left\{\theta, \tau\right\}\right\}$$
$$= \sum_{l=1}^{m}\left(\theta_{m+l}\tau_l + \theta_l\tau_{m+1}\right) + \theta_{m+1}\tau_{m+1}$$

where $m \geq 3$.

On the other hand, if no explicit acknowledgment of packet reception outcome is provided (this happens in the case of unreliable communications), the transmission parameters might be properly tuned in order to minimize the number of coded packets transmitted on a link basis, thereby lowering the end-to-end delay and overall power consumption.

In particular, the transmitted power level of different network nodes is preliminary optimized, pointing out that the basic principle of this approach (Chiti, 2010) can be considered as an ideal realization of the well-known Chase combining principle (Ahlswede, 2000) widely adopted in the case of ARQ systems to improve their performance both in terms of throughput and end-to-end delivery delay (Li, 2003).

The Chase combining approach is a method that suggests to use all the received replicas of the same packet (even if affected by errors); it is accomplished by means of a suitable combining scheme involving the decision variables of each bit of each received copy of a same packet (Cui, 2004). It is well known, almost until now, that in NC schemes, the Chase combining principle cannot be directly applied for two reasons:

- Due to the lack of ACK/NACK messages;
- Because the transmitting node randomly combines packets to be transmitted into different and independently encoded packets, so that the retransmission of an erroneous packet is not guaranteed.

In order to easily generalize this analysis to any DAG Chiti (2010) resorts to the concept of subtree decomposition introduced in (Nguyen, 2009): where a single-source multi-sink network coding problem can be modeled as a packing problem of network subtrees through which the same information flows (Fragouli, 2007). Each subgraph is a tree, rooted either at the coding point, or at the source node. This concept can be integrated within the optimization procedure described in this section since: i) the subtree decomposition simplifies power/delay optimization by focusing only on subtrees, and ii) as soon as the transmission inside any subtree is finished (i.e. all subtree destinations send feedback ACK to the subtree root) the subtree may be "turned off" and will not further participate in communication, resulting in significant power savings as compared to the traditional approach.

As a consequence, to discuss the optimization procedure proposed in (Chiti,2010), Figure 2 shows this reference network topology. In this case we have one source node (the node S), intermediate node I, which adopt a DNC scheme, and two destination nodes (the node D_1 and D_2). Each link is characterized by a different Packet Dropping Probability (PDP, namely $P_d^{(S,I)}$, $P_d^{(I,D1)}$, and $P_d^{(I,D2)}$).

First, we focus on a single link delay and power expenditure, and later extend to any subtree topology. Under the hypothesis that each coded packet transmitted is a linearly independent combination of the buffered packets, we have that the mean link delay $\bar{\delta}$ to correctly receive K coded packets is:

$$\bar{\delta} = \frac{K}{1 - P_d(m)}$$

where m represents the power control factor. Likewise, the mean power w invested in transmission of K coded packets over a single link is:

Figure 2. Reference butterfly network topology (Chiti, 2010)

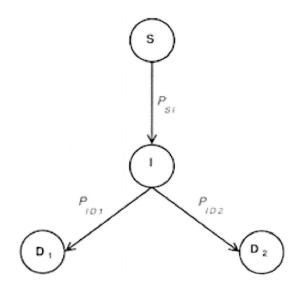

$$\overline{\Delta} = \max_{i \in D} \left\{ \max_{i,j \in p_i} \left[\frac{K}{1 - P_d^{(j,j)}(m)} \right] + \left| p_i - 1 \right| \right\}$$

In the above equation, $P_d^{(j,j)}(m)$ is PDP for the link (j, k) connecting two generic nodes j and k with power-level m applied at the transmitting node j, and $|p_i|$ is the number of links in the path p_i.

The mean total power $\overline{W}$ invested in communication process by all the transmitting network nodes is:

$$\overline{W} = \sum_{i \in S \cup I} \overline{w}_i$$

where for each i, we obtain $\overline{w}_i$ as:

$$\overline{w}_i = \frac{mE}{T} \max_{(i,j)} \left\{ \overline{\delta}_j \right\}$$

$$\overline{w} = \frac{K}{1 - P_d(m)} \frac{mE}{T} = \frac{mE}{T} \overline{\delta}$$

where E and T are the energy and time duration associated to each packet, respectively. For general subtrees, we similarly derive the mean End-two-End delay (E2E) $\overline{\Delta}$ and the mean total power consumption $\overline{W}$. Let the degree $d(i)$ of the node i in the subtree be the number of neighbors of I. For general subtree, we can divide the set of all nodes in the subtree into the three disjoint subsets: the source (or root) node S, the set of interior nodes I such that $\forall i \in$ I, $d(i) \geq 2$, and the set of destination (or leaf) nodes D such that $\forall i \in D$, $d(i) = 1$. Let P be the set of all paths from the source node S to any of the destination nodes in D, where $p_i \in P$ is the list of the links representing the unique path from S to the node i (note that $|P| = |D|$). Note that, in this case, in a general subtree, each destination node is connected to just one interior node or to the source node itself. Due to re-encoding at intermediate nodes, average E2E delay for data delivery of K source blocks from the source S to all the subtree destinations in D is:

and $\overline{\delta}_j$ is the delay over the link (i, j) for each "downstream" neighbour j of the node i. The previous derivations rely on the hypotheses that: i) BER's affecting each link are independent random variables and ii) PDP is independent over different packets. They are fully satisfied both for AWGN and fast fading channels (Lin, 1984).

With the above definitions of average E2E delay $\overline{\Delta}$ and total power expenditure $\overline{W}$ e are interested in the following optimization problem for a given subtree topology:

$$m^* = \arg \min_{m \in N^{|I|+1}} \left\{ \overline{\Delta}(m), \overline{W}(m) \right\}$$

where $m = \{m_S, m_I, \ldots, m_{|I|}\}$ is $|I| + 1$-vector containing m values associated to the source node and all the intermediate nodes $i \in$ I. However, joint optimization of $(\overline{\Delta}, \overline{W})$-pair is not possible since $\overline{\Delta}$ monotonically decreases with increasing m-values of nodes, which is not the case for $\overline{W}$. Therefore, the possible way to proceed is, for example, to find the *m*-values ($\hat{m}^*$) that optimize either $\overline{W}$ or $\overline{\Delta}$, while keeping the other parameter within a given "distance" away from its optimal value. In the following, we discuss some heuristic selections of $\hat{m}^*$ for simple link and subtree topologies discussed. Should be noted, that to find optimal values the perfect knowledge of the channel status is needed; in practice it can be accomplished by estimating the return link of each bidirectional link provided that it is symmetric.

Solutions and Recommendations

In accomplishing the performance evaluation for the case of acknowledged MAC-NC scheme, it has been supposed the presence of independent errors affecting packet transmissions, with a Signal to Noise Ratio (SNR) in the range between (4÷9) dB.

To complete the investigation, the average delay $\overline{\tau}$ comparison for DNC with (S)ARQ or without (S)ARQ has been provided for SNR = 9dB, as depicted in Figure 3. It could be noticed that NC+(S)ARQ always outperforms DNC alone due to minor impact of packet retransmissions to the decoding process. However, DNC profits of increased traffic load as the larger buffer occupancy provides more packets to be combined.

As detailed in (Chiti, 2009), the advantages of adopting packet retransmission outperform the classical ARQ schemes. In particular, a remarkable gain is provided for low-to-medium SNR levels which can be further improved by jointly adopting a simple soft combined ARQ scheme (SARQNC).

As a result, DNC alone performs worse than other schemes for all SNR and loading factor values, so that it is always preferable to retransmit uncorrect packet rather than merely relying on linear combination.

We start our discussion about the power adaptation optimized MAC-NC schemes with the performance analysis of a link communication for AWGN regime. In Figure 4 the delivery delay

$\overline{\delta}$ is presented as a function of SNR for the packet size of *n = 100bits*, *K* = 50 source packets and different values of $m \in N$. It can be noticed that the delay is decreasing at the increasing of *m*, while approaching asymptotic floor equal *K*.

Cut-off points (pointed out with circles in Figure 4) describe the *m*-values at which the delay drops to within 1% of its asymptotic value.

The overall power $\overline{w}$, presents a similar decreasing trend: it is evident that there is no m^* value that jointly minimizes $\overline{\delta}$ and $\overline{w}$, but there exist ($\hat{m}^*$) such that $\overline{w}$ is optimized, while $\overline{\delta}$ is close enough to its optimal value for a specific SNR interval, this representing a good heuristic.

In order to generalize the proposed approach to any topology, the performance for the simplest subtree case has been investigated, as any DAG can be decomposed into a set of subtrees. The total delay ($\overline{\Delta}$) has been presented in Figure 5 The values of $\overline{\Delta}$ is a function of $m = (m_S, m_I)$ values adopted by nodes S and I, and of different link SNR values (i.e., γ_{SI}, γ_{ID1}, γ_{ID2}). For the simplest subtree, the expressions for general subtree topologies reduce to the following expressions:

$$\overline{\Delta}\left(m_S, m_I\right) = \frac{K}{\min\left\{1 - P_d^{(S,I)}(m_S), 1 - P_d^{(I,Dx)}(m_I)\right\}}$$

where *x* can be either 1 or 2.

In addition, for the or the sake of clarity, it has been assumed that node S always selects the optimal m^* value, K = 100 source packets, and γ_{SI} = γ_{ID1} = γ_{ID2} = 3 [dB], representing a worst case scenario. Moreover, in Figure 4 and 5 the performance for the case of m_I = 1 and $m_I = m_I^* = m^*$ is compared, highlighting the advantages provided, as well as the impossibility of a strict joint optimization, since there is no pair (m_S^*, m_I^*) that jointly minimizes delay and power, but there exist ($\hat{m}^*_S$, $\hat{m}^*_I$) tuplets such that $\overline{\Delta}$ and $\overline{W}$ are close enough to their optimal values.

Figure 3. Mean normalized delay for both basic ARQ and SARQ schemes with ρ∈[0.01,0.5]and SNR = 9 dB (Chiti, 2009)

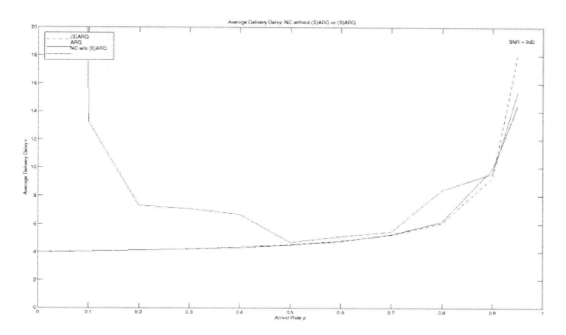

Figure 4. Mean normalized delay for both basic ARQ and SARQ schemes with ρ∈[0.01,0.5]and SNR = 9 dB (Chiti, 2010)

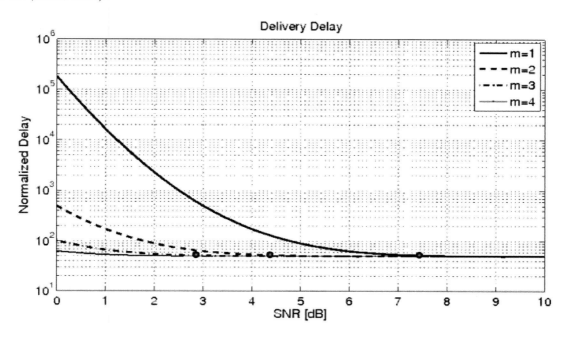

DF-PLNC in Multipath Fading

As stated before, PLNC is theoretically an interesting solution to increase the system throughput by reducing the resources needed for a bidirectional communications between two nodes connected by means of an intermediate node that acts as relay. However the expected gains are limited by the actual channel propagation conditions in wireless systems: multiple reflections and refractions lead to multiple paths between transmitter and receiver and hence random fluctuations of the received signal (i.e., multipath fading). In particular DF is a promising solution due to the noise level reduction. But when the multipath fading effect is taken into account the benefits of the method are significantly reduced.

In particular the two main problems concern with DF:

- The need of the whole channel knowledge that introduces significant signalization overhead;
- The need of imposing power constraints to limit the power emission.

In order to better explain these issues and then the proposed solutions, we refer to a Two-Way Relay Network based on OFDM (Orthogonal Frequency Division Multiplexing). OFDM is a multi-carrier modulation technique, with orthogonal sub-carriers, that has the capability of mitigating frequency-dependent distortion across the channel band and simplifying the equalization in a multipath fading environment. In addition the multicarrier nature of the OFDM transmission offers flexibility in adaptive resource allocation.

We consider an OFDM system where QPSK (Quadrature Phase Shift Keying) symbols are transmitted on K orthogonal sub-channels.

The communication channel is assumed to be a multipath fading channel with L taps where the fading coefficient on each subcarrier is modeled as a random variable Rayleigh distributed.

Assuming both source nodes $(T_{1,2})$ transmit on the same time slot (for sake of simplicity and without loss in generality we can consider the time slot equal to the OFDM symbol duration) and an ideal phase pre-compensation is applied, the signal received by the relay node (R) on subcarrier k is:

$$r_R[k] = \left\| H_1[k] \right\| s_{T_1}[k] + \left\| H_2[k] \right\| s_{T_2}[k] + n_R[k]$$

where:

- $H_i[k]$ is the i-th channel (i.e., between source node T_i and relay R) on k-th subcarrier
- $s_{Ti}[k]$ is the QPSK symbol transmitted on k-th subcarrier by the source node Ti
- n_R is the noise on k-th subcarrier at the relay (R).

The signal received by the relay is the superimposition of the two transmitted signals affected by the channel attenuation that is different in the two channels and for each subcarrier. For this reason a suitable threshold to limit the decision region should be addressed for each subcarrier. The threshold depends on the channel values, hence the relay should know both channels links ($H_1[k]$ and $H_2[k]$). For instance, simplified sub-optimal decision thresholds have been proposed in (Peh, 2008):

$$\gamma[k] = \frac{\sqrt{2}}{2} \max_i \left\{ \left\| H_i[k] \right\| \right\} i=1,2.$$

The relay performs a detection of the transmitted information. The signal received in each QPSK branch (i.e., phase and quadrature) is compared with the previous defined threshold: if it is inside the interval $[-\gamma[k], \gamma[k]]$ the relay decides that the two source nodes have transmitted different bits, otherwise they have transmitted the same bit. In the first case the decision is mapped in a bit "1",

Figure 5. Normalized E2E delivery delay as a function of (m_S^*, m_I^*) for SNR values $\gamma_{SI} = \gamma_{ID1} = \gamma_{ID2} = 3$ [dB] and n = 100bits (Chiti, 2010)

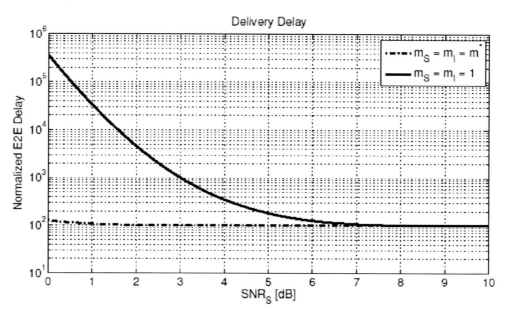

in the second case in a bit "0" and forwarded to the destination nodes.

At the receiving end, after the channel equalization, the node is able to recover the information transmitted by the other terminal by means of a *xor* operation between the received bit and the previously transmitted one.

This transmission/reception scheme works correctly if each terminal node knows the channel toward the relay (direct link) and the relay knows both channels. This introduces the need of a certain amount of signaling.

In order to counteract the multipath effects on the relay detection, pre-equalization can be adopted. Theoretically pre-equalization overcomes the fading effects and the system performance tends to the AWGN case. The power to be allocated to the subcarrier k-th by the source node i-th, $p_i[k]$, is calculated by inverting the channel gain $H_i[k]$. In that way higher power is assigned to the subcarrier that experiences higher attenuation. However this approach is not viable due to the power emission constraint needed in actual implementations. Assuming that the transmitted symbols are normalized (i.e., $\left\| s_{T_i}[k] \right\| = 1$), the coefficient $p_i[k]$ has to respect the following constraint:

$$\sum_{k=0}^{K-1} \left\| p_i[k] \right\|^2 \leq K \quad i = 1, 2$$

For this reason a normalization factor should be introduced (Bartoli, 2011):

$$p_i[k] = \frac{F_i}{H_i[k]}$$

where:

$$F_i = \sqrt{\frac{K}{\displaystyle\sum_{k=0}^{K-1} \frac{1}{\left\| H_i[k] \right\|^2}}}$$

Introducing the normalization factor, the error rate of the system increases significantly, making the communication less reliable. Figure 6 (Bartoli, 2011) shows the BER (Bit Error Rate) of the direct link (i.e., between the source node and the relay) when PLNC is applied or not.

The normalization factor is highly dependent on the most attenuated subcarriers, for this reason it usually assumes low values and, consequently, the signal level at the relay is very low.

Solutions and Recommendations

In this section we refer to the previously described OFDM system, where pre-equalization is performed adopting a normalization factor F_i at each source node ($i=1,2$). The received signal at the relay node can be expressed as:

$$r_R[k] = F_1 s_{T_1}[k] + F_2 s_{T_2}[k] + n_R[k]$$

The use of normalization factor introduces an important advantage, the same decision threshold can be used at the relay for each subcarrier:

$$\gamma[k] = \frac{\sqrt{2}}{2} \max_i \{F_i\} \quad i = 1, 2.$$

The relay needs to know only F_i values and not all the sub-channel gains of the two links. This reduces significantly the complexity and the signalization overhead. In fact the values F_1 and F_2 can be sent to the relay by means of a suitable signaling channel: for instance, two subcarriers may be reserved, one for each terminal node, to transmit pilot tones modulated by Fi (Bartoli, 2011).

In that way it is possible to reduce the signalization overhead but in order to overcome the communication unreliability due to small normalization factor suitable power allocation techniques should be adopted.

In particular Bartoli (2011) proposes a selective subcarrier suppression criterion. The channel gain of each subcarrier is compared with a fixed threshold, if it is lower the subcarrier is suppressed, i.e., it has assigned no power. The saved power is allocated to the other active subcarriers. In that way the normalization factor is calculated only on active subcarriers that are less attenuated. The normalization factor value increases with the threshold: higher is the threshold, lower is the number of active subcarriers.

In a conventional system (not NC) when a subcarrier is suppressed it is not used for transmission: the symbols are mapped only on active subcarriers with a consequent throughput reduction that increases with the threshold value. However, in PLNC schemes the decoding at the relay is made assuming both terminal nodes transmit simultaneously on the same frequency at the same time. Transmitting only on the active subcarriers requires both the relay node and the other terminal node know which subcarriers have been suppressed with an increase of the complexity and the signalization overhead and protocol. For this reason the subcarrier suppression method proposed in (Bartoli, 2011) maps the symbols of the incoming streaming on each subcarrier independently whether it is active or suppressed. It means there is no need of additional signaling because the system works exactly in the same way as the subcarrier suppression is not performed. From here the name *Blind Subcarrier Suppression* (BSS).

The bit error probability of the data transmitted on a suppressed subcarrier is the highest (of 50%), but the other subcarriers gain more power: as long the number of suppressed subcarriers N_{sup} is low, the performance of the system gets an improvement.

The threshold choice is based on a tradeoff between the need of increasing the normalization factor (and then the transmitting power of the active subcarriers) and the errors introduced by the suppressed subcarriers. For this reason the optimal

Figure 6. BER comparison between channel inversion scheme and traditional transmission (direct link) (Bartoli, 2011)

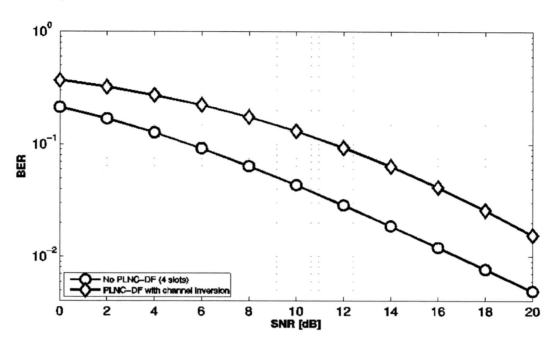

threshold value changes with the SNR (Bartoli, 2011): for high SNR the noise level is low and the errors introduced by the suppressed subcarriers become predominant with a consequent performance degradation that leads to a BER floor. Hence, low threshold values should be selected for high SNR channels in order to suppress only the most attenuated subcarriers.

The performance of the BSS method is presented in Figure 7 and 8 in terms of BER and throughput (the throughput is evaluated taking into account the overall data exchange: direct links and the links forwarded by the relay). It is possible to see that the proposed method achieves good performance either in terms of error rate or throughput. BER performance reaches value near to the single way communication system (i.e., only one node per time communicate with the relay and no signal superimposition occurs). The throughput reaches values that are very close to the ideal PLNC limit: double the system capacity.

FUTURE RESEARCH DIRECTIONS

NC is a promising technique whose practical implementation in wireless networks needs further investigation. For this reason there is much room for future contributions.

For what concern the RLNC, the method used to compute the coding matrix has a big impact on the overall system performance in terms of network throughput and computing power required (at the network node side) to combine and decode the several traffic flows. Some real implementations have been shown (Heide, 2011) but the real impact on complexity and power consumption is still an open issue. Implementative frameworks, developed for the main embedded operative system, could help to practically test the benefits of the RLNC. In addition it can be easily shown that the network throughput is directly related to the singularity probability of the random coding matrix: when this probability becomes big, also the number of replicas needed by each receiver to

Figure 7. BER evaluation of Blind Subcarrier Suppression for different threshold values (direct link)-(Bartoli, 2011)

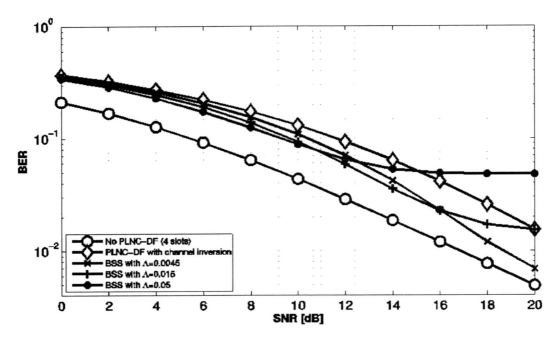

Figure 8. Overall throughput evaluation of blind subcarrier suppression for different threshold values - (Bartoli, 2011)

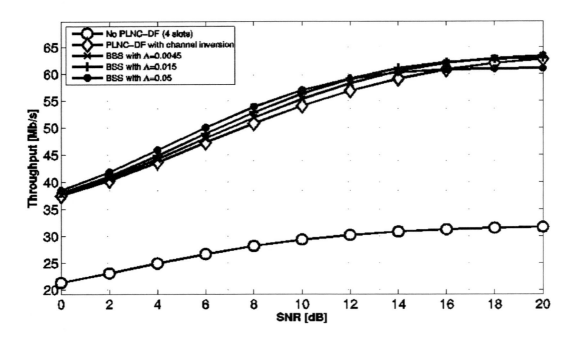

decode the original message set increases. When the elements of a coding matrix are equiprobable, the singularity probability can be exactly found (Siavoshani, 2011) but when the matrix is sparse this problem becomes a hard combinatorial problem. It has been provided some upper and lower bounds to the singularity probability in (Li & Mow, 2011) but this is a still open and challenging problem.

Also specific layer's issue should be further investigated.

The MAC-NC schemes more suitable for unreliable communications rely upon the integration of additional features with NC approach; in particular, it has been previously studied an approach leveraging on transmitted power adaptation on a link basis. A possible development could concern the application of NC in burst communications occurring over wireless network, where an explicit acknowledgment for each received packet is not provided. In this context an alternative implementation of the Chase algorithm could be proposed, suitable for applications in NC schemes that does not require significant system modifications. In addition the MAC-NC can be easily merged into the set of functionalities already provided by the MAC layers of the modern broadband wireless communication standards, like: IEEE 802.16 and the 3GPP Long Term Evolution. For instance MAC-NC schemes combined to the classical ARQ have been proposed for what concern the IEEE 802.16 communication protocol (Jin, 2008), but there are some open issues. The MAC layer of the modern broadband wireless communication standards is able to manage the power allocation, the modulation and the coding profile on a per-user basis. Unfortunately, until now, the integrity control task of the delivered traffic has been usually addressed independently to the power and rate adaptation problem; if it could be addressed in a cross-layer manner by a MAC-NC scheme this could lead to a closed (and possibly optimal) solution to this challenging issue.

The PLNC is based on the natural interference generated by the wireless medium when different signals are transmitted simultaneously. For this reason the PLNC needs suitable methods to remove the interference at the receiver. In current works a TWRN is considered where collision is caused by only two signals and the interference cancellation method is well designed. However when multiple sources transmit together and multiple-collisions occur suitable interference cancellation schemes should be investigated. In that cases a cross-layer approach should be needed in order to take into account also flow decomposition and scheduling. In addition PLNC works usually refer to QPSK modulation for which the coding scheme is known. Few papers address theoretically the extension to other modulation schemes but it still remains an open issue that should be considered and deeply analyzed. In general, PLNC should be extended to more complex and actual networks.

Finally, for its nature PLNC recalls cooperative networks concepts. For this reason specific NC schemes should be studied and analyzed to be applied in this specific contest. Particularly interesting could be the joint use of PLNC and MIMO (Multiple Input Multiple Output), either to provide spatial separation of the interfering signals (i.e., MIMO could be used as a techniques to reduce the collisions) or to provide diversity and hence additional freedom degrees.

CONCLUSION

In this chapter the NC principle has been discussed and specific approaches suitable for applications in wireless systems have been presented. After an overview of the state of the art the attention has been focused on critical issues as that concerning with data integrity in wireless communication systems. Some specific solutions have been outlined in order to acheve better performance in terms of energy consumption, delivery delay and throughput.

In particular, different MAC-NC approaches able to assure a reliable data multicasting have been described: a classical random linear network coding scheme, a linear network coding combined with a basic ARQ or, alternatively, with a soft combined ARQ scheme. In addition, it has been investigated the feasibility of applying MAC-NC to unreliable wireless communications scenarios in which the transmitted power level of different network nodes is optimized with the aim of minimizing the number of NC packets transmitted on a link basis, thereby lowering the end-to-end delay and overall power consumption.

Moreover a DF-NC approach has been also investigated showing its limits in multipath fading channels. Then a possible solution has been presented to overcome the problem of power imbalance of the channels while maintaining a low complexity and a low signalization overhead. By means a suitable power and subcarrier allocation is possible to reduce the total signaling overhead amount required to exchange channel information and in addition is possible to increase significantly the system performance either in terms of throughput or error rate.

REFERENCES

Ahlswede, R., Cai, N., Li, S.-Y. R., & Yeung, R. W. (2000). Network information flow. *IEEE Transactions on Information Theory*, 46, 1204–1216. doi:10.1109/18.850663

Bartoli, G., Fantacci, R., Marabissi, D., & Simoni, R. (in press). *Physical layer network coding in multipath channel: Effective precoding-based transmission scheme*. IEEE Global Telecommunications Conference 2011.

Bose, S. K. (2002). *An introduction to queueing systems*. New York, NY: Kluwer Academic/Plenum.

Chase, D. (1985). Code combining - A maximum likelihood decoding approach for combining an arbitrary number of noisy packets. *IEEE Transactions on Communications*, 33, 385–393. doi:10.1109/TCOM.1985.1096314

Chiti, F., & Fantacci, R., Johnson, R. A., Crnojević, V., & Vukobratović, D. (2009). *End-to-end delay analysis for reliable communications over lossy channels: Integrating network coding and ARQ schemes*. IEEE Globecom'09.

Chiti, F., Fantacci, R., & Vukobratović, D. (2010). *Joint discrete power-level and delay optimization for network coded wireless communications*. IEEE International Conference on Communications.

Chou, P. A., & Wu, Y. (2007). Network coding for the internet and wireless networks. *IEEE Signal Processing Magazine*, 24(5), 77–85. doi:10.1109/MSP.2007.904818

Cui, T., Gao, F., Ho, T., & Nallanathan, A. (2008). Distributed space-time coding for two-way wireless relay networks. *IEEE International Conference on Communications*, (pp. 3888–3892).

Cui, Y., Xue, Y., & Nahrstedt, K. (2004). Optimal distributed multicast routing using network coding: Theory and applications. *Proceedings of Sixth Workshop on MAthematical performance Modeling and Analysis (MAMA)*, Vol. 32, (pp. 47–49).

Ding, Z., Leung, K., Goeckel, D., & Towsley, D. (2009). On the study of network coding with diversity. *IEEE Transactions on Wireless Communications*, 8(3), 1247–1259. doi:10.1109/TWC.2009.07051022

Fragouli, C., Emina, S., & Shokrollahi, A. (2004). *Network coding as a coloring problem*. Conference on Information Sciences and Systems.

Fragouli, C., & Soljanin, E. (2006). Information flow decomposition for network coding. *IEEE Transactions on Information Theory*, 52(3), 829–8481. doi:10.1109/TIT.2005.864435

Fragouli, C., & Soljanin, E. (Eds.). (2007). *Network coding fundamentals*. Boston, MA: Publisher Inc.

Gacanin, H., & Adachi, F. (2010). Broadband analog network coding. *IEEE Transactions on Wireless Communications, 9*(5), 1577–1583. doi:10.1109/TWC.2010.05.091053

Gao, F., Zhang, R., & Liang, Y. C. (2009). Optimal channel estimation and training design for two-way relay networks. *IEEE Transactions on Communications, 57*(10), 3024–3033. doi:10.1109/TCOMM.2009.10.080169

Ghaderi, M., Towsley, D., & Kurose, J. (2008). Reliability gain of network coding in lossy wireless networks. *Proceedings of IEEE MILCOM,* (pp. 2171–2179).

Heide, J., Pedersen, M. V., Fitzek, F. H. P., & Larsen, T. (2011). *Network coding for mobile devices – Systematic binary random rateless codes*. IEEE International Conference on Communications, ICC Workshops.

Ho, T., & Lun, D. S. (Eds.). (2008). *Network coding. An introduction*. Cambridge, UK: Cambridge University Press. doi:10.1017/CBO9780511754623

Jin, J., & Li, B. (2008). *Adaptive random network coding in WiMAX*. IEEE International Conference on Communications.

Katti, S., Gollakota, S., & Katabi, D. (2007). Embracing wireless interference: Analog network coding. *Proceedings of the 2007 Conference on Applications, Technologies, Architectures, and Protocols for Computer Communications* (pp. 397–408).

Koetter, R., & Medard, M. (2003). An algebraic framework to network coding. *IEEE/ACM Transactions on Networking, 11*(5), 782–795. doi:10.1109/TNET.2003.818197

Koike-Akino, T., Popovski, P., & Tarokh, V. (2009). Adaptive modulation and network coding with optimized precoding in two-way relaying. *IEEE Global Telecommunications Conference,* (pp. 1–6).

Koike-Akino, T., Popovski, P., & Tarokh, V. (2009). Optimized constellations for two-way wireless relaying with physical network coding. *IEEE Journal on Selected Areas in Communications, 27*(5), 773–787. doi:10.1109/JSAC.2009.090617

Kötter, R., & Kschischang, F. R. (2008). Coding for errors and erasures in random network coding. *IEEE Transactions on Information Theory, 54*, 3549–3591.

Kurose, J. F., & Ross, K. W. (Eds.). (2006). *Computer networking*. Addison-Wesley Longman Incorporated.

Li, S.-Y. R., Yeung, R. W., & Cai, N. (2003). Linear network coding. *IEEE Transactions on Information Theory, 49*(2), 371–381. doi:10.1109/TIT.2002.807285

Li, X., Mow, W. H., & Tsang, F.-L. (2011). *Singularity probability analysis for sparse random linear network coding*. IEEE International Conference on Communications.

Li, Z., Xia, X., & Li, B. (2009). Achieving full diversity and fast ML decoding via simple analog network coding for asynchronous two-way relay networks. *IEEE Transactions on Communications, 57*(12), 3672–3681. doi:10.1109/TCOMM.2009.12.090005

Lin, D. J. C. S., & Miller, M. (1984). Automatic repeat request error control schemes. *IEEE Communications Magazine, 22*, 5–16. doi:10.1109/MCOM.1984.1091865

Liu, J. N., Goeckel, D., & Towsley, D. (2006). Bounds on the throughput gain of network coding in unicast and multicast wireless networks. *IEEE Journal on Selected Areas on communications, 27*, 582.592.

Lucani, D. E., Stojanovic, M., & Mdard, M. (2008). *Random linear network coding for time division duplexing: When to stop to talking and start listening.* CoRR, abs/0809.2350.

Maric, I., Goldsmith, A., & Medard, M. (2010). Analog network coding in the high-SNR regime. *IEEE Wireless Network Coding conference*, (pp. 1-6).

Nguyen, D., Tran, T., Nguyen, T., & Bose, B. (2009). Wireless broadcast using network coding. *IEEE Transactions on Vehicular Technology, 58*(2), 914–925. doi:10.1109/TVT.2008.927729

Papadimitriou, C. H., & Steiglitz, K. (Eds.). (1982). *Combinatorial optimization.* Mineola, NY: Dover Publications Inc.

Peh, E., Liang, Y. C., & Guan, Y. L. (2008). Power control for physical-layer network coding in fading environments. *IEEE 19th International Symposium on Personal, Indoor and Mobile Radio Communications,* (pp. 1–5).

Popovski, P., & Yomo, H. (2006). The antipackets can increase the achievable throughput of a wireless multihop network. *IEEE International Conference on Communications,* Vol. 9, (pp. 3885–3890).

Shiqiang, W., Qingyang, S., Xingwei, W., & Jamalipour, A. (2011). Power and rate adaptation for analog network coding. *IEEE Transactions on Vehicular Technology, 60*(5), 2302–2313. doi:10.1109/TVT.2011.2135869

Siavoshani, M. J., Mohajer, S., & Fragouli, C. (2011). On the capacity of non-coherent network coding. *IEEE Transactions on Information Theory, 57*(2), 1046–1066. doi:10.1109/TIT.2010.2094813

Tran, T., Nguyen, T., Bose, B., & Gopal, V. (2009). A hybrid network coding technique for single-hop wireless networks. *IEEE Journal on Selected Areas in Communications, 27*(5), 685–698. doi:10.1109/JSAC.2009.090610

Yeung, R. W. (2008). *Information theory and network coding.* New York, NY: Springer-Verlag.

Yeung, R. W., Li, S.-Y. R., Cai, N., & Zhang, Z. (2006). Network coding theory. *Foundation and Trends in Communications and Information Theory, 2*(4&5), 241–381.

Zhang, S., Liew, S. C., & Lam, P. P. (2006). Hot topic: Physical-layer network coding. *Proceedings of the 12th Annual International Conference on Mobile Computing and Networking* (pp. 358–365).

ADDITIONAL READING

Borade, S., Zheng, L., & Gallager, R. (2007). Amplify-and-forward in wireless relay networks: Rate, diversity and network size. *IEEE Transactions on Information Theory, 53*(10), 3302–3318. doi:10.1109/TIT.2007.904774

Cover, T., & Gamal, A. (1979). Capacity theorems for the relay channel. *IEEE Transactions on Information Theory, 25*(5), 572–584. doi:10.1109/TIT.1979.1056084

Deb, S., Effros, M., Ho, T., Karger, D. R., Koetter, R., & Lun, D. S. … Ratnakar, N. (2005). Network coding for wireless applications: A brief tutorial. *Proceedings of International Workshop Wireless Ad-hoc Sensor Network.*

Fragouli, C., & Soljanin, E. (Eds.). (2007). *Network coding applications*. Boston, MA: Publisher Inc.

Heindlmaier, M., Lun, D. S., Traskov, D., & Médard, M. (2011). *Wireless inter-session network coding – An approach using virtual multicasts*. IEEE International Conference on Communications.

Kang, Y., & Yuan, D. (2009). Joint design of physical network coding and source coding in two-way relying systems. *Vehicular Technology Conference Fall*, (pp. 1 – 5).

Katti, S. (2006). XORs in the air: Practical wireless network coding. *SIGCOM Computer and Communications Review*, *36*, 243–254. doi:10.1145/1151659.1159942

Laneman, J., Tse, D., & Wornell, G. (2004). Cooperative diversity in wireless networks: Efficient protocols and outage behavior. *IEEE Transactions on Information Theory*, *50*(12), 3062–3080. doi:10.1109/TIT.2004.838089

Li, S.-Y. R., Sun, Q. T., & Ziyu, S. (2011). Linear network coding: Theory and algorithms. *Proceedings of the IEEE*, *99*(3), 372–387. doi:10.1109/JPROC.2010.2093851

Louie, R. H. Y., Yonghui, L., & Vucetic, B. (2010). Practical physical layer network coding for two-way relay channels: performance analysis and comparison. Practical physical layer network coding for two-way relay channels: Performance analysis and comparison. *IEEE Transactions on Wireless Communications*, *9*(2), 764–777. doi:10.1109/TWC.2010.02.090314

Maric, I., & Yates, R. D. (2010). Bandwidth and power allocation for cooperative strategies in Gaussian relay networks. *IEEE Transactions on Information Theory*, *56*(4). doi:10.1109/TIT.2010.2040875

Médard, M., & Sprintson, A. (Eds.). (in press). *Network coding: Fundamentals and applications*. Academic Press.

Nazer, B., & Gastpar, M. (2011). Reliable physical layer network coding. *Proceedings of the IEEE*, *99*, 438–460. doi:10.1109/JPROC.2010.2094170

Parag, P., & Chamberland, J.-F. (2010). Queueing analysis of a butterfly network for comparing network coding to classical routing. *IEEE Transactions on Information Theory*, *56*(4), 1890–1908. doi:10.1109/TIT.2010.2040862

Peng, H., & Ibnkahla, M. (2011). A survey of physical-layer network coding in wireless networks. *IEEE 25th Biennial Symposium on Communications*, (pp. 311-314).

Popovski, P., & Yomo, H. (2007). Physical network coding in two-way wireless relay channels. *International Conference on Communications*, (pp. 707-712).

Rankov, B., & Wittneben, A. (2007). Spectral efficient protocols for half duplex fading relay channels. *IEEE Journal on Selected Areas in Communications*, *25*(2), 379–389. doi:10.1109/JSAC.2007.070213

Raymond, R., Li, S.-Y. R., & Zhang, Z. (Eds.). (2006). *Network coding theory*. Boston, MA: Publisher Inc.

Sung Hoon, L., Kim, Y.-H., Gamal, E. A., & Chung, S.-Y. (2011). Noisy network coding. *IEEE Transactions on Information Theory*, *57*(5), 3132–3152. doi:10.1109/TIT.2011.2119930

Wang, H., Wang, Y., & Wang, W. (2010). *A relay-based retransmission scheme via analog network coding in wireless cooperative communication systems*. International Conference on Computer Application and System Modeling.

Wu, Y. N. (2009). On practical design for joint distributed source and network coding. *IEEE Transactions on Information Theory, 55*(4), 1709–1720. doi:10.1109/TIT.2009.2013016

Xue, F., & Sandhu, S. (2007). PHY-layer network coding for broadcast channel with side information. *IEEE Information Theory Workshop*, (pp. 108 – 113).

Yazdi, S. M. S., Savari, S. A., & Kramer, G. (2011). Network coding in node-constrained line and star networks. *IEEE Transactions on Information Theory, 57*(7), 4452–4468. doi:10.1109/TIT.2011.2146450

Yuchul, K., & De Veciana, G. (2009). Is rate adaptation beneficial for inter-session network coding? *IEEE Journal on Selected Areas in Communications, 27*(5), 635–646. doi:10.1109/JSAC.2009.090606

Zhan, A., & He, C. (2008). Joint design of channel coding and physical network coding for wireless networks. *International Conference on Neural Networks and Signal Processing*, (pp. 512-516).

Zhang, D., & Narayan, M. (2001). *Resource allocation for multicast in an OFDMA network with random linear network coding*. IEEE International Conference on Computer Communications.

ENDNOTE

[1] Delay is normalized to the slot duration T that is equal to round trip time (RTT) if ACK are instantaneously received.

Chapter 6
Adaptation of Algebraic Space Time Codes to Frequency Selective Channel

Ahmed Bannour
Higher School of Communications of Tunis Sup'Com, Tunisia

Mohamed Lassaad Ammari
Higher School of Communications of Tunis Sup'Com, Tunisia

Yichuang Sun
University of Hertfordshire, UK

Ridha Bouallegue
Higher School of Communications of Tunis Sup'Com, Tunisia

ABSTRACT

The Algebraic Space Time Codes (ASTC) are constructed based on cyclic algebras; they showed a good spectral efficiency, a full diversity, and a full rate under non selective channel condition. However, the radio - mobile channel is a selective channel whose features vary during the time. This selectivity is owed to the multi-path phenomenon and generates interferences between symbols (IES). The overall objective of this chapter is to proof that ASTC is adapted to channel selectivity, in order to analyze and improve its performances in wide-band system.

INTRODUCTION

Communication using multiple antennas at both transmitter and receiver ends achieve a very high spectral efficiency over wireless channels. Therefore, a significant interest has been shown in developing systems that offer both high capacity and high data speed using multiple antennas. A variety of space-time codes have been proposed accordingly in the literature, among which a new family of codes based on cyclic division algebras are of particular interest.

The so called Quaternionic Space Time codes have good performance but they suffer from the non-uniform distribution of the energy in the codeword. To alleviate this problem, a new fam-

DOI: 10.4018/978-1-4666-1797-1.ch006

Copyright © 2012, IGI Global. Copying or distributing in print or electronic forms without written permission of IGI Global is prohibited.

ily of algebraic space time codes have been proposed in (J. C. Rekaya, 2005), which have a structure of full-rate and full diversity $2 \times 2, 3 \times 3, 4 \times 4$ and 6×6 space-time codes. These codes have a constant minimum determinant as the spectral efficiency increases. The name perfect space time codes, used for these codes, are suggested by the fact that they satisfy a large number of design criteria and only appear in a few special cases of the classical perfect error correcting codes, achieving the Hamming sphere packing bound. In this paper we will use 2×2 and 4×4 perfect codes.

Recently, there has been an increasing interest in providing high data rate services like video conference, multimedia over wideband channels. Algebraic Space Time Coding techniques, by their very nature, readily lend themselves to high data rate situations. Unfortunately, they require a flat fading channel to function correctly. Therefore, it becomes extremely necessary to harness their power for wideband systems.

Orthogonal frequency division multiplexing (OFDM) has been adopted in the wireless local-area network (WLAN) standards IEEE 802.11a (ISO/IEC) and g (standard) due to its high spectral efficiency and ability to deal with frequency selective fading. The combination of OFDM with spectral efficient multiple antenna techniques makes the OFDM as good candidate to overcome the frequency selective problems for the perfect 2×2 and 4×4 ASTC codes.

BACKGROUND

Despite the attractive features of both OFDM and ASTC they are very sensitive to the transmitter and receiver synchronization imperfections (A. Bannour M. A., 2010) (A. Bannour M. A., 2011). Thus, the synchronization is crucial for ASTC-MIMO-OFDM-based systems. Frequency synchronization errors destroy the orthogonality among the subcarriers which results in inter-carrier interference (ICI) (Renfors, 2007) (B.Swami, 2005) (Schlegel, 2002) (Peeters, 2002). Therefore an accurate CFO estimation is essential for OFDM receiver design. Various carrier synchronization schemes have been proposed for SISO OFDM systems. Some schemes rely on pilot or preamble data (Moose, 1994) (Cox, 2007) (Santella, 2002) (Mengali, An improved frequency offset estimator for OFDM applications, 2002) (S. Hyoung-Kyu, 2000) (Reggiannini, 2005) and some use the inherent structure of the OFDM symbol in either frequency (U. Tureli H. L., 1997) or time domain (J. J. van de Beek, 2002). For multiple antenna OFDM, data-aided schemes are proposed for receiver diversity and MIMO in (Czylwik, p. 1999) and (Stuber, 2001), respectively. A blind method for receiver diversity combined with OFDM is proposed in (U. Tureli D. K., 2001).

MAIN FOCUS OF THE CHAPTER

In this chapter, we propose a new CFO estimator to mitigate the degraded performance of most existing CFO estimators in highly frequency-selective fading channels. The proposed estimator utilizes both time and frequency domain symbols, hence it can be considered as a hybrid time and frequency domain estimator. The proposed CFO estimation technique is applied for MIMO-OFDM systems employing algebraic space time coding schemes with a fixed common CFO among all transmit and receive antenna pairs. This assumption is justifiable because the antennas in MIMO systems usually share a single radio frequency oscillator. Moreover, the differences in Doppler shift between all transmit and receive antenna pairs are small (Giannakis, 2005). By assuming that the channel response remains approximately constant over one ASTC-MIMO-OFDM symbol block, a CFO estimator is derived by extracting the frequency domain matrix perturbation from

Figure 1. MIMO-OFDM system employing perfect codes ASTC

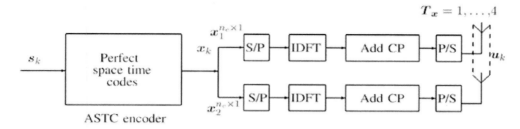

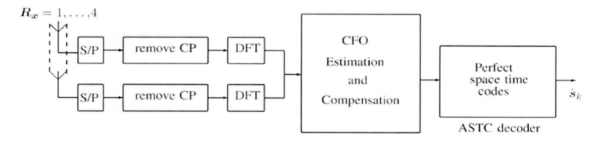

the MIMO-OFDM signal. The method is applicable for MIMO-OFDM CFO estimation with any ASTC scheme and without training symbol repetition.

In the following, superscripts $(.)+$, $(.)^H$, $\|.\|$, $\odot$ and $(.)^*$ stand for pseudo inverse, transpose Hermitian, the Frobenius norm of matrix, scalar product, and conjugate, respectively.

ASTC-MIMO-OFDM SYSTEM MODEL

Let us consider the baseband-equivalent ASTC-MIMO-OFDM system, with n_t transmit antennas and n_r receive antennas, depicted in Figure 1. The transmitted binary source sequence s_k is QPSK modulated.

Algebraic Space Time Coders

The QPSK symbols are then ASTC encoded. We note $\mathbf{v}_k = [s_{4k-3}, s_{4k-2}, s_{4k-1}, s_{4k}]^T$ and $\mathbf{d}_k = [\mathbf{v}_{4k-3}, \mathbf{v}_{4k-2}, \mathbf{v}_{4k-1}, \mathbf{v}_{4k}]^T$ the ASTC

encoder input. $\mathbf{C}_{k,2\times2}$, $\mathbf{C}_{k,4\times4}$, $\mathbf{C}_{k,T}, \mathbf{C}_{k,D}$ its output at time k, respectively for the perfect codes $(n_t = 2 \times n_r = 2)$ and the perfect codes $(n_t = 4 \times n_r = 4)$, given by

$$\mathbf{C}_{k,4\times4} = \sum_{n=0}^{n_t-1} \mathrm{diag}(\frac{1}{\sqrt{15}} \mathbf{Md}_k[n])\mathbf{E}^n \quad (1)$$

where

$$\mathbf{M} =$$

$$\begin{bmatrix} 0.2582-0.3122i & 0.3455-0.4178i & -0.4178+0.5051i & -0.2136+0.2582i \\ 0.2582+0.0873i & 0.4718+0.1596i & 0.1596+0.054i & 0.7633+0.2582i \\ 0.2582+0.2136i & -0.5051-0.4178i & -0.4178-0.3455i & 0.3122+0.2582i \\ 0.2582-0.7633i & -0.054+0.1596i & 0.1596-0.4718i & -0.0873+0.2582i \end{bmatrix}$$

and

$$\mathbf{E} = \begin{bmatrix} 0 & 1 & 0 & 0 \\ 0 & 0 & 1 & 0 \\ 0 & 0 & 0 & 1 \\ i & 0 & 0 & 0 \end{bmatrix}$$

$$\mathbf{C}_{k,2\times2} =$$

$$\frac{1}{\sqrt{5}} \begin{bmatrix} \alpha(\mathbf{v}_k[1] + \theta\mathbf{v}_k[2]) & \alpha(\mathbf{v}_k[3] + \theta\mathbf{v}_k[4]) \\ \bar{\alpha}(\mathbf{v}_k[3] + \bar{\theta}\,\mathbf{v}_k[4]) & \bar{\alpha}(\mathbf{v}_k[1] + \bar{\theta}\,\mathbf{v}_k[2]) \end{bmatrix}$$

$$(2)$$

where

$$\theta = \frac{1+\sqrt{5}}{2}; \bar{\theta} = \frac{1-\sqrt{5}}{2};$$

$$\alpha = 1 + i - i\theta; \bar{\alpha} = 1 + i - i\bar{\theta}$$

TAST Encoder

As shown in (J. C. Rekaya, 2005), the TAST code is a 2×2 space time algebraic code obtained using the integer algebra, with rate $R = n_t = 2$ Symbole/uc (used code word), and diversity $D = n_t \times n_r = 4$. Each space time layer is associated with his proper algebraic space φ in order to alleviate the problem of ISI (Inter-Symbol-Interferences). The code word is expressed as

$$\mathbf{C}_{k,T} =$$

$$\frac{1}{\sqrt{2}} \begin{pmatrix} (\mathbf{v}_k[1] + \theta\,\mathbf{v}_k[2]) & \varphi(\mathbf{v}_k[3] + \theta\,\mathbf{v}_k[4]) \\ \varphi(\mathbf{v}_k[3] - \theta\,\mathbf{v}_k[4]) & (\mathbf{v}_k[1] - \theta\,\mathbf{v}_k[2]) \end{pmatrix}$$

$$(3)$$

where

$$\theta = \exp(i\lambda); \qquad \lambda \in \Re; \qquad \varphi = \theta^2$$

DAST Encoder

The DAST code is a 2×2 diagonal space time algebraic code obtained using the turned constellations of integer algebra, with rate 1 Symbole/uc, and full diversity. The code word is described as follows

$$C_{K,D} = \mathbf{H}_{n_t} . diag(\mathbf{M}.\mathbf{v}_{n_t}) \qquad (4)$$

where

$$\mathbf{M} = \frac{1}{\sqrt{2}} \begin{pmatrix} 1 & \theta \\ 1 & -\theta \end{pmatrix} \qquad \theta = \exp(i\pi/4)$$

$$\mathbf{H}_{n_t} = Hadamard\ matrix\ of\ n_t\ degree$$

$\mathbf{M}$ is the rotation matrix of $n_t = 2$ degree.

ASTC-OFDM Modulation

The ASTC output is converted to a serial stream and then fed to n_t OFDM modulators with n_c subcarriers and a cyclic prefix (CP) of length n_g.

In order to simplify the discussion, let us define the kth MIMO-OFDM vector to be transmitted as $\mathbf{x}_k = [\mathbf{x}_{0,k}, \mathbf{x}_{1,k}, \dots, \mathbf{x}_{n_c-1,k}] \in \mathcal{C}^{n_c n_t \times 1}$ where $\mathbf{x}_{n,k} \in \mathcal{C}^{n_t \times 1}$ is the MIMO algebraic code word to be transmitted on the nth subcarrier at time k and by the qth antenna.

After a serial to parallel conversion, the OFDM modulator uses an IDFT module and a CP is added. The overall vector of length $(n_c + n_g)$ is transmitted over a frequency and time selective MIMO channel. The CP length n_g is assumed to be longer than the largest multi-path delay spread in order to avoid OFDM inter-symbol interference. The kth MIMO-OFDM symbol $\mathbf{u}_k \in \mathcal{C}^{n_t(n_c+n_g)\times 1}$ is then given by

$$\mathbf{u}_k = \xi_1 \sqrt{n_c} (\mathbf{F}^{-1} \otimes \mathbf{I}_{n_t}) \mathbf{x}_k \qquad (5)$$

where $\mathbf{F}^{-1}$ is the $\mathcal{C}^{n_c n_c \times 1}$ Fourier matrix, of which the $(n, k)^{th}$ element is $\exp(-j2\pi nk/n_c)$, $\otimes$ denotes the Kronecker product, $\mathbf{I}_{n_t}$ represents the n_t identity matrix, and $\xi_1 \in \mathcal{C}^{n_t(n_c+n_g)\times n_c n_t}$ is the CP adding matrix given by

$$\xi_1 = \left[\begin{bmatrix} 0 & \mathbf{I}_{n_g} \\ \mathbf{I}_{n_c} & \end{bmatrix} \otimes \mathbf{I}_{n_t} \right] \tag{6}$$

The $n_t(n_c + n_g)$ length MIMO-OFDM symbol is transmitted over a time and frequency selective channel. We assume that the channel taps remain constant during a packet transmission. Consequently, the channel impulse response (CIR) between q^{th} transmitting antenna and p^{th} receiving antenna is modeled by a tapped delay line as

$$\mathbf{h}_k^{p,q} = \sum_{l=0}^{L-1} h_k^{p,q}(l)\delta(k-l) \tag{7}$$

where $h_k^{p,q}(l)$ is the lth path from the qth transmitting antenna to p^{th} receiving antenna at time k and L is the largest order among all impulse responses. The channel taps sequence $\{h_k^{p,q}(l)\}$ is a correlated complex Gaussian process with zero mean, the same variance σ_h^2 and the autocorrelation function

$$E\{\mathbf{h}_k^{p,q}(l)[\mathbf{h}_{k-k'}^{m,n}(l')]^*\} = \\ \rho_{Rx}^{(m,p)}\rho_{Tx}^{(n,q)}J_0(2\pi f_m k')\delta(l-l') = P_h \tag{8}$$

where J_0 is the Bessel function with zero order, f_m is the normalized Doppler shift, $\rho_{Rx}^{(m,p)}$, $\rho_{Tx}^{(n,q)}$ refers respectively to the correlation coefficient between the received antennas (m,p) and the transmitted antennas (n,q).

The received signal at the pth receiving antenna during the kth MIMO-OFDM symbol is

$$\mathbf{y}_k^p = \sum_{q=1}^{n_T} \sum_{l=0}^{L-1} \mathbf{h}_k^{p,q}(l)\mathbf{u}_k^q(k-l) + \mathbf{w}_k^p \tag{9}$$

where $\mathbf{u}_k^q$ is the symbol vector transmitted by the qth antenna and $\mathbf{w}_k^p$ is a zero mean white Gaussian complex noise of variance $\dfrac{N_0}{2}$.

Let us introduce the $\mathcal{C}^{n_t(n_c+n_g)\times n_t(n_c+n_g)}$ time domain matrices $\mathbf{G}_k$ defined as the equivalent channel matrix

$$\mathbf{G}_k = \begin{bmatrix} \mathbf{h}_k(0) & 0 & \cdots & & \cdots & 0 \\ \mathbf{h}_k(1) & \ddots & & & & \vdots \\ \vdots & & \ddots & & & \\ \mathbf{h}_k(L-1) & \cdots & \cdots & \mathbf{h}_k(0) & & \\ 0 & \ddots & & & & \\ \vdots & & \ddots & & \ddots & \vdots \\ 0 & \cdots & \cdots & \mathbf{h}_k(L-1) & \cdots & \mathbf{h}_k(0) \end{bmatrix} \tag{10}$$

where $\mathbf{h}_k(l) = \mathbf{h}_k^{p,q}(l)$.

The transmitted signals is then up-converted to radio frequency centered at f^{T_x} and transmitted through the quasi-static multipath channel $\mathbf{G}_k$. We can thus express the received MIMO-OFDM signal in a matrix notation as

$$\mathbf{y}_k = \mathbf{G}_k\mathbf{u}_k + \mathbf{w}_k \tag{11}$$

where $\mathbf{y}_k \in \mathcal{C}^{n_r(n_c+n_g)\times 1}$ and $\mathbf{w}_k \in \mathcal{C}^{n_r(n_c+n_g)\times 1}$ represents the AWGN at time k. At the receiver, the signals are down converted to baseband with the local oscillator centered at f^{R_x}.

CAPACITY ANALYSIS OF ASTC-MIMO-OFDM SYSTEM

To obtain the analytic expression of the information capacity of ASTC-MIMO-OFDM system for a given channel matrix $\mathbf{H}$, the mutual information between transmitted code word $\mathbf{x}_k$ and received vector $\mathbf{z}_k$ should be determined. The mutual information is given by

$$I(\mathbf{x}_k, \mathbf{z}_k)$$
$$= H(\mathbf{z}_k) - H(\mathbf{z}_k \mid \mathbf{x}_k) \qquad (12)$$
$$= H(\mathbf{z}_k) - H(\mathbf{w}_k)$$

where $H(y)$ denotes the entropies of multivariate distribution y. The capacity equals the maximum mutual information. Maximizing $I(\mathbf{x}_k, \mathbf{z}_k)$ is equivalent to maximizing $H(\mathbf{Z}_k)$. Thus we can derive the capacity as

$$C = \max(H(\mathbf{z}_k)) - H(\mathbf{w}_k) \qquad (13)$$

We have to derive the exact expression of $H(\mathbf{z}_k)$ to obtain the capacity expression. The entropies of $\mathbf{z}_k$ is given by

$$H(\mathbf{z}_k) = -\int p(\mathbf{z}_k) \log_2 \left[p(\mathbf{z}_k) \right] d\mathbf{z}_k$$
$$= \log_2 \det(\pi \mathbf{Q}_z e) \qquad (14)$$

where $\mathbf{Q}_z$ is the covariance matrix of $\mathbf{z}_k$. From equation (0.1), we can derive the covariance relation-ship between the received signal $\mathbf{z}_k$ and the transmitted codeword $\mathbf{x}_k$ as

$$\mathbf{Q}_{z_k} = \mathbf{Q}_w + \mathbf{H}\mathbf{Q}_{x_k}\mathbf{H}^H \qquad (15)$$

where $\mathbf{Q}_{w_k} = \sigma_{w_k}^2 \mathbf{I}_{n_c n_t}$

The above analysis leads to the following capacity expression

$$C = \max(H(\mathbf{z}_k)) - H(\mathbf{w}_k)$$
$$= \log_2 \det(\pi \mathbf{Q}_{z_k} e) - \log_2 \det(\pi \mathbf{Q}_{w_k} e)$$
$$= \log_2 \det\left(\pi e(\mathbf{Q}_{w_k} + \mathbf{H}\mathbf{Q}_{x_k}\mathbf{H}^H)\right) + \log_2 \det(\pi \mathbf{Q}_{w_k} e)^{-1}$$
$$= \log_2 \det\left(\mathbf{I}_{n_c n_t} + \frac{1}{\sigma_{w_k}^2} \mathbf{H}\mathbf{Q}_{x_k}\mathbf{H}^H\right)$$
$$= \log_2 \det\left(\mathbf{I}_{n_c n_t} + \frac{1}{\sigma_{w_k}^2} \mathbf{Q}_{x_k}\mathbf{H}^H\mathbf{H}\right) bits/s/Hz \qquad (16)$$

We can derive the expression of the covariance matrix $\mathbf{Q}_{x_k}$ for the two transmitted code words as $\mathbf{Q}_{x_k} = E\left(\mathbf{x}_k\mathbf{x}_k^H\right) = E\left(\Phi \odot \mathbf{s}_k(\Phi \odot \mathbf{s}_k)^H\right)$, then the capacity expression will be

$$C = \log_2 \det\left(\mathbf{I}_{n_c n_t} + \frac{1}{\sigma_w^2} \Phi\Phi^H \mathbf{H}^H\mathbf{H}\right) \qquad (17)$$

Since the frequency domain channel $\mathbf{H}_{n,k}$ is a diagonal matrix we can derive the following expression

$$\mathbf{H}_k^{2} = \begin{pmatrix} \mathbf{H}_k(0)^{2} & & 0 \\ & \ddots & \\ 0 & & \mathbf{H}_k(n_c n_t)^{2} \end{pmatrix}$$
$$= \mathbf{H}_k\mathbf{H}_k^H = n_c n_t \, \mathbf{H}(n)^{2} \; \forall \; 1 \leq n \leq n_c n_t \qquad (18)$$

whereas

$$\mathbf{H}_k(n)^{2} = \sum_{l=0}^{L-1} \mathbf{h}_k(l) \exp\left(-j2\pi \frac{nk}{n_c}\right)^{2}$$
$$\leq \sum_{l=0}^{L-1} \mathbf{h}_k(l) \exp\left(-j2\pi \frac{nk}{n_c}\right)^{2}$$
$$\leq \sum_{l=0}^{L-1} \mathbf{h}_k(l)^{2} = L.P_h^2$$

where P_h denotes the mean power to each channel coefficient in time domain. If we derive the exact expression of $\Phi\Phi^H$ we get $\mathbf{I}_{n_c n_t}$. At this step, we can bound the last capacity by

$$C = \log_2 \det\left(\mathbf{I}_{n_c n_t}\left[1 + \frac{1}{\sigma_{w_k}^2} \mathbf{H}_k^{2}\right]\right)$$
$$= \log_2 \left(\left[1 + \frac{1}{\sigma_{w_k}^2} n_c n_t L \, \mathbf{H}_k^{2}\right]^{n_c n_t}\right)$$

Thus

$$C \leq \log_2 \left(\left[1 + \frac{1}{\sigma_{w_k}^2} n_c n_t L P_h^2 \right]^{n_c n_t} \right)$$

$$\leq n_c n_t \log_2 \left(\left[1 + \frac{1}{\sigma_{w_k}^2} n_c n_t L P_h^2 \right] \right)$$

If we average over the capacity of $n_c n_t$ narrowband channels we derive the following capacity

$$C \leq \log_2 \left(\left[1 + \frac{1}{\sigma_{w_k}^2} n_c n_t L P_h^2 \right] \right) \text{bits/s/Hz}$$

(19)

THE CHANNEL ESTIMATION

As shown in Equation (11), the signal correction needs the knowledge of the channel response which is generally unknown. In this section, we present a channel estimation method for OFDM systems using pilot symbols (Gagnon, 2007). For MIMO-OFDM systems, pilots are inserted in both time and frequency domains as it is shown in Figure 2. Let us denote p the pilot location order and O the number of pilots by an MIMO-OFDM symbol and introduce the vector $\mathbf{x}_k^{(o)}$ of length O defined as in Equations (1), (2) and (3) whose elements are the pilot symbols. A straightforward channel estimation method at pilot location, which is based on the LS and LMMSE criterion, is given by

$$\widehat{\mathbf{H}}_{ij,LS}(p) = \left[\mathbf{x}_i(p) \right]^+ \mathbf{Z}_j(p)$$

(20)

$$\widehat{\mathbf{H}}_{ij,LMMSE}(p) = \left[\mathbf{x}_i(p)^H \mathbf{x}_i(p) + \sigma_w^2 \right]^{-1} \mathbf{x}_i(p)^H \mathbf{Z}_j(p)$$

(21)

The channel frequency response at non-pilot positions is then estimated by interpolating the channel estimates at neighboring pilot symbol positions. Several efficient interpolation techniques for OFDM channel estimation have been investigated in (Morelli, 2001). In this work, we use the linear interpolation as

$$\widehat{\mathbf{H}} \left[p \times L_f + n \right] =$$

$$\frac{L_f - n}{L_f} \widehat{\mathbf{H}} \left[p \times L_f \right] + \frac{n}{L_f} \widehat{\mathbf{H}} \left[(p + n) \times L_f \right]$$

(22)

where

$$L_f = \frac{length \ of \ one \ MIMO - OFDM \ symbol}{number \ of \ pilots \ by \ one \ MIMO - OFDM \ symbol}$$

and

$$1 \leq n \leq L_f$$

PROPOSED CFO ESTIMATOR

To investigate the powerful ASTC technique of ASTC codes, we have to reduce the sensitivity of the codes to CFOs. For this reason accurate synchronization is important, preferably before reception of the data. Therefore the data packet is preceded by a section of predefined data, which is called the preamble. MIMO channel estimates are also drawn from the preamble.

The preamble is used for both frequency synchronization and channel estimation. For the proposed frequency synchronization algorithm a repetition of the training symbol is not required. The preamble is formed by orthogonal codes.

At the receiver, when CFO does not occur $\Delta f = f^{T_x} - f^{R_x} = 0$. After removing the CP, the signal is transformed back to the frequency domain

Figure 2. A pilot symbol insertion in both time and frequency domains

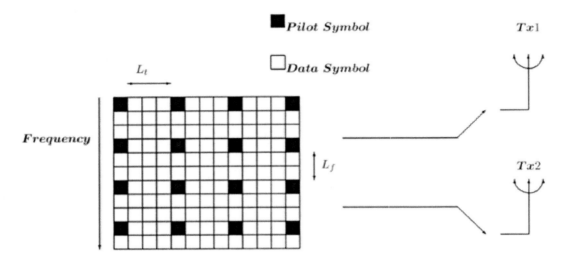

by means of a DFT process. The signal at the DFT output is then given by

$$\mathbf{z}_k = \frac{1}{\sqrt{n_c}}\left[(\mathbf{F} \otimes \mathbf{I}_{n_t n_r})\xi_2\right]\mathbf{y}_k \qquad (23)$$

where the CP removing matrix $\xi_2 \in \mathcal{C}^{n_c n_r \times (n_c n_g + 1)n_r}$, which discards the $n_g n_r$ first elements of $\mathbf{y}_k$, is defined as $\xi_2 = [\mathbf{0}_{n_c n_g}\ \mathbf{I}_{n_g}] \otimes \mathbf{I}_{n_g}$. By combining Equations (23) and (11), we can re-express the DFT output as

$$\mathbf{z}_k = \left[(\mathbf{F} \otimes \mathbf{I}_{n_t n_r})\xi_3(\mathbf{F}^{-1} \otimes \mathbf{I}_{n_t n_r})\right]\mathbf{x}_k + \mathbf{w}_k = \mathbf{H}_k \mathbf{x}_k + \mathbf{w}_k$$

where the block circulant matrix $\xi_3 \in \mathcal{C}^{n_t n_c \times n_r n_c}$ is defined as $\xi_3 = \xi_2 \mathbf{G}_k \xi_1$ and $\mathbf{w}_k$ is the frequency domain noise with zero mean and variance σ_w^2 and $\mathbf{H}_k$ is $\mathcal{C}^{n_t n_c \times n_c n_t}$ frequency domain matrix defined as

$$\mathbf{H}_k = \left[(\mathbf{F} \otimes \mathbf{I}_{n_t n_r})\xi_3(\mathbf{F}^{-1} \otimes \mathbf{I}_{n_t n_r})\right] \qquad (24)$$

When frequency offset occurs, $\Delta f \neq 0$. The received frequency domain signal is given by

$$\begin{aligned}\mathbf{r}_k &= \left(\mathbf{F} \otimes \mathbf{I}_{n_t n_r}\right)\xi_2 \mathbf{z}_k \\ &= \left(\mathbf{F} \otimes \mathbf{I}_{n_t n_r}\right)\xi_2 \mathbf{E}\mathbf{G}_k \xi_1 (\mathbf{F}^{-1} \otimes \mathbf{I}_{n_t n_r})\mathbf{x}_k + \mathbf{w}_k \\ &= (\mathbf{G}_{\Delta f} \otimes \mathbf{I}_{n_r})\mathbf{H}_k \mathbf{x}_k + \mathbf{w}_k \\ &= \mathbf{B}\mathbf{H}_k \mathbf{x}_k + \mathbf{w}_k\end{aligned} \qquad (25)$$

where $\mathbf{E} = \operatorname{diag}(e_0, e_1, \ldots, e_{n_c + n_g - 1}) \otimes \mathbf{I}_{n_r}$ denotes the phase rotation due to the CFO, with $e_m = \exp(j2\pi\Delta f T_s(n_c + n_g) + m)$. T_s denotes the sample time. It is clear that $\xi_2 \mathbf{E}\mathbf{G}_k \xi_1$ is no longer block circulant and can thus not be diagonalized by the DFT and IDFT operations. The $\mathcal{C}^{n_c n_r \times n_c n_r}$ matrix $\mathbf{B} = \mathbf{G}_{\Delta f} \otimes \mathbf{I}_{n_r}$ shows the influence of the CFO on the received frequency domain symbols, $\mathbf{G}_{\Delta f}$ is given by

$$\mathbf{G}_{\Delta f} = \begin{bmatrix} g_0 & g_{-1} & \cdots & g_{-(n_c-1)} \\ g_1 & g_0 & \cdots & g_{-(n_c-2)} \\ \vdots & \vdots & \ddots & \vdots \\ g_{n_c-1} & g_{n_c-2} & \cdots & g_0 \end{bmatrix} \quad (26)$$

where

$$g_q = \frac{\sin(\pi(\delta - q))}{n_c \sin(\frac{\pi}{n_c}(\delta - q))} \cdot \exp\left(j\frac{\pi(n_c - 1)}{n_c}(\delta - q)\right)$$

$$\times \exp(j\frac{2\pi\delta}{n_c}(n_c + 2n_g))$$

where $\delta = \Delta f n_c / f_s \ll 1$ is the frequency offset normalized to the subcarrier spacing. We clearly see the following effects of frequency offset: the wanted carriers multiplied with g_0 are rotated and their amplitude is reduced, and the other elements of $\mathbf{G}$, thus for $q \neq 0$, introduce cross terms which result in ICI. From the development in Appendix we have another expression of g_q under the consideration $n_g = n_c / 4$.

$$g_q =$$

$$\frac{\sin(\pi(\delta - q))\cos(4\pi\delta + \frac{\pi q}{n_c} - \frac{\pi\delta}{n_c})}{n_c \sin(\frac{\pi}{n_c}(\delta - q))}(1 \pm j\tan(\theta))$$

$$(27)$$

where $\theta = \frac{\pi}{n_c}(4\pi\delta + \frac{\pi q}{n_c})$. If we focus on g_q expression we find that $\Im\mathrm{m}(g_q) \simeq 0$ for $\delta \neq \pm\pi$. When n_c is enough important $\theta \simeq 0$ then $\tan(\theta) \simeq \theta$, thus, we do approximate θ to $\theta \approx \frac{\pi}{n_c}(4\pi\delta)$ the imaginary part of g_q. In the noise free case and by assuming that δ is sufficiently small, we can re-express the received signal $\mathbf{r}_k$ in (25) as

$$\mathbf{r}_k = \mathbf{B} \quad \exp(j\theta)\mathbf{H}_k\mathbf{x}_k\mathbf{r}_k \quad (28)$$

where θ denotes the approximated phase rotation of the CFO matrix. In order to estimate the module of the CFO matrix, we guess to use orthogonal training symbols which satisfy the orthogonality relation $\mathbf{x}_k\mathbf{x}_k^H = \mathbf{I}_{n_c n_t}$. Thus we can evaluate the expression of $\mathbf{B}$ as

$$\mathbf{B} = \left(\mathbf{r}_k \odot \mathbf{x}_k \quad \left[\mathbf{H}_k \right]^{-1}\mathbf{I}_{n_t n_c} \right) \quad (29)$$

or

$$\mathbf{H}_k^{\ 2} = \mathbf{H}_k\mathbf{H}_k^H$$
$$= \xi_2\mathbf{G}_k\xi_1(\xi_1^H\mathbf{G}_k^H\xi_2^H) \quad (30)$$
$$= \mathbf{G}_k^{\ 2}$$

If we focus on the shape of $\mathbf{G}_k$ matrix (see the proof in Appendix) we can derive $\mathbf{G}_k^{\ 2}$ as

$$\mathbf{G}_k^{\ 2} = \sum_{i,j}|\mathbf{h}_k(i,j)|^2 \approx \left(\frac{L^2}{2} + (\lambda - L)L\right)P_h \quad (31)$$

where $\lambda = (n_c + n_g)n_t$ and P_h denotes the power to each channel coefficient in time domain. Since the channel is selective and correlated we can estimate from (10) the power profile of the time domain channel $\mathbf{G}_k$. From (29) we evaluate $\mathbf{B}$ as

$$\widehat{\mathbf{B}} = \frac{1}{((\frac{L^2}{2} + (\lambda - L)L)P_h)^{\frac{1}{2}}}\left(\mathbf{r}_k \odot \mathbf{x}_k \right) \quad (32)$$

At this step we perform the phase of the CFO matrix. In fact when δ is sufficiently small, we approximate the phase rotation $\exp(j\theta)$ by Taylor series expansion up to second order term

$J_\theta = \exp(j\theta) \approx 1 + j\theta - \dfrac{1}{2}\theta^2$. From (28) we derive $J_{\hat\theta}$ as

$$
\begin{aligned}
&\mid J_{\hat\theta}\mid^2 \mathbf{I}_{n_t n_c}\\
&= \left[\;\widehat{\mathbf{B}}^{\,2}\right]^{-1}\;\left|\mathbf{r}_k \odot \mathbf{x}_k\right|^2 \left[\;\widehat{\mathbf{H}_k}^{\,2}\right]^{-1}\mathbf{I}_{n_t n_c}\\
&= \left(1+\dfrac{\hat\theta^4}{4}\right)^2 \mathbf{I}_{n_t n_c}\\
&= \hat\alpha \mathbf{I}_{n_t n_c}
\end{aligned}
\tag{33}
$$

Since $\hat\alpha$ is known we do estimate $\hat\theta$ as

$$
\hat\theta = \sqrt[4]{\hat\alpha - 1}
\tag{34}
$$

Then we could correct the received signal $\mathbf{r}_k$ to

$$
\widehat{\mathbf{r}_k} = \left[\widehat{\mathbf{B}}\,\exp(j\hat\theta)\right]^{-1}\mathbf{r}_k
\tag{35}
$$

At this step $\widehat{\mathbf{H}_k}$ is diagonalized by the IDFT and DFT operations and can be estimated using both $\widehat{\mathbf{r}_k}$ and the same pilots symbols as without any training symbol repetition.

$$
\widetilde{\mathbf{H}_k} = \mathrm{diag}(\mathbf{x}_k)^{+}\widehat{\mathbf{r}_k}
\tag{36}
$$

Table 1 summarizes all the above steps.

ASTC DECODER

Once the channel effect is compensated as $\hat{\mathbf{x}}_k = \widetilde{\mathbf{H}}_k^{+}\,\widetilde{r_k}$ the decision variable $\hat{\mathbf{x}}_k$ is passed for decoding. The maximum-likelihood perfect codes decoding can be performed using the sphere decoder or the Schnorr-Euchner algorithms. In this work, we propose to use the zero forcing sub-optimum decoder which reduces the nu-

merical complexity without significant performance loss. A serial to parallel module, at each DFT output, is used to reshape the signal $\hat{\mathbf{x}}_k$ and to provide the output signal $\widehat{\mathbf{s}}_k$. If we re-express the received code word $\hat{\mathbf{x}}_k$ in function of $\widehat{\mathbf{s}}_k$ we can derive the decoder matrix Φ for each algebraic space time code as

$$
\Phi_{2\times 2} = \frac{1}{\sqrt{5}}
\begin{bmatrix}
\alpha & \alpha\theta & 0 & 0\\
0 & 0 & i\bar\alpha & i\overline{\alpha\theta}\\
0 & 0 & \alpha & \alpha\theta\\
\bar\alpha & \overline{\alpha\theta} & 0 & 0
\end{bmatrix}
\tag{37}
$$

$$
\Phi_{4\times 4} = \begin{bmatrix}\phi_1 & \phi_2 & \phi_3 & \phi_4\end{bmatrix}
\tag{38}
$$

where ϕ_i is the decoder block matrix for each received symbol defined as

$$
\phi_1 = \begin{bmatrix}
a_1 & a_5 & a_9 & a_{13}\\
0 & 0 & 0 & 0\\
0 & 0 & 0 & 0\\
0 & 0 & 0 & 0\\
0 & 0 & 0 & 0\\
a_2 & a_6 & a_{10} & a_{14}\\
0 & 0 & 0 & 0\\
0 & 0 & 0 & 0\\
0 & 0 & 0 & 0\\
0 & 0 & 0 & 0\\
a_3 & a_7 & a_{11} & a_{15}\\
0 & 0 & 0 & 0\\
0 & 0 & 0 & 0\\
0 & 0 & 0 & 0\\
0 & 0 & 0 & 0\\
a_4 & a_8 & a_{12} & a_{16}
\end{bmatrix}
\qquad
\phi_2 = \begin{bmatrix}
0 & 0 & 0 & 0\\
0 & 0 & 0 & 0\\
0 & 0 & 0 & 0\\
ia_4 & ia_8 & ia_{12} & ia_{16}\\
a_1 & a_5 & a_9 & a_{13}\\
0 & 0 & 0 & 0\\
0 & 0 & 0 & 0\\
0 & 0 & 0 & 0\\
a_2 & a_6 & a_{10} & a_{14}\\
0 & 0 & 0 & 0\\
0 & 0 & 0 & 0\\
0 & 0 & 0 & 0\\
0 & 0 & 0 & 0\\
a_3 & a_7 & a_{11} & a_{15}\\
0 & 0 & 0 & 0
\end{bmatrix}
$$

$$
\phi_3 = \begin{bmatrix}
0 & 0 & 0 & 0\\
0 & 0 & 0 & 0\\
ia_3 & ia_7 & ia_{11} & ia_{15}\\
0 & 0 & 0 & 0\\
0 & 0 & 0 & 0\\
0 & 0 & 0 & 0\\
0 & 0 & 0 & 0\\
ia_4 & ia_8 & ia_{12} & ia_{16}\\
a_1 & a_5 & a_9 & a_{13}\\
0 & 0 & 0 & 0\\
0 & 0 & 0 & 0\\
0 & 0 & 0 & 0\\
a_2 & a_6 & a_{10} & a_{14}\\
0 & 0 & 0 & 0\\
0 & 0 & 0 & 0\\
0 & 0 & 0 & 0
\end{bmatrix}
\qquad
\phi_4 = \begin{bmatrix}
0 & 0 & 0 & 0\\
ia_2 & ia_6 & ia_{10} & ia_{14}\\
0 & 0 & 0 & 0\\
0 & 0 & 0 & 0\\
0 & 0 & 0 & 0\\
ia_3 & ia_7 & ia_{11} & ia_{15}\\
0 & 0 & 0 & 0\\
0 & 0 & 0 & 0\\
0 & 0 & 0 & 0\\
ia_4 & ia_8 & ia_{12} & ia_{16}\\
a_1 & a_5 & a_9 & a_{13}\\
0 & 0 & 0 & 0\\
0 & 0 & 0 & 0\\
0 & 0 & 0 & 0\\
0 & 0 & 0 & 0
\end{bmatrix}
$$

Table 1. The compensation steps of CFO

Steps	Operations
1	Estimate the module of the CFO Matrix
2	Estimate the phase of the CFO Matrix
3	Correct the received signal
4	Estimate the frequency domain channel

where **M** is re-defined as

$$\mathbf{M} = \begin{bmatrix} a_1 & a_5 & a_9 & a_{13} \\ a_2 & a_6 & a_{10} & a_{14} \\ a_3 & a_7 & a_{11} & a_{15} \\ a_4 & a_8 & a_{12} & a_{16} \end{bmatrix}$$

and

$$\phi_{TC} = \frac{1}{\sqrt{2}} \begin{pmatrix} 1 & \theta & 0 & 0 \\ 0 & 0 & \varphi & -\varphi\theta \\ 0 & 0 & \varphi & \varphi\theta \\ 1 & -\theta & 0 & 0 \end{pmatrix} \quad (39)$$

For DAST code case we decode each 2 symbols together, thus we slice the received symbol by 2 as

$$\phi_{DC} = \frac{1}{\sqrt{2}} \begin{pmatrix} 1 & \theta \\ 1 & -\theta \end{pmatrix} \quad (40)$$

The decision for the output signal $\hat{\mathbf{s}}_k$ will be

$$\hat{\mathbf{s}}_k = \begin{cases} \Phi_{2\times2}^+ \hat{\mathbf{x}}_k & \text{for } 2\times2 \text{ perfect code} \\ \Phi_{4\times4}^+ \hat{\mathbf{x}}_k & \text{for } 4\times4 \text{ perfect code} \\ \Phi_{DC}^+ \hat{\mathbf{x}}_k & \text{for } 2\times2 \text{ DAST code} \\ \Phi_{TC}^+ \hat{\mathbf{x}}_k & \text{for } 2\times2 \text{ TAST code} \end{cases} \quad (41)$$

SIMULATION RESULTS AND DISCUSSIONS

We consider an OFDM orthogonal pilot symbol with a total of $n_c = 128$ subcarriers and no virtual subcarriers. A cyclic prefix of length $n_g = n_c / 4$ is inserted. The discrete-time channel has 16 taps. The channel coefficients are assumed to be correlated Rayleigh with known mean power delay profile $P_h = |h(i,j)|^2$. We consider 1-user 2×2 and 4×4 MIMO system. The CFO was selected from a set of $[-0.5, 0.5]$. For all results 10000 independent realizations were simulated. The system parameters are summarized in Table 2.

CFO Analysis

To check the optimality of the algorithm we derived the Cramer-Rao Lower Bound (CRLB) for the MIMO frequency offset as a measure of accuracy for the CFO estimator, which can be considered as the theoretical value of the variance of the estimate. We assume that the noise used is AWGN, and the signal to be estimated is unbiased. The information to be estimated in our case is the CFO which is provided by the imaginary part of the approximated function J_δ. In the Appendix we give the derivation details of the following CRLB expression

$$\text{CRLB} \geq \frac{\sigma^2}{\sum_{p=1}^{(n_r n_c - 1)} \left[\frac{\partial \Im(J_\delta)}{\partial \delta} \right]^2} = \frac{n_c \sigma^2}{16\pi^4 n_r \delta^2}$$

where σ^2 is the variance of the AWGN used. The Cramer-Rao lower bound is equal to the theoretical value of the variance, which means that it is the Maximum-Likelihood estimator. The estimated CFO values in Figure 3 for high SNR fit with CRLB curves. The results show how accurate the proposed CFO estimator is. For both the 2×2

Table 2. Simulation parameters

System Parameter	Parameter Value
Modulation	QAM-4
Bandwidth	20MHz
Number of subcarriers	$n_c = 128, 48$
Cyclic prefix length	$n_g = \dfrac{n_c}{4} = 32$

and 4×4 configurations the variance follows asymptotically the CRLB.

It is clear from the results in Figure 5 that the implementation of the frequency synchronization causes some degradation in performance at low SNR, which can be explained by the poor estimation of the frequency offset at these SNR values. The use of the perfect codes with 4×4 configuration, increases notably the performance of the proposed MIMO-OFDM system at low SNR and correct significantly the frequency synchronization. In the BER range of interest, however, the degradation compared to perfect synchronization is very small, for both 2×2 and 2×2 ASTC. We note that for the perfect codes 2×2 the gain is about 2 dB, this is explained by the full rate, full diversity and good spectral efficiency of the 2×2 perfect codes.

Figure 6 shows the system performances for two normalized Doppler frequencies. In the Unmod case, when $f_d = 0.001$, the gain obtained is about 0.5 dB better than $f_d = 0.05$, at BER equal to 10^{-3}. However, in the perfect codes of 2×2 configuration, the gain difference is not noticeable anymore but the spectral efficiency is much more increased. It is noted that performances are better when the normalized fading rate f_d decreases. The 2×2 perfect codes perform the CFO synchronization implementation compared to the Un-mod configuration.

Capacity Analysis

We consider the case when $\mathbf{H}$ is chosen according to (8). We investigate 1000 independent channel realizations for a fixed number of $n_t \times n_r = 2$ antennas. The Cumulative Complementary Density Function (CCDF) is used as tool, to give the probability that the capacity $\mathbf{C}$ is larger than the abscissa $\mathbf{C}_x$.

The ergodic capacity as function of E_b / N_o per receive antenna, for both the analytic capacity expression, derived in (19) and the simulated expression using (16), is shown in Figure 7. The simulated curves of the two algebraic space time codes GC and TC, remain the same, this is clearly shown by the analytic capacity expression. It can be observed also that the match between the analytic and the simulated capacity, is more perfect for high E_b / N_o, mainly when $E_b / N_o \geq 16$ dB.

Figure 8, depict the CCDF of the capacity C developed in (19), respectively for GC codes. In the CCDF of the capacity is plotted for up to 10 dB. The results show that at 90% probability, the capacity is larger than 11 bits/s/Hz when the normalized Doppler frequency $f_d = 0.01$, and becomes larger than 11.5 bits/s/Hz when $f_d = 0.0001$, as expected. It can be observed that the capacity increase almost linearly when f_d decrease.

Channel Estimation

Figure 9 shows the performance of GC, TC, DC, for both LS and LMMSE channel estimation methods (A. Bannour M. L., 2011). The GC shows better performance than DC and TC at high SNR. The LS estimate suffers from a high mean-square error and does not take into account the channel correlation property. These drawbacks can be addressed by the LMMSE channel estimation

Figure 3. Theoretical and simulated MSE of the CFO estimation for MIMO configurations of 2 × 2 and 4 × 4

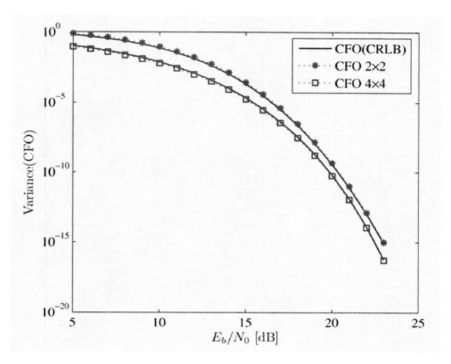

Figure 4. Performance of the proposed method using perfect (-*-) and implemented synchronization (–) for 2 × 2 and 4 × 4 configurations, n_c = 128 subcarriers, with an ASTC scheme

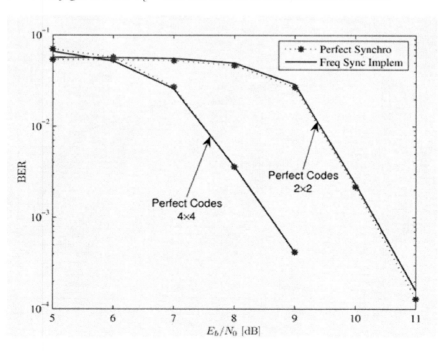

Figure 5. Doppler effects on MIMO-OFDM CFO compensation, perfect code $n_t = n_r = 4$ and $n_c = 128$ subcarriers, vehicle speed vh = 30km/h

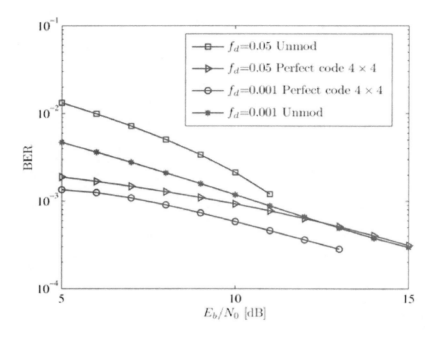

Figure 6. Doppler effects on MIMO-OFDM CFO compensation, perfect code $n_t = n_r = 2$ and $n_c = 128$ subcarriers, vehicle speed vh = 30km/h

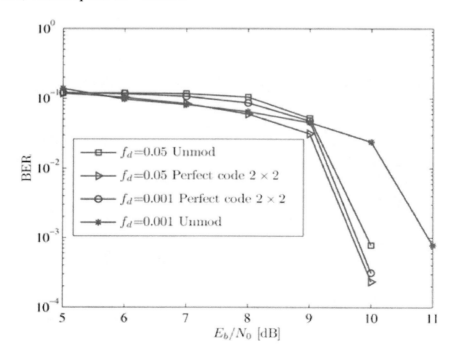

Figure 7. Ergodic capacity of GC and TC codes in MIMO-OFDM $n_t = n_r = 2$ and $n_c = 48$ subcarrier

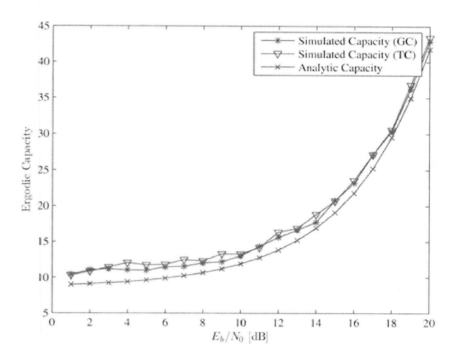

Figure 8. Doppler effects on the capacity for GC-MIMO-OFDM with $\sigma_w = 10\,dB$, $n_t = n_r = 2$

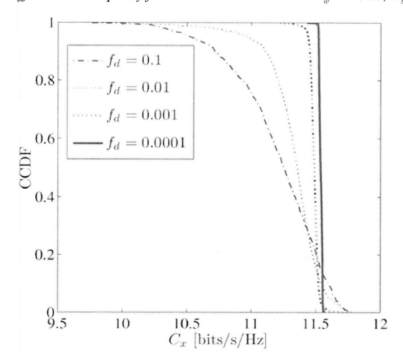

Figure 9. LS/LMMSE estimation for GC, TC and DC code. Frequency pilot spacing $L_f = 4$. $n_t = n_r = 2$ $n_c = 128$

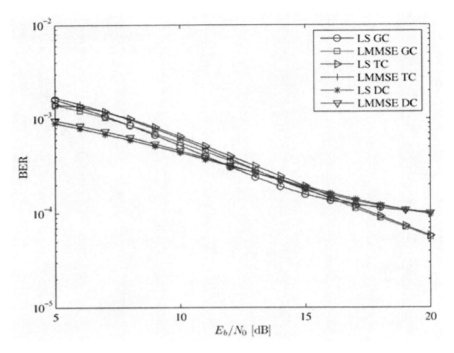

Figure 10. Geometry of the time domain matrix G

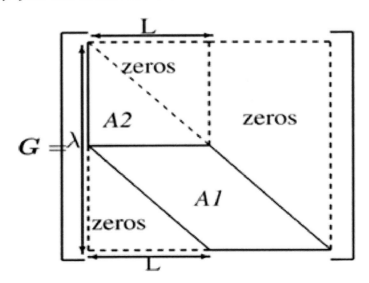

technique, which is capable of reducing the estimation error. For LS estimator, the BER for GC is close to 10^{-3} for SNR about 18 dB, however, in case of the LMMSE estimation method, at SNR 18 dB the BER is about 10^{-6}, so the gain is around 3 dB for the LMMSE estimator.

FUTURE RESEARCH DIRECTIONS

It has been shown, by their construction, the Algebraic Space Time Codes have a reasonable BER when working in a non selective channel thanks to their properties, full rank, full rate, and non-vanishing determinant for increasing rate. We have proved that it is possible to combine MIMO-OFDM system with ASTC encoder under a frequency-selective channel. Another interesting research area consists of applying the ASTC-MIMO-OFDM discussed in this chapter to the Ultra Wide Band (UWB) systems under a non coherent channel conditions.

CONCLUSION

The ASTC code is an optimal space time code with a full-rate and a full-diversity that has a maximal coding gain and good performance in flat fading channels. For a high bit-rate transmission over a multi-path channel, the received signal is affected by the channel ISI. In this chapter, we have considered the MIMO-OFDM system with ASTC, TAST and DAST coding. The OFDM technique allows to overcome the channel selectivity. Thus, the ASTC codes can still maintain their properties and achieve good capacity under frequency selective channels. Pilot-aided channel Estimation methods have been discussed and performances of ASTC-MIMO-OFDM systems have been evaluated using the channel estimation parameters of different ASTC codes. Computer simulations have demonstrated the efficiency of the proposed ASTC

encoder in terms of performance improvement. In this chapter we presented also a new algebraic CFO estimation technique for MIMO-OFDM systems over frequency-selective fading channels employing an algebraic space time coder. Knowing the time power profile, we estimate the frequency power profile which is a key point of the proposed method. The performance of the proposed CFO compensation method was evaluated using Monte Carlo simulation for different configurations mainly with the Doppler effect, ASTC, vehicular speed and compared to the empirical bound defined by the CRLB. The simulation results have demonstrated that the proposed method substantially reaches the empirical bound and the ASTC maintain their properties under a multi-path channel and achieve good BER.

REFERENCES

Bannour, M. A. (2010). Adaptation of golden codes with a correlated rayleigh frequency-selective channel in OFDM system with imperfect channel estimation. *2010 7th International Symposium of Wireless Communication Systems (ISWCS)*, York, (pp. 159–163).

Bannour, M. A. (2011). *On the capacity of ASTC-MIMO-OFDM system in a correlated rayleigh frequency-selective channel.* IEEE Vehicular Technology Conference Spring 2011, Budapest.

Bannour, M. L. (2011). *Pilot-aided channel estimation and performance of ASTC-MIMO-OFDM system in a correlated Rayleigh frequency-selective channel. 2011 Wireless Advanced (WiAd).* London, UK: IEEE.

Cox, T. M. (2007). Robust frequency and timing synchronization for OFDM. *IEEE Transactions on Communications, 45*(12), 1613–1621.

Czylwik, A. (1999). Synchronization for systems with antenna diversit. *Vehicular Technology Conference, 1999*, (pp. 728–732).

Gagnon, M. L. (2007). Iterative channel estimation and decoding of turbo-coded OFDM symbols in selective rayleigh channel. *Canadian Journal of Electrical and Computer Engineering, 32*(1), 9–18. doi:10.1109/CJECE.2007.364328

Giannakis, Y. Y. (2005). Blind carrier frequency offset estimation in SISO, MIMO, and multiuser OFDM systems. *IEEE Transactions on Communications, 53*(1), 173–183. doi:10.1109/TCOMM.2004.840623

Hyoung-Kyu, Y. Y.-H.-H.-S. (2000). Frequency-offset synchronization and channel estimation. *IEEE Communications Letters, 4*(3), 95–97. doi:10.1109/4234.831036

IEEE. (n.d.). *IEEE 802.11g standard, further higher-speed physical layer extension.*

ISO/IEC. (2000). IEEE *802.11a standard, ISO/IEC 8802-11:1999/Amd 1:2000(E).*

Mengali, M. M. (2001). A comparison of pilot-aided channel estimation methods for OFDM systems. *IEEE Transactions on Signal Processing, 49*(12), 3065–3073. doi:10.1109/78.969514

Mengali, M. M. (2002). An improved frequency offset estimator for OFDM applications. *IEEE Communications Letters, 3*(3), 75–77.

Moose, P. H. (1994). A technique for orthogonal frequency division multiplexing frequency offset correction. *IEEE Transactions on Communications, 42*(10). doi:10.1109/26.328961

Peeters, T. P. (2002). Synchronization with DMT modulation. *IEEE Communications Magazine, 37*(4), 80–86.

Reggiannini, M. L. (2005). Carrier frequency acquisition and tracking for OFDM systems. *IEEE Transactions on Communications, 44*(11), 1590–1598.

Rekaya, G. V. (2005). The golden code: A 2×2 full-rate space-time code with nonvanishing determinants. *IEEE Transactions on Information Theory, 51*(4), 1432–1436. doi:10.1109/TIT.2005.844069

Renfors, A. H.-D. (2007). Blind estimation of large carrier frequency offset in wireless OFDM systems. *IEEE Transactions on Vehicular Technology, 56*(2), 965–968. doi:10.1109/TVT.2007.891430

Santella, G. (2002). A frequency and symbol synchronization system for OFDM signals: Architecture and simulation results. *IEEE Transactions on Vehicular Technology, 49*(1), 254–275. doi:10.1109/25.820719

Schlegel, L. W. (2002). Synchronization requirements for multi-user OFDM on satellite mobile and two-path rayleigh fading channels. *IEEE Transactions on Communications, 43*(234), 887–895.

Stuber, A. N. (2001). Synchronization for MIMO OFDM systems. *Global Telecommunications Conference, 2001,* (pp. 509–513).

Swami, A. S. (2005). Doppler and frequency-offset synchronization in wideband OFDM. *IEEE Transactions on Wireless Communications, 4*(6), 2870–2881. doi:10.1109/TWC.2005.858337

Tureli, D. K. (2001). Multicarrier synchronization with diversity. *Vehicular Technology Conference, 2001,* (pp. 952–956).

Tureli, H. L. (1997). A high efficiency carrier estimator for OFDM communications. *Conference Record of the Thirty-First Asilomar Conference on Signals, Systems & Computers,* (pp. 505–509). Pacific Grove, CA, USA.

van de Beek, M. S. (2002). ML estimation of time and frequency offset in OFDM systems. *IEEE Transactions on Signal Processing, 45*(7), 1800–1805. doi:10.1109/78.599949

APPENDIX

Proof of CFO Approximation

$$g_q = \frac{\sin(\pi(\delta - q))}{n_c \sin(\frac{\pi}{n_c}(\delta - q))} \times \exp\left(j\frac{\pi(n_c - 1)}{n_c}(\delta - q)\right) . \exp\left(j\frac{2\pi\delta}{n_c}(n_c + 2n_g)\right)$$

$$= \frac{\sin(\pi(\delta - q))}{n_c \sin(\frac{\pi}{n_c}(\delta - q))} \times \exp\left(j\left[\frac{\pi(n_c - 1)}{n_c}(\delta - q) + \frac{2\pi\delta}{n_c}(n_c + 2n_g)\right]\right)$$

$$= \frac{\sin(\pi(\delta - q))}{n_c \sin(\frac{\pi}{n_c}(\delta - q))} \times \exp\left(j\frac{\pi}{n_c}\left[(n_c - 1)(\delta - q) + 2\delta(n_c + 2n_g)\right]\right)$$

$$= \frac{\sin(\pi(\delta - q))}{n_c \sin(\frac{\pi}{n_c}(\delta - q))} \times \exp\left(j\frac{\pi}{n_c}\left[4n_c\delta + q(1 - n_c) - \delta\right]\right)$$

$$= \frac{\sin(\pi(\delta - q))}{n_c \sin(\frac{\pi}{n_c}(\delta - q))} \times \exp\left(j\left[4\pi\delta + \frac{\pi q}{n_c}(1 - n_c) - \frac{\pi\delta}{n_c}\right]\right)$$

$$= \frac{\sin(\pi(\delta - q))}{n_c \sin(\frac{\pi}{n_c}(\delta - q))} \times \exp\left(j\left[4\pi\delta + \frac{\pi q}{n_c} - \pi q - \frac{\pi\delta}{n_c}\right]\right)$$

$$= \frac{\sin(\pi(\delta - q))}{n_c \sin(\frac{\pi}{n_c}(\delta - q))} \times \exp\left(j\left[4\pi\delta + \frac{\pi q}{n_c} - \frac{\pi\delta}{n_c} - \pi q\right]\right)$$

$$= \frac{\sin(\pi(\delta - q))\cos(4\pi\delta + \frac{\pi q}{n_c} - \frac{\pi\delta}{n_c} - \pi q)}{n_c \sin(\frac{\pi}{n_c}(\delta - q))} \times \left(1 + j\tan\left(4\pi\delta + \frac{\pi q}{n_c} - \frac{\pi\delta}{n_c} - \pi q\right)\right)$$

$$= \frac{\sin(\pi(\delta - q))\cos(4\pi\delta + \dfrac{\pi q}{n_c} - \dfrac{\pi\delta}{n_c}}{n_c \sin(\dfrac{\pi}{n_c}(\delta - q))} \times \left[1 \pm j \tan\left(4\pi\delta + \frac{\pi q}{n_c} - \frac{\pi\delta}{n_c} \right) \right]$$

$$= \frac{\sin(\pi(\delta - q))\cos(4\pi\delta + \dfrac{\pi q}{n_c} - \dfrac{\pi\delta}{n_c})}{n_c \sin(\dfrac{\pi}{n_c}(\delta - q))} \times \left[1 \pm j \tan\left(4\pi\delta + \frac{\pi q}{n_c} \right) \right]$$

$$= \frac{\sin(\pi(\delta - q))\cos(4\pi\delta + \dfrac{\pi q}{n_c} - \dfrac{\pi\delta}{n_c})}{n_c \sin(\dfrac{\pi}{n_c}(\delta - q))} \left(1 \pm j \tan(\theta) \right) = \frac{\sin(\pi(\delta - q))\cos(4\pi\delta + \dfrac{\pi q}{n_c} - \dfrac{\pi\delta}{n_c})}{n_c \sin(\dfrac{\pi}{n_c}(\delta - q))} \left(1 \pm j \tan(\theta) \right)$$

where $\theta = \dfrac{\pi}{n_c}(4\pi\delta + \dfrac{\pi q}{n_c}) \approx \dfrac{\pi}{n_c}(4\pi\delta)$. The same angle of CFOs for all antennas is used.

Proof of Power Channel Definition

$$A2 = \frac{L^2}{2} P_h \; ; \; A1 = (\lambda - L)L P_h \; ; \; P_h \approx |h(i,j)|^2$$

$$\mathbf{G}^2 = [A1 + A2] = \left[\sum_{i,j} |\mathbf{h}_k(i,j)|^2 \right] \approx \left[\left(\frac{L^2}{2} + (\lambda - L)L \right) P_h \right]$$

where $\lambda = (n_c + n_g)n_t$ and $A1, A2$ denote the used channel coefficient areas. We suppose that channel coefficients have roushy the same power which is almost the case with Rayleigh channel.

Derivation of CRLB

When the data is an AWGN signal,

$$x[n] = \Im(J_{\delta,n}) + w(n)$$

We could get a simple form for the CRLB. First write the likelihood function as

$$p(x, \delta) = \frac{1}{(2\pi\sigma^2)^{\frac{n}{2}}} \exp\left\{ \frac{-1}{\sigma^2} \sum_{n=0}^{N-1} (x[n] - \Im(J_{\delta,n})^2) \right\}$$

where σ^2 denotes the variance of the white gaussian noise. If we differentiate $\ln p(x, \delta)$ twice we get

$$\frac{\partial^2}{\partial \delta^2} \ln p(x, \delta) = \frac{1}{\sigma^2} \sum_{n=0}^{N-1} \left\{ (x[n] - \Im(J_{\delta,n})) \frac{\partial^2 \Im(J_{\delta,n})}{\partial \delta^2} - \left[\frac{\partial \Im(J_{\delta,n})}{\partial \delta} \right]^2 \right\}$$

Then when we average for all observations as

$$E \left\{ \frac{\partial^2}{\partial \delta^2} \ln p(x, \delta) \right\} = \frac{1}{\sigma^2} \sum_{n=0}^{N-1} \left\{ \underbrace{(E(x[n]) - \Im(J_{\delta,n}))}_{=0} \frac{\partial^2 \Im(J_{\delta,n})}{\partial \delta^2} - \left[\frac{\partial \Im(J_{\delta,n})}{\partial \delta} \right]^2 \right\} = -\frac{1}{\sigma^2} \sum_{n=0}^{N-1} \left[\frac{\partial \Im(J_{\delta,n})}{\partial \delta} \right]^2$$

Using these results the CRLB for CFO signals in AWGN is

$$\text{CRLB} \geq \frac{\sigma^2}{\sum_{p=1}^{(n_r n_c - 1)} \left[\frac{\partial \Im(J_\delta)}{\partial \delta} \right]^2} = \frac{n_c \sigma^2}{16 \pi^4 n_r \delta^2}$$

Acronyms Used

CP: Cycle Prefix

DFT: Discrete Fourier Transform

FO: Frequency Offset

GI: Gard Interval

IC: Inter-Carrier Interference

IDFT: Inverse Discrete Fourier Transform

IS: Inter-Symbol Interference

MIMO: Multi-Input Multi-Output

MSE: Mean Square Error

OFDM: Orthogonal Frequency Division Multiplexing

Chapter 7
Precoding for Multiuser MIMO

Elsadig Saeid
Universiti Teknologi PETRONAS, Malaysia

Varun Jeoti
Universiti Teknologi PETRONAS, Malaysia

Brahim Belhaouari Samir
Universiti Teknologi PETRONAS, Malaysia

ABSTRACT

Future Wireless Networks are expected to adopt multi-user multiple input multiple output (MU-MIMO) systems whose performance is maximized by making use of precoding at the transmitter. This chapter describes the recent advances in precoding design for MU-MIMO and introduces a new technique to improve the precoder performance. Without claiming to be comprehensive, the chapter gives deep introduction on basic MIMO techniques covering the basics of single user multiple input multiple output (SU-MIMO) links, its capacity, various transmission strategies, SU-MIMO link precoding, and MIMO receiver structures. After the introduction, MU-MIMO system model is defined and maximum achievable rate regions for both MU-MIMO broadcast and MU-MIMO multiple access channels are explained. It is followed by critical literature review on linear precoding design for MU-MIMO broadcast channel. This paves the way for introducing an improved technique of precoding design that is followed by its performance evaluation.

1. INTRODUCTION

Multiple Input Multiple Output technology has revolutionized the research in wireless systems. Today, the existence and realization of high capacity communication network backbones motivates researchers to investigate the following two directions, namely, development of new applications that utilize this huge capacity of backbone transport networks and on the other hand, development of reliable and spectrally efficient wireless access networks to take advantage of this huge capacity. The need for developing the high capacity wireless access network to support the emerging high data rate applications requires one to overcome the three fundamental limitations intertwined with each other, namely, bandwidth, power and system

DOI: 10.4018/978-1-4666-1797-1.ch007

Copyright © 2012, IGI Global. Copying or distributing in print or electronic forms without written permission of IGI Global is prohibited.

complexity. The goal to overcome all these challenges has ignited up a lot of research in the wireless communication that includes, among others, use of multiple antennas, cooperative networking, cross layer design, cognitive radio techniques and advanced relaying. Since the pioneering work in the multiple input multiple output (MIMO) that showed large room of improvement in the spectral efficiency and bandwidth utilization, MIMO and MU-MIMO have become one of the most attractive and rich area of investigation and a lot of research results and novel systems design proposals have since been reported.

These extremely novel results and features of MIMO systems have stirred up a lot of technical proposals to integrate MIMO into current and future wireless communication standards. The international telecommunication union (ITU) defines the general requirement of what is called ITU-R/IMT-advanced air interface for 4G systems, as well as for the next-generation wireless network to be flexible and able to fill up the rate gap between broadband transport network and the wireless access networks. Currently MIMO techniques have been proposed to be incorporated into many wireless communication standards such as IEEE 802.11n (XIAO, 2005) wireless LAN, IEEE 802.16e Mobile WiMAX and the next generation candidate mobile standards IEEE802.16m (WIMAX profile 2.0) and 3GPP E-UTRA-LTE Advanced (LTE-A)(Release 10) (Etemad, 2008; Li et al., 2010; Parikh & Basu, 2011). IEEE 802.11n wireless LAN standard incorporate MIMO-OFDM nice Features to enhance data rate. The first draft IEEE802.11n devices are capable of achieving throughput up to 300Mbps utilizing two spatial streams in 40MHz channel at 5GHz band. The MIMO techniques so adapted include both open loops spatial diversity (utilizing the STBC and cyclic shift diversity) and spatial multiplexing techniques which do not require any kind of channel state information (CSI) at the transmitter. In the IEEE 802.11n second draft

maximum of four spatial multiplexing streams are specified. Thus, a maximum throughput of 600Mbps can be achieved by using four spatial streams in a 40MHz channel bandwidth.

IEEE 802.16e is the first wireless wide area network standard that support both closed loop and open loop MIMO transmission. In closed loop MIMO where full or partial CSI is available at the transmitter through the feedback channel, the standard supports precoding for both spatial multiplexing and spatial diversity with space time coding. In open loop mode of transmission the standard supports up to four streams spatial multiplexing and spatial diversity based on Alamouti STBC technique. With the goal of backward compatibility, the techniques adopted or under development in IEEE 802.16m and the 3GPP/LTE – advanced include a wide range of spatial multiplexing with flexible assumptions on MIMO receiver complexity. Furthermore, both standards adopting MU-MIMO mode of operations under different CSI degree precision, code book and zero-forcing precoding method are just an example of two precoding candidate methods to be applied in the two wireless standards.

The rest of the chapter is organized into three parts: In section 2, sufficiently deep background is given that covers the basics of single user multiple input multiple output (SU-MIMO) links, its capacity, various transmission strategies, SU-MIMO link precoding and MIMO receiver structures. Section 3 starts with definition of MU-MIMO system model and maximum achievable rate regions for both the MU-MIMO broadcast and MU-MIMO multiple access channels. This is followed by critical literature review on linear precoder design for MU-MIMO broadcast channel. In section 4, an improved technique of precoding design is explained and the results of its performance are presented in the light of reported results of other techniques. The chapter is concluded with a section on conclusion.

Figure 1. Block diagram of single user MIMO system

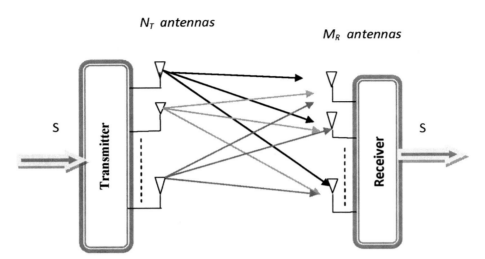

Figure 1. Block diagram of single user MIMO system

2. BACKGROUND

2.1 Single User MIMO (SU-MIMO) System Model

In the wireless communication system design, channel modeling is a central problem and starting point of understanding into the whole system. Most often, we differentiate between two types of wireless communication channels, frequency selective and frequency-flat channels. In frequency selective channel the link gain between transmit and receive antennas during the channel using time is described using a finite duration multiple tap impulse response sequence which is opposed to frequency flat fading where the impulse response is a single tap sequence with scalar channel gain. From practical system design point of view, the system designer can destroy the frequency selectivity effect in wideband system by using some kind of direct sequence spread spectrum technique as applied in 3G systems or subdividing the wideband into narrow sub-band using orthogonal frequency division multiplexing (OFDM) as applied in 4G systems (Goldsmith, 2005; Tse & Viswanath, 2005). Another conven-

tional method for mitigating the inter-symbol interference (ISI) effect of frequency selectivity is the use of channel frequency equalization techniques. In MIMO system research, the common assumption is that the channel gains between each pairs of transmits and receive antennas correspond to frequency flat channel. Figure 1, illustrates the SU-MIMO system with N_T transmit antenna and M_R receive antennas, the channel matrix of the frequency-flat narrowband link is given by:

$$H = \begin{bmatrix} h_{11} & \cdots & h_{1,N_T} \\ \vdots & \ddots & \vdots \\ h_{M_R,1} & \cdots & h_{M_R,N} \end{bmatrix} \in \mathbf{C}^{M_R \times N_T} \qquad (1)$$

where $h_{i,j}$ denotes the complex channel gain from the jth transmit antenna to the ith receive antenna, while $1 \leq j \leq N_T$, $1 \leq i \leq M_R$. We further assume that the channel bandwidth is B Hz. The received signal vector $y[n] \in \mathbf{C}^{M_R \times 1}$ at time instants $[n]$ is given by:

$$y[n] = HS[n] + V[n] \qquad (2)$$

where $S[n] \in C^{N_T \times 1}$ is the $N_T \times 1$ transmitted signal vector $S[n] = [s_1 \cdots s_{N_T}]^T$,

$V[n] \in C^{M_R \times 1} = [v_1 \cdots v_{M_R}]^T$ is the additive white Gaussian noise vector which is assumed to have independent complex Gaussian elements with zero mean and variance equal to $\delta_v^2 I_{M_R}$, there $\delta_v^2 = BN_\circ$ is the power spectral density of the noise. In all MIMO research, there is another common assumption that the elements of the channel matrix H are independent complex Gaussian random variable with zero mean and variance σ_h^2. This statistical distribution is very useful and reasonable assumption to model the effect of rich scattering environment where the angular bins are fully populated paths with sparsely spaced antennas. Justification for all the assumptions about MIMO channel model is very important in system design. As about the system bandwidth B, the common assumption in MIMO system design is that the channel frequency response through this bandwidth is flat because practically it is very hard to implement ISI equalization across MIMO system. Furthermore; the assumption is realizable with the utilization of OFDM where it is indeed true for individual sub-carriers. In physical scattering environment with proper antenna array spacing, the common assumption is that the elements of the Channel matrix are independent identically distributed (i.i.d). In practice, if there are any kinds of spatial correlation, consequently, this means that there will be a reduction in the MIMO channel degree of freedom which results in a decrease in the MIMO capacity gain. The assumptions of i.i.d channel can be partially realized by correctly separating the antennas in the MIMO. In some deployment scenarios, there are not enough scatterers in the propagation environment to provide what is called "uniform scattering" and the i.i.d assumption become inapplicable statistically and

instead of that correlated MIMO channel become more applicable. A part of the last decade research focussed on this kind of correlation study. In general, fading correlation between the elements of MIMO channel matrix H is separated into two independent components, namely, transmit correlation and receive correlation (Shiu, Foschini, Gans, & kahn, 2000). In this view, the common MIMO channel model H become as:

$$H = R_r^{1/2} H_w R_t^{1/2} \qquad (3)$$

where, H_w is a matrix whose element are i.i.d, and $R_r^{1/2}$ and $R_t^{1/2}$ are the receive and transmit correlation matrix factors, respectively.

2.2 MIMO Performance Gains

The key point to the additional performance gain in MIMO systems is the additional spatial degrees of freedom that are associated with the multiple antennas. These additional degrees of freedom can be exploited and utilized in the same way as frequency and time dimensions in the classical single input single output (SISO) systems. The initial promising capacity and spectral efficiency of MIMO ignited by the work of Telatar (Telatar, 1995) and Foschini (Foschoini, 1996) have demonstrated that by utilizing multiple antennas at the transmitter and receiver, the capacity of a MIMO system can scale linearly with the *min* (N_T, M_R). This capacity can be extracted by three techniques, spatial multiplexing, spatial diversity, and beam forming.

From classical communication and information theory, communication channel characterization has played a crucial rule in the communication system design that both transmitter and receiver design have heavily depended on it (Gallager, Fall 2006.). In MIMO systems, knowledge of the channel state information (CSI) is an important parameter in system design. CSIT and CSIR refer to the CSI at the transmitter and receiver respectively. In the state of art of communication system design, there is common assumption that the receiver has perfect CSIR. With this fair assumption, all MIMO performance gains are exploited. Furthermore, optimization of any MIMO performance gain depends largely on the availability and quality of CSI at the transmitter (Sampath, Stoica, & Paulraj, 2001). Thus, the accessibility and utilization of CSI at the transmitter is one of the most important classification criteria of MIMO research in the last decade. Next section gives brief overview of the most critical processing techniques and type of gains that we can extract from single user point-to-point MIMO link.

2.3 Single User MIMO Processing without CSI at the Transmitter

When there's no CSI available at the transmitter, also called open loop MIMO, there are two types of performance gain that can be extracted, multiplexing gain and diversity gain (Lozano & Jindal, 2010).

Multiplexing gain is the increase in the transmission rate at no cost of power consumption. This type of gain is achieved through the use of multiple antennas at both transmitter and receiver. In single user MIMO system with spatial multiplexing gain configuration, different data streams are transmitted from the different transmit antennas simultaneously. At the receiver, both linear and nonlinear MIMO decoders are used to decode the transmitted data vector. The multiplexing gain value is equal to the length of data vector and it is equivalent to the rank of H. When CSI is not known at the transmitter, this gain becomes more sensitive to long-deep MIMO channel fade. Thus, in such communication environment the designer should solve this problem by resorting to system design that can extract MIMO diversity gain with the aid and help of time domain or frequency domain design.

Diversity gain is the redundancy in the received signal. In SU-MIMO diversity gain is extracted when replicas of information signals are received through independent fading channel. Diversity gain increases the probability of successful transmission which in turn increases the communication link reliability. In SU-MIMO system, there are three types of diversity methods namely, transmit-receive diversity, receive diversity and transmit diversity. Both transmit and receive diversity is applicable on the system configuration where there are multiple antennas at both the transmitter and receiver and length of transmitted symbol equal to one. With system of N_T transmit and M_R receive antennas, the maximum diversity gain that can be extracted is equal to $N_T \times M_R$

Receive diversity is applied on sub-category of MIMO system where there is only one transmit antenna and multiple receive antennas. For system that has one transmit antenna and M_R receive antennas, this is also called single input multiple output (SIMO), the MIMO channel H is reduced to

$$H = h = [h_1 h_2 \cdots h_{M_R}] \qquad (4)$$

For s denoting the transmitted signal symbol, the received signal $y \in C^{M_R \times 1}$ can be expressed as

$$y = hs + v \qquad (5)$$

The received signal vector from all received antennas is combined using one of the various combining techniques such as selection combining (SC), maximal ratio combining (MRC) or equal gain combining (EGC) to enhance the received signal SINR. The most notable drawbacks of the receive diversity technique is the computational burden on the receiver site, which leads to high power consumption on the receiver, which is bad design trade-off.

Transmit diversity gain is extracted by what is called space time codes (STC) which require only simple linear processing at the receiver to decode the received signal. Space time codes are classified into space time block codes (STBC) and space time trellis codes (STTC) families. In general, STTC families achieve better performance than STBC families at the expense of more computational complexity. Well known example and starting point for investigation into these STBC diversity techniques is the basic Alamouti method (Alamouti, 1998) which has diversity gain of the order $2M_R$. The main drawback design limitation of the basic Alamouti method is the constraints on the number of transmit antennas to two. Latest advances in SU-MIMO transmit diversity gain enhancement relax this design constraint by allowing coding for MIMO channel with more than two transmit antennas through what is known as orthogonal space time block codes (OSTBC) (Gershman & Sidiropoulos, 2005; Mary, Mischa Dohler, Gorce, & Villemau, 2011; Tarokh, Jafarkhani, & Calderbank, 1999). In this method, the orthogonal structure of the code is used to achieve maximum likelihood decoding simply by decoupling of the signals transmitted from different antennas rather than using joint detection

2.4 SINGLE User MIMO System Capacity without Channel State Information

Without CSI at the transmitter, the MIMO channel capacity is given in (Telatar, 1995). For time-invariant communication channel, the MIMO capacity is defined as the maximum mutual information between the channel input and the channel output and it is given by:

$$C = B \log_2 \left\| I + \frac{1}{\sigma_v^2} HR_s H^* \right\| bit / s \qquad (6)$$

where:

B : Bandwidth in (Hz)

R_s : channel covariance matrix of the transmitted signal

$P_T = tr(R_s)$: The total power constraints.

For SU-MIMO channel with Gaussian random matrix and i.i.d elements, this channel capacity is maximized by averaging the total transmit power over all transmit antennas. Thus, the input covariance matrix R_s is selected as

$$R_s = \frac{P_T}{N_T} I_{N_T} \qquad (7)$$

with power constraints $Tr(R_s) \leq P_T$, where P_T is the total MIMO transmit power. Substituting the power constraints in the average capacity, Equation (6) can be rewritten such that:

$$C = B \log_2 \left\| I + \frac{1}{\sigma_v^2} \frac{p_T}{N_T} HH^* \right\| bit / s \qquad (8)$$

And for the case of SIMO configuration (one transmit antenna and multiple M_R receive antennas) the channel capacity reduces to:

$$C_{SIMO} = B \log_2 (1 + \frac{P}{\sigma_v^2} \|h\|_F^2) bit / s \qquad (9)$$

For the case of MISO configuration (N_T transmit antenna and one receive antennas) the channel capacity reduces to:

$$C_{SIMO} = B \log_2 (1 + \frac{1}{\sigma_v^2} \frac{p}{N_T} \|h\|_F^2) bit / s \qquad (10)$$

On the other hand, if the communication channel is time-variant SU-MIMO channel, the capacity become random or ergodic and is given by:

$$C_{ergodic} = E\left\{B\log_2\left\|I + \frac{1}{\sigma_v^2}\frac{p}{N_T}HH^*\right\|\right\} \qquad (11)$$

This kind of system capacity is hard to evaluate, and it has no significant practical meaning. Thus, in such cases, the system designer can use some kind of valuable system outage metric for system performance evaluations

2.5 Single User MIMO Processing with CSIT

When CSI is available at both transmitter and receiver, all kinds of MIMO gains (diversity, spatial multiplexing and beam forming) can be extracted and optimized. In practice, CSI can be acquired by the transmitter either through feedback channels in frequency division duplex (FDD) system or just taking the transpose of the received channel as an estimate of the transmit channel in the case of time invariant time division duplex (TDD) system. For spatial multiplexing gain, transmission is optimized by what is called channel precoding and decoding (Costa, 1983). In SU-MIMO channel with CSI available at the transmitter, the precoder is calculated and multiplied with user data and launched through N_T transmit antennas. At the receiver, the received signal vector from M_R received antennas is processed by the optimized linear decoder. The general form of the received signal can be written as:

$$y = HFS + V \qquad (12)$$

where F is the precoding matrix.

Different constraints and conditions were used to design this precoding matrix. Generalized method of joint optimum precoder and decoder for SU-MIMO system is given in (Sampath, et al., 2001). In this method, minimum mean square error performance criteria are used. As the name suggests, this framework is general. It solves for any QoS performance criteria like minimum BER or maximum information rate. Among the other simplest methods of precoding is to apply simple linear pre-equalizer like zero forcing, MMSE or code book based techniques. Spatial diversity is also optimized when the CSI is available at the transmitter. Precoding across the space time block code or transmit antenna selection is two of the most notable closed loop spatial diversity optimization techniques.

2.6 Single User MIMO with CSI Transmission Channel Capacity

The general capacity formula for the SU-MIMO system with CSI available at the transmitter is given by:

$$C = B\left[\log_2\left\|I + \frac{1}{\sigma_v^2}HR_sH^*\right\|\right]bit/S \qquad (13)$$

This capacity depend on the channel realization H and the input covariance matrix, thus from the assumption of the availability of CSI at the transmitter, for any channel realization, there exist an optimum choice of the input covariance matrix R_s such that the channel capacity is maximized under transmit power constraints. The maximum capacity is shown to be achieved by what is so-called water-filling solution which can be summarized as follows:

The SU-MIMO channel matrix is diagonalized using the eigenvalue decomposition

Figure 2. MIMO channel capacity with CSI available at transmitter and water filling power allocation for different numbers of transmit and receive antenna configuration

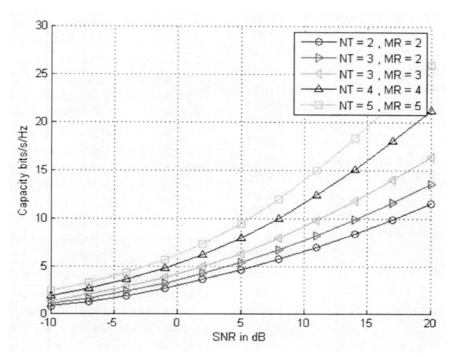

$$(HH^*) \Rightarrow V\Lambda V \qquad (14)$$

where:

$$\Lambda = \begin{bmatrix} \lambda_1 & 0 \cdots & 0 \\ 0 & \cdot & 0 \\ \vdots & \ddots & \vdots \\ 0 & 0 \dots & \lambda_{N_T} \end{bmatrix} \qquad (15)$$

where V is unitary.

For generalization, we assume that the rank of (HH^*) is (r), the power distribution policy is to allocate more power to the strongest Eigen mode and less power to the weak Eigen modes. Figure 2 shows the maximum capacity using the water filling algorithm for the point-to-point SU-MIMO link with different number of antenna configuration at transmitter and receiver.

2.7 MIMO Receiver Design

MIMO receiver design is one of the hot topics of wireless communication research in the last decade. Many receiving techniques were reported to decode this kind of transmission. Decoder design ranges from simple linear methods such as zero-forcing(ZF), minimum mean square error (MMSE) to complex sphere sub-optimal decoding and optimal maximum likelihood detections (MLD) (Tse & Viswanath, 2005).

Zero-forcing (ZF) method is a simple linear transform for the received symbol to remove the inter-channel interference by multiply the received signal by the inverse of the channel matrix (Wang et al., 2007). If perfect CSI (complex channel gain matrix) is available at the receiver, the zero-forcing estimate of the transmitted symbol vector can be written as:

$$\overline{y} = G(HS + V) = S + GV \qquad (16)$$

where the decoder is calculated from $G = (H^*H)^{-1}H^*$ which is the pseudo inverse of the MIMO channel matrix.

In ZF, the complexity reduction comes at the expense of noise enhancements which result in some performance loss compared to other MIMO receiving methods.

Minimum Mean Square Error (MMSE) Receiver is another simple receiver. The MMSE balances between interference mitigation and noise enhancement (Jiang, Varanasi, & L, 2011). Thus, at low SNR values MMSE outperform the ZF receiver. Using the CSIR, the MMSE MIMO receiver calculatea the decoding factor G which maximize the expectation criteria:

$$E\{[Gy - S][Gy - S]^*\} \tag{17}$$

Solving this MMSE criterion analytically gives:

$$G = (H^*H + \sigma_v^2 I)^{-1}H^* \tag{18}$$

Successive Interference Cancelation (SIC) method is a non linear receiver technique. Additional nonlinear steps like successive interference cancelation are added to the original ZF and MMSE equalizers. The resulting versions are ZF-SIC and MMSE-SIC decoding method. The idea of SIC receiver is as shown in Figure 3. The data layers symbols are decoded and subtracted successively from the next received data symbol starting with the highest SINR received signal at each decoding stage. The main drawback of this kind of receiver structure is the error propagations.

Maximum Likelihood (ML) decoding achieves the best performance in terms of BER among all the MIMO decoding techniques. The decoder searches for the input vector S that minimizes:

$$\|y - HS\|_F^2 \tag{19}$$

Here $\|.\|_F^2$ denote the Frobenius norm. The complexity of the decoder increases exponentially as the number of transmits antennas and receives antenna increase. In spite of it is good BER performance; ML decoding is not used in any practical system.

Sphere Decoding Family is a new type of decoding technique which aims to reduce the computational complexity of the ML decoding technique. In the sphere decoder, the received signal is compared with the closest lattice point. Since each codeword is represented by a lattice point, the number of lattice points scanned in a sphere decoder depends on the initial radius of the sphere and the correctness of the codeword is in turn dependent on the SNR of the system. The search in Sphere decoding is restricted by drawing a circle around the received signal in such a way so as to encompass small number of lattice points. This entails a search of sub-set of the code words in the constellation and allows only those code words to be checked that happen to fall within the sphere. All code words outside the sphere are not taken into consideration for decoding.

3. PRECODING LITERATURE REVIEW

3.1 Multi-User Multiple Input Multiple Outputs (MU-MIMO) Model

Multi-user multiple input multiple output system (MU-MIMO) refers to the system which has multiple antennas at the transmitter(s) and multiple antennas at the receiver (s) to improve the BER performance (diversity gain) or enhance the total sum rate (multiplexing gain). In general MU-MIMO system configuration scenario, N_T transmit antennas are located at the base station front end. The transmitter sends multiple K data vectors to a set of K individual users. Each individual user $i = 1, \cdots K$ is equipped with M_{R_i} re-

Figure 3. Successive interference cancelation decoding diagram for spatial multiplexed signal vector

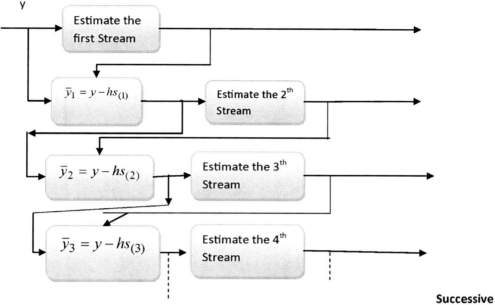

Successive

ceive antennas as shown in Figure 4. By taking the total number of antennas at the all user terminals to be equal to:

$$M_R = \sum_{i=1}^{K} M_{R_i} \qquad (20)$$

Using this basic system setting, the overall system parameters are defined as follows:

The MIMO channel from the base station to the ith user $H_i \in C^{M_{R_i} \times N_T}$ is given by:

$$H_i = \begin{bmatrix} h_{11} & \cdots & h_{1,N_T} \\ \vdots & \ddots & \vdots \\ h_{M_{R_i},1} & \cdots & h_{M_{R_i},N_T} \end{bmatrix} \in C^{M_{R_i} \times N_T} \qquad (21)$$

The combined channel matrix from the central node base station to the all users is given by:

$$H_c = [H_1^T H_2^T \cdots H_K^T]^T \in C^{M_R \times N_T} \qquad (22)$$

The downlink signal model form the central base station to user is given by:

$$y_c = M(H_c FX + V) \qquad (23)$$

where:

$X = [S_1^T S_2^T \cdots S_K^T]^T \in C^{D \times 1}$: is the combined transmit signals from the base stations to all K users.

$y_c = [y_1^T y_2^T \cdots y_K^T]^T \in C^{D \times 1}$: Is the combined received signal vectors for all the K users.

$V = [V_1^T V_2^T \cdots V_K^T]^T \in C^{M_R \times 1}$: is the combined additive white Gaussian noise at all receivers' front ends.

Figure 4. General block diagram of MU-MIMO system

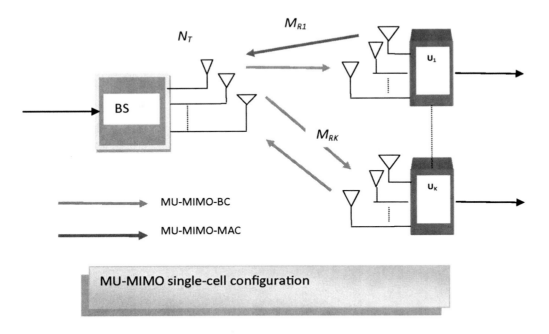

$$
M = \begin{bmatrix} M_1 & \cdots & 0 \\ \vdots & \ddots & \vdots \\ 0 & \cdots & M_k \end{bmatrix} \in C^{D \times M_R} : \text{ is the combined}
$$

decoding matrix for all users in the system
$F = [F_1 F_2 \cdots F_K] \in C^{N_T \times D}$: is the combined pre-coding matrix for all users

The vector $y_i \in C^{d_i \times 1}$ and $S_i \in C^{d_i \times 1}$ are the received and transmitted data vectors of the ith user respectively. An Important condition here is that the length of multiplexed data vector to the ith user should satisfy the individual user channel rank condition:

$$
d_i \leq rank(H_i) \tag{24}
$$

So the total length of data stream vector trans-mitted to all users in the MU-MIMO systems D is given by:

$$
D = \sum_{i=1}^{K} d_i \tag{25}
$$

$V_i \in C^{M_{R_i} \times 1}$ is the additive white Gaussian noise vector at the input of the ith user receive. And the matrices $M_i \in C^{d_i \times M_{R_i}}$, $F_i \in C^{N_T \times d_i}$ are the ith user decoding and precoding matrices respectively. By the same way similar to the downlink MU-MIMO channel definition, the uplink MU-MIMO reverse channel from all users to the central point base station can be modeled by:

$$
y = R(H_c^{T} EX + V_r) \tag{26}
$$

where V_r is the additive white Gaussian noise vector at the input of the base station antennas.

The combined matrices R and E are given by:

$$R = [R_1^T \cdots R_K^T]^T \in C^{D \times N_T}$$

$$E = \begin{bmatrix} E_1 & \cdots & 0 \\ \vdots & \ddots & \vdots \\ 0 & \cdots & E_k \end{bmatrix} \in C^{M_R \times D} \quad (27)$$

where $E_i \in C^{M_{R_i} \times d_i}$ and $R_i \in C^{d_i \times N_T}$ are the ith user precoding and decoding matrices on the MU-MIMO uplink respectively.

The received signal at any arbitrary user i is given by:

$$y_i = H_i F_{a_i} S_i + H_i \sum_{\substack{j=1 \\ J \neq i}}^{k} F_{a_j} S_j + V_i \quad (28)$$

Based on the system modeling in Equations 20-28 and the diagram in Figure 4, we can differentiate between two main types of multi-user MIMO channels:

- Reverse uplink multiple access MU-MIMO channel (MU-MIMO-MAC) (many-to-one transmission).
- Forward downlink Broadcast MU-MIMO channel (MU-MIMO-BC)(one-to-many transmission)

3.2 MU-MIMO Capacity Regions

In Shannon information theoretic sense, when CSI is available at the transmitter and receiver, the transmitter can adapt or precode the transmitted signal relative to the CSI. By definition, the Shannon channel capacity of time-invariant channel is defined as the maximum mutual information between channel input and channel output. In MU-MIMO system model of Figure 4, there are two communications channels namely, the MU-MIMO-MAC and the MU-MIMO-BC, the maximum achievable channel capacity or bit rate of these is characterized by what is called

sum rate region or capacity region. Next section describe the maximum achievable sum rate region for both the Gaussian MU-MIMO Multiple access (MU-MIMO-MAC) and the Gaussian MU-MIMO broadcast (MU-MIMO-BC), which is the maximum theoretical upper bound rate for any sub-optimal practical method.

3.2.1 The Maximum Rate Region for MU-MIMO MAC

It has been shown that the maximum Shannon information theoretic sum rate region for the Gaussian uplink MU-MIMO-MAC can be found from the solution of the individual power constraints information theoretic objective function as given in Equation 29 (COVER & THOMAS, 2006).

$$C_{MAC}(H_1^H, \cdots, H_k^H, P_{T_1} P_{T_2} \cdots P_{T_K})$$
$$= \max_{Tr(Q_i) \leq P_{T_i}} \log \left| I + \sum_{i=1}^{k} H_i^* Q_i H_i \right| \quad (29)$$

where Q_i is the uplink input covariance matrix for the ith user.

This objective function is concave over the covariance matrices, the constraints are separable (individual trace constraints on each user covariance matrix), there are many numerical method exist for solving this kind of convex optimization problem example of these methods are: Interior point method, mini-max method, A steepest descent method and Alternative dual decomposition(Boyd & Vandenberghe, 2008). The Iterative water-filling algorithm (Yu, Rhee, Boyd, & Cio, 2001) is one of the best algorithms proposed to solve this problem. In this algorithm, one user optimize it is covariance matrix while treating the signal from all other users as interference. In the next step, the next user in order optimize his covariance matrix while treating all other users including the updated covariance matrix of the previous user as interference and so on.

While maximum likelihood (ML) is the best optimal decoding method that can achieve this sum capacity recently it is also shown that minimum mean square error with successive interference cancelation (MMSE-SIC) can also achieve this maximum capacity. MMSE-SIC means that user's data are decoded sequentially, and for any user to be decoded treats all other users to be decoded as interference, and subtract the previously decoded users from the received signal.

3.2.2 The Maximum Rate Region for MU-MIMO Broadcast Channel

Information theoretic results shows that the maximum rate region for the downlink MU-MIMO-BC channel is achieved by dirty paper coding strategy (Caire & Shamai, 2003). Calculation of the maximum rate region from the Direct optimization over the transmit covariance matrix of the MU-MIMO-BC is computationally complex non-convex problem. Thus finding the optimal rates and optimum transmission policy is computationally hard and not trivial problem. This because the objective functions is not concave over the set of user's covariance matrices.

$$C_{BC}(H_1, \cdots, H_k, P_T) = \max_{\sum_{i=1}^{k} Tr(\Sigma_i) \leq P_T}$$
$$= \log\left|I + H_1\Sigma_1 H_1^*\right| + \log\frac{\left|I + H_2(\Sigma_1 + \Sigma_2)H_2^*\right|}{\left|I + H_2\Sigma_1 H_2^*\right|}$$
$$+ \cdots + \log\frac{\left|I + H_k(\Sigma_1 + \cdots + \Sigma_k)H_k^*\right|}{\left|I + H_k(\Sigma_1 + \cdots + \Sigma_{k-1})H_k^*\right|}$$

$$(30)$$

where Σ_i is the ith user input covariance matrix on the downlink.

The great duality theory presented by (Jindel, Rhee, Vishwanath, Jafar, & Goldsmith, 2005) transform this non-convex downlink MU-MIMO-BC problem into a convex sum power uplink MU-MIMO problem which is much simpler to solve.

$$C_{MAC/BC}(H_1^H, \cdots, H_k^H, P_T)$$
$$= \max_{\sum_{i=1}^{K} Tr(Q_i) \leq P_T} \log\left|I + \sum_{i=1}^{k} H_i^* Q_i H_i\right| \quad (31)$$

The Solution of this convex optimization problem by maximization over the uplink covariance matrices $Q_1 Q_2 \cdots Q_K$ subject to the total power constraints P_T is going to be trivial (concave problem). Simple algorithm utilizing the water-filling framework used to solve the individual power constraint MU-MIMO MAC is developed (Jindel, et al., 2005). This algorithm called the sum power iterative water-filling because it solves sum power constraints problem, instate if separable power constraint as in the NU-MIMO-MAC.

Sum power Iterative water-filling algorithm:

- Generate the effective channels for each user use

$$V_i = H_i(I + \sum_{J \neq i} H_j^* Q_j^{n-1} H_j)^{-1/2}$$

- Treating these effective channels as parallel non-interfering channels, find the concave matrix $\{S_i^n\}_{i=1}^k$ by water-filling with total power P

$$\{S_i^n\}_{i=1}^k =$$
$$\arg\max_{\{S_i\}_{i=1}^k, \sum_{i=1}^{K} tr(S_i) \leq P_T} \sum_{i=1}^{K} \log\left|I + (V_i^n)^* S_i V_i^n\right|$$

- Compute the updated covariance matrix Q_i^n as

$$Q_i^n = \frac{1}{K}S_i^n + \frac{K-1}{K}Q_i^{n-1}$$
$$i = 1, \cdots, K$$

By utilizing duality theory, we can transform the calculated uplink covariance matrices to the downlink covariance matrices to find the maximum rate region for the MU-MIMO-BC channel. To conclude, maximum upper bound capacity regions for MU-MIMO-MAC and MU-M IMO-BC are explained, both MMSE with SIC and Costa information theoretic dirty paper coding are maximum achieving rate strategies for MU-MIMO-MAC and MU-MIMO-BC respectively.

3.3 Linear Precoding Transmission Techniques for MU-MIMO-BC

Having in mind the computational complexity of the nonlinear DPC precoding methods, the research community gives much preference to investigations of simple computationally linear precoding techniques. Many performance measures and conditions were used to develop linear precoding methods for MU-MIMO downlink BC system that going to be very hard to survey all of them. Generally, one can divide the MU-MIMO linear precoding methods in the literature into two categories, namely, methods that formulate the design problem as an independent problem (Giang, Yang, Shu, & Gang, 2010; Joham,

Utschick, Nossek, & J.A., 2005; Park, Chun, & Park, 2009; Sadek, Tarighat, & Sayed, 2007b; Q. H. Spencer, Swindlehurst, & Haardt, 2004) and methods that jointly design both the precoding and decoding matrices (Lee & Oh, 2007; Schubert, Shi, Jorswiech, & Boche, 2005; Wiesel, Eldar, & Shamai, 2006). One more possible classification is to distinguish between formulations that provide closed-form solution expressions for the precoding matrix versus other formulations results in Iterative solutions which have higher computational complexity than other linear closed form solution method. Table 1, list and summarize a set of linear precoding methods along with their advantage and disadvantages of each method.

Generally precoding problem formulated as joint optimization of both precoding and decoding matrices have better results with more computational cost. In the next section, we discuss some linear precoding transmission methods namely the zero-forcing precoding (ZFP), Minimum mean square error (MMSE) precoding, Successive Minimum mean square error (SMMSE) precoding, regularized Block diagonalization (RBD) precoding and Signal to leakage plus noise ratio (SLNR) precoding methods.

Table 1. Linear precoding transmission techniques summary

Precoding Method	Merits	Demerits
Zero-forcing or (channel Inversion)(Q. H. Spencer, et al., 2004)	• Very Simple	• Total number of antennas at receivers constraints, • low performance
Minimum mean square error (MMSE) (M. Joham, Kusume, Gzara, Utschick, & Nossek, 2002)	• Simple • Related to QoS measures	• Total number of antennas at receivers constraints
Successive minimum mean square error (SMMSE) (Lee & Oh, 2007)	• related to QoS measures • No constraint on numbers of antennas at the receivers	• Complex in computations • Low performance
Regularized block Diagonalization (RBD) (V. Stankovic & Haardt, 2008)	• No constraint on numbers of antennas at the receivers	• Low performance
Signal to leakage noise ratio- Generalized eigenvalue decomposition (SLNR-GEVD) (Lim, Ghogho, & McLernon, 2007; Sadek, Tarighat, & Sayed, 2007a)	• Very Simple	• Suboptimal solution • Computational Problems

3.3.1 Zero-Forcing (ZF) Precoding

In zero-forcing precoding, the precoding matrix is designed to eliminate all inter-user interference at the user terminal (Joham, et al., 2005). In this method, the number of receive antennas at the user terminal is restricted to one. Thus, the total number of antennas at all users is equal to the number of users $K = M_R$. The precoding matrix is defined as $F = \chi f_a$, where the f_a unitary precoding matrix and the scaling factor χ are calculated from the following optimization:

$$f_a = \arg \min_{f_a} E\{\|Hf_a S - S\|_F^2\}$$
$$subject\ to: Hf_a = I_{M_R} \tag{32}$$

The scaling parameter χ is selected to fulfill the total power constraints such that:

$$\chi^2 \|f_a\|_F^2 \leq P_T \tag{33}$$

With an assumption of i.i.d complex data sample to be transmitted S, the solution of the optimization problem in Equation 32 is given by the Pseudo-inverse of the combined channel matrix of all users as follows:

$$f_a = H^*(HH^*)^{-1}\ and\ \chi = \sqrt{\frac{P_T}{\|f_a\|_F^2}} \tag{34}$$

In addition to it is constraints on the number of receive antennas, Zero-forcing precoding method suffer from noise enhancement at the receiver which require more transmit power to eliminate its effects.

3.3.2 Minimum Mean Square Error (MMSE) Precoding

The same like MMSE receiver, the MMSE precoder is designed to balance between the inter-user interference mitigation and noise enhancement to minimize the total BER (Schubert. & Boche, 2004). In MMSE method, the precoder is designed from the following optimization

$$f_a = \arg \min_{f_a} E\{\|\chi^{-1}y - S\|_F^2\}$$
$$subject\ to: \tag{35}$$
$$\chi^2 \|f_a S\|_F^2 \leq P_T$$

With an assumption of i.i.d complex sample vector transmitted data S the solution of the optimization problem in Equation (35) is given by

$$f_a = (H^*H + \varphi I_{N_T})^{-1} H^* \tag{36}$$

where the scaling parameters χ and φ are given by:

$$\varphi = \frac{\sigma_v^2 M_R}{P_T}\ and\ \chi = \sqrt{\frac{P_T}{\|f_a\|_F^2}} \tag{37}$$

The main drawbacks of the MMSE precoding method is it limitation and restriction in the number of receive antenna at any user terminal to one and the total number of receive antennas is equal to the number of users $K = M_R$ and should be less than or equal to the total number of transmit antennas $N_T \geq M_R$.

3.3.3 Successive Minimum Mean Square Error (SMMSE) Precoding Method

In the SMMSE precoding method the precoding matrix F_{a_i} is derived from the linear transmit MMSE optimization by neglecting the contribution of the interference between signal streams at one user to the total sum of the MSE. By another words, the interference of other co-channel users to the signal arriving at the ith e user j^{th} receive antenna is cancelled independently from the other antenna at the same user terminal. Thus, the jth column of the ith user precoding matrix is defined using the following optimization (Lee & Oh, 2007; Veljko Stankovic, 2007):

$$fa_i^j = \arg\min_{fa_i^j} E\{\left\|\bar{H}_i^j fa_i^j \bar{z}_i^j + \frac{\bar{v}^j}{\chi} - \bar{z}_i^j\right\|_F^2\}$$

$$(38)$$

Such that $\chi\|Fa_i\| \le P_T$ is the total power constraints, the matrix $\bar{H}_i^j$ and the vectors $\bar{Z}_i^j$ and $\bar{v}_i^j$ are corresponding to the ith users $i = 1, \cdots, K$ and the jth receive antenna $j = 1, \cdots, M_{R_i}$, which are defined by:

$$\bar{H}_i^j = \begin{bmatrix} h_i^{jT} \\ H_1 \\ \vdots \\ H_{i-1} \\ H_{i+1} \\ \vdots \\ H_K \end{bmatrix} \bar{z}_i^j = \begin{bmatrix} z_i^{jT} \\ z_1 \\ \vdots \\ z_{i-1} \\ z_{i+1} \\ \vdots \\ z_K \end{bmatrix} \text{ and } \bar{v}_i^j = \begin{bmatrix} v_i^{jT} \\ v_1 \\ \vdots \\ v_{i-1} \\ v_{i+1} \\ \vdots \\ v_K \end{bmatrix} \quad (39)$$

where

h_i^{jT} : Is the jth row of the ith user channel matrix,

$\bar{z}_i^j$: Is the jth element of the ith vector,

v_i^j : Is the noise at the input of the ith user j^{th} receive antenna.

By analytically solving the optimization in Equation 38, the column of the precoding matrix F_{a_i} is given by:

$$fa_i^j = (\bar{H}_i^{j*}\bar{H}_i^j + \varphi \ I_{N_T})^{-1}\bar{H}_i^{j*}$$

$$\chi = \frac{P_T}{\|Fa_i\|}$$

where

$$\varphi = \frac{\sigma_v^2 K}{P_T} \tag{40}$$

for any $i = 1 \cdots K$, and $j = 1 \cdots M_{R_i}$

After mitigation of the multi-user interference (MUI) by designing the matrix F_{a_i}, the interference domain of the MU-MIMO system is resolved to a set of parallel SU-MIMO channels. Further step can be taken to optimize the parallel SU-MIMO transmission by one of the well known SU-MIMO precoding method like what presented by (Sampath, et al., 2001).

The main advantage of SMMSE precoding method is the relaxation of the constraints on the number of the base station transmit antenna ($N_T \ge M_R$) to be greater than or equal to the sum of users receive antennas. On the other hand the method neglect to take into account the contribution of intra-user antenna interference which lead to poor performance, furthermore, calculating the precoding matrix vector by vector is also increase the computational load linearly with the sum number of receive antennas for all users.

3.3.4 Regularized Block Diagonalization (RBD) Precoding Method

RBD precoding method which is firstly proposed in (V. Stankovic & Haardt, 2008) is a generalization of block diagonalization (BD) method (Q. Spencer & Haardt, 2002). RBD relax the limitation condition of the BD method on the number of transmit antennas to be greater than or equal to the total number of all receiver antennas. Considering the MU-MIMO-BC system model, and the diagram in figure 4, for system consist of K simultaneous user, each with M_{R_i} receive antennas, for $i = 1, \cdots, K$. The total number of all user receive antennas is

$$M_R = \sum_{i=1}^{K} M_{R_i} \qquad (41)$$

In the RBD precoding method the precoding matrix $F_i = \chi F_{a_i} F_{b_i}$ is designed in two steps, in the first step, the matrix F_{a_i} is designed with the main goal to mitigate the inter-user interference at multiuser system level. In the second step, the matrix F_{b_i} is designed to optimize individual user transmission.

In RBD precoding, the matrix F_{a_i} and the scaling factor χ are calculated from the following optimization:

$$F_{a_i} = \arg \min_{F_a} E\{\|\chi^{-1} y - S\|_F^2\}$$

$$= \arg \min_{F_a} E\{\|(HF_a - I_{M_R})S\|_F^2 + \frac{\|V\|_F^2}{\chi}\}$$

$$\chi \|Fa_i F_{b_i}\| \leq P_T \qquad (42)$$

The parameter χ is used to fulfill the base station total transmit power constraints. The closed

form solution of the optimization function in Equation (42) taking into account the total system power constraints gives

$$F_a = \tilde{V}_l (\tilde{\Sigma}_i^T \tilde{\Sigma}_i + \frac{M_R \sigma_n^2}{P_T} I_{M_T})^{\frac{-1}{2}}$$

$$\chi = \frac{P_T}{\|Fa_i F_{b_i}\|} \qquad (43)$$

where $\tilde{V}_l$ and $\tilde{\Sigma}_i$ are the unitary and singular value matrices resulted from the singular value decomposition of the ith user interference domain matrix $\tilde{H}_i$ which constructed from.

$$\tilde{H}_i = [H_1^T \cdots H_{i-1}^T H_{i+1}^T \cdots H_K^T]^T \in C^{(M_R - M_{R_i}) \times N_T} \qquad (44)$$

After mitigation of MUI by designing the matrix F_a the interference domain of the MU-MIMO system is resolved to a set of parallel SU-MIMO channels. In the following step, any individual SU-MIMO performance optimization (BER, RATE, QoS, etc...) can be carried on to construct the matrix F_{b_i}. A generalized method for SU-MIMO precoding optimization is shown in (Sampath, et al., 2001).

3.3.5 Signal to Leakage Plus Noise Ratio Precoding Method

This precoding method is based on the novel signal to leakage plus noise ratio (SLNR) metric proposed by (Sadek, et al., 2007b). In MU-MIMO-BC, recall the received signal at the ith user can be written as:

$$y_i = H_i F_{a_i} S_i + H_i \sum_{\substack{j=1 \\ J \neq i}}^{k} F_{a_j} S_j + V_i \qquad (45)$$

The first term represent the desired signal to the ith user, the second term is the multi-user interference from the other user to the ith user, and the third term is the additive white Gaussian noise at the ith user antenna front end. In SLNR precoding method as shown in figure 5, the objective function is build such that the desired signal component to the ith user $\|H_i F_i\|_F^2$ is maximized with respect to the signal leaked from the ith user to all other users in the system $\sum_{\substack{j=1 \\ j \neq i}}^{K} H_j F_{a_i}$ plus the noise power at the ith user antennas front end, $M_{R_i} \sigma_v^2$. The SLNR objective function for the ith user can be written as:

$$SLNR_i = \frac{\|H_i F_{a_i}\|_F^2}{M_{R_i} \sigma_v^2 + \sum_{\substack{J=1 \\ j \neq i}}^{K} Hj F_{a_i}} \qquad (46)$$

By defining the auxiliary matrix $\tilde{H}_i$ as:

$$\tilde{H}_i = [H_1 \cdots H_{i-1} H_{i+1} \cdots H_K]^T$$

Assuming that the data vector symbols for each user are i.i.d with zero mean and unity variance and the $trace(F_{a_i} F_{a_i}^H) = M_{R_i}$. The optimization in Equation (47) can be rewritten as:

$$F_{a_i} = \arg\max_{F_{a_i}} \frac{(F_{a_i}^* H_i^* H_i F_{a_i})}{F_{ai}^* (\tilde{H}_i^* \tilde{H}_i + \sigma_v^2 I_{N_T}) F_{a_i}} \qquad (47)$$

Both Generalized Eigenvalue Decomposition (GEVD) and Generalized Singular Value Decomposition (GSVD) techniques were used to solve this fractional rational optimization problem (Park,

et al., 2009; Sadek, et al., 2007b). Like RBD, this method also relax the constraints on the number of transmit antennas and it has better BER performance than the RBD method. This method neglect to take into account the intra-user stream interference which results in limited performance.

Table 1 summarizes the reviewed Linear precoding methods that tends to have closed form solutions and the Figures 6, and 7 compare the BER performance of the RBD, SLNR-GEVD and PA-SLNR-FKT precoding transmission methods.

4. PROPOSED METHOD

4.1 Successive Per-Antenna Signal to Leakage Plus Noise Ratio (PA-SLNR) Maximization Precoding

The objective function originally proposed by (Sadek, et al., 2007a) maximizes SLNR of each user. This precoder is designed to cancel inter-user interference. The work in (Saeid, Jeoti, & Samir, 2011), however, proposes a new cost function that maximizes the per antenna SLNR (PA SLNR), which helps minimize inter-antenna interference and thus, the designed precoder has better performance than one that maximizes the overall SLNR per user. This is justified because per-antenna signal to leakage noise ratio as explained in Figure 6, takes into account the inter-antenna interference as well. For each ith user j^{th} receive antenna, The $PA - SLNR_i^j$, γ_i^j, is defined as ratio between the individual received antenna desired signal power to the interference introduced by the signal meant to that antenna to all other antennas in the system plus the noise power at the front of the receiving antenna. So for the ith user $i = 1, \cdots, K$, j^{th} receive antenna $j = 1, \cdots, M_{R_i}$, the signal to leakage noise ratio is given by:

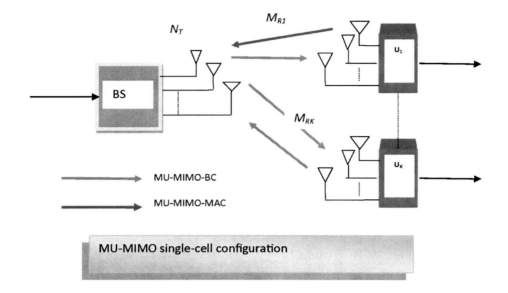

Figure 5. The definition of the desired signal and the leaked signal

$$\gamma_k^j = \frac{\left\| \hbar_i^j f_i^j \right\|_F^2}{\sum_{\substack{k=1 \\ k \neq i}}^{K} \left\| H_i f_i^j \right\|_F^2 + \sum_{\substack{m=1 \\ m \neq j}}^{M_{R_i}} \left\| \hbar_i^m f_i^j \right\|_F^2 + \sigma_{vi}^{2j}} \quad (48)$$

where $\hbar_i^m \in C^{1 \times N_T}$ is the ith user m^{th} antenna received row, $m = 1, \cdots, M_{R_i}, m \neq j$. If we define an auxiliary matrix $\tilde{\hbar}_i^j$ as the matrix contains user i received antennas rows except the jth antenna row as follows:

$$\tilde{\hbar}_i^j = \begin{vmatrix} h_k^{(1,1)} & h_k^{(1,2)} & \cdots & h_k^{(1,N_T)} \\ \vdots & \vdots & \vdots & \vdots \\ h_k^{(j-1,1)} & h_k^{(j-1,2)} & \cdots & h_k^{(j-1,N_T)} \\ h_k^{(j+1,1)} & h_k^{(j+1,2)} & \cdots & h_k^{(j+1,N_T)} \\ \vdots & \vdots & \vdots & \vdots \\ h_k^{(M_k,1)} & h_k^{(M_k,2)} & \cdots & h_k^{(M_k,N_T)} \end{vmatrix} \in C^{((M_{R_i}-1) \times N_T)}$$

$$(49)$$

and the combined channel matrix for all other system received antennas except the jth desired receive antenna channel row as:

$$\tilde{H}_i^j = [\tilde{\hbar}_k^{jT} H_1^T \cdots H_{k-1}^T H_{k+1}^T \cdots H_B^T]^T \quad (50)$$

From Equation (49) and Equation (50) the expression in (48) can be rewritten as:

$$\gamma_i^j = \frac{\left\| \hbar_i^j f_i^j \right\|_F^2}{\left\| \tilde{H}_i^j f_i^j \right\|_F^2 + \sigma_{vi}^{2j}} \quad (51)$$

Problem statement: For any receive antenna j of user i, select the precoding vector f_i^j, where $i = \{1, \cdots, K\}$, $j = \{1, \cdots, M_{R_i}\}$ such that the per-antenna signal to leakage noise ratio is maximized as

$$f_i^j = \arg \max_{f_i^j \in C^{N_T \times 1}} \frac{f_i^{jH} (\hbar_i^{jH} \hbar_i^j) f_i^j}{f_i^{jH} (\tilde{H}_i^{jH} \tilde{H}_i^j + \sigma_{vi}^{2j} I_{N_T}) f_i^j}$$

$$(52)$$

Figure 6. System model depicting all variables

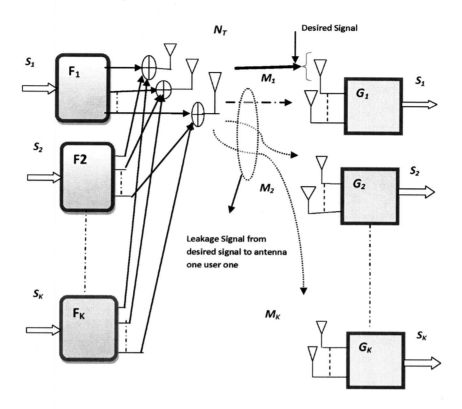

The optimization problem in Equation (52) deals with the jth antenna desired signal in the numerator and a combination of total leaked power from desired signal to antenna j to all other antennas plus noise power at the denominator. To calculate the precoding matrix for each user we need to calculate the precoding vector for each receive antenna independently. This requires solving the linear fractional optimization problem in Equation (52) $M_{R_i} \times K$ times using either GEVD as in (Sadek, et al., 2007a) or GSVD as in (Park, et al., 2009) which is high computational load to the base stations. In the next section, FKT transform based method for solving such series of linear fractional optimization problems is described and simple computational method for multi-streams MU-MIMO precoding algorithm is developed.

4.1.1 FKT Based Precoding Algorithm

As mentioned in (Fukunaga & Koontz, 1970; Zhang & Sim, 2006), for any given positive definite and symmetric (p.d.s) covariance matrices S_1 and S_2, the sum of these two matrices, i.e. S is still p.d.s and can be written as

$$S = S_1 + S_2 = \begin{bmatrix} U\, U_\perp \end{bmatrix} \begin{bmatrix} D & 0 \\ 0 & 0 \end{bmatrix} \begin{bmatrix} U^T \\ U_\perp^T \end{bmatrix} \quad (53)$$

Without loss of generality, S can be singular and $r = rank(S) < D$ .where $D = diag(\lambda_1, \cdots \lambda_r)$ and also $\lambda_1 \geq \cdots \geq \lambda_r > 0$ and $U \in C^{D \times r}$ is the set of eigenvectors that corresponds to the set of nonzero eigenvalues and $U_\perp \in C^{D \times (D-r)}$ is the orthogonal complement of U. From Equation

Figure 7. BER performance comparison of the MU-MIMO RBD, SLNR-GEVD and PA-SLNR transmission techniques under system configuration of $\left(N_T = 15, M_{R_i} = 5, K = 3 \right)$, a vector of 5 sample are QAM modulated and transmitted to each user

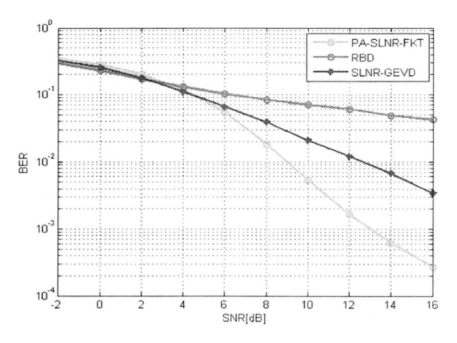

(53), Fukunaga Koontz transformation (FKT) matrix operator is defined as:

$$p = UD^{-1/2} \tag{54}$$

Using this transformation factor, the sum S can be whitened such that the whitening two matrices S_1 and S_2 gives the identity matrix as follows:

$$p^T S p = p^T (S_1 + S_2) p = \tilde{S}_1 + \tilde{S}_2 = I^{r \times r} \tag{55}$$

where $\tilde{S}_1 = p^T S_1 p$, $\tilde{S}_2 = p^T S_2 p$ are the transformed covariance matrices S_1 and S_2 respectively, and $I^{r \times r}$ is an identity matrix. If we suppose that v is an eigenvector of $\tilde{S}_1$ with corresponding eigenvalue λ_1 then $\tilde{S}_1 v = \lambda_1 v$ and since from

Equation (55) $\tilde{S}_1 = I - \tilde{S}_2$ thus, the following results can be pointed out:

$$\begin{aligned} (I - \tilde{S}_2) v &= \lambda_1 v \\ (I - \tilde{S}_2) v &= \lambda_1 v \end{aligned} \tag{56}$$

This means that $\tilde{S}_2$ has the same eigenvectors as $\tilde{S}_1$ but the corresponding eigenvalue $\lambda_2 = (1 - \lambda_1)$. Thus, we can conclude that the dominant eigenvectors of $\tilde{S}_1$ is the weakest eigenvectors of $\tilde{S}_2$ and vice versa. Based on the FKT transform analysis we see that $\tilde{S}_1$ and $\tilde{S}_2$ share the same eigenvectors reversely ordered and the sum of the two corresponding eigenvalues are equal to one. Thus we can write:

$$\tilde{S}_1 = V \Lambda_1 V^T \tag{57}$$

$$\tilde{S}_2 = V \Lambda_2 V^T \tag{58}$$

$$I = \Lambda_1 + \Lambda_2 \tag{59}$$

where $V \in C^{r \times r}$ is the matrix contains the sets of orthogonal eigenvectors and Λ_1, Λ_2 are the corresponding eigenvalues matrices. Thus, these given analyses conclude that FKT gives the best optimum solution of any fractional linear problem without going through any serious matrix inversion step.

By relating FKT transform analysis of the two covariance matrices, and the precoding design problem for MU-MIMO multiple streams (linear fractional optimization problem) and direct mapping of the optimization variable from Equation (52) to the FKT transform such as:

$$S_1 = \hbar_i^{jH} \hbar_i^{j} \tag{60}$$

$$S_2 = \tilde{H}_i^{jH} \tilde{H}_i^{j} + \sigma_i^{j} I_{N_T} \tag{61}$$

And consequently the sum of the two covariance matrices S becomes:

$$S = H_{com}^H H_{com} + \sigma_i^{j} I_N \tag{62}$$

According to the FKT analysis, we use Equation (62) to calculate the FKT factor and consequently we use this transformation factor to generate the shared eigenspace matrices $\tilde{S}_1$ and $\tilde{S}_2$ using the facts from Equation (57-59) for each receive antenna in the system. The shared eigen subspaces are orthogonal complement of each others, which means that the best principle eigenvectors of the first transformed covariance matrix ($\tilde{S}_1$) are the least principle eigenvector for the second transformed covariance matrix ($\tilde{S}_2$) and vice-versa. Thus, we can find the receive antenna precoding vector by simply multiply FKT factor

with the eigenvectors correspond to best eigenvalue of the transformed antenna covariance matrix or eigenvector that corresponding to the least eigenvalue of the transformed leakage plus noise covariance matrix. The most notable observation is that for the set of $M_{R_i} \times K$ receive antennas in the system, we need to compute the FKT transform factor one time only, which cuts down the computation load sharply. Algorithm 1 summarizes the computation steps of the precoding matrix for multiple K users in the system.

Algorithm 1. PA-SLNR MU-MIMO precoding based on FKT for multiple K independent users

Input: *all* **B** *users combined channel matrix*
$H_{com} = [H_1^T H_2^T \cdots H_K^T]^T$

Output: *multiple K users precoding matrices F_i such that,* $i = 1, \cdots, K$

    1.   *Compute the sum*
          $S = H_{com}^H H_{com} + \sigma_i^{j} I_{N_T}$

    2.   *Compute FKT factor* $P = UD^{-\frac{1}{2}}$ *from* $SVD(S)$

    3.   ***For*** *$i = 1$ to K*

    4.   ***For*** *$j = 1$ to M_{R_i}*

        ▪ *Transform the j receive antenna covariance matrix S_1 using the FKT factor P to $\tilde{S}_1$ and select the first eigenvector V_i^j from $\tilde{S}_1$*

        ▪ *The precoding vector correspond to the receive antenna j at user i is $f_i^j = P V_i^j$*

    5.   ***End***

        ▪ *The ith user precoding matrix is*
          $F_i = [f_i^1 \cdots f_i^{M_{R_i}}]$

    6.   ***End***

The algorithm takes the combined MU-MIMO channel matrix as well as the value of the noise covariance as inputs and outputs K users precoding matrices. The algorithm computes the FKT factor in step one and two and iterates K times from step three to six to calculate the precoding matrices for K number of users. For each user there are M_{R_i} sub-iteration operations from step four to five to calculate any user precoding matrix vector by vector.

4.2 Results and Discussions

The BER performance of the proposed PA-SLNR FKT MU-MIMO precoding scheme is evaluated through Monte-Carlo Integral simulation for different MU-MIMO broadcast system configurations. In each simulation setup, the entry of each kth user MIMO channel H_k is generated as complex white Gaussian entries with zero mean and unit variance. Also the vector of all users' data symbols are 4-QAM modulated and spatially multiplexed at the base station. At the receivers, matched filter is used to decode each user's data.

Figure 7 compares the BER performance of the proposed PA-SLNR precoding and the reference literature results of SLNR-GEVD as well as the RBD precoding schemes for the MU-MIMO broadcast system configurations of $\left(N_T = 15, M_{R_i} = 5, K = 3\right)$. In this configuration, the base station modulates, spatially multiplexes and precodes a vector of 5 symbols to each user. The BER is calculated over 2000 MU-MIMO channel realization for each algorithm.

The proposed method outperforms both SLNR-GEVD and RBD. At BER equal to 10^{-2} there is approximately 2.4dB performance gain difference between PA-SLNR-FKT and SLNR-GEVD.

Figure 8 compares the BER performance of the proposed PA-SLNR and the literature reference methods SLNR-GEVD and RBD precoding schemes for the MU-MIMO broadcast channel system configurations of

$$\left(N_T = 12, M_{R_i} = 4, K = 3\right).$$

In this configuration, the base station modulates, spatially multiplexes and precodes a vector of length 4 symbols to each user. The BER is calculated over 2000 MU-MIMO channel realization for each algorithm.

Here too, the proposed method outperforms SLNR-GEVD and RBD. At BER equal to 10^{-2} there are approximately 2.5dB performance gain difference between PA-SLNR-FKT and SLNR-GEVD method.

The performance improvement visible in both figure.7 and figure.8 is expected as it relates to minimization of antenna to antenna interference even for a given user in the formulation of the proposed technique. Furthermore, as discussed in (Saeid, et al., 2011), the outage probability of the proposed method is less than the outage probability of the literature reported method. Looking at the algorithm 1 of section 4.1.1, it can be argued that by computing FKT factor only once, the overall computational load is reduced.

5. CONCLUSION

In this book chapter, a detailed background on MIMO and an extensive survey on MU-MIMO precoding techniques are given. A new MU-MIMO precoding algorithm based on PA-SLNR and its solution based on Fukunaga and Koontz transform is proposed. This algorithm improves the BER performance of MU-MIMO. The method transforms MU-MIMO multiple stream channel in to a set of single antenna channels to effectively cancel inter-antenna interference and multiplex multiple data stream to each user. BER performance integral simulation results show that the proposed method outperforms the conventional method. And by making use of FKT transform computation the overall computational load of the proposed method is reduced.

Figure 8. BER performance comparison of the MU-MIMO RBD, SLNR-GEVD and PA-SLNR transmission techniques under system configuration of $\left(N_T = 12, M_{R_i} = 4, K = 3\right)$, a vector of 5 sample are QAM modulated and transmitted to each user

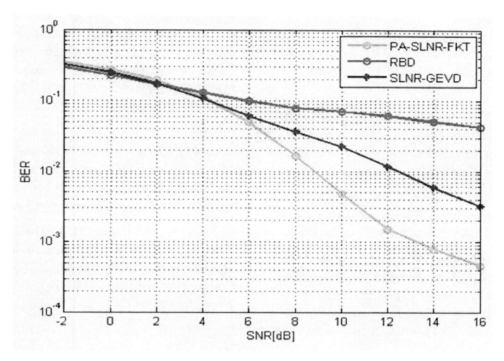

REFERENCES

Alamouti, S. M. (1998). A simple transmit diversity scheme for wireless communications. *IEEE Journal on Selected Areas in Communications*, *16*(8), 1451–1458. doi:10.1109/49.730453

Boyd, S., & Vandenberghe, L. (2008). *Convex optimization*. Cambridge, UK: Cambridge University Press.

Caire, G., & Shamai, S. (2003). On the achievable throughput of multi-antenna gaussian Broadcast Channel. *IEEE Transactions on Information Theory*, *49*(7), 1691–1706. doi:10.1109/TIT.2003.813523

Costa, M. (1983). Writing on dirt paper. *IEEE Transactions on Information Theory*, *29*(12), 439–441. doi:10.1109/TIT.1983.1056659

Cover, T. M., & Thomas, J. A. (2006). *Elements of information theory* (2nd ed.). John Wiley & Sons, Inc.

Etemad, K. (2008). Overview of mobile WiMAX technology and evolution. *IEEE Communications Magazine*, 31–40. doi:10.1109/MCOM.2008.4644117

Foschoini, G. J. (1996). Layered space-time architecture for wireless communication in a fading environment when using multi-element antennas. *Bell Labs Technical Iournals*, *1*(2), 41–49. doi:10.1002/bltj.2015

Fukunaga, K., & Koontz, W. L. G. (1970). Application of the Harhunen-loeve expansion to feature selection and ordering. *IEEE Transactions on Computers*, *19*(4), 311–317. doi:10.1109/T-C.1970.222918

Gallager, R. (Fall 2006). *Course materials for 6.450 principles of digital communications I.* MIT OpenCourseWare. Retrieved from http//ocw.mit.edu

Gershman, A. B., & Sidiropoulos, N. D. (2005). *Space-time processing for MIMO communications.* Johon Wiley & Sons, Ltd. doi:10.1002/0470010045

Giang, L., Yang, Y., Shu, F., & Gang, W. (2010). *SLNR precoding based on QBC with limited feedback in downlink CoMP system.* Paper presented at the Wireless Communications and Signal Processing Suzhou

Goldsmith, A. (2005). *Wireless communications.* Cambridge, UK: Cambridge University Press.

Jiang, Y., & Varanasi, M. K., & L, J. (2011). Performance analysis of ZF and MMSE equalizers for MIMO systems: An in-depth study of the high SNR regime. *IEEE Transactions on Information Theory, 57*(4), 2008–2026. doi:10.1109/TIT.2011.2112070

Jindel, N., Rhee, W., Vishwanath, S., Jafar, S. A., & Goldsmith, A. (2005). Sum power iterative water-filling for multi-antenna Gaussain broadcast channel. *IEEE Transactions on Information Theory, 51*(4), 1570–1580. doi:10.1109/TIT.2005.844082

Joham, M., Kusume, K., Gzara, M. H., Utschick, W., & Nossek, J. A. (2002). *Transmit Wiener filter for the downlink of TDDDS-CDMA systems.* Paper presented at the Spread Spectrum Techniques and Applications IEEE Seventh International Symposium.

Joham, M., Utschick, W., & Nossek, J. A. (2005). Linear transmit processing in MIMO communications systems. *IEEE Transactions on Signal Processing, 53*(8), 2700–2712. doi:10.1109/TSP.2005.850331

Lee, M., & Oh, S. K. (2007). *A per-user successive MMSE precoding technique in multiuser MIMO systems.* Paper presented at the Vehicular Technology Conference, VTC2007, Dublin.

Li, Q., Li, G., Lee, W., Lee, M.-I., Mazzarese, D., Clerckx, B., & Li, Z. (2010). MIMO techniques in WiMAX and LTE: A feature overview. *IEEE Communications Magazine, 48*(5), 86–92. doi:10.1109/MCOM.2010.5458368

Lim, M. C. H., Ghogho, M., & McLernon, D. C. (2007). *Spatial multiplexing in the multi-user MIMO downlink based on signal-to-leakage ratios.* Paper presented at the Global Telecommunications Conference, Washington Dc.

Lozano, A., & Jindal, N. (2010). Transmit diversity vs. spatial multiplexing in modern MIMO systems. *IEEE Transactions on Wireless Communications, 9*(1), 186–197. doi:10.1109/TWC.2010.01.081381

Mary, P., Mischa Dohler, Gorce, J.-M., & Villemau, G. (2011). Symbol error outage analysis of MIMO OSTBC systems over rice fading channels in shadowing environments. *IEEE Transactions on Wireless Communications, 10*(4), 1009–1014. doi:10.1109/TWC.2011.021611.091838

Parikh, J., & Basu, A. (2011). LTE advanced: The 4G mobile broadband technology. *International Journal of Computers and Applications, 13*(5), 17–21. doi:10.5120/1776-2449

Park, J., Chun, J., & Park, H. (2009, 14-18 June). *Efficient GSVD based multi-user MIMO linear precoding and antenna selection scheme.* Paper presented at the IEEE ICC 2009, Dresden.

Sadek, M., Tarighat, A., & Sayed, A. H. (2007a). Active antenna selection in multiuser MIMO communications. *IEEE Transactions on Signal Processing, 44*(4), 1498–1510. doi:10.1109/TSP.2006.888893

Sadek, M., Tarighat, A., & Sayed, A. H. (2007b). A leakage-based precoding scheme for downlink multi-user MIMO channels. *IEEE Transactions on Communications, 6*(5), 1711–1721. doi:doi:10.1109/TWC.2007.360373

Saeid, E., Jeoti, V., & Samir, B. B. (2011). *FKT based successive linear precoding for multiuser multiple input multiple output system.*

Sampath, H., Stoica, P., & Paulraj, A. (2001). Generalized linear precoder and decoder design for MIMO channels using the weighted MMSE criterion. *IEEE Transactions on Communications, 49*(12), 2198–2206. doi:10.1109/26.974266

Schubert, M., & Boche, M. (2004). Solution of the multiuser downlink beamforming problem with individual SINR constraints. *IEEE Transactions on Vehicular Technology, 53*(1), 18–28. doi:10.1109/TVT.2003.819629

Schubert, M., Shi, S., Jorswiech, E. A., & Boche, H. (2005). *Downlink sum-MSE transceiver optimization for linear multi-user MIMO systems.* Paper presented at the Signals, Systems and Computers, 2005.

Shiu, D.-S., Foschini, G. J., Gans, M. J., & Kahn, J. M. (2000). fading correlation and Its effect on the capacity of multielement antenna systems. *IEEE Transactions on Communications, 48*(3), 502–512. doi:10.1109/26.837052

Spencer, Q., & Haardt, M. (2002, November). *Capacity and downlink transmission algorithms for a multi-user MIMO channel.* Paper presented at the 36th Asilomar Conference on Signals, Systems, and Computers.

Spencer, Q. H., Swindlehurst, A. L., & Haardt, M. (2004). Zero-forcing methods for downlink spatial multiplexing in multiuser MIMO channels. *IEEE Transactions on Signal Processing, 52*(2), 461–471. doi:10.1109/TSP.2003.821107

Stankovic, V. (2007). Iterative successive MMSE multi-user MIMO transmit filtering. *Electrical Engineering in Japan, 20*(1), 45–55.

Stankovic, V., & Haardt, M. (2008). Generalized design of multi-user MIMO precoding matrices. *IEEE Transactions on Wireless Communications, 7*(3), 953–961. doi:10.1109/LCOMM.2008.060709

Tarokh, V., Jafarkhani, H., & Calderbank, A. R. (1999). Space–time block coding for wireless communications: Performance results. *IEEE Journal of Selected Topics in Communications, 17*(3), 451–460. doi:10.1109/49.753730

Telatar. (1995). *Capacity of multi-antenna Gaussian Channel.* ATT Bell Technical Memorandum.

Tse, D., & Viswanath, P. (2005). *Fundamentals of wireless communication.* Cambridge, UK: Cambridge university Press.

Wang, C., Au, E. K. S., Murch, R. D., Mow, W. H., Cheng, R. S., & Lau, A. V. (2007). *On the performance of the MIMO zero-forcing receiver in the presence of channel estimation error.* Paper presented at the Information Sciences and Interaction Sciences, Chengdu, China

Wiesel, A., Eldar, Y. C., & Shamai, S. (2006). Linear precoding via conic optimization for fixed MIMO receivers. *IEEE Transactions on Signal Processing, 54*(1), 161–176. doi:10.1109/TSP.2005.861073

Xiao, Y. (2005). IEEE 802.11N: Enhancements for higher throughput in wireless LANs. *IEEE Wireless Communications, 12*(6), 82–91. doi:10.1109/MWC.2005.1561948

Yu, W., Rhee, W., Boyd, S., & Cio, J. M. (2001). *Iterative water-filling for Gaussian vector multiple access channels.* Paper presented at the IEEE International Symposium on Information Theory, Washington DC.

Zhang, S., & Sim, T. (2006, 17-22 June). *When Fisher meets Fukunaga-Koontz: A new look at linear discriminants*. Paper presented at the IEEE Computer Society Conference on Computer Vision and Pattern Recognition (CVPR'06), New York.

ADDITIONAL READING

Alamouti, S. M. (1998). A simple transmit diversity scheme for wireless communications. *IEEE Journal on Selected Areas in Communications, 16*(8), 1451–1458. doi:10.1109/49.730453

Catreux, S., Driessen, P. F., & Greenstein, L. J. (2000). Simulation results for an interference-limited multiple-input multiple-output cellular system. *IEEE Communications Letters, 4*(11), 334–336. doi:10.1109/4234.892193

Costa, M. (1983). Writing on dirt paper. *IEEE Transactions on Information Theory, 29*(12), 439–441. doi:10.1109/TIT.1983.1056659

Khalid, F., & Speidel, J. (2010). Advances in MIMO techniques for mobile communications- A survey. *International Journal of Computer Network and Security, 3*(3), 213–252. doi:doi:10.4236/ijcns.2010.33031

Lee, J. (2006). *Dirty paper coding vs. linear precoding for MIMO broadcast channels*.

Sadek, M., Tarighat, A., & Sayed, A. H. (2007). A leakage-based precoding scheme for downlink multi-user MIMO channels. *IEEE Transactions on Communications, 6*(5), 1711–1721. doi:doi:10.1109/TWC.2007.360373

Schubert, M., & Boche, M. (2004). Solution of the multiuser downlink beamforming problem with individual SINR constraints. *IEEE Transactions on Vehicular Technology, 53*(1), 18–28. doi:10.1109/TVT.2003.819629

Spencer, Q., & Haardt, M. (2002, November). *Capacity and downlink transmission algorithms for a multi-user MIMO channel*. Paper presented at the 36th Asilomar Conference on Signals, Systems, and Computers.

Spencer, Q. H., Swindlehurst, A. L., & Haardt, M. (2004). Zero-forcing methods for downlink spatial multiplexing in multiuser MIMO channels. *IEEE Transactions on Signal Processing, 52*(2), 461–471. doi:10.1109/TSP.2003.821107

Tarokh, V., Jafarkhani, H., & Calderbank, A. R. (1999). Space–time block coding for wireless communications: Performance results. *IEEE Journal of Selected Topics in Communications, 17*(3), 451–460. doi:10.1109/49.753730

Telatar. (1995). *Capacity of multi-antenna Gaussian channel*. ATT Bell technical memorandum.

Section 3
Network Design

Chapter 8
Creating Realistic Vehicular Network Simulations

Kun-chan Lan
National Cheng Kung University, Taiwan

Chien-Ming Chou
National Cheng Kung University, Taiwan

Che-Chun Wu
National Cheng Kung University, Taiwan

ABSTRACT

A key component for Vehicular Ad-Hoc Network (VANET) simulations is a realistic vehicular mobility model, as this ensures that the conclusions drawn from simulation experiments will carry through to the real deployments. Node mobility in a vehicular network is strongly affected by the driving behavior such as route choices. While route choice models have been extensively studied in the transportation community, the effects of preferred route and destination on vehicular network simulations have not been discussed much in the networking literature. In this chapter, the authors describe the effect of route choices on vehicular network simulation. They also discuss how different destination selection models affect two practical ITS application scenarios: traffic monitoring and event broadcasting. The chapter concludes that selecting a sufficient level of detail in the simulations, such as modeling of route choices, is critical for evaluating VANET protocol design.

INTRODUCTION

Vehicular Ad-Hoc Network (VANET) communication has recently become an increasingly popular research topic in the area of wireless networking, as well as in the automotive industry. The goal

of VANET research is to develop a vehicular communication system to enable the quick and cost-efficient distribution of data for the benefit of passengers' safety and comfort.

While it is crucial to test and evaluate protocol implementations in a real world environment, simulations are still commonly used as a first step

DOI: 10.4018/978-1-4666-1797-1.ch008

Copyright © 2012, IGI Global. Copying or distributing in print or electronic forms without written permission of IGI Global is prohibited.

in the protocol development for VANET research. Several communication networking simulation tools already exist to provide a platform to test and evaluate network protocols, such as ns-2 (Breslau, 2000), OPNET (Chang, 1999) and Qualnet (http://www.scalable-networks.com/). However, these tools are designed to provide generic simulation scenarios, without being particularly tailored for applications in the transportation environment. In addition, simulations also play an important role in the field of transportation. A variety of simulation tools, such as PARAMICS (Cameron, 1996), CORSIM (Halati, 1997) and VISSIM (Fellendorf, 1994), have been developed to analyze transportation scenarios at the micro- and macro-scale levels. However, to date there have been only few attempts (Saha, 2004; Mahajan, 2006; Baumann, 2007; Dressler, 2010) to create communication scenarios in a realistic transportation simulation environment.

One of the most important parameters in simulating vehicular networks is the node mobility. It is important to use a realistic mobility model so that results from the simulation correctly reflect the real world performance of a VANET, as shown in some prior studies (Saha, 2004; Heidemann, 2001). Node mobility in a vehicular network is strongly affected by the drivers' behavior, which can change road traffic at different levels. Drivers' preferences in path and destination selection can further affect the overall network topology. It has been shown that drivers tend to use certain regular routes for their daily routines (Abdel-aty, 1994), and only 15.5% of commuters reported that they did not always choose the same exact route to work. Once a commuter has settled on a habitual route, the route choice strategies they deploy might possibly descend to a subconscious level, unless there are external factors (e.g., accidents or traffic jams) that bring the choice of route back to the conscious level (Tawfik, 2010). Furthermore, some commuters might select their routes based on the suggestions of some travel

guidance system, such as variable message signs. Once a commuter has had a good experience with using a travel guidance system, they might increase their reliance on such advice the next time they travel (Zhao, 2010). While most current navigation systems use the shortest path to the destination for selecting routes, some commuters use faster paths instead of shorter ones to avoid congestion and reduce travel time. Some studies also show that path selection could possibly change on a temporal basis (Li, 2005; Chen, 1993). For example, when driving in the evening commuters usually have more flexibility in selecting alternate routes than when they drive to work in the morning.

In this chapter, we discuss the effect of path selection (for a particular destination) and destination selection on vehicular network simulations. We also consider two application scenarios in which we assume cars are equipped with sensors and can collect road information. In the first scenario, we consider the situation in which some road-side units (RSUs) are deployed so that cars can push their sensor data online via the help of such units, which we assume are connected to servers on the Internet. In other words, each car can upload its sensor data to the Internet when it encounters a RSU. We also assume that the sensor data can be sent to a RSU even when it is far away if there exists a multi-hop path between the source and the RSU. In the second scenario, we consider the case in which cars want to disseminate their sensor information over the vehicular network via vehicle-to-vehicle communication only.

RELATED WORK

Details in the mobility model may have a critical effect on the fidelity, and thus the usefulness, of the resulting network simulations. Zhang *et al.* (Zhang, 2007) used traces taken from the UMassDieselNet project (Burgess, 2006) to study the effect of mobility models on the performance of Delay-tolerant networking (DTN). They showed that a finer-grained route-level model of inter-contact times is able to predict performance much more accurately than a coarser-grained all-bus-pairs aggregated model, which suggests caution should be taken in choosing the right level of detail when modeling vehicle mobility.

Many different route choice models have been proposed. For example, Dia and Panwai (Dia, 2007) used fuzzy logic to model the impact of traveler information system on route choices. Liu and Huang (Liu, 2007) investigated day-to-day route paths and modeled them with the logit-based stochastic user equilibrium state. In addition, Shenpei and Xinping (Shenpei, 2008) discussed how route choices are affected by signal split, while Zhao and Li (Zhao, 2010) proposed a route choice model that considers human memory and traffic information factors. Guo *et al.* (Guo, 2010) proposed a path choice model based on game theory, and assumed that drivers obey traffic information to select their alternate routes. Dingus *et al.* (Dingus, 1996) discussed how route choices are affected by human factors such as efficiency (e.g., fastest route vs. shortest route), problem avoidance (e.g., safer routes) and road condition (e.g., number of traffic lights). They showed a shortest path is not necessarily the driver's first choice when selecting routes, and that very often commuters use faster paths to avoid congestion and reduce travel time (Jan, 2000). Finally, Tawfik *et al.* (Tawfik, 2010) showed that drivers' perceptions are significantly different from their actual experiences, and drivers' choices can be better explained by the former rather than the latter.

While there are a huge amount of works that model driving behavior in the transportation literature, there are only a few studies in the networking literature that described the impact of driving behavior on vehicular network simulations. For example, Viriyasitavat *et al.* (Viriyasitavat, 2009) provided an analysis of how traffic lights affect network topology and connectivity. Dressler and Sommer (Dressler, 2010) evaluated route choice strategies via different route choices to show their impact on average speed. They did not consider the effect of route choice on the performance of network communication though.

Simulation Environment

To understand the effect of preferred route and destination on vehicular network simulation, we use MOVE (http://lens.csie.ncku.edu.tw/MOVE/) to simulate various driving behaviors. MOVE runs on top of an open-source micro-traffic simulator called SUMO (Krajzewicz, 2002), and allows users to simulate road dynamics on the fly by utilizing the Traffic Control Interface (TraCI) (Wegener, 2008). More details about MOVE can be found in the prior work (Karnadi, 2007). MOVE also supports modeling obstacles on roads by allowing users to specify the shape of the obstacle and their penetration loss. We used Cramer's Rule (Leon, 2006) to check if there is an obstacle between the sender and the receiver and adjust the radio signal attenuation accordingly based on the obstacle's penetration loss. The roads in simulations have two lanes and are bi-directional. Traffic light is simulated at each intersection. Each simulation runs for 2,000 seconds and the maximum radio transmission range is 250m. We enabled CSMA/CA in simulations and used the TwoRayGround model to simulate the radio propagation. The road topology generated in the simulation is based on the TIGER database (Marx, 1986) using real-world traces. All nodes employ 802.11 MAC operating at 2Mbps.

Preferred Route and Destination

Mobility models play an important role in VANET simulations and driving behavior could strongly affect the mobility model. Since a truly realistic simulation is very challenging to produce, as human behavior and unexpected events are difficult if not impossible to model, simulation designers need to understand what level of detail is appropriate to the research questions they are examining. In this section, we discuss the effects of driving behavior on VANET simulations in two different cases, including path selection and destination selection.

Path Selection

Path selection is highly dependent on an individual's personal perceptions, experiences, preferences, and so on. The decision of path selection could have an effect on road congestion and clustering of vehicles. In this section, we demonstrate the effect of path selection with two examples: turning decisions at an intersection and the choice of the preferred path to the destination. We use AODV (Perkins, 1999) to route packets from the sender to the receiver in the following experiments. In simulations, we consider the packet delivery ratio (PDR) of a network, defined as

$$PDR = \frac{Packets\ received\ by\ all\ receivers}{Packets\ sent\ by\ all\ senders}$$

1. Turning Decisions at an Intersection: In the real world, a driver normally has to decide which way to move at an intersection, choosing to either go straight, turn left, or turn right. To illustrate the effect of turning decisions at the intersection we ran a simple experiment using MOVE, which allows users to define the turning probability for different directions at each intersection (e.g., a probability of 0.5 to turn left, 0.3 to go straight and 0.2 to turn right). In other words, users can set different turning probabilities at each intersection, according to different requirements, such as avoiding road congestion.

2. Fastest Path vs. Shortest Path: A driver may choose a path based on different criteria, such

as travel time, distance, personal habit, and so on. Still, most people choose paths which have the shortest distance to their destinations. However, if everybody chooses the "same" shortest path, it might actually lead to more congestion on the road, and, as a result, a longer travel time. Consequently, the fastest path to destination might not necessarily be the shortest one, since a faster path might include road segments which are longer but less congested. Intuitively, the choice of a path to the destination could affect node density and the network topology.

Specifically, while drivers choosing the same shortest path might lead to more congestion, it also creates a network with a higher node density. On the other hand, when the shortest travel time is considered, the vehicles could be potentially more uniformly distributed over the whole area, which results in a sparser network. To understand the effect of different preferred paths, we randomly picked a source-destination pair and created a constant bit rate (CBR) connection between the source and the destination. As shown in Figure 1, we observe that the network performance is significantly better when the shortest path is used as the route choice to the destination. When the fastest path is selected, it may result in a sparser network, in which link breakages are more likely to occur, since the inter-node distance is potentially larger. However, as we increase the number of nodes in the network, the differences between different route selection mechanisms becomes less significant. Note that the packet delivery ratio is saturated at some point (around 0.9 for using the shortest path and 0.8 for using the fastest path), which is due to that the distance between some intersections are greater than the radio range, leading to unavoidable link breakages and packet losses in simulations.

3. Rerouting when Encountering an Accident or Traffic Jam: Traffic jams or car accidents

Figure 1. The effect of different preferred path choices

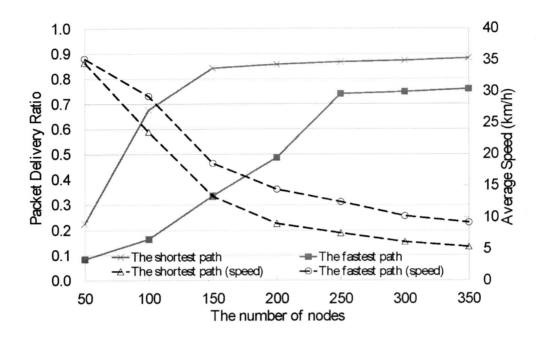

could create incentives for drivers to change their routes in order to reduce travel time. However, the reaction to re-route could potentially affect the network topology. To be more specific, car accidents tend to create road congestion, which results in a higher network density, and leads to a better packet delivery ratio. To illustrate the effect of re-routing, we create an accident in the simulation and use TraCI to change the vehicle mobility on-the-fly when it encounters the incident. As shown in Figure 2, as we increase the number of cars that decide to re-route when they approach an accident (from 0%, 50% to 100% of the total cars), the network performance becomes worse, although the average travel time is reduced. Note that, although re-routing when encountering a traffic jam is a common practice for drivers in the real world, its effects have been rarely discussed in the literature (Lo, 2009; Lai, 2009; Leontiadis, 2007). Routing protocols

that predict the next hop based only on history or the use of navigation system might perform poorly when such a driving behavior is considered.

DESTINATION SELECTION

As described previously, drivers tend to exhibit a bias in their destination selection (Abdel-aty, 1994), and thus some locations could potentially be visited more often than others. Different destination selection patterns will result in different network topologies and levels of connectivity. To simplify the discussion, let us assume that the selection of destinations follows a certain probability distribution. Here we consider three different probability distributions: pareto, exponential, and uniform.

When the selection of destinations follows a uniform distribution, it suggests that the probability of a car visiting any location on the map is

Figure 2. Effect of rerouting

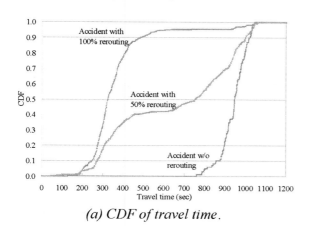

(a) CDF of travel time.

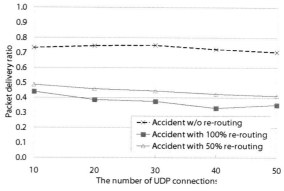

(b) The packet delivery ratio.

Figure 3. Comparison of the effect in the three node distributions

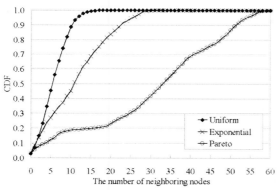

(a) Comparison of the number of neighboring nodes for the three node distributions.

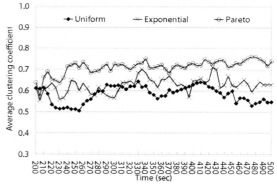

(b) Comparison of the average cluster coefficient for the three node distributions.

uniformly distributed. On the other hand, when the selection of destination follows a pareto distribution, it implies that some locations are visited much more often than others. To understand the effects of destination selection, we setup a simulation using a 4x4 grid map with 100 cars. The length of the road segment is 400m. As shown in Figure 3, when cars pick their destination following a pareto destination, the network will have a larger cluster coefficient (Fiore, 2008) over time and every car will have more neighboring nodes, as compared

to the cases when cars choose their destinations following an exponential or uniform distribution.

However, this is not unexpected, as when more cars select the same destination (e.g., when students select their school as the destination), the chance that some road segments in their selected paths to the destination overlap will become higher. More overlapping road segments suggest a higher node density, shorter inter-car distance and a lower moving speed, which typically leads to a better network connectivity.

CASE STUDY FOR DESTINATION SELECTION

In order to illustrate how the route choice could potentially affect the performance of ITS applications, in this section we consider two scenarios. In the first scenario, we assume that, for traffic monitoring purposes, vehicles can collect road information using their sensors (e.g., GPS), and then periodically send the sensor data to the RSUs within their radio range (Wischhof, 2005; Eisenman, 2006). In the second scenario, we consider the case when a vehicle wants to disseminate information about a certain event (such as a car accident) over the whole network via vehicle-to-vehicle communication (Nadeem, 2004; Uichin, 2009).

Application A: Traffic Monitoring

For the traffic monitoring scenario, we use a 4x4 grid map. The length of each grid is 400m. We place a RSU at the center of the map. Each car periodically (i.e., every 5 seconds) broadcasts the sensor information it has collected. Nodes overhearing the sensor data will rebroadcast the packet (i.e., via flooding). We employ simple MAC in ns-2 as the underlying MAC protocol. Simple MAC supports CSMA (without the backoff mechanism when data needs to be retransmitted). In this scenario, we consider the packet reception ratio at RSUs when different destination selection models are used (i.e., with the uniform, exponential, and pareto distributions). The packet reception ratio (PRR) is defined as

$$PRR = \frac{The\ number\ of\ packets\ received\ by\ any\ RSU}{The\ number\ of\ packets\ sent\ by\ the\ cars}$$

In the simulations, many cars' destinations fall in the bottom part of the map when pareto and exponential distributions are used. Note that a packet will be discarded immediately if it cannot be forwarded to RSU through flooding. We do not considered a store-and-forward mechanism used by the car to temporarily store the packets in this scenario.

As shown in Figure 4a, when cars select their destinations following a uniform distribution, the application performance is better than when the other two distributions are employed. The reason is that lots of the cars tend to use routes in the bottom half of the map when selecting their destinations following an exponential or pareto distribution. In fact, when pareto distribution is used, many cars choose the same route to their destinations. Therefore, some roads become very congested, while others have only a few cars. In other words, cars tend to cluster in a certain area when their destination selection follows a pareto distribution. If the center of the cluster is far away from a RSU, it is very likely that cars cannot find a path (either single-hop or multi-hop) to send their data to the RSU at the time when the sensor data is broadcast. As shown in Figure 4b, there are more packets that cannot find a path to a RSU when the destination selection follows a pareto distribution as compared to when the other two distributions are used. As shown in Figure 5, when cars select their destinations following a uniform distribution, most of the MAC-layer collisions occur at the intersections and the central part of the map. In contrast, when cars select destinations following an exponential or pareto distribution, more than 90% of collisions happen in the bottom part of the map.

On the other hand, if the center of the cluster is close to a RSU, the application can be greatly improved when cars select their destinations following a pareto or exponential distribution. For example, as the results show in Figure 6, if we change the location of the RSU from the center of the map to the bottom left corner, the packet reception ratio for the exponential and pareto distributions are significantly improved, as compared to the results in Figure 4a. Note that the

Figure 4. Effects of destination selection on traffic monitoring application

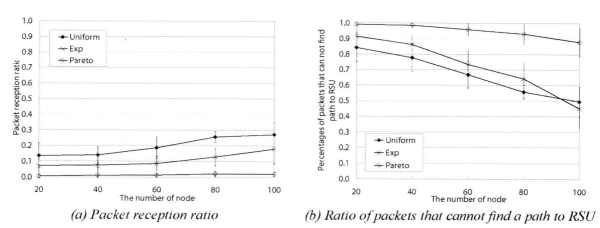

(a) Packet reception ratio   *(b) Ratio of packets that cannot find a path to RSU*

Figure 5. Distributions of MAC-layer collisions when different destination selection models are used

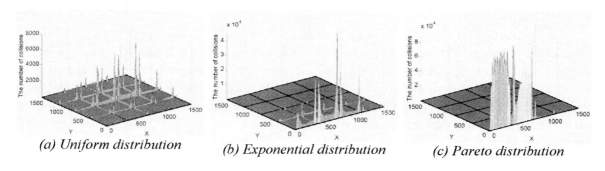

(a) Uniform distribution   *(b) Exponential distribution*   *(c) Pareto distribution*

application performance when the destination selection follows a uniform distribution is reduced since half of the cars traveling to the upper part of the map are not able to find a path to the RSU. Similarly, if cars select their destinations following a uniform distribution while RSUs are located on a remote part of the map (e.g., the corner), the preferred destination has only little effect on the performance of the application. The above insight suggests that how to select connection pairs in simulations could be very important, since the results might be totally different when different mobility models are employed. Most of the vehicular network simulations in the literature tend to select their node destinations uniformly, which will favor the scenario when RSUs are located near the center of the map. In addition,

from the perspective of network efficiency, our observation provides an incentive to consider users' preferred routes and destinations when one wants to deploy some RSUs for ITS applications in the real world, as previously observed by Ding and Xiao (Ding, 2010).

Application B: Event Broadcasting

Next, we look at the effect of destination selection on disseminating data in a vehicular network. We consider a scenario in which a car wants to broadcast an event (e.g., a car accident) over the whole network via vehicle-to-vehicle communication in a flooding-like fashion (e.g., using epidemic routing (Vahdat, 2000)). Unlike the previous scenario, here we consider that the store-and-forward

Figure 6. The combined effects of driver destination selection and the location of RSU

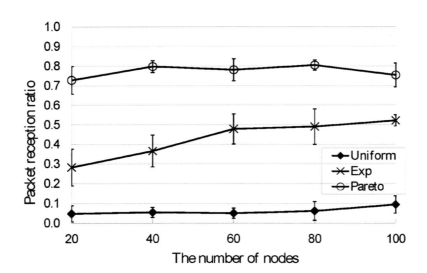

mechanism is employed so that a car can carry a packet around when it cannot immediately find the next forwarder. The performance metric we are interested in here is how long the message takes to reach every car in the network. The road topology is the same as that for application A, and the sender is randomly selected. For simplicity, here we only consider three different node densities: 20, 80, and 140. Generally speaking, the delay in data dissemination is a function of the inter-contact time of vehicles. Here we define data dissemination delay as the duration from when the originating car sends out the event until when the other cars receives the event, and inter-contact time as the time interval between two contacts (i.e., the duration from when one car encounter finishes and the next one begins). Karagiannis *et al.* (Karagiannis, 2007) showed that inter-contact time tends to follow a power law and exponential decay distribution.

As shown in Figure 7 (each point in the graph is the result from one simulation), we find that the average inter-contact time and dissemination delay are larger when cars choose their destinations

following a uniform distribution, as compared to when they follow an exponential or pareto distribution. This is because many cars might cluster together as their selected destinations and the paths to them are similar when they choose destinations following either of these distributions. As a result, the inter-contact distance between cars will be shorter and, consequently, the inter-contact time and dissemination delay are smaller. In addition, we observe that the dissemination delay is not significantly affected by the changing node density when the node density is high (e.g., when nodes=80 and 140), if the selected destinations follow a pareto distribution (i.e., most of the cars are in the same cluster). Note that some large delays in Figure 7 (e.g., > 130 seconds) are because we happened to select a sender that was far from all the other nodes in that simulation.

DISCUSSION

Selecting an appropriate level of details for the mobility model used in VANET simulation is a

Figure 7. Effect of different destination selection models on data dissemination delay

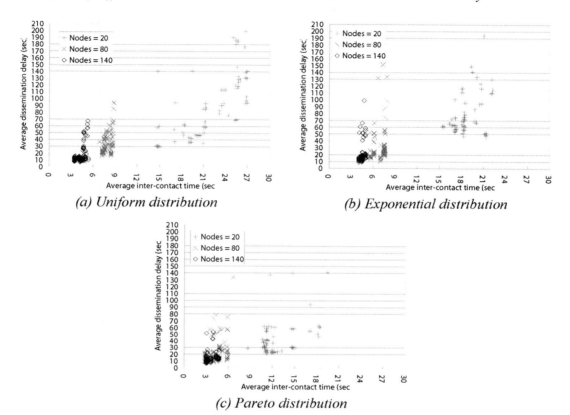

(a) Uniform distribution

(b) Exponential distribution

(c) Pareto distribution

challenging task. Unrealistic mobility models can produce misleading or incorrect results. On the other hand, adding details requires more time to implement and debug the system. In this section, we discuss the interaction between the route choice and other parameters in VANET simulations. Specifically, we describe how different route choice models are affected by the simulation of traffic lights.

As shown in the prior work (Lan, 2008), traffic lights can potentially create clustering effects at the intersections and affect network connectivity. Intuitively, when the inter-cluster distance is larger than the radio range, the probability of link breakages may increase as the number of clusters rises, as shown in Figure 8a. Here we define a cluster as a group of nodes that can find at least one multipath route to each other. We find that this

observation is applicable to all three destination selection models we tested, as shown in Figure 8b. The results for cases without traffic lights are generally better than when traffic lights are simulated. Note that, when the vehicles select destinations following the pareto distribution, the results are similar whether we simulate the traffic lights or not. This is not surprising though, since cars are clustered anyway with or without the traffic lights when their mobility follows a pareto distribution. In addition, people tend to put the RSU on the traffic light for practical reasons (Lan, 2007). For the traffic monitoring application discussed in the previous section, we observe that as we put more and more RSUs in the simulation, the effects of the destination selection models become less and less significant. As shown in Figure 8c, as the number of extra RSUs (as compared to the original case,

Figure 8. Discussion the effects of traffic light

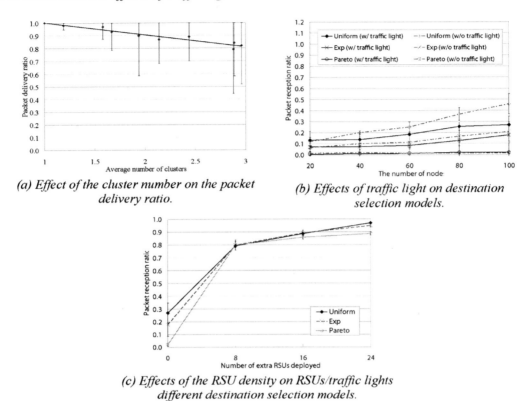

(a) Effect of the cluster number on the packet delivery ratio.

(b) Effects of traffic light on destination selection models.

(c) Effects of the RSU density on RSUs/traffic lights different destination selection models.

when there was only one RSU at the center of map) becomes greater than 8, the results for the three destination selection models are similar.

CONCLUSION AND FUTURE WORK

Performing a realistic VANET simulation is challenging, since many factors could affect the node mobility in real life situations. In this chapter, we discuss the effect of preferred route and destination on the network topology and application performance.

We observe that the network performance is generally better when one models drivers' route choice using the shortest path model, as compared to using the fastest path model which might actually occur more frequently in real life

though. Finally, we show that when drivers pick their destinations following a pareto distribution, the network performance is generally better, as compared to when cars choose their destinations following an exponential or uniform distribution. Furthermore, we observe that simulation results are not significantly affected by different node density settings when cars pick their destination following a pareto distribution. To sum up, selecting an appropriate level of details in the mobility model for a VANET simulation is important.

REFERENCES

Abdelaty, M. A., Vaughn, K. M., Kitamura, R., Jovanis, P. P., & Mannering, F. L. (1994). Models of commuters' information use and route choice: Initial results based on southern California commuter route choice survey. *Transportation Research Record, 1453*, 46–55.

Baumann, R., Heimlicher, S., & May, M. (2007). *Towards realistic mobility models for vehicular ad-hoc networks.* In the 2007 Mobile Networking for Vehicular Environments.

Breslau, L., Estrin, D., Fall, K., Floyd, S., Heidemann, J., & Helmy, A. (2000). Advances in network simulation. *Computer, 33*(5), 59–67. doi:10.1109/2.841785

Burgess, J., Gallagher, B., Jensen, D., & Levine, B. N. (2006). *MaxProp: Routing for vehicle-based disruption-tolerant networks.* In the 25th IEEE International Conference on Computer Communications.

Cameron, G. D. B., & Duncan, G. I. D. (1996). Paramics: Parallel microscopic simulation of road traffic. *The Journal of Supercomputing, 10*(1), 25–53. doi:10.1007/BF00128098

Chang, X. (1999). Network simulations with OPNET. In *Simulation Conference Proceedings.*

Chen, P.-T., & Mahmassani, H. S. (1993). Dynamic interactive simulator for studying commuter behavior under real-time traffic information supply strategies. *Transportation Research Record, 1413*, 12–21.

Dia, H., & Panwai, S. (2007). Modelling drivers' compliance and route choice behaviour in response to travel information. *Nonlinear Dynamics, 49*(4), 493–509. doi:10.1007/s11071-006-9111-3

Ding, Y., & Xiao, L. (2010). SADV: Static-node-assisted adaptive data dissemination in vehicular networks. *IEEE Transactions on Vehicular Technology, 59*(5), 2245–2255.

Dingus, T., Hulse, M., Jahns, S., Alves-Foss, J., Confer, S., Rice, A., et al. (1996). *Development of human factors guidelines for advanced traveler information systems and commercial vehicle operations: Literature review.* Federal Highway Administration, Report FHWA-RD-95-153.

Dressler, F., & Sommer, C. (2010). *On the impact of human driver behavior on intelligent transportation systems.* In the 2010 IEEE 71st Vehicular Technology Conference (2010-Spring).

Eisenman, S. B., Lane, N. D., Miluzzo, E., Peterson, R. A., Ahn, G.-S., & Campbell, A. T. (2006). *Metrosense project: People-centric sensing at scale.* In Workshop on World-Sensor-Web.

Fellendorf, M. (1994). *VISSIM: A microscopic simulation tool to evaluate actuated signal control including bus priority.* In the 64th Institute Transportation Engineers Annual Meeting.

Fiore, M., & Härri, J. (2008). The networking shape of vehicular mobility. In the 9th ACM International Symposium on Mobile ad hoc Networking and Computing, Hong Kong, China.

Guo, D., Li, X., Liu, M., & Zhang, L. (2010). *Model of traffic path choice based on game theory and induction mechanism.* In 2010 Ninth International Symposium on Distributed Computing and Applications to Business Engineering and Science.

Halati, A., Lieu, H., & Walker, S. (1997). Corsim-corridor traffic simulation model. In the Traffic Congestion and Traffic Safety in the 21st Century Conference.

Heidemann, J., Bulusu, N., Elson, J., Intanagonwiwat, C., Lan, K. C., Xu, Y., & Govindan, R. (2001). *Effects of detail in wireless network simulation.* In the Society for Computer Simulation International Multiconference on Distributed Simulation.

Jan, O., Horowitz, A. J., & Peng, Z.-R. (2000). Using global positioning system data to understand variations in path choice. *Transportation Research Record, 1725*, 37–44. doi:10.3141/1725-06

Karagiannis, T., Boudec, J.-Y. L., & Vojnović, M. (2007). *Power law and exponential decay of inter contact times between mobile devices*. In the 13th Annual ACM International Conference on Mobile Computing and Networking.

Karnadi, F. K., Mo, Z. H., & Lan, K.-C. (2007). *Rapid generation of realistic mobility models for VANET*. In IEEE Wireless Communications and Networking Conference.

Krajzewicz, D., Hertkorn, G., Rössel, C., & Wanger, P. (2002). *SUMO (simulation of urban mobility): An open-source traffic simulation*. In the 4th Middle East Symposium on Simulation and Modelling.

Lai, P., Wang, X., Lu, N., & Liu, F. (2009). *A reliable broadcast routing scheme based on mobility prediction for VANET*. In 2009 IEEE Intelligent Vehicles Symposium.

Lan, K. C., & Chou, C.-M. (2008). *Realistic mobility models for vehicular ad hoc network (VANET) simulations*. In the 8th International Conference on ITS Telecommunications.

Lan, K. C., Wang, Z., Hassan, M., Moors, T., Berriman, R., & Libman, L. (2007). Experiences in deploying a wireless mesh network testbed for traffic control. *ACM SIGCOMM Computer Communication Review, 37*(5), 17–28. doi:10.1145/1290168.1290171

Leon, S. J. (2006). *Linear algebra with applications*. New Jersey: Pearson.

Leontiadis, I., & Mascolo, C. (2007). *Opportunistic spatio-temporal dissemination system for vehicular networks*. In the 1st International MobiSys Workshop on Mobile Opportunistic Networking, San Juan, Puerto Rico.

Li, H., Guensler, R., & Ogle, J. (2005). *An analysis of morning commute route choice patterns using GPS based vehicle activity data*. In the 84th Annual Meeting of the Transportation Research Board.

Liu, T.-L., & Huang, H.-J. (2007). *Multi-agent simulation on day-to-day route choice behavior*. In the third International Conference on Natural Computation.

Lo, S.-C., & Lu, W.-K. (2009). *Design of data forwarding strategies in vehicular ad hoc networks*. In the IEEE 69th Vehicular Technology Conference (2009- Spring).

Mahajan, A., Potnis, N., Gopalan, K., & Wang, A.-I. A. (2006). Urban mobility models for VANETs. In the Second IEEE International Workshop on Next Generation Wireless Networks, Bangalore, India.

Marx, R. W. (1986). The tiger system: Automating the geographic structure of the United States census. *Government Publications Review, 13*(2), 181–201. doi:10.1016/0277-9390(86)90003-8

Nadeem, T., Dashtinezhad, S., Liao, C., & Iftode, L. (2004). TrafficView: Traffic data dissemination using car-to-car communication. *ACM SIGMOBILE Mobile Computing and Communications Review, 8*(3), 6–19. doi:10.1145/1031483.1031487

Perkins, C. E., & Royer, E. M. (1999). *Ad-hoc on-demand distance vector routing*. In the 2nd IEEE Workshop on Mobile Computing Systems and Applications.

Saha, A. K., & Johnson, D. B. (2004). *Modeling mobility for vehicular ad-hoc networks*. In the 1st ACM International Workshop on Vehicular ad hoc Networks, Philadelphia, PA, USA.

Shenpei, Z., & Xinping, Y. (2008). *Driver's route choice model based on traffic signal control*. In the 3rd IEEE Conference on Industrial Electronics and Applications.

Tawfik, A. M., Rakha, H. A., & Miller, S. D. (2010). *Driver route choice behavior: Experiences, perceptions, and choices*. In 2010 IEEE Intelligent Vehicles Symposium.

Uichin, L., Magistretti, E., Gerla, M., Bellavista, P., & Corradi, A. (2009). Dissemination and harvesting of urban data using vehicular sensing platforms. *IEEE Transactions on Vehicular Technology, 58*(2), 882–901. doi:10.1109/TVT.2008.928899

Vahdat, A., & Becker, D. (2000). *Epidemic routing for partially-connected ad hoc networks. Technical Report*. Duke University.

Viriyasitavat, W., Tonguz, O. K., & Fan, B. (2009). *Network connectivity of VANETs in urban areas*. In the 6th Annual IEEE Communications Society Conference on Sensor, Mesh and Ad Hoc Communications and Networks.

Wegener, A., & Piórkowski, M. EPFL, M. R., Hellbrück, H., Fischer, S., & Hubaux, J.-P. (2008). *TraCI: An interface for coupling road traffic and network simulators*. In the 11th Communications and Networking Simulation Symposium, Ottawa, Canada.

Wischhof, L., Ebner, A., & Rohling, H. (2005). Information dissemination in self-organizing intervehicle networks. *IEEE Transactions on Intelligent Transportation Systems, 6*(1), 90–101. doi:10.1109/TITS.2004.842407

Zhang, X., Kurose, J., Levine, B. N., Towsley, D., & Zhang, H. (2007). *Study of a bus-based disruption-tolerant network: Mobility modeling and impact on routing*. In the 13th Annual ACM International Conference on Mobile Computing and Networking.

Zhao, D., & Shao, C. (2010). *Empirical study of drivers' learning behavior and reliance on VMS*. In 2010 13th International IEEE Conference on Intelligent Transportation Systems.

Zhao, J., & Li, Q. (2010). *A method for modeling drivers' behavior rules in agent-based traffic simulation*. In the 18th International Conference on Geoinformatics.

ADDITIONAL READING

Baumann, R., Heimlicher, S., & May, M. (2007). *Towards realistic mobility models for vehicular ad-hoc networks*. In the 2007 Mobile Networking for Vehicular Environments.

Boban, M., Vinhoza, T. T. V., Ferreira, M., Barros, J., & Tonguz, O. K. (2011). Impact of vehicles as obstacles in vehicular ad hoc networks. *IEEE Journal on Selected Areas in Communications, 29*(1), 15–28. doi:10.1109/JSAC.2011.110103

Bojin, L., Khorashadi, B., Haining, D., Ghosal, D., Chen-Nee, C., & Zhang, M. (2009). VGSim: An integrated networking and microscopic vehicular mobility simulation platform. *IEEE Communications Magazine, 47*(5), 134–141. doi:10.1109/MCOM.2009.4939289

Burgess, J., Gallagher, B., Jensen, D., & Levine, B. N. (2006). *MaxProp: Routing for vehicle-based disruption-tolerant networks*. In the 25th IEEE International Conference on Computer Communications (INFOCOM 2006).

Ding, Y., & Xiao, L. (2010). SADV: Static-node-assisted adaptive data dissemination in vehicular networks. *IEEE Transactions on Vehicular Technology, 59*(5), 2245–2255.

Dressler, F., & Sommer, C. (2010). *On the impact of human driver behavior on intelligent transportation systems*. In the 2010 IEEE 71st Vehicular Technology Conference (2010-Spring).

Fan, L., & Yu, W. (2007). Routing in vehicular ad hoc networks: A survey. *IEEE Vehicular Technology Magazine, 2*(2), 12–22. doi:10.1109/MVT.2007.912927

Fiore, M., & Härri, J. (2008). *The networking shape of vehicular mobility*. In the 9th ACM International Symposium on Mobile ad hoc Networking and Computing, Hong Kong, China.

Harri, J., Filali, F., & Bonnet, C. (2009). Mobility models for vehicular ad hoc networks: A survey and taxonomy. *IEEE Communications Surveys & Tutorials, 11*(4), 19–41. doi:10.1109/SURV.2009.090403

Heidemann, J., Bulusu, N., Elson, J., Intanagonwiwat, C., Lan, K. C., Xu, Y., & Govindan, R. (2001). *Effects of detail in wireless network simulation*. In the Society for Computer Simulation International Multiconference on Distributed Simulation.

Hong-Yu, H., Pei-En, L., Minglu, L., Da, L., Xu, L., Wei, S., & Min-You, W. (2007). Performance evaluation of SUVnet with real-time traffic data. *IEEE Transactions on Vehicular Technology, 56*(6), 3381–3396. doi:10.1109/TVT.2007.907273

Jan, O., Horowitz, A. J., & Peng, Z.-R. (2000). Using global positioning system data to understand variations in path choice. *Transportation Research Record, 1725,* 37–44. doi:10.3141/1725-06

Karagiannis, T., Boudec, J.-Y. L., & Vojnović, M. (2007). *Power law and exponential decay of inter contact times between mobile devices*. In the 13th Annual ACM International Conference on Mobile Computing and Networking.

Krajzewicz, D. (2010). Traffic simulation with SUMO - Simulation of urban mobility. In Barcelo, J. (Ed.), *Fundamentals of traffic simulation* (pp. 269–294). Springer International Series in Operations Research and Management Science. doi:10.1007/978-1-4419-6142-6_7

Lan, K. c., Wang, Z., Hassan, M., Moors, T., Berriman, R., & Libman, L. (2007). Experiences in deploying a wireless mesh network testbed for traffic control. *ACM SIGCOMM Computer Communication Review, 37*(5), 17–28. doi:10.1145/1290168.1290171

Lan, K. C., & Chou, C.-M. (2008). *Realistic mobility models for vehicular ad hoc network (VANET) simulations*. In the 8th International Conference on ITS Telecommunications.

Nadeem, T., Dashtinezhad, S., Liao, C., & Iftode, L. (2004). TrafficView: Traffic data dissemination using car-to-car communication. *ACM SIGMOBILE Mobile Computing and Communications Review, 8*(3), 6–19. doi:10.1145/1031483.1031487

Saha, A. K., & Johnson, D. B. (2004). *Modeling mobility for vehicular ad-hoc networks*. In the 1st ACM International Workshop on Vehicular ad hoc Networks, Philadelphia, PA, USA.

Shenpei, Z., & Xinping, Y. (2008). *Driver's route choice model based on traffic signal control*. In the 3rd IEEE Conference on Industrial Electronics and Applications.

Sommer, C., & Dressler, F. (2008). Progressing toward realistic mobility models in VANET simulations. *IEEE Communications Magazine, 46*(11), 132–137. doi:10.1109/MCOM.2008.4689256

Sommer, C., German, R., & Dressler, F. (2011). Bidirectionally coupled network and road traffic simulation for improved IVC analysis. *IEEE Transactions on Mobile Computing, 10*(1), 3–15. doi:10.1109/TMC.2010.133

Tawfik, A. M., Rakha, H. A., & Miller, S. D. (2010). *Driver route choice behavior: Experiences, perceptions, and choices*. In 2010 IEEE Intelligent Vehicles Symposium.

Uichin, L., Magistretti, E., Gerla, M., Bellavista, P., & Corradi, A. (2009). Dissemination and harvesting of urban data using vehicular sensing platforms. *IEEE Transactions on Vehicular Technology, 58*(2), 882–901. doi:10.1109/TVT.2008.928899

Vahdat, A., & Becker, D. (2000). *Epidemic routing for partially-connected ad hoc networks. Technical Report*. Duke University.

Wegener, A., & Piórkowski, M. EPFL, M. R., Hellbrück, H., Fischer, S., & Hubaux, J.-P. (2008). *TraCI: An interface for coupling road traffic and network simulators*. In the 11th communications and networking simulation symposium, Ottawa, Canada.

Wenjing, W., Fei, X., & Chatterjee, M. (2009). Small-scale and large-scale routing in vehicular ad hoc networks. *IEEE Transactions on Vehicular Technology*, *58*(9), 5200–5213. doi:10.1109/TVT.2009.2025652

Chapter 9
CORM:
A Concern–Oriented Approach and Model to Computer Network Design

Hoda Mamdouh Hassan
American University in Cairo, Egypt

ABSTRACT

Designing future computer networks dictates an eclectic vision capable of encompassing ideas and concepts developed in contemporary research unfettered by today's operational and technological constraints. However, unguided by a clear articulation of core design principles, the process of network design may be at stake of falling into similar pitfalls and limitations attributed to current network realizations. This chapter presents CORM: a clean-slate Concern-Oriented Reference Model for architecting future computer networks. CORM stands as a guiding framework from which several network architectures can be derived. CORM represents a pioneering attempt within the network realm, and to the author's knowledge, CORM is the first reference model that is bio-inspired, accounts for complex system characteristics, and applies a software engineering approach to network design. Moreover, CORM's derivation process conforms to the Function-Behavior-Structure (FBS) engineering framework, which is credited to be applicable to any engineering discipline for reasoning about, and explaining the process of design.

INTRODUCTION

Current research in computer networks is at a critical turning point. The research community is endeavoring to devise future network architectures that address the deficiencies identified in present network realizations, acknowledge the need for a trustworthy IT infrastructure, and

satisfy the society's emerging and future requirements (Clark, 2010). Considering the lessons from the past, and evaluating the outcomes and contributions of contemporary research literature, the community concluded that the advent of a trustworthy future Internet cannot be achieved by the current trajectory of incremental changes and point solutions to the current computer networks, but rather more revolutionary paths need to be

DOI: 10.4018/978-1-4666-1797-1.ch009

Copyright © 2012, IGI Global. Copying or distributing in print or electronic forms without written permission of IGI Global is prohibited.

explored (Clark, 2010; Feldmann, 2007). Proposed network architectures need to be grounded on well-articulated design principles that account for network operational and management complexities, embrace technology and application heterogeneity, regulate network inherent emergent behavior, and overcome shortcomings attributed to present network realizations.

Present computer network realizations are the outcome of incremental research efforts and endeavors exerted during the inchoative stage of computer network design. Back then, the aim was to interconnect architecturally disparate networks into one global network. Such inter-network connection was achieved through the introduction of the Transmission Control Protocol (TCP) (Cerf, & Kahn, 1974). TCP was introduced as a flexible protocol that sustains inter-process communication across networks, while hiding any underlying inter-network differences. TCP was later split into TCP and IP leading to the derivation of the layered Internet TCP/IP suite. As such, the TCP/IP suite defined the Internet system, which was regarded as a vehicle to interconnect diverse types of networks. However, the astounding success of the TCP/IP suite in interconnecting networks resulted in adopting the TCP/IP suite as the de facto standard for inter-computer communication within a single network, as well as across multiple networks. An initiative that undermined the need for independent research efforts addressing the requirements and specifications for internally designing computer networks. Focusing primarily on interconnection, TCP/IP networks possessed intelligence at the network edges, while regarding the network core as a "dump forwarding machine," thus introducing the end-to-end (E2E) design principle; a fundamental principle for TCP/IP networks (Saltzer, Reed, & Clark, 1984). Influenced by TCP/IP-layered architecture and the E2E design principle, network designers and protocol engineers conformed to a top-down design strategy as the approach to architect networks. Moreover, with the introduction of the layered OSI model,

the top-down layered approach in network design and protocol engineering was emphasized further, in spite of the fact that the OSI was primarily developed as an "Interconnection Architecture," i.e. an architecture facilitating the interaction of heterogeneous computer networks rather than an architecture for building computer networks (Zimmermann, 1980).

Despite the outstanding success of its realizations, we argue that the Internet-layered model was deficient in representing essential network aspects necessary for network design and subsequent protocol engineering. First, the traditional "cloud model" derived from the E2E principle abstracts the Internet layout as core and edge, thus it fails to express the network topological, social, and economical boundaries. Second, resource management as a function is absent form the Internet-layered model. Consequently, network designers and engineers introduced several point solutions to handle resource-management functions such as admission control, traffic engineering, and quality of service. Third, the Internet-layered model prohibits vertical function integration, thus it hinders the efficient engineering of performance aspects that need to span several layers. A requirement that was accentuated when operating in wireless environments, and resulted in numerous proposals for cross-layer designs. Finally, the Internet-layered model does not express network behavior nor allow for its customization according to context and requirements. A deficiency that led to two undesirable effects. First, IP-based networks exhibit a defining characteristic of unstable complex systems— a local event can have a destructive global impact (Greenberg, et al., 2005). Second, lack of support for mobility, security, resilience, survivability, etc., which are considered main features for a pervasive trustworthy infrastructure.

In response to observed computer network liabilities, research efforts have sprouted a plethora of architectural proposals aiming to overcome shortcomings evident in computer network realizations. Two main approaches can be identified. The first preserves the layered protocol structure, yet allows for vertical integration between protocols operating at different layers to induce context awareness and adaptability. The second approach targets clean-slate designs, primarily ignoring the need for backward compatibility. Nevertheless, we argue that the majority of contemporary architectural proposals remain idiosyncratic, satisfying a particular service model, tailored to a specific set of requirements, or fettered by implicit assumptions (Khoury, Abdallah, & Heileman, 2010). Targeting causes rather than symptoms, we opine that deficiencies apparent in current network realizations can be traced back to the following underlying causes;

1. The general trend towards network science and engineering lacks a systematic formalization of core principles that expresses essential network features required to guide the process of network design and protocol engineering;
2. The prevalence of a top-down design approach for computer network architecture demonstrated as confining intelligence to network edges, and maintaining a dump core; and
3. The absence of a general reference model that embodies core network design principles and acknowledges the multidimensionality in design entailed in architecting computer networks that reach beyond core networking requirements.

Taking a broader view on the community's architectural quest, we present CORM, a clean-slate Concern-Oriented Reference Model for architecting future computer networks. CORM reflects our vision on how the process of network design need to proceed guided by, and adapting to the conventional engineering process. CORM stands as a guiding framework from which several network architectures can be derived according to specific functional, contextual, and operational requirements or constraints. CORM represents a pioneering attempt within the network realm, and to our knowledge, CORM is the first reference model that is bio-inspired, accounts for complex system characteristics, and applies a software engineering approach to network design. Moreover, CORM's derivation process conforms to the Function-Behavior-Structure (FBS) engineering framework developed by the Australian design scientist John Gero and his colleagues (Gero, 1990). We aspire that CORM presentation motivates the derivation, as well as the experimentation of CORM-based network architectures in an attempt to construct evolvable future computer networks.

This chapter presents CORM. The chapter starts by overviewing relevant background and related work. CORM's design principles and approach are then presented, followed by a detailed description of CORM's components and distinctive features. CORM is validated using the FBS engineering framework. A conjecture of a file transfer protocol engineered according to a CORM-based architecture is then presented, before the chapter concludes by pointing out future directions and open research areas.

BACKGROUND AND RELATED WORK

CORM's related work and background encompasses several areas of research. This section overviews three main areas that have profoundly affected the path to CORM. The first subsection introduces our definition of a reference model and how it differs from an architecture. Our definitions are based, in part, on the definitions presented by MacKenzie, et al. (2006). The second subsection introduces the FBS engineering framework introduced by Gero (1990). The FBS is used to validate CORM and the derivation of its basic abstraction unit. The last subsection overviews contemporary architectural proposals to computer networks.

Reference Model vs. Architecture

MacKenzie, et al. (2006) states that "a reference model is an abstract framework for understanding significant relationships among the entities of some environment. It enables the development of *specific* reference or concrete architectures using consistent standards or specifications supporting that environment." This statement accentuates the key difference between a reference model and an architecture. A reference model expresses requirements at the highest level of abstractions. These requirements will be refined as the specifications of the model are further revealed, passing through several stages where the reference model yields a reference architecture and eventually a concrete architecture. As an illustration, consider concepts as eating areas and hygiene areas when modeling buildings. These concepts represent requirements at the higher level of abstraction that might be applied differently as further building specifications are revealed; for example in case of residential housing the concept of eating area will be realized as a kitchen and a dining room, while in case of a school building, the concept of eating area could be realized as a kitchen and a cafeteria. Similarly, in computer networks, a reference model for computer networks need to express the most fundamental design principles for engineering computer networks at the highest level of abstraction. These design principles will be further materialized and detailed in a network architecture that is derived to operate in a specific context, or to satisfy a particular set of performance requirements and constraints.

The Function-Behavior-Structure Framework

The Function-Behavior-Structure framework (FBS) has been developed by the Australian design scientist John Gero and his colleagues (Gero, 1990). It is credited to be applicable to any engineering discipline, for reasoning about and explaining the nature and process of design (Kruchten, 2005). According to Gero, the metagoal of design is to transform a set of functions F (generally referred to as requirements) into a design description D. The purpose of D is to transform sufficient information about the designed artifact so that it can be manufactured, fabricated, or constructed. However, translating requirements, expressed as F, to an artifact's design description D, is not a straightforward task. Thus further explorations are required to attain the transformation F to D denoted as follows

$$F \rightarrow D.$$

On the other hand, the artifact, to be produced using D, will be realized in the physical world. Thus D needs to express the artifact in terms of composing elements and their relationships. The description of the artifact's elements and their relationships is referred to as the artifact's structure S. Thus the design description D of an artifact, can be partially derived by delineating the artifact's structure S, yielding the below transformation

$$S \rightarrow D$$

Another way of deriving the structure of an artifact S is by using a catalog lookup, where we find a structure associated to a certain function providing the direct transformation

$$F \rightarrow S$$

However, this transformation occurs at the element level of an artifact, and it does not represent the general case of design. Nevertheless, both F and S can be defined within the context of the target artifact behavior. The behavior of structure B_s can be directly derived from structure yielding the transformation

$$S \rightarrow B_s$$

Figure 1. John Gero's function-behavior-structure framework (adapted from [Gero 1990; Kruchten, 2005])

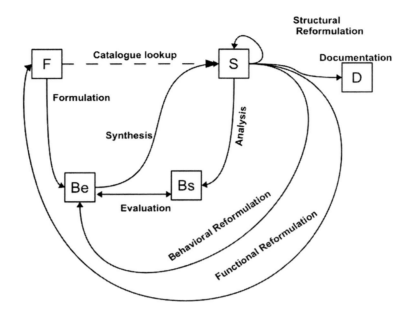

while F can be expressed in terms of expected behavior Be, where Be provides the syntax by which the semantics represented by F can be achieved

$$F \rightarrow Be$$

Comparing Bs to Be determines the appropriateness of S in fulfilling F yielding the following transformations

$$F \rightarrow Be \rightarrow S \rightarrow Bs \rightarrow D$$

Here, requirements specified through a set of functions F, will be expressed in terms of expected behavior Be. This expected behavior Be is used in the selection and combination of structure S based on a knowledge of the behavior Bs produced by S to be defined in D. However, when S is synthesized, its accompanying Bs might not be quite what was expected, leading to several reformulations of all elements of the model (F, Be, S, Bs, and D). Figure 1 illustrates the design

activity encompassing FBS elements and the different processes involved, while Table 1 lists the eight processes of the FBS model.

Architectural Innovations

Several alternatives to the layered architecture have been proposed even before the advancements of new wireless technologies, and the introduction of new services that request support for a wide range of media (voice, video, graphics, and text) and access patterns (interactive, bulk transfer, real-time rendering, opportunistic). The argument presented back then was that layering may not be the most effective modularity for implementation, since it unnecessarily constrains or complicates the engineering alternatives available to the implementer (Clark & Tennenhouse, 1990). However, the reluctance to change working implementations and long-standing inter-layer interfaces often led designers to apply short-term solutions by inserting functionalities between existing layers,

Table 1. The eight steps of the FBS model (adapted from [Gero 1990; Kruchten, 2005])

Process	Transformation	Explanation
Formulation	F → Be	Transformation of the posited functions into behaviors that are expected to enable these functions.
Synthesis	Be → S	Transformation of these expected behaviors into a structure that is intended to exhibit these behaviors.
Analysis	S → Bs	Derivation of the actual behaviors of the structure
Evaluation	Bs ↔ Be	Comparison of the actual and expected behaviors
Documentation	S → D	Production of Design description
Structural Reformulation	S → S'	Changes in design state space in terms of structural variables or their values expressing structural evolution and refinement over time
Behavioral Reformulation	S → Be'	Changes in the design state space in terms of behavioral variables or their values leading to changes/evolution of expected behavior
Functional Reformulation	S → F'	Changes in design state space in terms of functional variables or their values illustrating evolution of requirements

rather than modifying them. Nevertheless, the proliferation of wireless communication and demanding needs of new Internet services motivated individual researchers to propose alternatives to the layered architecture. Some presented point solutions, while others aimed at providing a general framework for network design. Some preserved the layered structure, while others took a "clean-slate" approach to their design. In this respect, the US NSF FIND (FIND, 2011) and EU FIRE (FIRE, 2011) initiatives can be considered the most influential research attempting architectural innovations aimed at Future Internet.

Following is a survey of the different proposals presented in contemporary research literature. Proposals will be discussed from two points of views; the first classifies the presented designs as incremental, add-on, or clean-slate. The second view classifies the design according to the network dimension addressed. We identify two network dimensions along which most architectural proposals can be classified; a vertical dimension addressing structure and configuration of protocols, and a horizontal dimension addressing communication in terms of routing functions.

Cross-Layer Design

Cross-Layer Designs (CLD) defy the strict layered architecture and allow protocols at nonadjacent layers to interact and communicate. CLD concept was motivated by the severe performance deterioration of traditional protocols when operating in wireless environments. In order to cope with the unique and dynamic nature of wireless links, a protocol architecture that incorporates CLD has been frequently proposed. The majority of CLD presented in the research literature address a specific requirement of the wireless communication such as QoS, TCP performance, mobility, resource management, etc. However several general designs that targeted the network architecture as a whole were also presented and those are the designs that will be considered here.

The first attempt to incorporate a degree of layer interaction was proposed by Larzon, Bodin, & Schelen, (2002) through the use of Hints and Notifications (HAN). HAN are exchanged between layers above and below the network layer. Exchange was done using option fields in the IP header and ICMP messages. Hints are provided by upper layers to the link layer to guide it in its choice of error coding, modulation techniques and retransmission policies. Notifications, on the other hand, are passed from link layer to the upper layer indicating the reasons for packet drops as well as the level of link congestion experienced. All exchanges are done at the network layer.

Wang, and Abu-Rgheff (2003) present a more comprehensive cross layer interaction scheme which is referred to as Cross-LAyer Signaling Shortcuts (CLASS). The basic idea of CLASS was to break the layer ordering constraints, while keeping the layering structure and propagating cross-layer messages through local out-band signaling shortcuts.

Interlayer Coordination Model (Carneiro, Ruela, & Ricardo, 2004) was the first to present a cross-layer framework for the layered architecture, where a central entity manages the different layer interactions. Four planes are identified along which interactions are required across the protocol stack. These are Security plane, QoS plane, mobility plane and link adaptation plane. Protocols at different layers, whose operations will be affected, or can affect the operation at the previously mentioned planes, expose their internal state to the management entity (ME), which on its turn, responds with the appropriate action.

ÉCLAIR, introduced by Raisinghani and Iyer (2006), is an architecture for an asynchronous cross layer feedback system where protocol adaptation is done out of phase with the protocol operation. ÉCLAIR splits the cross layer system into two subsystems; Tuning Layers (TL) and Optimizing Subsystem (OSS). A TL is an extension appended to each layer of the protocol stack, and is aware of the data structures used to store the control information of each protocol within a given layer. OSS is composed of several Protocol Optimizers (POs). Each PO contains the algorithm for a particular cross layer optimization. TL exports an API to PO, which, on its turn, needs to register with the TL for information about a specific event. On receiving feed back from the TL, the PO executes

the required optimizing code to modify protocol behavior.

CLDs target the network vertical dimension addressing primarily the configuration of the on node network stack. CLDs aim to preserve the layered architecture, yet, reduce the rigid order imposed by the layered paradigm, as well as alleviate the constraint imposed on vertical layer integration. CLDs are aimed primarily at wireless environments, and address the need for inducing adaptability in face of the unstable wireless link conditions, by allowing protocols at nonadjacent layers to communicate and expose their internal states. Preserving the layered architecture, CLDs are compatible with the current network realizations, which ease their integration into the TCP/IP suite. Yet, Kawadia and Kumar (2005) argue that integrating several CLDs with the Internet protocol suite may work at cross purposes, leading to unintended side effects that eventually deteriorates overall performance. Moreover, CLD stifles future development, since changes can no longer be confined to one layer.

FIND Proposals

SILO architecture (Baldine, et al. 2007) aims to integrate cross-layer designs and optimizations into the Future Internet. The SILO architecture main components are services, a control agent, and a set of rules and constraints that dictates services associations and orderings. In SILO a service is an abstract fine-grained, well-defined, self-contained, atomic function to be performed on application data relevant to a specific communication task. A service is described using an ontology of functions, interfaces, and control parameters called knobs. A service implementation is called a method. Several methods (implementations) could exist for the same service. Methods are ordered to build vertical stacks called silo. The control agent is an entity that resides inside a node hosting the SILO architecture. The control agent dynamically custom-builds a silo for each initiated connection according to service associations and ordering rules, while taking into consideration requirements, policies and resources. Each instantiated silo is associated with a given traffic stream, and possesses a state that is a union of all constituents methods states, as well as any shared state resulting from cross method interactions. A silo persists for the duration of the connection. The control agent is capable of adjusting the knobs of an instantiated silo during runtime to optimize performance. Moreover, the control agent may optionally be able to communicate with other control agents residing on other nodes in the network in order to further optimize a silo behavior.

Recursive Network Architecture (RNA) (Touch, Wang, & Pingali, 2006)is an architectural proposal based on recursive composition of a single configurable protocol structure. RNA avoids recapitulation of implementation as well as encourages a cleaner cross-layer interaction. RNA uses a single meta-protocol as a generic protocol layer. This meta-protocol includes a number of basic services, as well as hooks to configurable capabilities. This meta-protocol provides the building block from which layers are instantiated forming dynamic stacks. Each layer of the stack is tuned to the properties of the layers below it. RNA uses a MultiDomain Communications Model (MDCM), which is a structured abstract template to delineate both next-hop and next-layer resolution, where either can be chosen at runtime.

SILO and RNA have been presented as clean-slate architectural attempts towards Future Internet. However, layering, as a design paradigm, is still the prevailing model. An essential goal of both proposals is to gracefully embrace cross layering into the present network stack. In SILO, Baldine, et al. (2007) argue in favor of layering for modularization and abstraction. They propose "rejuvenating the layering concept" by relaxing the traditional rigid boundaries and strict ordering among layers and allowing any set of services to be selected dynamically for a particular task. While in RNA the protocol layering is still the basic design, but it provides freedom in protocol organization to create dynamic custom-build stacks. Although considered clean-slate architectures, we argue that by adhering to layered stacks as the underlying model, both proposals might suffer form shortcomings attributed to the Internet model. First, both architectures do not give guidance to engineers as how to handle cross interests among composed protocols: The single control agent in SILO, as presented, is a monolithic unit representing a single point of failure for all protocols working under its control, as well as imposing scalability problem as service diversity, granularity, and operational parameters increase. Needless to say the expected code complexity, since it is required to be aware of all services, their compositional logic, polices and constrains. As for RNA MDCM, we note that confining the logic for horizontal and vertical interlayer communication into a single entity is a very challenging task that is error prone. Furthermore, it lacks explicit representation for interactions leaving it to be decided-on at runtime. This allows for implicit assumptions to creep into protocol design and implementations. Second, both architectures have undermined monitoring and resource management failing to express both functions as first class architectural constructs. Finally, as presented, both architectures focus on the vertical dimension of the network without suggesting how the horizontal dimension will be incorporated.

FIRE Proposals

ANA (Keller, Hossmann, May, Bouabene, Jelger, &Tschudin, 2008) is an EU initiative aiming to frame autonomic networking principles and architecture, as well as to build a prototype for autonomic networks. ANA main architectural abstractions are, Functional Blocks (FB), Information Dispatch Point (IDP), Information Channels (IC), and network and node Compartments. ANA architecture is built on the concept of indirection manifested through the use of IDPs. An IDP represents the entry point to all ANA's abstractions and allows for transparent change in the data flow path. An FB in ANA is an information processing unit that implement data transmission function, or additional functionalities such as traffic monitoring. FBs existing within local scope of each other exchange data through the IDPs attached to each directly. While for remote FBs, each FB's IDP need to be first attached to the IDP of an IC. To support communication between any pair of networking functionalities, ANA's constructs export a generic API. Scope in ANA is defined using the concept of a compartment, which represents a set of FBs, IDPs and ICs with some commonly agreed set of communication principles, protocols and policies. Two types of compartments are defined in ANA. The node compartment represents a local and private execution environment for ANA clients, while the network compartment represents a network instance encompassing several ANA nodes, and involve communication across an underlying network infrastructure. ANA's network compartments exist at the waist of the TCP/IP model and provides the means to federate multiple heterogenous networks. Internally, a network compartment has a variety of choices regarding naming, addressing policies, packet headers, etc. Externally, each network compartment supports a generic compartment API, which provides the glue that permits to build complex network stacks and packet processing paths.

Indirection in ANA gives a solution to data flow flexibility. However, the ANA's framework does not give guidance as to how each network internally should be built, reasoning that, leaving internals unspecified, provides flexibility and accounts for future change. In contrast, we argue that, to support future changes, the com-

munity's compelling need is a clear definition of ground network design principles and specifications, according to which all networks need to be developed and synthesized. These ground principles and specifications will be common to all networks regardless of network's heterogeneity in terms of purpose, size, underlying technology, or running applications. Defining network core-design principles will promote global network system integrity leading to seamless integration and federation. Furthermore, although developed primarily towards autonomic behavior, ANA's abstractions do not enforce, or even imply monitoring activities, which is a principal functionality for supporting autonomic behavior.

Haggle (Scott, Huiy, Crowcrofty, and Diot, 2006) is a FIRE architectural proposal targeting Pocket Switched Networks. Haggle is a non-layered architecture that enables applications to be infrastructure-independent. Haggle architecture targets mobile node configuration. It divides the on-node communication functionalities into four modules; delivery, user data, protocols, and resource management. Haggle architecture is motivated by the need to support mobile applications. An important concept that Haggle introduces is the Application Data Unit (ADU). ADU is the unit of transmission in the Haggle architecture, and as the name suggests an ADU is a data item meaningful to the end application. Haggle was presented at an abstract level with no details on realizations in terms of protocols and their interactions.

BIONETS (BIONETS, 2011) is another EU research project that focuses on the definition of a biologically-inspired design toolkit for autonomic networks and services. At the network level, the BIONETS system is composed of clouds of mobile nodes that are connected among themselves, but potentially disconnected from any IP network or backbone, in addition to any number of sensors or embedded sources of contextual data. At the application and user level, the BIONETS system is comprised of users interacting with each other, and with a range of services and applications that are supported by the local cloud and by the other sensors. BIONETS overcomes device heterogeneity and achieves scalability via an autonomic and localized peer-to-peer communication paradigm. Services in BIONETS are also autonomic, and evolve, like living organisms, by natural selection to adapt to their surrounding environment. Biologically-inspired concepts permeate the network and its services, blending them together, so that the network moulds itself to the services it runs, and services, in turn, become a mirror image of the social networks of users they serve.

BIONETS project provide very useful and interesting insights into different aspects of computer communication. BIONETS research highlights the social dimension of technology in supporting sustainable business models. In addition, it incorporates biological, physical and mathematical models into the design of user level, service level and network level protocols. BIONETS does not provide a standalone framework for network design and protocol engineering. However, we, conjecture that BIONETS contribution in terms of bio-inspired theoretical foundations, principles and protocols can be further culminated if incorporated within a bio-inspired network architecture.

Cognitive Networks

Cognitive networks is a research area in computer networks that draws on multidisciplinary fields including communication, artificial intelligence, learning and decision making. Thomas, DaSilva, & MacKenzie, (2005) defines cognitive networks as

a network with a cognitive process that can perceive current network conditions, and then plan, decide and act on those conditions. The network can learn from these adaptations and use them to make future decisions, all while taking into account end-to-end goals.

Observing the end-to-end goals of communication is the main feature that differentiates cognitive networks from other smart, self modifying, cognitive communication technologies. The central mechanism of the cognitive network is the cognitive process. The design of the cognitive process is based on a feedback loop model. A simple model of a feedback loop, called OODA, was first put forward by Col John Boyd USAF (Thomas, et al. 2005). OODA stands for Observe, Orient, Decide and Act, which represent the four stages required for a decision making process. Although missing a learning stage, simple feedback loops as the OODA can operate in a highly complex environment. This is because, as Thomas, et al. (2005) argue, complex systems have a structure that may not be apparent from the outside analysis but an attempt to approximate it can be made through iterative cycles of a test-response feedback loop.

Thomas proposes a framework for the cognitive network composed of the following

1. **User/Application/ Resource Requirements:** This is the top level component of the cognitive networks. Observing the end-to-end goals of communication as put forth by the users, applications, or resources, is what sets a cognitive network apart from other cognitive communication mechanisms.

2. **Cognitive Process:** The cognitive process is composed of three components: the specification language, cognition layer, and network input. The cognition layer observe the status of network elements from the network input component through sensors. While the top-level user requirements is fed to the cognition layer through the specification language component which acts as an interface layer. Being aware of the network status, as well as the end-to-end requirements and goals, the cognition layer performs required adaptations

3. **Software Adaptable Network (SAN):** The SAN depends on a network that has one or more tunable elements. The SAN provides the cognitive layer with an interface to the tunable network elements. It also reports to the cognition layer the operating state of the network elements.

Cognitive networks highlights the significance of observing the end-to-end goals while conducting adaptations. However, as presented, the cognitive network is an add on to the computer network were the feedback loop operates outside the network stack. This layout renders cognition in cognitive networks as an extrinsic feature rather being an intrinsic feature of the operating network elements or protocols. The framework proposed adopts a layered paradigm, and does not clearly express the structure of the cognition layer leaving it to be decided upon during the implementation stage. Moreover, the framework proposed, although targeting the horizontal dimension of the network by observing the end-to-end goals, concentrates on the components to be instantiated at the vertical dimension and fails to delineate the interactions required to establish cognitive communication paths.

CORM DESIGN PRINCIPLES

In crafting CORM design principles, we aimed to address computer network design at the highest level of abstraction. On the one hand, distributed computer networks, such as the Internet, stand as a typical example of complex systems (Mitchell, 2006 ; Park and Willinger 2005). On the other hand, the operations performed by computer networks rely fundamentally on protocols, which can be described as distributed software running on different nodes constituting the network. Therefore, computer networks are a typical example of distributed software-dependent systems. From these two observations, we assert that a computer network is a software-dependent complex system. This leads to our two ground design principles to be detailed in the following subsections.

Principle I: A Computer Network is a Complex System

The study of complex systems has been the focus of interdisciplinary research. Its importance rises from the fact that different diverse social, natural, economic and physical systems have been shown to exhibit several commonalities. Such commonalities have promoted the interest of researchers to come up with a unified framework within which different complex systems can be analyzed and formulated. So far there is no consensus on the definition of *complex systems* in the literature although their general properties are well recognized. Informally, complex systems can be defined as a large network of relatively simple components with no central control in which emergent complex behavior is exhibited as a result of component interactions. "The complexity of the system's global behavior is typically characterized in terms of the patterns it forms, the information processing that it accomplishes, and the degree to which this pattern formation and information processing are adaptive for the system - that is, increase its success in some evolutionary or competitive context." (Mitchell, 2006, pp. 2). This definition highlights three characteristics for complex systems.

1. Complex systems are composed of relatively large number of autonomous entities. This property implies the distributed control and structure of complex systems, as well as their indeterminate nature. Entities in a complex system exist independent of each other (no implied global structure or imposed hierarchy). Yet, act interdependently, affecting and getting affected by each other;
2. Complex systems exhibit complexity. Quantitatively, complexity refers to the amount of information required to depict

the system at the micro and macro levels (Mitchell, 2006). Complexity arises, not only from the myriad intricate interactions occurring at the micro level among the system components, but more notably, form the feedback and influence of the macro level resultant behavior on decisions taken at the micro level. In other words, the mapping from individual actions to collective behavior is non-trivial giving the system its discernible emergent behavior property; and

3. Complex systems exhibit emergent behavior. Emergent behavior refers to the ability of the system's components to change/evolve their structures and/or functions without external intervention as a result of their interactions, and/or in response to changes in their environment (Mitchell, 2006). Emergent behavior results in global level system stability, in spite of possible local level disequilibrium. Therefore, complex systems are frequently described as being at the "edge of chaos" (Mogul, 2006). A metaphor used to describe the system's reaction to minor context/environmental changes, by shifting from one state of order to another to better cope with the induced changes. Emergent behavior can be further classified as self-organization, adaptation or evolution (Rihani, 2001)

   a. Self-organization refers to changes in the individual behavior of a component due to inter-component communication.

   b. Adaptation refers to changes in components' behavior in response to changes in the surrounding environment. Both self-organization and adaptation imply information propagation and adaptive processing through feedback mechanisms.

   c. Evolution refers to a higher form of intelligent adaptation and/or self organization of components in response to changes by accounting on previously recorded knowledge from past experience(s). Evolution usually implies the presence of memory elements, as well as monitoring functions in evolvable components.

After delineating the properties of complex systems, we need to highlight the following points:

1. We have previously pointed out that current network realizations, based on the Internet model, have been cited as an example of complex systems. However, in contrast to complex-system's emergent behavior, present network realizations are characterized by emergent ill-behavior, where a local event may have a destructive global effect realized as cascading meltdowns that might require human intervention for correct network operation (Greenberg, et al., 2005; Mogul, 2006). Furthermore, up to our knowledge, adaptation in present network realizations is crude (e.g. TCP aggressive cut down on congestion window size regardless of the reason for packet drops). It lacks the evolvability capability intrinsic to all complex systems. This renders the network to be oblivious to changing patterns and trends in operating conditions and performance requirements. In the literature, the term Adaptive Complex System (CAS) has been used to designate systems that exhibit emergent behavior in contrast to those that exhibit emergent ill-behavior, and likewise we will be using the term CAS hereafter to refer to complex systems that possess emergent behavior (Dooley, 1996).

2. In context of CAS, stability is different from equilibrium. Stability refers to the ability of the system to maintain stable global patterns, in spite of the unpredictable interactions occurring at the local level. These overall stable patterns are a direct consequence of the local chaotic agitation, where elements

composing the system operate at conditions that are far from equilibrium (Rihani, 2001). In other words, for CAS to be stable, its components' states alternate between order and chaos.

3. CAS strive to fit their context. However, fitness within the context of CAS means to be able to find approximate solutions to difficult problems, rather than being able to find the best solution. Finding the best solution may be impossible due to the multitude of possibilities, limited time allowed for reaching a decision, and restricted vision of context (Stirling, 2005).

Principle II: A Computer Network is a Distributed Software System

Software Engineering (SE) refers to using systematic, disciplined, quantifiable approaches to the development, operation and maintenance of software (Wikipedia, 2011). To manage software functional complexity, SE defines the concept of Separation of Concerns (SoC), which is a general problem-solving technique that addresses complexity by cutting down the problem space into smaller, more manageable, loosely-coupled, and easier to solve sub-problems. Thus SoC allows for better problem understanding and design (Mili, et al., 2004). SoC is a dual facet concept addressing concerns from two different views. The first view identifies concerns according to the system requirement specifications. It classifies concerns into core concerns and crosscutting concerns. Core concerns refer to core functional requirements of a system that can be identified with clear cutting boundaries. Hence, can be represented in separable modules or components resulting in loosely coupled systems. On the other hand, crosscutting concerns are nonfunctional aspects of the system that span over multiple modules or components, trying to manage or optimize the core concerns, and if not carefully represented, result in scattering and tangling of system behavior (Mili, et al.,

2004). In that respect, concerns will be identified according to the domain in which the system will operate. The second view of the SoC concept addresses system configuration. It differentiates between system components and system connector (Gacemi1, et al., 2004). System components represents loci of computations, decisions and states, while system connectors, represents component interactions that facilitates information flow and state communication.

CORM METHODOLOGY: CONCERN-ORIENTED BOTTOM-UP DESIGN APPROACH

Our proposed Concern-Oriented Bottom-Up[1] design approach follows directly from our design principles. The Bottom-Up approach is derived from property 1 in Principle I, and the second view of SoC concept in Principle II. Both accentuated the significance of the basic building block or entity composing the network system. The Concern-Oriented paradigm represents our vision in network functional and structural decomposition.

Computer networks need to be designed along two main dimensions; a vertical dimension that addresses structure and configuration of network building blocks, and a horizontal dimension that addresses communication and interactions among the previously formulated building blocks. In adopting a Bottom-Up approach, our main focus will be the vertical network dimension delineating the network building block responsibilities and capabilities. From a CAS perspective, these network building blocks need to possess adaptability, self-organization and evolvability as intrinsic features. The network will then be constructed by composition from these building blocks. From a SE perspective, applying the second view of the SoC principle, network building blocks will represent the loci of computation, decisions and states encompassing the network concerns (core as well as crosscutting concerns), while their interactions and communications identify network connectors instantiating the network horizontal dimension.

Our Concern-Oriented Bottom-Up design methodology does not differentiate between network core and network edge in terms of capabilities, thus it contradicts the End-to-End (E2E) principle that has been central to the Internet design. The E2E principle dictates that mechanisms should not be placed in the network if they can be placed at the end nodes, and that the core of the network should provide a general service, not one that is tailored to a specific application (Saltzer, et al., 1984). It has been argued that the E2E principle has served the Internet well by keeping the core general enough to support a wide range of applications. However, we contend that, taken as an absolute rule, the E2E principle constrained core evolvability rather than fostered its capabilities rendering the Internet biased to those applications that can tolerate its oblivious nature, and forcing designers and protocol engineers to adopt point solutions to compensate for core deficiencies (Hassan, Eltoweissy, & Youssef, 2008). Another consequence to our proposed bottom-up network composition is contradicting the prevailing misconception of abstracting a network in terms of an inter-network. Adopting a bottom-up approach to network composition implies recursive construction of the inter-networks from networks, which are likewise recursively constructed form network components, which are constructed from one or more network building blocks.

CORM: A CONCERN-ORIENTED REFERENCE MODEL FOR COMPUTER NETWORKS

A network reference model is an abstract representation of the network. It conveys a minimal set of unifying concepts, axioms, and relationships to be realized within the network (MacKenzie,

et al., 2006). For expressing a multi-dimensional system such as a computer network, multiple abstract representations are required to capture the network from different perspectives. CORM abstracts a computer network in terms of requirement specifications, structure, and interactions, represented as the network-concerns conceptual framework, the network structural template, and the information flow model respectively. Focusing primarily on the vertical dimension of the network, the two following subsections detail the first two components of CORM; the concern-oriented conceptual framework and the network structural template. As for the horizontal network dimension, the third subsection provides a synopsis of the information flow model.

ACRF: The Conceptual Framework for Network Concerns

CORM's conceptual framework for network concerns was derived according to our interpretation of the network requirement specifications. We postulate that the basic requirement for computer networks can be expressed by the following statement: *The network is a communication vehicle allowing its users to communicate using the available communication media.* Accordingly, we identify the network users, the communication media, and the communication logic as the primary requirements, which the network design need to address and plan for. Applying the concept of SoC to our analysis, we identify four main network concerns; Application Concern (ACn), Communication Concern (CCn), Resource Concern (RCn), and Federation Concern (FCn). The first three are core network concerns encompassing the network functional requirements, while the fourth is a crosscutting concern (non-functional requirement) representing the area of intersection or common interests among core concerns. Elaborating on each concern we have:

- The ACn encompasses the network usage semantics; the logic and motivation for building the network, where different network-based end-applications (network users) can be manifested.
- The CCn addresses the need for network-route binding to provide an end-to-end communication path allowing network elements to get connected (communication logic)
- The RCn focuses on network resources, whether physical or logical, highlighting the need for resource management to efficiently address different trade-offs for creating and maintaining network resources (communication media).
- Finally, FCn orchestrates interactions, resolves conflicts and manages cross interests, where areas of overlap exist among the aforementioned concerns.

These four network concerns are manifested as CORM conceptual framework for network concerns, referred to hereafter as ACRF. The ACRF represents the blueprint for the network functional design that need to be realized along both network dimensions, vertically on the network components and horizontally among network components.

Analyzing the Internet model (vertical dimension) and the present network realizations (horizontal dimension) with respect to the ACRF framework, we note that both the RCn and the FCn are absent. Vertically, the Internet-layered model accounts for ACn and CCn. However, the model did not apply the correct concern separation; a single concern was split along two layers. Refer to Figure 2 that maps the ACRF to the Internet-layered model. Moreover, by applying a strict layered paradigm for functional decomposition, inter-layer communication was reduced to a minimum set of primitives conducted by the use of protocol headers. Such layout curtailed all possibilities for considering FCn (Clark & Tennenhouse, 1990). As for RCn, it was assumed that resource-management functionalities, in general, are either applications of specific type and thus will be overlaid on top of the protocol stack (Zimmermann, 1980), or are to be handled locally by the physical media. As with respect to the horizontal dimension, present network realizations account for both ACn and CCn, while the RCn and FCn are usually realized as point solutions.

Figure 2. ACRF mapping to the internet layered model

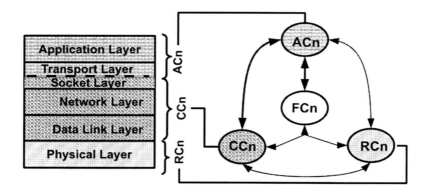

Servers and server farms represent ACn, while routers, switches, and DNS represent CCn. As for RCn and FCn, both are implemented as add on functionalities conducted by the use of protocols for network management and traffic engineering.

NST: Network Structural Template

CORM networks are composed of network components that communicate through a communication substrate. The network components are composed of one or more active network building-blocks, where computations and decisions take place, while the communication substrate represents a passive media for information flow and exchange. Being the primary constituents of a software-dependent complex system, CORM-based network building-blocks need to possess adaptability, self-organization and evolvability as intrinsic features, thus mimicking bacterial cells in a bacterial colony; our adopted model of CAS (Ben-Jacob & Levine, 2005). Accordingly, we define the Network Cell (NC), the CORM-based network building-block, as a self-contained computational/decision entity capable of monitoring its state, adapting to perceived conditions, inferring decisions, recording its experience, and eventually evolving through self-learning and intelligent adaptations. One or more NCs make up a Network Component (Ncomp), which we define as the basic network entity capable of end-to-end communication. The internal structure of an NC and the bottom-up network composition template are detailed in the following subsections.

The Network Cell

The Network Cell structure and behavior are inspired by observations recorded in a recent study on primordial bacteria that provided a vivid representation of the main features that need to be present in entities composing a self-engineering

CAS (Ben-Jacob & Levine, 2005). According to this study the following four cell capabilities are essential to attain emergent behavior.

1. The cell should be aware of its surrounding environment as well as of its inner states;
2. The cell should be able to reason about its perceived states and decide on its course of action that best serves its goal function;
3. The cell should be able to memorize previously inferred decisions and learn from past experience; and
4. The cell should be able to communicate and cooperate with other cells to achieve the high level goals of the whole system.

To beget these capabilities in a CORM network, the NC is constructed out of four units: the Interface Unit (IU), the Monitoring Unit (MU), the Regulatory Unit (RU) and the Execution Unit (EU). NC structure is shown in Figure 3, which represents the structure of a generic NC. By generic we mean that this structure will be common to all NCs, regardless of their assigned responsibilities or roles. The NC has two modes of concurrent operations; intrinsic operation and functional operation. The intrinsic operation is again common to all NCs and represents the NC's genetic blueprint that can be regarded as the sequence of actions and rules that the NC must obey throughout its lifetime. On the other hand, the functional operation of the NC is assigned to it on its creation and prescribes the role that the NC must perform. This includes the function to be realized and the corresponding instruction set that is to be executed by all units. Once the NC is assigned a functional role, it turns to be a specialized NC. Therefore, the generic NC is just a template out of which all specialized NC can be derived. It is also possible for a specialized NC to change its function during its lifetime or alternate between different functions depending

Figure 3. The network cell

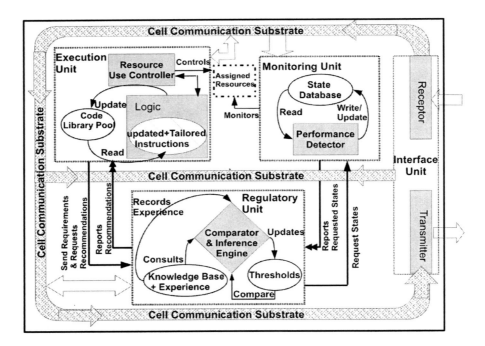

on its assigned role(s). Once an NC materializes by assuming a functional role, it will be assigned a portion of the system resources according to its functional needs.

Following is an outline for the intrinsic operation of each of the units shown in Figure 3:

- Interface Unit (IU): The IU is the NC boundary allowing it to communicate with the outside world (environment or peer NCs). Through the IU the NCs receive and transmit different forms/representations of data (states, instructions, control, content, etc.).
- Monitoring Unit (MU): The MU is responsible for monitoring the different states of an NC. This includes monitoring all input and/or output communication flows directed into or out of the NC, all internal communications among the NC units, as well as the usage level of assigned recourses.

The MU will extract state information and represent this information in a quantifiable format. These quantified states are then stored in the state database to be retrieved upon requests received form Regulatory Unit.

Regulatory Unit (RU): The RU has two regulatory cycles one is inherent and the other is initiated. The inherent cycle is always in operation, and checks that the resource usage levels and performance parameters are always within the set thresholds. The initiated cycle is either triggered by requests received from the Execution Unit (EU is described below) asking for advices and/or recommendations for performance enhancement, or due to performance deterioration realized through monitoring. Accordingly, the RU inspects environmental/performance parameters to infer the reasons that accounted for performance deterioration. This step may

Figure 4. ACRF realization within CORM-NC

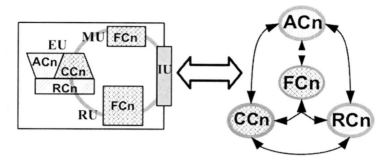

lead to communication with neighboring peers requesting their views of the environment. The RU has the capability of gaining knowledge and learning from past experience, which it records in the Knowledge/Experience database. Therefore, the RU provides educated recommendations to the EU to optimize its operation. In addition, the RU may update some of the threshold levels according to its inferred decisions.

- Execution Unit (EU): The EU is responsible for executing the function(s) assigned to the NC. Function(s) assigned to an NC are usually accompanied by a pool of libraries that can be used to formulate different ways of accomplishing the required function. The EU is composed of two main components; the Logic Component (LC) and the Resource Use Controller Component (RUCC). The LC is the part responsible for performing the NC function. The LC starts by creating a set of instructions that best accomplishes the required function using the code library pool. It also requests the RU's recommendations, thus incorporating both the RU knowledge and experience, as well as accounting for environmental alterations. Once the LC receives feedback recommendations from the RU, it might update its tailored instruc-

tion set to fit the inferred operational status. The RUCC, on the other hand, is responsible for managing resources assigned to the NC. The RUCC works together with the LC to ensure optimal internal resource usage and distribution. The RUCC is also responsible for estimating the required level of resources for the NC operation as a whole, and thus requests the estimated resources from the system

All the NC units communicate through the cell communication substratum (CCS) that represents the media into which information is temporarily deposited to be later consumed. The function assigned to a specialized NC will further identify operational aspects of each of the NC units, such as the parameters to be monitored and states to be recorded by the MU, the threshold values to be used by the RU, and the code library pool out of which the logic will be tailored and then executed by the EU. Recalling that the ACRF represents the network functional blueprint to be realized throughout the network, and that the NC represents the basic building-block to encompass the network-concern space for CORM networks, we note that any functional role assigned to the NC will be decomposed according the ACRF as illustrated in Figure 4.

Network Compositional Logic

Network compositional logic defines the bottom-up network construction out of network entities and identifies the different interaction boundaries that can occur among network entities. Network entities can be classified into computational/decision building-blocks (NC and/or Ncomp) that produce and/or consume network data, and a passive communication substrate, where network data can flow. Network Compositional Logic stems from our bottom-up definition of network and inter-network construction. We define a computer network as two or more Ncomp connected by a communication substratum, where Ncomp interactions are sustained, despite the heterogeneity of the hardware, middleware, and software of the connected Ncomps. While a computer inter-network is defined as two or more computer networks connected by communication substrate, where interactions among Ncomps residing within each of the connected networks are sustained, despite the heterogeneity of the hardware, middleware, and software employed by the Ncomp composing the connected networks. Ncomps communicating over the inter-network perceive the connected networks as a single network. Integrating NC, Ncomp, network and inter-network definitions into the Network Composition Logic we derive CORM NST and define it, using EBNF, as follows:

CORM NST EBNF formal Definition:

- Notations
  - Trailing * means repeat 0 or more times
  - Trailing + means repeat 1 or more times
- Abbreviations
  - NC = Network Cell
  - CCS = Cell Communication Substratum
  - Ncomp = Network Component
  - Net = Network
  - NCS = Network Communication Substratum
  - INet = Inter-network
- Grammar Definitions
  - NC = MU RU EU IU CCS
  - Ncomp = NC (CCS NC)*
  - Net = Ncomp (NCS Ncomp)+
  - INet = Net (NCS Net)+ = Ncomp (NCS Net NCS)+ Ncomp

IFM: The Information Flow Model

Information exchange is the essence of computer communication bringing life to the network. It is the activity to be observed, measured and evaluated indicating network behavior. Information exchange incorporates two main aspects; the first deals with the "meaning" or content of information, and the second deals with actual exchange or "communication" identifying the communicating points and path.

The Information Flow model (IFM) represents the horizontal dimension of the network allowing for interactions among network entities, giving rise to the emergent behavior required for network adaptation and evolution. The IFM captures the aspects of information exchange by defining two sub-models: Data Representation sub-model (DR) and Data Communication sub-model (DC). Data representation and communication in CORM exist at both the vertical and horizontal network dimensions. Vertically, data representation and communication occurs within an NC between the NC-units, and between different NCs making up a Ncomp. Horizontally, data representation and communication occurs between Ncomps in the same network or across networks. DR will provide categorization for the different types of information flowing in the system abiding by the ACRF framework. Therefore, DR is mainly concerned with the "meaning" of information flowing within the network system. DR need to handle complexity in terms of the amount of information required to depict the system states

Table 2. CORM vs. layered network models

Features/Network Models	CORM	Layered Models
BAU	CORM-NC (NC+ACRF)	Layer
Operation of BAU	Independent: CORM-NC can exist and operate by itself	Dependent: a single layer can never exist or operate by itself
BAU responsibilities	-Execution of assigned network function -Self-monitoring and regulation	-Execution of assigned network function
BAU Relationships	Interdependent: NC realizes other NCs and cooperate to maximize the over all performance by adapting to context	Incognizant: A layer at one level uses services from the layer below and provides services to the layer above. However, it is unaware of the state of adjacent layers nor realizes the presence of other layers that are more than one level further
System level awareness	Global awareness: CORM-NCs have a sense of global system goal	Unaware of the global system: Awareness is restricted to layer boundaries
Network Composition	Bottom up recursive	Top-down incremental overlaying

at the macro and micro level, taking decisions on the details that need to be exposed and those that need to be suppressed. DC, on the other hand, is concerned with communication aspects including interface compatibilities, data formating across different communication boundaries and majorly routing functions including addressing, naming and forwarding. Similar to DR, the DC will need to address characteristics of complex systems, such as the free scale small world layout (Mitchell, 2006), when devising the routing functions. DC represents a major part of the CCn to be realized by CORM NCs and Ncomps.

CORM FEATURES

Being developed according to a software-dependent CAS paradigm, CORM refutes the long endorsed concept of layering, presenting the CORM-NC as a novel abstraction unit. To our knowledge, CORM is the first reference model that addresses the need for engineering for emergent behavior by accentuating monitoring, knowledge acquisition, and regulation as first class intrinsic features of the basic abstraction unit. Furthermore, we argue that CORM maintains system integrity due to network construction

congruency, where Ncomps, networks and inter-networks are defined recursively in terms of the basic abstraction unit (BAU) – the CORM-NC. In addition to the previously mentioned features, CORM facets acknowledge the multidimensionality of the networks, and accounts for concepts and notions proposed by contemporary designs and architectures including protocol composability out of fine-grained micro-protocols, dynamic protocol adaptation, protocol extensibility and flexibility, cross interest management and control, context awareness through monitoring, resource management as a standalone requirement, and inspired biological behavior and evolution. Table 2 highlights the differences between CORM and the more conventional layered network models (e.g. Internet, OSI, ATM, etc...)

CORM VALIDATION

CORM validation is a challenging task. We posit that models can be classified into definitional and descriptive. A definitional model is more typical of conventional engineering-it expresses required characteristics of a system at an appropriate level of abstraction (Polack, Hoverd, Sampson, Stepney & Timmis, 2008). A descriptive model, on the other hand, captures observed high-level behavior of a system (Polack, et al., 2008). Being a reference model for computer networks, CORM can be considered a definitional model. CORM expresses the required CAS characteristics and network functional decomposition through its basic abstraction unit (NC and ACRF), and enforces them to be synthesized into the network fabric by construction. Therefore, we resorted to validate CORM and the derivation of its basic abstraction unit using an engineering model. For this purpose we used the Function-Behavior-Structure (FBS) engineering framework, which is applicable to any engineering discipline, for reasoning about and explaining the nature and process of design (Gero,1990; Kruchten, 2005).

Derivation Process for CORM Basic Abstraction Unit

Our derivation process of CORM-NC coincides with the design steps proposed by the FBS framework. The inception point of our design activity was marked by our design principles. According to which, computer networks need to be designed as software-dependent complex adaptive systems that exhibit emergent behavior. CORM design principles formed our first set of requirements F_1 and the corresponding expected behavior Be_1 as follows

F_1 = Complex adaptive systems (autonomous entities, complexity)

Be_1 = Emergent Behavior (adaptation, self-organization, evolution)

Shifting to the structure that can deliver F_1 and Be_1, we attempted a catalog lookup by exploring natural complex systems, and studying their structure (S), and the individual behavior of their components (Bs). Our research led us to a recent study on primordial bacterial colonies and their fascinating capabilities in self-engineering (Ben-

Jacob & Levine, 2005). This point of our research marked our first functional reformulation, where we needed to formulate new requirements F_2 for designing a network cell that mimics the bacterium cell behavior Be_2. Accordingly, we synthesized the structure S_2 from Be_2 presenting the NC.

F_2 = Self-engineering NC

$F_2 \rightarrow Be_2$

Be_2 = Bacterium cell behavior (Self-monitoring, Self-regulation and decision-making, experience recording and memorization, communication and cooperation with peers and environment to perform high level goals of the whole colony)

$Be_2 \rightarrow S_2$

S_2 = IU, MU, RU, EU, CCS

However, F_2, Be_2, and S_2 needed further reformulation to detail network requirements. At this point we defined the network requirement specification that led to the derivation of the ACRF framework for network concerns yielding a new set of requirements F_3.

F_3 = ACn, CCn, RCn, FCn

F_3 was integrated with F_2, and superimposed over our previously defined Be_2, and S_2 to customize each towards computer network context in which they all will be realized. This led to the derivation of CORM-NC illustrated in Figure 4, where F_3, F_2 and Be_2 are encompassed within the NC structure S_2

CORM-NC delineates the basic abstraction unit (BAU) from which the network can be recursively built. However, at this point of our research, we still have not completely defined Bs for CORM-NC, since this will involve defining performance variables and their range of values for the software code that will be running within each unit of the CORM-NC structure. Nevertheless, we accounted for Bs by defining the IFM that constitutes a major part of our future work.

ARCHITECTURE PROTOTYPE FOR CORM-BASED NETWORKS

To derive a network architecture based on CORM, network specifications regarding operational context, performance requirements, and/or constraints need to be identified. For the purpose of prototype illustration, we will derive in this section a rudimentary reference architecture featuring a single networking task. Our main focus will be to illustrate the shift in protocol engineering paradigm required to acknowledge both the NC structure and the ACRF framework. We identify the requirements for a CORM-based network architecture that provides different levels of reliable file transfer as follows:

1. Minimal architecture that provides file transfer functionality (functional specification).
2. Supports several levels of reliability (behavioral specifications).
3. Defines modular architectural abstractions that encapsulate the required functions into modules with clear defined interfaces (structural specifications).

Guided by CORM's abstractions (NST and ACRF) and the above requirements, a CORM-based Reliable File Transfer (CRFT) network architecture will be composed of two or more CRFT-Ncomps. We define the CRFT-Ncomp to be composed of three CORM-NCs, each of which are specialized to instantiate the core concerns indicated by the ACRF. Accordingly, the CRFT-Ncomp will be composed of an Application network Cell (Acell), a Communication network cell (Ccell), and a Resource network cell (Rcell). Protocols running on the CRFT-Ncomp are also classified according to the ACRF framework, and are executed by the corresponding concern-specialized NC. Moreover, the task performed by each protocol (or concern-specialized NC) will be internally classified according to the ACRF (refer to the CORM-NC configuration in Figure 4). To clarify this recursive assignment of the ACRF framework, we present the configuration of a file transfer operation in CRFT. We note that this is a high level presentation that illustrates a conjecture of how protocols might be engineered in CRFT. In context of our presentation, the term end user may refer to a human user, the OS, or any other end-application. The operational parameters we refer to in this presentation, are a subset of the actual parameters that need to be involved in a tunably-reliable file transfer operation, and their use here is just for the purpose of illustrating our perception.

According to the ACRF, preparing a file for network transfer is an application concern (ACn). In CRFT, an ACn will be handled by the Acell in the CRFT-Ncomp (see Figure 5). Preparing a file for network-transfer involves several subtasks such as, preparing the transmission endpoints, disassembling and reassembling of file content, handling retransmissions and acknowledgement, etc... These subtasks will be recursively classified according to the ACRF. Following is an example of such recursive classification.

- Acell-ACn: The code for the ACn will be executed in the Logic Component (LC) of the EU in the Acell. We presume that the Acell-ACn will receive from the end user an application profile that depicts the file transfer instantiation. This will specify, among other things, the level of reliability required for the file transfer. The level of reliability will thus indicate how the transport service will be tailored from micro-transport-protocols. According to the reliability level, several operational factors

Figure 5. Managing cross-interests in CRFT-Ncomp

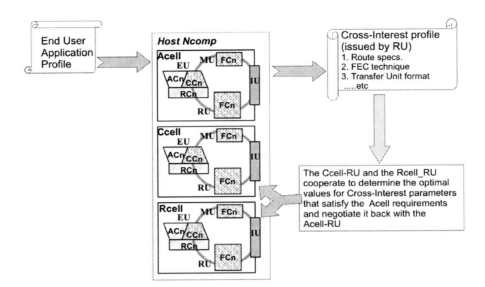

will be decided upon. Such operational factors include: the size of the file-transfer-unit, the Forward Error Correction (FEC) technique to be used, formating of the file-transfer-unit, the retransmission and acknowledgement policy, and the procedure of handling corrupted packets.

- CCn: The code for the CCn will be executed in the Logic Component (LC) of the EU in the Acell. The Acell-CCn will read from the application profile the destination of file transfer. Accordingly, the CCn will prepare a communication profile to be fed to the Ccell on the host Ncomp indicating the specifications of the end-to-end path required for the file transfer. Parameters to be included in the communication profile might include the quality of the route to be discovered in terms of bandwidth and error rate, an upper threshold on the transfer duration, and the priority of the transfer.

- RCn: The code for the RCn will be executed in the Resource Use Controller Component (RUCC) of the EU in the Acell. It is responsible for estimating and managing the resources assigned by the OS to the instantiated Acell among its internal units.

- FCn: The execution of the FCn code is distributed between the MU and the RU. The MU will be responsible for monitoring all performance parameters. These parameters could be specific to the file transfer, such as the rate of lost packets, or general parameters reflecting the operation of the EU. These monitored parameters are specified once the Acell gets specialized, and are subject to adjustments/amendments if required. The RU, on the other hand, will constantly check the performance of the file transfer operation in specific, and the EU operation in general, by comparing the values of the monitored parameters to thresholds values. Part of the threshold values are fed into the RU when the NC is specialized, and part are to be negotiated with other NCs, as will be explained shortly. The RU interferes to adjust the EU operations, in case the monitored values fall below the indicated thresholds. Furthermore, the RU will decide on any optimizations required for improving performance, resolving any cross interests that might rise among the core concerns within the Acell, or among the Acell and other NCs (the Ccell and the Rcell). In this presented case of file transfer, the size of the file-transfer-unit, the FEC technique and the file-transfer-unit format, represent a cross-interest among the Acell, the Ccell and the Rcell, since the values of these parameters are affected by the link technology used, the type of the file to be transferred, the level of reliability required, and the available resources in terms of power, memory and CPU cycles. Accordingly the RU, in conjunction with the EU, will prepare a profile indicating that the values of these cross-interest parameters need to be negotiated among the three NCs residing on the host Ncomp. In case that the optimal values for these parameters require consulting equivalent NCs residing on the Ncomps along the path to the destination, the RU will communicate with the corresponding RUs along the path to the destination to reach to a decision. The agreed upon values for these parameters will then be adopted as the operational values to be used in the file transfer among all involved NCs (whether on the host Ncomp, or on the Ncomps along the path to the destination).

FUTURE RESEARCH DIRECTIONS

CORM future work draws on multidisciplinary research areas, the main focus of which will be to derive the IFM component of CORM. IFM derivation poses several open research issues outlined as follows:

1. Network system profiling: A major constituent of the DR sub-model is devising network knowledge-base (NKB) schema for profiling network entities, protocols, and interactions. Entities can be represented in terms of their capabilities and resources, protocols can be expressed in terms of their performance parameters, and interactions can be modeled in terms of patterns they form (out of which behavioral descriptors can be identified). Out of these elements, key performance indicators (KPI) will be extracted for measurements and evaluation.

2. Network system profile representation: Devise a representation schema for the NKB to be the base for interface design and engineering. The schema needs to address the variability, diversity, and immensity of information existing within the NKB. The representation schema is required to address the need for information abstraction and hiding to handle complexity without disrupting system awareness and sensitivity to context. Furthermore, the representation schema needs to be expressive with no implicit assumptions about the information format or contents. In other word, the design of the representation schema needs to adopt a minimal architecture approach.

3. Devise network evaluation schema: What cannot be measured cannot be evaluated. Accordingly, elements of the derived NKB need to be quantified and measured. Thus, measurement procedures as well as evaluation calibration techniques need to be devised.

4. CORM-compliant protocols: CORM-compliant protocols require a paradigm shift in protocol engineering methodologies. As such, we invite SE practitioners to provide their insights in developing concepts, tools, and methodologies to assist in engineering CORM-compliant protocols.

5. Designing the DC sub-model: A plethora of proposals have addressed the challenging area of network routing in terms of naming addressing and forwarding functions. In

CORM, we need to tackle these topics from a FBS perspective taking into considerations the DR sub-model, derived NKB, and representation schema, (behavioral aspects) as well as complex system layout models (structural aspect of CAS) that have already been identified in CAS research literature.

6. Modeling CAS structure: The NST derived in this research work expresses mainly point-to-point connections. We need to expand our NST grammar definition to present other forms of communication including point-to-multipoint and multipoint-to-multipoint connections.

7. Evaluating CORM-derived architectures using Formal Methods: Formal Methods is an approach in SE to assess the correction of software specifications, and design. Formal methods can be used to assess architectures based on CORM as well as verifying derived protocols.

8. CORM prototyping: CORM-compliant platforms and devices are required for testing and evaluating CORM-based networks and architectures. We conjecture, that CORM-based network simulation results will motivate the interest in constructing CORM-compliant platforms where comparisons of CORM-based network realizations can be performed to test and evaluate proposals for trustworthy future computer networks.

CONCLUSION

This chapter presents CORM, a concern-oriented reference model for future computer networks. CORM conceives computer networks as a software-dependent complex system whose design need to be attempted in a concern-oriented bottom-up approach along two main dimensions: a vertical dimension addressing structure and configuration of network building blocks; and a horizontal dimension addressing communication and interactions among the previously formulated building blocks. CORM addresses this multidimensionality in networks by detailing the network in terms of function, structure, and behavior, represented as network-concerns conceptual framework (ACRF), the network structural template (NST), and the information flow model (IFM) respectively. This chapter focused on the vertical dimension of the network, thus presented the first two components of CORM: ACRF and NST. As for the horizontal network dimension, we provided a synopsis of the information flow model, which represents a major area of our future work. Being developed according to a complex system paradigm, CORM refutes the long endorsed concept of layering, intrinsically accounts for emergent behavior, and ensures system integrity and stability. CORM, as a reference model, was validated using the FBS engineering framework. We aspire that CORM presentation will motivate the derivation as well as experimentation of CORM-based network architectures in an attempt to construct evolvable future computer networks.

REFERENCES

Baldine, I., Vellala, M., Wang, A., Rouskas, G., Dutta, R., & Stevenson, D. (2007). *A unified software architecture to enable cross-layer design in the future internet*. Retrieved from http://net-silos.net/joomla/index.php?option=com_docman&task=doc_view&gid=100&Itemid=39

Ben-Jacob, E., & Levine, H. (2005). Self-engineering capabilities of bacteria. *Journal of the Royal Society, 3*(6), 197–214. doi:doi:10.1098/rsif.2005.0089

BIONETS. (2011). *BIONETS*. Retrieved from http://www.bionets.eu/index.php?area=11

Carneiro, G., Ruela, J., & Ricardo, M. (2004). Cross-layer design in 4G wireless terminals. *IEEE Wireless Communication Magazine, 11*(2), 7–13. doi:10.1109/MWC.2004.1295732

Cerf, V., & Kahn, R. (1974). A protocol for packet network intercommunication. *IEEE Transactions on Communications, 22*(5). doi:10.1109/TCOM.1974.1092259

Clark, D. (2010). *NSF Future Internet Summit, meeting summary*, Washington, DC October 12-15, 2009. Version 7.0. Retrieved from http://www.nets-find.net/Summit-summary-7.pdf

Clark, D., & Tennenhouse, D. (1990). Architectural considerations for a new generation of protocols. *ACM SIGCOMM Computer Communication Review, 20*(4). doi:10.1145/99517.99553

Dooley, K. (1996). A nominal definition of complex adaptive systems. *The Chaos Network, 8*(1), 2-3. Retrieved from http://www.public.asu.edu/~kdooley/papers/casdef.PDF

Feldmann, A. (2007). Internet clean-slate design: What and why? *ACM SIGCOMM Computer Communication Review, 37*(3). doi:10.1145/1273445.1273453

FIND -NSF NeTS FIND Initiative. (2011). *National Science Foundation*. Retrieved from http://www.nets-find.net/index.php

FIRE - Future Internet Research & Experimentation. (2011). *European Commission ICT Research in FP7*. Retrieved from http://cordis.europa.eu/fp7/ict/fire/home_en.html

Gacemi1, A., Senail, A., & Oussalah, M. (2004). Separation of concerns in software architecture via a multiviews description. *Proceedings of the IEEE International Conference on Information Reuse and Integration*, (pp. 60-65). doi:10.1109/IRI.2004.1431437

Gero, J. S. (1990). Design prototypes: A knowledge representation schema for design. *AI Magazine, 11*(4), 26–36. http://portal.acm.org/citation.cfm?id=95793

Greenberg, A., Gisli, H., Maltz, D., Myers, A., Rexford, J., & Xie, G. (2005). A clean slate 4D approach to network control and management. *ACM SIGCOMM Computer Communication Review, 35*(5). doi:doi:10.1145/1096536.1096541

Hassan, H., Eltoweissy, M., & Youssef, M. (2008). *Towards a federated network architecture* (pp. 1–4). IEEE INFOCOM Workshops.

Kawadia, V., & Kumar, P. (2005). A cautionary perspective on cross layer design. *IEEE Wireless Communication, 12*(1), 3–11. doi:10.1109/MWC.2005.1404568

Keller, A., Hossmann, T., May, M., Bouabene, G., Jelger, C., & Tschudin, C. (2008). A system architecture for evolving protocol stacks (invited paper). *IEEE Proceedings of the 17th International Conference on Computer Communications and Networks (ICCCN)*, (pp. 144-150). doi: 10.1109/ICCCN.2008.ECP.44

Khoury, J., Abdallah, C., & Heileman, G. (2010). Towards formalizing network architectural descriptions. In Frappier, M., Glässer, U., Khurshid, S., Laleau, R., & Reeves, S. (Eds.), *Abstract State Machines, Alloy, B and Z* (*Vol. 5977*, pp. 132–145). Lecture Notes in Computer Science Berlin, Germany: Springer. doi:10.1007/978-3-642-11811-1_11

Kruchten, P. (2005). Casting software design in the function-behavior-structure framework. *IEEE Software, 22*(2), 52–58. doi:10.1109/MS.2005.33

Larzon, L., Bodin, U., & Schelen, O. (2002). Hints and notifications. *Proceedings of IEEE Wireless Communications and Networking Conference (WCNC), 2*, (pp. 635-641). doi: 10.1109/WCNC.2002.993342

MacKenzie, C. M., Laskey, K., McCabe, F., Brown, P., Metz, R., & Hamilton, B. A. (Eds.). (2006). Reference model for service oriented architecture 1.0. *OASIS SOA Reference Model Committee Specification 1*. Retrieved from http://docs.oasis-open.org/soa-rm/v1.0/soa-rm.pdf

Mili, H., Elkharraz, A., & Mcheick, H. (2004). Understanding separation of concerns. *Aspect-Oriented Software Development*. Retrieved from http://www.latece.uqam.ca/publications/mili-kharraz-mcheick.pdf

Mitchell, M. (2006). Complex systems: Network thinking. *Artificial Intelligence, 170*(18), 1194–1212. doi:10.1016/j.artint.2006.10.002

Mogul, J. (2006). Emergent (mis)behavior vs. complex software systems. *ACM SIGOPS Operating Systems Review, 40*(4), 293–304. doi:10.1145/1218063.1217964

Park, K., & Willinger, W. (Eds.). (2007). The internet as a large-scale complex system. *Journal of the Royal Statistical Society. Series A, (Statistics in Society), 170*(1), 260. doi:10.1111/j.1467-985X.2006.00455_12.x

Polack, F., Hoverd, T., Sampson, A. T., Stepney, S., & Timmis, J. (2008). Complex systems models: Engineering simulations. *Artificial Life, 11*, 482–489. Retrieved from http://www.cosmos-research.org/docs/alife2008-engineering.pdf

Raisinghani, V., & Iyer, S. (2006). Cross-layer feedback architecture for mobile device protocol stacks. *IEEE Communications Magazine, 44*(1), 85–92. doi:10.1109/MCOM.2006.1580937

Rihani, S. (2001). *Nonlinear systems*. Retrieved May 14, 2010, from http://www.globalcomplexity.org/NonlinearSystems.htm

Saltzer, J., Reed, D., & Clark, D. (1984). End-to-end arguments in system design. *ACM Transactions on Computer Systems, 2*(4), 277–288. doi:10.1145/357401.357402

Scott, J., Huiy, P., Crowcrofty, J., & Diot, C. (2006). Haggle: A networking architecture designed around mobile users. *Proceedings of the Third Annual Conference on Wireless On-demand Network Systems and Services*, (pp. 78-86). Retrieved from http://www.cl.cam.ac.uk/~ph315/publications/haggle-wons06-editforxtoff.pdf

Software Engineering. (2011). *Wikipedia, the free encyclopedia*. Retrieved from http://en.wikipedia.org/wiki/Software_engineering

Stirling, D. (2005). *Modeling complex systems*. Retrieved from http://www.learndev.org/dl/BtSM2005-Stirling-Complexity.pdf

Thomas, R., DaSilva, L., & MacKenzie, A. (2005). *Cognitive networks* (pp. 352–360). New Frontiers in Dynamic Spectrum Access Networks.

Touch, J., Wang, Y., & Pingali, V. (2006). *A recursive network architecture*. Retrieved from http://www.isi.edu/touch/pubs/isi-tr-2006-626/

Wang, Q., & Abu-Rgheff, M. (2003). Cross-layer signaling for next generation systems. *IEEE Wireless Communications and Networking Conference (WCNC), 2*, (pp. 1084-1089). doi: 10.1109/WCNC.2003.1200522

Zhang, Z., & Jia, L. Chai1, Y., & Guo, M. (2008). A study on the elementary control methodologies for complex systems. *Control and Decision Conference*, (pp. 4455-4460). doi:10.1109/CCDC.2008.4598172

Zimmermann, H. (1980). OSI reference model-The ISO model of architecture for open systems interconnection. *IEEE Transactions on Communications, 28*(4), 425–432. doi:10.1109/TCOM.1980.1094702

KEY TERMS AND DEFINITIONS

ACRF: CORM's conceptual framework for network concerns. The ACRF identifies four network concerns, which are the Application Concern (ACn), the Communication Concern (CCn), the Resource Concern (RCn) and the Federation Concern (FCn)

Cell Communication Substrate (CCS): The Communication Substrate that exist within an NC connecting the NC-units.

Computer Inter-Network: Two or more Computer Networks connected by a Network Communication Substrate, where interactions among Ncomps residing within each of the connected networks are sustained, despite the heterogeneity of the hardware, middleware, and software employed by the Ncomp composing the connected networks. Ncomps communicating over the Computer Inter-network perceive the connected networks as a single network.

Computer Network: Two or more Ncomp connected by a Network Communication Substratum, where Ncomp interactions are sustained, despite the heterogeneity of the hardware, middleware, and software of the connected Ncomps.

Computer Network Requirement Specifications: The network is a communication vehicle allowing its users to communicate using the available communication media.

Communication Substrate: A passive media connecting CORM network entities, where network data can flow.

CORM Basic Abstraction Unit (BAU): The basic abstraction unit of CORM networks represented as the CORM NC encompassing the framework for network concerns (ACRF)

Network Cell (NC): The building-block of CORM-networks, which is a self-contained computational/decision entity capable of monitoring its state, adapting to perceived conditions, inferring decisions, recording its experience, and eventually evolving through self-learning and intelligent adaptations.

Network Communication Substrate: A Communication Substrate that connects Ncomps in a Computer Network or in a Computer Inter-network

Network Component (Ncomp): The basic network entity capable of end-to-end communication in CORM networks. It is made of one or more NCs.

ENDNOTE

[1]   In the context of this research work the terms bottom-up and top-down refer to network composability as opposed to their more frequent use to refer to layer organization in the Internet layered architecture.

Section 4
Cognitive Radio Networking

Chapter 10
Spectrum Sensing and Throughput Analysis for Cognitive Radio:
An Overview

M. A. Matin
Institut Teknologi Brunei, Brunei Darussalam

M Ahmed
North South University, Bangladesh

N. Ferdous
North South University, Bangladesh

ABSTRACT

Cognitive radio (CR) is a new technology introduced to deal with the issues of spectrum scarcity and underutilization. Since the spectrum is limited, the unlicensed secondary users (CR users) opportunistically access the underutilized spectrum allocated to the licensed primary users (PUs) of the network. This chapter first gives a brief overview on spectrum sensing and its impact on the system throughput in a cognitive radio network. Later, cooperative relays are introduced in the network to improve spectrum efficiency and mitigate interference to PU. A detailed analysis of power allocation is demonstrated where the transmit power of CR is kept within such limit so that it can maintain low interference to PU. This optimal power allocation can achieve high throughput, which is also presented in this chapter.

INTRODUCTION

Cognitive radio is a promising new technology which provides the scope of a more reliable, flexible and efficient spectrum sharing scheme with better utilization of the radio spectrum us-

ing signal processing and adaptive procedures. As pointed out by Cabric et al. (2004), there is a spectrum scarcity at frequencies that can be economically used for wireless communications. A recent survey made by Federal Communications Commission's (FCC) Spectrum Policy Task Force (FCC, 2002) has shown that the actual licensed spectrum is largely underutilized in vast temporal

DOI: 10.4018/978-1-4666-1797-1.ch010

Copyright © 2012, IGI Global. Copying or distributing in print or electronic forms without written permission of IGI Global is prohibited.

and geographic dimensions. Indeed, if portions of the radio spectrum are scanned, it reveals that some frequency bands in the spectrum are largely unoccupied most of the time; some other frequency bands are only partially occupied while the remaining bands are heavily used. The underutilization of the electromagnetic spectrum leads us to a term *spectrum hole*, which is a band of frequencies assigned to a primary user (licensed) but at a particular time and specific geographic location, the band is not being utilized by the user.

Basically CR is an intelligent radio that can first perceive its radio environment through wide-band spectrum sensing and then adapts its transmission and reception parameters such as, the operating frequency, modulation scheme, code rate, and transmission power in real time with two primary objectives in mind: highly reliable communication whenever and wherever needed and efficient utilization of radio spectrum. CR improves the spectrum utilization by allowing secondary users to share the same licensed band allowed by the primary users. The secondary user or CR user first senses the spectrum band for any spectrum holes and if it finds one then it starts its transmission; otherwise it waits for the next time slot to repeat its actions. Coexistence of primary user (PU) and CR often leads to harmful interference to PU. In such a case spectrum sharing to the CR can only be allowed under tolerable interference limits. Cooperative relays can be used to mitigate the interference and improve spectrum utilization.

Two of the major functions of CR are sensing and transmit-power control. This chapter basically focuses on the transmit-power control of a relay assisted CR system. At first it gives a general idea of spectrum sensing and presents the tradeoff relationship between sensing time and cognitive system throughput. A study of optimal approach of power allocation is done to maximize throughput using subgradient method, a part of which is later modified with ellipsoid method that ensures faster convergence rate. Furthermore, an alternative iterative approach for power allocation and throughput maximization of the CR system is shown which provides a near-optimal performance but reduces the computational complexity significantly.

BACKGROUND

One of the main reasons for the birth of Cognitive Radio in the wireless world is to fight against the problems of spectrum scarcity (Haykin, 2005) and spectrum underutilization (Neel, 2006). On one hand the radio spectrum is scarce and on the other hand the licensed users do not use their spectrum fully which results in underutilization of the band (FCC, 2003a). To mitigate the problem of underutilization, unlicensed users better known as secondary users (SU) are introduced in the wireless network to utilize the unused band by the PU. The secondary users are also referred to as Cognitive Radios (CR) which was first introduced by Mitola and Maguire (1999).

CR's main task is to sense its operational electromagnetic environment and dynamically and autonomously adjust its radio operating parameters to modify system operation such as maximize throughput, mitigate interference, facilitate interoperability and access secondary market (Neel, 2006). To carry out these tasks cognitive radios are constructed from the next generation of software-defined radios (SDR) with the additional ability to sense its surrounding environment, to track potential spectra changes, and to adapt according to the findings (Ulversoy, 2010). SDR technology brings the flexibility, cost efficiency and power to drive communications forward, with wide-reaching benefits realized by service providers and product developers through to end users. So SDR is an ideal platform for the realization of CR as majority of CR functions will be implemented on modified software components that run on flexible and powerful processing.

CR users need to sense the environment at regular time interval for sharing the spectrum band of the primary users and once they find the spectrum idle, they start their transmission through it. Even while transmitting they need to continue the sensing process so that they can leave the spectrum immediately whenever they find a PU wanting to use the band. Moreover, since CR users share the same spectrum band with PU, it has the chance of causing harmful interference to PU. So in the presence of PU the CR user is allowed to use the spectrum until it guarantees no harmful interference with PU. For that CR must control its transmission parameters to operate within limited interference limit. Letaief and Zhang (2009) have introduced relays in the CR network to mitigate this interference. The effect of such cooperative techniques in CR systems on spectrum sharing and sensing is further investigated by Ganesan and Li (2005).

Therefore, by exploiting the benefit of cooperative relay, throughput of the system can be greatly increased as cooperative transmission between CR users improve both spatial and spectrum diversity (Zhang, Jia and Zhang, 2009). There has been some recent work in the field of resource allocation in cooperative CR network. In Jia et al. (2009) work, power allocation and relay selection has been done by selfish optimization of resource to maximize system throughput without considering potential interference with primary users. During the same year, Yan and Wang (2009) proposed a power allocating algorithm using amplified-forward (AF) cooperative protocol to maximize SNR at the destination of the CR system. Later Liu et al. (2010) considered the interference limits caused to PUs and proposed an alternative cooperative protocol which uses Maclaurin series to formulate the problem to enhance the system throughput.

This was later covered by Li et al. (2011) where relay selection and power allocation has been investigated with interference limitation.

However the optimal approach that they proposed for power allocation and throughput maximization has a very high computational complexity. Keeping interference limitation in mind, Ferdous et al. (2011) investigated power allocation, using a new approach which maintains high throughput and lowers computational complexity.

SPECTRUM SENSING

Cognitive radios are essentially the unlicensed secondary users utilizing the licensed bands of the primary users. However they can utilize it only when PU is absent and they have to vacate it as soon as the PUs start using the band. Therefore the CR users must continuously keep on sensing the spectrum to identify and access unutilized bands and also to detect the presence of a new PU signal as quickly as possible. In practice, the available spectrum bands for secondary users vary with time and location. A region of location-time-frequency that is not utilized by PU is called a *spectrum hole*. The coexistence of CR and PU is done by accessing these *spectrum holes.* Thus spectrum sensing is very important and crucial in the development of CR (Unnikrishnan and Veeravalli, 2007). Generally, the spectrum sensing techniques can be classified as transmitter detection, cooperative detection, and interference-based detection, as shown in Figure 1.

Cabric et al. (2004) talked about the three traditional signal detection techniques that are used by CR for local spectrum sensing. They are: matched filter, cyclostationary feature detector and energy detector. If the structure of the primary signal is known and if the secondary system is limited to operate in a few primary bands, the optimal detector in stationary Gaussian noise is a matched filter followed by a threshold test. If some features of the primary signal such as its carrier frequency or modulation type are known,

Figure 1. Spectrum sensing techniques

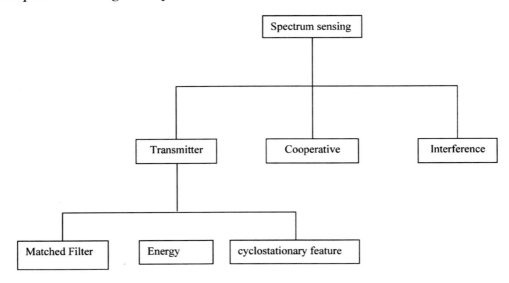

feature detectors may be employed. Since the spectral correlation properties of different signals are usually unique, feature detection allows a cognitive radio to detect a specific primary signal buried in noise and interference. Among these energy detector is the most popular technique used in fading channels (Digham et al., 2007). An energy detector simply measures the energy received on a primary band during an observation interval and declares a *spectrum hole* if the measured energy is less than a certain threshold (Ghasemi and Sousa, 2008).

Spectrum sensing is associated with two parameters: probability of false alarm, P_f and probability of detection, P_d (Zhang et al., 2009). The probability of false alarm refers to the probability of detecting primary signal even though it is silent in the sensed spectrum band. On the other hand the probability of detection is the probability of detecting primary signal when the PU is actually active in the sensed spectrum band. Low P_f ensures throughput maximisation of CR system. Moreover, while low sensing time keeps the PU less protected, it increases the CR system throughput. Therefore, there exists a tradeoff

between the sensing duration and the throughput of the CR system (Hamdi and Letaief, 2009).

To further study the relationship between sensing time and throughput a simple pair of cognitive transmitter-receiver can be taken that shares the same frequency band with a PU. The popular spectrum sensing scheme, energy detection technique is used to sense PU in this CR model. We assume τ_s to be the duration of sensing and τ_f the total frame period. During sensing the received SNR of PU at the CR transmitter has the following two hypotheses,

$$y[n] = \begin{cases} n_0 \\ hx[n] + n_0 \end{cases},$$
$$H_0(\text{PU is absent}) \qquad (1)$$
$$H_1(\text{PU is present})$$

where $y[n]$ is the observed signal at the CR transmitter with variance σ_x^2, $x[n]$ is the PU signal and h is the complex channel gain of the sensing channel between PU and CR transmitter. For simplicity h is assumed to be 1 under hypothesis H1 and 0 under hypothesis H0. The noise n_0 is

Figure 2. A MAC time slot

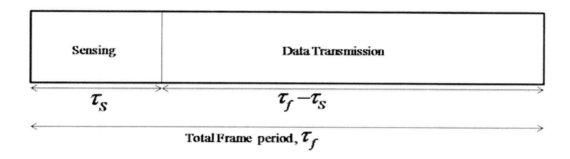

assumed to be AWGN with zero mean and variance σ_n^2. The main purpose of the spectrum sensing scheme is to decide between the two hypotheses.

CR can only access the spectrum when the sensing result is idle. Hence from a general form of throughput an expression for average throughput of CR in relation to the sensing time can be written as follows,

$$\mathscr{C} = \left(\frac{\tau_f - \tau_S}{\tau_f} \right) \Pr(C) \mathrm{E}\left(\log_2 \left(1 + \frac{P \, |\, h\, |^2}{N_o} \right) \right)$$

(2)

where P is the transmit power at the cognitive user, $\mathrm{E}(\bullet)$ denotes statistical expectancy of $\bullet$ and $\Pr(C)$ refers to the probability that CR doesn't sense any PU when PU is actually absent.

In Figure 2, frame structure of a MAC (media access control) time slot, τ_f, is shown where, τ_S unit of time is initially used to sense the spectrum and the remaining $\tau_f - \tau_S$ unit of time is used for data transmission if the user finds the spectrum idle. Therefore, there exists a tradeoff between the duration of spectrum sensing and data transmission. Since the primary signal under detection are very weak and therefore may lead to high sensing times that would have a harmful effect on the system throughput of the cognitive radio network. The continuous communication in spectrum sharing CR networks would get disrupted in the presence of PU which too decreases their throughput by a factor of $\dfrac{\tau_f - \tau_S}{\tau_f}$ as shown in Equation (2) (Stotas and Nallanathan, 2010).

After spectrum sensing and accessing, CR's next job is to transmit its data in the licensed frequency band. At this point, the challenge of efficient power allocation and optimization of throughput arises in the CR network. For a certain value of the sensing time τ_S for which the throughput is optimized, we dedicate the rest of the chapter on the work of power allocation and throughput analysis for a relay-assisted cognitive network. Before introducing our model, an overview of benefits of relays in a CR network is drawn.

THE PROBLEM OF UNBALANCED RESOURCE

Cognitive radio has been introduced in the network as a secondary user to increase the spectrum efficiency by exploiting the spectrum holes. However, at this point the challenge of efficient spectrum allocation arises in the secondary network. The problem of resource unbalance is much more severe in a cognitive radio network than in the conventional wireless networks.

The cognitive users have heterogeneous spectrum availability mainly due to differences in the relative locations of primary and secondary users, dynamic traffic of primary users and opportunistic spectrum access nature of secondary users. On the other hand, the traffic demand of the cognitive user is also random. As a result the question arises of how to allocate the spectrum to meet the demand of the users and at the same time achieve high spectrum utilization, especially when there is a mismatch between the traffic demand and spectrum availability (Li et al., 2011).

Role of Relay in Increasing Spectrum Utilization

To address the problem mentioned in the previous section the concept of relays has been introduced in the network (Ganesa and Li, 2005). Here relays are referred to the cognitive users who do not need to use their entire available spectrum as they have low traffic demand. So these users can now help to relay the traffic of other cognitive users with their otherwise wasted spectrum (Atapattu, Tellambura and Jiang, 2009). Hence the spectrum utilization is effectively increased.

Role of Relay in Improving the System Performance

In Figure 3 a three node secondary network is shown where two secondary users CU2 and CU3

Figure 3. Transmission without relaying

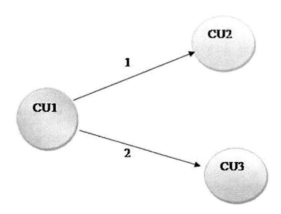

receive data from another secondary user CU1 via channel 1 and 2 respectively. Orthogonal Frequency division Multiplexing Access (OFDMA) has been used and we assume that each channel between any two pair of nodes can provide 100 Kbps of data rate. However, CU2 needs only 50 Kbps whereas CU3 needs 150 Kbps. Thus the demand of CU3 is not met while channel 1 experiences an underutilization of resource.

To mitigate the above mentioned problem cooperative relay is introduced. This scheme is divided into two time slots as shown in Figure 4. In the first time slot, CU3 receives its data through channel 2. On the other hand, CU2 receives its own data through channel 1 and CU3's data through channel 3. In the second time slot, CU3 receives data from CU1 through channel 2 and from CU2 through channel 4. Therefore, the average data rates after the two time slots are 150 Kbps and 50 Kbps for CU3 and CU2 respectively. Thus relay plays a role in enhancing the performance of the system.

Relay-Assisted Transmission

By using OFDM, data can be modulated into different orthogonal subcarriers (Olfat, Farrokhi and Liu, 2005). Numbers of adjacent subcarriers together form each channel and guard bands are allocated between neighboring channels to prevent interference. This enables multiple channels to be transmitted at the same time using the same radio frequency.

As shown in Figure 5 the CR transmitter, CRtx has two available channels CH1 and CH2 and the CR receiver, CRrx has the available channels CH1 and CH3. The other channels are occupied by primary users so they cannot be accessed. Thus only channel CH1 can be used for tramsmitting data between CRtx and CRrx since it is the only channel common between. In such a case a relay can prove to be of much help in transmission if it has channels common to CRtx and CRrx. For example a relay, CRR, which has both channels CH2 and CH3 available, can help in the transmis-

Figure 4. Cooperative relay transmission: (a) In the first time slot; (b) In second time slot

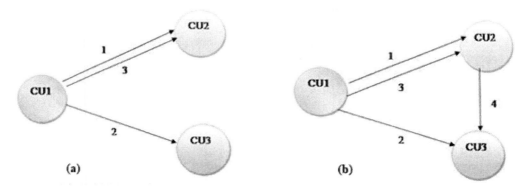

(a)   (b)

sion. During the first time slot CRtx sends data packet 1 to CRrx and data packet 2 to CRR via CH1 and CH2 respectively. During second time slot CRtx sends packet 3 to CRrx via CH1 and CRR forwards packet 2 to CRrx via CH3. Therefore with the help of relay we can send three packets in two time slots as opposed to only one packet per slot in case of transmission without relay. Hence, with relay the throughput has increased by 50%.

Criterions of Being a Relay

To be able to act as a relay CR user needs to satisfy certain conditions. CR transmitter should send signal to the cognitive radio relay (CRR) without interfering with PU (i.e relay should be closer to the transmitter than to PU) and CRR should forward signal to CR receiver without interfering with PU (i.e. relay should be closer to receiver than the PU). Interference to PU can be reduced if CR is at a short transmission range, is with a low transmit power and/or has directional/ multiple antennas with beamforming. Moreover in a CR network, whether a CR link can be assisted by relay depends on the position of PU and the density of the CR users.

Multi-Hop Transmission

Figure 6 shows a network where primary users and secondary users coexist. There is a pair of

cognitive transmitter and receiver surrounded by P number of primary users and C number of CR users available as possible relay stations. Each CR user is with directional transmitting and omnidirectional abilities. Direction of transmission is assumed to be random. Before transmitting, the CR transmitter senses the spectrum band for the coverage of its directional antenna by varying the direction of transmission randomly. In case of idle sensing result, if the CR receiver is within the coverage of CR transmitter, a direct link between them can be established else relay stations can be used to assist the CR communication.

CR users have to sense the available spectrum bands before relay selection and data transmission. This is done by varying the antenna beamwidth. Antenna beamwidth is referred to as the angle θ of the antenna beam over which the relative power is at or above 50% of the peak power. Hence we can say that normalized beamwidth, ς is $\theta/360^0$. It denotes the probability that PU is within the coverage of CR transmitter. The probability that CR transmitter can access the spectrum coverage is $(1 - \varsigma)$. Therefore, for P number of PUs, the probability of idle sensing result at CR transmitter can be obtained by

$$pr_{idle} = (1 - \varsigma)^p \tag{3}$$

Figure 5. Three-node relay-assisted transmission

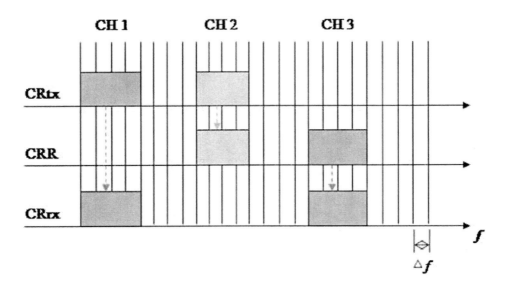

The probability of the one-hop direct communication between the CR transmitter and receiver is given by

$$pr_1 = \varsigma(1 - \varsigma)^P \tag{4}$$

Using the concept of moment generating function (Irwin, p. 19) the average probability of successful secondary transmission (PSST) of two hop relay can be obtained by

$$pr_2 = pr_{idle} \cdot pr_{relay} = (1 - \varsigma)^P [1 - (1 - \varsigma + \varsigma(1 - pr_1))^C]. \tag{5}$$

Similarly PSST of m-hop transmission can be obtained as

$$pr_m = (1 - \varsigma)^P \left[1 - (1 - \varsigma pr_{m-1})^C \right] \tag{6}$$

Since pr_1 and pr_2 are independent, the PSST of a maximum of 2-hop relay communication, is given as

$$\xi_2 = 1 - (1 - pr_1)(1 - pr_2). \tag{7}$$

As shown by Ferdous et al. (2011), Figure 7 presents maximum PSST of CR, ς, versus normalized beamwidth ξ_2 for different number of CRR, C. It is assumed in this case that the two PUs are communicating with each other in the area and a maximum of two hops relay can be used for relay-assisted directional transmission scheme, i.e., P = 2 and M = 2. As shown in the Figure 7 ς increases with the number of CR users,C. This is because more number of CR users can now exploit spatial spectrum holes more sufficiently. Moreover, we notice the CR antenna beamwidth gets narrower as the number of CR users increases. A possible explanation for it can be that large CR users refers to the fact that CRtx can find a proper relay station easily now and the interfernce from the PUs will be the bottleneck for PSST. Thus a narrow antenna beamwidth is required to avoid the interfernce with PUs and therefore acheives a higher PSST. On the contrary, when the number of CR users is small, lacking of relay stations will be the bottleneck and therefore a large antenna beamwidth can help the CRtx to find a relay station easily.

Figure 6. Relay-assisted CR transmission using directional antennas

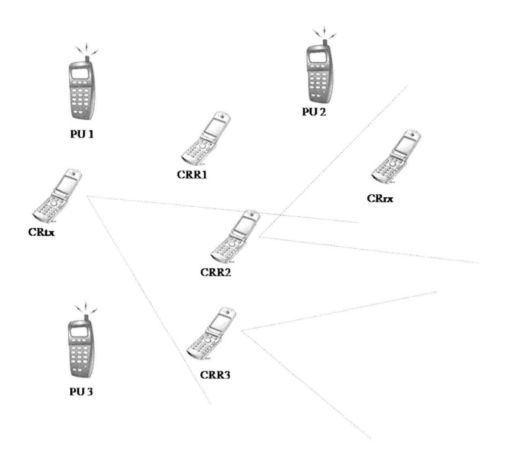

SYSTEM MODEL

In this three node channel, Figure 8 each node uses orthogonal channels. A CR user is assigned as relay to each CR transmitter and receiver. The CR transmitter sends data simultaneously via CH0 and CH1 to CR receiver and relay respectively. The relay then in turn forwards the data to the CR receiver via CH2. Channel gains are assumed to be known by the CR source and relays, and are constant during a data frame. The relays use amplify-and-forward (AF) protocol. Unit channel bandwidth is considered for simplicity. The received signal is corrupted by additive white Gaussian noise (AWGN) with zero mean and σ^2 variance for each channel.

Problem Formulation

After choosing a relay, while allocating power potential interference should be taken into account so that no harmful interference occurs with the PU. The interference with PU happens either due to mis-detection of PU or during coexistence with PU using limited transmission power. In order to prevent interference the following conditions regarding the power of the three nodes must be satisfied:

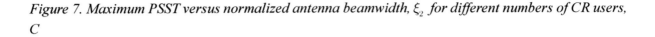

Figure 7. Maximum PSST versus normalized antenna beamwidth, ξ_2 for different numbers of CR users, C

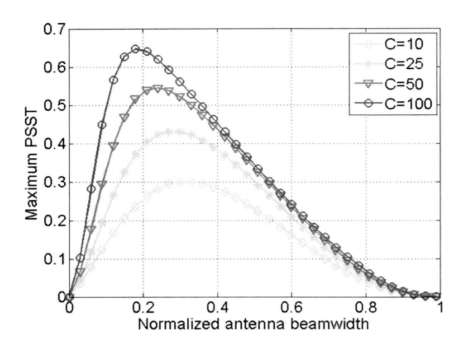

$$P_{CR} \mid h_{CR,P} \mid^2 \leq \gamma, \tag{8}$$

where P_{CR} is the transmission power from the transmitter to the receiver over Ch 0, $h_{CR,P}$ is the channel gain between transmitter and PU for Ch 0, and γ is acceptable interference power of PUs.

$$P_{\overline{CR}} \mid h_{\overline{CR},P} \mid^2 \leq \phi, \tag{9}$$

where $P_{\overline{CR}}$ is the transmission power from the transmitter to the relay over Ch 1, $h_{\overline{CR},P}$ is the channel gain between transmitter and PU for Ch 1, and ϕ is acceptable interference power of PUs.

$$P_{RELAY} \mid h_{RELAY,P} \mid^2 \leq \varpi, \tag{10}$$

where P_{RELAY} is the transmission power from the relay to the receiver over Ch 2, $h_{RELAY,P}$ is the channel gain between relay and PU for Ch 2, and ϖ is acceptable interference power of PUs.

The constraint of the battery capacity of the transmitter and relay also should be considered

$$P_{CR} + P_{\overline{CR}} \leq \Psi,, \tag{11}$$

$$P_{RELAY} \leq \Theta, \tag{12}$$

where Ψ is the overall power limit for the CR transmitter and Θ is the maximum transmission power allowed by each relay.

The received power signal, noise and hence SNR at the receiver from relay can be given as follows:

Figure 8. Cooperative cognitive radio network with relay

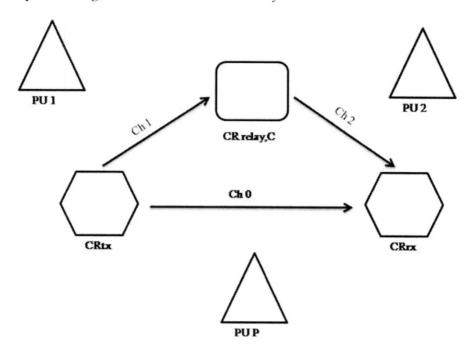

$$P_S = \frac{P_{RELAY} P_{\overline{CR}} \mid h_{T,RELAY} \mid^2 \mid h_{RELAY,R} \mid^2}{2 P_{RELAY} \mid h_{T,RELAY} \mid^2 + \sigma^2}$$

(13)

$$P_n = \left(\frac{P_{RELAY} \mid h_{RELAY,R} \mid^2}{P_{\overline{CR}} \mid h_{T,RELAY} \mid^2 + \sigma^2} + 1 \right) \sigma^2$$

(14)

$$SNR = \frac{P_S}{P_n} = \frac{P_{RELAY} P_{\overline{CR}} \mid h_{T,RELAY} \mid^2 \mid h_{RELAY,R} \mid^2}{\left(P_{RELAY} \mid h_{RELAY,R} \mid^2 + P_{\overline{CR}} \mid h_{T,RELAY} \mid^2 + \sigma^2 \right) \sigma^2}$$

(15)

where $h_{T,RELAY}$, $h_{T,R}$ and $h_{RELAY,R}$ are the channel gains between the transmitter and the relay, the transmitter and the receiver, and the relay and the receiver respectively.

Therefore, the overall system throughput can be shown as,

$$T(P_{CR}, P_{\overline{CR}}, P_{RELAY}) = (1 - \alpha) \log_2 \left(1 + \frac{P_{CR} \mid h_{T,R} \mid^2}{\sigma^2} \right)$$

$$+ (1 - \alpha) \log_2 \left(1 + \frac{P_{RELAY} P_{\overline{CR}} \mid h_{T,RELAY} \mid^2 \mid h_{RELAY,R} \mid^2}{\left(P_{RELAY} \mid h_{RELAY,R} \mid^2 + P_{\overline{CR}} \mid h_{T,RELAY} \mid^2 + \sigma^2 \right) \sigma^2} \right)$$

(16)

where α is the mis-detection probability for spectrum sensing. If interference during transmission takes place then data is considered to be lost.

OPTIMAL APPROACH

An optimal approach is used that maximizes the system throughput. Here the power is optimized which in turn maximizes the throughput using dual domain optimization (Wei and Lui, 2006).

213

Constrained Optimization Problem

First the problem is expressed as a constrained optimization problem,

$$Maximize \quad T(P_{CR}, P_{\overline{CR}}, P_{RELAY}) \qquad (17a)$$

Subject to

$$P_{CR} + P_{\overline{CR}} \leq \Psi, \qquad (17b)$$

$$P_{RELAY} \leq \Theta, \qquad (17c)$$

$$0 \leq P_{CR} \mid h_{CR,P} \mid^2 \leq \gamma, \qquad (17d)$$

$$0 \leq P_{\overline{CR}} \mid h_{\overline{CR},P} \mid^2 \leq \phi, \qquad (17e)$$

$$0 \leq P_{RELAY} \mid h_{RELAY,P} \mid^2 \leq \varpi. \qquad (17f)$$

Since the throughput T increases with

$$P_{RELAY}, P_{RELAY}^* = \min \left\{ \frac{\phi}{\mid h_{RELAY,P} \mid^2}, \Theta \right\}$$

Unconstrained Optimization Problem

In order to solve this we introduce the Lagrangian function (see Box 1).

Where λ s are the Lagrangian multipliers. To solve many constrained problem in unconstrained

form Lagrangian multipliers are used (Boyd and Vandenberghe, 2004).

The main idea of here is to solve the constrained optimization problem (17) in the dual domain (Cendrillon et al, 2006). For that a dual objective function, $g(\lambda_1, \lambda_2, \lambda_3)$, is defined as an unconstrained maximization of Lagrangian,

$$g(\lambda_1, \lambda_2, \lambda_3) = \max L(P_{CR}, P_{\overline{CR}}, \lambda_1, \lambda_2, \lambda_3)$$
$$(19)$$

To obtain the optimal solution of (17) it is required to minimize $g(\lambda_1, \lambda_2, \lambda_3)$ directly by updating all components of the Lagrangian multipliers at the same time along some search direction. Since $g(\lambda_1, \lambda_2, \lambda_3)$ is convex, a gradient type search is guaranteed to converge to the global optimum. The problem arises when $g(\lambda_1, \lambda_2, \lambda_3)$ is non differentiable. In such a case we bring a vector d in the scenario on the basis of which the search direction can be found. The vector d is a subgradient of $g(\lambda_1, \lambda_2, \lambda_3)$.

Differentiating Equation (19) we can find,

$$d = \begin{bmatrix} \Psi - P_{CR} - P_{\overline{CR}} \\ \gamma - P_{CR} \mid h_{CR,P} \mid^2 \\ \phi - P_{\overline{CR}} \mid h_{\overline{CR},P} \mid^2 \end{bmatrix}. \qquad (20)$$

Let P_{CR} and $P_{\overline{CR}}$ be the optimizing variable in $g(\lambda_1, \lambda_2, \lambda_3)$

Box 1.

$$L(P_{CR}, P_{\overline{CR}}, P_{RELAY}, \lambda_1, \lambda_2, \lambda_3) = (1 - \alpha) \log_2 \left(1 + \frac{P_{CR} \mid h_{T,R} \mid^2}{\sigma^2} \right)$$

$$+ (1 - \alpha) \log_2 \left(1 + \frac{P_{RELAY} P_{\overline{CR}} \mid h_{T,RELAY} \mid^2 \mid h_{RELAY,R} \mid^2}{\left(P_{RELAY} \mid h_{RELAY,R} \mid^2 + P_{\overline{CR}} \mid h_{T,RELAY} \mid^2 + \sigma^2 \right) \sigma^2} \right) + \lambda_1 \left(\Psi - P_{CR} - P_{\overline{CR}} \right)$$

$$+ \lambda_2 \left(\gamma - P_{CR} \mid h_{CR,P} \mid^2 \right) + \lambda_3 \left(\phi - P_{\overline{CR}} \mid h_{\overline{CR},P} \mid^2 \right) \qquad (18)$$

Table 1. Comparison between optimal and proposed scheme complexity

Approach	Complexity	comment
Optimal approach	$O(T_2 B^K)$.	Exponential in K
Iterative approach	$O(T_1 T_2 BK)$	Linear in K

To solve the Langrangian function problem, we take the help of Karush-Kuhn-Tucker (KKT) conditions. According to Boyd and Vandenberghe(2004), in KKT conditions the gradient of the Lagrangian should equal zero. Hence, we can write,

$$\frac{\partial L}{\partial P_{CR}} = 0, \frac{\partial L}{\partial P_{\overline{CR}}} = 0. \tag{21}$$

Thus differentiating the Lagrangian function (16) and solving for P_{CR} and $P_{\overline{CR}}$ gives,

$$P_{CR} = \left[\frac{1-\alpha}{\left(\lambda_1 + \lambda_2 \mid h_{CR,P} \mid^2\right)\ln 2} - \frac{\sigma^2}{\mid h_{T.P} \mid^2} \right]^+, \tag{22}$$

$$P_{\overline{CR}} =$$

$$\left[\frac{P_{RELAY}^2 \mid h_{RELAY,R} \mid^4 + 4 P_{RELAY} \mid h_{RELAY,R} \mid^2 \mid h_{T,RELAY} \mid^2 \Lambda}{2 \mid h_{T,RELAY} \mid^2} - \frac{P_{RELAY} \mid h_{RELAY,R} \mid^2 + 2\sigma^2}{2 \mid h_{T,RELAY} \mid^2} \right]^+. \tag{23}$$

where $\Lambda = \dfrac{1-\alpha}{\ln 2\left(\lambda_1 + \lambda_3 \mid h_{\overline{CR},P} \mid^2\right)}$ and $[.]+=\max$ $(.,0)$.

DUAL UPDATE METHODS

λ basically gives the price of the resource i.e. power in our case. If the power constraint is exceeded, the price goes up, otherwise it decreases. Hence it plays a role in allocating the resource in the system and so a systematic update of λ is required. Although λ update methods have been used in joint routing and resource allocation problems by Xiao et al. (2004) in Digital subscribers line (DSL) and by Shen et al. (2003) in OFDM wireless system, but it is relatively new in cognitive radio.

Subgradient Method

The subgradient method is a simple algorithm for minimizing a nondifferentiable convex function. The method looks very much like the ordinary gradient method for differentiable functions, but with several notable exceptions. For example, the subgradient method uses step lengths that are fixed ahead of time, instead of an exact or approximate line search as in the gradient method. Unlike the ordinary gradient method, the subgradient method is not a descent method; the function value can and often does increase (Boyd, 2004).

The subgradient method is far slower than other methods, but is much simpler and can be applied to a far wider variety of problems. By combining the subgradient method with primal or dual decomposition techniques, it is sometimes possible to develop a simple distributed algorithm for a problem.

The subgradient method basically updates λ in the subgradient direction on the basis of a step size sequence sk. Generally the iteration used by subgradient method can be expressed as

$$\lambda_l^{k+1} = \left[\lambda_l^k - s^k d_l^k\right]^+, \text{ for } l = \{1,2,...,L\} \tag{24}$$

where k is the number of iterations, $[.]^+$ denotes max$(.,0)$, L is the number of Lagrangian multipliers and s^k is a sequence of scalar step sizes. For our case $l = 1, 2, 3$ and d_l represents the l th row of d matrix expressed in (19). Hence, we can write λ_1, λ_2 and λ_3 as follows,

$$\lambda_1^{k+1} = \left[\lambda_1^k - s^k \left(\Psi - P_{CR} - P_{\overline{CR}}\right)\right]^+, \tag{25a}$$

$$\lambda_2^{k+1} = \left[\lambda_2^k - s^k \left(\gamma - P_{CR} \mid h_{CR,P} \mid^2\right)\right]^+, \tag{25b}$$

$$\lambda_3^{k+1} = \left[\lambda_3^k - s^k \left(\phi - P_{\overline{CR}} \mid h_{\overline{CR},P} \mid^2\right)\right]^+. \tag{25c}$$

Step sizes are fixed ahead of time. Several different types of step size rules are used all of which ensures convergence.

Constant Step Size:

$$s^k = h \tag{26a}$$

where h is a constant and is independent of k.

Constant Step Length:

$$s^k = \frac{h}{\|d_l^k\|_2} \tag{26b}$$

Therefore,

$$\|\lambda_l^{k+1} - \lambda_l^k\|_2 = h \tag{27}$$

Square Summable but not Summable:
The step sizes satisfy,

$$\sum_{k=1}^{\infty} (s^k)^2 < \infty \text{ and} \tag{28}$$

$$\sum_{k=1}^{\infty} s^k = \infty \tag{29}$$

One typical example is $s^k = \dfrac{a}{(b+k)}$, where $a > 0$ and $b \geq 0$.

Nonsummable Diminishing:
The step sizes must satisfy,

$$\lim_{k \to \infty} s^k = 0, \tag{30}$$

and

$$\sum_{k=1}^{\infty} s^k = \infty. \tag{31}$$

Step sizes that satisfy this condition are called diminishing step size rules. A typical example is $s^k = \dfrac{a}{\sqrt{k}}$ and $a > 0$.

Ellipsoid Method

In this section an update method is shown that has a faster convergence than the method discussed in the previous section. The idea here is to localize the set of candidate λ's in a minimalized ellipsoid region. Then by evaluating the subgradient of $g(\lambda_1, \lambda_2, \lambda_3)$ at the center of the ellipsoid, roughly half of the ellipsoid is sliced away from the candidate set. The iteration continues as the size of the candidate set diminishes until it converges to an optimal set of λ. An ellipsoid can be defined as,

$$E = \left\{x \mid (x - z)^T A(x - z) \leq 1\right\}, \tag{32}$$

where z is the center and A is a semidefinite matrix that gives the size and orientation of E.

The initial ellipsoid should be chosen so that it bounds all the λ's. As Ferdous et al. (2011) has shown, by considering the KKT conditions and differentiating the Lagrangian function we get Equations (33a) and (33b) (see Box 2 for Equation (33c).

$$\lambda_1 = \frac{1 - \alpha}{\ln 2} \frac{\mid h_{T,R} \mid^2}{(\sigma^2 + P_{CR} \mid h_{T,R} \mid^2)}, \tag{33a}$$

$$\lambda_2 = \frac{1-\alpha}{\ln 2} \frac{\mid h_{T,R} \mid^2}{(\sigma^2 + P_{CR} \mid h_{T,R} \mid^2) \mid h_{CR,P} \mid^2},$$

(33b)

To enclose a region where the optimal λ may reside, we choose an initial ellipsoid using the above results,

$$A_0^{-1} = \begin{bmatrix} N\left(\frac{(1-\alpha)\lambda_1}{2}\right)^2 & 0 & 0 \\ 0 & N\left(\frac{(1-\alpha)\lambda_2}{2}\right)^2 & 0 \\ 0 & 0 & N\left(\frac{(1-\alpha)\lambda_3}{2}\right)^2 \end{bmatrix},$$

(34)

$$z_0 = \left[\frac{(1-\alpha)\lambda_1}{2} \quad \frac{(1-\alpha)\lambda_2}{2} \quad \frac{(1-\alpha)\lambda_3}{2} \right]^T.$$

(35)

The update algorithm is as follows,

$$d_{n+1} = \frac{d_n}{\sqrt{d_n^T A_n^{-1} d_n}},$$

(36)

$$z_{n+1} = z_n - \frac{1}{N+1} A_n^{-1} d_{n+1},$$

(37)

$$A_{n+1}^{-1} = \frac{N^2}{N^2-1}\left(A_n^{-1} - \frac{2}{N+1} A_n^{-1} d_{n+1} d_{n+1}^T A_n^{-1} \right).$$

(38)

The stopping criterion can be defined as follows,

$$\sqrt{d_n^T A_n^{-1} d_n} \leq \varepsilon,$$

(39)

The ellipsoid method is a better update method than subgradient method because it converges λ to the optimal faster.

In Figure 9(a) a comparison between subgradient and ellipsoid method in updating lagrangian multiplier $\lambda_1, \lambda_2, \lambda_3$ in the optimal approach has been demonstrated. It's seen that the two update methods give similar output. The interferences are taken to be 0.0001 W and Ψ is 1 W. This graph shows that we can also use the ellipsoid method instead of subgradient method without hampering the performance and at the same time reap the advantage of ellipsoid update of having a faster convergence of the Lagrangian multipliers.

Figure 9(b) shows the comparison of the convergence of the Lagrangian multiplier between the subgradient method and ellipsoid method. As it is shown, ellipsoid method converges faster i.e. it requires less iteration number as compared to the subgradient method. On the other hand the convergence of the subgradient is high because it depends heavily on the choice of step size. Since the computational cost per iteration for both the methods is similar, the total computational cost of ellipsoid method is lower than the subgradient method.

Box 2.

$$\lambda_3 = \frac{1-\alpha}{\ln 2} \cdot \frac{\left(P_{RELAY} \mid h_{RELAY,R} \mid^2 \mid h_{T,RELAY} \mid^2 \sigma^2\right)\left(P_{RELAY} \mid h_{RELAY,R} \mid^2 + \sigma^2\right)}{\left[\left(P_{RELAY} \mid h_{RELAY,R} \mid^2 + P_{\overline{CR}} \mid h_{T,RELAY} \mid^2 + \sigma^2\right)\sigma^2 + P_{RELAY}P_{\overline{CR}} \mid h_{T,RELAY} \mid^2 \mid h_{RELAY,R} \mid^2\right] \mid h_{\overline{CR},P} \mid^2}$$

(33c)

Figure 9. (a) Performance of subgradient method and ellipsoid method (b) Convergence comparison of the Lagrangian multiplier

(a)

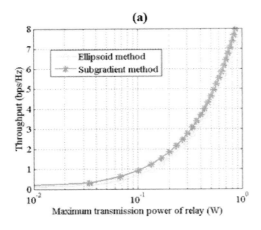

(b)

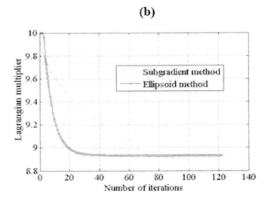

APPROACHES TO SOLVE OPTIMIZATION PROBLEMS

So far we have shown how an efficient allocation of power in a CR system can be used to achieve maximized system throughput. However, such a scheme has a high computational complexity. This is a very common problem in wireless systems where optimal approaches are often accompanied with high level of complexities. In such cases it is seen that lowering the complexity often involves the sacrifice of the systems performance. Still such trade-off is acceptable as it is always desirable to keep our complexity as low as possible. Ferdous et al. (2011) has implemented a new scheme in CR system that has a very low complexity compared to the optimal approach discussed earlier and yet it provides near-optimal results. Before going into details of this scheme, let us have an overview of how the scheme has been developed from the other conventional schemes.

Iterative Waterfilling

Iterative waterfilling (IW) is one of the pioneer approaches to solve dual optimization problems.

Here each user tries to iteratively maximize its own achievable rate. Each user iteratively maximizes its own achievable rate by performing a single-user waterfilling with the crosstalk interference from all other users treated as noise. Therefore, it converges to a "selfish optimum" instead of seeking a "global optimum" of the entire system. Each user participates in a non-cooperative game, and the convergence point of the iterative water-filling process corresponds to a competitive equilibrium. IW is a low-complexity approach since its complexity scales linearly with the number of users in the system (Yu and Cioffi, 2006).

Optimal Approach

Another approach is the optimal approach discussed previously in this chapter. It has been developed after IW to find the true global optimal solution of the optimization problem. It transforms the spectrum optimization problem into the dual domain by forming the Lagrangian dual of the primal optimization. This approach provides significant performance improvement as compared to IW. However, unlike IW, the computational complexity of optimal approach is exponential to the number of users in the system.

Near-optimal Low Complexity Iterative Approach

As seen so far IW is a greedy approach that can't converge to the global optimum of the system despite having low complexity and on the other hand, the optimal approach, which can seek a global optimal solution, has a high complexity (Lui and Yu, 2005). To address these problems, an iterative approach known new in CR system has been proposed which is a middle ground between the iterative waterfilling and the optimal approach. This approach reaps the advantage of both the dual formulation of the optimal approach and the low-complexity of IW. Therefore, unlike IW, the iterative approach reaches a global optimum by optimizing the objective function that includes the joint rate of all users. It differs from iterative water-filling in the following two key aspects. First, unlike the iterative waterfilling approach where each user maximizes its own rate in each step of the iteration, the iterative approach optimizes an objective function that includes the joint rates of all users. Thus, the new approach has the potential to reach the social optimum. Second, the power constraint in the iterative waterfilling process is handled in an ad-hoc basis, while the new approach dualizes the power constraint in an optimal fashion.

Methodology

Here the main objective is to evaluate $g\left(\lambda_1, \lambda_2, \lambda_3\right)$ with a complexity that is linear to the number of users. This can be done by,

$$\max L(P_{CR}, P_{\overline{CR}}, \lambda_1, \lambda_2, \lambda_3) \triangleq \max h\left(P_{CR}, P_{\overline{CR}}\right). \quad (40)$$

The optimization of $h\left(P_{CR}, P_{\overline{CR}}\right)$ is done in an iterative water filling fashion via coordinate descent. Here, for each fixed set of ($\lambda_1, \lambda_2, \lambda_3$) the power levels $P_{CR}, P_{\overline{CR}}, P_{RELAY}$ are optimized individually where in each case the other power levels are kept constant. For each fixed set of ($\lambda_1, \lambda_2, \lambda_3$), this approach first finds the optimal P_{CR} while keeping $P_{\overline{CR}}$ and P_{RELAY} fixed, then optimizes $P_{\overline{CR}}$ keeping P_{CR} and P_{RELAY} fixed, and so on. Note that when optimizing each power, only a small finite number of power levels (corresponding to a finite number of integer bits) need to be searched. Further, such an iterative process is guaranteed to converge because each iteration strictly increases the objective function. The convergence point must have integer bit values for all users, and it is guaranteed to be at least a local maximum for $\max h\left(P_{CR}, P_{\overline{CR}}\right)$. The correct dual variables, λ's, are then used in the following search method,

$$\lambda_m^{k+1} = \left[\lambda_m^k - s^k d_m\right]^+, \text{ for m=1, 2, 3} \quad (41)$$

where s^k is the step size sequence and d_m denotes the mth row in the subgradient matrix, d given in (20).

Complexity Analysis

It can be shown that the total computational complexity of this scheme is lower than that of optimal approach. Here, in the evaluation of $h\left(P_{CR}, P_{\overline{CR}}\right)$ each iteration has a computational complexity that is linear to the number of users. The number of iterations needed to evaluate each $h\left(P_{CR}, P_{\overline{CR}}\right)$ is T1 and the number of subgradient update needed in the optimal approach algorithm is T_2. Therefore the total computational complexity of our scheme is $O\left(T_1 T_2 BK\right)$, where B is the maximum number of bits per channel and K is the total number of users. On the other hand, the complexity of the optimal scheme is exponential in K, the total computational complexity of the optimal scheme is $O(T_2 B^K)$. The comparison between the existing and proposed scheme has been shown in Table 1.

Figure 10 shows a comparison between optimal approach and iterative low-complexity approach. In this simulation we have taken the values of the interference limits $\gamma = \phi = \varpi = 0.001\,W$. The total power limit of the cognitive transmitter, Ψ is $0.5\,W$. The standard deviation of shadowing is taken to be 3.98. As shown in the graph, the low-complexity scheme implemented in CR system has actually achieved a performance very much similar to high-complexity optimal approach. We see that the throughput of the system increases exponentially with the increase in the maximum power of the relay, Θ. This shows

that the throughput is dependent on the relay power when the total power of the CR transmitter is constant.

FUTURE RESEARCH DIRECTIONS

Cognitive radios offer the promise of being a disruptive technology innovation that will enable the future wireless world. It is expected that CR technology will soon emerge from early stage laboratory trials to become a general purpose programmable radio that will provide solutions to the "traffic jam" problem and serve as a universal platform for wireless system development. Significant new research is required to address the many unexplored fields of cognitive radio networking. These can include further details analysis in power allocation approaches on larger

Figure 10. Performance comparison of optimal approach and iterative approach

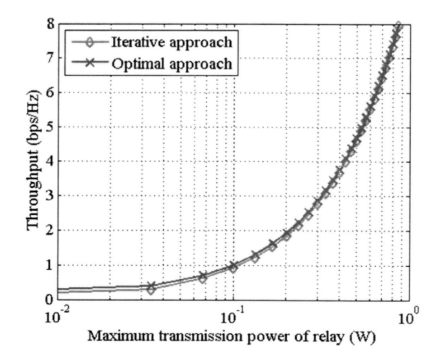

and more complex CR network. More realistic results can be obtained if practical channel conditions like fading, shadowing, varying of channel gains during data transmission and other factors are considered in future research. In case of relay selection and assignment, security issues must be considered and more work has to be done in preserving the integrity of the CR data during multi hop transmission. Coexistence of CR and PU results in harmful interference. It's always desirable to lower the interference level, hence bright scopes of research lies there. Moreover spectrum sensing itself is a vast area in CR and much work can be done in improving the existing detection techniques or in combining different techniques and come up with a better sensing scheme.

CONCLUSION

In this chapter, a brief discussion on spectrum sensing is done to show the effect of sensing time on CR throughput. The transmit power optimization issue of the cognitive radio network is considered to ease the coexistence of CR network with the primary network keeping the interference to the PU by the CR users to an acceptable limit. In such scenario, it is very important to assign relays to convey transmission of the CR source to its destination as relay exploits the diversity. So we have shown that after assigning relays in the CR system, the system throughput increases and also it helps to keep control on the interference limit. The relay-based cognitive network further faces obstacles like controlling transmit power which is solved by many conventional optimal techniques. Ellipsoid method is shown, which enhances the system performance in comparison to the subgradient method of the optimal approach. As with every conventional technique comes the trade-off between system performance and

computational complexity. Thus, a near-optimal iterative approach is shown which not only lessens the trade off but also reduces the computational complexity to great extent. Thus it can be concluded that iterative approach efficiently reduces the computational complexity in comparison to the optimal approach.

REFERENCES

Atapattu, S., Tellambura, C., & Jiang, H. (2009). Relay based cooperative spectrum sensing in cooperative radio networks. In *Proceedings of IEEE GLOBECOM.*

Boyd, S. (2004). *EE392o course notes.* Stanford, CA: Stanford University. Retrieved April 11, 2011, from http://www.stanford.edu/class/ee392o

Boyd, S., & Vandenberghe, L. (2004). *Convex optimization.* Cambridge University Press.

Cabric, D., Mishra, S. M., & Brodersen, R. W. (2004). Implementation issues in spectrum sensing for cognitive radios. In *Proceedings of the Asilomar Conference on Signals, Systems, and Computers.*

Cabric, D., Tkachenko, A., & Brodersen, R. (2006). Spectrum sensing measurements of pilot, energy, and collaborative detection. In *Proceedings IEEE Military Communication Conference,* Washington, DC, USA (pp. 1-7).

Cendrillon, R., Yu, W., Moonen, M., Verlinden, J., & Bostoen, T. (2006). Optimal multiuser spectrum balancing for digital subscriber lines. *IEEE Transactions on Communications,* 54(5), 922–933. doi:10.1109/TCOMM.2006.873096

Digham, F., Alouini, M., & Simon, M. (2003, May 5). On the energy detection of unknown signals over fading channels. In *Proceedings of IEEE ICC 2005*, Vol. 5 (pp. 3575–3579).

FCC. (2002). *Spectrum policy task force 1/8, an interleaver report*. ET Docket No. 02-155, Nov 02, 2002.

FCC 03-289. (2003). *ET docket No.03-237*. Retrieved April 10, 2011, from http://hraunfoss.fcc.gov/edocs_public/attachmatch/FCC-03-289A1.pdf

Ferdous, N., Ahmed, M., Matin, M. A., & Habiba, U. (2011). Efficient algorithm for power allocation in relay-based cognitive radio network. *Radio Engineering Journal, 20*(4).

Ganesan, G., & Li, Y. G. (2005). Agility improvement through cooperative diversity in cognitive radio networks. In *Proceedings of IEEE GLOBECOM*.

Ghasemi, A., & Sousa, E. S. (2008). Spectrum sensing in cognitive radio networks: requirements, challenges and design trade-offs [cognitive eradio communications]. *IEEE Communications Magazine, 4*, 32–39. doi:10.1109/MCOM.2008.4481338

Hamdi, K., & Letaief, K. B. (2009). Power, sensing time and throughput tradeoffs in cognitive radio systems: A cross-layer approach. In *Proceedings IEEE WCNC 2009*, Budapest, Hungary.

Haykin, S. (2005). Cognitive radio: Brain-empowered wireless communications. *IEEE Journal on Selected Areas in Communications, 23*(2), 201–220. doi:10.1109/JSAC.2004.839380

Irwin, M. E. (2006). *Moment generating function* (p. 19). Retrieved April 13, 2011, from http://www.markirwin.net/stat110/Lecture/Section45.pdf

Jia, J., Zhang, J., & Zhang, Q. (2009). Cooperative relay for cognitive radio networks. In *Proceedings IEEE INFOCOM*, (pp. 2304–2312).

Letaief, K. B., & Zhang, W. (2009). Cooperative communications for cognitive radio networks. *Proceedings of the IEEE, 97*(5), 878–893. doi:10.1109/JPROC.2009.2015716

Li, L., Zhou, X., Xu, H., Li, G. Y., Wang, D., & Soong, A. (2011). Simplified relay selection and power allocation in cooperative cognitive radio systems. *IEEE Transactions on Wireless Communications, 10*(1), 33–36. doi:10.1109/TWC.2010.101810.100311

Liu, Z., Xu, Y., Zhang, D., & Guan, S. (2010). *An efficient power allocation algorithm for relay assisted cognitive radio network. Wireless Communications and Signal Processing* (pp. 1–5). WCSP.

Lui, R., & Yu, W. (2005). Low-complexity near-optimal spectrum balancing for digital subscriber lines. In *Proceedings IEEE International Conference Communication*, 3, (pp. 1947-1951).

Mitola, J., III, & Maguire, G. Q. (1999). Cognitive radio: making software radios personal. *IEEE Personal Communication, 6*(4), 13-18.

Neel, J. O. (2006). *Analysis and design if cognitive radio network and distributed radio resource management algorithms.* Unpublished doctoral dissertation, Virginia Polytechnic Institute and State University, Blacksburg, VA.

Olfat, M., Farrokhi, F. R., & Liu, K. J. R. (2005). Power allocation for OFDM using adaptive beamforming over wireless networks. *IEEE Transactions on Communications, 53*(3), 505–514. doi:10.1109/TCOMM.2005.843438

Shen, Z., Andrews, V., & Evans, B. L. (2003). Optimal power allocation in multiuser OFDM systems. In *Proceedings of IEEE Global Communication Conference*, (pp. 337-341).

Stotas, S., & Nallanathan, A. (2010). On the throughput maximization of spectrum sharing cognitive radio networks. In *Proceedings of IEEE Globecom*.

Ulversoy, T. (2010). Software defined radio: Challenges and opportunities. *IEEE Communication Surveys Tutorials, 12*(4), 531–550. doi:10.1109/SURV.2010.032910.00019

Unnikrishnan, J., & Veeravalli, V. V. (2007). *Cooperative sensing and detection for cognitive radio*. Paper presented at IEEE Globecom, Washington DC.

Wei, Y., & Lui, R. (2006). Dual methods for nonconvex spectrum optimization of multicarrier systems. *IEEE Transactions on Communications, 54*(7), 1310–1322. doi:10.1109/TCOMM.2006.877962

Xiao, L., Johansson, M., & Boyd, S. P. (2004). Simultaneous routing and resource allocation via dual decomposition. *IEEE Transactions on Communications, 52*(7), 1136–1144. doi:10.1109/TCOMM.2004.831346

Yan, S., & Wang, X. (2009). Power allocation for cognitive radio systems based on nonregenerative OFDM relay transmission. In *Proceedings of IEEE Wicom*, (pp. 1-4).

Yu, D. D., & Cioffi, J. M. (2006). Iterative water-filling for optimal resource allocation in OFDM multi-access and broadcast channels. In *Proceedings of IEEE Global Telecommunication Conference*, San Francisco, CA, (pp. 1-5).

Zhang, Q., Jia, J., & Zhang, J. (2009). Cooperative relay to improve diversity in cognitive radio networks. *IEEE Communications Magazine, 47*(2), 111–117. doi:10.1109/MCOM.2009.4785388

Zhang, W., Mallik, R., & Letaief, K. (2009). Optimization of cooperative spectrum sensing with energy detection in cognitive radio networks. *IEEE Transactions on Wireless Communications, 8*(12), 5761–5766. doi:10.1109/TWC.2009.12.081710

ADDITIONAL READING

Bengtsson, M., & Ottersten, B. (1999). Optimal downlink beamforming using semidenite optimization. in Proceeding.*37th Annual Allerton Conference on Communication, Control and Computing*.

Bletsas, A., Lippman, A., & Reed, D. (2005). A simple distributed method for relay selection in cooperative diversity wireless networks, based on reciprocity and channel measurements. In *Proceedings of the IEEE 61st Vehicular Technology Conference*.

Chalise, B. K., & Czylwik, A. (2004). *Robust uplink beamforming based upon minimum outage probability criterion*. IEEE Globecom.

Czylwik, A. (1996). Adaptive OFDM for wideband radio channels. In *Proceedings of IEEE GLOBECOM*, London, UK, (pp. 713–718).

Gao, F., Cui, T., & Nallanathan, A. (2008). On channel estimation and optimal training design for amplify and forward relay networks. *IEEE Transactions on Wireless Communications, 7*(5), 1907–1916. doi:10.1109/TWC.2008.070118

Ghasemi, & Sousa, E. S. Fundamental limits of spectrum-sharing in fading environments. *IEEE Transaction Wireless Communication, 6*(2), 649–658.

Jing, Y., & Jafarkhani, H. (2007). Network beamforming using relays with perfect channel information. *IEEE International Conference on Acoustics, Speech and Signal Processing*, Honolulu, Hawaii.

Laneman, J. N., Tse, D. N. C., & Wornell, G. W. (2004). Cooperative diversity in wireless networks: Efficient protocols and outage behavior. *IEEE Transactions on Information Theory, 50*(12), 3062–3080. doi:10.1109/TIT.2004.838089

Liang, Y. C., Zeng, Y., Peh, E., & Hoang, A. T. (2008). Sensing-throughput tradeoff for cognitive radio networks. *IEEE Transactions on Wireless Communications, 7*(4), 1326–1337. doi:10.1109/TWC.2008.060869

Madsen, A., & Zhang, J. (2005). Capacity bounds and power allocation for wireless relay channels. *IEEE Transactions on Information Theory, 51*(6), 2020–2040. doi:10.1109/TIT.2005.847703

Mitola, J. III. (2009). Cognitive radio architecture evolution. *Proceedings of the IEEE, 97*(4), 626–641. doi:10.1109/JPROC.2009.2013012

Pentz, B., Chen, R., & Peterson, K. (n.d.). *IEEE 802.22 WRAN (cognitive radio).* Retrieved from http://ecee.colorado.edu/~ecen4242/cognitive/index.html

Rohling, H., & Grunheid, R. (1996). Performance of an OFDM-TDMA mobile communication system. In *Proceedings of IEEE Vehicular Technology Conf. (VTC'96)*, Atlanta, GA, (pp. 1589–1593).

Verdu, S. (2002). Spectral efficiency in the wideband regime. *IEEE Transactions on Information Theory, 48*(6). doi:10.1109/TIT.2002.1003824

Zou, Y., Yao, Y. D., & Zheng, B. (2010). Cognitive transmissions with multiple relays in cognitive radio networks. *IEEE Transaction Wireless Communication, 10*(2). Retrieved from http://personal.stevens.edu/yzou1/TWC~Cog Multi2010.pdf

KEY TERMS AND DEFINITIONS

Cognitive Radio (CR): An intelligent radio device that changes its transmitting parameters based on its interaction with its surrounding electromagnetic environment.

Constrained Optimization: The conversion of a primal problem i.e. the original form of a optimization problem to a dual form, which is termed a *dual problem*. Usually *dual problem* refers to the *Lagrangian dual problem*.

Lagrangian Multiplier: A method that provides a strategy for finding the maxima and minima of a function subject to constraints.

Primary Users (PU): The licensed users that have the rights to use specific parts of the spectrum band.

Probability of Successful Secondary Transmission (PSST): The probability that there would be a successful data transmission from the cognitive radio transmitter to the cognitive radio receiver either directly or via single/multiple relays.

Secondary Users (SU): The unlicensed users that have cognitive capabilities to sense the licence bands of primary users and access it when the band is idle.

Spectrum Hole (SH): A region of location-time-frequency that is not utilized by PU.

Spectrum Sensing: The technique of detecting the presence of primary signal in a scanned frequency band.

Chapter 11
Spectrum Sensing in Cognitive Radio Networks

Danda B. Rawat
Eastern Kentucky University, USA

Gongjun Yan
Indiana University-Kokomo, USA

Bhed Bahadur Bista
Iwate Prefectural University, Japan

ABSTRACT

The rising number and capacity requirements of wireless systems bring increasing demand for RF spectrum. Cognitive radio (CR) system is an emerging concept to increase the spectrum efficiency. CR system aims to enable opportunistic usage of the RF bands that are not occupied by their primary licensed users in spectrum overlay approach. In this approach, the major challenge in realizing the full potential of CR systems is to identify the spectrum opportunities in the wide band regime reliably and optimally. In the spectrum underlay approach, CR systems enable dynamic spectrum access by co-existing and transmitting simultaneously with licensed primary users without creating harmful interference to them. In this case, the challenge is to transmit with low power so as not to exceed the tolerable interference level to the primary users. Spectrum sensing and estimation is an integral part of the CR system, which is used to identify the spectrum opportunities in spectrum overlay and to identify the interference power to primary users in spectrum underlay approach. In this chapter, the authors present a comprehensive study of signal detection techniques for spectrum sensing proposed for CR systems. Specifically, they outline the state of the art research results, challenges, and future perspectives of spectrum sensing in CR systems, and also present a comparison of different methods. With this chapter, readers can have a comprehensive insight of signal processing methods of spectrum sensing for cognitive radio networks and the ongoing research and development in this area.

DOI: 10.4018/978-1-4666-1797-1.ch011

Copyright © 2012, IGI Global. Copying or distributing in print or electronic forms without written permission of IGI Global is prohibited.

1. INTRODUCTION

Most of the current spectrum assignment rules in existing wireless communication networks around the world challenge the dynamic spectrum access aspects due to static RF spectrum assignment to the service providers for exclusive use on a long term basis. The exclusive spectrum licensing by government regulatory bodies, such the Federal Communications Commission (FCC) in the United States, and its counterparts around the world, is for interference mitigation among different service providers and their service users. However, the static spectrum assignment to particular service provider leads to inefficient use of spectrum since most portion of the spectrum remains under-utilization (Akyildiz et al., 2006). This implies that the scarcity of spectrum is not because of lack of natural spectrum but result of static spectrum allocation which leads to serious bottleneck for deployment of larger density of wireless systems. Advancements in integrated circuits and transceiver technology results in increasing demand of RF spectrum. Cognitive radio (CR) system is an emerging concept to increase the spectrum efficiency which uses the spectrum opportunities dynamically without creating harmful interference to licensed users. CR system may have two situations. One is with both licensed primary users and unlicensed secondary CR users occupying the same spectrum like in licensed band scenarios. The next situation is with no primary users and every CR user contends for spectrum with other CR users and non-CR users as in the unlicensed band scenario. In this paper, we deal with the situation where primary and secondary CR users are active, and the aim is to present signal processing techniques for spectrum sensing to avoid the disturbance to primary user transmissions while CR users use the band dynamically.

The dynamic spectrum access for spectrum sharing in CR systems has two basic approaches (Akyildiz et al., 2006, Haykin, 2005). One is *spectrum overlay* technique whereby a unlicensed CR users require to sense and identify the spectrum opportunities in licensed bands before using them for given time and geographic location, and exploit those opportunities dynamically. Whenever the primary users are active in given frequency band for given time and location, secondary CR users are not allowed to use that band. Once they find the spectrum opportunities they can use those opportunities dynamically until the primary systems want to use them and the CR users have to leave the band as quickly as possible (Poor, H.V. and Hadjiliadis, O., 2009, Haykin, 2005). The other is *spectrum underlay* approach where secondary CR users coexist and transmit simultaneously with primary users sharing the licensed bands but CR users are not allowed to transmit with high power as they have to respect the active primary user transmissions. In this approach, secondary CR users do not have to sense the spectrum for opportunities however they are not allowed to transmit with higher than the preset power mask even if the primary system is completely idle. It is worth to note that the main goal in both approaches is to access the licensed spectrum dynamically and/or opportunistically without disturbing the primary user transmissions. In spectrum overlay approach, the major challenge to realize the full potential of CR systems is to identify the spectrum opportunities in the wide band regime reliably and optimally. And in spectrum underlay approach, the challenge is to transmit with low power so as not to exceed the tolerable interference level at primary users.

In order to realize the full potential of CR system, the detection of primary user signal is of vital importance (Rawat and Yan, 2009, Rawat and Yan, 2011). Generally, in CR system, devices detect each other's presence as interference and try to avoid the interference by changing their behavior accordingly. For CR systems, different techniques for spectrum sensing have been proposed in the literature to identify the spectrum opportunities for CRs. (Zeng and Liang, 2009, Cabric et al., 2006, De and Liang, 2007, Tang, 2005, Cabric et al., 2004, ¨Oner and Jondral, 2007,Urkowitz, 1967,Y. Zhuan and Grosspietsch, 2008, Challapali et al., 2004, Tian and Giannakis, 2006,Wild and Ramchandran, 2005,Farhang-Boroujeny and Kempter, 2008,Ganesan and Li, 2007a,Ganesan and Li, 2007b,Han et al., 2009).

Our main goal in this chapter is to present the state-of-the-art research results of signal detection techniques for spectrum sensing. We also present the comparison of transmissions in spectrum overlay and spectrum underlay in terms of Bit-Error-Rate (BER) and distance between two communicating CR devices. Furthermore, we present the comparison of different signal detection techniques for spectrum sensing which are used to identify the spectrum opportunities to operate CR users in spectrum overlay.

Spectrum Overlay vs. Spectrum Underlay

Bit-Error-Rate (BER) of CR user transmission with respect to distance (CR transmitter receiver pair distance) is compared in spectrum overlay and spectrum underlay approaches. For spectrum underlay, we consider the simulations with UWB signaling and the channel model CM3 as in (Molisch et al., 2004) which models the office environment with line-of-site (LOS). The other simulation parameters are listed on Table 1. For this scenario, we have plotted the BER vs. the distance (in meter) as shown in Figure 1.

We then performed the simulation for spectrum overlay approach considering two scenarios: in the first scenario we vary the distances of CR transmitter-receiver pair from 15 m to 160 m, and consider that the spectrum opportunities are available in this range. The second scenario, we consider that the spectrum opportunities are available only for the transmitter-receiver pair distances of 15 m to 120 m. We consider that there are no spectrum opportunities for the distance range of 120 m to 160 m and thus the CR users would not be able to

Table 1. List of simulation parameters

Parameter	Value
Channel model	Office LOS (CM3)
Reference path loss	35.4db
-10db Bandwidth	500 MHz
Throughput	20 Mbps
Frequency range	3.1 GHz-3.6 GHz
Path loss exponent	1.63
Receive Antenna Noise Figure	17dB
Implementation loss	3dB
Geometric center frequency	3.34 GHz

use the spectrum to transmit their information in spectrum overlay approach. Then we plotted the BER vs. the distance for both scenarios of spectrum overlay in the same Figure 1.

From Figure 1, we note that the BER is increasing with the CR transmitter-receiver pair distance as expected in spectrum underlay approach because there will be external interference from primary users for larger distances. However, the BER is almost constant (regardless of distance between transmitter and receiver pairs) in the case of spectrum overlay compared to that of spectrum underlay approach. We note that, in spectrum underlay approach, no matter whether there are spectrum opportunities or not, CR users are able to communicate but in spectrum overlay approach, the CR users are allowed to transmit their information only when the spectrum opportunities are present.

Overlay spectrum sharing is an interference technique typical of IEEE 802.22 networks where cognitive radio (unlicensed) users only access the network using portions of spectrum that have not been occupied by a licensed primary user. This method avoids interference to primary users. Underlay spectrum sharing exploits spread spectrum techniques developed for cellular networks where cognitive radio user transmits messages at a specific power level and at a specific point in

Figure 1. BER vs. distance between nodes for spectrum underlay (UWB like) and spectrum overlay scenarios

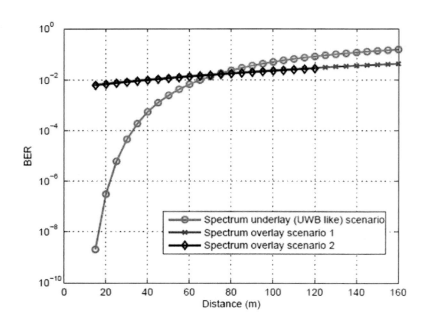

the spectrum so that it is regarded as noise by a licensed primary user.

It is noted by stating that the CR users should be able to switch between spectrum underlay and overlay approaches so that the device can transmit their information one way or the other based on their operating RF environment. In other words, if spectrum opportunities are present, CR users would be using those opportunities dynamically in spectrum overlay, and if spectrum opportunities are not available to CR users, then they can switch to spectrum underlay approach for their transmissions. This mechanism will lead to efficient utilization of spectrum to increase the overall efficiency and the system capacity with a bit device complexity.

Capabilities of Cognitive Radios

Basically, in spectrum overlay based communications, a cognitive radio users should be able to jump in and out of free spaces in spectrum bands,

avoiding pre-existing users. Whereas in spectrum underlay, cognitive radio should transmit with low power so as not to disturb primary transmissions.

Cognitive radio technology is regarded as emerging technology for efficient spectrum use in dynamic fashion. The main capabilities of cognitive radios can be categorized according to their functionality based on the definition of the cognitive radio in (Haykin, 2005) as follows:

- **Sense the Environment**: Which is cognitive capability, where a CR sense the spectrum either to identify the frequency band not used by licensed primary users or to make sure that the cognitive radio is not creating harmful interfere to primary users. In order to sense the environment, it will first discover the network around it. Furthermore, cognitive radio will identify its location in order to choose the transmission parameters according to its position.

- **Analyze and Learn Sensed Information**: Which is self-organized capability, in which CR should be able to self-organize their communication based on sensed information.
- **Adapt to the Operating Environment**: Which is re-configurable capability, for which the CR will choose best transmission parameters such as operating frequency, modulation, transmission power and so on.

Main capabilities of CR users depend on sensed information from which they analyze and learned and then adapt their own operating parameters accordingly. All functionality of cognitive radio networks rely on sensed information. Therefore spectrum sensing is a fundamental task in CR system, which is the subject matter of the following section.

2. SPECTRUM SENSING METHODS

Spectrum sensing and estimation is the first step to implement the CR system. In this paper, as mentioned, we deal with the situation where primary and secondary CR users are present, and the aim is to identify the spectrum opportunities to operate CR users in spectrum overlay and to identify the interference power created by CR users to primary users while operating in spectrum underlay approach. There are many signal processing techniques in the literature. We can categorize them into *direct* method which is recognized as frequency domain approach where the estimation is carried out directly from signal and *indirect* method which is known as time domain approach where the estimation is performed using autocorrelation of the signal. Another way of categorizing the spectrum sensing and estimation methods is by making group into model based *parametric* method and periodogram based *non-parametric* method (Proakis and Manolakis, 2007). Without

loss of generality, the spectrum sensing techniques can be categorized as follows:

- **Spectrum Sensing for Spectrum Opportunities**
  - ◦ **Primary Transmitter Detection:** In this case, the detection of primary users is performed based on the received signal at CR users. This approach includes matched filter (MF) based detection (Cabric et al., 2004, Proakis, 2000), energy based detection (Urkowitz, 1967,Y. Zhuan and Grosspietsch, 2008,De and Liang, 2007), covariance based detection (Zeng and Liang, 2009), waveform-based detection (Tang, 2005), cyclo-stationarity based detection ("Oner and Jondral, 2007), radio identification based detection (Farnham et al., 2000), and random Hough Transform based detection (Challapali et al., 2004)
  - ◦ **Cooperative and Collaborative Detection:** In this approach the primary user signal for spectrum opportunities are detected reliably by interacting or cooperating with other users (Cabric et al., 2006, Ganesan and Li, 2007a, Ganesan and Li, 2007b), and the method can be implemented as either centralized access to spectrum coordinated by a spectrum server (Yates et al., 2006) or distributed approach implied by the spectrum load smoothing algorithm (Berlemann et al., 2006) or external detection (Han et al., 2009),
- **Spectrum Sensing for Interference Detection**
  - ◦ **Interference Temperature Detection:** In this approach, CR system works as in the ultra-wide band (UWB) technology where the

secondary users coexist with primary users and are allowed to transmit with low power and restricted by the interference temperature level so as not to cause harmful interference to primary users (Xing et al., 2007,Bater et al., 2007).

- ◦ **Primary Receiver Detection:** In this method, the interference and/or spectrum opportunities are detected based on primary user-receiver's local oscillator leakage power (Wild and Ramchandran, 2005).

Different techniques for spectrum sensing are also listed in Figure 2.

2.1 Primary Transmitter Detection

In this section, we present the spectrum sensing techniques which base on the received signal (transmitted by primary users) at secondary CR user in its vicinity. These methods are aimed on detecting the weakest signal from a primary user but not the strongest. The idea of detecting the weakest signal of primary transmitter is to deal with the furthest one from the CR user but still susceptible to interference from CR user, and thus the approach would easily be able to detect the strong signals. In the following subsections, we present the signal detection methods for spectrum sensing to identify the opportunities to operate the CR users in spectrum overlay approach.

2.1.1 System Model

We consider the scenario where primary and secondary CR users are present, and the aim is to identify the spectrum opportunities based on sensed information. We consider the received signal at CR user in continuous time as

$$r(t) = g\, s(t) + w(t) \tag{1}$$

where $r(t)$ is the received signal at CR user, g is channel gain between primary transmitter to CR user receiver, $s(t)$ is the primary user's signal (that is to be detected by CR users), and $w(t)$ is the additive Gaussian white noise (AWGN) that corrupts the transmitted signal.

In order to represent the received signal (1) in terms of its sampled version (to use the signal processing methods for spectrum sensing), we consider the signal in the frequency band with central frequency fc and bandwidth W, and sample the received signal at a sampling rate fs, where $fs > W$, and $Ts = 1/fs$ is the sampling period. Then we define $r(n) = r(nTs)$ as the samples of the received signal, $s(n) = s(nTs)$ as the samples of the primary signal and $w(n) = w(nTs)$ as the noise samples. We then write the sampled received signal in (1) as follows

$$r(n) = gs(n) + w(n) \tag{2}$$

If we consider the channel gain $g = 1$ (i.e., ideal case) between the terminals then (2) becomes

$$r(n) = s(n) + w(n) \tag{3}$$

We use two possible hypotheses for primary user detection as follows:

- $H0$ to denote that the signal $s(n)$ is not present, that is, Null-hypothesis which represents that there is no licensed primary users signal in a certain band and
- $H1$ to denote that the signal $s(n)$ is present, that is, alternative hypothesis which indicates that there exists some licensed primary signal in the band.

We can also write the received signal samples under the two hypotheses as (Ghasemi and Sousa, 2005)

$$H0: r(n) = w(n)$$

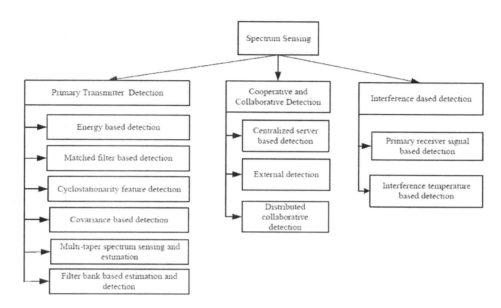

Figure 2. Spectrum sensing techniques in cognitive radio systems

H1: r(n) = gs(n) + w(n) or r(n) = s(n) + w(n)

$$(4)$$

In the case of primary transmitter detection, we consider the system model either in Equation (2) or in (3) where appropriate along with the given two hypotheses (4). We note that if the signal component *s(n) = 0* in Equation (3) implies that the particular frequency band may be idle (if the detection is error free) and the signal *s(n) ≠ 0* in Equation (3) implies that the particular frequency band is in use and there is no spectrum opportunities for given time and location.

We present different methods for spectrum sensing which base on the hypothesis in (4) in the following subsections.

2.1.2 Energy Detection

Energy detection method bases on energy level of received signal. This is the most common method of detection because of its low computational and implementation complexities (Cabric et al., 2004). In energy detection, the receivers do not need any prior knowledge of the primary users' signals as in matched filtering based approach. The working principle of energy detection is to compare the output of energy detector with a given threshold value (Urkowitz, 1967), and the observed energy is less than the threshold implies that the band is idle otherwise the band is occupied by primary user. Proper choice of threshold value is very important and it can be adapted based on the noise floor.

In energy based detection method, for given system model in Equation (3), we can compute the signal energy (or decision metric) as

$$D = \sum_{n=0}^{N} | r(n) |^2 \qquad (5)$$

By considering the AWGN with variance σ_n and the signal with variance σ_s (this assumption can be made with the help of Central limit theorem), the decision metric D follows chi-square distribution with 2N degrees of freedom $(\chi_{2N})^2$ (Urkowitz, 1967), and can be modeled two hypotheses as follows

$$D = \begin{cases} \dfrac{\sigma_W^2}{2} \chi_{2N}^2 & H_0 \\[4mm] \dfrac{\sigma_W^2 + \sigma_S^2}{2} \chi_{2N}^2 & H_1 \end{cases}$$

(6)

Then, comparing the computed energy level D value with given threshold value λ_T, CR users can identify whether the band is idle or not. The detection of the signal can be performed based on following probabilities

$$P_T = \Pr(D > \lambda|H1)$$
$$P_F = \Pr(D > \lambda|H0)$$

(7)

That is, by calculating the false alarm probability, P_F, and true detection probability, P_T, using Equation (6), one can easily identify whether the spectrum opportunities is available.

This method is simple to implement however has some disadvantages such as identifying the proper threshold value, poor performance under low Signal-to-Noise-Ratio (Tang, 2005), and inability to differentiate between interference from licensed users and noise. This approach also does not work optimally for detecting spread spectrum, such as CDMA, signals (Cabric et al., 2004).

2.1.3 Matched Filtering Based Detection

Matched filtering (MF) is another approach of detecting the signal. This method needs prior knowledge of transmitted signal to detect primary users signal optimally (Proakis, 2000) since it maximizes received signal-to-noise ratio (SNR). The working principle of matched filter is to correlate a known signal (or template) with an unknown signal and detect the presence of the template in the unknown signal (which is received

signal sn). the biggest advantage of the matched filter is that it requires less time to achieve a high processing gain because of its coherency (Akyildiz et al., 2006).

However, MF has many disadvantages such as it requires perfect knowledge of the primary user signaling features (such as modulation type, operating frequency, etc.) of primary users which in a real world situation for CR systems may not be available. It has high implementation complexity of detection unit (Cabric et al., 2004) because CR system needs receivers for all signal types of wide band regime, and it needs more power which will be consumed to execute such several detection processes. As a consequence the MF based detection is most accurate but the most complex to implement in CR devices.

2.1.4 Cyclostationarity-Based Detection

This is another approach for signal detection which takes advantage of cyclostationarity properties of the received signals (Oner and Jondral, 2007, Gardner, 1991) to detect primary user transmissions. In general, the transmitted signals are stationary random process however they bear cyclostationarity features because the modulated signals are coupled with sine wave carriers, repeating spreading code sequences, or cyclic prefixes which results in a built-in periodicity. The mean and autocorrelation of the signal exhibit periodicity which is characterized as being cyclostationary. We note that the noise, on the other hand, is Wide-Sense Stationary process. Therefore, this method can differentiate primary users' signals from noise (Oner and Jondral, 2007). In this method, cyclic spectral correlation function (SCF) is used for detecting signals present in a given frequency band, and it is possible to differentiate modulated signal energy from noise energy and thereby detect whether a primary user is present or not. The cyclic SCF of received signal in Equation (3) can be calculated as (Oner and Jondral, 2007, Gardner, 1991)

$$S_{yy}^{\alpha}(f) = \sum_{t=-\infty}^{\infty} R_{yy}^{\alpha}(t)e^{-j2\pi f}$$

where $R_{yy}^{\alpha}(t)$ is the cyclic autocorrelation function which is obtained from the conjugate time varying autocorrelation function of s(n), which is periodic in n. When the parameter α, which is the cyclic frequency, is equal to zero the SCF becomes power spectral density. This method gives the peak in cyclic SCF implying that the primary user is present in a given band. When there is no such peak, the given spectrum band is idle. This method is applicable to wide variety of wireless standards including CDMA and OFDM wireless systems.

2.1.5 Covariance Based Detection

The central idea of the covariance based signal detection technique (Zeng and Liang, 2009) is that to exploit the covariance of signal and noise. Generally, the statistical covariance of signal and noise are different. To apply this method for spectrum sensing, the received signal (2) is expressed in vector form as (Zeng and Liang, 2009)

$$\mathbf{r} = \mathbf{G}\,\mathbf{s} + \mathbf{w} \qquad (8)$$

where G is channel matrix between a primary user-transmitter and a secondary CR user-receiver through which the signal travels. The covariance matrices corresponding to the received signal, transmitted signal and noise can be written as

$$\begin{aligned} \mathbf{R}_r &= E[(\mathbf{rr}^{\mathbf{T}})] \\ \mathbf{R}_s &= E[(\mathbf{ss}^{\mathbf{T}})] \\ \mathbf{R}_n &= E[(\mathbf{ww}^{\mathbf{T}})] \end{aligned} \qquad (9)$$

As we consider the noise as AWGN, all the elements of $\mathbf{R}_n$ are zero except the main diagonal. We note that $\mathbf{R}_s = 0$ when the primary signal is not present (i.e., $\mathbf{s}_n = 0$). Therefore, the off-diagonal elements of $\mathbf{R}_r$ are all zeros when the primary signal is absent. The signal samples are correlated and the matrix Rs is not a diagonal matrix when the signal is present (i.e., $\mathbf{s}_n \neq 0$) which results in some of the off-diagonal elements of $\mathbf{R}_r$ should not be zeros. This methods usages this technique and identifies the spectrum opportunities with the help of covariance matrices of the received signal and the noise. Unlike the other methods, this method can detect the spread spectrum (CDMA) signals.

2.1.6 Multi-Taper Spectrum Sensing and Estimation

Multi Taper spectrum estimation (MTSE) has proposed by (Thomson, 1982) before the CR concept was introduced. In this method the last N received samples are collected in a vector form and represented them as a set of Slepian base vectors (Thomson, 1982). The main idea of this method is that the Fourier transforms of Slepian vectors have the maximal energy concentration in the bandwidth $f_c - W$ to $f_c + W$ under finite sample-size constraints (Thomson, 1982, Haykin, 2005). By exploiting this feature, CR user can easily identify the spectrum opportunities in given band. As MTSE uses multiple prototype filters (Thomson, 1982, Haykin, 2005), it is better for small sample spaces since the computational complexity increases with large samples (Farhang-Boroujeny and Kempter, 2008).

2.1.7 Filter Bank Based Spectrum Sensing

Filter bank based spectrum estimation (FBSE) is regarded as the simplified version of MTSE which uses only one prototype filter for each band and has been proposed for multi-carrier modulation based CR systems by using a pair of matched-root Nyquist-filter (Farhang-Boroujeny and Kempter, 2008). As mentioned, FBSE, is simplified version of MTSE, uses the same concept of maximal energy concentration in the bandwidth $f_c - W$ to $f_c + W$.

Exploiting this information, CR user identifies the spectrum occupancy and hence the spectrum opportunities. MTSE is better for small samples whereas FBSE is better for large number of samples (Farhang-Boroujeny and Kempter, 2008).

2.2 Cooperative and Collaborative Detection

The detection procedure which bases on sensing by single CR user might be erroneous because of many problems such as hidden terminal (primary user) problem and signal fading (or blocking) which results in increase in both probability of miss-detection and false alarms. In order to deal with these problems, recently the cooperative and collaborative approach for detection of spectrum occupancy has been proposed (Cabric et al., 2006, Ganesan and Li, 2005). In this approach, the spectrum estimation is done by interacting or collaborating among many participating wireless users in order to get reliable and accurate information regarding spectrum opportunities.

In CR systems, the cooperative and collaborative based spectrum sensing can be implemented in the following three different ways.

2.2.1 Centralized Server Based Detection

In this approach, a central unit (i.e., a spectrum server) which does not sense the spectrum itself but collects all the spectrum occupancy information from participating CR users, is used. Then this central unit (spectrum server) aggregates the collected information centrally, and broadcasts the aggregated spectrum status to all CR users.

The aggregation help to reduce the probability of miss detection and false alarms. Once the CR users receive the spectrum occupancy information from central server they can adapt their transmission parameters accordingly (Yates et al., 2006). We note that the spectrum server is assumed to be just a facilitator and information collector without having spectrum sensing capability and this method needs to have a spectrum server or central unit like a base station in cellular telecommunication systems.

2.2.2 External Detection

External detection technique for spectrum sensing is another approach used in cooperative and collaborative detection. Similar to the spectrum server based cooperative detection; the CR users obtain the spectrum occupancy information from external agent (Han et al., 2009). However, in this method, the external agent performs the spectrum sensing, and broadcasts the spectrum occupancy information to CR users. Unlike the previous cooperative method, the CR devices will not have spectrum sensing capabilities. As a result, this method is regarded as an efficient in terms of spectrum and power consumptions from the prospective of CR users since they do not spend time and power for signal detection (Han et al., 2009). Similar to previous method, this method also help to overcome hidden terminal (primary user) problem as well as the uncertainty due to shadowing and fading (Han et al., 2009). This method also needs to have installed external agent like a base station in cellular telecommunication systems, which might be seen as a major drawback of this approach.

2.2.3 Distributed Detection

This is an alternative approach of above two methods. Unlike the centralized and external detection methods, the CR users make their own decision based on the spectrum occupancy information received from other interacting or collaborating users.

The main advantage of this approach is that we do not need any high capacity centralized backbone infrastructure. However there are some issues related to reliability, security and authenticity. Generally, the distributed detection are implemented by using spectrum load smoothing algorithms (Berlemann et al., 2006).

(Shankar, 2005) pointed out that cooperative and collaborative detection are network resource hungry methods since CR users take on the dual role of both spectrum sensing (sensor network for cooperative spectrum sensing) and data transmission (operational network). Furthermore, when the location of the primary receiver is not known, (Akyildiz et al., 2006) state that the primary receiver uncertainty problem is still unsolved even if with cooperative sensing methods.

2.3 Interference Based Detection

In this section, we present interference based detection so that the CR users would operate in spectrum underlay (UWB like) approach.

2.3.1 Primary Receiver Detection

In general, primary receiver emits the local oscillator (LO) leakage power from its RF front-end while receiving the data from primary transmitter. (Wild and Ramchandran, 2005) have suggested a method to detect a primary user by mounting a low-cost sensor node close to a primary user's receiver in order to detect the local oscillator (LO) leakage power emitted by the RF front-end of the primary user's receiver which are within the communication range of CR system users. The local sensor then reports the sensed information to the CR users so that they can identify the spectrum occupancy status.

We note that this method can also be used to identify the spectrum opportunities to operate CR users in spectrum overlay.

2.3.2 Interference Temperature Management

Unlike the primary receiver detection, the basic idea behind the interference temperature management (as depicted in Figure 3 (FCC, 2003)) is to set up an upper interference limit for given frequency band in specific geographic location such that the CR users are not allowed to cause harmful interference while using the specific band in specific area (Xing et al., 2007, Bater et al., 2007). Typically, CR user-transmitters control their interference

Figure 3. Interference temperature model

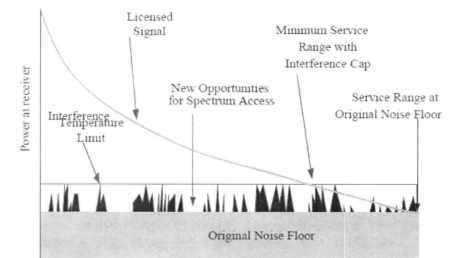

by regulating their transmission power (their out-of-band emissions) based on their locations with respect to primary users. This method basically concentrates on measuring interference at the receiver. The working principle of this method is like an UWB technology where the CR users' are allowed to coexist and transmit simultaneously with primary users using low transmit power that is restricted by the interference temperature level so as not to cause harmful interference to primary users (Xing et al., 2007,Bater et al., 2007).

In this method, CR users do not need to perform spectrum sensing for spectrum opportunities and can transmit right way with specified preset power mask. However, the CR users cannot transmit their data with higher power even if the licensed system is completely idle since they are not allowed to transmit with higher than the preset power to limit the interference at primary users. It is noted that the CR users, in this method, are required to know the location and corresponding upper level of allowed transmit power levels. Otherwise they will interfere the primary user transmissions.

3. OTHER SIGNAL PROCESSING APPROACHES

Wavelet based detection is popular in image processing for edge detection. (Tian and Giannakis, 2006) have proposed this approach in spectrum sensing where wavelets are used for detecting edges in the power spectral density (PSD) of a wideband channel. This process is applied to find the edges in PSD which are the boundary between spectrum holes and occupied bands. Based on this information, CR can identify the spectrum opportunities. *Random Hough transform based detection* is also widely used for pattern (such as lines, circles) detection in image processing. Recently, (Challapali et al., 2004) have proposed to perform Random Hough transform of received signal $r(n)$ to identify the presence of radar pulses

in the operating channels of IEEE 802.11 wireless systems. *Radio identification based detection* techniques are used in the context of European Transparent Ubiquitous Terminal (TRUST) project (Farnham et al., 2000) which bases on several extracted features such as transmission frequency, transmission range, modulation technique, etc. Once the features are extracted from the received signal $r(n)$ in (3), CR users exploit those features and can select suitable transmission parameters for them.

4. COMPARISON: DIFFERENT SPECTRUM SENSING TECHNIQUES VS. ACCURACIES AND COMPLEXITIES

In this section, we present the comparison of different transmitter detection techniques for spectrum sensing to find the spectrum opportunities. The comparison presented in Figure 4 is not drawn to scale.

We note that matched filter based detection is complex to implement in CRs (because of its many drawbacks as mentioned previously) but has highest accuracy. Similarly, the energy based detection is least complex to implement in CR system and least accurate compared to other approaches because of its drawbacks as mentioned previously. And other approaches are in the middle of these two approaches as shown in Figure 4.

5. CONCLUSION

In this paper we have presented the survey of signal processing techniques for next generation CR systems. In order to realize the CR systems with full potential for efficient utilization of scarce spectrum, the interference detection for spectrum underlay approach and spectrum sensing for spectrum opportunities for spectrum overlay should

Figure 4. Comparison of different techniques for spectrum sensing methods for spectrum overlay in terms of sensing accuracies and implementation complexities

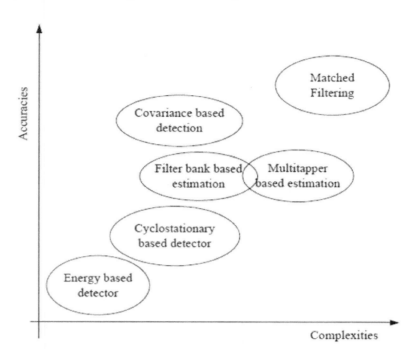

be reliable and prompt so that the primary user transmissions would not be suffered from CR users. We have presented the in-depth survey of signal processing techniques for spectrum sensing applicable to CR system to operate in both spectrum overlay and underlay approaches. We have also presented the comparison in terms of BER for CR user transmissions in spectrum overlay and underlay. We note that the efficient utilization of spectrum could be obtained when CR user are able to switch from spectrum overlay to underlay and vice versa, according to available spectrum opportunities. We have also made comparison of signal processing techniques for spectrum sensing based on their advantages and disadvantages, and concluded that the MF gives most accurate result but with highest implementation complexity for CR devices. Similarly the energy based detection

is least complex and least accurate. Other approaches are in the middle of these two methods.

We have noted that the licensed user can claim their frequency bands at any time while CR system is operating on the band opportunistically. In this case, the CR users should be able to vacate the band as quickly as possible (Poor, H.V. and Hadjiliadis, O., 2009) in order not to disturb the primary user transmissions. The proposed signal detection methods have limitations in terms of time and frequency resolution. The CR system is still in its early stage of development, there are number of challenges to be addressed in terms of primary user signal detection time, hardware and computational complexities. Furthermore, the "spread spectrum primary user" (e.g. for CDMA) detection is also difficult since the energy is spreaded over wider frequency range for a user.

REFERENCES

Akyildiz, I. F., Lee, W.-Y., Vuran, M. C., & Mohanty, S. (2006). Next generation/dynamic spectrum access/cognitive radio wireless networks: A survey. *Computer Networks, 50*(13), 13–18. doi:10.1016/j.comnet.2006.05.001

Bater, J., Tan, H.-P., Brown, K., & Doyle, L. (2007). Modelling interference temperature constraints for spectrum access in cognitive radio networks. In *Proceeding of IEEE International Conference on Communications, 2007, ICC '07,* (pp. 6493–6498).

Berlemann, L., Mangold, S., Hiertz, G. R., & Walke, B. H. (2006). Spectrum load smoothing: Distributed quality-of-service support for cognitive radios in open spectrum. *European Transactions on Telecommunications, 17*, 395–406. doi:10.1002/ett.1121

Cabric, D., Mishra, S., & Brodersen, R. (2004). Implementation Issues in Spectrum Sensing for Cognitive Radios. In *ASILOMAR Conference on Signals, Systems and Computers,* (pp. 772–776). Pacific Grove, CA.

Cabric, D., Tkachenko, A., & Brodersen, R. (2006). Spectrum sensing measurements of pilot, energy, and collaborative detection. In *Proceedings IEEE Military Communication Conference,* (pp. 1–7).

Challapali, K., Mangold, S., & Zhong, Z. (2004). Spectrum agile radio: Detecting spectrum opportunities. In *Proceedings of the International Symposium on Advanced Radio Technologies,* Boulder, CO.

De, P., & Liang, Y.-C. (2007). Blind Sensing algorithms for cognitive radio. In *IEEE Radio and Wireless Symposium, 2007,* (pp. 201–204).

Farhang-Boroujeny, B., & Kempter, R. (2008). Multicarrier communication techniques for spectrum sensing and communications in cognitive radios. *IEEE Communications Magazine, 48*(4).

Farnham, T., Clemo, G., Haines, R., Seidel, E., Benamar, A., & Billington, S. ... Mangold, P. (2000). IST-TRUST: A perspective on the reconfiguration of future mobile terminals using software download. In *Proceedings of IEEE International Symposium on Personal, Indoor and Mobile Radio Communication,* (pp. 1054–1059). London, UK.

FCC. (2003). *ET docket number 03-237, Notice of inquiry and notice of proposed rulemaking,* November 2003.

Ganesan, G., & Li, Y. (2005). Cooperative spectrum sensing in cognitive radio networks. In *IEEE International Symposium on New Frontiers in Dynamic Spectrum Access Networks,* (pp. 137–143).

Ganesan, G., & Li, Y. (2007a). Cooperative spectrum sensing in cognitive radio, part I: Two user networks. *IEEE Transactions on Wireless Communications, 6*(6), 2204–2213. doi:10.1109/TWC.2007.05775

Ganesan, G., & Li, Y. (2007b). Cooperative spectrum sensing in cognitive radio, part II: Multiuser networks. *IEEE Transactions on Wireless Communications, 6*(6), 2214–2222. doi:10.1109/TWC.2007.05776

Gardner, W. (1991). Exploitation of spectral redundancy in cyclostationary signals. *IEEE Signal Processing Magazine, 8*(2), 14–36. doi:10.1109/79.81007

Ghasemi, A., & Sousa, E. S. (2005). Collaborative spectrum sensing for opportunistic access in fading environment. In *Proceedings of IEEE DySPAN 2005.*

Han, Z., Fan, R., & Jiang, H. (2009). Replacement of spectrum sensing in cognitive radio. *IEEE Transactions on Wireless Communications, 8*(6), 2819–2826. doi:10.1109/TWC.2009.080603

Haykin, S. (2005). Cognitive radio: Brain-empowered wireless communications. *IEEE Journal on Selected Areas in Communications, 3*(2), 201–220. doi:10.1109/JSAC.2004.839380

Molisch, A., Balakrishnan, K., Chong, C. C., Emami, S., Fort, A., & Karedal, J. … Siwiak, K. (2004). *IEEE 802.15.4a channel model - Final report* (Online). Retrieved from http://www.ieee802.org/15/pub/TG4a.html

Oner, M., & Jondral, F. (2007). Air interface identification for software radio systems. *AEÜ. International Journal of Electronics and Communications, 61*(2), 104–117. doi:10.1016/j.aeue.2006.03.005

Poor, H. V., & Hadjiliadis, O. (2009). *Quickest detection*. Cambridge, UK: Cambridge University Press.

Proakis, J., & Manolakis, D. G. (2007). *Digital signal processing: Principles, algorithms, and applications* (4th ed.). Upper Saddle River, NJ: Prentice Hall Inc.

Proakis, J. G. (2000). *Digital communications* (4th ed.). Boston, MA: McGraw Hill.

Rawat, D. B., & Yan, G. (2009). Signal processing techniques for spectrum sensing in cognitive radio systems: Challenges and perspectives. In *Proceedings of IEE/IFIP AH-ICI 2009*, Kathmandu, Nepal.

Rawat, D. B., & Yan, G. (2011). Spectrum sensing methods and dynamic spectrum sharing in cognitive radio networks: A survey. *International Journal of Research and Reviews in Wireless Sensor Network, 1*(1), 1–13.

Shankar, S. (2005). Spectrum agile radios: Utilization and sensing architecture. In *Proceedings of IEEE DySPAN 2005*, Baltimore, MD.

Tang, H. (2005). Some physical layer issues of wide-band cognitive radio systems. In *IEEE International Symposium on New Frontiers in Dynamic Spectrum Access Networks*, (pp. 151–159). Baltimore, MD.

Thomson, D. J. (1982). Spectrum estimation and harmonic analysis. *Proceedings of the IEEE, 20*, 1055–1096. doi:10.1109/PROC.1982.12433

Tian, Z., & Giannakis, G. B. (2006). A wavelet approach to wideband spectrum sensing for cognitive radios. In *Proceedings of IEEE International Conference of Cognitive Radio Oriented Wireless Networks and Communications (Crowncom)*, (pp. 1054–1059). Mykonos, Greece.

Urkowitz, H. (1967). Energy detection of unknown deterministic signals. *Proceedings of the IEEE, 55*, 523–531. doi:10.1109/PROC.1967.5573

Wild, B., & Ramchandran, K. (2005). Detecting primary receivers for cognitive radio applications. In *Proceeding of IEEE Dynamic Spectrum Access Networks, DySPAN 2005*, (pp. 124–130).

Xing, Y., Mathur, C. N., Haleem, M., Chandramouli, R., & Subbalakshmi, K. (2007). Dynamic spectrum access with QoS and interference temperature constraints. *IEEE Transactions on Mobile Computing, 6*(4), 423–433. doi:10.1109/TMC.2007.50

Yates, R., Raman, C., & Mandayam, N. (2006). Fair and efficient scheduling of variable rate links via a spectrum server. In *Proceeding of IEEE International Conference on Communications, ICC'06*, (pp. 5246 – 5251).

Zeng, Y., & Liang, Y.-C. (2009). Spectrum-sensing algorithms for cognitive radio based on statistical covariances. *IEEE Transactions on Vehicular Technology, 58*(4), 1804–1815. doi:10.1109/TVT.2008.2005267

Zhuan, G. M., & Grosspietsch, J. (2008). PHY 28-1 - Energy detection using estimated noise variance for spectrum sensing in cognitive radio networks. In *IEEE Wireless Communications and Networking Conference, WCNC 2008*, (pp. 711–716).

KEY TERMS AND DEFINITIONS

Cognitive Radio User: Wireless user with software defined radio and some artificial intelligence to act according to its operating environment.

Cooperative Spectrum Detection: Spectrum opportunities detection by interacting with other wireless users.

Receiver Detection: Spectrum opportunity detection based on receiver leaking signal.

Spectrum Underlay: Secondary users coexist and transmit simultaneously with primary users sharing the licensed bands.

Spectrum Overlay: Secondary users coexist but avoid the frequency bands that are used by primary users.

Transmitter Detection: Spectrum opportunity detection based on transmit signal.

Chapter 12
Spectrum Access and Sharing for Cognitive Radio

Raza Umar[1]
King Fahd University of Petroleum and Minerals, Saudi Arabia

Asrar U. H. Sheikh
King Fahd University of Petroleum and Minerals, Saudi Arabia

ABSTRACT

Cognitive radio (CR) has emerged as a smart solution to spectrum bottleneck faced by current wireless services, under which licensed spectrum is made available to intelligent and reconfigurable secondary users. CR technology enables these unlicensed secondary users to exploit any spectrum usage opportunity by adapting their transmission parameters on the run. In this chapter, the authors discuss the characteristic features and main functionality of CR oriented technology. Central to this chapter is Spectrum sensing (SS), which has been identified as a fundamental enabling technology for next generation wireless networks based on CR. The authors compare different SS techniques in terms of their sensing accuracy and implementation and computational complexities along with merits and demerits of these approaches. Various challenges facing SS have been investigated, and possible solutions are proposed.

INTRODUCTION

New wireless services and applications are being introduced day by day, resulting in insatiable demand for radio spectrum. Currently, the wireless networks are being regulated by government agencies that sell exclusive rights of radio frequencies over large geographical region to wireless system operators. This policy worked well in past as it provided an optimal solution that avoided interference between active wireless users. However, with steadily growing number of wireless subscribers and operators, fixed assignment of radio spectrum is proving to be a hurdle in the deployment of new wireless services or even enhancing existing services and applications to meet the requirements of wireless market. As a result Federal

DOI: 10.4018/978-1-4666-1797-1.ch012

Copyright © 2012, IGI Global. Copying or distributing in print or electronic forms without written permission of IGI Global is prohibited.

Communications Commission (FCC) carried out a number of studies that investigated current spectrum scarcity with goal to optimally manage available radio resources. Recent measurements have revealed that a large portion of assigned spectrum is sporadically utilized. According to FCC (2003a) notice of proposed rulemaking and order, spectrum utilization varies from 15% to 85% with wide variance in time and space. This suggests that the root cause of current spectrum scarcity is not the physical shortage of spectrum rather it is inefficient fixed spectrum allocation. This fact questioned the effectiveness of traditional spectrum policies and opened doors to a new communication paradigm to exploit radio resources dynamically and opportunistically.

Dynamic and Opportunistic Spectrum Access (DOSA) is proposed to be the solution for inefficient spectrum utilization wherein unlicensed users are allowed to opportunistically access the un-used licensed spectrum without interfering with the existing users with legacy rights to that spectrum. In essence, these NeXt Generation (xG) wireless networks based on DOSA techniques will meet the requirements of wireless users over heterogeneous wireless architectures by making them intelligently interact with their radio environment. The key technology that enables xG network to use the spectrum dynamically and opportunistically is the *Cognitive radio* (CR) technology.

The key component of CR technology is the ability to measure, sense and ultimately adapt to the radio's operating environment. In CR terminology, the users with legacy rights on the usage of specific part of the spectrum are called *primary users* (PU) while the term *secondary users* (SU) is reserved for low-priority un-licensed users which are equipped with a cognitive capability to exploit this spectrum without being noticed by PU. Therefore, the fundamental task of SU (also termed as simply CR in literature) is to reliably sense the spectrum with an objective to identify a vacant band and to update its transmission pa-

rameters to exploit the unused part of the spectrum in such a way that it does not interfere with PU.

This chapter presents an introductory tutorial on Cognitive radio. It defines cognitive functionality, identifies its objectives and highlights characteristic features of CR to meet cognition requirements. Being the focus of this chapter, we identify *Spectrum sensing* (SS) as the key cognitive functionality. Spectrum sensing in essence is the task of obtaining awareness about the spectrum usage at a specific time in a given geographical region. Intuitively this awareness can be obtained by using beacons or geolocation and database. These approaches though appear simple but are practically infeasible because of prohibitively large infrastructure requirements and implementation complexity. Here, we focus on local spectrum sensing at CR based on primary transmitter detection. Various challenges associated with local spectrum sensing are discussed and sensing methodologies to meet these challenges are proposed. An in-depth performance comparison of these sensing methods is presented. The concept of local sensing is then extended to cooperative sensing and we highlight advantages, disadvantages and challenges faced in cooperative detection. This is followed by an Interference based detection approach which allows CR to use a frequency band as long as its transmissions keep the interference at primary receivers within a tolerance limit. Finally, we conclude the chapter with conclusions.

BACKGROUND

Cognitive radio is essentially an evolution of Software Defined Radio (SDR) whose communication functions are implemented in software so that when it interacts with its environment, it reacts upon its findings in order to dynamically exploit any available spectrum usage opportunities. The term CR has been coined by Mitola (2000) where the main focus was on how the

Figure 1. CR operation

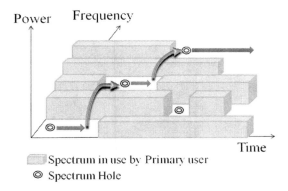

Spectrum in use by Primary user

Spectrum Hole

CR can enhance the flexibility of personal wireless services using so called Radio Knowledge Representation Language (RKRL). Lately, FCC formally defined CR as: "A Cognitive radio is a radio that can change its transmitter parameters based on interaction with the environment in which it operates" (FCC, 2002)

In essence, this means that CR introduces intelligence to conventional radio such that it senses the information from its environment by monitoring spectrum bands and capturing temporal and spatial variations. In this way, CR tracks a *spectrum hole* defined as "a licensed band not being used by a licensed user at a particular time over a selected area". With an objective to exploit this spectrum availability, CR adjusts its transmitter parameters e.g. modulation, frequency, access technique etc on the fly and makes use of the available band as long as the licensed i.e. Primary user, resumes its transmission. In that case, CR which behaves like a low priority Secondary user, must move to another spectrum hole if available or to reconfigure itself (by changing its transmission power, modulation scheme etc) to avoid presenting any noticeable interference to PU.

The ultimate objective of CR is to utilize un-used spectrum. As most of the spectrum is already assigned to PUs with legacy rights, the most important challenge is to share licensed spectrum without interfering with primary trans-

missions. Hence the main task of CR is to track the spectrum hole. Spectrum usage opportunity is exploited by CR as long as no spectrum activity is detected. If this band is further acquired by PU, CR being SU shifts to another spectrum hole as shown in Figure 1.

In summary: cognitive functionality enables the wireless user to:

1. Determine which portions of the spectrum are vacant and identify any PU that becomes active in its licensed band (**Spectrum sensing**)
2. Select best available channel (**Spectrum Management**)
3. Coordinate access to available best channel with other SUs (**Spectrum Sharing**)
4. Vacate the occupied channel if PU is detected in that band (**Spectrum Mobility**)

Cognitive Radio Characteristics

Cognitive functionality described above is achieved by two main characteristics of CR namely, *Cognitive Capability* and *Reconfigurability*.

Cognitive Capability refers to the ability of radio technology to interact with its radio environment in real time to identify and scavenge "un-occupied" licensed spectrum bands. These unoccupied licensed frequency bands are the spectrum holes which are termed as *white spaces* by Haykin (2005). Generally, based on observations published by FCC (2003a), spectrum holes can be classified into two categories: *temporal spectrum holes* and *spatial spectrum holes*. This gives rise to two secondary communication scenarios (Jun Ma, Li & Juang, 2009) of exploiting spectrum opportunity in time and space domain which are depicted in Figure 2 (a) and (b) respectively.

A **temporal spectrum hole** means that no primary transmission has been detected over the scanned frequency band for a reasonable amount of time and hence this frequency band is available for secondary communication in current time slot. In the scenario shown in Figure 2 (a), SU with

Figure 2. (a) Temporal spectrum hole; (b) Spatial spectrum hole

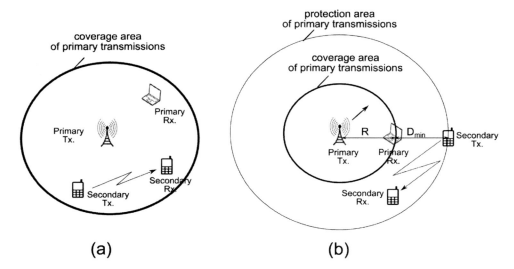

(a)   (b)

cognitive capability is located in the coverage area of PU and hence requires detection sensitivity similar to primary receivers in order to detect any ongoing primary communication. Hence, it is relatively easy to detect any primary user activity.

A **spatial spectrum hole** is created when the primary transmissions are confined to a certain area and hence this frequency band is available for secondary communication (may be in the same time slot) well outside the coverage area of PU to avoid any possible interference with primary communication. In comparison to the utilization of temporal spectrum holes, SU benefitting from spatial spectrum opportunity must lie outside the PU coverage area. This is emphasized in Figure 2 (b). This means that SU must be equipped with sophisticated detection capability/sensitivity higher than the primary receivers' sensitivity by a large margin in order to successfully detect any PU activity. More importantly, SU in this case, though lie outside the coverage area of PU (transmitter) yet it may possibly be quite near to primary receiver. Hence, secondary communication over the spatially available licensed band is allowed if and only if it does not interfere with

presumably nearby primary receiver. This puts a stringent requirement on SU to be able to successfully detect PU at any location where secondary transmission may cause intolerable interference to primary communication. Therefore, Sahai, Hoven and Tandra (2004) define a protection area of PU wherein SU must be able to detect any PU activity to avoid harmful interference with primary receiver D_{min} apart from SU.

As pointed out by Yucek and Arslan (2009), the cognitive capability is not limited to only monitoring power in some frequency band rather it demands multidimensional spectral awareness. Typically, CR operation involves sophisticated techniques to capture real time spectrum awareness to determine appropriate communication parameters and adapt to the dynamic radio environment. The steps required in this regard are:

1. **Spectrum Sensing:** Identify a spectrum hole.
2. **Spectrum Analysis:** Analysis of detected spectrum hole(s) to estimate its characteristics, in particular, predict the channel capacity to be used by CR for its secondary transmissions.

3. **Spectrum Decision:** Determine the data rate, transmission mode, transmission bandwidth etc and choose best available spectrum hole according to spectrum characteristics and SU requirements.

Haykin (2005) called these tasks to form a *Cognitive cycle*.

In this way, cognitive capability enables SU to acquire best available spectrum and set appropriate communication parameters for its transmissions. However, dynamic nature of radio environment requires CR to be adaptive in its selection of spectrum and communication parameters. This is called Reconfigurability characteristics of CR and is explained in the following.

Cognitive Reconfigurability enables CR to adapt to its radio environment on the fly during transmission when CR switches from one spectrum hole to other. This necessitates that transmission parameters of CR must be dynamically adjustable in software (making CR an evolution of SDR) such that it may adapt its transmitting power, carrier frequency, modulation scheme, access technology etc (FCC, 2003a) to the available spectrum resource.

KEY TO COGNITION: SPECTRUM SENSING

Cognitive radio is widely expected to be the enabling technology for future wireless networks. The key concept in Cognitive radio is the provision of dynamic and opportunistic spectrum access of licensed frequency band to unlicensed users. Hence, the main functionality of CR lies in efficient Spectrum sensing so that whenever an opportunity of unused spectrum band is identified, CR may make use of it. The objective of this chapter is to explore various dimensions of spectrum sensing with an aim to review ongoing trends in SS and compare different SS techniques.

Challenges in Spectrum Sensing

In order to analyze spectrum sensing problem, it is appropriate to first investigate the practical challenges associated with it. In this section, we discuss some of the key issues that must be taken into account before exploring different spectrum estimation techniques.

A.   Restricted Sensing Ability

CRs need to sense their radio environment with limited sensing ability. In the most general case, CRs have no information regarding the possible primary communication over a licensed band. This makes spectrum sensing for cognitive radio a very challenging task.

Possible way out to enhance sensing capability might be cooperative communication between secondary users but this may not be always feasible and simple along with possible delays and other overheads.

B.   Hardware Requirements

In principle, CRs are required to sense relatively wide frequency band for identifying vacant spectrum opportunities. The wide operating bandwidth imposes stringent requirements on RF front end of cognitive radio including wideband antennas, power amplifiers, high resolution analog to digital converters (ADCs) with large dynamic range and high speed DSPs or FPGAs with relatively low delay.

Different approaches are suggested in literature to combat CR hardware requirements. Shankar, Cordeiro and Challapali (2005) have proposed two different SS architectures based on *single radio* and *dual-radio chains*. In single radio architecture, only a specific time slot is allocated to CR for SS. Limiting sensing time results in degraded reliability of spectrum occupancy decision. Also, spectrum efficiency is decreased as some portion of the time slot (sensing period) is used in SS while remaining time (transmission period) is used for data transmission. The obvious advantage is simplicity and low cost. In the dual radio architecture, one radio chain is dedicated for spectrum monitoring while the other radio chain transmits and receives secondary data. In this way, disadvantages of single radio architecture are combated at the cost of increased power consumption and hardware cost and complexity.

Sahin and Arslan (2006) have shown to tackle the hardware requirements of CR by allowing the CR to scan only limited spectrum. In this way, they propose to prevent single type of CR to exploit majority of the available spectrum usage opportunities.

C.   PU Detection Sensitivity Requirements

In a typical wireless environment, severe multipath fading and shadowing cause high attenuation of transmitted signal such that the required SNR at CR for PU detection may be practically as low as -20 dB. Poor CR detection sensitivity in this case, results in missed detection of PU (transmitter), ending up in secondary transmissions offering unacceptable interference to PU receiver. This problem is handled by Ganesan and Li (2005) using cooperative sensing approach where more than one CR coordinates to increase the reliability of PU activity in their coverage area.

It is important to point out here that these detection sensitivity requirements are practically more demanding and generally required to be raised by additional 30-40 dB. This is because CR has no information regarding PU transmitter and receiver locations and hence bases PU detection on its local channel measurements to a PU transmitter rather measuring channel between PU transmitter and receiver (Cabric, Mishra & Brodersen, 2004). Sonnenschein and Fishman (1992) have shown that SS is further challenged by noise/interference power variations which are dependent on both time and space. Same findings have been verified by Sahai and Cabric (2005).

D.   Detecting Spread Spectrum PUs

PUs employing spread spectrum signaling spread their transmitted power over wide bandwidth. This may be a single band in the case of Direct Sequence Spread Spectrum (DSSS) or multiple bands for Frequency Hopping Spread Spectrum (FHSS). Cabric et al. (2004) have shown that in both the cases, SS becomes difficult and needs some *apriori* information regarding hopping patterns and synchronization pulses.

E.   Sensing Duration and Sensing Frequency

The key to efficient spectrum utilization is rapid and reliable spectrum sensing. However, sensing time reduction is always traded off with sensing reliability.

Similarly, sensing frequency (i.e. how often spectrum sensing is performed) is another design parameter that must be selected very carefully. Optimum value of spectrum frequency depends on CR capabilities and PU temporal characteristics in the radio environment.

An important thing to note is that a channel that is being used by SU cannot be used for sensing. This requires SU to interrupt their data transmission for possible PU identification on that channel. As a result, spectrum efficiency of the overall system is decreased. To combat this situation, a method known as Dynamic frequency hopping (DFH) has been proposed by Wendong et al. (2007). DFH is based on the assumption of having more than one channel. During operation on a working channel, intended channel is sensed simultaneously and if its availability is reported, the intended channel becomes the working channel. In this way, spectrum efficiency can be improved to some extent though some of the time would still be wasted in sensing the intended channel which can otherwise be used for secondary transmissions.

F. SS in Multiuser Environment

Usually, CRs reside in a multiuser environment consisting of users with and without exclusive rights for frequency spectrum. In addition, CRs can be co-located with other secondary networks competing for the same spectrum resource. Under these situations, SUs may interfere with each other making PU detection a difficult task. The presence of a second secondary network affects the detection capability of a CR in two ways:

1. A secondary signal may be detected as a primary signal
2. A secondary signal may mask the primary signal thus deteriorating the PU detection capability of CR

In order to solve the multiuser problem, cooperative sensing has been proposed which exploits the spatial diversity inherent in multiuser environment.

G. Security

In CR, specifically, in a multiuser environment, legitimacy of PU is an important aspect to consider where a selfish or malicious SU may mimic a PU. Such a behavior is investigated by Chen and Ruiliang (2006) and is called Primary user emulation (PUE) attack. Public key encryption based security mechanism has also proposed in this scenario but it has its own requirements and limitations.

H. Other Challenges

For the sake of completeness of topic, some of the other challenges related to CR are indicated:

1. In CR networks, multiple non-contiguous spectrum bands may be used for secondary transmission. Multi-spectrum transmission offer less quality degradation during spectrum handoff as compared to conventional single band transmission. It also benefits from low power in each spectrum band. However, multi-spectrum transmission makes spectrum sharing model a very challenging issue as all available spectrum in non-contiguous bands need to be shared among CRs for optimal system performance.
2. Spectrum sharing solutions typically assume a common control channel (CCCH) for information sharing. However, when a PU becomes active this control channel also needs to be vacated. This requires that local CCCHs should be exploited for clusters of nodes.
3. Spectrum handoffs need to be tackled carefully to avoid excessive delays and loss of service. New mobility management approaches need to be investigated in this regard for seamless transfer of services from one spectrum hole to another.

In the following section, we highlight different spectrum sensing approaches to meet the above mentioned challenges.

SPECTRUM SENSING TECHNIQUES

Spectrum sensing is the task of obtaining spectrum usage awareness. This awareness can be obtained using geolocation and database, by listening to Cognitive pilot channel (CPC) or PU beacons, or by local SS at CR. The most efficient and simple approach to identify spectrum opportunity with low infrastructure requirement is to detect Primary receiver within coverage area of CR. Practically, however, it is not feasible as CR cannot locate PU receiver. Hence, most of the recent work in SS focuses on Primary transmitter detection based on local observations at SU.

Before looking into the details of spectrum sensing methods, following subsection presents the classification of sensing techniques.

Classification of SS Techniques

There are mainly three different ways in which SS techniques can be classified as shown in Figure 3.

1. Transmitter Detection / Cooperative Detection / Interference based Detection

In primary **transmitter detection** approach, CR bases its decision about the presence or absence of PU on locally observed primary transmitter signal (Akyildiz et al., 2006). This technique is based on the assumption that the locations of PU are unknown to SU due to absence of signaling between them. Hence, in transmitter detection, CR relies only on weak primary transmitter signals to detect any spectrum usage opportunity. This approach is simple but it cannot detect PU activity when CR lies outside the primary transmitter range. As a result, with transmitter detection, CR offers unavoidable interference to Primary receivers particularly when CR lies close to them. This situation is called *primary receiver uncertainty problem* and depicted in Figure 4(a). A similar scenario occurs even when CR lies inside the primary transmitter range but observes shadowing or deep fading resulting in *hidden primary transmitter problem*, shown in Figure 4(b). Consequently, reliable PU detection calls for collaboration among CRs.

Transmitter detection, where CRs detect PU independently through their local observations, falls under the category of non-cooperative sensing. In comparison, **cooperative detection** refers to SS methods where multiple CRs cooperate in a centralized or decentralized manner to decide about the spectrum hole (Akyildiz, Lo & Balakrishnan, 2011). Each cooperating node in Cognitive radio Oriented Wireless Network (CROWN) may apply any sensing method based

on transmitter detection approach locally, and then share its raw/refined sensing information with other node(s), depending on the cooperation strategy.

The third category of PU detection namely, **Interference based detection**, defines a new model, introduced by FCC (2003b), for measuring interference level at primary receiver (Brown, 2005; Kolodzy, 2006). Figure 5 illustrates this model by showing the operative range of PU as the distance at which the received power approaches the noise floor. As additional interfering signals appear, possibly under the practical situations shown in Figure 4(a) and (b), the noise floor increases at various points within the service area, as indicated by peaks above the noise floor. The new interference model defines *Interference temperature limit* as the maximum amount of interference that the primary receiver can tolerate. Thus, as long as CRs do not exceed this interference temperature limit, by their transmissions in a particular frequency band, they can use this spectrum band.

2. Proactive / Reactive Sensing

Another broad approach to classify SS techniques is *proactive* and *reactive sensing*. In **proactive sensing**, spectrum is periodically sensed and information is maintained while **reactive sensing** calls for on-demand spectrum sensing when CR has some data to transmit. Any sensing technique based on transmitter detection in a cooperative/non-cooperative fashion can be invoked in a proactive or reactive manner depending upon CROWN requirements.

3. Non-blind / Semi-blind / Total Blind Spectrum Sensing

Apriori information required for PU detection is another important criterion upon which different SS methods can be classified (Zeng et al., 2010). In this category, different transmitter detection based sensing techniques can be categorized as *non-blind*

Figure 3. Classification of spectrum sensing techniques

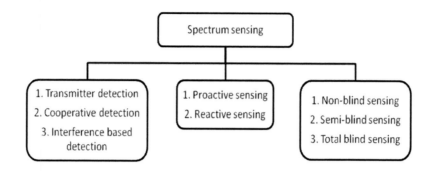

Figure 4. Transmitter detection problems: (a) Rx. Uncertainty problem; (b) Hidden primary Tx. problem

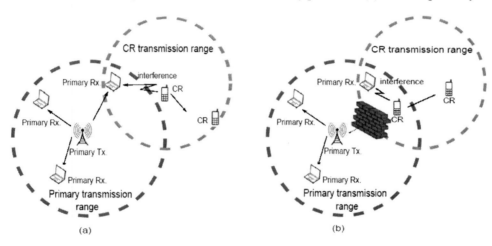

(Haykin, 2005; Tian and Giannakis, 2006, 2007; Kim, 2007; Cabric, Tkachenko and Brodersen, 2006; Tandra and Sahai, 2005), *semi-blind* (Sahai, Hoven and Tandra 2004) or *total blind* (Zeng, Y. H. & Liang Y. C., 2007, 2008, 2009). **Non-blind** schemes require primary signal signatures as well as noise power estimation to reliably detect PU. **Semi-blind** schemes are relaxed in the sense that they need only noise variance estimate to detect a spectrum hole. However, most practical sensing techniques are supposed to be **total blind**, requiring no information on source signal or noise power to decide about PU activity.

Here, we focus on transmitter detection sensing approach based on received primary signal observations at CR. Figure 6 illustrates the SS classification and groups some of the representative SS techniques into their respective categories.

SS: TRANSMITTER DETECTION (NON-COOPERATIVE DETECTION)

Transmitter detection approach is based on the detection of weak PU signal at CR. A variety of sensing methods are proposed in this regard to identify spectrum hole. In some techniques, *apriori* information about primary transmissions is used to identify spectrum utilization (non-blind approach), while other methods rely partially or

Figure 5. Interference temperature model

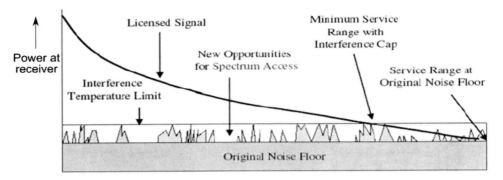

Figure 6. Enabling spectrum sensing techniques

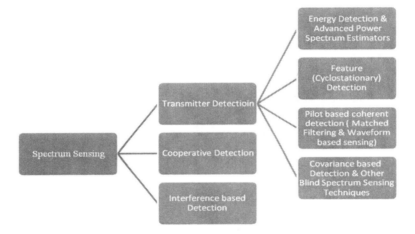

solely on incoming signal at CR to opportunistically exploit any un-used frequency band making them semi-blind or total- blind.

In general, no matter whether transmitter detection is non-blind, semi-blind or total blind, basic hypothesis model is defined as follows:

$$x(t) = \begin{cases} n(t), & 0 < t \le T \quad H_0 \\ h \cdot s(t) + n(t), & 0 < t \le T \quad H_1 \end{cases} \quad (1)$$

where $x(t)$ is the signal received by CR during observation window T, $n(t)$ represents the noise signal assumed to be Additive White Gaussian Noise (AWGN) with mean 0 and variance σ^2,

$s(t)$ represents the transmitted signal from primary user which is to be detected and h is the channel gain. This is a classic binary signal detection problem in which CR has to decide between two Hypothesis, H_0 and H_1. H_0 corresponds to the absence of primary signal in scanned spectrum band while H_1 indicates that some licensed user is occupying the frequency of interest. The performance of detection algorithm is gagged with its *sensitivity* and *specificity* (Yucek & Arslan, 2009) which are measured by Probability of detection P_d and Probability of false alarm P_f, respectively. P_d is the probability of correctly detecting the signal when the PU signal is actually present in the considered frequency band. In terms of hypothesis, it is given as

$$P_d = \Pr(\text{signal is detected} \mid H_1) \qquad (2)$$

P_f is the probability that the detection algorithm falsely decides that PU is active in the scanned frequency band when it actually is silent, and it is written as

$$P_f = \Pr(\text{signal is detected} \mid H_0) \qquad (3)$$

Thus, we target at maximizing P_d while keeping P_f at minimum. Another important probability of interest in analyzing the performance of detection algorithm is Probability of missed detection P_m which is the complement of P_d. P_m indicates the likelihood of not detecting the primary transmission when PU is active in the band of interest and can be formulated as

$$P_m = 1 - P_d = \Pr(\text{signal is not detected} \mid H_1) \qquad (4)$$

Total probability of making a wrong decision on spectrum occupancy is given by the weighted sum of P_f and P_m. Hence the key challenge in transmitter detection approach is to keep both P_f and P_m under maximum allowed limit as high P_f corresponds to poor spectrum utilization/exploitation by CR and high P_m results in increased interference at primary receiver.

A number of different methods have been proposed for identifying any spectrum usage opportunity in the scanned frequency band ranging from very simple energy detection to quite advanced cyclostationary feature extraction and waveform based sensing. Recent work in SS mainly focuses on further sophistication of these basic techniques with an aim to make sensing results more robust and accurate at the same time. The following subsections provide a brief overview of funda-mental spectrum sensing techniques based on the observation of PU signal at CR. This overview aims at providing a one-stop reference to ongoing trends in SS for CR providing reference to key publications for in-depth reading without going into the mathematical details. We classify each approach as non-blind, semi-blind and total blind and identify prominent merits and demerits of each scheme to obtain a comprehensive comparison between different sensing methods.

A. ENERGY DETECTION

Energy detection is the simplest signal detection approach which is referred in classical literature as *radiometry*. In practice, Energy detector (ED) is especially suitable for wideband SS when CR cannot gather sufficient information about the PU signal. First, received signal is pre-filtered with a band pass filter (BPF) of bandwidth W to get the sub-band of interest. Filtered signal is then squared and integrated over observation window of length T. This gives an estimated energy content of signal which is then compared with a threshold value depending on noise floor to decide about the presence of PU signal in scanned sub-band (Urkowitz, 1967). When the spectral environment is analyzed in frequency domain and Power Spectral Density (PSD) of the observed signal is estimated, this approach is termed as *periodogram*.

Advantages of Energy Detection

The implementation simplicity and low computational complexity of ED are its key advantages which have motivated most of the recent work in SS for CR towards enhanced energy detection algorithms and its combinations with other robust and accurate SS methods. Also, it needs to estimate only the noise power to set its threshold and does not require any information about primary transmission characteristics. This makes energy detection based sensing a semi-blind approach. Moreover, as shown by Sahai, Hoven and Tandra (2004), ED is an optimal technique for detecting IID primary transmissions especially when PU signal features are unknown to CR.

Disadvantages of Energy Detection

The key challenge in ED based SS is optimal threshold setting. The value of threshold strongly depends on the noise power. As a result, the performance of ED is highly susceptible to uncertainties in noise variance as noise level may change with time and location making it practically very difficult to obtain accurate noise power estimate at any given time and location.

Noise Power Uncertainty

In practice what we really know is the average/expected noise power. Let us denote it by $\tilde{\sigma}_n^2$. In fact, the actual noise power σ_n^2 could be different from the expected noise variance i.e. $\tilde{\sigma}_n^2$. This implies that, practically, there always exists noise power uncertainty by some factor α such that;

$$\tilde{\sigma}_n^2 = \alpha \times \sigma_n^2 \tag{5}$$

Zeng et al. (2009) has called this factor α as *noise uncertainty factor*. The upper bound on noise uncertainty factor (in dB) is defined as;

$$B = sup\left\{10log_{10}\alpha\right\} \tag{6}$$

The parameter B is used to quantify the amount of uncertainty in the noise power. In order to take care of worst case scenario, α (in dB) is assumed to be uniformly distributed over the interval [-B, B], thus allowing ± B dB of uncertainty in the estimated noise power (Tandra and Sahai, 2008). The parameter B is referred to as *noise uncertainty bound* or simply *noise uncertainty*. Shellhammer

& Tandra (2006) have shown that in practice, noise uncertainty of a receiving device is around 1 dB without considering the interference/environment noise uncertainty.

The performance of ED under 0.5 dB noise uncertainty is analyzed for different sample size N and compared with no noise uncertainty case. The simulation results targeting 10% probability of false alarm are presented in Figure 7 which clearly indicate that, if there is no uncertainty ($B = 0$), ED performs remarkably i.e. sensing based on energy detection can reach any probability of detection and probability of false alarm requirements at any given SNR by increasing the sensing time. This makes ED *unlimitedly reliable* under no noise uncertainty as pointed out by Zeng et al. (2009). However, noise uncertainty drastically degrades the performance of ED and detection requirements may not be met at some given SNR even with unlimited number of samples.

Tandra and Sahai (2005) have investigated the fundamental limits on detection in low SNR under noise uncertainty for different sample size and indicated the presence of SNR wall. SNR wall defines the minimum SNR below which the performance of ED remains unreliable even for infinite sensing duration (unlimited sample size).

Setting the right threshold value is of critical importance. The key problem in this regard is illustrated in Figure 8 which shows probability density function of received signal with and without active PU. If Γ represents the test statics in the form of energy content of the received signal, energy detection differentiates between the two hypotheses H_0 and H_1 by comparing Γ with threshold voltage γ as:

$$\Gamma \geq \gamma => H_1, \quad \Gamma < \gamma => H_0 \tag{7}$$

Hence if γ is kept too low, $Pr(\Gamma \geq \gamma|H_0)$ increases, hence increasing P_f which results in low spectrum utilization. On the other hand, if γ is kept unnecessarily high, $Pr(\Gamma < \gamma|H_1)$ in-

Figure 7. Performance of energy detector under noise uncertainty

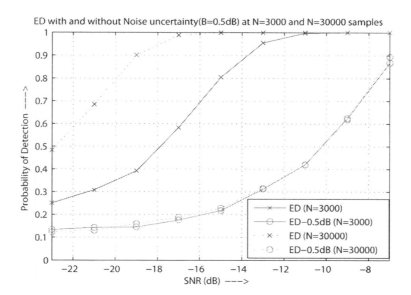

creases, corresponding to increased P_m which makes the CR susceptible to interfere with active PU. Therefore, a careful trade off has to be considered while setting the threshold value for ED. In practice, if a certain spectrum re-use probability of unused spectrum is targeted, P_f is fixed to a small value (e.g. $\leq 5\%$) and P_d is maximized. This is referred to as Constant False alarm Rate (CFAR) detection principle. However, if the CROWN is required to guarantee a given non-interference probability, P_m is set at a minimum value (or equivalently P_d is fixed to a high value (e.g. $\geq 95\%$) and P_f is minimized. This requirement is known as Constant Detection Rate (CDR) principle.

Imani, Dehkordi & Kamarei (2011) have proposed an adaptive procedure to find a spectrum hole which is less sensitive to energy threshold value.

It is important to highlight that ED is unable to differentiate interference from PU (modulated) signals and noise which appears as a cost of semi-blind signal detection. This may result in false detection triggered by un-intended signals. Also

because of this inability to differentiate between signal types, adaptive signal processing techniques for interference cancelation are not applicable to ED. Other demerits include its poor performance under low SNR (resulting from shadowing and fading) and inability to detect spread spectrum signals. All these factors characterize ED with less robustness and low accuracy/reliability and call for ED based on advanced power estimation techniques which is the subject of next subsection.

ED Based on Advanced Power Estimation Techniques

Accurate power estimation is vital to reliable detection of idle frequency band. Keeping in view the fact that simple ED approach does not exploit any available knowledge about PU signal, a number of more sophisticated power estimation techniques are proposed in recent literature with an aim to improve over all sensing performance specially under scanning of wide frequency band. These include *filter bank approach, multitaper spectrum estimation, wavelet based spectrum sensing* and *spectrum detection employing compressed sens-*

Figure 8. Threshold setting in ED: Trade-off between P_m and P_f

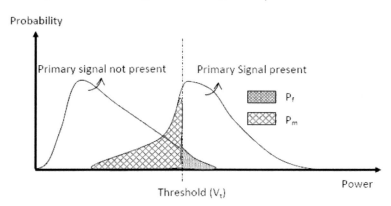

ED Using Filter Banks

Filter bank power spectrum estimation technique is based on periodogram spectral estimator in which a bank of N sub-filters is used to divide whole frequency band of interest into N sub-bands. The, i-th sub-filter of the bank

$$h_i(n) = h(n)e^{j2\pi f_i n}, \quad 0 \le i \le (N-1) \quad (8)$$

is used to extract spectral information from the i-th sub-band of interest with normalized center frequency $f_i = \dfrac{i}{N}$ where, $h(n)$, the low pass filter used to realize *zero*-th sub-band is termed as *prototype filter* of the filter bank. Frequency response specifically bandwidth and shape of transfer function of this prototype filter influences the quality of estimated power in the sub-band. Hence, a prototype filter with small side lobes can be designed in order to minimize the power leakage from the neighboring sub-bands to the sub-band of interest (Boroujeny, 2008).

It is important to note that the simple periodogram approach discussed earlier employs rectangular window as prototype filter which has large side lobes in frequency domain giving high power leakage. This indicates room of improvement in power estimation by preprocessing the received signal before FFT operation with window functions having small side lobes. This preprocessing is popularly known as *tapering* in signal processing language.

Multitaper Spectrum Estimation

Tapering effectively improves the performance of conventional ED by minimizing the power leakage from the neighboring sub-bands to the sub-band of interest, however, it do so by truncating the time domain windowing which results in information loss. This information loss increases the variance of power spectrum estimate and hence severely degrades the accuracy and reliability of sensing results. Multiple prototype filters or multiple tapers may be used in power spectrum estimation to reduce the variance of the estimate. The algorithm proposed by Thomson (1982) employing multiple tapers is shown to be an approximation to maximum likelihood (ML) PSD estimator which behaves nearly optimal for wideband signals and at the same time it turns out to be computationally feasible. Because of this reason, Haykin (2005) has recommended this approach as a promising power spectrum estimation technique for wide band SS based on ED.

ing. In the following, we present a brief overview of these sensing methodologies.

Wavelet Based SS

In comparison to ED using filter banks and multitaper spectrum estimation, where multiple narrowband BPFs are used for wideband SS, wavelet approach is based on detecting variations in the power level of the received wideband signal at CR. Wavelet based SS models the entire wide spectrum of interest as a train of consecutive frequency sub-bands and assumes PSD within each sub-band to be almost flat, exhibiting a discontinuous change between adjacent sub-bands. These changes in power spectral characteristics are treated as irregularities and wavelet transform is applied to identify corner frequencies of each sub-band within wide band of interest (Tian and Giannakis, 2006). Once the sub-bands are identified, power level within each sub-band is estimated to decide about the spectrum hole. It is important to point out here that under the assumption of zero mean additive white ambient noise and *apriori* known fact that at least one frequency band is vacant in the scanned frequency range; the minimum power level in a frequency sub-band can be treated as noise variance. This noise floor is then subtracted from observed power level in each sub-band to get an estimate of signal power level in that sub-band. In this way, wavelet approach gives highly accurate sensing results even in low SNR. Moreover, it also outperforms conventional wideband SS based on multiple narrowband BPFs, in terms of both implementation costs and flexibility in adapting to dynamic PSD structures over dynamic frequency sub-bands.

Spectrum Detection Based on Compressed Sampling

Tian and Giannakis (2007) have extended their approach of wavelets to wideband SS using sub-Nyquist sampling by exploiting the *sparse* nature of wireless signals in frequency domain. The sparsity results due to the low percentage of spectrum occupancy by PUs. This technique relies on the maximum sparsity order to determine the fundamental limit on the sampling rate which turns out to be unnecessarily high for the desired sensing performance and hence wasteful of sensing resources. To alleviate wasteful sampling, a Two Step Compressed spectrum sensing (TS-CSS) scheme is proposed recently by Wang and Tian (2010). The first step estimates the actual sparsity order, given by the number of non-zero elements in the received wideband primary signal vector at CR, using a small number of samples, and the second step uses the estimated sparsity order to adaptively decide about the number of additional samples required to accurately reconstruct the wideband spectrum and identify any spectrum hole. In this way, TS-CSS achieves the desired sensing accuracy at considerably lower average sampling rate.

B. FEATURE (CYCLOSTATIONARY) DETECTION

The idea of feature detection is based on capturing a specific signature of PU signal. Wireless (modulated) signals are in general coupled with sine wave carriers, pulse trains, repeating spreading or hopping sequences or cyclic prefixes, which induce periodicity in the signal making them cyclostationary i.e. their statistics (mean and autocorrelation) exhibit periodicity. This periodicity may result from modulation or even be intentionally produced to aid channel estimation (regularly transmitted pilot sequences) and synchronization (preambles, mid-ambles etc). Cyclostationary feature detection exploits in-built periodicity of received signal to detect primary transmissions (with certain modulation type) in a background of noise and other modulated signals. Features that can be extracted include sine wave carrier, symbol rate and modulation type etc.

The inherent periodicity in cyclostationary signals causes key statistical characteristics of PU signal like mean and correlation to repeat after regular time intervals. This results in correlation between widely separated frequency components of the received signal which is identified in cyclostationary detection by analyzing Cyclic Autocorrelation Function (CAF) (Dandawate and Giannakis, 1994) of the received signal, or, equivalently in frequency domain by its Cyclic Spectral Density (CSD), also known as Spectrum Correlation Function (SCF) (Gardner, 1991).

Advantages of Feature Detection

The salient property of cyclostationary detection is its ability to differentiate PU signal from interference and noise and even distinguish among different types of PUs. This stems from the fact that noise is in general (white) uncorrelated while every PU signal has a specific cyclostationary feature. Another important advantage is robustness to noise uncertainty which allows cyclostationary detector to identify primary transmissions more than 30 dB below the noise floor. Therefore, feature detector outperforms ED especially in low SNR regime. Hidden PU problem occur much less likely than with ED because of its high Probability of detection.

Disadvantages of Feature Detection

High accuracy of cyclostationary detection comes at the cost of increased implementation complexity in terms of high processing requirements which results in large sensing time. Specifically, this processing is required to extract cyclic frequencies (if not known *apriori*) from received primary transmissions which in turn also makes this approach non-blind. Also, short duration spectral opportunities cannot be exploited efficiently using this approach because of the requirement of large observation time.

Recent work by Cabric et al. (2004) and Maleki, Pandharipande and Leus (2010) has reported to combine ED with feature detection to benefit from complementary advantages of both the schemes

by doing coarse detection using ED which is then made more reliable by fine detection employing cyclostationary detection.

C. COHERENT SENSING: PILOT BASED DETECTION

Coherent sensing makes use of known patterns in PU signal to coherently detect the presence of active PU. These known patterns, sometimes termed as *pilot signals*, are usually transmitted periodically by PU to assist channel estimation and achieve time and frequency synchronization at primary receiver. When CR has *apriori* knowledge of these known signal patterns in primary transmission, it can detect the PU signal by either passing the received signal at CR through a filter (Matched filter: MF) having impulse response matched to the incoming signal or correlating it with a known copy of itself. Thus there are two main approaches of coherent sensing namely: *Matched filtering* and *Correlation (Waveform-based) detection*.

Matched Filtering

Matched filtering is an optimal detection approach as it maximizes the output SNR. The output of MF is compared with a threshold to decide about the presence or absence of PU signal.

Waveform Based Sensing

Waveform based approach is less complex as compared to MF and consists of a correlator which exploits the known patterns in PU signal by correlating the received primary signal at CR with its own copy. Similar to MF, correlator output is compared with a fixed threshold to identify spectrum hole.

Advantages of Pilot Based Detection

The main advantage of pilot based sensing lies in its high processing gain which is achieved in comparatively very short time because of coherent detection. For matched filtering, Tandra and Sahai (2005) have shown that the required number of samples grows as $O(1/SNR)$ to achieve given probability of false alarm at low SNRs. As is the case of cyclostationary feature detection, coherent detection exploits *apriori* knowledge about PU signals to be able to distinguish them from interference and noise and thus detecting PU in very low SNR. Moreover, it has less complexity and higher agility when compared with cyclostationary detection. Tang (2005) has shown that performance of waveform based sensing is better than ED in terms of reliability and convergence time and improves further with increasing length of known signal patterns.

Disadvantages of Pilot Based Detection

Pilot based detection requires CR to demodulate the signal to be detected. As a result, it requires perfect knowledge of PU transmission parameters like carrier frequency, bandwidth, modulation type and order, frame format, pulse shaping etc. This makes this scheme non-blind and detection performance degrades dramatically in case of inaccurate PU signal information or synchronization errors. A significant drawback of MF is its stringent requirement of dedicated receivers for all PU signal types. This makes implementation complexity of MF impractically large as pointed out by Cabric et al. (2004). MF also suffers from high power consumption as quite large number of receiver algorithms need to be executed for PU detection. Waveform based detector is also very sensitive to synchronization errors (Tang, 2005).

D. COVARIANCE BASED DETECTION

Covariance based detection exploits the inherent correlation in received PU signal samples at CR. These received PU signal samples are usually correlated in time because of time dispersive nature of wireless channel and oversampling of received signal. If CR uses multiple antennas, received PU signal samples happen to be spatially correlated as well. Spatial correlation results from the fact that the received signal samples at different antennas/secondary receivers are generated from the same source (primary) signals.

In multiple-antenna CR, multiple copies of the received PU signal(s) can be coherently combined to maximize the SNR of received (combined) signal. This diversity combining approach is known as Maximum Ratio Combining (MRC). Although, MRC gives optimal detection performance, yet it is only applicable when channel between transmitter (primary) and receiver (secondary) is known at the receiver which is not the case in most practical scenarios. Practically, blind detection calls for Equal Gain Combining (EGC) or Blind Combining (BC). Zeng, Liang and Zhang (2008) have analyzed the combining strategies for PU signal samples received at different CR antennas during different time intervals. They have shown that an optimal combining approach (MRC) requires *apriori* information about the primary signal and channel in the form of eigenvector corresponding to maximum eigenvalue of the received source (primary) signal covariance matrix. However, this eigenvector can be estimated using the received signal (source signal plus noise) samples only without requiring any information of primary transmitted signal. In this way, temporal spatial combining of received samples may be achieved blindly. After combining, ED is used to identify any vacant spectrum band in the received wideband signal. Zeng et al. (2008) called MRC based ED as Optimally combined energy detection (OCED) and BC based ED as Blindly combined energy detection (BCED).

There are other possible ways to utilize eigenvalues of received sample covariance matrix for SS. For example, signal space dimension estimation based on the number of significant eigenvalues is directly related to presence/absence of data in received signal and may be exploited to identify vacant spectrum bands (Zayen, Hayar and Kansanen, 2009). Similarly, various test statistics based on the eigen values of received sample covariance matrix like the ratio of Maximum eigenvalue to minimum eigenvalue (MME) and the ratio of average eigenvalue (Energy of received signal) to Minimum Eigenvalue (EME) may be used to detect the presence of primary signal (Zeng and Liang, 2007, 2008, 2009). Spectrum sensing based on eigenvalues of received signal sample covariance matrix is known as *eigenvalue based detection* (EBD) and falls under the category of blind sensing. In general, EBD algorithm can be summarized as:

EBD Algorithm

Step 1. Compute the sample covariance matrix of the received signal as:

$$\tilde{R}_x(N) = \frac{1}{N} \sum_{n=0}^{N} x(n) x^T(n) \qquad (9)$$

where $x(n)$ is received signal vector obtained by stacking the samples over space and time (from M receive antennas over L time instants) i.e.

$$x(n) =$$
$$\begin{bmatrix} x_1(n) \cdots x_M(n) x_1(n-1) \\ \cdots x_M(n-1) \\ \cdots x_1(n-(L-1)) \\ \cdots x_M(n-(L-1)) \end{bmatrix}^T \qquad (10)$$

Step 2. Obtain the test statistic Γ based on eigenvalues of $\tilde{R}_x(N)$. For example maximum eigenvalue of $\tilde{R}_x(N)$ or Trace of $\tilde{R}_x(N)$ corresponding to average energy of received signal etc.

Step 3. Compute the threshold γ for selected test statistic. In general, the test threshold γ can be decomposed into γ_1 and $\Gamma_0(x)$ as:

$$\gamma = \gamma_1 \Gamma_0(x) \qquad (11)$$

Where γ_1 is related to sample size N and targeted probability of false alarm P_f while $\Gamma_0(x)$ is the statistic related to noise distribution under H_0. In practice, when noise power is known *apriori* or can be estimated

$$\Gamma_0(x) = \sigma_n^2 \qquad (12)$$

and when there is no *apriori* knowledge of the noise power, we use, minimum eigenvalue of $\tilde{R}_x(N)$ to estimate the noise variance

$$\Gamma_0(x) = \tilde{\lambda}_{min}^2 \qquad (13)$$

On the other hand, the parameter γ_1 is set analytically based on the distribution of the selected test statistic under H_0. Random matrix theory (RMT) is often proved to be useful in evaluating γ_1 as demonstrated by Zeng, Liang and Zhang (2010).

Step 4. Decision: if $\Gamma > \gamma$ signal exists; otherwise, there is spectral hole available for SU to exploit.

As evident from the EBD approach, this sensing technique captures the inherent temporal and spatial correlation in primary signals to be de-

Figure 9. Performance comparison of EBD algorithms

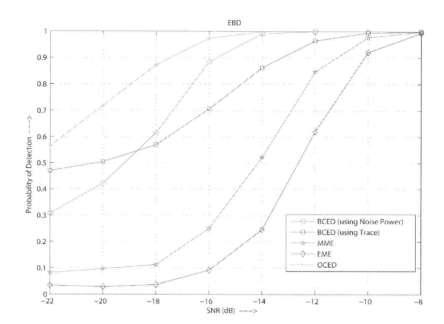

tected. More significantly, EBD, being total blind, uses minimum eigenvalue of $R_x(N)$ to estimate the noise variance and hence is robust to *noise uncertainty*.

Figure 9 indicates the performance comparison of variety of blind EBD algorithms. These results are obtained for IID source signal samples which are BPSK modulated. There are $M = 4$ receiver antennas (on SU with cognitive capability) and one primary user ($K = 1$). For simplicity, we consider the smoothing factor incorporating temporal correlation between received samples to be unity i.e. ($L = 1$). We assume that each multipath channel has eight taps and all the channel taps are independent with equal power. These channel taps are generated as normally distributed random numbers and different for different Monte Carlo realizations. We compare the detection performance of different EBD algorithms targeting 10% probability of false alarm for $N=10000$ samples and average the detection probability over 2000 Monte Carlo realizations.

Kortun et al. (2011) have investigated the performance of EBD in a cooperative CROWN and evaluated exact decision threshold for MME detector using RMT. Li, Wang and Kuang (2011) have proposed a hybrid sensing approach by combining ED with EBD. ED is employed for coarse detection at first stage. If it does not detect any primary signal, fine sensing is performed using maximum eigenvalue based detection to finally decide about any vacant spectrum opportunity.

Generalizing the concept of EBD, if the signals exhibit time correlation as well, the concept of EBD can be extended to incorporate joint space time processing. This approach constructs the test statistics based on actual elements of received signal sample covariance matrix (in comparison to eigenvalues) and is generally known as *covariance based detection*. It is evident that EBD is in fact one special case of covariance based detection where the eigenvalues of received signal sample covariance matrix are used for PU signal detection.

Advantages of Covariance Based Detection

Generally covariance based detection works without using any information about the primary signal or noise and hence falls into the category of blind spectrum sensing. However, if some *apriori* information about primary signal correlation is available, this may assist in choosing corresponding elements in sample covariance matrix making the decision test statistic more efficient. Most importantly, covariance based detection does not need conventional noise power estimation as the threshold is related to P_f and sample size N of the received signal at CR only. Hence this approach is inherently robust to noise uncertainty which is unavoidable in practical scenario. Also it outperforms semi-blind ED and non-blind SS methods based on feature extraction and pilot based detection for highly correlated signals.

Disadvantages of Covariance Based Detection

Performance of covariance based detection strongly depends on statistics of received primary signal which degrades if primary signal tends to be uncorrelated.

Other Blind Spectrum Sensing Techniques

Blind spectrum sensing approach is not limited to only covariance based detection rather other promising techniques have also been reported in recent literature. Cui et al. (2010) have investigated moments of received PU signal to identify any vacant spectral opportunity. Model selection tools such as Akaike information criterion (AIC) and Akaike weights (Akaike, 1973) are applied to SS by Zayen, Hayar and Nussbaum (2008) where they have modeled the noise using Gauss-

ian distribution and analyzed Akaike weights to decide if the distribution of received signal at CR fits the noise distribution or not. Blind SS algorithm based on oversampling the received signal or employing multiple antennas at CR has been proposed by De and Liang (2008). In this approach, linear prediction is used in conjunction with QR decomposition of the received signal matrix to compute two signal statistics whose ratio indicates the presence/absence of primary signal in the scanned frequency band. Shen et al. (2011) have formulated the blind spectrum sensing as Student's *t*-distribution testing problem. They have analyzed their sensing scheme over flat fading channel with noise uncertainty and showed that their blind approach outperforms semi-blind ED at about 4 dB gain.

Blind source separation (BSS) techniques have also been discussed for the CR system model with multiple antennas to simultaneously detect active PUs in the scanned spectrum. Instantaneous linear mixture of various active PU signals is separated and identified by CR incorporating BSS. A low complexity, non-iterative BSS approach for multiuser detection in CR environment is proposed by Liu, Tan and Anghuwo (2009). Recently, Kurtosis metric has been used inside BSS algorithm based on Independent component analysis (ICA). A new framework for SS has been proposed by Khajavi, Sadeghi & Sadough (2010) that combines BSS based SS with conventional blind SS techniques employing EBD. In this approach, sensing accuracy is tremendously increased as SS can be performed even when the cognitive transmitter is in operation.

COMPARISON OF SENSING METHODS

Transmitter detection makes a wide generic class of spectrum sensing methods. A concluding comparison of these techniques is presented in Figure 10.

Figure 10. Comparison of spectrum sensing methods

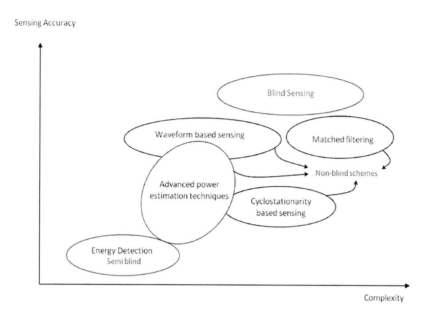

Different SS methods discussed above are compared in terms of their implementation, computational complexities and sensing accuracies. When nothing is known about the PU signal, ED happens to be most simple approach but it fails in practical fading environment and noise uncertainties. Advanced power spectrum estimation techniques achieve accuracy sacrificing the simplicity of energy detection. As a matter of fact, some *apriori* knowledge about primary transmissions is necessary to differentiate primary signal from interference and noise. Processing of this known information achieves reliability in detection at the cost of additional implementation and computational complexities. Such schemes are classified as non-blind and detection approach depends on what sort of information is known about primary signal. In particular, cyclostationary detector is suitable when cyclic frequencies associated with primary transmissions are known before hand; coherent detection is applicable when pilot transmissions of primary system are known

with waveform based sensing outperforming MF based coherent detection in terms of required implementation complexity. Blind sensing based on received signal covariance matrix and other approaches achieve high accuracy especially under noise uncertainty, with its computational complexity dependent on sensing algorithm used.

As a representative comparison, Figure 11 presents the detection performance of total blind EBD schemes (MME and EME) and semi-blind ED under 0.5 dB noise uncertainty for considerably large sample size (N = 100000). These results verify that EBD is a more reliable sensing approach under practical channel conditions.

Hence, selection of sensing method comes with a tradeoff between accuracy and complexity while keeping in view the required sensing time. PU signal characteristics are the main factor in deciding about the sensing mechanism. Other factors include network requirements and economics.

Figure 11. Comparison of ED with EBD under 0.5 dB noise uncertainty

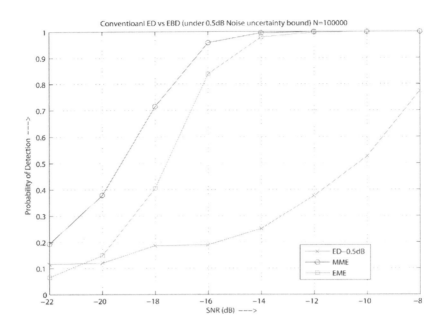

SS: COOPERATIVE DETECTION

The most serious limitation of transmitter detection approach is its degraded performance in multi-path fading and shadowed environments. This problem can be solved by exploiting the inherent spatial diversity in a multi-user environment resulting from the fact that if some SUs are in deep fade or observe severe shadowing, there might be other SUs in the network that may have a good line-of-sight to Primary transmitter. Consequently, combining the sensing information from different CRs results in more reliable spectrum awareness. This gives rise to the concept of cooperative spectrum sensing wherein CRs employing different technologies, exchange information about the time and frequency usage of spectrum to exploit any vacant spectrum opportunity efficiently (Ganesan and Li, 2007a, 2007b).

Cooperation among CRs can be implemented in two different forms: *Centralized* and *Decentralized*

In **centralized cooperation**, a central unit, also called *fusion center*, decides about the spectrum hole after collecting local sensing results from co-operating SUs. This spectrum opportunity is then either broadcasted to all CRs or central unit itself controls the CR traffic by managing the detected spectrum usage opportunity in an optimum fashion. This central node is an *Access Point* (*AP*) in a Wireless Local Area Network (WLAN) or a *Base Station* (*BS*) in a cellular network. On the other hand, in **distributed cooperation**, each cooperating CR decides about the spectrum opportunity locally after gathering spectrum observations from other CRs in the network. The shared spectrum observations may be in the form of *soft sensing* results or *quantized* (*binary/hard*) version of local decisions about spectrum hole availability.

From the working principle of centralized and decentralized cooperation, it is evident that in both cooperation strategies, the decision about spectrum opportunity is made internally in CR network (either at one central entity for all CR or locally at each CR itself). Thus, both centralized and distributed sensing fall under the category of *Internal sensing*, which results in suboptimal utilization of spectrum opportunity as both the spectrum sensing and subsequent data transmission on the detected frequency band are collocated in single CR. Another approach for cooperative PU detection is *External sensing;* where in a CR network architecture constitutes of two distinct networks i.e. the *sensor network* and an *operational network* (Shankar et al., 2005). In **external sensing**, a dedicated network composed of only spectrum sensing nodes is used to sense the wideband spectrum continuously or periodically. The sensing results are then communicated to a central node in this external network which optimally combines the sensing data and shares the spectrum occupancy information in the sensed area with operational network. In this way, CRs in the operational network do not spend time for spectrum sensing rather simply use the information from external sensor network for selecting the appropriate bands and time duration for secondary transmissions. As a result, external sensing not only solves the shadowing/fading and hidden PU problems but also increases spectrum efficiency by allowing CRs to acquire available spectrum usage opportunity with minimum delay.

In cooperative sensing, CRs need a control channel to share local spectrum sensing results and frequency band allocation information with each other. This control channel, depending upon system requirements, can be implemented using a dedicated band, an un-licensed band such as ISM or an underlay system such as Ultra Wide Band (UWB) (Cabric et al., 2005).

Advantages of Cooperative Detection

Cooperative detection mitigates the multipath fading and shadowing effects which are the key issues in transmitter detection. In this way, cooperative detection results in much improved sensing performance of CR network by improving the detection probability while simultaneously decreasing the probabilities of mis-detection and false alarms. In addition, cooperative detection solves the hidden PU problem. This results in decreased sensitivity requirements for CR added with improved agility (Ganesan and Li, 2005).

Disadvantages of Cooperative Detection

While cooperative sensing provides high sensing accuracy, they are not feasible on resource-constrained networks due to the additional infrastructure, overhead control traffic and operations. Also, primary receiver location uncertainty problem as indicated by Figure 4(b), is still un-addressed in cooperative sensing.

Challenges in Cooperative Detection

Key challenge in cooperative sensing is finding efficient information sharing approach. This problem in itself is manifold and becomes very critical when the number of CRs in CROWN become large, requiring prohibitively large control channel band width along with added complexity. First challenge in this regard is to optimize the local sensing results, both in terms of size and reliability. Sun, Zhang and Letaief (2007) have proposed to meet this challenge by using two thresholds in conventional energy detector to reliably detect a spectrum hole. Then, CRs with only reliable sensing information share their scanning results in the form of one bit hard decision. The next important aspect to consider is imperfect reporting channel which has also been analyzed by Sun et al. (2007). Sensing time is another challenge in cooperative detection. Delays in cooperation need to be very short and signaling overhead in distributing sensing information must be kept at minimum to save temporal resources for secondary data transmission. To achieve this, fast physical layer signaling is proposed by Weiss et al. (2003). Cooperative sensing is most effective when cooperating nodes observe independent fading and shadowing. Ghasemi and Sousa (2007) have studied the effect of correlated shadowing which results in increased probability of missed detection hence degrading the overall sensing performance.

Optimally choosing the number of cooperating CRs is another challenge which has been investigated by Peh and Liang (2007) who showed that CRs with high PU's SNR give optimum sensing performance rather employing all SUs in CROWN to cooperate. Xia et al. (2010) have adopted binary particle swarm optimization (BPSO) algorithm to find suitable cooperative nodes and showed improved sensing performance when compared with the case that all neighboring nodes participate in sensing.

Similarly, choosing between the centralized and de-centralized cooperation is another important decision to make which mainly depends on system requirements and available resources. Last but not the least, the overall sensing performance of cooperative network strongly depends on information fusion criterion which has been investigated by Chair and Varshney (1986).

SS: INTERFERENCE BASED DETECTION

Key requirement in CROWN is that secondary transmissions must not harm PUs with legacy rights of the spectrum. This means that CRs are allowed to use licensed spectrum band as long as secondary transmissions by these CRs, added to the existing interference level at the primary receiver in the vicinity of CROWN, do not increase the noise floor above the interference temperature limit as shown in Figure 5. This requires that CRs must adjust their transmission parameters to comply with FCC requirements such that interference temperature remains within limit at primary receiver(s) (FCC 2003b).

Advantages of Interference Based Detection

The main advantage of Interference based detection is its ability to tremendously increase spectrum utility by even exploiting spectrum opportunities which are not classified as spectrum holes. Moreover, it is not sensitive to hidden PU problem.

Disadvantages of Interference Based Detection

CR must measure or estimate the effect of its transmissions on nearby primary receivers. However, primary receivers being passive are difficult to locate by CR and hence it cannot measure the effect of its transmission on PU receiver to adjust its transmission parameters. As a result, a true measurement of interference temperature is a very difficult task for CR. Practically, it can only sense primary transmissions locally and adjust its transmission power to minimum required to achieve desired range and data rate.

Challenges in Interference Based Detection

Interference temperature measurement is the key challenge in this approach. Kolodzy (2006) has discussed various approaches to effectively measure the interference temperature but they more or less demand changes to be done in primary system. In summary, recent work in interference based detection attempts to measure interference temperature in a very limited scenario but no practical way of measuring interference temperature at all primary receivers has been reported in literature by now to the best of our knowledge.

FUTURE RESEARCH DIRECTIONS

Emerging trends in spectrum sensing for CR applications target at sensing methodologies that provide user specified sensing accuracy while requiring minimum *apriori* information about PU transmissions to be detected. Future research directions include analysis of these sensing techniques under practical channel conditions taking into consideration fading, shadowing and time varying effects of wireless environment. Specifically, sensing duration requirements of different sensing approaches need to be compared with reliability of sensing decisions to choose the best suitable sensing technique under given user and channel constraints. Different sensing methods can be combined in this regard to come up with a hybrid sensing algorithm to achieve optimal detection.

Another research avenue to explore is to keep track of interference level enhancement by secondary transmissions of CR. Accurate interference temperature measurement is the key to deal with spectrum scarcity which is hindering the progress of xG wireless networks.

CONCLUSION

In this chapter, we have examined various aspects of CR and identified its key tasks. Variety of SS techniques have been studied, compared and classified. We have found that blind transmitter detection sensing techniques give highly accurate results and their implementation complexity can be made practically realizable by employing a non-iterative blind sensing algorithm. However, sensing duration increases remarkably to outperform semi-blind schemes such as ED. Another important observation is that the performance of all such methods degrades drastically in multipath fading environment which is unavoidable in wireless communication. Hence, for all practical scenarios, CROWN must be equipped with cooperative sensing ability which would ensure high detection probability while keeping probability of mis-detection under acceptable limit.

For optimal performance without relying on any *apriori* information about source signals, we recommend to employ blind spectrum detection at each sensing node. However, when we have some prior information about the primary signals, we may benefit from it by making a more efficient test statistic that would result in much improved sensing performance. Local decisions about the spectrum hole can then be combined to make a global decision for any spectrum opportunity. Open research challenges in this scenario are devising efficient information sharing approach with minimum control channel overhead (e.g. short-listing reliable CRs to cooperate, minimizing information to share etc.) and information fusion criteria.

REFERENCES

Akaike, H. (1973). Information theory and an extension of the maximum likelihood principle. In *Proceedings of 2nd International Symposium on Information Theory*, (pp. 267-281).

Akyildiz, I. F., Lee, W. Y., Vuran, M. C., & Mohanty, S. (2006). NeXt generation/dynamic spectrum access/ cognitive radio wireless networks: A survey. *Computer Networks Journal*, *50*(13), 2127–2159. doi:10.1016/j.comnet.2006.05.001

Akyildiz, I. F., Lo, B. F., & Balakrishnan, R. (2011). Cooperative spectrum sensing in cognitive radio networks: A survey. *Physical Communication Journal*, *4*(1), 40–62. doi:10.1016/j.phycom.2010.12.003

Boroujeny, F. (2008). Filter bank spectrum sensing for cognitive radios. *IEEE Transactions on Signal Processing*, *56*(5), 1801–1811. doi:10.1109/TSP.2007.911490

Brown, T. X. (2005). An analysis of unlicensed device operation in licensed broadcast service bands, *First IEEE International Symposium on Dynamic Spectrum Access Networks (DySPAN '05)* (pp. 11-29).

Cabric, D., Mishra, S., Willkomm, D., Brodersen, R., & Wolisz, A. (2005). A cognitive radio approach for usage of virtual unlicensed spectrum. In *Proceedings of IST Mobile and Wireless Communications Summit*, Dresden, Germany.

Cabric, D., Mishra, S. M., & Brodersen, R. W. (2004). Implementation issues in spectrum sensing for cognitive radios. In *Proceedings of Asilomar Conference*, (pp. 772-776).

Cabric, D., Tkachenko, A., & Brodersen, R. W. (2006). Spectrum sensing measurements of pilot, energy, and collaborative detection. *IEEE International Conference on Military Communications (MILCOM '06)*, (pp. 1-7).

Chair, Z., & Varshney, P. K. (1986). Optimal data fusion in multiple sensor detection systems. *IEEE Transactions on Aerospace and Electronic Systems*, 22(1), 98–101. doi:10.1109/TAES.1986.310699

Chen, R., & Ruiliang, J. M. (2006). Ensuring trustworthy spectrum sensing in cognitive radio networks. In *Proceedings of IEEE Workshop on Networking Technologies for Software Defined Radio Networks (held in conjunction with IEEE SECON '06)*, (pp. 110-119).

Cui, T. T., Jia, G., & Feifei Tellambura, C. (2010). Blind spectrum sensing in cognitive radio. *Wireless Communications and Networking Conference (WCNC '10)*, (pp. 1-5).

Dandawate, A. V., & Giannakis, G. B. (1994). Statistical tests for presence of cyclostationarity. *IEEE Transactions on Signal Processing*, 42, 2355–2369. doi:10.1109/78.317857

De, P., & Liang, Y. C. (2008). Blind spectrum sensing algorithms for cognitive radio networks. *IEEE Transactions on Vehicular Technology*, 57(5), 2834–2842. doi:10.1109/TVT.2008.915520

FCC. (2002). Notice of proposed rulemaking and order. *ET Docket No. 02-135*.

FCC. (2003a). Notice of proposed rulemaking and order. *ET Docket No. 03-222*.

FCC. (2003b). Notice of proposed rulemaking and order. *ET Docket No. 03-289*.

Ganesan, G., & Li, Y. (2005). Cooperative spectrum sensing in cognitive radio networks. *First IEEE International Symposium on Dynamic Spectrum Access Networks (DySPAN '05)*, (pp. 137-143).

Ganesan, G., & Li, Y. (2007a). Cooperative spectrum sensing in cognitive radio, part I: Two user networks. *IEEE Transactions on Wireless Communications*, 6(6), 2204–2213. doi:10.1109/TWC.2007.05775

Ganesan, G., & Li, Y. (2007b). Cooperative spectrum sensing in cognitive radio, part II: Multiuser networks. *IEEE Transactions on Wireless Communications*, 6(6), 2214–2222. doi:10.1109/TWC.2007.05776

Gardner, W. A. (1991). Exploitation of spectral redundancy in cyclostationary signals. *IEEE Signal Processing Magazine*, 8(2), 14–36. doi:10.1109/79.81007

Ghasemi, A., & Sousa, E. S. (2007). Asymptotic performance of collaborative spectrum sensing under correlated log-normal shadowing. *IEEE Communications Letters*, 11(1), 34–36. doi:10.1109/LCOMM.2007.060662

Haykin, S. (2005). Cognitive radio: Brain-empowered wireless communications. *IEEE Transactions on Communications*, 3(2), 201–220.

Imani, S., Dehkordi, A. B., & Kamarei, M. (2011). Adaptive sub-optimal energy detection based wideband spectrum sensing for cognitive radio. *IEEE International Conference on Electrical, Control and Computer Engineering*, (pp. 22-26).

Jun, M., Li, G. Y., & Juang, B. H. (2009). Signal processing in cognitive radio. *Proceedings of the IEEE, 97*(5), 805–823. doi:10.1109/JPROC.2009.2015707

Khajavi, N. T., Sadeghi, S., & Sadough, S. M. (2010). An improved blind spectrum sensing technique for cognitive radio systems. In *Proceedings of 5th International Symposium on Telecommunications (IST '10)*, (pp. 13-17).

Kim, K., Akbar, I. A., Bae, K. K., Urn, J. S., Spooner, C. M., & Reed, J. H. (2007). Cyclostationary approaches to signal detection and classification in cognitive radio. *IEEE International Symposium on Dynamic Spectrum Access Networks (DySPAN '07)*, (pp. 212-215).

Kolodzy, P. J. (2006). Interference temperature: A metric for dynamic spectrum utilization. *International Journal of Network Management, 16*, 103–113. doi:10.1002/nem.608

Kortun, A., Ratnarajah, T., Sellaathurai, T., Zhong, C., & Papadias, C. B. (2011). On the performance of eigenvalue based cooperative spectrum sensing for cognitive radio. *IEEE Journal of Selected Topics in Signal Processing, 5*(1), 49–55. doi:10.1109/JSTSP.2010.2066957

Li, Z., Wang, H., & Kuang, J. (2011). A two-step spectrum sensing scheme for cognitive radio networks. *International Conference on Information Science and Technology (ICIST '11)*, (pp. 694-698).

Liu, X., Tan, X., & Anghuwo, A. A. (2009). Spectrum detection of cognitive radio based on blind signal separation. *IEEE Youth Conference on Information, Computing and Telecommunication (YC-ICT '09)*, (pp. 166-169).

Maleki, S., Pandharipande, A., & Leus, G. (2010). Two-stage spectrum sensing for cognitive radios. *IEEE International Conference on Acoustic, Speech and Signal Processing (ICASSP '10)*, (pp. 2946-2949).

Mitola, J., III. (2000). *Cognitive radio: An integrated agent for software defined radio.* Doctoral dissertation, Royal Institute of Technology (KTH), Stockholm, Sweden.

Peh, E., & Liang, Y. C. (2007). Optimization for cooperative sensing in cognitive radio networks, *Wireless Communications and Networking Conference (WCNC '07)*, (pp. 27-32).

Sahai, A., & Cabric, D. (2005). *Spectrum sensing: Fundamental limits and practical challenges.* First IEEE International Symposium on Dynamic Spectrum Access Networks (DySPAN '05).

Sahai, A., Hoven, N., & Tandra, R. (2004). Some fundamental limits in cognitive radio. In *Proceedings of Allerton Conference on Communications, Control and Computing.*

Sahin, M. E., & Arslan, H. (2006). System design for cognitive radio communications. In *Proceedings of the International Conference on Cognitive Radio Oriented Wireless Networks and Communications (CROWNCOM '06).*

Shankar, N. S., Cordeiro, C., & Challapali, K. (2005). Spectrum agile radios: Utilization and sensing architectures, *First IEEE International Symposium on Dynamic Spectrum Access Networks (DySPAN '05)* (pp. 160-169).

Shellhammer, S., & Tandra, R. (2006). *Performance of the power detector with noise uncertainty.* IEEE 802.22-06/0134r0. IEEE P802.22 Wireless RANs.

Shen, L., Wang, H., Zhang, W., & Zhao, Z. (2011). Blind spectrum sensing for cognitive radio channels with noise uncertainty. *IEEE Transactions on Wireless Communications, 10*(6), 1721–1724. doi:10.1109/TWC.2011.040511.101559

Sonnenschein, A., & Fishman, P. M. (1992). Radiometric detection of spread-spectrum signals in noise of uncertain power. *IEEE Transactions on Aerospace and Electronic Systems*, *28*(3), 654–660. doi:10.1109/7.256287

Sun, C., Zhang, W., & Letaief, K. B. (2007). Cooperative spectrum sensing for cognitive radios under bandwidth constraints. *Wireless Communications and Networking Conference (WCNC '07)*, (pp. 1-5).

Tandra, R., & Sahai, A. (2005). Fundamental limits on detection in low SNR under noise uncertainty, *in Proceedings of the International Conference on Wireless Networks, Communications and Mobile Computing (wirelessCom '05)*, (pp. 464-469).

Tandra, R., & Sahai, A. (2008). SNR walls for signal detection. *IEEE Journal on Selected Topics in Signal Processing*, *2*(1), 4–17. doi:10.1109/JSTSP.2007.914879

Tang, H. (2005). Some physical layer issues of wide-band cognitive radio systems. *First IEEE International Symposium on Dynamic Spectrum Access Networks (DySPAN '05)*, (pp. 151-159).

Thomson, D. J. (1982). Spectrum estimation and harmonic analysis. *Proceedings of the IEEE*, *70*(9), 1055–1096. doi:10.1109/PROC.1982.12433

Tian, Z., & Giannakis, G. B. (2006). A wavelet approach to wideband spectrum sensing for cognitive radios. In *Proceedings of the International Conference on Cognitive Radio Oriented Wireless Networks and Communications (CROWNCOM '06)*.

Tian, Z., & Giannakis, G. B. (2007). Compressed sensing for wideband cognitive radios. *IEEE International Conference on Acoustic, Speech and Signal Processing (ICASSP '10)*, (pp. 1357-1360).

Urkowitz, H. (1967). Energy detection of unknown deterministic signals. *Proceedings of the IEEE*, *55*(4), 523–531. doi:10.1109/PROC.1967.5573

Wang, Y., Tian, Z., & Feng, C. (2010). A two-step compressed spectrum sensing scheme for wideband cognitive radios. *IEEE Global Telecommunications Conference (GLOBECOM '10)*, (pp. 1-5).

Weiss, T., Hillenbrand, J., Krohn, A., & Jondral, F. (2003). Efficient signaling of spectral resources in spectrum pooling systems. In *Proceedings of 10th Symposium on Communication and Vehicular Technology*.

Wendong, H., Willkomm, D., Abusubaih, M., Gross, J., Vlantis, G., Gerla, M., & Wolisz, A. (2007). Cognitive radios for dynamic spectrum access - Dynamic frequency hopping communities for efficient IEEE 802.22 operation. *IEEE Communications Magazine*, *45*(5), 80–87. doi:10.1109/MCOM.2007.358853

Xia, W., Yuan, W., Cheng, W., Liu, W., Wang, S., & Xu, J. (2010). Optimization of cooperative spectrum sensing in ad-hoc cognitive radio networks. *IEEE Global Telecommunications Conference (GLOBECOM '10)*, (pp. 1-5).

Yucek, T., & Arslan, H. (2009). A survey of spectrum sensing algorithms for cognitive radio applications. *IEEE Communications Surveys and Tutorials*, *11*(1), 116–130. doi:10.1109/SURV.2009.090109

Zayen, B., Hayar, A., & Kansanen, K. (2009). Blind spectrum sensing for cognitive radio based on signal space dimension estimation. *IEEE International Conference on Communications (ICC '09)*, (pp. 1-5).

Zayen, B., Hayar, A. M., & Nussbaum, D. (2008). Blind spectrum sensing for cognitive radio based on model selection. In *Proceedings of the International Conference on Cognitive Radio Oriented Wireless Networks and Communications (CROWNCOM '08)*, (pp. 1-4).

Zeng, Y. H., & Liang, Y. C. (2007). *Maximum-minimum eigenvalue detection for cognitive radio*. 18th IEEE International Symposium on Personal, Indoor and Mobile Radio Communications (PIMRC '07).

Zeng, Y. H., & Liang Y. C. (2008). Eigenvalue based sensing algorithms. *IEEE 802.22-06/0118r0*.

Zeng, Y. H., & Liang, Y. C. (2009). Eigenvalue-based spectrum sensing algorithms for cognitive radio. *IEEE Transactions on Communications*, *57*(6), 1784–1793. doi:10.1109/TCOMM.2009.06.070402

Zeng, Y. H., Liang, Y. C., Hoang, A. T., & Peh, E. (2009). Reliability of spectrum sensing under noise and interference uncertainty. *IEEE International Conference on Communications Workshops (ICC Workshops '09)*, (pp. 1-5).

Zeng, Y. H., Liang, Y. C., & Zhang, R. (2008). Blindly combined energy detection for spectrum sensing in cognitive radio. *IEEE Signal Processing Letters*, *15*, 649–652. doi:10.1109/LSP.2008.2002711

Zeng, Y. H., Liang, Y. C., & Zhang, R. (2010). A review on spectrum sensing for cognitive radio: Challenges and solutions. *EURASIP Journal on Advances in Signal Processing*, 2010.

ADDITIONAL READING

Arshad, K., & Moessner, K. (2009). Collaborative spectrum sensing for cognitive radios. *IEEE International Conference on Communications Workshops (ICC Workshops '09)*, (pp. 1-5).

Astaneh, S. A., & Gazor, S. (2011). Relay assisted spectrum sensing in cognitive radio. *International Workshop on Systems, Signal Processing and their Applications (WOSSPA '11)*, (pp. 163-166).

Cabric, D., & Brodersen, R. W. (2005). Physical layer design issues unique to cognitive radio systems. *16th IEEE International Symposium on Personal, Indoor and Mobile Radio Communications (PIMRC '05)*, (pp. 759-763).

Cui, T., Gao, F., & Nallanathan, A. (2011). Optimization of cooperative spectrum sensing in cognitive radio. *IEEE Transactions on Vehicular Technology*, *60*(4), 1578–1589. doi:10.1109/TVT.2011.2116815

Digham, F., Alouini, M. S., & Simon, M. K. (2003). On the energy detection of unknown signals over fading channels. *5th IEEE International Conference on Communications (ICC '03)*, (pp. 3575-3579).

Fehske, A., Gaeddert, J., & Reed, J. H. (2005). A new approach to signal classification using spectral correlation and neural networks. *First IEEE International Symposium on Dynamic Spectrum Access Networks (DySPAN '05)*, (pp. 144-150).

Frank, H. P. Fitzek & Marcos, D. K. (2007). *Cognitive wireless networks: concepts, methodologies and visions inspiring*, Springer.

Ghasemi, A., & Sousa, E. (2007). Opportunistic spectrum access in fading channels through collaborative sensing. *The Journal of Communication*, *2*(2), 71–82.

Ghasemi, A., & Sousa, E. S. (2008). Spectrum sensing in cognitive radio networks: Requirements, challenges and design trade-offs. *IEEE Communications Magazine*, *46*(4), 32–39. doi:10.1109/MCOM.2008.4481338

Ghozzi, M., Marx, F., Dohler, M., & Palicot, J. (2006). Cyclostationarity-based test for detection of vacant frequency bands. In *Proceedings of the International Conference on Cognitive Radio Oriented Wireless Networks and Communications (CROWNCOM '06)*, (pp. 1-5).

Hulbert, A. P. (2005). Spectrum sharing through beacons. *16th IEEE International Symposium on Personal, Indoor and Mobile Radio Communications (PIMRC '05)*, (pp. 989-993).

Jens, P. E., Braun, M., Holger, J., & Jondral, F. K. (2009). Compressed spectrum estimation for cognitive radios. In *Proceedings of 19th Virginia Tech Symposium on Wireless Communications*, (pp. 1-4).

Kim, S. J., & Giannakis, G. B. (2010). Sequential and cooperative sensing for multi-channel cognitive radios. *IEEE Transactions on Signal Processing, 58*(8), 4239–4253. doi:10.1109/TSP.2010.2049106

Kundargi, N., & Tewfik, A. (2010). A performance study of novel sequential energy detection methods for spectrum sensing. *IEEE International Conference on Acoustics Speech and Signal Processing (ICASSP '10)*, (pp. 3090-3093).

Lee, S., & Kim, S. L. (2011). Optimization of time-domain spectrum sensing for cognitive radio systems. *IEEE Transactions on Vehicular Technology, 60*(4), 1937–1943. doi:10.1109/TVT.2011.2132157

Maleki, S., & Leus, G. (2011). Censored truncated sequential spectrum sensing for cognitive radio networks. *IEEE International Conference on Digital Signal Processing*, (pp. 1-8).

Maleki, S., Pandharipande, A., & Leus, G. (2011). Energy-efficient distributed spectrum sensing for cognitive sensor networks. *IEEE Sensors Journal, 11*(3), 565–573. doi:10.1109/JSEN.2010.2051327

Mishra, S. M., Sahai, A., & Brodersen, R. W. (2006). Cooperative sensing among cognitive radios. *IEEE International Conference on Communications (ICC '06)*, (pp. 1658-1663).

Mohammad Karimi, M., Mahboobi, B., & Ardebilipour, M. (2011). Optimal spectrum sensing in fast fading Rayleigh channel for cognitive radio. *IEEE Communications Letters, 15*(10).

Rao, R., Cheng, Q., & Varshney, P. K. (2011). Subspace-based cooperative spectrum sensing for cognitive radios. *IEEE Sensors Journal, 11*(3), 611–622. doi:10.1109/JSEN.2010.2052800

Taherpour, A., Nasiri-Kenari, M., & Gazor, S. (2010). Multiple antenna spectrum sensing in cognitive radios. *IEEE Transactions on Wireless Communications, 9*(2), 814–823. doi:10.1109/TWC.2009.02.090385

Thomas, R. W., DaSilva, L. A., & MacKenzie, A. B. (2005). *Cognitive networks: New frontiers in dynamic spectrum access networks.* First IEEE International Symposium on Dynamic Spectrum Access Networks (DySPAN '05).

Xin, Y., Zhang, H., & Rangarajan, S. (2009). SSCT: A simple sequential spectrum sensing scheme for cognitive radio. *IEEE Global Telecommunications Conference (GLOBECOM '09)*, (pp. 1-5).

Zeng, Y. H., & Liang, Y. C. (2007). Covariance based signal detections for cognitive radio. *Proceedings of the 2nd IEEE International Symposium on New Frontiers in Dynamic Spectrum Access Networks (DySPAN '07)*, (pp. 202-207).

Zeng, Y. H., & Liang, Y. C. (2009). Spectrum sensing algorithms for cognitive radio based on statistical covariances. *IEEE Transactions on Vehicular Technology, 58*(4), 1804–1815. doi:10.1109/TVT.2008.2005267

Zhao, J., Zheng, H., & Yang, G. H. (2005). Distributed coordination in dynamic spectrum allocation networks. *First IEEE International Symposium on Dynamic Spectrum Access Networks (DySPAN '05)*, (pp. 259-268).

Zhuan, Y., Memik, G., & Grosspietsch, J. (2008). Energy detection using estimated noise variance for spectrum sensing in cognitive radio networks. *Wireless Communications and Networking Conference (WCNC '08)*, (pp. 711-716).

Zou, Q., Zheng, S., & Sayed, A. H. (2010). Cooperative sensing via sequential detection. *IEEE Transactions on Signal Processing, 58*(12), 6266–6283. doi:10.1109/TSP.2010.2070501

KEY TERMS AND DEFINITIONS

Blind Sensing (BS): A spectrum sensing approach that does not require any information on primary signal or noise power to decide about primary user activity.

Cognitive Radio (CR): An intelligent reconfigurable device that can interact with its radio environment and update its transmission parameters (in software) on the run to optimally benefit from the available radio resources.

Interference Temperature: Temperature equivalent of the maximum amount of interference that the primary receiver can tolerate.

Primary User (PU): High priority licensed user with legacy rights on usage of specific part of frequency spectrum.

Probability of Detection (P_d): Probability of correctly detecting the primary signal when the primary user is actually active in the scanned frequency band.

Probability of False Alarm (P_f): Probability of falsely detecting the primary signal when the primary user is actually silent in the scanned frequency band.

Secondary User (SU): Low priority unlicensed user equipped with cognitive capability to exploit any vacant spectrum band without interfering with the primary user

Spectrum Hole: A licensed frequency band not being used by a primary user at a particular time over a certain geographical area under consideration.

Spectrum Sensing (SS): The ability to determine which portion(s) of the scanned frequency band are vacant and identify any primary user activity.

Transmitter Detection: A spectrum sensing approach of identifying primary transmissions based on local observations of the primary user signal at cognitive radio/secondary user.

ENDNOTE

[1]   On study leave from Department of Electrical Engineering, University of Engineering and Technology, Lahore, Pakistan.

Section 5
Services and Applications

Chapter 13
Localizing Persons Using Body Area Sensor Network

Cheng Guo
Delft University of Technology, The Netherlands

R. Venkatesha Prasad[1]
Delft University of Technology, The Netherlands

Jing Wang
Delft University of Technology, The Netherlands

Vijay Sathyanarayana Rao
Delft University of Technology, The Netherlands

Ignas Niemegeers
Delft University of Technology, The Netherlands

ABSTRACT

Context awareness is an important aspect in many ICT applications. For example, in an intelligent home network, location of the user enables session transfer, lighting, and temperature control, et cetera. In fact, in a body area sensor network (BASN), location estimation of a user helps in realizing realtime monitoring of the person (especially those who require help) for better health supervision. In this chapter the authors first introduce many localization methods and algorithms from the literature in BASNs. They also present classification of these methods. Amongst them, location estimation using signal strength is one of the foremost. In indoor environments, the authors found that the signal strength based localization methods are usually not accurate, since signal strength fluctuates. The fluctuation in signal strength is due to deficient antenna coverage and multi-path interference. Thus, localization algorithms usually fail to achieve good accuracy. The authors propose to solve this problem by combining multiple receivers in a body area sensor network to estimate the location with a higher accuracy. This method mitigates the errors caused by antenna orientations and beam forming properties. The chapter evaluates the perfor-mance of the solution with experiments. It is tested with both range-based and range-free localization algorithm that we developed. The chapter shows that with spatial diversity, the localization accuracy is improved compared to using single receiver alone. Moreover, the authors observe that range-based algorithm has a better performance.

DOI: 10.4018/978-1-4666-1797-1.ch013

Copyright © 2012, IGI Global. Copying or distributing in print or electronic forms without written permission of IGI Global is prohibited.

BODY AREA SENSOR NETWORK AND LOCALIZATIONS

With a number of devices equipped with sensors, micro-controllers and radio components, important parameters, such as body temperature, momentum, glucose levels, blood pressure or heart rate of the person can be monitored. In the meanwhile ambient intelligence (Ducatel, 2010; Aarts, 2003) is seen to be penetrating our daily lives. Being a way to realize ambient intelligence, the rapid development of these wireless sensor networks also extend to body area networks. Wireless sensors can be placed on persons, on cloths, etc. to monitor diverse vital health parameters of the persons. These devices form a Body Area Sensor Network (BASN). Such networks provide many novel applications in healthcare, fitness, and entertainment, which enable better quality of life of persons. A large amount of BASN applications are in healthcare domain. A BASN can help patients in hospitals gain more freedom. Wireless sensors can replace wired sensors monitoring patients. Thus they can move freely instead of being bonded to beds. More than in the hospitals, chronically ill patients or those are in recovery may return to their normal life at home with their physical conditions closely monitored by the doctors remotely. Another application of such body area sensor networks is helping senior citizens to manage their life in houses or even in public places without any support. In the above applications, context information has to be generated to provide control systems some form of context awareness. In case of emergency, data collected from sensors have to be collected and then processed in a control center to make a decision for actuation. Among the context information, location is an important one. No matter in hospital, home or in public area, locations of the patience have to be known so that first-aid can be provided timely. Moreover, the location information also provides doctors with the movement patterns of patients so that their living habits can be analyzed and used for disease prevention and diagnosis. Especially, people with Alzheimer disease should be monitored with wearable sensors and their house is equipped with other sensors for monitoring temperature, humidity, smoke or other hazardous gas and cameras for security surveillance. Some areas are dangerous such as kitchen where there are some sharp tools, gas stoves and electrical appliances. When the patient is moving in the house, sand moves into the kitchen his location should be known to the monitoring systems so that a video-camera in the kitchen is activated. An alarm and the video are sent to caretakers so that help can be provided timely in case required.

APPLYING WIRELESS SENSOR NETWORKS FOR LOCALIZATIONS

One of the most well-known localization systems is the Global Positioning System (GPS). However, due to poor penetration of the radio signals this system is not suitable for indoor localization (Savvides, 2001). A revolving technique in indoor environment is to use already deployed wireless sensor devices (in hospitals, buildings and other indoor area), together with wearable BASN to estimate the locations of the persons wearing them. This technique is highly practical and cost effective since all the sensors are already deployed and connected wirelessly for their usual tasks. Hence, localization does not add any additional investment on hardware infrastructure. There are a few requirements for reliable localization system. The localization system must have the features such as: (1) Accuracy: although many applications do not require localization to be accurate to centimeter, in many applications in home, buildings or hospitals, a monitoring system has to know where a user is, e.g. a living room or bed room. (2) Low complexity: in an indoor environment, location information is likely to be provided without dedicated hardware to avoid extra cost. Localization is expected to be an additional service on other devices, such as access points and environmental sensors. These devices work with embedded devices which can even be worn on the body. Computational and memory resource are limited on these devices. The localization algorithm or method must be as simple as possible and work inconspicuously to the users (Ducatel, 2010). (3) Real-time operation: location information has to be estimated in real time following the movement of the person. Therefore it has to be updated periodically at appropriate intervals. These intervals have to be decided by the speed of the users. Since we have the indoor environment as our user scenario, walking speed of 1 to 2 m/s is considered as a moderate mobility in these scenarios. Therefore, locations shall be updated every a few seconds. In the literature, there are many approaches designed for different applications. Taxonomy for identifying location techniques in general was developed in (Hightower, 2001). The techniques are classified into Angle-of-Arrival (AoA), Time-of-Arrival (ToA), and the radio signal strength, which is frequently represented by Received Signal Strength Indicator (RSSI). Different techniques focus on different sensing data that is collected (Mutukrishnan, 2005). It has been shown that AoA and ToA methods are very accurate in ranging thus they estimate location with high accuracy. Especially when Ultra Wide Band (UWB) are combined with ToA method (Yu, 2004; Savvides, 2001) or both ToA and AoA (Deng, 2000), the accuracy can be improved even higher. A survey on UWB based localization methods is provided in (Gezici, 2005). Nevertheless, UWB requires extra hardware as reference points and all the devices have to have higher computational frequency so that the differences between ToA can be identified. Therefore it is not suitable for a BASN since the devices required by UWB methods are too large and consumes substantial power in wearable devices. Furthermore, the cost of a UWB system is much higher than that of a BASN. It is well known from many studies that the radio propagation is essentially related to the

transmission distance. Given the transmitted signal power, RSSI is highly influenced by the distance. However, distance is not the only factor deciding RSSI. Both (Cox, 1984) and (Bernhardt, 1987) suggested that the distribution of receiving signal strength is a random and log normally distributed random variable with a distance dependent mean value. It is decided by a path loss exponent and a zero mean Gaussian distributed random variable accounting the effect of shadowing. Most of RSSI-based localization systems take advantage of existing indoor network devices such as WLAN or RFIDs (Jin, 2006). Along with the development of WSNs, RSSI-based methods use such a network more and more. The WSNs in most scenarios are implemented for monitoring environmental parameters such as temperature, humidity, presence, illumination etc. Together with a BASN, the two networks can cooperate to locate a person. A review of existing RSSI-based methods is provided in the next section.

LOCALIZATION TECHNIQUES USING RSSI

RSSI-based positioning algorithms are generally divided into two categories according to the classification in (Liu, 2004): range-based and range-free. The former makes use of the absolute distance or angle calibrated from the pre-measured RSSI map, which can be a set of "signatures" or RSSI to distance/angle relation. The latter, rather than using the information concerning the absolute distance, utilizes the geographic relationship between target motes and anchor motes.

RADAR (Bahl, 2000) and MoteTrack (Lorincz, 2005) are the examples of using the "signatures" for localization. Both protocols utilize a large set of pre-measured reference points on a map. Firstly the localization systems in the two protocols have a set of anchors. Then a mobile node is put at different points, which location is know, in the deployed area to measure the RSSIs to different anchors. The RSSIs are used latter for deciding a target mote's location. Afterwards the target node's RSSI to anchors are compared the neighboring reference points' RSSI to the same anchors. The closet reference points are selected. Location of these reference points form an area of which the gravity center is considered as the estimated location of the mobile node.

An enhanced RSSI-based localization system is proposed in (Lau, 2008). Although it is also range-based, it does not use "signatures". Instead, triangulation with Minimum Mean Square Error (MMSE) estimation is used to calculate the target node's location. The authors proposed a better ranging algorithm which assumes the target's current location is not far away from a previous one. Thus the two RSSIs should be highly correlated. So the current RSSI is averaged with the EWMA method.

APIT (He, 2003) is a good example of range-free localization protocol. The authors assume a lot of nodes are available in the area where the localization is needed. Nodes can exchange their RSSIs observations of three anchors. The three anchors form a triangle. If a node in the target node's neighborhood has RSSIs to the anchors larger than the target node's, then the target node must be outside the triangle formed by the anchors. Otherwise it is inside. Changing another three anchors, another triangle can be formed. The whole localization area is divided into small areas; once a triangle is formed the possible areas where the target node may be are given more weight. After all the combination of anchors is tried, the highest weighted areas' gravity center is estimated as the target node's location. ROCRSSI (Liu, 2004) is similar to APIT. However, the rings are used to replace triangles. The RSSI p from the target to an anchor is compared to the RSSIs from the anchor to other anchors. We can always find a pair RSSIs between anchors that p is larger than one is smaller than the other one. Then a ring can be drawn that

the target node is possibly inside. Again several rings add weights to the possible small areas the target node may reside. The estimation location is the gravity center of the highest weight area.

Received Signal Strength Indicator (RSSI) is widely exploited for localization in the literature. However, because of the small size, wearable characteristics and cost restrictions, health care wireless sensor devices normally use an on-chip antenna which in turn has no perfect omnidirectional beam properties. As a consequence, the antenna orientation of the devices has a large influence on the received signal strength. Factors such as complex indoor radio propagation and the movement of people usually cause RSSI-based localization algorithms to fail to achieve a good accuracy. In this chapter, we propose a method, which takes advantage of multiple wireless devices in a BASN to improve the accuracy of estimates of location of a person in an indoor environment. The highlights of this method are: (a) nullifying the effects of antenna orientation by using multiple devices; (b) using the spatial redundancy in the estimations; and (c) implementation of the system to show our method performs better under similar circumstances.

LOCALIZATION WITH MULTIPLE DEVICES

Range-based localization algorithms usually fail to achieve good accuracy due to deficient antenna embedded, fading, shadowing, and people movements. In this chapter, we try to solve the first two problems by combining multiple wireless devices in a BASN. Their diverse antenna orientations and small distance can be exploited to increase the localization accuracy. Moreover, it was shown in the literature that the relation between RSSI and range is not one to one. Transceivers apart of different distances, sometimes up to 10s of meters, can receive packets with the same RSSI (Aguayo, 2004; Zhao, 2003). Therefore, absolute distance estimation is tricky.

Although range-free algorithms avoid using absolute distance estimation between anchor and target nodes, it has to use relative distances between anchors. If the antennas on the anchors also have the problem on orientation, the relative positions of anchors are not precise anymore thus the location estimated is not accurate. We will combine the multiple-devices-solution with representatives from both categories to test how much this solution can improve performance of the protocols.

In the following, we firstly introduce the advantages of using multiple devices for localization. For completeness, we introduce the two representatives from range-based and range-free algorithms that we proposed in (An, 2006; Wang, 2006).

Localization with Multiple Devices in a BASN

Small BASN devices normally transmit with on-chip antennas. These antennas' transmission pattern is far from perfect omnidirectional (Tmote sky datasheet, 2006). We verified the deficient coverage of the antenna by putting the transmitting and receiving motes 4m apart within the line-of-sight (An, 2006). We measured the RSSI values at 8 different antenna directions in steps of 45°. In Figure 1, we show that the antenna has the strongest strength of -50 dBm at 0° and the smallest signal strength of about -65 dBm at 90°. We observed that RSSI varies in a range of around 15dBm for the static case.

This problem can be solved by continuously rotating the antenna direction and taking the average of the RSSI values received from different directions. However, this method is neither agile

Figure 1. Antenna orientation effect (An, 2006)

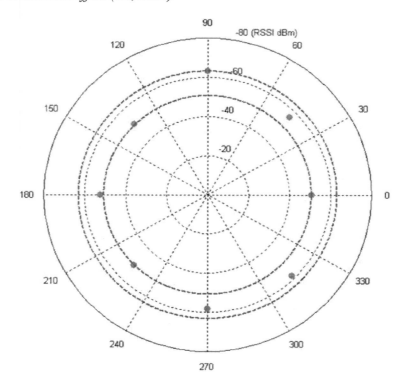

Figure 2. Empirical relation curve (An, 2006)

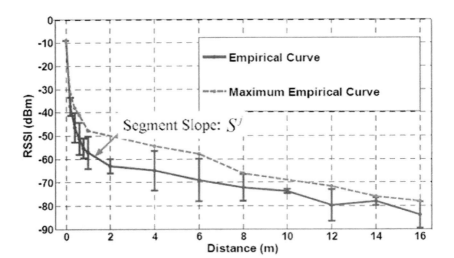

nor feasible. Since there may be many wireless sensor devices in a BASN, we can actually use the RSSI from different devices to calculate the location with the average RSSI. Or we can let the devices calculate the location independently and take the average of the calculated locations. Both ways may mitigate the estimation error induced by the deficient antenna radiation pattern. We will show the performance of both methods in Section V.

Using multiple devices can also reduce the estimation error caused by fading, since the signal is transferred in different paths. We can use the so-called micro diversity, which refers to that the antennas are at a distance of an order of a wavelength, to combat fading.

Range-Based Localization Algorithm

We proposed an enhanced triangulation algorithm in (An, 2006). The optimization is that we give anchors which have higher RSSI to a target higher weight so that they are trusted more and used firstly to calculated a location. The next question is how large weight we shall assign to an anchor. Since we do not know the reliability of any measure

RSSI it is hard to assign the weight. We proposed to use the following way. We firstly have to plot out an empirical curve showing relation between RSSI and distance, as shown in Figure 2. All the distances were estimated by this relation with received RSSIs. We can see from Figure 2 that the higher the RSSI the steep of the curve is. We use the slopes of the curve as the weight of an anchor. To be specific, we record all the RSSIs received from anchor i and mapped them to the empirical relation curve. For each of them we have a slope of the mapped segment, i.e. if we have a RSSI of -68 dBm then we can get the slope of segment 4 meter to 6 meter. We get the weight of the anchor when it receives the j RSSI as

$$W_i = \frac{Slope_i^j}{\max(Slope_i^j)}$$

Then we try to find the position of the target mote by minimizing

$$\Delta = \left(\sum_{i=1}^{N} W_i \Delta_i^2 \right)^{1/2}$$

Where Δ_i is the error calculated by

$$f_i(x_e, y_e) = \left| d_i - \sqrt{(x_i - x_e)^2 + (y_i - y_e)^2} \right|. \text{ In}$$

the last equation, d_i is the estimated distance between the target mote and the anchor mote i, which is located at $(x_i; y_i)$. For more details about the algorithm, please refer to (An, 2006).

Range-Free Localization Algorithm

Range-free localization algorithms utilize the relative position to decide the possible region where the target mote may reside (Wang, 2006). Take for example, Figure 3, Anchor A receives packets from Anchor B and estimates RSSI, so as Anchor C, and Target T. Thus we may expect the relationship $RSSIAB > RSSIAT > RSSIAC$. Therefore, we can conclude that the Target T is most likely to be in the grey ring. We can derive a series of such grey areas so that the estimated position is decided as the gravity center of the final intersectional area.

We extend this basic algorithm by ensuring more credibility to the measured RSSI. The same theory as the range-based algorithm is used. If the distance between transceivers is small, the RSSI rapidly changes with a tiny increment or decrement of the distance. Contrarily, a large change of distance may only lead to an imperceptible change of RSSI if the distance is large. Therefore, we assign lower credibility if the RSSI has lesser value which corresponds to a bigger estimation error, i.e., a longer distance. In our algorithm, each anchor node has a neighbor list sorted in descending order based on the received RSSI. We briefly explain the algorithm with an example. In Table 1, Anchor 6 decides that Target T is in the ring between Anchor 5 and Anchor 7. However, if $d_{65} > d_{67}$, the ring cannot be generated. Therefore, we refer to Target T's neighbor list. Target T also has a sorted neighbor list based on the RSSI from the anchor nodes, which is also shown in Table I. In Target T's list, the RSSI from Anchor 5 is higher than the RSSI from Anchor 7.

Figure 3. An illustration of range-free localization algorithm (Wang, 2006)

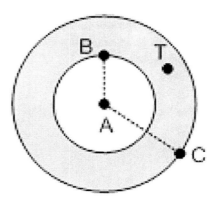

Thus, we envisage that RSSI from Anchor 5 has a higher reliability than the RSSI from Anchor 7. Therefore, we ignore Anchor 7 and move to Anchor 3. If Anchors 5 and 3 can generate a ring, we proceed to the next step. If Anchor 5 and 3 still cannot generate a ring, we go back to trust Anchor 7 and ignore Anchor 5. If Anchor 2 and 7 can generate a ring, then algorithm proceeds further. The accuracy of the process is based on the assumption that, the majority of RSSI are reliable. Although RSSI is disturbed by a multitude of factors, the above assumption is usually true in most of the situations when averaged over a small duration.

After generating a series of rings, we count the number of times an area is covered. Every time a ring covers an area, the counter of the area increases by one. Then, we calculate the gravity center of the area to find the location. However, since we already know that higher RSSIs have higher credibility, we give overlapping areas with a higher RSSI more weight. If an area is covered by a ring, the increase of the area counter is related with the reliability weight of the ring. For Anchor I, the reliability weight is defined as:

$$w_{TI} = \left(\frac{1}{RSSI_{TI}} \right)^n$$

where, $RSSI_{TI}$ is the RSSI received by Anchor I from Target T and n is the exponential index of the radio propagation model. Now we use the refined RSSI conceived from multiple sensors (acting as a bunch of targets) into the above expression to get a better accuracy.

EXPERIMENTAL SETUP AND RESULTS

Setup

We conducted a series of experiments at the 19th floor of our faculty. The devices used in the experiments were TMote-Sky sensors with 2.4 GHz IEEE 802.15.4 compliant Texas Instruments CC2420 transceivers (CC2420 RF transceiver datasheet, 2008). The transceiver provides RSSI in a range of 100 dBm for every received packet, which is the received strength signal reading averaged over eight symbol periods. IEEE 802.15.4 (Gutierrez, 2001) uses 2.4 GHz DSSS RF modulation with a data rate of 250 kbps. In our experiment, the IEEE 802.15.4 packet header and payload of 17 bytes and 9 bytes were used resulting in 26 bytes packet.

We bound four motes oriented in four directions on a 30 cm high platform made of polystyrene. The distance between any two motes was about 6 cm, which is half the wavelength of 2.4 GHz radio. We expected that distance may help us to combat the effects of fading. The four motes were connected to a PC via USB cables. Thus, the received packets were directly relayed to the PC, which acts as the sink of the BASN. The environment was checked to be Wi-Fi free. All the experiments were carried out during weekends minimizing the effect of human movements and other activities.

We deployed in total 11 anchors on a straight line in the middle of the corridor. All the anchors were also lifted with the 30 cm high polystyrene.

Table 1. Example of selecting reliable RSSI

Neighbor list of Target (ID 1)		Neighbor list of Target (ID 6)	
Anchor ID	RSSI (dBm)	Node ID	RSSI (dBm)
2	-54.387	4	-64.7273
3	-83.801	8	-66.3333
4	-73.778	2	-76.4667
5	-65.529	5	-78.5714
6	-80.029	1	-80.0294
7	-82.002	7	-82.7143
8	-85.791	3	-88.6316

The distance between any two anchors was 4 m. All the anchors were powered by external DC supply to avoid the fluctuation in power supply due to different battery levels. The arrangement of the motes is shown in Figure 4. The blue nodes in the figure are anchors and the red nodes represent the positions of target nodes. The horizontal distances between the anchors and the targets are 2 m. We tested 10 target positions in line with the anchor nodes, called Scenario-A and another 9 positions which were close to the wall, called Scenario-B. With Scenario-B, we want to check the influence of reflections from the wall on the accuracy.

In each target location, we run an experiment for 60s. During each experiment, the anchors randomly sent a beacon message every second and the target randomly selected one in each 1 s interval. Hence, for each measurement, 60 beacon messages were sent by every anchor mote. Meanwhile, the target motes reported the received packets to the sink and the anchors recorded the beacons they received into their local memory. Afterwards, one of the target motes polled all the anchors of the recorded data. For each received beacon, sender, receiver, packet identifier, and RSSI were collected and gathered at the PC for further computations and analysis. Then, all the motes were reset and we moved the target motes to the next location.

Figure 4. Location of anchors and targets

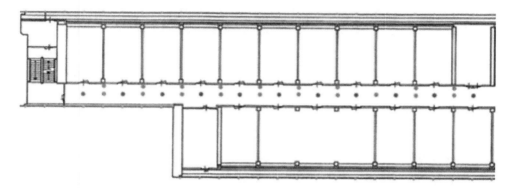

Results

We will show in this section the performance of using multiple devices for localization. Both range-based and range-free algorithms are tested. We take the averaged RSSI from the target motes to estimate a location. Then the estimation error is compared with the error using the RSSI from each target and the maximum RSSI among all target nodes. The joint performance of using multiple devices with range-based is compared to that with range-free algorithm to select a winner. We are also curious about whether averaging RS-SIs collected from a longer period may improve localization accuracy. Furthermore, instead of averaging RSSIs from multiple devices, we can also take the average of estimated positions from individual target device or the gravity center of the estimated positions. We will show which way may improve the localization accuracy the most.

Considering the requirements of a real-time indoor person tracking system, it is then important that location updates are done frequently. Hence, for a moving person, we must typically not use more than 5 samples. Therefore, we firstly use 5 samples for estimation. Figure 5 shows the estimation result with range-free algorithm. It compares the sample RSSI averaged on four target motes and the RSSI from each target mote. Figure 8 shows the case with range-based algorithm. Please note

that in the two figures, the scale of estimation error is different. We can see that in both cases, using the averaged RSSI still gives best estimation with an largest error about 3 m, which is indicated by the thick red line in the figures. The range-based algorithm performs better in 90% positions where errors are less than half meter. The only exception happens in one location where the error is only a bit large than 3 m.

Secondly, all the 60 beacons collected by each target mote were used for the estimation. The application scenario can be that a person stands in a location for some time. We want to see whether averaged RSSI from a longer period may reduce the estimation error. Again Figure 7 shows the estimation result with range-free algorithm and Figure 7 shows the case with range-based algorithm. In general, using the average still gives higher accuracy. Compared to the 5 samples case, all the estimation errors are below 2 m. It means that averaging RSSIs from longer period indeed removes some jittering in the RSSI values.

However, the case is not always true. In the added 55 samples, some may add larger errors. Therefore 90% of estimation errors are smaller than half meters in the 5 samples case, but only 40% are smaller than haft meter in the 60 samples case. This time a large exception in estimation error happens with range-free algorithm. Since the complex nature of radio propagation and lo-

Figure 5. Estimation error comparison with range-free algorithm in scenario-A: 5 samples each target

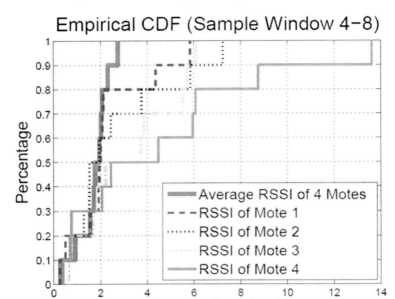

Figure 6. Estimation error comparison with range-based algorithm in scenario-A: 5 samples each target

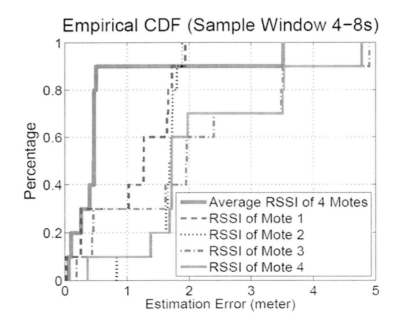

Figure 7. Estimation error comparison with range-free algorithm in scenario-A: 60 samples each target

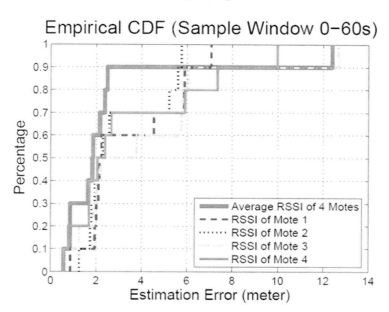

calization algorithms, it is hard to explain why the exception happens sometimes with range-based algorithm, but happens with range-free algorithm the other times. A possible reason may be that the accuracy of range-free algorithm does not depend on the magnitude of RSSI deviation. As long as rings can be formed, even a large RSSI deviation may be ruled out by other rings. But in some cases, even a small deviation may cause a serious error since rings can not be formed anymore or formed wrongly. Compared to range-free algorithm, the accuracy of range-based algorithm depends on the RSSI deviation. Averaging RSSIs from longer period reduced the deviation hence large estimation errors are removed.

For Scenario-B, the estimation results when using 60 beacons is drawn in Figure 9. In general, the average method outperforms and provides better accuracy than using an individual target mote. However, due to extra reflections and shadowing, the median error is around 2m and in the 90% of the cases the errors are below 6m.

We are also interested in the comparisons in estimations between 5 beacons case (4 s to 8 s)

and 60 beacons case. In Figure 10, which is plotted with data from Scenario-A, we can see that the estimation accuracy is generally the same except for the exception introduced in Figure 9.

Another method to utilize the RSSI from multiple devices is to estimate the location of each individual targets and then calculate the average location. In Figure 10, we investigate the accuracy of this method. However, we can see that the average RSSI method outperforms the average position method in general.

This is due to the fact that an individual measurement going haywire can pull the location farther away since slight change in RSSI contributes to higher distance when the target is away. Thus it is better to use averaged RSSI than averaged estimated location.

For the estimation using a small number of beacons, we also examined the estimation stability on the time scale. We divided the whole 60s data into 12 estimations of 5s each. The 10 locations in Scenario-A and the 9 locations in Scenario-B are all plotted in Figure 11 with both algorithms. The curves show the average estimation error of

Figure 8. Estimation error comparison with range-based algorithm in Scenario-A: 60 samples each target

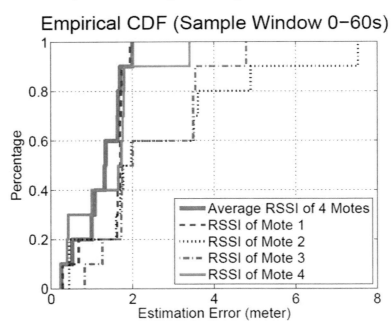

Figure 9. Estimation error comparison with range-free algorithm in Scenario-B: 60 samples each target

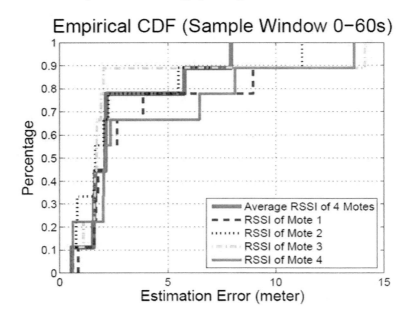

Figure 10. Estimation error comparison: 5 samples each target

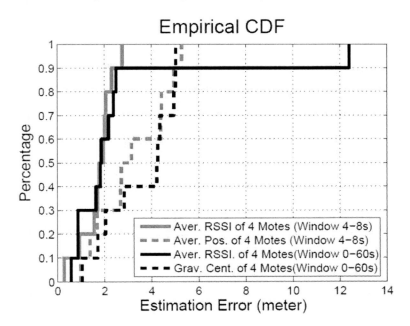

the 12 estimations and the bars show the standard deviation. We can see that the stability of range-based algorithm is better than that of range-free algorithm. Most of the estimation errors of range-based algorithm in different locations are less than 2 m. The estimation variations in most locations are so small that are hardly observed. Even the estimation errors in Scenario-B are small. With range-free algorithm, the largest error is more than 5.5m in Scenario-A. Due to the structure of the floor, some places have more obstacles than others and thus suffer more from shadowing effect, which degrades the estimation accuracy. The estimation errors also vary with time. Interestingly, the locations with larger error also have larger deviations due to the complex structures around the location. In Scenario-B, the average error is a little less than 7m and the standard deviation is more than 4.5 m.

In general, the estimation of Scenario-B is worse than Scenario-A. This is due to the fact that target positions in Scenario-B are very close

to the walls, therefore RSSI measurements are expected to have higher influence from radio reflections and shadowing.

Except for the average RSSI from 4 target motes, the other option is to use the largest RSSI among the four. We use the same setup as used in Figure 11 to compare the performance of using average RSSI and maximum RSSI. The results are plot in Figure 12 and Figure 13 for range-free algorithm and range-based algorithm respectively. With range-free algorithm the maximum RSSI performs worse than the average RSSI in both scenarios in most locations. This is due to that we use the same antenna in anchors thus they are not omni-directional. Thus the maximum RSSI does not really show the actual distance between target mote and anchors. With range-based algorithm the difference of estimation error between average RSSI and maximum RSSI is smaller. Only in a few locations we can see a clear gap between curves where maximum RSSI still performs a bit worse than average RSSI. Almost all the estima-

Figure 11. Variation of estimation error on time scale: comparison between range-based and range-free algorithm

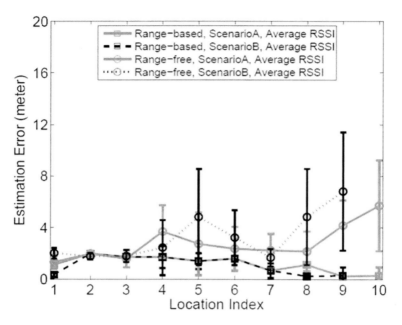

Figure 12. Variation of estimation error on time scale with range-free algorithm

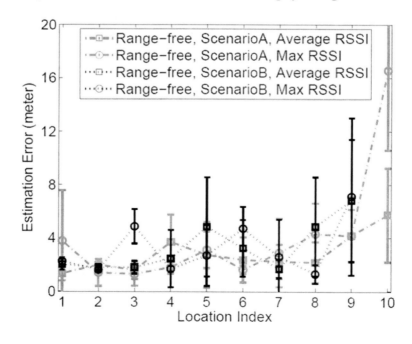

Figure 13. Variation of estimation error on time scale with range-based algorithm

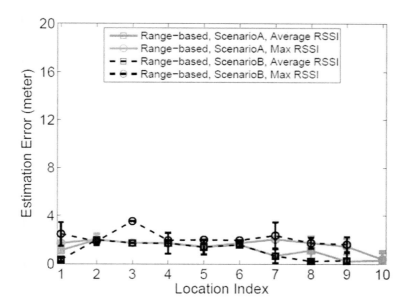

tion errors are below 2m except one error with maximum RSSI in Scenario-B is close to 4 m. We can conclude from the experimental results in the two figures that average RSSI performs better than maximum one.

CONCLUSION

In this chapter we first introduced the localization with BASN. Such network provides many novel health monitoring applications for users. In these applications, especially in health care domain, location of the user is essential context information for providing first-aid or to analyze the movement pattern of users. To eliminate the cost of standalone localization we exploit RSSI based localization in of WSNs and BASN that is frequently used as the source for localization estimation. Many RSSI-based localization methods are proposed in the literature. One common assumption in these methods is that the devices have omni-directional antennas, which is normally not true in practice. Due to their small size and

low cost, the antennas on BASN devices are far from omni-directional. Therefore, we proposed a new method to improve localization accuracy by mitigating the errors caused by deficient antennas and combating fading with spatial diversity. The method uses multiple receivers in a BASN to locate the person who carries them. The method used here has a real application since a person may carry several wireless device in the future. We introduced the method and our range-based and range-free algorithms in this chapter. We investigated the performances of the method with both algorithms through experiments. With the experimental results, we show that the method can improve localization accuracy from a single receiver with both range-based and range-free algorithms. We also show that the accuracy may change over time significantly with range-free algorithm but rather stable with range-based algorithm. The latter algorithm also has a smaller localization error as well. Thus we can recommend with confidence that range-based algorithm works better with the multiple receiver method as long as the empirical curve is also plotted with multiple receivers. The comparison between using maximum and average RSSI suggests that average RSSI works better. Furthermore, average RSSI from a longer duration does not improve the accuracy much.

ACKNOWLEDGMENT

This work was supported by Dutch Freeband PNP 2008 project and Dutch IOP GenCom Future Home Networks project.

REFERENCES

Aarts, E., & Marzano, S. (2003). *The new everyday - Views on ambient intelligence*. Philips Design.

Aguayo, D., Bicket, J., Biswas, S., Judd, G., & Morris, S. (2004). Link level measurements from an 802.11b mesh network. In *Proceedings ACM SIGCOMM'04*, Portland, OR, USA.

An, X., Wang, J., Prasad, R. V., & Niemegeers, I. G. M. M. (2006). Opt - Online person tracking system for context-awareness in wireless personal network. In *Proceedings of ACM SIGMOBILE REALMAN Workshop*. Florence, Italy.

Bahl, P., & Padmanabhan, V. N. (200). Radar: An in-building rf-based user location and tracking system. In *Proceedings IEEE INFOCOM 2000*, Tel-Aviv, Israel.

Bernhardt, R. C. (1987). Macroscopic diversity in frequency reuse radio systems. *IEEE Journal on Selected Areas in Communications, 5*(5), 862–870. doi:10.1109/JSAC.1987.1146594

CC2420. (2008). *Texas Instruments RF transceiver datasheet*. Retrieved from http://focus.ti.com/docs/prod/folders/print/cc2420.html

Cox, D. C., Murray, R., & Norris, A. W. (1984). 800 MHz attenuation measured in and around suburban houses. *AT & T Bell Laboratories Technical Journal, 63*(6), 921–954.

Deng, P., & Fan, P. Z. (2000). An AoA assisted ToA positioning system. In *WCC - ICCT 2000: Proceedings of IEEE International Conference on Communication Technology*, Beijing, China.

Ducatel, K., et al. (2001). *Scenarios for ambient intelligence in 2010*. Brussels, Belgium: IST Advisory Group (ISTAG), European Commission. Retrieved from www.cordis.lu/ist/istag.html

Gezici, S., Tian, Z., Biannakis, G. B., Kobayashi, H., Molisch, A. F., Poor, H. V., & Sahinoglu, Z. (2005). Localization via ultra-wideband radios. *IEEE Signal Processing Magazine, 22*(4), 70–84. doi:10.1109/MSP.2005.1458289

Gutierrez, J., Naeve, M., Callaway, E., Bourgeois, M., Mitter, V., & Heile, B. (2001). IEEE 802.15.4: A developing standard for low-power low cost wireless personal area networks. *IEEE Network, 15*(5), 12–19. doi:10.1109/65.953229

He, T., Huang, C., Blum, B. A., Stankovic, J. A., & Abdelzaher, T. (2003). Range-free localization schemes for large scale sensor networks. In *MobiCom '03: Proceedings of the 9th Annual International Conference on Mobile Computing and Networking*, New York, NY, USA (pp. 81-95).

Hightower, J., & Boriello, G. (2001). Location systems for ubiquitous computing. *IEEE Computer, 34*(5), 57–66. doi:10.1109/2.940014

Jin, G., Lu, X. Y., & Park, M. (2006). An indoor localization mechanism using active RFID tag. In *SUTC 2006: Proceedings of IEEE International Conference on Sensor Networks, Ubiquitous, and Trustworthy Computing*, Taichung, Taiwan.

Lau, E. E. L., Lee, B.-G., & Chung, W.-Y. (2008). Enhanced RSSI based high accuracy real-time user location tracking system for indoor and outdoor environments. *International Journal on Smart Sensing and Intelligent Systems, 1*(2), 534–548.

Liu, C., Wu, K., & He, T. (2004). Sensor localization with ring overlapping based on comparison of received signal strength indicator. In *Proceedings of IEEE International Conference on Mobile Ad-hoc and Sensor Systems*. Florida, USA.

Lorincz, K., & Welsh, M. (2005). Motetrack: A robust, decentralized approach to RF-based location tracking. In *Proceedings of International Workshop on Location- and Context-Awareness (LoCA 2005)*, Oberpfaffenhofen, Germany.

Mutukrishnan, K., Lijding, M., & Havinga, P. (2005). Towards smart surroundings: Enabling techniques and technologies for localization. In *LoCA 2005: Proceedings of Location- and Context-Awareness: First International Workshop*, Oberpfaffenhofen, Germany.

Savvides, A., Han, C. C., & Srivastava, M. B. (2001). Dynamic fine-grained localization in ad-hoc networks of sensors. In *Proceedings ACM MobiCom 2001*, Rome, Italy.

Tmote Sky Datasheet. (2006). *Mote IV Corporation*. Retrieved from http://www.moteiv.com/products/docs/tmote-skydatasheet.pdf

Wang, J., An, X., Prasad, R. V., & Niemegeers, I. (2006). A range-free online person tracking system. In *Proceedings of the First International Conference on Pervasive Computing Technologies for Healthcare*, Innsbruck, Austria.

Yu, K., & Oppermann, I. (2004). Performance of UWB position estimation based on time-of-arrival measurements. In *UWBST: Proceedings of IEEE Conference on Ultra wideband System and Technology*, Kyoto, Japan.

Zhao, J., & Govindan, R. (2003). Understanding packet delivery performance in dense wireless sensor networks. In *Proceedings ACM SenSys '03*, Los Angeles, CA, USA.

ENDNOTE

[1]   *Corresponding author*

Chapter 14
Deployment of a Wireless Mesh Network for Traffic Control

Kun-chan Lan
National Cheng Kung University, Taiwan

Zhe Wang
University of New South Wales, Australia

Mahbub Hassan
University of New South Wales, Australia

Tim Moors
University of New South Wales, Australia

Rodney Berriman
National ICT Australia, Australia

Lavy Libman
National ICT Australia, Australia

Maximilian Ott
National ICT Australia, Australia

Bjorn Landfeldt
National ICT Australia, Australia

Zainab Zaidi
National ICT Australia, Australia

Ching-Ming Chou
National Cheng Kung University, Taiwan

ABSTRACT

Wireless mesh networks (WMN) have attracted considerable interest in recent years as a convenient, new technology. However, the suitability of WMN for mission-critical infrastructure applications remains by and large unknown, as protocols typically employed in WMN are, for the most part, not designed for real-time communications. In this chapter, the authors describe a wireless mesh network architecture to solve the communication needs of the traffic control system in Sydney. This system, known as SCATS and used in over 100 cities around the world — from individual traffic light controllers to regional computers and the central TMC —places stringent requirements on the reliability and latency of the data exchanges. The authors discuss experience in the deployment of an initial testbed consisting of 7 mesh nodes placed at intersections with traffic lights, and share the results and insights learned from measurements and initial trials in the process.

DOI: 10.4018/978-1-4666-1797-1.ch014

Copyright © 2012, IGI Global. Copying or distributing in print or electronic forms without written permission of IGI Global is prohibited.

INTRODUCTION

Adaptive traffic control systems are employed in cities worldwide to improve the efficiency of traffic flows, reduce average travel times and benefit the environment via a reduction in fuel consumption. One of the main and most common functions of such systems lies in adaptive control of traffic lights. This ranges from simple lengthening or shortening of green and red light durations in an intersection according to the actual presence of cars in the respective lanes, to coordination of green light phases among neighboring intersections on main thoroughfares. This adaptivity is made possible with the use of sensors (typically in the form of magnetic loop detectors embedded under the road pavement) that feed data to roadside traffic light controllers, and a communications infrastructure that connects among the intersections and a traffic management centre, as well as, in some cases (typically in large cities), a hierarchy of regional computers (RC) that perform the control decisions for respective portions of the system.

Traditionally, the communications layer of traffic control systems has been based on wired connections, either private or leased from public telecommunications operators. While for many years such leased lines (operating at 300bps) have served their purpose well, they have several shortcomings, such as a significant operating cost, inflexibility, and difficulty of installation in new sites. In certain cases, alternative solutions, operating over public infrastructure, have been deployed for specific sites where private or leased lines were not a viable option; these ranged from ADSL, regular dialup, or cellular (GPRS). However, using public network for traffic control could suffer from inconsistent delay jitters and reliability issues. For example, previous experimental studies (Chakravorty, 2002) have shown GRPS links could have very high RTTs (>1000ms), fluctuating bandwidths and occasional link outages.

In recent years, there has been considerable interest in wireless mesh networks and their deployment in metropolitan areas, from both a commercial and a research perspective (Lundgren, 2006). Trials in several major cities in the US (e.g., Philadelphia, New Orleans, Tropos networks (http://www.tropos.com), and Locust world (http://www.locustworld.com)) and worldwide (e.g., M-Taiwan (http://www.nici.nat.gov.tw/content/application/nici/english/)) have shown mesh networks to be a viable technology that can compete well with alternative "last-mile" connectivity solutions to the public. Correspondingly, most of the research on metropolitan-area wireless mesh networks (MAWMN) has focused on maximising the throughput that can be extracted from them, in the anticipation that their major use will be public, for purposes such as accessing the Internet or conducting voice calls (Ganguly, 2006). On the other hand, little attention has been directed to the aspects of reliability and latency, which are most important if MAWMN are to be considered for replacement of mission-critical infrastructure, such as traffic control system communications.

In this chapter, we describe a testbed (Lan, 2007) that has been built with a goal to develop protocols that enhance the reliability and reduce the latency of mesh networks, and thereby enable them to be used as the communications layer of traffic control systems. Our initial testbed covers seven traffic lights in the suburban area of Sydney. These intersections are chosen because they represent a typical suburban area with lots of traffic, foliages, pedestrians and high-rise residential buildings. In addition, the inter-node distance (ranging from 200 to-500m) is representative of 90% of the distance between traffic controllers in the Sydney CBD (Central Business District) area. The nodes have been custom-built to meet the need of research.

In this chapter, we describe the first efforts to study the feasibility of using wireless mesh networking for traffic control and the details of testbed implementation and some experiences we gained during the deployment of the testbed in an urban environment. We also present some initial measurement study of link characteristics of different wireless and wired technologies used in our testbed (including the use of 900MHz, 2.4GHz and 3.5GHz radios and Ethernet-over-powerline). Although these results are still very preliminary, they are useful to serve as a reality check toward the goal of applying wireless mesh networking to traffic control applications.

SCATS OVER WIRELESS

In this section, we first describe the details of SCATS (Sydney Coordinated Adaptive Traffic System) and its communication requirements. We then discuss the benefits and research challenges when running SCATS on a wireless mesh network.

The SCATS Traffic Management System

Developed and maintained by the Roads and Traffic Authority (RTA, formerly Department of Main Roads) of the state of New South Wales, the Sydney Coordinated Adaptive Traffic System (SCATS) is one of the most popular traffic management systems used worldwide. Its main task is to adjust, in real time, signal timings in response to variations in traffic demand and system capacity. Real-time data from traffic controllers are collected and transported to a central traffic management centre (TMC) for analysis and optimum control of road traffic. The performance of SCATS, therefore, depends critically on the capabilities of the underlying communication system that transports roadside data to and from the TMC.

The existing communication system of SCATS relies strongly on third-party wired infrastructure (provided by Telstra, Australia's largest telco). The bulk of the communications to the intersections, namely the traffic light controllers and vehicle detectors, are predominantly made using serial point-to-point connections over standard voice-grade telephone lines, using 300bps modems. This is also the most common method of connecting between the TMC and other low bandwidth devices, including variable message signs, variable speed limits, ramp meters, and over-height detectors. At the core of the SCATS operation is a periodic exchange of messages between the controlling computer and each and every intersection (via the point-to-point links). This exchange happens every 1sec, and is initiated by the computer which sends to the intersection's local controller a command message, instructing it about the next phase it should switch to and the timing of that switch. The controller, in turn, is required to reply with an acknowledgement, which includes information from the intersection's sensors. If an acknowledgement is not received within 1sec from the time the command message is sent, it is retried once; after the second time an acknowledgement fails to arrive, the communications link is declared failed, and SCATS instructs all controllers at the respective cluster of intersections to fall back into a 'default' self-controlling mode, where decisions about the timing of green light phases are made locally and independently. Likewise, a controller will fall back to this mode upon not receiving a command message. Once triggered, a controller will stay in the self-controlling mode for at least 15 minutes; if another communications failure happens during this time, the duration of this mode will be extended by another 15 minutes, and so on. Obviously, the self-controlling mode, where the decisions at intersections are uncoordinated, can lead to a severely suboptimal traffic control, particularly in a busy thoroughfare during rush hour. Accordingly, though the bandwidth required from the communication links is quite low (comfortably handled by 300bps modems), the 1sec latency is critical for an efficient operation of the system.

The currently used SCATS infrastructure, based on wired communications, suffers from the following problems:

- **Slow Installation and Inflexibility:** In most cases, installing a new line at a road site (especially a remote site) involves earth excavation, which is very slow and with adverse effects on existing infrastructure.
- **High Capital and Operating Cost:** The installation of a wired connection at a new site, or repairs at an existing one, carries a high cost due to the material and labour required. More importantly, the ongoing fees for leasing the wires from the telephone company run very high; currently, RTA pays nearly A$40 million annually to Telstra in leasing fees for connecting the traffic signals and other roadside devices to SCATS.
- **Low Bandwidth:** Modem-based leased lines support bandwidth less than 32 Kbps. While these low-bandwidth telephone lines are adequate for connecting traffic signal sensors, they cannot provide adequate support for connecting high-bandwidth applications, e.g. high-resolution video cameras, that increasingly becoming necessary to effectively monitor traffic pattern on our roads.

Going Wireless

With wireless solutions, there is no cabling involved. Wireless can therefore provide fast installation and exceptional flexibility. Cost can be reduced significantly by building a private wireless network, because there will be no monthly charges to be paid to telephone company (some small license fee may apply). Moreover, the installation cost will be low because there will be no cabling-related labour. The cost issue is, in fact, the major concern for most road authorities as well as the main factor that motivated RTA and us to start this work. Finally, it should be noted that recent advances in wireless technology provide bandwidth that is more than adequate for con-

necting many high-resolution roadside cameras to SCATS.

One possible option for going wireless is to build a dedicated RTA wireless network using widely available, standards-based, low-cost wireless technologies, e.g. IEEE 802.11x and 802.16x. 802.11x equipment is cheaper, less complex, and operates entirely in the unlicensed spectrum (no licensing fee). On the other hand, 802.16x is more reliable (has multiple carrier frequencies to avoid interference), has longer range, and better features to cater for a diverse range of communication needs of future roadside equipment. In addition, it is possible to operate 802.16x in both license and unlicensed spectrums.

Despite of its enormous benefits, there are several challenges when roadside ITS equipment are connected via wireless media:

- **Latency:** Wireless can potentially increase latency. For example, IEEE 802.11x, uses a common wireless channel (it is cheaper to share channel) among many contending devices causing potential conflict. To avoid such conflicts, some form of medium access control (MAC) is implemented by these technologies. MAC introduces some delay before data can be transmitted on the wireless channel.
- **Reliability:** Wireless signals are susceptible to interference from other signals in the vicinity operating in the same or adjacent spectrum. Given that ITS equipment is deployed in public area, such interference will be the norm rather than exception. Interference can corrupt messages transmitted over the wireless medium. Some frequencies do not work well (or at all) if there is no direct line-of-sight between the two communicating end points. In a dynamic context of public roads, roadside equipment may frequently face line-of-sight problems due to transient obstructions, e.g. a high vehicle carrying a

tall crane etc. Also in vehicle-to-roadside communications, a car in the near-lane may obstruct communication between a far-lane car and the roadside equipment. Temporary outages, i.e., periods when no wireless signal is available, therefore, is a real issue to deal with.

- **Security:** What makes wireless so vulnerable is the fact that the attacker does not have to gain physical access to the channel from any predefined access point. Roadside wireless components are well within the wireless range of passing motorists and pedestrians, which make them vulnerable to intrusion, denial of service, and other forms of security threats.

- **Scalability:** As mentioned earlier, wireless systems are sensitive to interference from other communicating devices operating in the vicinity. Additionally, if a common wireless channel is shared among all devices within a given area (cell), the MAC delay increases rapidly as the number of competing devices increases. Another scalability issue arises from the processing overhead that is required at a central radio base-station. The more remote radios there are in communication with the central radio, the more processing that must take place. The radio controller at the base-station will simply not be able to process all incoming radio signals if there are too many of them.

RELATED WORK

Roofnet (Bicket, 2005; Sombrutzki, 2006) are an experimental 802.11b/g mesh network built by MIT and humboldt university. Each node in Roofnet has an antenna installed on the roof of a building. Aguayo *et al.* (Aguayo, 2004) analyzed the link-layer behavior on the Roofnet testbed and described the impact of distance, SNR and trans-mission rate on the packet loss. While Roofnet's propagation environment is characterized by its strong Line-of-Sight component, our work differs from the prior work in that our links are generally heavily obstructed[1]. In addition, our planned deployment strategy is different from the unplanned topology in Roofnet.

Similar to our work, The WAND project (Weber, 2003) has built a multi-hop wireless testbed in the centre of Dublin. They have 11 nodes mounted on traffic lights along a 2km route in urban area. However, their topology is simpler than ours (i.e., a chain topology) and the measurements they performed on their testbed were relatively limited.

TFA project (Camp, 2006) aimed to provide broadband access to low income community in Houston area via wireless mesh network technology. Their architecture consist of two wireless tiers: an access tier to connect homes, businesses, and mobile users to the infrastructure, and a backhaul tier to forward traffic to and from the wired entry point. The architecture of two wireless tiers is widely used in community mesh network such as (Sombrutzki, 2006; Ishmael 2008).

Jardosh *et al.* (Jardosh, 2005) discussed the correlation of link reliability with the frame retransmissions, frame sizes and data rate by collecting trace data from a structured 802.11b network during an international conference. They concluded that sending smaller frames and using higher data rates with a fewer number of frames improves the performance of congested network. Gupta *et al.* (Gupta, 2009) built a testbed based on 802.11b/g structures in IIT Bombay to observe link qualities using different received signal strength indications (RSSIs) and data rates. This testbed has 9 nodes with links varying from 90 m to 1.2 km. This work built a radio map to help the link planning of 802.11g mesh network. Since our work directly deployed nodes on traffic lights, in order to increase system reliability, we employed multi-radio systems (Adya, 2004) for back-haul connection to increase capacity and flexibility of a traffic control system.

All the previous studies have been centered around maximization of available bandwidth for non-real-time applications such as broadband access for the general public. On the other hand, to the best of our knowledge, our work is the first to focus on using wireless mesh networking for traffic control, which places stringent requirements on the reliability and latency of the data exchanges.

AN INTRODUCTION TO WIRELESS MESH NETWORK

Wireless communication is no doubt a very desirable service as demonstrated by the tremendous growth in both cellular and wireless local area networks (WLANs) (primarily, the ones that are compliant with the IEEE 802.11 family of standards, widely known as Wi-Fi). However, these two radically different technologies address only one part of the spectrum of connectivity needs, and there are many other applications that can benefit from wireless connectivity. The cellular networks offer wide area coverage, but the service is in general expensive and offers low data rates: even the third generation of cellular networks (3G) only offers at best up to 2Mbps which is low as compared to WLANs (>50Mbps for IEEE 802.11a and 802.11g and 100Mbps for 802.11n). On the other hand, the WLANs have rather limited coverage which typically is less than a couple of hundred meters (and therefore poor support for mobility). Furthermore, in order to increase the coverage of WLANs, a wired backbone connecting multiple access points is a must. Wireless metropolitan area networks (WMANs) (e.g., the family of IEEE 802.16 standards or long term evolution [LTE]), was proposed to bridge this gap, offering high data rates with guaranteed QoS to a potentially large customer base (theoretically can cover up to tens of miles from the base station). The main problem with WMANs such as 802.16d is their poor mobility support and the line of sight (LOS) requirement: if a customer does not have a clear LOS to the WMAN base station, it is very like that he quality of service is poor. In an urban environment when a high density of obstructions (high-rise buildings or trees) exist, many customers cannot be served due to the LOS requirement.

In its simplest form, a wireless mesh network (WMN) connects a stationary base stations as well as mobile clients and optionally provides access to the Internet. The unique characteristic of a WMN is that the nodes at the core of the network can collaborate with the other nodes and forward the data to and from the clients in a multi-hop fashion. In that aspect, WMN is a subset of the well-known mobile ad hoc network (MANET). Beyond the multi-hop requirement, there are no other restrictions on the design of a WMN, which offers considerable flexibility and versatility. This versatility allowed many companies to enter the mesh networking market with different products and applications. For example, the Internet access links can be wired (e.g., T1, Ethernet, etc.) or wireless (either point to point or point to multipoint). Some WMN technologies have been proposed for high-speed mobility (100mph), some for casual roaming in a small area, while others are only meant to be used by stationary clients. The wireless links used to connect the mobile clients can be of the same type as the intra-mesh wireless links or can be a completely different technology. Many different implementations allow mobile nodes to connect to the WMN while the nodes are in the radio range; their packets can be forwarded in the same multi-hop manner as the ones of the stationary nodes (similarly, although not always preferable, the mobile nodes can also forward packets on behalf of other nodes). Not all nodes have to support client nodes; the service provider can employ several relay nodes to increase the coverage of the wireless mesh network or to improve its performance, as the relays can allow some clients to reach their destinations in fewer hops (theoretically more hops could reduce the available bandwidth for the client).

Due to their versatility, WMNs can efficiently satisfy the needs of many different applications. Today, most of the Internet broadband connections rely either on cable or digital subscriber lines (DSL) (satellite connection is another option, but it is typically far more expensive). Unfortunately, a significant percentage of the population (especially in a large rural environments like some villages in India or China, but also in large cities, even in some developed countries) do not have the necessary broadband infrastructure (either through TV cable or a good quality phone cable) to connect the home computers to the Internet. Furthermore, installing the required infrastructure (in particular, installing new cables) is prohibitively expensive and labor-consuming even for the largest Internet Service Providers (ISPs). Several ISP companies realized the potential of WMNs as an Internet access solution and has produced a broad range of related products to support WMNs. WMNs offer considerable advantages as another option for an Internet broadband access technology such as low upfront investments, large customer coverage, fast deployment and high reliability.

Since there are no need to install any cable, the significant upfront investments typically associated with building the infrastructure for cable and DSL services can be bypassed. A bare-bones WMN providing minimal coverage can be used to service the seeding customers; and as the number of customers gradually increases, the network can be upgraded incrementally. In addition, due to the WMN's multi-hop routing ability, the requirement to have line of sight to a single base station is less serious here; as long as a client has connectivity to any other client, it can obtain Internet access through the forwarding of the other client. Many field tests have shown that, especially for scenarios with significant obstructions such as trees or high-rise buildings, WMN can significantly improve the radio coverage in comparison with a point-to-multipoint (e.g., IEEE 802.16) solution. Furthermore, adding a new client to an existing WMN can take several hours instead of several

months, the typical delay for installing new wires for cable or DSL service. Finally, when multiple gateways are used, all single point-of-failures are eliminated and the reliability of the network can be improved. A responsive routing protocol can quickly detect the failure and route around failed links or nodes; and, in the case of a gateway failure, it can dynamically redistribute the orphaned nodes to neighboring gateways.

The popularity of IEEE 802.11 compatible WLANs also showed one of its most unpleasant aspects of this technology: in order to provide coverage to all the buildings, multiple access points (APs) are required in each of the building. In addition, all of these access points (AP) have to be connected to a distribution system (typically a wired network), commonly a wired Ethernet network. To overcome this restriction, several companies leveraged the multi-hop capabilities of WMNs to eliminate the need for deploying cables. In such a deployment, at least one of the WMN routers can be connected to the external network (such as the Internet) and, hence, becomes a gateway. All of the other WMN routers can be used as APs and forward the data from (and to) the wireless clients to the gateway. Another form of WMN is formed by using the bridging features of some models of commercial access points which offer the capability to forward each others' packets. The main problems for these types of products are the potentially larger number of required APs and the APs have to be in the wireless range of each other. Furthermore, because all of the APs have to be on the same channel (to be able to forward each other's data) and, due to forwarding induced inefficiencies, the resulting network capacity can be several times smaller than the capacity of a traditional WLAN. Theoretically, the network capacity will become smaller as more number of hops are required to forward the data to the destination. To mitigate these problems, some company proposed to replace the numerous wired APs with only a few larger, more powerful (and also more expensive) APs and locate them at the *exterior* of the building. In addition, to increase its network capacity, many new features are added to these powerful APs. For example, these wireless routers typically use directional antennas to increase signal power as well as reduce the interference. Multiple radios are also employed to efficiently utilize the entire 2.4 GHz ISM band.

The third generation of cellular systems, known as 3G, claim to be able to offer relatively high-speed connections (up to 2Mbps for static users and 144kbps for highly mobile users in a macro cell). However, full deployment of 3G, especially in the rural area, will take several years to happen. In the mean time, some mobile users seeking Internet connectivity when outside the sparse coverage of WLAN hot spots have to settle for the slow GPRS connection (usually 20-30kbps - theoretical maximum 171.2kbps). For example, many bus and traffic light systems in the world today still use GPRS to report bus schedule and traffic light information. A properly designed WMNs can easily provide higher bandwidth than the current best 3G technology. For example, the Mesh Networks (http://www.themeshnet.com) was one of the first companies that demonstrates connectivity and seamless handovers are possible at highway speeds. Thus, all of the support of 3G technology (bandwidth, mobility, and voice quality) can be accommodated by WMNs with lower upfront investments as discussed previously (and possibly without expensive spectrum licenses, which as a result, can reduce the operation cost). This makes WMNs a serious competitor to 3G cellular systems.

Sometimes, providing network connectivity can be cumbersome, expensive, time consuming or unsightly. As an example, Firetide (http://www.firetide.com) is one of the companies that constructs WMNs specifically focus on providing connectivity. Each of their WMN routers have an available Ethernet port; all WMN routers form a wireless "cloud" that can be seen from outside as one big Ethernet switch. In their design, the Internet access and mobile user access are optional (for example, IEEE 802.11 APs can be connected to the WMN nodes if WLAN coverage is desired). The main advantages of their products, when compared with traditional Ethernet wiring are: (1) If fast deployment is required (e.g., a quick deployment of a access network in conferences, shows, etc.), plugging WMN routers in the power sockets in the appropriate places is all that is needed in order to obtain network connectivity. Furthermore, even if fast deployment is not required, many large companies cannot afford to shut down for wires to be installed (e.g., a network in the airport). (2) In many place, people might not be able to endure the sighting of ugly wires associated with Ethernet networks (e.g., hotel lobbies, show halls, airports, and so on.). Moreover, in some buildings (e.g., historic), drilling holes for the networking cables is not allowed altogether. Using WMNs can avoid all these troubles.

A SIMPLE ANALYSIS OF THE SYDNEY TRAFFIC LIGHT TOPOLOGY

This analysis was based on data provided by RTA, indicating the latitude and longitude of traffic controllers. Figure 1a shows points at each traffic controller location. There are around 70 controllers in a 4km × 6km area.

To understand the effect of radio range on the degree of connectivity when the traffic controllers are forming a mesh network, we calculate the shortest distance (assuming that the radio has a circular radio range and have perfect coverage in that range) between every pair of traffic controllers, and the output was then sorted so that for each controller, its neighbours were listed (from nearest to furthest) with the distance to each neighbour. We then processed this data to deter-

Figure 1. Simple analysis case in Sydney

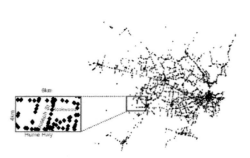

(a) Location of traffic controllers.

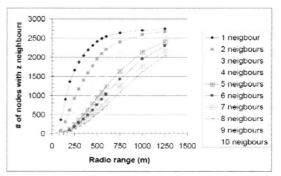

(b) Numbers of neighbours within certain radio range of RTA controllers.

mine how many neighbours of each traffic controller were within a specified range (from 100m to 1250m). The results of this analysis are shown in Figure 1b, which shows on the y-axis how many traffic controllers had 0, 1, 2, 3, . . . neighbours when a given radio range is assumed (x-axis).

The results shown in Figure 1b provide a rough indication of what radio range is needed if we are aiming to interconnect a certain number of nodes with each node having a certain degree (number of neighbours within range). For example, if we seek to interconnect 90% of the nodes (accepting that some alternative technology may be needed for the minority 10% of nodes) and require that each node has three neighbours (to provide redundancy and hence fault tolerance), then we require a radio technology with range of at least 1km. Note that, while city environments may have large densities of traffic controllers in both (lat/long) dimensions, in suburban environments controllers (particularly those that are important to synchronise with communication links) often lie linearly along main arterial roads, with few controllers in close range orthogonal to the main arteries. Neighbours that form a line would not provide the same level of fault tolerance as those that are better separated angularly around a controller, since the links are less likely to fail independently.

TESTBED

In this section, we provide the details of our testbed. We first describe the environment that the testbed is located. Next, the hardware used for the initial seven nodes and the software installed on each of these nodes are discussed.

Environment

The testbed is located in the Sydney CBD (Central Business District) area. We selected seven intersections initially to deploy the testbed, as shown in Figure 2a (specifically, intersection number m1 to m7). We plan to extend our testbed to 15-20 nodes in the next phase. We use a number of custom-build embedded PCs with multiple wireless interfaces. The nodes are mounted on the traffic lights at a height of about 2-3m from the ground, and distributed along the streets in the form of rectangle covering an area of 500 × 1000 square metres at a distance of 200-500m apart.

None of the nodes is in a clear line of sights of its neighboring nodes. The node at intersection m1 is connected to a gateway node in University of Sydney.

The streets where the network is deployed are about 10- 20m wide and surrounded by building

Figure 2. The scenario of testbed deployment

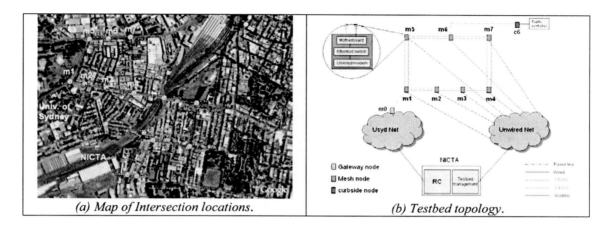

(a) Map of Intersection locations.   *(b) Testbed topology.*

at least two stories high. The majority of these buildings are made of concrete and steel that block the propagation of radio signals into the neighboring streets. All these streets have busy public traffic during business hours. Most of the vehicles on the street have a height of less than 2.5m. But some double-decker buses (such as Sydney Explorer Bus) or truck can have a height of more than 5m.

Channel Characteristics

Wireless channels can be coarsely characterized by its path loss exponent. Path loss described the attenuation experienced by a wireless signal as a function of distance. The amount of variations in path loss between similar propagation scenarios is called shadowing. In other words, shadowing represents the difference between the signal power at different points in the same environment with the same estimated path loss. Prior study (Rapport, 1996) showed that shadowing can be modeled as a zero-mean Gaussian random variable. Specifically, one can predict the received signal power at a given distance d with the following formula:

$$P_{dBm}\left(d\right) = P_{dBm}\left(d_0\right) - 10\alpha \log_{10}\left(\frac{d}{d_0}\right) + \varepsilon$$

where α is the path loss exponent, ε is the shadowing and d_0 is the reference distance.

The prior work (Rapport, 1996) suggested that the path loss can range from 2 to 5 for outdoor urban environment. To accurately estimate the range and reliability of mesh links, we performed extensive measurements at various locations and distances to find our environment's path loss exponent and shadowing. Such physical level measurements are important for an efficient deployment (i.e., overestimating path loss can result in overprovisioning network while underestimating path loss can produce disconnected network). By using linear regression, we find our environment has a path loss α =3.1 and shadowing ε = 7.2. Note that the observed path loss in our environment is significantly lower than the suggested urban path loss of 4 in the literature (Rapport, 1996).

Hardware

The hardware components used for the nodes of our initial testbed are all off-the-shelf products

Figure 3. Hardware component

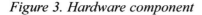

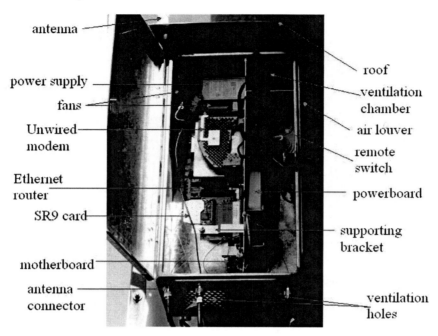

including the following, as shown in Figure 3. All the components are mounted on two sides of a metal plate for easy maintenance (for example, we can simply swap an old plate with a new plate when we want to upgrade the node). A custom-built enclosure is made to house this component plate.

- **Motherboard:** A VIA MB720F Mini-ITX motherboard featuring an 1GHz processor and 1G memory is employed as the core in our system.
- **Storage:** The traffic pole sometimes vibrates a lot due to the passing traffic. Since that our node is mounted on a traffic pole, instead of using a hard-drive, we employ a 2G USB flash drive for storing OS and data. Unlike a hard-drive, a flash drive does not have a highspeed spinning platter and is less failure-prone.
- **Wireless Interfaces:** Each node has two wireless interfaces to connect to its neighboring nodes, as shown in Figure 2b. To

allow the testbed users to experiment with different radio technologies, two different radio frequencies are currently used on our testbed: 2.4GHz (802.11b/g) and 900MHz radios. Specifically, the nodes at intersection m2, m3 and m6 are installed with two 2.4GHz mini-PCI wireless cards from Ubiquiti (SR2). The nodes at intersections m1 and m5 are equipped with one 2.4GHz Ubiquiti SR2 card (with a transmission power of 400mW) and one 900MHz Ubiquiti SR9 card (with a transmission power of 700mW). Finally, the nodes at intersections m4 and m7 are installed with two Ubiquiti SR2 cards. One of these two SR2 cards is connected to a 2.4GHz-to-900MHz converter (from RFlinx) to send 2.4GHz signal output by the wireless card on 900MHz band. Due to its better penetration rate for buildings and trees, theoretically the use of 900MHz radios could result in a better connectivity than 2.4GHz radios (i.e., 802.11x). Hence, we decided to install 900MHz radios on the nodes for intersection pairs m1-m5 and m4-m7. These two intersection pairs have a longer distance (i.e., 400m and 500m respectively) than the other intersection pairs.

- **Back-Haul Connection:** In addition to the two Ubiquiti wireless cards, each node is equipped an "Unwired" modem (http://www.unwired.com.au/) to establish a back-haul link for the purpose of remote management, as shown in Figure 2b. Unwired is a Sydney-based metropolitan wireless ISP. The Unwired modem uses a proprietary protocol but claims to be a variant of WiMAX and operates in a licensed 3.5GHz band.

- **Ethernet Router:** A Linux-based Ethernet router (Diamond Digital R100) is installed in each node. We employ this Ethernet router for several purposes. First, it is used as an Ethernet switch to connect the motherboard and the Unwired modem (and any IP-based devices such as a camera in the future). The Unwired modem is connected to the WAN port of the router, thus the router get a public Internet IP address. The motherboard has an Ethernet connection with the router's 4-port switch. Second, the Diamond Digital router has an USB port which allow the motherboard to have a serial connection with the router's USB port through an USB-to-serial adapter. Being able to establish a serial link to the motherboard allows the user to remotely login into the serial console for troubleshooting when the Ubiquiti wireless interfaces are not responding. Third, given that the router is a Linux box itself (runs on openWRT), we can run all the existing software (e.g., we are currently running DNS, NTP and VPN clients on it). Finally, the Diamond Digital router has an 802.11 wireless interface which can be used as an alternative

link to remotely connect the mesh node in addition to Unwired and Ubiquiti links.

- **Power:** As shown in Figure 3, we use an off-the-shelf power-board (with surge protector and fuse) and a PC power-supply to provide the power to all the components in the node. The power-board takes a 240AC power from the traffic light.

- **Antenna:** Nodes on our testbed are all installed with omni-directional antennas due to the following
  - **Cost:** An omni-directional antenna is typically cheaper than a directional antenna. In addition, for a node which has n neighbors, n directional antennas are needed. On the other hand, one omni-directional antenna per intersection is sufficient to cover all the neighbors.
  - **Mounting:** The space on the traffic light for the mounting of antennas is quite limited. It is comparatively more difficult to mount a directional antenna on the traffic pole in practice.

- We use an 8dBi omni-directional antenna for the 2.4GHz wireless card and an 6dBi omni-directional antenna for the 900MHz wireless card.

- **Weatherproof:** The temperature in the summer can be above 40 Celsius degree in Sydney. The temperature inside the node can be even higher. As shown in Figure 3, to provide enough air circulation inside the node, we drilled many holes on the bottom of the enclosure and made some air louvres on the side. Two temperature-controlled fans are used in the node to dissipate the hot air out through the louvres. In addition, we mount a roof on top of the enclosure to shield the enclosure from direct sunlight and rain.

- **Remote Recovery:** Due to the fact that the testbed is deployed in an outdoor environment, it is time consuming to visit the nodes when something goes wrong. In addition, given that our nodes are mounted on the traffic lights which is a public asset, visiting any node on the testbed required calling out the RTA maintenance crew to gain access to the node. Therefore, some means of remote recovery are necessary. Currently, we have one wireless remote switch installed on each node (runs in the unlicensed 433MHz band), which allows us to reboot the node on-site when accessing the node via the 2.4GHz or 3.5GHz links fails.

The ultimate goal is to control traffic lights using wireless mesh networks. However, due to practical consideration, we do not connect the mesh node directly to the real traffic controller initially. A "dummy" traffic controller board is used instead. The main difference between the real traffic controller and the dummy traffic controller is that the data coming from the dummy traffic controller is fake data (and not the real sensor data coming from the road-side sensor). A pair of power-over- Ethernet adapters (Netcomm NP285) are used to connect the node to a dummy traffic controller board in the curbside housing through the powerline. The dummy traffic controller board sends and receives data via a serial interface. Hence, a serial-to-IP conversion is required for the communication between the dummy traffic controller and the testbed (which runs IP). We mount the traffic controller board inside an embedded PC and connect the traffic controller board to the embedded PC's motherboard's (VIA MB770F) serial port. A serial-to-IP converter software is written and run on the PC to encasuplate the SCATS data from the serial port of the traffic controller board into an IP packet as well as to descapsulate the IP packet from the regional computer and send its payload to the serial interface.

In order to connect the testbed to the regional computer which is located at our facility, we deploy a gateway node at University of Sydney.

The gateway node has a reasonable line-of-sight to intersection m1 and connects to the m1 node with a 802.11 link. Note that we do not use the Unwired links to connect the regional computer (RC) to the testbed due to the consideration of reliability, latency and cost issues. More details about the characteristics of Unwired links are described later. The RC is connected to the gateway node via AARNet (http://www.aarnet.edu.au/). The round-trip delay between RC and the gateway is about 1.2ms, and the throughput is typically over 100Mbps.

Software

We use a custom-built Linux OS image that consists of the following components:

- The image size is small enough to be fit into an USB flash drive. And run completely in RAM (1GB). This allows us to enable 'clean' reboots uncontaminated by previous experiments.
- We add some kernel modifications for various driver support for USB, madwifi and PXE reboot.
- We modify Grub to activate the watchdog timer at the time of boot-loading so that the watchdog timer can be started before any program start. Watchdog timer is used to reboot the motherboard when the system fails.
- We include various tools including timesync, Open- VPN, some network support tools and software from Orbit project (Raychaudhuri, 2005) in our image. The image is built to be Debian-based for the compatibility with Orbit software.

We build our OS image based on DSL-N (http://www.damnsmalllinux.org/dsl-n/). DSL-N provides most of the software support we need out of the box. The default syslinux bootloader of DSL-N is replaced with grub. We use OML

Figure 4. Observation round-trip delay

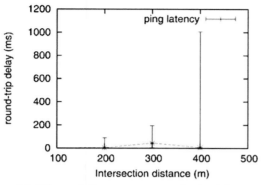

(a) Effect of distance on round-trip delay.   *(b) Latency of powerline communication.*

software (Singh, 2005) from Orbit project to build the measurement collection infrastructure for the testbed. Two security mechanism is currently implemented on our testbed. First, OpenVPN is used for the Unwired links to each of the mesh nodes. Second, ssh and friends are used on all network interfaces. We plan to implement host-based and certificate-based access in the next phase. In addition, root access is disabled on all the machines.

LINK CHARACTERISTCS

In this section, we describe some preliminary results of measured link characteristics from the testbed. Specifically, we discuss some statistics of the wireless link performance in terms of round-trip delay, loss and throughput. We use ping to measure the round-trip delay and iperf for the throughput measurement.

Link Latency

The round-trip delay increases as the number of hops increases on the 802.11 links. In addition, the variation also increases significantly when there are more hops. We do not observe such a strong correlation between distance and link latency though. As shown in Figure 4a, the latency does not increase from 300m to 400m. However, the variation increase significantly as the distance increases. One possibility is that there are more retries at 300m than at 400m due to different line-of-sight conditions. We are currently investigating this issue. We next examine the efficiency of powerline communication. As suggested in Figure 4b, given a distance of 100m, the link latency of powerline communication is excellent. The average round-delay is about 3.6ms and the variations are very small. In addition, the largest delay for such a distance is less than 8ms.

As previously mentioned, we use the Unwired network to carry out our back-haul traffic. To understand the expected latency of running management traffic over the Unwired network, we measured the round-trip delay to the mesh node. As shown in Figure 5a, the average delay of sending traffic over the Unwired network to the mesh node is about 400ms. However, there is a large variation (the delay can be as long as 3 seconds) and significant number of outages. We find that the delay and outages over the Unwired network are mostly contributed by the wireless link between the mesh node and the Unwired base station. As shown in Figure 5b, the average delay of the

Figure 5. Round-trip delay over the unwired network

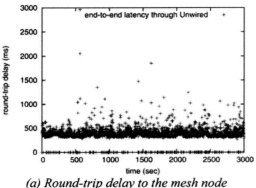

(a) Round-trip delay to the mesh node

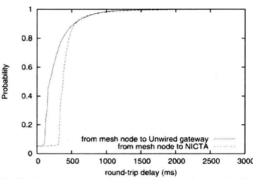

(b) CDF comparison between the end-to-end delay and the Unwired wireless link delay (from mesh node to Unwired gateway)

Figure 6. Effect of number of hops on consecutive packet loss

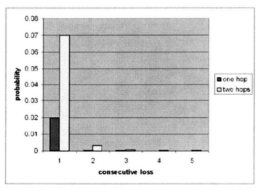

(a) Effect of number of hops on consecutive packet loss.

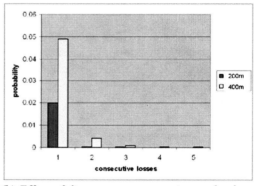

(b) Effect of distance on consecutive packet loss.

Unwired wireless link is about 200ms. The large delay variations and significant number of outages suggest that a public-shared wireless network like Unwired is not suitable for operating SCATS traffic.

Losses

As shown in Figure 6, the packet loss seems to be distributed uniformly over time. However, the loss becomes more bursty as the number of hops

and distance increase. Note that Figure 6 is based on the results from a low probing rate (i.e., one-packet-per-second ping). The loss pattern might change if we change the probing rate. In addition, we do not find there is a strong correlation between packet loss and the distance. The line-of-sight condition (which is location-dependent) plays a more important role on the packet loss. We find the use of 900MHz radio results in a much lower loss rate (0.5%) than 2.4GHz radio (20%), which is not surprising though since 900MHz radio have a better penetration rate than 2.4GHz radio. Finally, for a distance of 100m, the loss rate of powerline communication is almost negligible (less than 0.1%).

Throughput

As shown in Figure 7, the use of 900MHz radio results in a better throughput than when 2.4GHz radio is employed, even for a longer distance. However, we also observe there is a larger variation when using 900MHz radio, which might be due to MAC-layer retransmission. The throughput of Ethernet-over-powerline communication is very stable and typically maintained at about 600Kps.

Discussion

In this work, we built a testbed using off-the-shelf hardware within unlicensed bands. However, our initial results are somewhat discouraging since our system does not perform to the requirements of a traffic control system. Specifically, based on Figure 4a, the dimension of the network will not be able to scale up to more than 20-hop assuming an average delay of 50ms. In addition, as shown in Figure 6a, the loss is pretty significant (2% for 1-hop and 7% for 2-hop) as compared to the typi-

Figure 7. Comparison of throughput for different technologies

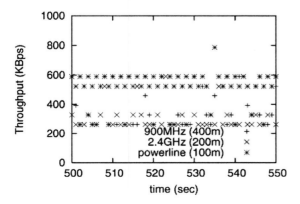

cal loss rate that one will see on a wired network. Needless to say, there are many research challenges that need to be addressed before our mesh network can be used in a live system for traffic control. We are currently developing innovative multi-path routing and cross-layer techniques to address these issues.

EXPERIENCES

In this section, we discuss some experiences we gained in terms of the deployment and maintenance of our testbed in an urban environment.

Deployment

- **Hardware:** We observed that many antenna connectors were held on by weak glue or crimp. Gradual stress (e.g., vibration) could eventually loosen the plug and degrade the signal before it is transmitted into the air. Some protection of the antenna plug might be necessary be necessary for an operational network to ensure there is no signal leakage from the antenna connector. In addition, while the appearance of the hardware might look identical, it is safer to check if the hardware does comply to the specification before starting using it. For example, during our experiments we found some of our Senao wireless cards does not output a transmission power of 200mW as they should according to the specification.
- **Software:** Most of the wireless measurements are based on readings from the wireless cards. However, while the hardware can be identical, different firmwares and drivers could introduce inaccuracy in the measurement results. We strongly suggest, if possible, one should try to validate the readings from a wireless card against the results from a spectrum analyser.

- **Antenna Locations:** In our testbed, each node is equipped with three antennas, including two 2.4GHz (or one 2.4GHz and one 900MHz) omni-directional antennas and one 3.5GHz directional antenna. To facilitate the ease of mounting, we first mount all three antennas on a pole and then mount this pole on the traffic light. Specifically, one omni-directional antenna is pointing upward and the other is pointing downward while the directional antenna is mounted in between. We found the location of antenna can have an effect on the link performance. Figure 8 shows the round-trip delays from node m2 to its neighboring node m3 using the omni-directional antennas. The use of the lower antenna results in a higher loss and a larger variation. One possible explanation is that the upper antenna might be less obstructed and hence have a better connectivity. At 2.4GHz, a quarter wavelength is approximately 30cm. Antenna position changes in the range 10-30 cm can cause dramatic changes in signal strength, presumably due to the presence of standing waves in the vicinity of the traffic light pole or more specifically in the vicinity of metal stop signs and the like! If multiple antennas are deployed, it is essential to have a means for independently adjusting their position.

Maintenance

- **Remote Management:** Remote management is challenging. Currently we provide the following ways to allow the user to access the nodes.
    - **To Access the Linux-Based Ethernet Router:** The router can be connected via the Unwired link over OpenVPN. In the case when the OpenVPN connection can not be established, given

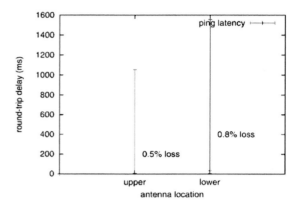

Figure 8. Effect of antenna locations on round-trip delay

that a public IP address is obtained for each router from Unwired, one can connect to the router via its public IP address, although this could introduce a dependency on a dynamic DNS lookup. In addition, one can connect to the mesh node first and then connect to the router via the Ethernet or USB-to-serial link between the router and the motherboard.

- **To Access the Mesh Node:** One can connect to the mesh node (i.e., the motherboard) by first connecting to the router and then connect to the motherboard via the Ethernet or USB-to-serial link. Being able to access the motherboard via its serial port is important since the Ethernet link might fail for various reasons. In addition, one can access the motherboard via its 802.11 interfaces from any reachable neighboring nodes.

In addition, the following mechanisms are currently implemented to recover the system from failure. First, and the default way to recover from a failure is to login to the offending router or motherboard using one of the above methods, analyse the problem and/or reboot the node. Second, the watchdog timer support on the MB720 is used. In addition, Grub is setup to fall back to a stable backup image which is installed in a separate partition in case when the default image fails. Finally, the BIOS is configured to give top priority to PXE network boot but we configure DHCP server in a way that it does not provide PXE boot information in the default case. Therefore the node defaults to its second priority, which is to boot from the USB flash drive. However, in the event of a node failure (for example, due to a bad image) the DHCP server can be quickly reconfigured to support the PXE boot. Having rebooted the node using PXE, a new working disk image can be distributed to the node via frisbee (http://www.emulab.net/software.php3) or FTP. In practice, we use FTP instead of frisbee since that frisbee introduce more control traffic overhead on the Unwired links, where we are charged for every bits send to the nodes.

- **Security:** Security is a major concern especially when our wireless mesh testbed is sharing public spectrum with an average of 50+ external APs at each intersection. Furthermore, our testbed is effectively connected to the Internet via Unwired network, and exposed to various password attacks. In a live deployment for traffic control, the mesh security should be integrated with the traffic control system security model, which may include e.g. segmentation to contain the damage of a denial of service or break-in attack, combined with multiple levels of fallback to local control.

CONCLUSION

Although WMNs can be built up based on existing technologies, field trials and experiments with existing WMNs prove that the performance of WMNs is still far below expectations. There still remain many research problems. Among them, the most important and urgent ones are the scalability and the security. Based on existing MAC, routing, and transport protocols, network performance is not scalable with either the number of nodes or the number of hops in the network. This problem can be alleviated by increasing the network capacity through using multiple channels/radios per node or developing wireless radios with higher transmission speed. However, these approaches do not truly enhance the scalability of WMNs, because resource utilization is not actually improved. Therefore, in order to achieve scalability, it is essential to develop new MAC, routing, and transport protocols for WMNs. In addition, WMNs are vulnerable to security attacks in various protocol layers. Current security approaches may be effective

to a particular attack in a specific protocol layer. However, there still exists a need for a comprehensive mechanism to prevent or counter attacks in all protocol layers. Moreover, self-organization and self-configuration capability is a desired feature in WMNs. It requires protocols in WMNs to be distributive and collaborative. However, current WMNs can only partially realize this objective. Furthermore, current WMNs still have very limited capabilities of integrating heterogeneous wireless networks, due to the difficulty in building multiple wireless interfaces and the corresponding gateway/bridge functions in the same mesh router. In this chapter, we discuss our experiences in deploying a testbed as a first step towards creating a fully functional wireless mesh network-based traffic control system. In addition, we describe some initial results of link characteristics of different technologies used on our testbed. While wireless mesh networks have been used in public safety and residential broadband for years, there are several research challenges such as latency, reliability, security and scalability that need to be addressed.

REFERENCES

Adya, A., Bahl, P., Padhye, J., Wolman, A., & Zhou, L. (2004). *A multi-radio unification protocol for IEEE 802.11 wireless networks.* In the First International Conference on Broadband Networks, California, USA.

Aguayo, D., Bicket, J., Biswas, S., Judd, G., & Morris, R. (2004). *Link-level measurements from an 802.11b mesh network.* In the 10th Annual International Conference on Mobile Computing and Networking, Philadelphia, PA, USA.

Bicket, J., Aguayo, D., Biswas, S., & Morris, R. (2005). *Architecture and evaluation of an unplanned 802.11b mesh network.* In the 11th Annual International Conference on Mobile Computing and Networking, Cologne, Germany.

Camp, J., Robinson, J., Steger, C., & Knightly, E. (2006). *Measurement driven deployment of a two-tier urban mesh access network.* In the 9th International Conference on Mobile Systems, Applications, and Services, Uppsala, Sweden.

Chakravorty, R., & Pratt, I. (2002). Performance issues with general packet radio service. *Journal of Communications and Networks, Special Issue on Evolving from 3G Deployment to 4G Definition, 4,* 266-281.

Ganguly, S., Navda, V., Kim, K., Kashyap, A., Niculescu, D., & Izmailov, R. (2006). Performance optimizations for deploying VOIP services in mesh networks. *IEEE Journal on Selected Areas in Communications, 24*(11), 2147–2158. doi:10.1109/JSAC.2006.881594

Gupta, P., Jain, B., Raman, B., & Kulkarni, P. (2009). *Link-level measurements of outdoor 802.11g links.* In the 6th Annual IEEE Communications Society Conference on Sensor, Mesh and Ad Hoc Communications and Networks Workshops, Rome, Italy.

Ishmael, L., Bury, S., Pezaros, D. P., & Race, N. J. (2008). Deploying rural community wireless mesh networks. *IEEE Internet Computing Magazine, 12*(4), 22–29. doi:10.1109/MIC.2008.76

Jardosh, A., Ramachandran, K., Almeroth, K. C., & Belding-Royer, E. M. (2005). *Understanding congestion in IEEE 802.11b wireless networks.* In the 5th ACM Special interest Group on Data Communication conference on Internet Measurement, Berkeley, CA.

Kolar, V., Razak, S., Mahonen, P., & Abu-Ghazaleh, N. B. (2010). *Measurement and analysis of link quality in wireless networks: An application perspective.* In INFOCOM IEEE Conference on Computer Communications Workshops, Orlando, Florida, USA.

Lan, K.-c., Wang, Z., Hassan, M., Moors, T., Berriman, R., Libman, L., . . . Zaidi, Z. (2007). Experiences in deploying a wireless mesh network testbed for traffic control. *ACM Special interest Group on Data Communication Computer Communication Review, 37*(5), 17-28.

Lundgren, H., Ramachandran, K., Belding-Royer, E., Almeroth, K., Benny, M., & Hewatt, A. (2006). Experiences from building and using the UCSB meshnet testbed. *IEEE Wireless Network, 13*(2), 18–29.

Rapport, T. S. (1996). *Wireless communications principles and practice.* Prentice Hall PTR.

Raychaudhuri, D., Seskar, I., Ott, M., Ganu, S., Ramachandran, K., & Kremo, H. . . . Singh, M. (2005). *Overview of the orbit radio grid testbed for evaluation of next-generation wireless network protocols.* In the IEEE Wireless Communications and Networking Conference, New Orleans, LA, USA.

Singh, M., Ott, M., Seskar, I., & Kamat, P. (2005). *Orbit measurements framework and library (OML): Motivations, design, implementation, and features*. In IEEE First International Conference on Testbeds and Research Infrastructures for the development of networks and communities, Trento, Italy.

Sombrutzki, R., Zubow, A., Kurth, M., & Redlich, J.-P. (2006). *Self-organization in community mesh networks: The Berlin RoofNet*. In the 1st Workshop on Operator-Assisted (Wireless Mesh) Community, Berlin, Germany.

Weber, S., Cahill, V., Clarke, S., & Haahr, M. (2003). Wireless ad hoc network for Dublin: A large-scale ad hoc network test-bed. *ERCIM News, 54.*

ADDITIONAL READING

Aguayo, D., Bicket, J., Biswas, S., Judd, G., & Morris, R. (2004). Link-level measurements from an 802.11b mesh network. *In the 10th Annual International Conference on Mobile Computing and Networking*, Philadelphia, PA, USA.

Barolli, L., Ikeda, M., Xhafa, F., & Duresi, A. (2010). A testbed for MANETs: Implementation, experiences and learned lessons. *IEEE Systems Journal, 4*(2), 243–252. doi:10.1109/JSYST.2010.2047174

Bernardi, G., Buneman, P., & Marina, M. K. (2008). *Tegola tiered mesh network testbed in rural Scotland*. In the 2008 ACM Workshop on Wireless Networks and Systems for Developing Regions, San Francisco, California, USA.

Bicket, J., Aguayo, D., Biswas, S., & Morris, R. (2005). *Architecture and evaluation of an unplanned 802.11b mesh network*. In the 11th Annual International Conference on Mobile Computing and Networking, Cologne, Germany.

Cheng-Yuan, H., Fu-Yu, W., Chien-Chao, T., & Ying-Dar, L. (2011). NAT-compatibility testbed: An environment to automatically verify direct connection rate. *IEEE Communications Letters, 15*(1), 4–6. doi:10.1109/LCOMM.2010.102810.101700

Das, S. M., Pucha, H., Koutsonikolas, D., Hu, Y. C., & Peroulis, D. (2006). DMesh: Incorporating practical directional antennas in multichannel wireless mesh networks. *IEEE Journal on Selected Areas in Communications, 24*(11), 2028–2039. doi:10.1109/JSAC.2006.881631

Elrakabawy, S. M., Frohn, S., & Lindemann, C. (2010). A scalable dual-radio wireless testbed for emulating mesh networks. *Wireless Networks, 16*(8), 2191–2207. doi:10.1007/s11276-010-0253-3

Gurewitz, O., Mancuso, V., Jingpu, S., & Knightly, E. W. (2009). Measurement and modeling of the origins of starvation of congestion-controlled flows in wireless mesh networks. *IEEE/ACM Transactions on Networking, 17*(6), 1832–1845. doi:10.1109/TNET.2009.2019643

Iqbal, M., Wang, X., & Wertheim, D. (2010). Reliable multimedia multicast communications over wireless mesh networks. *IET Communications, 4*(11), 1288–1299. doi:10.1049/iet-com.2009.0134

Ishmael, J., Bury, S., Pezaros, D., & Race, N. (2008). Deploying rural community wireless mesh networks. *IEEE Internet Computing, 12*(4), 22–29. doi:10.1109/MIC.2008.76

Jardosh, A., Ramachandran, K., Almeroth, K. C., & Belding-Royer, E. M. (2005). *Understanding congestion in IEEE 802.11b wireless networks*. In the 5th ACM Special Interest Group on Data Communication Conference on Internet Measurement, Berkeley, CA.

Jeongkeun, L., Sung-Ju, L., Wonho, K., Dae-hyung, J., Taekyoung, K., & Yanghee, C. (2009). Understanding interference and carrier sensing in wireless mesh networks. *IEEE Communications Magazine, 47*(7), 102–109. doi:10.1109/MCOM.2009.5183479

Kyu-Han, K., & Shin, K. G. (2009). On accurate and asymmetry-aware measurement of link quality in wireless mesh networks. *IEEE/ACM Transactions on Networking, 17*(4), 1172–1185. doi:10.1109/TNET.2008.2008001

Lei, J., Yates, R., Greenstein, L., & Hang, L. (2009). Mapping link SNRs of real-world wireless networks onto an indoor testbed. *IEEE Transactions on Wireless Communications, 8*(1), 157–165. doi:10.1109/T-WC.2009.070330

Lundgren, H., Ramachandran, K., Belding-Royer, E., Almeroth, K., Benny, M., & Hewatt, A. (2006). Experiences from building and using the UCSB meshnet testbed. *IEEE Wireless Network, 13*(2), 18–29.

Maltsev, A., Khoryaev, A., Lomayev, A., Maslennikov, R., Antonopoulos, C., & Avgeropoulos, K. (2010). MIMO and multihop cross-layer design for wireless backhaul: A testbed implementation. *IEEE Communications Magazine, 48*(3), 172–179. doi:10.1109/MCOM.2010.5434390

Muthukumar, S. C., Li, X., Liu, C., Kopena, J. B., Oprea, M., Correa, R., et al. (2009). *RapidMesh: Declarative toolkit for rapid experimentation of wireless mesh networks.* In the 4th ACM international Workshop on Experimental Evaluation and Characterization, Beijing, China.

Pan, L., Scalabrino, N., Yuguang, F., Gregori, E., & Chlamtac, I. (2009). How to effectively use multiple channels in wireless mesh networks. *IEEE Transactions on Parallel and Distributed Systems, 20*(11), 1641–1652. doi:10.1109/TPDS.2008.256

Ramachandran, K., Sheriff, I., Belding, E. M., & Almeroth, K. C. (2008). A multi-radio 802.11 mesh network architecture. *Mobile Networks and Applications, 13*(1-2), 132–146. doi:10.1007/s11036-008-0026-8

Rapport, T. S. (1996). *Wireless communications principles and practice.* Prentice Hall PTR.

Riggio, R., Miorandi, D., Chlamtac, I., Scalabrino, N., Gregori, E., Granelli, F., & Yuguang, F. (2008). Hardware and software solutions for wireless mesh network testbeds. *IEEE Communications Magazine, 46*(6), 156–162. doi:10.1109/MCOM.2008.4539480

Singh, S. R., & Motani, M. (2010). *Mesh testbed for multi-channel MAC development: Design and experimentation.* In the 5th ACM International Workshop on Wireless Network Testbeds, Experimental Evaluation and Characterization, Chicago, Illinois, USA.

Subramanian, A. P., Gupta, H., Das, S. R., & Jing, C. (2008). Minimum interference channel assignment in multiradio wireless mesh networks. *IEEE Transactions on Mobile Computing, 7*(12), 1459–1473. doi:10.1109/TMC.2008.70

Weber, S., Cahill, V., Clarke, S., & Haahr, M. (2003). Wireless ad hoc network for Dublin: A large-scale ad hoc network test-bed. *ERCIM News, 54.*

Zaidi, Z. R., Hakami, S., Landfeldt, B., & Moors, T. (2010). Real-time detection of traffic anomalies in wireless mesh networks. *Wireless Networks, 16*(6), 1675–1689. doi:10.1007/s11276-009-0221-y

ENDNOTE

[1]   For example, the antenna is mounted at a height of about 4 meters from the ground. But the trees on the road are typically higher than 7 meters.

Compilation of References

Aarts, E., & Marzano, S. (2003). *The new everyday - Views on ambient intelligence*. Philips Design.

Abdelaty, M. A., Vaughn, K. M., Kitamura, R., Jovanis, P. P., & Mannering, F. L. (1994). Models of commuters' information use and route choice: Initial results based on southern California commuter route choice survey. *Transportation Research Record, 1453*, 46–55.

Adya, A., Bahl, P., Padhye, J., Wolman, A., & Zhou, L. (2004). *A multi-radio unification protocol for IEEE 802.11 wireless networks*. In the First International Conference on Broadband Networks, California, USA.

Aggarwal, V., Sankar, L., Calderbank, A. R., & Poor, H. V. (2009). Secrecy capacity of a class of orthogonal relay eavesdropper channels. *EURASIP Journal on Wireless Communications and Networking, 2009*.

Aguayo, D., Bicket, J., Biswas, S., Judd, G., & Morris, R. (2004). *Link-level measurements from an 802.11b mesh network*. In the 10th Annual International Conference on Mobile Computing and Networking, Philadelphia, PA, USA.

Ahlswede, R., Cai, N., Li, S.-Y. R., & Yeung, R. W. (2000). Network information flow. *IEEE Transactions on Information Theory, 46*, 1204–1216. doi:10.1109/18.850663

Akaike, H. (1973). Information theory and an extension of the maximum likelihood principle. In *Proceedings of 2nd International Symposium on Information Theory*, (pp. 267-281).

Akyildiz, I. F., Lee, W. Y., Vuran, M. C., & Mohanty, S. (2006). NeXt generation/dynamic spectrum access/cognitive radio wireless networks: A survey. *Computer Networks Journal, 50*(13), 2127–2159. doi:10.1016/j.comnet.2006.05.001

Akyildiz, I. F., Lo, B. F., & Balakrishnan, R. (2011). Cooperative spectrum sensing in cognitive radio networks: A survey. *Physical Communication Journal, 4*(1), 40–62. doi:10.1016/j.phycom.2010.12.003

Alamouti, S. M. (1998). A simple transmit diversity scheme for wireless communications. *IEEE Journal on Selected Areas in Communications, 16*(8), 1451–1458. doi:10.1109/49.730453

An, X., Wang, J., Prasad, R. V., & Niemegeers, I. G. M. M. (2006). Opt - Online person tracking system for context-awareness in wireless personal network. In *Proceedings of ACM SIGMOBILE REALMAN Workshop*. Florence, Italy.

Atapattu, S., Tellambura, C., & Jiang, H. (2009). Relay based cooperative spectrum sensing in cooperative radio networks. In *Proceedings of IEEE GLOBECOM*.

Awduche, D., Berger, L., Gan, D., Li, T., Srinivasan, V., & Swallow, G. (2001). *RFC 3209 (proposed standard), RSVP-TE: Extensions to RSVP for LSP tunnels*. Retrieved from http://www.ietf.org/rfc/rfc3209.txt

Bacheldor, B. (2009, February 2). Tego launches 32-Kilobyte EPC RFID tag. *RFID Journal*. Retrieved June 1, 2011, from http://www.rfidjournal.com/article/view/4578

Bahl, P., & Padmanabhan, V. N. (200). Radar: An in-building rf-based user location and tracking system. In *Proceedings IEEE INFOCOM 2000*, Tel-Aviv, Israel.

Baker, M., & Rozema, G. (2011). *OpenWRT, wireless freedom*. Retrieved from https://openwrt.org/

Baldi, M., Giacomelli, R., & Marchetto, G. (2009). Time-driven access and forwarding for industrial wireless multihop networks. *IEEE Transactions on Industrial Informatics, 5*(2), 99–112. doi:10.1109/TII.2009.2017523

Baldine, I., Vellala, M., Wang, A., Rouskas, G., Dutta, R., & Stevenson, D. (2007). *A unified software architecture to enable cross-layer design in the future internet.* Retrieved from http://net-silos.net/joomla/index.php?option=com_docman&task=doc_view&gid=100&Itemid=39

Bannour, M. A. (2010). Adaptation of golden codes with a correlated rayleigh frequency-selective channel in OFDM system with imperfect channel estimation. *2010 7th International Symposium of Wireless Communication Systems (ISWCS),* York, (pp. 159–163).

Bannour, M. A. (2011). *On the capacity of ASTC-MIMO-OFDM system in a correlated rayleigh frequency-selective channel.* IEEE Vehicular Technology Conference Spring 2011, Budapest.

Bannour, M. L. (2011). *Pilot-aided channel estimation and performance of ASTC-MIMO-OFDM system in a correlated Rayleigh frequency-selective channel. 2011 Wireless Advanced (WiAd).* London, UK: IEEE.

Barros, J., & Rodrigues, M. R. (2006). Secrecy capacity of wireless channels. In *Proceedings of the IEEE International Symposium on Information Theory (ISIT2006),* (pp. 1054–1059). Seattle, USA.

Bartoli, G., Fantacci, R., Marabissi, D., & Simoni, R. (in press). *Physical layer network coding in multipath channel: Effective precoding-based transmission scheme.* IEEE Global Telecommunications Conference 2011.

Bater, J., Tan, H.-P., Brown, K., & Doyle, L. (2007). Modelling interference temperature constraints for spectrum access in cognitive radio networks. In *Proceeding of IEEE International Conference on Communications, 2007, ICC '07,* (pp. 6493–6498).

Baumann, R., Heimlicher, S., & May, M. (2007). *Towards realistic mobility models for vehicular ad-hoc networks.* In the 2007 Mobile Networking for Vehicular Environments.

Beaulieu, N. C., & Cheng, C. (2005). Efficient Nakagami-m fading channel simulation. *IEEE Transactions on Vehicular Technology, 54*(2), 413–424. doi:10.1109/TVT.2004.841555

Ben-Jacob, E., & Levine, H. (2005). Self-engineering capabilities of bacteria. *Journal of the Royal Society, 3*(6), 197–214. doi:doi:10.1098/rsif.2005.0089

Berlemann, L., Mangold, S., Hiertz, G. R., & Walke, B. H. (2006). Spectrum load smoothing: Distributed quality-of-service support for cognitive radios in open spectrum. *European Transactions on Telecommunications, 17,* 395–406. doi:10.1002/ett.1121

Bernhardt, R. C. (1987). Macroscopic diversity in frequency reuse radio systems. *IEEE Journal on Selected Areas in Communications, 5*(5), 862–870. doi:10.1109/JSAC.1987.1146594

Bicket, J., Aguayo, D., Biswas, S., & Morris, R. (2005). *Architecture and evaluation of an unplanned 802.11b mesh network.* In the 11th Annual International Conference on Mobile Computing and Networking, Cologne, Germany.

BIONETS. (2011). *BIONETS.* Retrieved from http://www.bionets.eu/index.php?area=11

Bloch, M., Barros, J., Rodrigues, M. R. D., & McLaughlin, S. W. (2008). Wireless information-theoretic security. *IEEE Transactions on Information Theory, 54*(6), 2515–2534. doi:10.1109/TIT.2008.921908

Borgonovo, F., Capone, A., Cesana, M., & Fratta, L. (2004). AdHoc MAC: New MAC architecture for ad hoc networks providing efficient and reliable point-to-point and broadcast services. *Wireless Networks, 10*(4), 359–366. doi:10.1023/B:WINE.0000028540.96160.8a

Boroujeny, F. (2008). Filter bank spectrum sensing for cognitive radios. *IEEE Transactions on Signal Processing, 56*(5), 1801–1811. doi:10.1109/TSP.2007.911490

Bose, S. K. (2002). *An introduction to queueing systems.* New York, NY: Kluwer Academic/Plenum.

Boyd, S. (2004). *EE392o course notes.* Stanford, CA: Stanford University. Retrieved April 11, 2011, from http://www.stanford.edu/class/ee392o

Boyd, S., & Vandenberghe, L. (2008). *Convex optimization.* Cambridge, UK: Cambridge University Press.

Braden, R., Zhang, L., Berson, S., Herzog, S., & Jamin, S. (1997). *RFC 2205 (proposed standard), resource reservation protocol (RSVP) – Version 1 functional specification.* Retrieved from http://www.ietf.org/rfc/rfc2205.txt

Breslau, L., Estrin, D., Fall, K., Floyd, S., Heidemann, J., & Helmy, A. (2000). Advances in network simulation. *Computer, 33*(5), 59–67. doi:10.1109/2.841785

Brown, T. X. (2005). An analysis of unlicensed device operation in licensed broadcast service bands, *First IEEE International Symposium on Dynamic Spectrum Access Networks (DySPAN '05)* (pp. 11-29).

Burgess, J., Gallagher, B., Jensen, D., & Levine, B. N. (2006). *MaxProp: Routing for vehicle-based disruption-tolerant networks.* In the 25th IEEE International Conference on Computer Communications.

Cabric, D., Mishra, S. M., & Brodersen, R. W. (2004). Implementation issues in spectrum sensing for cognitive radios. In *Proceedings of Asilomar Conference,* (pp. 772-776).

Cabric, D., Mishra, S., Willkomm, D., Brodersen, R., & Wolisz, A. (2005). A cognitive radio approach for usage of virtual unlicensed spectrum. In *Proceedings of IST Mobile and Wireless Communications Summit,* Dresden, Germany.

Cabric, D., Tkachenko, A., & Brodersen, R. W. (2006). Spectrum sensing measurements of pilot, energy, and collaborative detection. *IEEE International Conference on Military Communications (MILCOM '06),* (pp. 1-7).

Caire, G., & Shamai, S. (2003). On the achievable throughput of multi-antenna gaussian Broadcast Channel. *IEEE Transactions on Information Theory, 49*(7), 1691–1706. doi:10.1109/TIT.2003.813523

Cameron, G. D. B., & Duncan, G. I. D. (1996). Paramics: Parallel microscopic simulation of road traffic. *The Journal of Supercomputing, 10*(1), 25–53. doi:10.1007/BF00128098

Camp, J., Robinson, J., Steger, C., & Knightly, E. (2006). *Measurement driven deployment of a two-tier urban mesh access network.* In the 9th International Conference on Mobile Systems, Applications, and Services, Uppsala, Sweden.

Carlson, E., Bettstetter, C., Karl, H., Prehofer, C., & Wolisz, A. (2004). *Distributed MAC for real-time traffic in multi-hop wireless networks.* IEEE Conference on Sensor and Ad Hoc Communications and Networks (SECON 04).

Carlson, E., Prehofer, C., Bettstetter, C., Karl, H., & Wolisz, A. (2006). A distributed end-to-end reservation protocol for IEEE 802.11-based wireless mesh networks. *IEEE Journal on Selected Areas in Communications, 24*(11), 2018–2027. doi:10.1109/JSAC.2006.881633

Carneiro, G., Ruela, J., & Ricardo, M. (2004). *Cross-layer design in 4G wireless terminals* (pp. 7–13). IEEE Wireless Communication Magazine.

Casetti, C., & Chiasserini, C. (2004). Improving fairness and throughput for voice traffic in 802.11e EDCA. *IEEE Personal, Indoor and Mobile Radio Communications Symposium (PIMRC 04)* (pp. 525-530).

CC2420. (2008). *Texas Instruments RF transceiver datasheet.* Retrieved from http://focus.ti.com/docs/prod/folders/print/cc2420.html

Cendrillon, R., Yu, W., Moonen, M., Verlinden, J., & Bostoen, T. (2006). Optimal multiuser spectrum balancing for digital subscriber lines. *IEEE Transactions on Communications, 54*(5), 922–933. doi:10.1109/TCOMM.2006.873096

Cerf, V., & Kahn, R. (1974). A protocol for packet network intercommunication. *IEEE Transactions on Communications, 22*(5). doi:10.1109/TCOM.1974.1092259

Chair, Z., & Varshney, P. K. (1986). Optimal data fusion in multiple sensor detection systems. *IEEE Transactions on Aerospace and Electronic Systems, 22*(1), 98–101. doi:10.1109/TAES.1986.310699

Chakravorty, R., & Pratt, I. (2002). Performance issues with general packet radio service. *Journal of Communications and Networks, Special Issue on Evolving from 3G Deployment to 4G Definition, 4,* 266-281.

Challapali, K., Mangold, S., & Zhong, Z. (2004). Spectrum agile radio: Detecting spectrum opportunities. In *Proceedings of the International Symposium on Advanced Radio Technologies,* Boulder, CO.

Chang, X. (1999). Network simulations with OPNET. In *Simulation Conference Proceedings.*

Chase, D. (1985). Code combining - A maximum likelihood decoding approach for combining an arbitrary number of noisy packets. *IEEE Transactions on Communications, 33*, 385–393. doi:10.1109/TCOM.1985.1096314

Chen, R., & Ruiliang, J. M. (2006). Ensuring trustworthy spectrum sensing in cognitive radio networks. In *Proceedings of IEEE Workshop on Networking Technologies for Software Defined Radio Networks (held in conjunction with IEEE SECON '06)*, (pp. 110-119).

Chen, P.-T., & Mahmassani, H. S. (1993). Dynamic interactive simulator for studying commuter behavior under real-time traffic information supply strategies. *Transportation Research Record, 1413*, 12–21.

Chiti, F., & Fantacci, R., Johnson, R. A., Crnojević, V., & Vukobratović, D. (2009). *End-to-end delay analysis for reliable communications over lossy channels: Integrating network coding and ARQ schemes.* IEEE Globecom'09.

Chiti, F., Fantacci, R., & Vukobratović, D. (2010). *Joint discrete power-level and delay optimization for network coded wireless communications.* IEEE International Conference on Communications.

Chou, P. A., & Wu, Y. (2007). Network coding for the internet and wireless networks. *IEEE Signal Processing Magazine, 24*(5), 77–85. doi:10.1109/MSP.2007.904818

Clark, D. (2010). *NSF Future Internet Summit, meeting summary*, Washington, DC October 12-15, 2009. Version 7.0. Retrieved from http://www.nets-find.net/Summit-summary-7.pdf

Clark, D., & Tennenhouse, D. (1990). Architectural considerations for a new generation of protocols. *ACM SIGCOMM Computer Communication Review, 20*(4). doi:10.1145/99517.99553

Clausen, T., & Jacquet, P. (2003). *RFC 3626 (experimental), optimized link state routing protocol (OLSR).* Retrieved from http://www.ietf.org/rfc/rfc3626.txt

Corbet, J. (2003). *Kobjects and Sysfs.* Retrieved from http://lwn.net/Articles/54651/

Corbet, J. (2006). *The high-resolution timer API.* Retrieved from http://lwn.net/Articles/167897/

Costa, M. (1983). Writing on dirt paper. *IEEE Transactions on Information Theory, 29*(12), 439–441. doi:10.1109/TIT.1983.1056659

Cover, T. M., & Thomas, J. A. (2006). *Elements of information theory* (2nd ed.). John Wiley & Sons, Inc.

Cox, D. C., Murray, R., & Norris, A. W. (1984). 800 MHz attenuation measured in and around suburban houses. *AT & T Bell Laboratories Technical Journal, 63*(6), 921–954.

Cox, T. M. (2007). Robust frequency and timing synchronization for OFDM. *IEEE Transactions on Communications, 45*(12), 1613–1621.

Cui, T. T., Jia, G., & Feifei Tellambura, C. (2010). Blind spectrum sensing in cognitive radio. *Wireless Communications and Networking Conference (WCNC '10)*, (pp. 1-5).

Cui, T., Gao, F., Ho, T., & Nallanathan, A. (2008). Distributed space-time coding for two-way wireless relay networks. *IEEE International Conference on Communications*, (pp. 3888–3892).

Cui, Y., Xue, Y., & Nahrstedt, K. (2004). Optimal distributed multicast routing using network coding: Theory and applications. *Proceedings of Sixth Workshop on MAthematical performance Modeling and Analysis (MAMA)*, Vol. 32, (pp. 47–49).

Czylwik, A. (1999). Synchronization for systems with antenna diversit. *Vehicular Technology Conference, 1999*, (pp. 728–732).

Dandawate, A. V., & Giannakis, G. B. (1994). Statistical tests for presence of cyclostationarity. *IEEE Transactions on Signal Processing, 42*, 2355–2369. doi:10.1109/78.317857

De, P., & Liang, Y.-C. (2007). Blind Sensing algorithms for cognitive radio. In *IEEE Radio and Wireless Symposium, 2007*, (pp. 201–204).

Deng, P., & Fan, P. Z. (2000). An AoA assisted ToA positioning system. In *WCC - ICCT 2000: Proceedings of IEEE International Conference on Communication Technology*, Beijing, China.

De, P., & Liang, Y. C. (2008). Blind spectrum sensing algorithms for cognitive radio networks. *IEEE Transactions on Vehicular Technology, 57*(5), 2834–2842. doi:10.1109/TVT.2008.915520

Department of Defense. (2006). *National industrial security program operating manual*, February 2006.

Dia, H., & Panwai, S. (2007). Modelling drivers' compliance and route choice behaviour in response to travel information. *Nonlinear Dynamics, 49*(4), 493–509. doi:10.1007/s11071-006-9111-3

Digham, F., Alouini, M., & Simon, M. (2003, May 5). On the energy detection of unknown signals over fading channels. In *Proceedings of IEEE ICC 2005*, Vol. 5 (pp. 3575–3579).

Dingus, T., Hulse, M., Jahns, S., Alves-Foss, J., Confer, S., Rice, A., et al. (1996). *Development of human factors guidelines for advanced traveler information systems and commercial vehicle operations: Literature review*. Federal Highway Administration, Report FHWA-RD-95-153.

Ding, Y., & Xiao, L. (2010). SADV: Static-node-assisted adaptive data dissemination in vehicular networks. *IEEE Transactions on Vehicular Technology, 59*(5), 2245–2255.

Ding, Z., Leung, K., Goeckel, D., & Towsley, D. (2009). On the study of network coding with diversity. *IEEE Transactions on Wireless Communications, 8*(3), 1247–1259. doi:10.1109/TWC.2009.07051022

Dooley, K. (1996). A nominal definition of complex adaptive systems. *The Chaos Network, 8*(1), 2-3. Retrieved from http://www.public.asu.edu/~kdooley/papers/casdef.PDF

Dressler, F., & Sommer, C. (2010). *On the impact of human driver behavior on intelligent transportation systems*. In the 2010 IEEE 71st Vehicular Technology Conference (2010-Spring).

Ducatel, K., et al. (2001). *Scenarios for ambient intelligence in 2010*. Brussels, Belgium: IST Advisory Group (ISTAG), European Commission. Retrieved from www.cordis.lu/ist/istag.html

Eisenman, S. B., Lane, N. D., Miluzzo, E., Peterson, R. A., Ahn, G.-S., & Campbell, A. T. (2006). *Metrosense project: People-centric sensing at scale*. In Workshop on World-Sensor-Web.

Emond, J. P. (2008). The cold chain. In Miles, S. B., Sarma, S. E., & Williams, J. R. (Eds.), *RFID technology and applications* (pp. 144–156). New York, NY: Cambridge University Press. doi:10.1017/CBO9780511541155.012

EPCglobal. (2008) *EPC™ radio-frequency identity protocols class-1 generation-2 UHF RFID protocol for communications at 860 MHz – 960 MHz version 1.2.0*. EPCglobal Inc.

EPCglobal. (2010). *Tag data standards version 1.5*. EPCglobal Inc.

Erez, U., Litsyn, S., & Zamir, R. (2005). Lattices which are good for (almost) everything. *IEEE Transactions on Information Theory, 51*, 3401–3416. doi:10.1109/TIT.2005.855591

Etemad, K. (2008). Overview of mobile WiMAX technology and evolution. *IEEE Communications Magazine*, 31–40. doi:10.1109/MCOM.2008.4644117

Facchini, C., Granelli, F., & Fonseca, N. L. S. (2010). Identifying relevant cross-layer interactions in cognitive processes. *IEEE Global Telecommunications Conference (GLOBECOM 2010)* (pp. 1-6).

Farhang-Boroujeny, B., & Kempter, R. (2008). Multicarrier communication techniques for spectrum sensing and communications in cognitive radios. *IEEE Communications Magazine, 48*(4).

Farnham, T., Clemo, G., Haines, R., Seidel, E., Benamar, A., & Billington, S. … Mangold, P. (2000). IST-TRUST: A perspective on the reconfiguration of future mobile terminals using software download. In *Proceedings of IEEE International Symposium on Personal, Indoor and Mobile Radio Communication*, (pp. 1054–1059). London, UK.

FCC 03-289. (2003). *ET docket No.03-237*. Retrieved April 10, 2011, from http://hraunfoss.fcc.gov/edocs_public/attachmatch/FCC-03-289A1.pdf

FCC. (2002). Notice of proposed rulemaking and order. *ET Docket No. 02-135*.

FCC. (2002). *Spectrum policy taskforce 1/8, an interleaver report*. ET Docket No. 02-155, Nov 02, 2002.

FCC. (2003). *ET docket number 03-237, Notice of inquiry and notice of proposed rulemaking*, November 2003.

FCC. (2003a). Notice of proposed rulemaking and order. *ET Docket No. 03-222*.

FCC. (2003b). Notice of proposed rulemaking and order. *ET Docket No. 03-289*.

Feldmann, A. (2007). Internet clean-slate design: What and why? *ACM SIGCOMM Computer Communication Review, 37*(3). doi:10.1145/1273445.1273453

Fellendorf, M. (1994). *VISSIM: A microscopic simulation tool to evaluate actuated signal control including bus priority.* In the 64th Institute Transportation Engineers Annual Meeting.

Ferdous, N., Ahmed, M., Matin, M. A., & Habiba, U. (2011). Efficient algorithm for power allocation in relay-based cognitive radio network. *Radio Engineering Journal, 20*(4).

FIND -NSF NeTS FIND Initiative. (2011). *National Science Foundation.* Retrieved from http://www.nets-find. net/index.php

Finkenzeller, K. (2003). *RFID handbook: Fundamentals and applications in contactless smart cards and identification.* Chichester, UK: John Wiley & Sons Ltd.

Fiore, M., & Härri, J. (2008). The networking shape of vehicular mobility. In the 9th ACM International Symposium on Mobile ad hoc Networking and Computing, Hong Kong, China.

FIRE - Future Internet Research & Experimentation. (2011). *European Commission ICT Research in FP7.* Retrieved from http://cordis.europa.eu/fp7/ict/fire/ home_en.html

Foschoini, G. J. (1996). Layered space-time architecture for wireless communication in a fading environment when using multi-element antennas. *Bell Labs Technical Journals, 1*(2), 41–49. doi:10.1002/bltj.2015

Fragouli, C., Emina, S., & Shokrollahi, A. (2004). *Network coding as a coloring problem.* Conference on Information Sciences and Systems.

Fragouli, C., & Soljanin, E. (2006). Information flow decomposition for network coding. *IEEE Transactions on Information Theory, 52*(3), 829–8481. doi:10.1109/ TIT.2005.864435

Fragouli, C., & Soljanin, E. (Eds.). (2007). *Network coding fundamentals.* Boston, MA: Publisher Inc.

Fukunaga, K., & Koontz, W. L. G. (1970). Application of the Harhunen-loeve expansion to feature selection and ordering. *IEEE Transactions on Computers, 19*(4), 311–317. doi:10.1109/T-C.1970.222918

Gacanin, H., & Adachi, F. (2010). Broadband analog network coding. *IEEE Transactions on Wireless Communications, 9*(5), 1577–1583. doi:10.1109/ TWC.2010.05.091053

Gacemi1, A., Senail, A., & Oussalah, M. (2004). Separation of concerns in software architecture via a multiviews description. *Proceedings of the IEEE International Conference on Information Reuse and Integration*, (pp. 60-65). doi:10.1109/IRI.2004.1431437

Gagnon, M. L. (2007). Iterative channel estimation and decoding of turbo-coded OFDM symbols in selective rayleigh channel. *Canadian Journal of Electrical and Computer Engineering, 32*(1), 9–18. doi:10.1109/ CJECE.2007.364328

Gallager, R. (Fall 2006). *Course materials for 6.450 principles of digital communications I.* MIT OpenCourseWare. Retrieved from http//ocw.mit.edu

Ganeriwal, S., Kumar, R., & Srivastava, M. B. (2003). Timing-sync protocol for sensor networks. *ACM International Conference on Embedded Networked Sensor Systems (SenSys 2003)* (pp. 138–149).

Ganesan, G., & Li, Y. (2005). Cooperative spectrum sensing in cognitive radio networks. *First IEEE International Symposium on Dynamic Spectrum Access Networks (DySPAN '05)*, (pp. 137-143).

Ganesan, G., & Li, Y. G. (2005). Agility improvement through cooperative diversity in cognitive radio networks. In *Proceedings of IEEE GLOBECOM.*

Ganesan, G., & Li, Y. (2007a). Cooperative spectrum sensing in cognitive radio, part I: Two user networks. *IEEE Transactions on Wireless Communications, 6*(6), 2204–2213. doi:10.1109/TWC.2007.05775

Ganesan, G., & Li, Y. (2007b). Cooperative spectrum sensing in cognitive radio, part II: Multiuser networks. *IEEE Transactions on Wireless Communications, 6*(6), 2214–2222. doi:10.1109/TWC.2007.05776

Ganguly, S., Navda, V., Kim, K., Kashyap, A., Niculescu, D., & Izmailov, R. (2006). Performance optimizations for deploying VOIP services in mesh networks. *IEEE Journal on Selected Areas in Communications, 24*(11), 2147–2158. doi:10.1109/JSAC.2006.881594

Gao, F., Zhang, R., & Liang, Y. C. (2009). Optimal channel estimation and training design for two-way relay networks. *IEEE Transactions on Communications, 57*(10), 3024–3033. doi:10.1109/TCOMM.2009.10.080169

Gardner, W. (1991). Exploitation of spectral redundancy in cyclostationary signals. *IEEE Signal Processing Magazine, 8*(2), 14–36. doi:10.1109/79.81007

Gero, J. S. (1990). Design prototypes: A knowledge representation schema for design. *AI Magazine, 11*(4), 26–36. http://portal.acm.org/citation.cfm?id=95793

Gershman, A. B., & Sidiropoulos, N. D. (2005). *Space-time processing for MIMO communications*. Johon Wiley & Sons, Ltd.doi:10.1002/0470010045

Gezici, S., Tian, Z., Biannakis, G. B., Kobayashi, H., Molisch, A. F., Poor, H. V., & Sahinoglu, Z. (2005). Localization via ultra-wideband radios. *IEEE Signal Processing Magazine, 22*(4), 70–84. doi:10.1109/MSP.2005.1458289

Ghaderi, M., Towsley, D., & Kurose, J. (2008). Reliability gain of network coding in lossy wireless networks. *Proceedings of IEEE MILCOM*, (pp. 2171–2179).

Ghasemi, A., & Sousa, E. S. (2005). Collaborative spectrum sensing for opportunistic access in fading environment. In *Proceedings of IEEE DySPAN 2005*.

Ghasemi, A., & Sousa, E. S. (2007). Asymptotic performance of collaborative spectrum sensing under correlated log-normal shadowing. *IEEE Communications Letters, 11*(1), 34–36. doi:10.1109/LCOMM.2007.060662

Ghasemi, A., & Sousa, E. S. (2008). Spectrum sensing in cognitive radio networks: requirements, challenges and design trade-offs [cognitive eradio communications]. *IEEE Communications Magazine, 4*, 32–39. doi:10.1109/MCOM.2008.4481338

Ghosh, A., Ratasuk, R., Mondal, B., Mangalvedhe, N., & Thomas, T. (2010). LTE-advanced: Next generation wireless broadband technology. *IEEE Wireless Communications Magazine, 17*(3), 10–22. doi:10.1109/MWC.2010.5490974

Giang, L., Yang, Y., Shu, F., & Gang, W. (2010). *SLNR precoding based on QBC with limited feedback in downlink CoMP system*. Paper presented at the Wireless Communications and Signal Processing Suzhou

Giannakis, Y. Y. (2005). Blind carrier frequency offset estimation in SISO, MIMO, and multiuser OFDM systems. *IEEE Transactions on Communications, 53*(1), 173–183. doi:10.1109/TCOMM.2004.840623

Goldsmith, A. (2005). *Wireless communications*. Cambridge, UK: Cambridge University Press.

Gopala, P. K., Lai, L., & Gamal, H. E. (2008). On the secrecy capacity of fading channels. *IEEE Transactions on Information Theory, 54*(10), 4687–4690. doi:10.1109/TIT.2008.928990

Gradshteyn, I. S., & Ryzhik, I. M. (2007). *Table of integrals, series, and products* (7th ed.). San Diego, CA: Academic.

Greenberg, A., Gisli, H., Maltz, D., Myers, A., Rexford, J., & Xie, G. (2005). A clean slate 4D approach to network control and management. *ACM SIGCOMM Computer Communication Review, 35*(5). doi:doi:10.1145/1096536.1096541

Guo, D., Li, X., Liu, M., & Zhang, L. (2010). *Model of traffic path choice based on game theory and induction mechanism*. In 2010 Ninth International Symposium on Distributed Computing and Applications to Business Engineering and Science.

Gupta, P., Jain, B., Raman, B., & Kulkarni, P. (2009). *Link-level measurements of outdoor 802.11g links*. In the 6th Annual IEEE Communications Society Conference on Sensor, Mesh and Ad Hoc Communications and Networks Workshops, Rome, Italy.

Gutierrez, J., Naeve, M., Callaway, E., Bourgeois, M., Mitter, V., & Heile, B. (2001). IEEE 802.15.4: A developing standard for low-power low cost wireless personal area networks. *IEEE Network, 15*(5), 12–19. doi:10.1109/65.953229

Halati, A., Lieu, H., & Walker, S. (1997). Corsim-corridor traffic simulation model. In the Traffic Congestion and Traffic Safety in the 21st Century Conference.

Hamdi, K., & Letaief, K. B. (2009). Power, sensing time and throughput tradeoffs in cognitive radio systems: A cross-layer approach. In *Proceedings IEEE WCNC 2009*, Budapest, Hungary.

Han, Z., Fan, R., & Jiang, H. (2009). Replacement of spectrum sensing in cognitive radio. *IEEE Transactions on Wireless Communications*, *8*(6), 2819–2826. doi:10.1109/TWC.2009.080603

Hassan, H., Eltoweissy, M., & Youssef, M. (2008). *Towards a federated network architecture* (pp. 1–4). IEEE INFOCOM Workshops.

Hawrylak, P. J., & Mickle, M. H. (2009). EPC Gen-2 standard for RFID. In Y. Zhang, L. T. Yang, & J. Chen (Eds.), *RFID and sensor networks: Architectures, protocols, security and integrations* (pp. 97-124). Boca Raton, FL: Taylor & Francis Group, CRC Press.

Hawrylak, P. J., Cain, J. T., & Mickle, M. H. (2007). Analytic modeling methodology for analysis of energy consumption for ISO 18000-7 RFID networks. *International Journal of Radio Frequency Identification Technology and Applications*, *1*(4), 371–400. doi:10.1504/IJRFITA.2007.017748

Hawrylak, P. J., Cain, J. T., & Mickle, M. H. (2008). RFID tags. In Yan, L., Zhang, Y., Yang, L. T., & Ning, H. (Eds.), *The Internet of things: From RFID to pervasive networked systems* (pp. 1–32). Boca Raton, FL: Auerbach Publications, Taylor & Francis Group. doi:10.1201/9781420052824.ch1

Haykin, S. (2005). Cognitive radio: Brain-empowered wireless communications. *IEEE Journal on Selected Areas in Communications*, *23*(2), 201–220. doi:10.1109/JSAC.2004.839380

He, T., Huang, C., Blum, B. A., Stankovic, J. A., & Abdelzaher, T. (2003). Range-free localization schemes for large scale sensor networks. In *MobiCom '03: Proceedings of the 9th Annual International Conference on Mobile Computing and Networking*, New York, NY, USA (pp. 81-95).

Heide, J., Pedersen, M. V., Fitzek, F. H. P., & Larsen, T. (2011). *Network coding for mobile devices – Systematic binary random rateless codes*. IEEE International Conference on Communications, ICC Workshops.

Heidemann, J., Bulusu, N., Elson, J., Intanagonwiwat, C., Lan, K. C., Xu, Y., & Govindan, R. (2001). *Effects of detail in wireless network simulation*. In the Society for Computer Simulation International Multiconference on Distributed Simulation.

Hightower, P. (2008). Motion effects on GPS receiver time accuracy. *Instrumentation Technology Systems*. Retrieved from http://www.itsamerica.com/

Hightower, J., & Boriello, G. (2001). Location systems for ubiquitous computing. *IEEE Computer*, *34*(5), 57–66. doi:10.1109/2.940014

Ho, T., & Lun, D. S. (Eds.). (2008). *Network coding. An introduction*. Cambridge, UK: Cambridge University Press. doi:10.1017/CBO9780511754623

Hyoung-Kyu, Y. Y.-H.-H.-S. (2000). Frequency-offset synchronization and channel estimation. *IEEE Communications Letters*, *4*(3), 95–97. doi:10.1109/4234.831036

IEEE. (2010). *IEEE 802.11p standard, wireless access in vehicular environments*.

IEEE. (2011). *IEEE 802.11s draft 8.0, draft amendment: ESS mesh networking*.

IEEE. (n.d.). *IEEE 802.11g standard, further higher-speed physical layer extension*.

Imani, S., Dehkordi, A. B., & Kamarei, M. (2011). Adaptive sub-optimal energy detection based wideband spectrum sensing for cognitive radio. *IEEE International Conference on Electrical, Control and Computer Engineering*, (pp. 22-26).

International Organization for Standardization. (2009). *ISO/IEC 18000-7 Information technology -- Radio frequency identification for item management -- Part 7: Parameters for active air interface communications at 433 MHz*.

International Organization for Standardization. (2010). *ISO/IEC 18000-6:2010 FDIS information technology -- Radio frequency identification for item management -- Part 6: Parameters for air interface communications at 860 MHz to 960 MHz*.

Irwin, M. E. (2006). *Moment generating function* (p. 19). Retrieved April 13, 2011, from http://www.markirwin.net/stat110/Lecture/Section45.pdf

Ishmael, L., Bury, S., Pezaros, D. P., & Race, N. J. (2008). Deploying rural community wireless mesh networks. *IEEE Internet Computing Magazine, 12*(4), 22–29. doi:10.1109/MIC.2008.76

ISO/IEC International Standard 7498-1. (1994). *Information Technology – Open systems interconnection – Basic reference model: The basic model.*

ISO/IEC. (2000). IEEE *802.11a standard, ISO/IEC 8802-11:1999/Amd 1:2000(E).*

Jan, O., Horowitz, A. J., & Peng, Z.-R. (2000). Using global positioning system data to understand variations in path choice. *Transportation Research Record, 1725,* 37–44. doi:10.3141/1725-06

Jardosh, A., Ramachandran, K., Almeroth, K. C., & Belding-Royer, E. M. (2005). *Understanding congestion in IEEE 802.11b wireless networks.* In the 5th ACM Special interest Group on Data Communication conference on Internet Measurement, Berkeley, CA.

Jia, J., Zhang, J., & Zhang, Q. (2009). Cooperative relay for cognitive radio networks. In *Proceedings IEEE INFOCOM,* (pp. 2304–2312).

Jiang, Y., & Varanasi, M. K., & L, J. (2011). Performance analysis of ZF and MMSE equalizers for MIMO systems: An in-depth study of the high SNR regime. *IEEE Transactions on Information Theory, 57*(4), 2008–2026. doi:10.1109/TIT.2011.2112070

Jin, G., Lu, X. Y., & Park, M. (2006). An indoor localization mechanism using active RFID tag. In *SUTC 2006: Proceedings of IEEE International Conference on Sensor Networks, Ubiquitous, and Trustworthy Computing,* Taichung, Taiwan.

Jin, J., & Li, B. (2008). *Adaptive random network coding in WiMAX.* IEEE International Conference on Communications.

Jindel, N., Rhee, W., Vishwanath, S., Jafar, S. A., & Goldsmith, A. (2005). Sum power iterative water-filling for multi-antenna Gaussain broadcast channel. *IEEE Transactions on Information Theory, 51*(4), 1570–1580. doi:10.1109/TIT.2005.844082

Joham, M., Kusume, K., Gzara, M. H., Utschick, W., & Nossek, J. A. (2002). *Transmit Wiener filter for the downlink of TDDDS-CDMA systems.* Paper presented at the Spread Spectrum Techniques and Applications IEEE Seventh International Symposium.

Joham, M., Utschick, W., & Nossek, J. A. (2005). Linear transmit processing in MIMO communications systems. *IEEE Transactions on Signal Processing, 53*(8), 2700–2712. doi:10.1109/TSP.2005.850331

Juels, A., & Brainard, J. (2004). Soft blocking: Flexible blocker tags on the cheap. In *Proceedings of the 2004 ACM Workshop on Privacy in the Electronic Society,* (pp. 1-7).

Juels, A., Rivest, R. L., & Szydlo, M. (2003). The blocker tag: Selective blocking of RFID tags for consumer privacy. In *Proceedings of the 10th ACM Conference on Computer and Communications Security,* (pp. 103-111).

Juels, A. (2006, February). RFID security and privacy: A research survey. *IEEE Journal on Selected Areas in Communications, 24*(2), 381–394. doi:10.1109/JSAC.2005.861395

Juels, A., & Pappu, A. (2003). In Wright, R. (Ed.), *Squealing Euros: Privacy-protection in RFID-enabled banknotes* (*Vol. 2742,* pp. 103–121). Lecture Notes in Computer Science Berlin, Germany: Springer.

Juels, A., & Weis, S. A. (2009, November). Defining strong privacy for RFID. *ACM Transactions on Information and System Security, 13*(1). doi:10.1145/1609956.1609963

Jun, M., Li, G. Y., & Juang, B. H. (2009). Signal processing in cognitive radio. *Proceedings of the IEEE, 97*(5), 805–823. doi:10.1109/JPROC.2009.2015707

Karagiannis, T., Boudec, J.-Y. L., & Vojnović, M. (2007). *Power law and exponential decay of inter contact times between mobile devices.* In the 13th Annual ACM International Conference on Mobile Computing and Networking.

Karnadi, F. K., Mo, Z. H., & Lan, K.-C. (2007). *Rapid generation of realistic mobility models for VANET.* In IEEE Wireless Communications and Networking Conference.

Katti, S., Gollakota, S., & Katabi, D. (2007). Embracing wireless interference: Analog network coding. *Proceedings of the 2007 Conference on Applications, Technologies, Architectures, and Protocols for Computer Communications* (pp. 397–408).

Katz, D., Kompella, K., & Yeung, D. (2003). *RFC 3630 (proposed standard), traffic engineering (TE) extensions to OSPF version 2.* Retrieved from http://www.ietf.org/rfc/rfc3630.txt

Kawadia, V., & Kumar, P. (2005). A cautionary perspective on cross layer design. *IEEE Wireless Communication, 12*(1), 3–11. doi:10.1109/MWC.2005.1404568

Keller, A., Hossmann, T., May, M., Bouabene, G., Jelger, C., & Tschudin, C. (2008). A system architecture for evolving protocol stacks (invited paper). *IEEE Proceedings of the 17th International Conference on Computer Communications and Networks (ICCCN),* (pp. 144-150). doi: 10.1109/ICCCN.2008.ECP.44

Khajavi, N. T., Sadeghi, S., & Sadough, S. M. (2010). An improved blind spectrum sensing technique for cognitive radio systems. In *Proceedings of 5th International Symposium on Telecommunications (IST '10),* (pp. 13-17).

Khoury, J., Abdallah, C., & Heileman, G. (2010). Towards formalizing network architectural descriptions. In Frappier, M., Glässer, U., Khurshid, S., Laleau, R., & Reeves, S. (Eds.), *Abstract State Machines, Alloy, B and Z (Vol. 5977,* pp. 132–145). Lecture Notes in Computer Science Berlin, Germany: Springer. doi:10.1007/978-3-642-11811-1_11

Kim, K., Akbar, I. A., Bae, K. K., Urn, J. S., Spooner, C. M., & Reed, J. H. (2007). Cyclostationary approaches to signal detection and classification in cognitive radio. *IEEE International Symposium on Dynamic Spectrum Access Networks (DySPAN '07),* (pp. 212-215).

Koetter, R., & Medard, M. (2003). An algebraic framework to network coding. *IEEE/ACM Transactions on Networking, 11*(5), 782–795. doi:10.1109/TNET.2003.818197

Koike-Akino, T., Popovski, P., & Tarokh, V. (2009). Adaptive modulation and network coding with optimized precoding in two-way relaying. *IEEE Global Telecommunications Conference,* (pp. 1–6).

Koike-Akino, T., Popovski, P., & Tarokh, V. (2009). Optimized constellations for two-way wireless relaying with physical network coding. *IEEE Journal on Selected Areas in Communications, 27*(5), 773–787. doi:10.1109/JSAC.2009.090617

Kolar, V., Razak, S., Mahonen, P., & Abu-Ghazaleh, N. B. (2010). *Measurement and analysis of link quality in wireless networks: An application perspective.* In INFOCOM IEEE Conference on Computer Communications Workshops, Orlando, Florida, USA.

Kolodzy, P. J. (2006). Interference temperature: A metric for dynamic spectrum utilization. *International Journal of Network Management, 16,* 103–113. doi:10.1002/nem.608

Kortun, A., Ratnarajah, T., Sellaathurai, T., Zhong, C., & Papadias, C. B. (2011). On the performance of eigenvalue based cooperative spectrum sensing for cognitive radio. *IEEE Journal of Selected Topics in Signal Processing, 5*(1), 49–55. doi:10.1109/JSTSP.2010.2066957

Koscher, K., Juels, A., Brajkovic, V., & Kohno, T. (2009). EPC RFID tag security weaknesses and defenses: Passport cards, enhanced drivers licenses, and beyond. In *Proceedings of the 16th ACM Conference on Computer and Communications Security* (CCS '09), (pp. 33-42). New York, NY: ACM.

Kötter, R., & Kschischang, F. R. (2008). Coding for errors and erasures in random network coding. *IEEE Transactions on Information Theory, 54,* 3549–3591.

Krajzewicz, D., Hertkorn, G., Rössel, C., & Wanger, P. (2002). *SUMO (simulation of urban mobility): An open-source traffic simulation.* In the 4th Middle East Symposium on Simulation and Modelling.

Kruchten, P. (2005). Casting software design in the function-behavior-structure framework. *IEEE Software, 22*(2), 52–58. doi:10.1109/MS.2005.33

Kurose, J. F., & Ross, K. W. (Eds.). (2006). *Computer networking.* Addison-Wesley Longman Incorporated.

Lai, P., Wang, X., Lu, N., & Liu, F. (2009). *A reliable broadcast routing scheme based on mobility prediction for VANET.* In 2009 IEEE Intelligent Vehicles Symposium.

Lai, L., El Gamal, H., & Poor, H. V. (2009). Authentication over noisy channels. *IEEE Transactions on Information Theory, 55,* 906–916. doi:10.1109/TIT.2008.2009842

Lan, K. C., & Chou, C.-M. (2008). *Realistic mobility models for vehicular ad hoc network (VANET) simulations.* In the 8th International Conference on ITS Telecommunications.

Lan, K.-c., Wang, Z., Hassan, M., Moors, T., Berriman, R., Libman, L.,... Zaidi, Z. (2007). Experiences in deploying a wireless mesh network testbed for traffic control. *ACM Special interest Group on Data Communication Computer Communication Review, 37*(5), 17-28.

Lan, K. C., Wang, Z., Hassan, M., Moors, T., Berriman, R., & Libman, L. (2007). Experiences in deploying a wireless mesh network testbed for traffic control. *ACM SIGCOMM Computer Communication Review, 37*(5), 17–28. doi:10.1145/1290168.1290171

Larzon, L., Bodin, U., & Schelen, O. (2002). Hints and notifications. *Proceedings of IEEE Wireless Communications and Networking Conference (WCNC), 2*, (pp. 635-641). doi: 10.1109/WCNC.2002.993342

Lau, E. E. L., Lee, B.-G., & Chung, W.-Y. (2008). Enhanced RSSI based high accuracy real-time user location tracking system for indoor and outdoor environments. *International Journal on Smart Sensing and Intelligent Systems, 1*(2), 534–548.

Lavine, G. (2008, August). RFID technology may improve contrast agent safety. *American Journal of Health-System Pharmacy, 65*(15), 1400–1403. doi:10.2146/news080064

Law, M. K., Bermak, A., & Luong, H. C. (2010, June). A sub-W embedded CMOS temperature sensor for RFID food monitoring application. *IEEE Journal of Solid-state Circuits, 45*(6), 1246–1255. doi:10.1109/JSSC.2010.2047456

Lee, M., & Oh, S. K. (2007). *A per-user successive MMSE precoding technique in multiuser MIMO systems*. Paper presented at the Vehicular Technology Conference, VTC2007, Dublin.

Lee, J.-W., Vo, D. H. T., Huynh, Q.-H., & Hong, S. H. (2011, June). A fully integrated HF-band passive RFID tag IC using 0.18-μm CMOS technology for low-cost security applications. *IEEE Transactions on Industrial Electronics, 58*(6), 2531–2540. doi:10.1109/TIE.2010.2060460

Leon, S. J. (2006). *Linear algebra with applications*. New Jersey: Pearson.

Leontiadis, I., & Mascolo, C. (2007). *Opportunistic spatio-temporal dissemination system for vehicular networks*. In the 1st International MobiSys Workshop on Mobile Opportunistic Networking, San Juan, Puerto Rico.

Letaief, K. B., & Zhang, W. (2009). Cooperative communications for cognitive radio networks. *Proceedings of the IEEE, 97*(5), 878–893. doi:10.1109/JPROC.2009.2015716

Leung-Yan-Cheong, S. K., & Hellman, M. E. (1978). The Gaussian wire-tap channel. *IEEE Transactions on Information Theory, 24*, 451–456. doi:10.1109/TIT.1978.1055917

Li, H., Guensler, R., & Ogle, J. (2005). *An analysis of morning commute route choice patterns using GPS based vehicle activity data*. In the 84th Annual Meeting of the Transportation Research Board.

Li, X., Mow, W. H., & Tsang, F.-L. (2011). *Singularity probability analysis for sparse random linear network coding*. IEEE International Conference on Communications.

Li, Z., Wang, H., & Kuang, J. (2011). A two-step spectrum sensing scheme for cognitive radio networks. *International Conference on Information Science and Technology (ICIST '11)*, (pp. 694-698).

Li, L., Zhou, X., Xu, H., Li, G. Y., Wang, D., & Soong, A. (2011). Simplified relay selection and power allocation in cooperative cognitive radio systems. *IEEE Transactions on Wireless Communications, 10*(1), 33–36. doi:10.1109/TWC.2010.101810.100311

Lim, M. C. H., Ghogho, M., & McLernon, D. C. (2007). *Spatial multiplexing in the multi-user MIMO downlink based on signal-to-leakage ratios*. Paper presented at the Global Telecommunications Conference, Washington Dc.

Lin, D. J. C. S., & Miller, M. (1984). Automatic repeat request error control schemes. *IEEE Communications Magazine, 22*, 5–16. doi:10.1109/MCOM.1984.1091865

Li, Q., Li, G., Lee, W., Lee, M.-I., Mazzarese, D., Clerckx, B., & Li, Z. (2010). MIMO techniques in WiMAX and LTE: A feature overview. *IEEE Communications Magazine, 48*(5), 86–92. doi:10.1109/MCOM.2010.5458368

Li, S.-Y. R., Yeung, R. W., & Cai, N. (2003). Linear network coding. *IEEE Transactions on Information Theory, 49*(2), 371–381. doi:10.1109/TIT.2002.807285

Liu, C., Wu, K., & He, T. (2004). Sensor localization with ring overlapping based on comparison of received signal strength indicator. In *Proceedings of IEEE International Conference on Mobile Ad-hoc and Sensor Systems*. Florida, USA.

Liu, J. N., Goeckel, D., & Towsley, D. (2006). Bounds on the throughput gain of network coding in unicast and multicast wireless networks. *IEEE Journal on Selected Areas on communications, 27*, 582.592.

Liu, T.-L., & Huang, H.-J. (2007). *Multi-agent simulation on day-to-day route choice behavior*. In the third International Conference on Natural Computation.

Liu, X., Tan, X., & Anghuwo, A. A. (2009). Spectrum detection of cognitive radio based on blind signal separation. *IEEE Youth Conference on Information, Computing and Telecommunication (YC-ICT '09)*, (pp. 166-169).

Liu, R., & Poor, H. V. (2009). Secrecy capacity region of a multiple-antenna Gaussian broadcast channel with confidential messages. *IEEE Transactions on Information Theory, 55*(3), 1235–1249. doi:10.1109/TIT.2008.2011448

Liu, T., & Shitz, S. S. (2009). A note on the secrecy capacity of the multiple-antenna wiretap channel. *IEEE Transactions on Information Theory, 55*(6), 2547–2553. doi:10.1109/TIT.2009.2018322

Liu, Z., Xu, Y., Zhang, D., & Guan, S. (2010). *An efficient power allocation algorithm for relay assisted cognitive radio network. Wireless Communications and Signal Processing* (pp. 1–5). WCSP.

Li, Z., Xia, X., & Li, B. (2009). Achieving full diversity and fast ML decoding via simple analog network coding for asynchronous two-way relay networks. *IEEE Transactions on Communications, 57*(12), 3672–3681. doi:10.1109/TCOMM.2009.12.090005

Lo, S.-C., & Lu, W.-K. (2009). *Design of data forwarding strategies in vehicular ad hoc networks*. In the IEEE 69th Vehicular Technology Conference (2009- Spring).

Lorincz, K., & Welsh, M. (2005). Motetrack: A robust, decentralized approach to RF-based location tracking. In *Proceedings of International Workshop on Location- and Context-Awareness (LoCA 2005)*, Oberpfaffenhofen, Germany.

Lozano, A., & Jindal, N. (2010). Transmit diversity vs. spatial multiplexing in modern MIMO systems. *IEEE Transactions on Wireless Communications, 9*(1), 186–197. doi:10.1109/TWC.2010.01.081381

Lucani, D. E., Stojanovic, M., & Mdard, M. (2008). *Random linear network coding for time division duplexing: When to stop to talking and start listening*. CoRR, abs/0809.2350.

Lui, R., & Yu, W. (2005). Low-complexity near-optimal spectrum balancing for digital subscriber lines. In *Proceedings IEEE International Conference Communication, 3*, (pp. 1947-1951).

Lundgren, H., Ramachandran, K., Belding-Royer, E., Almeroth, K., Benny, M., & Hewatt, A. (2006). Experiences from building and using the UCSB meshnet testbed. *IEEE Wireless Network, 13*(2), 18–29.

MacKenzie, C. M., Laskey, K., McCabe, F., Brown, P., Metz, R., & Hamilton, B. A. (Eds.). (2006). Reference model for service oriented architecture 1.0. *OASIS SOA Reference Model Committee Specification 1*. Retrieved from http://docs.oasis-open.org/soa-rm/v1.0/soa-rm.pdf

Magableh, A. M., & Matalgah, M. M. (2008). Capacity of SIMO system over non-identically independent Nakagami-m channel. In *Proceedings of the IEEE Sarnoff Symposium*, (pp. 1–5). Princeton, NJ.

Maguire, Y., & Pappu, R. (2009, January). An optimal Q-algorithm for the ISO 18000-6C RFID protocol. *IEEE Transactions on Automation Science and Engineering, 6*(1), 16–24. doi:10.1109/TASE.2008.2007266

Mahajan, A., Potnis, N., Gopalan, K., & Wang, A.-I. A. (2006). Urban mobility models for VANETs. In the Second IEEE International Workshop on Next Generation Wireless Networks, Bangalore, India.

Maillart, L. M., Kamrani, A., Norman, B. A., Rajgopal, J., & Hawrylak, P. J. (2010). Optimizing RFID tag-inventorying algorithms. *IIE Transactions, 42*(9), 690–702. doi:10.1080/07408171003705714

Maleki, S., Pandharipande, A., & Leus, G. (2010). Two-stage spectrum sensing for cognitive radios. *IEEE International Conference on Acoustic, Speech and Signal Processing (ICASSP '10)*, (pp. 2946-2949).

Mangold, S., Sunghyun, C., Hiertz, G., Klein, O., & Walke, B. (2003). *Analysis of IEEE 802.11e for QoS support in wireless LANs* (pp. 40–50). IEEE Wireless Communication Magazine.

Maric, I., Goldsmith, A., & Medard, M. (2010). Analog network coding in the high-SNR regime. *IEEE Wireless Network Coding conference*, (pp. 1-6).

Maròti, M., Kusy, B., Simon, G., & Lèdeczi, A. (2004). The flooding time synchronization protocol. *ACM International Conference on Embedded Networked Sensor Systems (SenSys 2004)* (pp. 39–49).

Marx, R. W. (1986). The tiger system: Automating the geographic structure of the United States census. *Government Publications Review, 13*(2), 181–201. doi:10.1016/0277-9390(86)90003-8

Mary, P., Mischa Dohler, Gorce, J.-M., & Villemau, G. (2011). Symbol error outage analysis of MIMO OSTBC systems over rice fading channels in shadowing environments. *IEEE Transactions on Wireless Communications, 10*(4), 1009–1014. doi:10.1109/TWC.2011.021611.091838

Matin, M. A. (2010). Ultra wideband preliminaries. In Lembrikov, B. (Ed.), *Ultra wideband*. Intech Publisher. doi:10.5772/10059

Maurer, U. (2000). Authentication theory and hypothesis testing. *IEEE Transactions on Information Theory, 46*, 1350–1356. doi:10.1109/18.850674

Mengali, M. M. (2001). A comparison of pilot-aided channel estimation methods for OFDMsystems. *IEEE Transactions on Signal Processing, 49*(12), 3065–3073. doi:10.1109/78.969514

Mengali, M. M. (2002). An improved frequency offset estimator for OFDM applications. *IEEE Communications Letters, 3*(3), 75–77.

Mickle, M. H., Mats, L., & Hawrylak, P. J. (2008). Resolution and integration of HF and UHF. In Miles, S. B., Sarma, S. E., & Williams, J. R. (Eds.), *RFID technology and applications* (pp. 47–60). New York, NY: Cambridge University Press. doi:10.1017/CBO9780511541155.005

Mili, H., Elkharraz, A., & Mcheick, H. (2004). Understanding separation of concerns. *Aspect-Oriented Software Development*. Retrieved from http://www.latece.uqam.ca/publications/mili-kharraz-mcheick.pdf

Mills, D. (1991). Internet time synchronization: The network time protocol. *IEEE Transactions on Communications, 39*(10), 1482–1493. doi:10.1109/26.103043

Mirowski, L., Hartnett, J., & Williams, R. (2009, October). An RFID attacker behavior taxonomy. *IEEE Pervasive Computing / IEEE Computer Society and IEEE Communications Society, 8*(4), 79–84. doi:10.1109/MPRV.2009.68

Mitchell, M. (2006). Complex systems: Network thinking. *Artificial Intelligence, 170*(18), 1194–1212. doi:10.1016/j.artint.2006.10.002

Mitola, J., III, & Maguire, G. Q. (1999). Cognitive radio: making software radios personal. *IEEE Personal Communication, 6*(4), 13-18.

Mitola, J., III. (2000). *Cognitive radio: An integrated agent for software defined radio*. Doctoral dissertation, Royal Institute of Technology (KTH), Stockholm, Sweden.

Mitrokotsa, A., Rieback, M., & Tanenbaum, A. (2010). Classifying RFID attacks and defenses. *Information Systems Frontiers, 12*(5), 491–505. doi:10.1007/s10796-009-9210-z

Mogul, J. (2006). Emergent (mis)behavior vs. complex software systems. *ACM SIGOPS Operating Systems Review, 40*(4), 293–304. doi:10.1145/1218063.1217964

Molisch, A., Balakrishnan, K., Chong, C. C., Emami, S., Fort, A., & Karedal, J. … Siwiak, K. (2004). *IEEE 802.15.4a channel model - Final report* (Online). Retrieved from http://www.ieee802.org/15/pub/TG4a.html

Moose, P. H. (1994). A technique for orthogonal frequency division multiplexing frequency offset correction. *IEEE Transactions on Communications, 42*(10). doi:10.1109/26.328961

Moy, J. (2008). *RFC 2328 (Standard), OSPF version 2*. Retrieved from http://www.ietf.org/rfc/rfc2328.txt

Mutukrishnan, K., Lijding, M., & Havinga, P. (2005). Towards smart surroundings: Enabling techniques and technologies for localization. In *LoCA 2005: Proceedings of Location- and Context-Awareness: First International Workshop*, Oberpfaffenhofen, Germany.

Nadeem, T., Dashtinezhad, S., Liao, C., & Iftode, L. (2004). TrafficView: Traffic data dissemination using car-to-car communication. *ACM SIGMOBILE Mobile Computing and Communications Review, 8*(3), 6–19. doi:10.1145/1031483.1031487

Neel, J. O. (2006). *Analysis and design if cognitive radio network and distributed radio resource management algorithms.* Unpublished doctoral dissertation, Virginia Polytechnic Institute and State University, Blacksburg, VA.

Nguyen, D., Tran, T., Nguyen, T., & Bose, B. (2009). Wireless broadcast using network coding. *IEEE Transactions on Vehicular Technology*, *58*(2), 914–925. doi:10.1109/TVT.2008.927729

O'Connor, M. C. (2011). Ultracapacitor offers 75-foot read range for passive tags. *RFID Journal*. Retrieved July 6, 2011, from http://www.rfidjournal.com/article/view/8565

Olfat, M., Farrokhi, F. R., & Liu, K. J. R. (2005). Power allocation for OFDM using adaptive beamforming over wireless networks. *IEEE Transactions on Communications*, *53*(3), 505–514. doi:10.1109/TCOMM.2005.843438

Oner, M., & Jondral, F. (2007). Air interface identification for software radio systems. *AEÜ. International Journal of Electronics and Communications*, *61*(2), 104–117. doi:10.1016/j.aeue.2006.03.005

Oppermann, I. (2004). *An overview of UWB activities within PULSERS.* Paper presented in Ultra- Wideband Seminar in Singapore.

Papadimitriou, C. H., & Steiglitz, K. (Eds.). (1982). *Combinatorial optimization.* Mineola, NY: Dover Publications Inc.

Parikh, J., & Basu, A. (2011). LTE advanced: The 4G mobile broadband technology. *International Journal of Computers and Applications*, *13*(5), 17–21. doi:10.5120/1776-2449

Park, J., Chun, J., & Park, H. (2009, 14-18 June). *Efficient GSVD based multi-user MIMO linear precoding and antenna selection scheme.* Paper presented at the IEEE ICC 2009, Dresden.

Park, K., & Willinger, W. (Eds.). (2007). The internet as a large-scale complex system. *Journal of the Royal Statistical Society. Series A, (Statistics in Society)*, *170*(1), 260. doi:10.1111/j.1467-985X.2006.00455_12.x

Peeters, T. P. (2002). Synchronization with DMT modulation. *IEEE Communications Magazine*, *37*(4), 80–86.

Peh, E., & Liang, Y. C. (2007). Optimization for cooperative sensing in cognitive radio networks, *Wireless Communications and Networking Conference (WCNC '07)*, (pp. 27-32).

Peh, E., Liang, Y. C., & Guan, Y. L. (2008). Power control for physical-layer network coding in fading environments. *IEEE 19th International Symposium on Personal, Indoor and Mobile Radio Communications*, (pp. 1–5).

Perkins, C. E., & Royer, E. M. (1999). *Ad-hoc on-demand distance vector routing.* In the 2nd IEEE Workshop on Mobile Computing Systems and Applications.

Polack, F., Hoverd, T., Sampson, A. T., Stepney, S., & Timmis, J. (2008). Complex systems models: Engineering simulations. *Artificial Life*, *11*, 482–489. Retrieved from http://www.cosmos-research.org/docs/alife2008-engineering.pdf

Poor, H. V., & Hadjiliadis, O. (2009). *Quickest detection.* Cambridge, UK: Cambridge University Press.

Popovski, P., & Yomo, H. (2006). The antipackets can increase the achievable throughput of a wireless multihop network. *IEEE International Conference on Communications*, Vol. 9, (pp. 3885–3890).

Pries, R., Menth, S., Staehle, D., Menth, M., & Tran-Gia, P. (2008). Dynamic contention window adaptation (DCWA) in 802.11e wireless local area networks. *IEEE International Conference on Consumer Electronics (ICCE 08)* (pp. 92–97).

Proakis, J. G. (2000). *Digital communications* (4th ed.). Boston, MA: McGraw Hill.

Proakis, J., & Manolakis, D. G. (2007). *Digital signal processing: Principles, algorithms, and applications* (4th ed.). Upper Saddle River, NJ: Prentice Hall Inc.

Raisinghani, V., & Iyer, S. (2006). Cross-layer feedback architecture for mobile device protocol stacks. *IEEE Communications Magazine*, *44*(1), 85–92. doi:10.1109/MCOM.2006.1580937

Rapport, T. S. (1996). *Wireless communications principles and practice.* Prentice Hall PTR.

Ratnarajah, T., & Vaillancourt, R. (2005). Quadratic forms on complex random matrices and multiple-antenna systems. *IEEE Transactions on Information Theory, 51*(8), 2976–2984. doi:10.1109/TIT.2005.851778

Ravilla, S. R., Ogirala, A., Murari, A., Hawrylak, P. J., & Mickle, M. H. (2011). Anti-collision policy for RFID systems: Fast predict tags in field algorithm. *International Journal of Radio Frequency Identification Technology and Applications, 3*(3), 215–228. doi:10.1504/IJRFITA.2011.040995

Rawat, D. B., & Yan, G. (2009). Signal processing techniques for spectrum sensing in cognitive radio systems: Challenges and perspectives. In *Proceedings of IEE/IFIP AH-ICI 2009*, Kathmandu, Nepal.

Rawat, D. B., & Yan, G. (2011). Spectrum sensing methods and dynamic spectrum sharing in cognitive radio networks: A survey. *International Journal of Research and Reviews in Wireless Sensor Network, 1*(1), 1–13.

Raychaudhuri, D., Seskar, I., Ott, M., Ganu, S., Ramachandran, K., & Kremo, H. ... Singh, M. (2005). *Overview of the orbit radio grid testbed for evaluation of next-generation wireless network protocols*. In the IEEE Wireless Communications and Networking Conference, New Orleans, LA, USA.

Raymond, D. R., Marchany, R. C., Brownfield, M. I., & Midkiff, S. F. (2009, January). Effects of denial-of-sleep attacks on wireless sensor network MAC protocols. *IEEE Transactions on Vehicular Technology, 58*(1), 367–380. doi:10.1109/TVT.2008.921621

Reggiannini, M. L. (2005). Carrier frequency acquisition and tracking for OFDM systems. *IEEE Transactions on Communications, 44*(11), 1590–1598.

Rekaya, G. V. (2005). The golden code: A 2×2 full-rate space-time code with nonvanishing determinants. *IEEE Transactions on Information Theory, 51*(4), 1432–1436. doi:10.1109/TIT.2005.844069

Renfors, A. H.-D. (2007). Blind estimation of large carrier frequency offset in wireless OFDM systems. *IEEE Transactions on Vehicular Technology, 56*(2), 965–968. doi:10.1109/TVT.2007.891430

Rieback, M. R., Crispo, B., & Tanenbaum, A. S. (2005). Keep on blockin' in the free world: Personal access control for low-cost RFID tags. In B. Christianson, B. Crispo, J. A. Malcolm, & M. Roe (Eds.), *Proceedings of the 13th International Conference on Security Protocols* (pp. 51-59). Berlin, Germany: Springer-Verlag.

Rieback, M. R., Crispo, B., & Tanenbaum, A. S. (2006, March). The evolution of RFID security. *Pervasive Computing, 5*(1), 62–69. doi:10.1109/MPRV.2006.17

Rihani, S. (2001). *Nonlinear systems*. Retrieved May 14, 2010, from http://www.globalcomplexity.org/NonlinearSystems.htm

Romdhani, L., Ni, Q., & Turletti, T. (2003). Adaptive EDCF: Enhanced service differentiation for IEEE 802.11 wireless ad-hoc networks. *IEEE Wireless Communications and Networking Conference (WCNC 03)* (pp. 1373–1378).

Rosenbaum, U. (1993). A lower bound on authentication after having observed a sequence of messages. *Journal of Cryptology, 6*(3), 135–156. doi:10.1007/BF00198462

Rotter, P. (2008, April-June). A framework for assessing RFID system security and privacy risks. *IEEE Pervasive Computing / IEEE Computer Society and IEEE Communications Society, 7*(2), 70–77. doi:10.1109/MPRV.2008.22

Sadek, M., Tarighat, A., & Sayed, A. H. (2007a). Active antenna selection in multiuser MIMO communications. *IEEE Transactions on Signal Processing, 44*(4), 1498–1510. doi:10.1109/TSP.2006.888893

Sadek, M., Tarighat, A., & Sayed, A. H. (2007b). A leakage-based precoding scheme for downlink multi-user MIMO channels. *IEEE Transactions on Communications, 6*(5), 1711–1721. doi:doi:10.1109/TWC.2007.360373

Saeid, E., Jeoti, V., & Samir, B. B. (2011). *FKT based successive linear precoding for multiuser multiple input multiple output system.*

Saha, A. K., & Johnson, D. B. (2004). *Modeling mobility for vehicular ad-hoc networks*. In the 1st ACM International Workshop on Vehicular ad hoc Networks, Philadelphia, PA, USA.

Sahai, A., & Cabric, D. (2005). *Spectrum sensing: Fundamental limits and practical challenges*. First IEEE International Symposium on Dynamic Spectrum Access Networks (DySPAN '05).

Sahai, A., Hoven, N., & Tandra, R. (2004). Some fundamental limits in cognitive radio. In *Proceedings of Allerton Conference on Communications, Control and Computing.*

Sahin, M. E., & Arslan, H. (2006). System design for cognitive radio communications. In *Proceedings of the International Conference on Cognitive Radio Oriented Wireless Networks and Communications (CROWNCOM '06).*

Saltzer, J., Reed, D., & Clark, D. (1984). End-to-end arguments in system design. *ACM Transactions on Computer Systems, 2*(4), 277–288. doi:10.1145/357401.357402

Sampath, H., Stoica, P., & Paulraj, A. (2001). Generalized linear precoder and decoder design for MIMO channels using the weighted MMSE criterion. *IEEE Transactions on Communications, 49*(12), 2198–2206. doi:10.1109/26.974266

Santella, G. (2002). A frequency and symbol synchronization system for OFDM signals: Architecture and simulation results. *IEEE Transactions on Vehicular Technology, 49*(1), 254–275. doi:10.1109/25.820719

Sarkar, M. Z. I., & Ratnarajah, T. (2011). Secrecy capacity and secure outage performance for Rayleigh fading SIMO channel. In *Proceedings IEEE 36th International Conference on Acoustics, Speech and Signal Processing,* Prague, Czech Republic.

Sarkar, M. Z. I., & Ratnarajah, T. (2011). Secure communication through Nakagami-m fading MISO channel. In *Proceedings of IEEE International Conference on Communications (ICC 2011),* Kyoto, Japan.

Savvides, A., Han, C. C., & Srivastava, M. B. (2001). Dynamic fine-grained localization in ad-hoc networks of sensors. In *Proceedings ACM MobiCom 2001,* Rome, Italy.

Schenato, L., & Gamba, G. (2007). A distributed consensus protocol for clock synchronization in wireless sensor network. *IEEE Conference on Decision and Control (CDC 07)* (pp. 2289–2294).

Schlegel, L. W. (2002). Synchronization requirements for multi-user OFDM on satellite mobile and two-path rayleigh fading channels. *IEEE Transactions on Communications, 43*(234), 887–895.

Schubert, M., Shi, S., Jorswiech, E. A., & Boche, H. (2005). *Downlink sum-MSE transceiver optimization for linear multi-user MIMO systems.* Paper presented at the Signals, Systems and Computers, 2005.

Schubert, M., & Boche, M. (2004). Solution of the multiuser downlink beamforming problem with individual SINR constraints. *IEEE Transactions on Vehicular Technology, 53*(1), 18–28. doi:10.1109/TVT.2003.819629

Scopigno, R., & Cozzetti, H. A. (2009). Mobile slotted aloha for VANETs. *IEEE Vehicular Technology Conference (VTC Fall 2009)* (pp. 1-5).

Scopigno, R., & Vesco, A. (2011). A distributed bandwidth management scheme for multi-hop wireless access networks. *IEEE Communications Society Conference on Sensor, Mesh and Ad Hoc Communications and Networks (IWCMC 2011)* (pp. 534–539).

Scott, J., Huiy, P., Crowcrofty, J., & Diot, C. (2006). Haggle: A networking architecture designed around mobile users. *Proceedings of the Third Annual Conference on Wireless On-demand Network Systems and Services,* (pp. 78-86). Retrieved from http://www.cl.cam.ac.uk/~ph315/publications/haggle-wons06-editforxtoff.pdf

Sellathurai, M., Ratnarajah, T., & Guinand, P. (2007). Multirate layered space-time coding and successive interference cancellation receivers in quasi-static fading channels. *IEEE Transactions on Wireless Communications, 6*(12), 4524–4533. doi:10.1109/TWC.2007.060399

Shakkottai, S., Rappaport, T. S., & Karlsson, P. C. (2003). Cross-layer design for wireless networks. *IEEE Communications Magazine,* (n.d), 74–80. doi:10.1109/MCOM.2003.1235598

Shankar, N. S., Cordeiro, C., & Challapali, K. (2005). Spectrum agile radios: Utilization and sensing architectures, *First IEEE International Symposium on Dynamic Spectrum Access Networks (DySPAN '05)* (pp. 160-169).

Shankar, S. (2005). Spectrum agile radios: Utilization and sensing architecture. In *Proceedings of IEEE DySPAN 2005,* Baltimore, MD.

Shannon, C. E. (1949). Communication theory of secrecy systems. *The Bell System Technical Journal, 28,* 656–715.

Shellhammer, S., & Tandra, R. (2006). *Performance of the power detector with noise uncertainty.* IEEE 802.22-06/0134r0. IEEE P802.22 Wireless RANs.

Shen, Z., Andrews, V., & Evans, B. L. (2003). Optimal power allocation in multiuser OFDM systems. In *Proceedings of IEEE Global Communication Conference,* (pp. 337-341).

Shen, L., Wang, H., Zhang, W., & Zhao, Z. (2011). Blind spectrum sensing for cognitive radio channels with noise uncertainty. *IEEE Transactions on Wireless Communications, 10*(6), 1721–1724. doi:10.1109/TWC.2011.040511.101559

Shenpei, Z., & Xinping, Y. (2008). *Driver's route choice model based on traffic signal control.* In the 3rd IEEE Conference on Industrial Electronics and Applications.

Shiqiang, W., Qingyang, S., Xingwei, W., & Jamalipour, A. (2011). Power and rate adaptation for analog network coding. *IEEE Transactions on Vehicular Technology, 60*(5), 2302–2313. doi:10.1109/TVT.2011.2135869

Shiu, D.-S., Foschini, G. J., Gans, M. J., & Kahn, J. M. (2000). fading correlation and Its effect on the capacity of multielement antenna systems. *IEEE Transactions on Communications, 48*(3), 502–512. doi:10.1109/26.837052

Siavoshani, M. J., Mohajer, S., & Fragouli, C. (2011). On the capacity of non-coherent network coding. *IEEE Transactions on Information Theory, 57*(2), 1046–1066. doi:10.1109/TIT.2010.2094813

Singh, M., Ott, M., Seskar, I., & Kamat, P. (2005). *Orbit measurements framework and library (OML): Motivations, design, implementation, and features.* In IEEE First International Conference on Testbeds and Research Infrastructures for the development of networks and communities, Trento, Italy.

Software Engineering. (2011). *Wikipedia, the free encyclopedia.* Retrieved from http://en.wikipedia.org/wiki/Software_engineering

Sombrutzki, R., Zubow, A., Kurth, M., & Redlich, J.-P. (2006). *Self-organization in community mesh networks: The Berlin RoofNet.* In the 1st Workshop on Operator-Assisted (Wireless Mesh) Community, Berlin, Germany.

Sonnenschein, A., & Fishman, P. M. (1992). Radiometric detection of spread-spectrum signals in noise of uncertain power. *IEEE Transactions on Aerospace and Electronic Systems, 28*(3), 654–660. doi:10.1109/7.256287

Spencer, Q., & Haardt, M. (2002, November). *Capacity and downlink transmission algorithms for a multi-user MIMO channel.* Paper presented at the 36th Asilomar Conference on Signals, Systems, and Computers.

Spencer, Q. H., Swindlehurst, A. L., & Haardt, M. (2004). Zero-forcing methods for downlink spatial multiplexing in multiuser MIMO channels. *IEEE Transactions on Signal Processing, 52*(2), 461–471. doi:10.1109/TSP.2003.821107

Stankovic, V. (2007). Iterative successive MMSE multiuser MIMO transmit filtering. *Electrical Engineering in Japan, 20*(1), 45–55.

Stankovic, V., & Haardt, M. (2008). Generalized design of multi-user MIMO precoding matrices. *IEEE Transactions on Wireless Communications, 7*(3), 953–961. doi:10.1109/LCOMM.2008.060709

Stevenson, C. R., Chouinard, G., Lei, Z., Hu, W., Shellhammer, S., & Caldwell, W. (2009). IEEE 802.22: The first cognitive radio wireless regional area network standard. *IEEE Communications Magazine, 47*(1), 130–138. doi:10.1109/MCOM.2009.4752688

Stirling, D. (2005). *Modeling complex systems.* Retrieved from http://www.learndev.org/dl/BtSM2005-Stirling-Complexity.pdf

Stotas, S., & Nallanathan, A. (2010). On the throughput maximization of spectrum sharing cognitive radio networks. In *Proceedings of IEEE Globecom.*

Stuber, A. N. (2001). Synchronization for MIMO OFDM systems. *Global Telecommunications Conference, 2001,* (pp. 509–513).

Sun, C., Zhang, W., & Letaief, K. B. (2007). Cooperative spectrum sensing for cognitive radios under bandwidth constraints. *Wireless Communications and Networking Conference (WCNC '07),* (pp. 1-5).

Sun, Y., Hawrylak, P. J., Mao, Z.-H., & Mickle, M. H. (2010, March). Collision resolution in ISO 18000-6c passive RFID. *Applied Computational Electromagnetics Society (ACES) Journal, Special Issue: Computational and Experimental Techniques for RFID Systems and Applications, 25*(3).

Suzuki, H. (1977). A statistical model for urban radio propagation. *IEEE Transactions on Communications, 25*(7), 673–680. doi:10.1109/TCOM.1977.1093888

Swami, A. S. (2005). Doppler and frequency-offset synchronization in wideband OFDM. *IEEE Transactions on Wireless Communications, 4*(6), 2870–2881. doi:10.1109/TWC.2005.858337

Tandra, R., & Sahai, A. (2005). Fundamental limits on detection in low SNR under noise uncertainty, *in Proceedings of the International Conference on Wireless Networks, Communications and Mobile Computing (wirelessCom '05)*, (pp. 464-469).

Tandra, R., & Sahai, A. (2008). SNR walls for signal detection. *IEEE Journal on Selected Topics in Signal Processing, 2*(1), 4–17. doi:10.1109/JSTSP.2007.914879

Tang, H. (2005). Some physical layer issues of wide-band cognitive radio systems. *First IEEE International Symposium on Dynamic Spectrum Access Networks (DySPAN '05)*, (pp. 151-159).

Tarokh, V., Jafarkhani, H., & Calderbank, A. R. (1999). Space–time block coding for wireless communications: Performance results. *IEEE Journal of Selected Topics in Communications, 17*(3), 451–460. doi:10.1109/49.753730

Tawfik, A. M., Rakha, H. A., & Miller, S. D. (2010). *Driver route choice behavior: Experiences, perceptions, and choices*. In 2010 IEEE Intelligent Vehicles Symposium.

Telatar. (1995). *Capacity of multi-antenna Gaussian Channel*. ATT Bell Technical Memorandum.

Thomas, R., DaSilva, L., & MacKenzie, A. (2005). *Cognitive networks* (pp. 352–360). New Frontiers in Dynamic Spectrum Access Networks.

Thomson, D. J. (1982). Spectrum estimation and harmonic analysis. *Proceedings of the IEEE, 20*, 1055–1096. doi:10.1109/PROC.1982.12433

Tian, Z., & Giannakis, G. B. (2006). A wavelet approach to wideband spectrum sensing for cognitive radios. In *Proceedings of IEEE International Conference of Cognitive Radio Oriented Wireless Networks and Communications (Crowncom)*, (pp. 1054–1059). Mykonos, Greece.

Tian, Z., & Giannakis, G. B. (2007). Compressed sensing for wideband cognitive radios. *IEEE International Conference on Acoustic, Speech and Signal Processing (ICASSP '10)*, (pp. 1357-1360).

Tmote Sky Datasheet. (2006). *Mote IV Corporation.* Retrieved from http://www.moteiv.com/products/docs/tmote-skydatasheet.pdf

Todd, B., Phillips, M., Schultz, S. M., Hawkins, A. R., & Jensen, B. D. (2009, April). Low-cost RFID threshold shock sensors. *IEEE Sensors Journal, 9*(4), 464–469. doi:10.1109/JSEN.2009.2014410

Touch, J., Wang, Y., & Pingali, V. (2006). *A recursive network architecture*. Retrieved from http://www.isi.edu/touch/pubs/isi-tr-2006-626/

Tran, T., Nguyen, T., Bose, B., & Gopal, V. (2009). A hybrid network coding technique for single-hop wireless networks. *IEEE Journal on Selected Areas in Communications, 27*(5), 685–698. doi:10.1109/JSAC.2009.090610

Tse, D., & Viswanath, P. (2005). *Fundamentals of wireless communication*. Cambridge, UK: Cambridge university Press.

Tureli, D. K. (2001). Multicarrier synchronization with diversity. *Vehicular Technology Conference, 2001*, (pp. 952–956).

Tureli, H. L. (1997). A high efficiency carrier estimator for OFDM communications. *Conference Record of the Thirty-First Asilomar Conference on Signals, Systems & Computers*, (pp. 505–509). Pacific Grove, CA, USA.

Uichin, L., Magistretti, E., Gerla, M., Bellavista, P., & Corradi, A. (2009). Dissemination and harvesting of urban data using vehicular sensing platforms. *IEEE Transactions on Vehicular Technology, 58*(2), 882–901. doi:10.1109/TVT.2008.928899

Ulversoy, T. (2010). Software defined radio: Challenges and opportunities. *IEEE Communication Surveys Tutorials, 12*(4), 531–550. doi:10.1109/SURV.2010.032910.00019

Unnikrishnan, J., & Veeravalli, V. V. (2007). *Cooperative sensing and detection for cognitive radio.* Paper presented at IEEE Globecom, Washington DC.

Urkowitz, H. (1967). Energy detection of unknown deterministic signals. *Proceedings of the IEEE, 55*(4), 523–531. doi:10.1109/PROC.1967.5573

Vahdat, A., & Becker, D. (2000). *Epidemic routing for partially-connected ad hoc networks. Technical Report.* Duke University.

van de Beek, M. S. (2002). ML estimation of time and frequency offset in OFDM systems. *IEEE Transactions on Signal Processing, 45*(7), 1800–1805. doi:10.1109/78.599949

Vesco, A., & Scopigno, R. (2009). Time-division access priority in CSMA/CA. *IEEE Personal, Indoor and Mobile Radio Communications Symposium (PIMRC 09)* (pp. 1–6).

Vesco, A., & Scopigno, R. (2011). Advances on time-division unbalanced carrier sense multiple access. *IEEE Workshop on Flexibility in Broadband Wireless Access Networks (FlexBWAN 2011), in conjunction with IEEE International Conference on Computer Communications and Networks (ICCCN 2011)* (pp. 1–6).

Vesco, A., Abrate, F., & Scopigno, R. (2011). Convergence and performance analysis of leaderless synchronization in Wi-Fi networks. ACM Workshop on Performance Monitoring, Measurement, and Evaluation of Heterogeneous Wired and Wireless Mobile Networks (PM2HW2N 2011), in conjunction with ACM International Conference on Modeling, Analysis and Simulation of Wireless and Mobile Systems (MSWiM 2011).

Viriyasitavat, W., Tonguz, O. K., & Fan, B. (2009). *Network connectivity of VANETs in urban areas.* In the 6th Annual IEEE Communications Society Conference on Sensor, Mesh and Ad Hoc Communications and Networks.

Walker, M. (1990). Information theoretic bounds for authentication schemes. *Journal of Cryptology, 2*(3), 131–143. doi:10.1007/BF00190800

Wang, C., Au, E. K. S., Murch, R. D., Mow, W. H., Cheng, R. S., & Lau, A. V. (2007). *On the performance of the MIMO zero-forcing receiver in the presence of channel estimation error.* Paper presented at the Information Sciences and Interaction Sciences, Chengdu, China

Wang, J., An, X., Prasad, R. V., & Niemegeers, I. (2006). A range-free online person tracking system. In *Proceedings of the First International Conference on Pervasive Computing Technologies for Healthcare,* Innsbruck, Austria.

Wang, Q., & Abu-Rgheff, M. (2003). Cross-layer signaling for next generation systems. *IEEE Wireless Communications and Networking Conference (WCNC), 2,* (pp. 1084-1089). doi: 10.1109/WCNC.2003.1200522

Wang, Y., Tian, Z., & Feng, C. (2010). A two-step compressed spectrum sensing scheme for wideband cognitive radios. *IEEE Global Telecommunications Conference (GLOBECOM '10),* (pp. 1-5).

Weber, S., Cahill, V., Clarke, S., & Haahr, M. (2003). Wireless ad hoc network for Dublin: A large-scale ad hoc network test-bed. *ERCIM News, 54.*

Wegener, A., & Piórkowski, M. EPFL, M. R., Hellbrück, H., Fischer, S., & Hubaux, J.-P. (2008). *TraCI: An interface for coupling road traffic and network simulators.* In the 11th Communications and Networking Simulation Symposium, Ottawa, Canada.

Weiss, T., Hillenbrand, J., Krohn, A., & Jondral, F. (2003). Efficient signaling of spectral resources in spectrum pooling systems. In *Proceedings of 10th Symposium on Communication and Vehicular Technology.*

Wei, Y., & Lui, R. (2006). Dual methods for nonconvex spectrum optimization of multicarrier systems. *IEEE Transactions on Communications, 54*(7), 1310–1322. doi:10.1109/TCOMM.2006.877962

Wendong, H., Willkomm, D., Abusubaih, M., Gross, J., Vlantis, G., Gerla, M., & Wolisz, A. (2007). Cognitive radios for dynamic spectrum access - Dynamic frequency hopping communities for efficient IEEE 802.22 operation. *IEEE Communications Magazine, 45*(5), 80–87. doi:10.1109/MCOM.2007.358853

Wiesel, A., Eldar, Y. C., & Shamai, S. (2006). Linear precoding via conic optimization for fixed MIMO receivers. *IEEE Transactions on Signal Processing, 54*(1), 161–176. doi:10.1109/TSP.2005.861073

Wild, B., & Ramchandran, K. (2005). Detecting primary receivers for cognitive radio applications. In *Proceeding of IEEE Dynamic Spectrum Access Networks, DySPAN 2005,* (pp. 124–130).

Wischhof, L., Ebner, A., & Rohling, H. (2005). Information dissemination in self-organizing intervehicle networks. *IEEE Transactions on Intelligent Transportation Systems, 6*(1), 90–101. doi:10.1109/TITS.2004.842407

Wroclawski, J. (1997). *RFC 2210 (proposed standard), the use of RSVP with IETF integrated services.* Retrieved from http://www.ietf.org/rfc/rfc2210.txt

Xia, W., Yuan, W., Cheng, W., Liu, W., Wang, S., & Xu, J. (2010). Optimization of cooperative spectrum sensing in ad-hoc cognitive radio networks. *IEEE Global Telecommunications Conference (GLOBECOM '10)*, (pp. 1-5).

Xiao, L., Greenstein, L., Mandayam, N., & Trappe, W. (2008). A physical-layer technique to enhance authentication for mobile terminals. In *Proceedings IEEE International Conference on Communications (ICC)*, (pp. 1520–1524). Beijing, China.

Xiao, L., Johansson, M., & Boyd, S. P. (2004). Simultaneous routing and resource allocation via dual decomposition. *IEEE Transactions on Communications, 52*(7), 1136–1144. doi:10.1109/TCOMM.2004.831346

Xiao, Y. (2005). IEEE 802.11N: Enhancements for higher throughput in wireless LANs. *IEEE Wireless Communications, 12*(6), 82–91. doi:10.1109/MWC.2005.1561948

Xing, Y., Mathur, C. N., Haleem, M., Chandramouli, R., & Subbalakshmi, K. (2007). Dynamic spectrum access with QoS and interference temperature constraints. *IEEE Transactions on Mobile Computing, 6*(4), 423–433. doi:10.1109/TMC.2007.50

Yan, S., & Wang, X. (2009). Power allocation for cognitive radio systems based on nonregenerative OFDM relay transmission. In *Proceedings of IEEE Wicom*, (pp. 1-4).

Yates, R., Raman, C., & Mandayam, N. (2006). Fair and efficient scheduling of variable rate links via a spectrum server. In *Proceeding of IEEE International Conference on Communications, ICC'06*, (pp. 5246 – 5251).

Yeung, R. W. (2008). *Information theory and network coding.* New York, NY: Springer-Verlag.

Yeung, R. W., Li, S.-Y. R., Cai, N., & Zhang, Z. (2006). Network coding theory. *Foundation and Trends in Communications and Information Theory, 2*(4&5), 241–381.

Yu, D. D., & Cioffi, J. M. (2006). Iterative water-filling for optimal resource allocation in OFDM multi-access and broadcast channels. In *Proceedings of IEEE Global Telecommunication Conference*, San Francisco, CA, (pp. 1-5).

Yu, K., & Oppermann, I. (2004). Performance of UWB position estimation based on time-of-arrival measurements. In *UWBST: Proceedings of IEEE Conference on Ultra wideband System and Technology,* Kyoto, Japan.

Yu, W., Rhee, W., Boyd, S., & Cio, J. M. (2001). *Iterative water-filling for Gaussian vector multiple access channels.* Paper presented at the IEEE International Symposium on Information Theory, Washington DC.

Yucek, T., & Arslan, H. (2009). A survey of spectrum sensing algorithms for cognitive radio applications. *IEEE Communications Surveys and Tutorials, 11*(1), 116–130. doi:10.1109/SURV.2009.090109

Zayen, B., Hayar, A. M., & Nussbaum, D. (2008). Blind spectrum sensing for cognitive radio based on model selection. In *Proceedings of the International Conference on Cognitive Radio Oriented Wireless Networks and Communications (CROWNCOM '08)*, (pp. 1-4).

Zayen, B., Hayar, A., & Kansanen, K. (2009). Blind spectrum sensing for cognitive radio based on signal space dimension estimation. *IEEE International Conference on Communications (ICC '09)*, (pp. 1-5).

Zeng, Y. H., & Liang Y. C. (2008). Eigenvalue based sensing algorithms. *IEEE 802.22-06/0118r0.*

Zeng, Y. H., & Liang, Y. C. (2007). *Maximum-minimum eigenvalue detection for cognitive radio.* 18th IEEE International Symposium on Personal, Indoor and Mobile Radio Communications (PIMRC '07).

Zeng, Y. H., Liang, Y. C., Hoang, A. T., & Peh, E. (2009). Reliability of spectrum sensing under noise and interference uncertainty. *IEEE International Conference on Communications Workshops (ICC Workshops '09)*, (pp. 1-5).

Zeng, Y. H., & Liang, Y. C. (2009). Eigenvalue-based spectrum sensing algorithms for cognitive radio. *IEEE Transactions on Communications, 57*(6), 1784–1793. doi:10.1109/TCOMM.2009.06.070402

Zeng, Y. H., Liang, Y. C., & Zhang, R. (2008). Blindly combined energy detection for spectrum sensing in cognitive radio. *IEEE Signal Processing Letters, 15,* 649–652. doi:10.1109/LSP.2008.2002711

Zeng, Y. H., Liang, Y. C., & Zhang, R. (2010). A review on spectrum sensing for cognitive radio: Challenges and solutions. *EURASIP Journal on Advances in Signal Processing,* •••, 2010.

Zeng, Y., & Liang, Y.-C. (2009). Spectrum-sensing algorithms for cognitive radio based on statistical covariances. *IEEE Transactions on Vehicular Technology, 58*(4), 1804–1815. doi:10.1109/TVT.2008.2005267

Zhang, S., & Sim, T. (2006, 17-22 June). *When Fisher meets Fukunaga-Koontz: A new look at linear discriminants.* Paper presented at the IEEE Computer Society Conference on Computer Vision and Pattern Recognition (CVPR'06), New York.

Zhang, S., Liew, S. C., & Lam, P. P. (2006). Hot topic: Physical-layer network coding. *Proceedings of the 12th Annual International Conference on Mobile Computing and Networking* (pp. 358–365).

Zhang, X., Kurose, J., Levine, B. N., Towsley, D., & Zhang, H. (2007). *Study of a bus-based disruption-tolerant network: Mobility modeling and impact on routing.* In the 13th Annual ACM International Conference on Mobile Computing and Networking.

Zhang, Z., & Jia, L. Chai1, Y., & Guo, M. (2008). A study on the elementary control methodologies for complex systems. *Control and Decision Conference,* (pp. 4455-4460). doi:10.1109/CCDC.2008.4598172

Zhang, Q., Jia, J., & Zhang, J. (2009). Cooperative relay to improve diversity in cognitive radio networks. *IEEE Communications Magazine, 47*(2), 111–117. doi:10.1109/MCOM.2009.4785388

Zhang, Q., Yang, F., & Zhu, W. (2005). Cross-layer QoS support for multimedia delivery over wireless Internet. *EURASIP Journal on Applied Signal Processing,* (n.d), 2005.

Zhang, W., Mallik, R., & Letaief, K. (2009). Optimization of cooperative spectrum sensing with energy detection in cognitive radio networks. *IEEE Transactions on Wireless Communications, 8*(12), 5761–5766. doi:10.1109/TWC.2009.12.081710

Zhao, D., & Shao, C. (2010). *Empirical study of drivers' learning behavior and reliance on VMS.* In 2010 13th International IEEE Conference on Intelligent Transportation Systems.

Zhao, J., & Govindan, R. (2003). Understanding packet delivery performance in dense wireless sensor networks. In *Proceedings ACM SenSys '03,* Los Angeles, CA, USA.

Zhao, J., & Li, Q. (2010). *A method for modeling drivers' behavior rules in agent-based traffic simulation.* In the 18th International Conference on Geoinformatics.

Zhu, H., Cao, G., Yener, A., & Mathias, A. (2004). EDCF-DM: A novel enhanced distributed coordination function for wireless ad hoc networks. *IEEE International Conference on Communications (ICC 04)* (pp. 3866–3890).

Zhuan, G. M., & Grosspietsch, J. (2008). PHY 28-1 - Energy detection using estimated noise variance for spectrum sensing in cognitive radio networks. In *IEEE Wireless Communications and Networking Conference, WCNC 2008,* (pp. 711–716).

Zimmermann, H. (1980). OSI reference model-The ISO model of architecture for open systems interconnection. *IEEE Transactions on Communications, 28*(4), 425–432. doi:10.1109/TCOM.1980.1094702

About the Contributors

Mohammad A Matin is currently working at the department of Electrical and Electronic Engineering, ITB Brunei Darussalam as an Associate Professor. He obtained his BSc. degree in Electrical and Electronic Engineering from BUET (Bangladesh), MSc degree in Digital Communication from Loughborough University, UK and PhD degree in Wireless Communication from Newcastle University, UK. He has taught several courses in Communications, Electronics, and Signal Processing at KUET, Khulna University, and BRAC University during his career. From January to March 2008, Dr. Matin was the visiting Lecturer at the National University of Malayisa.He has published over 50 refereed journals and conference papers. He is the author of two academic books and three book chapters. He has presented invited talks in Bangladesh and Malaysia and has served as a member of the program committee for more than 50 international conferences like ICCSIT'09, IDCS'09, ICCSN'10, ICCSIT'10, ICCSN'11, et cetera. He also serves as a referee of a few renowned journals, keynote speaker and technical session chair of a few international conferences like MIC-CPE 2008, ICCIT 2008, ICMMT 2010, ICCIT 2010, IEEE GLOBECOM 2010, ICCIT 2011, et cetera. He is currently serving as a member of editorial board of several international journals such as *IET Wireless Sensor Systems* (IET-WSS), *IJCTE, JECE*, et cetera, and Guest Editor of special issue of *IJCNIS*. Dr. Matin is a member of IEEE, IEEE Communications Society (IEEE ComSoc), and several other international organizations. He is the Secretary of IEEE Communication Society, Bangladesh Chapter. He has received a number of Prizes and Scholarships including the Best student prize (Loughborough University), Commonwealth Scholarship and Overseas Research Scholarship (ORS). He has been fortunate enough to work in WFS Project with Wireless Fibre Sytems Ltd, UK as an expert. His current research interests include UWB communication, wireless sensor networks, cognitive radio, EM modeling, and antenna engineering.

* * *

Mohamed Lassaad Ammari was born in Mahdia, Tunisia, in 1972. He received the Engineering degree from the Ecole Supèrieure des Communications, Tunis, Tunisia, in 1995, and the M.Sc. and Ph.D. degrees from Universite Laval, Quebec, Quebec, Canada, in 2000 and 2003, respectively. From 2003 to 2005, he was a Research Associate with the Laboratory of Communications and Integrated Microelectronics (LACIME), ´Ecole de Technologie Superieure, Montreal, Quebec, Canada. He is currently an Assistant Professor at the Ecole Nationale d'Ingenieurs de Sousse. His research interests include channel equalization, OFDM systems, turbo detection, and adaptive modulation.

Ahmed Bannour was born in Moknine, Tunisia, in 1982. He received the Engineering degree and the M.Sc respectively in Telecommunications in 2006 and in Communications System in 2008 from the National Engineering School of Tunis, Tunisia. From 2006 to 2009, he was a Research Associate with the Laboratory of Communications System, Higher School of Communications of Tunis, Sup'Com Universite at Carthage, Tunisia. He is currently an Assistant Professor at the High Institute of Computer Science Mahdia. His research interests include MIMO, OFDM systems, algebraic space time code, and channel estimation.

Bhed Bahadur Bista received the B.Eng. degree in Electronics from the University of York, England and the M.S. and Ph.D. degrees in Information Science from Tohoku University, Japan. After his Ph.D., he worked at the Miyagi University, Japan, for one year as a Research Associate and moved to the Iwate Prefectural University, also in Japan in 1998 as an Assistant Professor. Currently, he is an Associate Professor with the Department of Software and Information Science at the same university. His research interests include computer networks, vehicular networks, sensor networks, ad hoc, and cognitive radio networks. He has organized international workshops and has actively taken part as an area chair and a program committee member in international conferences.

Ridha Bouallegue is Professor at the National Engineering School of Tunis, Tunisia (ENIT); he practices at the Superior School of Communications of Tunis (Sup'Com). He founded in 2005, and is Director of the Research Unit "Telecommunications Systems." He is founded in 2005, and is Director of the National Engineering School of Sousse. He received his PhD in 1998 then HDR in 2003 on multiuser detection in cellular radio systems of the next generation. His research and fundamental development, focus on the physical layer of telecommunication systems in particular on digital communications systems, MIMO, OFDM, CDMA, UWB, WiMAX, LTE, SDR, et cetera. He has published 2 book chapters, 75 articles in refereed conference lectures, and 15 journal articles (2009).

Giulio Bartoli (S'10) born in Montevarchi, Italy. He received the M.Sc. in Telecommunication Engineering from the University of Florence in 2010, and he is now a Ph.D. student at the Electronic and Telecommunications Department at University of Florence. His research interests lay in physical layer of communications, such as: OFDM/OFDMA systems, MIMO systems, physical layer network coding, mobile channel modeling, digital, and statistical signal processing. He has been involved in some national projects (SINTESIS) as well as European projects (SESAR, CORASMA). He has been author of technical papers published in international symposia.

Rodney Berriman received his B.E. degrees in University of Queensland (honours in Control Systems) and his M.S. degrees in Deakin University (Management of Innovation). Long list of R&D projects delivered at Nortel Wollongong & Ottawa, Alcatel France, Marconi UK, Telstra Sydney, Foxboro / Leeds and Northrup control systems, Crosfield Laser-Gravure London. He is currently a Research Engineer at the NICTA, Australia.

Francesco Chiti (M'01) received the degree in Telecommunications Engineering and the PhD degrees in Informatics and Telecommunications Engineering from the University of Florence in 2000 and 2004. His current research topics are devoted to MAC, LLC, and NET layers protocols design for both public and private wireless communications systems together with ad hoc and sensor networks. He took part in several European research projects as the IP GoodFood, STREP DustBot and AgroSense, the NoEs Nexway, SatNex, Newcom and CRUISE, the SESAR JU "Airport Surface Data Link System," the Galileo JU "TWIST," the ETSI STF179, and the COST 289 action.

Chine-Ming Chou received his B.S. degree in Department of Computer Science and Information Engineering from Vanung University of Technology on 2005/6 and M.S. degree in Department of Information and Communication Engineering from Chaoyang University of Technology on 2007/8. He is currently working for his Ph.D degree in Department of Computer Science and Information Engineering, National Cheng Kung University. His research interests include network simulation, network measurement, opportunistic routing, WiMAX and DSRC protocol, and mobility model.

Romano Fantacci, born in Pistoia, Italy, since 1999 is a full Professor of Computer Networks at the University of Florence, Florence, Italy. His current research interests are digital communications, computer communications, queuing theory, wireless broadband communication networks, and ad-hoc and sensor networks. He has been involved in several national and international research projects and author of numerous articles published in prestigious communication science journals. He guest edited special issues in IEEE journals and magazines and served as symposium chair of several IEEE conferences, including VTC, ICC, and Globecom. Professor Fantacci was the recipient of the IEE IERE Benefactor premium (1990) and IEEE COMSOC Award Distinguished Contributions to Satellite Communications (2002). He was Associate Editor for *Telecommunication Systems, IEEE Transactions in Communications*, and funding Area Editor for *IEEE Transactions on Wireless Communications*. He is currently serving as Associated Editor for *International Journal of Communication Systems*. Professor Fantacci is an IEEE Fellow (2005).

Cheng Guo received his Bachelor degree in Telecommunications from Beijing University of Posts and Telecommunications, China in 2003 and Master degree in 2005 from Delft University of Technology, The Netherlands. From 2005 to 2009, he worked as a PhD candidate in Wireless and Mobile Communication Group, Telecommunication Department, TU Delft and got his Ph.D. degree at 2010. From 2010 till date he is a researcher at DIMES, TU Delft. Cheng Guo has published about 20 papers in international peer-reviewed conferences and journals. He has worked in several Dutch and European research and industrial projects. His current research interest is on intelligent lighting systems and complex lighting system integrations.

John Hale is a Professor of Computer Science in the Tandy School of Computer Science and faculty researcher in the Institute for Information Security at the University of Tulsa. He received his Bachelor of Science in 1990, Master of Science in 1992, and Doctorate degree in 1997, all in Computer Science from the University of Tulsa. Dr. Hale has overseen the development of one of the premier information assurance curricula in the nation while at iSec. In 2000, he earned a prestigious National Science Foundation CAREER award for his education and research initiatives at iSec. His research interests include cyber attack modeling, analysis and visualization, enterprise security management, secure operating systems, distributed system verification, and policy coordination.

Hoda Hassan is an adjunct Assistant Professor at the American University in Cairo, Egypt. Dr. Hassan received her BSc '92 and MSc '05 in Computer Science from the American University in Cairo (AUC), and her PhD '10 in Computer Engineering from Virginia Tech, Blacksburg, Virginia. During her PhD she has worked at the Advanced Research Institute, Arlington, Virginia as a graduate research assistant. Her research interests are computer network design and engineering, and software engineering.

Mahbub Hassan (M'91 - SM'00) is a full Professor in the School of Computer Science and Engineering, University of New South Wales, Sydney, Australia, where he leads a research program on mobile and wireless systems. He earned his PhD in Computer Science from Monash University, Melbourne, Australia (1997), MSc in Computer Science from University of Victoria, Canada (1991), and BSc in Computer Engineering (with High Honor) from Middle East Technical University, Turkey (1989). He has co-authored and co-edited three books on computer networking. His recent book, titled "High Performance TCP/IP Networking" (Prentice Hall, 2004) has been widely adopted across the world with translations published in foreign languages.

Peter J. Hawrylak, is an Assistant Professor in the Electrical Engineering department at The University of Tulsa (TU), is vice-chair of the AIM RFID Experts Group (REG), and chair of the Healthcare Initiative (HCI) sub-group of the AIM REG. Dr. Hawrylak is a member of The University of Tulsa's Institute for Information Security (iSec), which is a NSA (U.S. National Security Agency) Center of Excellence. Peter has four (4) issued patents in the RFID space and numerous academic publications. Peter's research interests are in the areas embedded system security, RFID, embedded systems, and low power wireless systems. He is Associate Editor of the *International Journal of Radio Frequency Identification Technology and Applications* (IJRFITA) journal published by InderScience Publishers, which focuses on the application and development of RFID technology.

Varun Jeoti received his Ph.D. degree from Indian Institute of Technology Delhi India in 1992. He worked on several sponsored R&D projects in IIT Delhi and IIT Madras during 1980 to 1989 developing Surface Acoustic Wave Pulse Compression filters, underwater optical receivers, et cetera. He was a Visiting Faculty in Electronics department in Madras Institute of Technology for about 1 year during 1989 to 1990 and joined Delhi Institute of Technology for next 5 years till 1995. He moved to Electrical & Electronic Engineering (E&E Engg) department of Universiti Sains Malaysia in 1995 and joined E&E Eng of Universiti Teknologi PETRONAS in 2001. His research interests are in signal processing and wireless communication relating to wireless LAN and MAN technologies, cognitive radio, maritime communication, distributed video coding, and security.

Kun-Chan Lan received his PhD degree from Computer Science at University of Southern California in 2004, advised by Professor John Heidemann. He received his Master degree in Computer Science from SUNY at Stony Brook in 1997, advised by Professor Tzi-cker Chiueh. He received his B.A. in Industrial Management Science from National Cheng Kung University in Taiwan. Kun-chan's research interests include realistic network simulation, network measurement, communication for intelligent transport system, sensor network, and multimedia over wireless network. From 2004 to 2007, Kun-chan joined the Network and Pervasive Computing Program at NICTA (National ICT Australia) in Sydney as a researcher and lead the effort of building one of the world's first outdoor wireless testbeds for traffic light communication in the context of STaR (Smart Transport and Roads) project (STaR in press). He is currently an Assistant Professor at the Department of Computer Science and Information Engineering of National Cheng Kung University.

Bjorn Landfeldt started his studies at the Royal Institute of Technology in Sweden. After receiving a B.Sc. equivalent, he continued studying at The University of New South Wales where he received his Ph.D. in 2000. In parallel with his studies in Sweden he was running a mobile computing consultancy company and after his studies he joined Ericsson Research in Stockholm as a Senior Researcher where he worked on mobility management and QoS issues. In November 2001, Dr. Landfeldt took up a position as a CISCO Senior Lecturer in Internet Technologies at the University of Sydney with the School of Electrical and Information Engineering and the School of Information Technologies. Dr. Landfeldt's research interests include mobility management, QoS, performance-enhancing middleware, wireless systems, and service provisioning.

Lavy Libman received his B.Sc. degrees in Electrical Engineering and in Computer Engineering, and his M.Sc. and Ph.D. degrees in Electrical Engineering, from the Technion - Israel Institute of Technology, Haifa, Israel, in 1992, 1997, and 2003, respectively. He is a Senior Lecturer in the School of Information Technologies, University of Sydney, which he joined in February 2009, and a member of the Centre for Distributed and High-Performance Computing. He also continues to be associated with the Networked Systems research group at NICTA (formerly National ICT Australia), where he was a researcher since September 2003. Dr. Libman is an Associate Editor of the *IEEE Transactions on Wireless Communications*, and was an Editor of the Academy Publisher *Journal of Communications* (JCM) between 2009-2011. He is a publicity co-chair of IEEE Infocom 2012.

Dania Marabissi was born in Chianciano, Italy. She received the degree in Telecommunications Engineering and the PhD degree in Informatics and Telecommunications Engineering from the University of Florence in 2000 and 2004, respectively. She joined the Electronic and Telecommunications Department at University of Florence in 2000 where now works as Assistant Professor. She currently conducts research on physical and MAC layers design for broadband wireless systems. In particular her interests include LTE, WiMAX, and OFDM systems, resource allocation strategies, channel estimation and synchronization. She has been involved in several national and European research projects and is author of technical papers published in international journals and conferences.

Tim Moors is a Senior Lecturer in the School of Electrical Engineering and Telecommunications at the University of New South Wales, in Sydney, Australia. He researches transport protocols for wireless and optical networks, wireless LAN MAC protocols that support bursty voice streams, communication system modularity, and fundamental principles of networking. Previously, he was with the Center for Advanced Technology in Telecommunications at Polytechnic University in New York, and prior to that, with the Communications Division of the Australian Defence Science and Technology Organization. He received his PhD and BEng (Hons) degrees from universities in Western Australia (Curtin and UWA).

Ignas G. M. M. Niemegeers got a degree in Electrical Engineering from the University of Gent, Belgium, in 1970. In 1972 he received a M.Sc.E. degree in Computer Engineering and in 1978 a Ph.D. degree from Purdue University in West Lafayette, Indiana, USA. From 1978 to 1981 he was a designer of packet switching networks at Bell Telephone Mfg. Cy, Antwerp, Belgium. From 1981 to 2002 he was a Professor at the Computer Science and the Electrical Engineering Faculties of the University of Twente, Enschede, The Netherlands. From 1995 to 2001 he was Scientific Director of the Centre for Telematics and Information Technology (CTIT) of the University of Twente, a multi-disciplinary research institute on ICT and applications. Since May 2002 he holds the chair Wireless and Mobile Communications at Delft University of Technology, where he is heading the Centre for Wireless and Personal Communication (CWPC) and the Telecommunications Department. He was involved in many European research projects, e.g., the EU projects MAGNET and MAGNET Beyond on personal networks, EUROPCOM on UWB emergency networks and, eSENSE and CRUISE on sensor networks. He is a member of the Expert group of the European technology platform eMobility and IFIP TC-6 on Networking. He is also chairman of the HERMES Partnership, an organization of leading European research institutes and universities in telecommunications. His present research interests are 4G wireless infrastructures, future home networks, ad-hoc networks, personal networks, and cognitive networks.

Maximilian Ott received a Ph.D. in Electrical Engineering from the University of Tokyo, Japan, an M.S. from the Technical University Vienna, Austria, and an excellent foundation from the HTBLA Steyr. He is a Sr. Principal Researcher and Research Theme Manager, Networked Systems at NICTA where he is currently involved in the TEMPO, Structural Health Monitoring and CAMP project. He also heavily involved in many of the worldwide experimental research facility activities, such as GENI (US) and FIRE with many testbeds adopting our award-winning OMF control and management framework. Before coming to NICTA he founded Semandex, which is a pioneer provider of Content-Based Networks, a new generation of Enterprise Information Integration and Knowledge Management systems.

Mauricio Papa is an Associate Professor for the Tandy School of Computer Science at The University of Tulsa. He also serves as Faculty Director of the Institute for Information Security, which supports a multi-disciplinary program of study and research tackling cyber security issues on a global scale. Dr. Papa received his Bachelor of Science in Electrical Engineering from Universidad Central de Venezuela in 1992, and his Master of Science in Electrical Engineering and Doctorate Degree in Computer Science from TU in 1996 and 2001, respectively. His primary research area is critical infrastructure protection. His team has designed and constructed process control testbeds to support cyber security efforts in critical infrastructure protection He also conducts research in distributed systems, network security, cryptographic protocol verification, and intelligent control systems.

R. Venkatesha Prasad received his Bachelor's degree in Electronics and Communication Engineering and M.Tech degree in Industrial Electronics from University of Mysore, India in 1991 and 1994. He received a PhD degree in 2003 from Indian Institute of Science, Bangalore India. During 1996 he was working as a consultant and project associate for ERNET Lab of ECE at Indian Institute of Science. While pursuing the Ph.D degree, from 1999 to 2003 he was also working as a consultant for CEDT, IISc, Bangalore for VoIP application developments as part of Nortel Networks sponsored project. In 2003 he was heading a team of engineers at the Esqube Communication Solutions Pvt. Ltd. Bangalore for the development of various real-time networking applications. Currently, he is a part time consultant to Esqube. From 2005 till date he is a senior researcher at Wireless and Mobile Communications group, Delft University of Technology working on the EU funded projects MAGNET/MAGNET Beyond and PNP-2008 and guiding graduate students. He is an active member of TCCN, IEEE SCC41, and reviewer of many transactions and journals. He is on the TPC of many conferences including ICC, GlobeCom, ACM MM, ACM SIGCHI, et cetera. He is the TPC co-chair of CogNet workshop in 2007, 2008, and 2009 and TPC chair for E2Nets at IEEE ICC-2010. He is also running PerNets workshop from 2006 with IEEE CCNC. He is the Tutorial Co-Chair of CCNC 2009 & 2011 and Demo Chair of IEEE CCNC 2010. He is an invited member of IEEE ComSoc Standards Board.

Vijay S. Rao received his B.E. degree in Information Science and Engineering from Visvesvaraya Technological University, India in 2004. He worked as Senior Software Engineer for 3 years with ES-QUBE Communications in the area of Voice over Internet Protocol. In 2007, he joined Delft University of Technology for Masters in Telecommunications, and obtained the degree in 2009. During his study, he worked with cognitive radios and personal networks. He is currently pursuing his Ph.D. in Wireless and Mobile Communications group, Delft University of Technology in the area of Wireless Sensor Networks.

Danda B. Rawat is currently working as an Assistant Professor of Network Security and Electronics in Eastern Kentucky University. He received his Ph.D. in Electrical and Computer Engineering from Old Dominion University in December 2010, M.S. in Information and Communication Engineering and B.E. in Computer Engineering from Institute of Engineering, Tribhuvan University. His research interests include design, analysis, and evaluation of computer networks, network security, wireless systems, cognitive radio networks, mobile and vehicular ad-hoc networks, wireless sensor networks, wireless LAN, and smart grid. He has over 50 research publications including journal articles, conference proceedings and book chapters in these areas. He served as an Editor-in-Chief, an Editor or Guest Editor, and an Editorial Board Member for numerous international journals. He has worked as a co-organizer and TPC member for numerous international workshops and conferences. Dr. Rawat has previously worked for the Government of Nepal and Center for Information Technology as a Lead Technical Member for Computer Network and System Administration. He also held an academic position at the Old Dominion University, USA and Institute of Engineering, Tribhuvan University, Nepal. He is the member of ATMAE, IEEE, ACM, IEEE Computer Society, IEEE Communication Society, and IEEE Vehicular Technology Society.

Elsadig Saeid received his B.Sc in Telecommunications Engineering and M.Sc in Telecommunications and Networks from Sudan University of Science and Technology, Sudan in 2003 and 2006, respectively. He worked on several telecommunication networks and telecontrol projects with National Electricity Corporation (NEC) Sudan during 2005 to 2008. In 2009 he received Universiti Teknologi PETRONAS Graduate Assistantship and he joined Electrical & Electronic Engineering (E&E Engg) Department of Universiti Teknologi PETRONAS as PhD candidate. His research interests are in the areas of wireless communications, signal processing, information theory, system modeling, and optimization.

Brahim Belhaouari Samir received his M.Sc degree in Networks and Telecommunications from School of Toulouse (ENSEEIHT), France and Ph.D degree in Mathematical Sciences from Federal Polytechnic School of Lausanne, (EPFL) Switzerland in 2000 and 2006, respectively. He joined Electrical &

Electronic Engineering (E&E Engg) department of Universiti Teknologi PETRONAS as Senior Lecturer in 2007. In 2009 he moved to the Fundamental Applied Science Department of Universiti Teknologi PETRONAS. His research interests are in the areas of signal processing, pattern recognition, modeling, and analysis of stochastic systems.

Md. Zahurul Islam Sarkar received the B.Sc. Engg. and M. Sc. Engg. degrees in Electrical and Electronic Engineering from Rajshahi University of Engineering & Technology, Bangladesh, in 1996 and 2000, respectively. He is an Assistant Professor, Department of Electrical and Electronic Engineering, Rajshahi University of Engineering & Technology, Bangladesh. From September 2007 to December 2008, Mr. Sarkar worked as a Research Assistant at the Communications and Coding Theory Laboratory (CCTLAB), Kyung Hee University, South Korea. He received the Best Paper Award at the 67th IEEE Vehicular Technology Conference (VTC2008-Spring). At present, he is working as a researcher at the Institute of Electronics, Communications and Information Technology (ECIT) of Queen's University Belfast, United Kingdom. His research interest includes the information theoretic security aspects of fading channels, cognitive radio channels, and wireless multicasting.

Riccardo Scopigno, PhD, has matured a 15-year working experience in the TLC field, obtaining, in the meantime his Ph.D. His skills cover telecommunication architectures, from theory to practice, as matured from his variegate working experience. He was a hardware designer for TLC systems in Italtel-Siemens (1997-1999); in Marconi (2000-2003), he achieved a good expertise in IP network design (as certified network engineer). He is currently active in advanced research on wireless networks– he is Director of MultiLayer Wireless Dept. of ISMB. He is ISMB's representative in ETSI ITS (the working group on intelligent transportation systems) and within ERTICO and Car-to-Car Communication Consortium. He is author of papers on WiFi and vehicular communications at IEEE conferences acting also as TPC and author of 3 patent pending techniques for VANETs (on synchronous MAC, georouting MapCast, and CSMA/CA QoS).

Asrar Ul Haq Sheikh graduated from the University of Engineering and Technology (UET), Lahore, Pakistan in 1964 and received his M.Sc. and Ph.D. degrees from the University of Birmingham, England, in 1966 and 1969 respectively. He held positions in Pakistan, Iran, UK, Libya and Canada before joining KFUPM as Bugshan/Bell Lab Chair in Telecommunications in 2000. Dr. Sheikh is the author of a book, Wireless Communications - Theory & Techniques published by Springer, USA in 2004. He also contributed a chapter on wireless communications in a book on Telecommunications in 1986. He was an editor of *IEEE Transaction on Wireless Communications* (2003-05), and was a Technical Associate Editor of *IEEE Communication Magazine* (2000-01). He is on the Editorial Board of several technical journals. Dr. Sheikh is listed in Marquis's Who's Who in Science and Engineering. He is a Fellow of the IEEE and a Fellow of the IET (London).

Yichuang Sun received his PhD degree from the University of York, UK in 1996. He is currently a Professor in the School of Engineering and Technology of the University of Hertfordshire, UK. His research interests fall into two major areas: (1) Wireless and Mobile Communications including MIMO, MIMO-OFDM, cooperative communications, cognitive communications, and green radio; (2) microelectronic circuits and systems including RF, analogue and mixed-signal circuits, continuous-time filters, automatic antenna tuning, and mixed-signal test. Professor Sun has published some 220 technical papers and contributed eight chapters in edited books. He has also published four text and research books including Wireless Communication Circuits and Systems, IEE Press, 2004. He has been a Series Editor of *IEE Circuits, Devices and Systems* Book Series. He is Associate Editor of *IEEE Transactions on Circuits and Systems-I* and Editor of *ETRI Journal*. He has also been Guest Editor of five IEE journal special issues including the *Issue on MIMO Wireless and Mobile Communications* in *IEE Proceedings: Communications,* 2006.

Andrea Tassi was born in Figline Valdarno (Italy) on 1984. He received the Master's degree in Computer Engineering (summa cum laude) from the University of Florence in 2010, with a thesis on "Routing strategies for pervasive grid applications." He won a scholarship for graduate student at University of Florence with the following topic: routing schemes for distributed computing environments. He's working at the Telecommunication Networks Laboratory (LaRT), Department of Electronics and Telecommunications as Ph.D. student. His research interests are mainly focused on resource allocation strategies for broadband wireless networks, distributed and pervasive computing, and MANET-based routing schemes.

Raza Umar received his B.Sc. degree in Electrical Engineering from the University of Engineering and Technology (UET), Lahore, Pakistan in 2000. He received his M.Sc. degree from the University of Stuttgart, Germany in 2005. He is an Assistant Professor in the Department of Electrical Engineering, UET Lahore, Pakistan. Before joining academia, he was with Alcatel Germany where he was involved in the evaluation of MIMO schemes for 3.5 G (HSDPA) during 2004-2005. He worked as a Senior Design Engineer in DSP Software Optimization Group at Avaz Networks, formerly Communications Enabling Technologies, a leading R&D company based in Islamabad, Pakistan from 2000 to 2003. Currently he is pursuing his Ph.D. degree under the supervision of Prof. Asrar U. H. Sheikh at KFUPM, Dhahran Saudi Arabia. His current research interests include next generation wireless systems, cognitive radio networks, and signal processing for optimum detection and estimation.

Jing Wang received her BSc degree in Electrical Engineering from Beijing University of Aeronautics and Astronautics, China, in 2003. In 2005 she received MSc degree on Telecommunications from Delft University of Technology, the Netherlands. In 2006, she joined in Wireless and Mobile Networks (WMC) group in Delft University of Technology on Dutch IOP GenCom "Future Home Networks" project, focusing on wireless mesh networks, high data rate wireless personal networks, wireless sensor networks, cognitive networking, and self-organization systems. In 2011, she received her PhD degree with dissertation "Networking Technologies for Future Home Networks Using 60 GHz Radio." She is currently working as system engineer for Technology Solutions Network group in Cisco Systems, the Netherlands, focusing on Borderless Networks and Unified Communications.

Andrea Vesco, PhD, received the M.S.Degree in Telecommunication Engineering from the Politecnico di Torino in 2003. He also received the Ph.D. in Computer and System Engineering from the Politecnico di Torino, under the supervision of prof. Mario Baldi, in 2009. He was a Post-Doc Researcher with the Control and Computer Engineering Department as a member of the Computer Networks Group at the Politecnico di Torino in 2009. He is with the Multi-Layer Wireless Solutions Department at the

Istituto Superiore Mario Boella (ISMB) from 2010. His main research interests are in Time-Based QoS over Packet Switched Networks and Wireless Access Networks. Moreover he carries on joint research activities with the SLD research group at Columbia University in the City of New York on QoS over Network-on-Chip (NoC). As part of his extensive research activity he is involved in various research projects, involving universities and industrial partners, funded by European Union, local government, and research institutions.

Gongjun Yan received his Ph.D. in Computer Science from Old Dominion University in 2010. He is currently an Assistant Professor in Indiana University and has been working on the issues surrounding vehicular ad-hoc networks, sensor networks, and wireless communication. His main research areas include intelligent vehicles, security, privacy, routing, and healthcare. In years, Dr. Yan applies mathematical analysis to model behavior of complex systems and integrates existing techniques to provide comprehensive solutions. He had more than 50 publications including journal/conference papers, book chapters, and patents.

Zainab Zaidi is a Researcher in Network Systems group in NICTA. Before joining NICTA in 2006. She taught in NED University of Engg. and Technology, Karachi, Pakistan, in 2005 and worked as a post doctoral fellow in Network Architecture Lab of George Mason University, Virginia, USA in 2004. Her research interests include different network layer issues in wireless mesh networks, such as robust routing, anomaly detection, cooperative/opportunistic routing, efficiency of link metrics, quality-of-service, et cetera, besides mobility tracking and its applications in mobile wireless networks.

Index

CPSIA information can be obtained at www.ICGtesting.com
Printed in the USA
BVOW050745140512

290035BV00008B/8/P